Business
and the Law

SOUTHERN CALIFORNIA CONSORTIUM

Business
and the Law
Telecourse Study Guide

Michael D. Hiscox
Vicki L. Spandel
Mary L. Lewis, J.D.
Interwest Applied Research, Inc.
Beaverton, Oregon

with contributions from Marilyn Averill, J.D.;
Lynn Darroch; Jeff Kuechle; and Richard Sanders

PWS-KENT Publishing Company
A Division of Wadsworth, Inc.
Boston, Massachusetts

PWS–KENT
Publishing Company

Preface

A telecourse study guide is a special kind of document. As its name implies, it must literally guide a student through a telecourse—help the student to focus his or her thinking, identify key ideas, monitor progress, and so on. In addition, it should strive to establish a context for learning so that the other course materials will be more effective. A telecourse study guide that actually accomplishes these things helps the student in much the same way that a private tutor would.

Research on learning theory indicates that students tend to learn more—and feel they get more out of a course—when their higher-level thinking skills are tapped. Without this element, a course becomes either a tedious and ineffective memorization of facts or so boring that the content is not studied with enthusiasm. Obviously, neither outcome is acceptable when trying to teach students to understand the conceptual underpinnings of the law. But how can a study guide lead students through the intricacies of business law while simultaneously forcing students to think for themselves?

Several tactics can be used. One is to introduce new material in a way that helps a student establish a kind of mental framework, to make connections with his or her own current and anticipated experience and with other previous learning. Without this connection, newly introduced material may seem irrelevant, or even incomprehensible. Research has shown that we all learn by integrating new information with our previous experiences. The overview within each telecourse study guide lesson is intended, then, to establish a basis for forming this framework. It highlights key legal elements and themes from the text, but does so in a way that shows how the material introduced has relevance in the business world.

Also, we tend to learn best when we see a purpose to that learning. Part of the function of the overview, therefore, is to demonstrate to students why they should care about pursuing the subject any further. The overviews try to give the message that "This is important material. It has implications for your business, for the way you think. It will help you make business decisions that avoid legal problems."

But because of the need for a more personal, more experienced-based approach to the content, the overview cannot simply replicate the text in content, format or tone. While it needs to cover most of the same topics, it should be more personal, more immediate. To these ends, the overview is constructed largely of scenarios that clearly illustrate the points under discussion—without extraneous legal complexities or the complicated language that is sometimes found in the explanations of actual court decisions.

Further, the telecourse study guide—and the **Business and the Law** telecourse in general—profits from having a well-established set of objectives. The function of learning objectives, of course, is to identify the purpose of any instruction. By reviewing the objectives, students see what it is they're supposed to learn, what skills they need to attain before leaving a lesson. Indeed, mastering the objectives is an important goal for students. It is not the only goal, however; the deeper purpose of any course is — or ought to be — to prepare students to engage in the same kind of mental networking and higher thinking that provides a context for the course in the first place. In other words, we've constructed the telecourse guide to cause the student to ask, "How can I apply these legal concepts when making business and personal decisions? How can I use this information to reduce the possibility of legal disputes?"

As one might suspect, each lesson of the **Business and the Law** telecourse is designed to increase opportunities for students to leave the course with more than just memorized knowledge. Specifically, each chapter contains six sections, each designed to assist the student in a particular way, as follows:

- First, the objectives for the lesson establish a structure for learning, suggesting what elements of the course require particular attention.

- Second, the overview introduces the lesson concepts and presents them in a practical context, all the while heightening the students' interest in and understanding of the legal system.

- Third, the assignments show students how to proceed through the learning activities of the lesson most efficiently.

- Fourth, a list of key terms alerts students to the important concepts covered in the lesson.

- Fifth, a self-test shows students what progress they've made in assimilating the material and learning to apply it. (Students and instructors will notice that a significant portion of the self-test questions require higher-level thinking skills.)

- Sixth, a "Your Opinion, Please" section asks students to apply legal concepts, integrate different principles, make choices, and synthesize and evaluate options in order to decide the outcome of a pair of hypothetical court cases.

Once all these steps have been completed, students should be prepared to both conduct additional activities assigned by the instructor and answer the test items from the accompanying course examination bank. Like a portion of the self-test questions, some examination bank items require the students to show considerable skill in analyzing and applying the legal concepts of the lesson and, on many occasions, evaluating and synthesizing the relative merit of alternative actions.

In summary, we've attempted to provide a telecourse study guide that is interesting, that provokes new learning, that allows the student some mental elbow room for evaluating the implications of legal concepts, and that accomplishes these tasks with just enough structure to complement the text. If we've succeeded, the document will serve instructors and students well.

Michael D. Hiscox
Vicki L. Spandel
Mary L. Lewis, J.D.

Contents

1

Law and the Businessperson

LEARNING OBJECTIVES

Upon completing your study of this lesson, you should be able to

- Explain the meaning of *law* and give examples of the law in terms of rules and social conduct.
- Describe the effect of law on business, with particular emphasis on the law's role in limiting and structuring transactions.
- Identify the ten portions of the law which are considered to comprise *business law*.
- Discuss the importance of a businessperson understanding the law in terms of the law's removal of discretion in business dealings.
- Provide hypothetical business-oriented examples of the consequences of a business-person not knowing the law.

An old saying suggests that what you don't know can't hurt you. In the case of business law, however, what you don't know can hurt you very much indeed. And what you *assume*—should your assumptions turn out to be even slightly inaccurate—can hurt you even more.

Unfortunately, too many businesspeople get their legal information second-hand—often from the recounted experiences of business associates. The value of such information can be extremely limited—first, because each situation is a little different, and second, because the person providing the information may have a hard time being objective, especially if the law seems, for the moment at least, to have somehow "favored" the other side.

So, how does one go about becoming better informed? Consulting an attorney is an obvious answer and at some times is absolutely crucial. We'll talk later in this lesson about the value of using an attorney as an ongoing business advisor. But from a practical perspective, it's a rare businessperson who can afford the luxury of having an attorney right at his or her elbow all the time. While it's a comfort to know that sound legal advice is only a phone call away, there are still moments in each business day when executives must rely on their own judgment. So, what other alternatives exist for ensuring legally sound business decisions?

Some businesspeople go so far as to enroll in night classes at a local law school. But for most, that solution is less than practical—though an occasional seminar on a point of interest might be in order. Perusing law books during off hours isn't a realistic option either. As anyone who has visited a law library can attest, written law now fills miles of shelves. For the novice, it's hard to know how or where to begin. Small wonder that some businesspeople wind up fatalistically shrugging the whole thing off—"Well, if I really get into trouble, that will be the time to consult an attorney and get details." The problem is, by then it's often too late. There *is*, however, a practical solution, and it's what this course is all about.

It is quite possible—and practical—for today's businessperson to learn enough about business law to feel fairly comfortable in his or her own situation. Most business executives, for example, do not need, on a daily basis at any rate, information about criminal laws pertaining to homicide, armed robbery, and treason. They don't need, for business purposes, an in-depth understanding of legal history or a thorough knowledge of recent child custody legislation. But they *do* need to know something about the ten major components of business law, which today include contracts, agency relationships, sales, property, commercial paper (e.g., checks, certificates of deposit), secured transactions, the nature of different types of business organization (e.g., partnerships, corporations), insurance, product liability, and business-related torts.

This course, then, takes a very focused approach, addressing those issues that are likely to be of primary concern to the businessperson in today's world. This doesn't mean that the businessperson who learns a bit about business law won't need an attorney any longer. On the contrary; one of the most important reasons for studying business law as a layperson is to recognize how and when you might require the services of a good attorney and how you might make the best possible use of such professional help.

In addition, studying business law can help the businessperson strike a good balance between caution and confidence. On the one hand, it's foolhardy to imagine that good intentions are all that are needed to keep the businessperson out of trouble. They're a beginning, but they're not enough. On the other hand, it's also a mistake to suppose that business laws have been created just for the purpose of making life difficult, for entangling enterprising businesspeople in sticky procedural webs that only complicate their business transactions. In fact, as we shall see, business laws are designed primarily to protect the just interests on both sides of any business dealing. No matter which side you happen to be on at the moment — employer or employee, consumer or manufacturer, purchaser or supplier — there are laws created specifically to guard your rights.

OVERVIEW

We've already made the point that what you don't know of the law *can* hurt you — seriously, in some cases. Let's consider a specific example to illustrate just how easily this can occur. Suppose that Blanford, executive director of an accounting firm, orders a new computer system for his office from Gamma Computer Systems, Inc. Gamma delivers the new system one day before Blanford is scheduled to leave town on vacation. He conducts a cursory inspection of the new equipment, tells the delivery person that "everything seems to be in order," requests that the business office issue the first payment to Gamma, and then leaves on vacation, confident that the situation is well in hand.

During his absence, Blanford's own employees install the system. But they encounter some problems. First, the software does not seem to be functioning as it should. During the printing of one report, an unexplained malfunction causes a significant loss of information crucial to the company's own tax statement. Further, the printed financial reports are full of sections where the information is garbage — it looks like the printers simply printed random characters instead of the numbers.

Upon returning from vacation, Blanford is told of the various difficulties and immediately phones Gamma to demand that the printers be replaced. He is dismayed to discover, however, that according to the terms of their agreement, his behavior prior to leaving on vacation constitutes acceptance of the equipment. Therefore, his complaints — coming so late — can no longer be honored in full. In short, Gamma will not replace the printers or any of the other equipment without additional charge. They *will* review the installation and modify anything that has been done incorrectly, but Blanford must take up his printer problems with the printer manufacturer.

Blanford further discovers that the limited warranty, which he failed to read in detail, will not extend to equipment that the buyer installs personally. With minor exceptions, Gamma disavows any responsibility for repairing or replacing computer equipment that Blanford's employees have installed and used for thirty days or longer. Had Blanford read the fine print, he would have known all this. But he didn't. And he's now in the awkward position of trying to show that the difficulties his company is experiencing are due to inherent problems in the equipment itself — problems *he could not have been expected to discover through inspection* — and not to the way in which it was installed or the way in which it has been operated.

Suppose Blanford becomes desperate enough to sue Gamma and try to recover his losses in that way. What are the odds that the court will see things from Blanford's side and require Gamma to repair or replace the equipment? Not good. As a buyer, Blanford had a duty to inspect the goods he purchased to ensure they were free of all defects — except those that might be hidden and therefore undetectable through reasonable inspection. But he was in a hurry to leave on his vacation and so didn't take the time for a thorough inspection. Too bad. The law makes no provision for this type of "special" circumstances.

Further, Blanford had a duty to read thoroughly any warranty provided by the seller. But he didn't. Either he was too busy or he assumed he knew what sort of information the warranty would contain. That sort of assumption can be costly — as Blanford is now discovering. He might also have protected his position by having the seller install the equipment. But he chose to save some money by installing it himself, and now he's suffering the consequences of having compromised his warranty rights through this sort of false economy.

In summary, Blanford has little or no support for his position, other than — probably — an overwhelming sense that the whole thing seems very unfair. But as this scenario illustrates, the law must make every effort to look at a situation impartially, to protect the rights on *both* sides. The court cannot *just* consider how things look from Blanford's vantage point, but must see things through Gamma's eyes, too. Gamma delivered the computer components in good faith and was told everything was satisfactory. Must they be responsible then if the buyer later changes his mind and decides things are not so satisfactory? The law says no. In failing to fulfill the legal duties of a buyer, Blanford waived some of his rights, and he cannot now reinstate them. Not this time around. Chances are he'll be wiser next time, though.

A Definition of "Law"

As we looked at Blanford's situation, we spoke about his duties and obligations and what *the law* required. But let's backtrack a moment and look at what we meant by the term "law." In our day-to-day lives, we use the word "law" in different ways and in different contexts. There are the laws of logic that parents always seem to know better than their children, and the law of averages keeps us believing that our favorite baseball player's ten-game hitting slump will end with the very next at-bat. There are also those perverse laws of nature that make it rain every year on our town's Founder's Day Parade.

But in this course, when we use the word *law*, we're referring to *the body of rules that establishes the acceptable level of social conduct for those living in our society*. These rules are both made by and enforceable by the society. And a violation or *breach* of those rules leaves the violator open to whatever sanction or punishment the society has determined is appropriate for the violation.

As you'll learn, exactly who within the society creates any particular rule will vary with the subject matter and how the issue came to be of concern to society. But it's the society as a whole—through its recognition of the need for the rule, the concept of the rule, and the severity of punishment—that ultimately determines when people's principles of behavior, ideals, morals, and plain old sense of "the right thing to do" become law.

While there are a seemingly unlimited number of topics about which one could have a law, a law will tend to fall into one of four categories:

- laws that set out certain affirmative standards to meet (for example, the requirements that an agreement must meet to be a formal contract, enforceable in court),
- laws that forbid certain conduct (for example, entering a building without the owner's permission and removing property of the owner is a crime),
- laws that recognize duties between private citizens and allow recovery if one is harmed by the other (for example, cancelling the purchase of goods that were intentionally described differently than they were manufactured), or
- laws of procedure that say how a legal dispute must be presented to the courts or decisionmaker.

Violations of society's laws are punishable as the society determines in the law. For violations of some laws, a person may be subject to time in jail; laws may also set out monetary fines that must be paid to the government. Some laws allow a private person to sue a violator and recovery money directly from the wrongdoer. And in some instances, the wrongdoer can be ordered to act in ways the wrongdoer does not want to act—or be forbidden to act as the wrongdoer wants to. In all instances, though, it is the society that determines the permissible scope the punishment can take, with the judge or jury in any one case deciding the particular punishment for the violation.

As we go through the course, you'll be introduced to the wide variety of laws that affect modern business conduct—laws that do different things, apply in different situations, and have different punishments But in spite of these differences, never lose sight of what each individual law represents: a portion of rules that society has established for itself to define and enforce the acceptable level of social conduct for those living in the society.

The Effect of Law on Business Operations

Because of the widespread nature of business operations, the law affects the nature of every business transaction. It places legal limits on what a businessperson can and cannot do. It structures how certain transactions are done. If the activities a typical business engages in are analyzed, it becomes apparent that there is very little that is not in some way influenced by the law: creating contracts, selling goods and services, initiating checks to pay for these goods and services, and even providing the purchaser with a warranty on the product. The law also affects business by providing specific meanings for everyday words. In addition to these areas, the law has other effects.

Protection for a Business Investment

The law is a system of rules, some of which are quite complex, and many of which are difficult to understand without the assistance of an attorney. Nevertheless, the rules are not meant to confuse or perplex the businessperson nor to bog down commerce. Instead, the primary purpose of business law is to create a system that will ensure maximum fairness to both sides and help create the kind of economic environment in which businesses of all types can thrive. Such an environment benefits each individual business, large or small, but—even more important—it's good for the economy as a whole. And that's the real point. If the law were to take a more narrow, more biased position, it might be good for one individual or one company in the short run, but in the long run, all of us would suffer.

For example, if a company like Gamma had to replace all the computer components that buyers installed incorrectly or operated inappropriately, it might soon go out of business. And if too many Gamma's go out of business, economic productivity falls, investment declines, unemployment shoots up. Thus, the law takes the position that it must protect consumers' rights, but not to the extent that businesses can no longer function or make a profit. Similarly, the law cannot protect the business owner or manager *at the consumer's expense*. If consumers become too apprehensive, too distrustful, they won't buy as many goods and services, and that can also put Gamma and others like it out of business.

Conflicting Perspectives

It may occur to you that in its role of preserving the social good, the law stands a little at odds with the needs and goals of the entrepreneur. In some respects, this is so. After all, the successful businessperson has a highly competitive spirit. In making most decisions, the businessperson will ask, "Is this in the best interests of the *company*?" That's as it should be—to a certain extent. But such a position is too limited for the law, which must always ask, "Is this in the best interests of the *society* that our system of law serves?" And sometimes these interests are in conflict. This is not to suggest that businesspeople tend to be ruthless or lacking in social conscience. Nevertheless, all good business managers recognize that priorities must be set, and the shrewd business manager will always have an eye on trimming costs and maximizing profits.

For example, suppose that Alchemy Chemical Company is polluting the rivers of the city with waste products from its main plant. Most of us would probably view this as socially irresponsible behavior. Yet, if Alchemy is required to clean up this waste or to discontinue manufacturing certain products, its profits could be threatened. Perhaps some employees would lose their jobs. The plant might even be forced to close. Further, certain of Alchemy's products on which other manufacturers depend would be discontinued; jobs could be lost in these other companies as well. Thus, looking at things strictly from Alchemy's side, continuing to pollute the river—while admittedly not desirable—might seem to be the "optimum" business decision for now, even if it's a decision that makes Alchemy managers and others a bit uncomfortable.

The legal perspective is a little different. The law must weigh the cost of having Alchemy lose profits or even go out of business against the cost of forcing society to deal with a polluted water source. And the law may well take the position that in the long run, it is not reasonable to protect Alchemy's rights at the cost of what is seen as the greater social good.

Similarly, manufacturers may go only so far, legally, in cutting corners to reduce product costs. Many laws exist to protect consumers' safety and their rights to a product or service that lives up to reasonable expectations. Employers are also expected to maintain hazard-free work environments for employees and to treat them fairly. They may not legally, for instance, cram hundreds of workers into cramped, unventilated quarters in order to save money, nor may they neglect to repair faulty safety equipment just to avoid unwanted expense. Make no mistake: The law supports the right of business to make a profit. But it also sets up boundaries within which profits cannot legally be made at the expense of employees or consumers.

What Is "Business Law"?

In truth, all types of laws affect all businesspeople. There are embezzlers and robbers who steal from businesses. There are thefts and destruction of merchandise—hijackings, arson, and so on. And there are, regrettably, a few businesses that use violence and threats of violence to get their way. Fortunately, these and similar situations, while covered by criminal laws and punishable by time in jail, are not the daily concern of most businesspeople.

There are, however, areas of the law that businesspeople—even those never confronted by a criminal act—have to deal with on a periodic basis. These areas can be conveniently classified into the following ten categories:

1. The Law of Contracts: The lifeblood of business is buying and selling, and agreements to buy and to sell are contracts. Over the centuries, the resolution of innumerable disputes between two or more businesses and between businesses and consumers has created an extensive body of law specifying how society expects contracting parties to act and how society will resolve disputes that the parties themselves cannot resolve.

2. The Law of Agency: Most businesses include workers besides the owner. And any time you have a situation other than one business owner dealing directly with another business owner, the rules of agency law come into play. When will an employee (the agent) legally bind an employer (the principal) to a course of action? What commitment and responsibility can a principal expect from an agent? Can a third party who wants to sell lamps to a motel chain reasonably rely upon the representations of the purchasing agent of the chain, or must the lamp salesperson eventually speak to the president of the motel chain about the transaction? Agency law provides the rules for answering these and related questions.

3. The Law of Sales: Today's merchant, whether selling paper clips or jet airplanes, sells his or her products in accordance with a body of laws controlling sales. Indeed, the sale of goods — that is, tangible and movable items — is such a major part of business affairs that a set of special rules — the Uniform Commercial Code — has been adopted across the United States. Designed to facilitate the free flow of commerce, the UCC allows businesspeople more leeway in creating, working under, and enforcing contracts than do the traditional common-law rules of contract law applicable to nongoods contracts.

4. The Law of Property: Private property ownership has special importance in our society, and there are special rules for the purchase and sale and handling of property. Both real property (land) and personal property (movable items like furniture, cars, or stereos) are deemed unique enough that they require precise laws governing their transfer from one party to another. Property law spells out how these transactions are handled.

5. The Law of Commercial Paper: Modern business practice — and most people's personal financial affairs for that matter — would be quite chaotic if all purchases had to be paid for with cash. But in our society, checks, promissory notes, loans, and credit cards are commonplace. These creations of convenience for the business community required a new body of law to set out the respective rights and responsibilities of the different parties involved in handling this new type of "money" — the law of commercial paper.

6. Laws Governing Business Organization: Historically, when a person had a business, the person and the business were inseparable. The problems and rewards of "the business" were the problems and rewards of the individual who had the business, and vice versa. With expansion of commerce, however, new forms of business ownership were created. Partnerships, limited partnerships, for-profit corporations, nonprofit corporations, and cooperatives all were created to meet certain needs and provide certain opportunities to the participating individuals. The laws governing business formation provide the necessary standards and guidance — not only for resolving disputes arising with these new business forms but for creating the business form appropriate for a given business enterprise in the first place.

7. The Law of Secured Transactions: If every business and every consumer paid for all their purchases in full, there would be no debtors and creditors. But modern commerce extends credit in a wide variety of circumstances, so special laws have evolved to regulate the relationships and rights and responsibilities of debtors and creditors.

8. Product Liability Laws: "Let the buyer beware!" Probably every adult has heard this historic phrase, born when a buyer's cautious attitude was the only protection available to the purchaser. But today, both businesses and individual consumers benefit from laws that can hold manufacturers or sellers responsible for the damages of improperly tested or dangerous or unsafe products. Product liability law is, as you'll see, one of the most rapidly evolving areas of law in modern society.

9. Insurance Law: There are many risks inherent in business life, risks that can be reduced by the purchase of insurance. The rules governing insurance — including coverage, claims presentation, and claims processing — and the standards for determining when insurance is necessary are all within the purview of insurance law and are an element of business law.

10. Tort Law: Any business, no matter how carefully and intelligently run, can be the victim of another's unscrupulous business practices. And any business can also find itself accused, rightly or wrongly, of perpetrating some wrongdoing. When the wrongdoing is civil, not criminal, the wrongdoing may fit within the boundaries of tort law. Efforts to assure that one's business neither intentionally nor unintentionally conducts itself in a tortious manner will be worth the effort; a wise businessperson needs to know the types of conduct that society will not tolerate between one private entity and another.

The crucial point in this classification is not that there are ten areas — another author might have nine, or eleven — or even what the names of the areas are, although they're moderately important. Rather, the key concept is that there is a sizable body of law that every businessperson *has* to deal with, like it or not. It's not a question of being "law abiding" or avoiding "criminal" behavior; business law encompasses matters that businesspeople must address in conducting business on a day-to-day basis. In this sense, business law is more akin to motor vehicle law than to criminal law. And just as you shouldn't drive a car without following the established laws for operating a motor vehicle, you shouldn't expect to conduct business without knowing and following the body of rules defined as "business law."

The Law and Personal Fairness

Most of us, like Blanford in our earlier scenario, tend to define "fairness" in terms of how a situation affects us personally. The law cannot afford to be personal, however. And in its efforts to be fair to both sides, it may appear grossly unfair to one side or the other. Take Blanford's experience with the computer equipment, for instance. Perhaps he didn't take the time he should have to thoroughly inspect the goods he'd ordered because he presumed that if anything went wrong, the law would be on his side. Perhaps it offended Blanford's personal sense of right and wrong to even imagine that the law would take the side of a large, profitable company like Gamma Computer over that of a small, struggling, privately owned business like his own. But that isn't how the law looks at things.

The courts cannot afford a sentimental perspective, however insensitive their objectivity may sometimes appear. Nor can they afford to become embroiled in lengthy debates over individual values — debates that may or may not have any final resolution. Laws must be clear and precise, must be enforceable, and must be capable of consistent interpretation. This doesn't mean, of course, that the details of the situation will never be considered; they certainly will. If Gamma Computer Company neglected to provide Blanford with a written warranty, or if the problem with the computers related to some internal malfunction that Blanford could not hope to have discovered through inspection, the whole scenario might well have turned out differently. Nevertheless, the issue isn't whether Big Bad Gamma took unfair advantage of Small Struggling Blanford. The issue concerns how each side behaved and how the law defines the relative rights of each in interpreting that behavior.

The law does not demand that the individual businessperson abandon his or her personal sense of ethics, naturally. But it does require that each person make his or her behavior conform to what the law says is just—regardless of whether the law seems to reflect one's *personal* sense of right and wrong. As society's values or perspectives begin to change, the law and courts also begin to look at old situations in a new light, reflecting those changes in societal values. If enough people come to view a given law as unfair or not reflective of values now seen as important, the law will most likely change.

The Consequences of Incorrect Assumptions About the Law

Even people who have never studied law or even looked inside a law book generally have some personal, private notions about how the law functions. Unfortunately, these beliefs—even when they're widely held within a business community—often reflect misconceptions that can create real problems for the businessperson. Here are just a few commonly held beliefs and attitudes that could get a businessperson into real trouble.

Assumption 1: The courts can't expect me to know every law. It may seem more than a little unreasonable, but in fact, the court can and does expect citizens to "know" the law. Wait a minute here, you say: Do attorneys and judges really suppose that laypeople spend all their free moments boning up on fine points of business law? Of course not. But it doesn't matter—ignorance of the law won't save you. Again, consider Blanford with his computers. Perhaps he didn't know that buyers have a duty to inspect purchased goods within a reasonable time. Does that ignorance then free him from that responsibility—and require Gamma Computer to keep its repair agreement open until whatever time Blanford gets around to inspecting the equipment? Not at all. The court takes the position that Blanford must either know the duties of buyer and seller under the law or suffer the consequences until he makes it his business to find out.

Similarly, many a businessperson may be hard-pressed to define the terms of a *bona fide offer*, may not know when a contract is binding, or may not know what constitutes discrimination in hiring practices. The court has no tolerance for this kind of ignorance. Of course, the employer who, for instance, practices discrimination quite unintentionally may get by with it—for a time, at least. But if she is sued, she cannot use ignorance of the law as a defense. Some persons—including her employees — may see her conduct as somewhat less reprehensible than if she had acted deliberately and maliciously. But in the eyes of the law, her guilt is defined by the law, not by her intentions.

Assumption 2: If it's in writing, it's binding; otherwise, it isn't. Potentially wrong on both counts — though in many ways, business life would be simpler if this common assumption were true. The fact is, however, some clauses within a written contract may be viewed by the court as too vague or unclear to be enforceable; or they may be viewed as unconscionably unfair to one party or the other. For instance, suppose Simmons agrees to sell Hutton a house for $50,000 cash. But one clause of their sales agreement stipulates that if Hutton is ever late with a payment, the cost of the house will double. Even if Hutton rashly agrees to such a promise, the court will probably not enforce it. Penalty clauses — especially those that enforce severe penalties for relatively small infractions — are rarely upheld even when fully, knowingly agreed to.

Conversely, an oral agreement may be fully enforceable even though it isn't backed by any written agreement. First, let's clarify one thing: A verbal agreement is a *real* contract. It isn't a "precontract" or an "imitation" contract or any such thing. It's real. The question is, is it provable and enforceable? And often the answer is no. This doesn't mean that the court will conclude that no contract exists. Sometimes, the behavior of the two parties will suggest to the court that a real contract exists, all right; the question is, what are the terms of that contract? And in the absence of any written documentation, the court will piece those terms together as best it can, recreating the contract, so to speak.

Of course, it may occur to you that the court-imposed terms could be extremely unacceptable to one or both sides. Quite right. So the moral of this story is, unless you want the court to define the terms of your contract for you in the event of a dispute, it's always best to put those terms in writing. And sometimes — depending on the nature of the contract — the contract *must* be in writing for the contract to be enforceable.

Let's suppose, for instance, that Bristol hires Chelsea as an office manager. Chelsea agrees to accept the position for $2,000 a month, and they seal the deal with a handshake. There is nothing in writing, however. In two weeks, Chelsea reports for work, as agreed, only to be told that sorry, the position has been filled by someone else — at the rate of $1,500 per month. Has Bristol breached a contract? Almost certainly. Can Chelsea prove it to the court's satisfaction? Well, that's much less certain. And even if she can, was she adversely affected by the breach of contract so that damages can be collected?

That she reported for work in the first place puts a point on Chelsea's side; it's not much to go on, true, but it will suggest to the court that Chelsea at least believed an agreement existed. But what would help even more is a letter from Bristol to Chelsea confirming the terms of their employment agreement and asking Chelsea to respond in writing if there were any misunderstanding. Were Chelsea able to produce such a document in court, Chelsea would have a very strong case indeed. In short, written documentation is highly desirable in confirming the terms of a verbal agreement. But in the absence of such documentation, and where the law allows it to do so, the court will use whatever evidence it can—including past behavior of the parties involved, or the behavior of other persons in the industry—to put the puzzle together. The implications are clear: Anyone who seals an agreement with a handshake believing that the contract isn't real unless it's written is playing a dangerous game. Prudent businesspeople do not agree either in writing *or* orally to any terms they do not intend to fulfill.

Assumption 3: Don't worry—a smart lawyer can always find a way out of trouble. Attorneys are sometimes viewed (rather ungraciously!) as crafty manipulators who can always find a loophole for those who are sufficiently desperate. Perhaps this perspective, however undeserved and unflattering, comes in part from attorneys' ability to make sense of a legal system that often seems to outsiders incomprehensible and mysterious. They routinely interpret and clarify the inscrutible. And when the interpretation works to our advantage, we tend to appreciate their cleverness. When it goes against us, we tend to see that same cleverness as manipulative.

The simple truth is, however, that putting all responsibility for our legal fates on an attorney's head is really a distortion of reality. Say a businessperson, Lawford, decides to purchase a tract of land as an investment, and agrees within the terms of the contract that the land will not be used for mining or any form of mineral resource development. Later, Lawford receives an enticing offer from an oil company that would like to do some exploratory drilling on the property—if only Lawford could get out of that pesky clause! Is it the competence of Lawford's attorney that holds the key to his fame and fortune? Of course not. It's the agreement itself. Lawyers can interpret the law. They can explain the extent to which an agreement is binding, and define the consequences for violating an agreement. And sometimes, true enough, they can go so far within the bounds of law as to find a new way of viewing an arrangement that one party believes is quite unfair. But they cannot legalize the illegal. Nor can they erase existing agreements or replace them with new ones unless both sides want it that way.

Assumption 4: If anything goes wrong, we'll just sue. Many of us, at one time or other—perhaps in a moment of extreme anger—have threatened to sue someone. We may not even voice the threat out loud—just think it. And usually, we don't really mean it. In a cooler moment, we recognize the threat for what it is—just a way of letting off steam.

Sometimes, though, the threat gets serious. It's important for the businessperson to recognize that suing the other guy isn't the solution to most business disputes. In the first place, suit is only appropriate when there are sufficient grounds to support it. And these are carefully defined under the law. For example, office manager Hillocks—given sufficient provocation—might sue her employer Hammond for defamation of character or for discrimination on the job or for failure to fulfill an employment contract. She cannot, however, sue Hammond because he's rude to her on the job or because he seems to favor all other employees with better work assignments or because she generally disagrees with the way he runs the company for which she works. All these things may anger her—justifiably, perhaps, from a social or ethical perspective. But rudeness and incompetence rarely provide justification for lawsuit.

Second, even when sufficient grounds for suit exist, that is no guarantee the court will see things the plaintiff's way. Hillocks may feel, for instance, that her being passed over for more challenging work assignments constitutes a form of sexual discrimination. Perhaps it does—or perhaps not. Maybe her employer, Hammond, really does favor his male employees with the more challenging and interesting work assignments. But unless Hillocks can prove that her perception is accurate and that she has comparable qualifications, her case is unlikely to hold up in court, *even if* she feels capable of handling the work and *even if* Hammond isn't always equitable in assigning projects to employees. Courts do not try to probe inside people's heads; they look at proof—of actions and intentions—in making their rulings.

And finally, even when the plaintiff wins the case, the cost of the whole thing may make him wonder whether the effort was worthwhile. Suppose Bentley sells Larson a desk for $2,000. Larson pays $1,300, but never comes up with the rest of the money. Should Bentley sue to recover it? Well, if he's sufficiently enraged over the unfairness of the whole thing, suing Larson might be one way of venting that rage—but it could prove an expensive way. If small claims court is not an option, Bentley will have to hire an attorney, pay the court costs, pay the administrative costs associated with actually filing the suit, writing up the complaint, and so forth. In the end, perhaps Bentley will spend $1,000 or more to recover $700—a questionable bargain at best. Small wonder that even attorneys themselves tend to look on suit as a kind of last resort, most often advising and helping clients to work out settlements or find some other means of resolving their differences if possible.

Assumption 5: I'll never be sued; I try to treat people fairly and have only good intentions. Of course, the nagging fear of getting into legal trouble haunts most cautious businesspeople. Nevertheless, many cling to the faith that if they really intend to do right by everyone, nothing so devastating as a lawsuit will befall them personally. Surely lawsuits, like accidents, happen mostly to "those other people."

Probably it's fair to say that if you try to deceive or cheat others, your chances of being sued are far greater. At the same time, though, acting with the very best of intentions will not free you from all liability if a problem does arise between you and a business associate or customer.

It's important to realize that most lawsuits arise out of a misunderstanding that the parties are unable to resolve on their own. Thus, saying you'll never be sued is a little like saying you'll never be involved in a disagreement. Maybe you never will—*if* you deal only with people who think as you do, *if* you get everything in writing, and *if* you make up your mind that in the event a disagreement does occur, you will be the one to compromise. Most businesspeople find that that is at least one *if* too many.

Remember, too, that a lawsuit is not meant as a form of civilized revenge. It's a carefully structured means by which the court has the opportunity to hear both sides of a dispute and render whatever verdict is called for under the facts and law of the case. To see in simple terms how this might work, picture two small children fighting over one apple. The parent resolves the conflict in an expedient and (from the parent's perspective) fair manner by slicing the apple in two. Note, however, that while the parent is happy with this outcome, neither child may see the fairness in it. Neither got the "verdict" she wanted. Law can be like that. The law promises that in the event of a conflict, both sides will be heard and the court will make every attempt at a fair resolution in light of the law. It does not promise, however, that the position of either side will be upheld in full, nor that either side will be happy with the results.

Acquiring Sound Legal Advice

Knowing the consequences of incorrect assumptions is not enough in the business world. A more proactive approach is to practice preventive maintenance just as you would on your car. One recommendation is to consider using a lawyer as an ongoing legal advisor. If you own or manage a business, you're likely to face questions like these every day:

- What sorts of product warranties must be provided to customers?
- What steps must be taken to ensure the safety of customers or employees?
- How should an employment agreement be written up?
- What elements should be included in a contract with clients, buyers, or vendors?
- If someone breaches a contract, what options are open?
- If I am sued, how do I defend myself?
- When a disagreement arises, when is a lawsuit the best option and when are other options preferable?
- What sorts of insurance—and how much insurance—do I need to protect my business interests?

Most businesspeople have some idea how to answer all or most of these questions. But partial information isn't good enough to establish a secure legal position. As we've seen, even minor misunderstandings can cause problems—problems that sometimes cannot be settled out of court.

It's also wise to use an attorney who specializes in business law. These days, with laws changing and evolving, with new laws being created constantly, no lawyer can specialize in every phase of law. An attorney who specializes in divorce cases is not usually the best person to see about drafting an employment agreement.

It's common practice, of course, to hire an attorney once there's a real problem to deal with. But from a planning perspective, that's like installing a sprinkler system after a fire breaks out. Why not select an attorney before problems and questions arise, when there is still time to reflect and make a good choice?

An interview is a good place to begin. During the interview, the businessperson can ask questions—just as he or she would of any other prospective employee. Questions about fees and experience, for instance, are best settled in advance. It's also perfectly appropriate to request references. An attorney is among the most important employees any business can have, and there is nothing wrong with ensuring that the person is both competent and appropriate for the position.

You can, of course, fire your attorney if all does not go well. But it can be a hassle. It's a little like starting over with a new physician. All the files, all the records, must be transferred. New forms must be completed, new working arrangements established. Sometimes all this is necessary, but it's always preferable to make the best possible decision the first time around.

SOME PRACTICAL ADVICE

First, if you're in the position of being a business owner or manager, consider getting a legal check-up from an attorney. In most cases, the fee you'll pay will be more than offset by the peace of mind gained through having something other than your own memory and imagination to rely upon for sound legal advice.

Once you've decided on which attorney to establish a working relationship with, make good use of his or her time. Ask the attorney to review *major* written documents associated with the business—not every letter or memo the company produces, but certainly new contract forms and any formal regulations or policies. An attorney who specializes in business law can, of course, create contracts or other needed documents from scratch, but it isn't always necessary or cost-effective to do so. Models abound, and some common documents—sales agreements, for instance—may look quite similar from one company to the next.

It's a good idea to get a realistic picture of any liabilities relating to the products or services provided by a company. These may be modest or quite dramatic. For instance, a business that rents horses for overnight trail rides in the mountains likely faces greater liabilities relating to consumer safety than one that rents video tapes. But virtually all businesses have liabilities of one sort or another, so assuming otherwise is risky. Similarly, it's often wise to determine what sort of insurance a business needs and how much insurance makes for a sound business investment. An attorney can provide such information.

Finally, don't approach the law with fear and trembling. If you do, you may not approach it at all. And if that happens, you'll be like the patient who avoids diagnosis, entrusting the future of your life (or business life) to chance. The prudent businessperson is intimidated just enough to be prompted into getting good information. Legal surprises *can* be nasty. It's wise to be prepared. But keep in mind— as we'll try to emphasize—that the law exists primarily to support the efforts of the well-intentioned businessperson and to ensure a social and commercial environment that is conducive to business success.

A WORD TO THE STUDENT

For purposes of this course, we ask that you put yourself, mentally and psychologically, in the position of a businessperson. Ask yourself as you go through the lessons, "From the businessperson's perspective, how would this situation look?" Of course, you may not ever actually own or manage your own business. But if you do, you'll have a good sense of how the law looks through the eyes of a businessperson. Further, even if you never become a business manager, it's almost inevitable that you will — more than once — find yourself in the position of client, customer, or employee. And even in these roles, you're likely to find some knowledge of legal rights and responsibilities more than modestly helpful.

Ultimately, however, this course is designed to provide particular assistance to the present or future businessperson who needs to know how business law can and should influence the operations of his or her business.

HOW TO USE THIS STUDY GUIDE

This study guide serves several purposes. First, as its name suggests, it is intended to guide you through the course in a structured way by laying out information and assignments much as a teacher might do within the classroom. The study guide specifies which pages of the textbook will be covered in each lesson, which video pertains to the lesson, and so forth. It also provides an overview that highlights key points that will be covered within the textbook and helps clarify or expand difficult concepts.

The study guide is in no way intended to replace the textbook, and if you use it in this way, you are likely to miss very important information. However, the material covered in the textbook should be more approachable and understandable if you first read the learning objectives and overview in the corresponding study guide lesson.

The study guide contains a number of different sections related to each lesson. The following paragraphs describe how each should be used.

Assignments. The study guide is the first place you will turn when beginning a lesson. As mentioned, the overview contained in the study guide is designed to give you a good start on the content of the lesson. But you can't master the course content using only the study guide as your information source. You will also need to view the accompanying video program and read the appropriate sections in the textbook.

At the end of each overview, you'll find the assignments for that lesson, including the reading assignment in the textbook. The assignment section will tell you how to proceed with the rest of your study. Here, as an example, is the assignment for Lesson 1.

- Before you watch the video program for Lesson 1, be sure you've read through the preceding overview, familiarized yourself with the learning objectives for this lesson, reviewed the key terms, and looked over each of the explanatory sections which follow. Then, read Chapter 1 (pages 4-7) and Chapter 6 (pages 92-95) of the book, Davidson et al., *Business Law: Principles and Cases*, 3rd edition.

- When you have read all the remaining sections of the study guide for this first lesson, watch the video program for Lesson 1.

Key Terms. Pay close attention to the key terms for each lesson. In some cases, exam questions will ask you to define one or more of these key terms. But even more important, understanding the key terms will make your reading much simpler.

Self-Test. Except for this introductory lesson, each study guide chapter includes a self-test—a set of ten questions that broadly cover the material presented in that lesson's video, study guide overview, and textbook assignment. These questions are intended to test your general knowledge of the information presented. (You will see examples of the types of questions used in the description of the examination bank below.)

The self-test questions are not meant to be tricky or particularly difficult. If you've read through the study guide overview and key terms, studied the textbook assignment thoroughly, and watched the video program carefully, you should find them relatively simple. If you miss one or two, don't be too concerned; simply note the textbook pages referenced for the item in the answer key at the back of the study guide, reread the relevant textbook and study guide overview information, and look at the question again. In most cases, the correct answer should now be quite obvious. But if you miss more than two or three self-test questions, consider reviewing the entire lesson again.

Your Opinion, Please. At the end of each study guide lesson, you'll be asked to give your opinion—your "legally informed" opinion, based on thoughtful consideration of what you've learned in the lesson—relating to hypothetical situations presented in scenario form. In most cases, one of the scenario characters will (or will want to) sue another, and you will be asked to comment on the appropriateness of this action and predict the outcome. We have tried to present the scenarios in such a way that there is no immediately obvious right or wrong response, though in most cases, one party will have a somewhat stronger position than another. This is another way of saying that one position is likely to be more *supportable* than another, but (as is common in real life) the facts do not lead to an immediately obvious verdict. It is your job to sort out the legal details and determine the most probable outcome.

You should prepare your answers to the *Your Opinion, Please* scenarios as if you were going to use them as the basis for an essay. In fact, your instructor may sometimes choose to have you use them in this way and may ask you to expand your responses in writing. The *Your Opinion, Please* scenarios are given at the end of each study guide lesson; be sure to review the questions at the end of each scenario.

THE EXAM BANK

A multiple-choice exam bank has been prepared for each lesson in *Business and the Law*. Questions are based on information presented in the textbook, study guide, and video. Your instructor will select from this exam bank those questions he or she feels are most important and relevant when it's time for a course examination.

Both the exam bank and the self-tests include questions written on several different levels of complexity. Level 1 questions test your recall and your attentiveness to important details presented in the study guide, video, or textbook. Level 2 questions require you to interpret, summarize, or consolidate information. Level 3 questions require that you apply what you have learned to a hypothetical situation, often involving fictional characters in a business context. Level 4 questions also require application of information but with considerable analysis required. You may need to integrate several different bits of information or do some comparing. Level 5 questions—the most sophisticated and challenging—require that you synthesize information from multiple sources and use that information in evaluating a situation or predicting outcomes.

It may sound strange, but some of the questions don't have a *correct* answer. What they all have is a *best* answer, and that's the option you should choose. A major concept of this course is that very little is absolutely clear-cut in the law—and the items are designed to reflect that concept. Often, you'll be asked to choose the *best* option, or identify what *probably* would happen, or determine what principle would *likely* apply. But if you approach the items thinking that knowing important legal principles will always lead you to a single, obviously correct answer to every question, you're likely to be disappointed.

The self-test and exam bank questions are not intended to trick you, but neither are the best answers always obvious. In order to do well on the tests, you will have to consider how you would apply the principles presented in the lesson in real life situations. Memorizing facts will help you only in a limited way. Though a few questions are fact-based, the vast majority require you to use your thinking skills to analyze, apply, synthesize, and evaluate the information presented in the lesson.

The answer keys for the self-test questions in this study guide and the exam bank questions your instructor may choose to use often contain explanations that will help you understand why the answer given as correct is the best choice. When you don't understand why the proposed answer is best, reading the explanation provided can help you see the reasoning behind the answer and better understand how to apply the principles learned during the lesson.

Here are a few sample questions to illustrate the various levels of complexity. The correct answer for each of these questions is indicated by an asterisk, but the answers to the self-test questions for all the other lessons are given in the answer keys at the end of the study guide.

1. Today, the law of business includes the study of all but one of the following. Which of the following is not considered a component of business law?

   a. Contracts
   b. Sales
   c. Partnerships
   d. Divorce and custody settlements (*)

   (Level 1, Study Guide) Notice that this question is phrased almost word for word as it appears in the first part of the study guide overview.

2. From the businessperson's perspective, which of the following most accurately describes the underlying purpose of our business law system? This legal system serves *mainly* to

   a. punish lawbreakers.
   b. create an economic environment in which business can thrive. (*)
   c. sufficiently complicate business transactions so that commerce does not proceed too rapidly.
   d. protect the rights of consumers.

   (Level 2, Study Guide) This information must be extracted through careful reading of the study guide lesson. It isn't directly stated in just this way anywhere; rather, it's a paraphrasing of ideas emphasized throughout the reading.

3. Emerson hires Wilcox to care for his horses while Emerson is out of town. They have no written contract but do shake hands to seal their detailed oral agreement. Do they have an actual contract, according to information presented in the study guide overview?

   a. No, definitely not; handshakes are never binding.
   b. Yes, they do. (*)
   c. We cannot say without knowing whether a court of law would *enforce* their agreement.

   (Level 3, Study Guide) True, the agreement between Wilcox and Emerson might not be enforceable just in the way they intended, but an oral agreement can be just as binding as a written contract. Notice that in a Level 3 question, you are often asked to *apply* the information presented in the lesson to a hypothetical situation.

4. Washington is uncertain whether a particular test his company gives to screen applicants for employment is discriminatory. The test is very useful in selecting applicants, but Washington doesn't want to get himself or his company into trouble. He could consult an attorney, but that might prove expensive, and no one has complained about the test so far. At this point, Washington should probably

   a. discontinue the test even if it's useful; it's better to give it up than take any chances.

b. continue using the test unless someone complains; after all, Washington cannot really get into trouble if he doesn't *know* the test is discriminatory.

c. consult an attorney about reviewing the test—even though it will mean some investment of time and money. (*)

(Level 4, Study Guide) Notice that in this Level 4 question you must integrate several kinds of information. There is more than one issue involved: Is the test discriminatory? If Washington doesn't know it's discriminatory and it is, can he still get himself or his company into trouble? Is it worth the trouble and expense to consult an attorney *before* anything really goes wrong? And the answer, of course, is that since ignorance of the law is no excuse for violating the law, Washington is taking a big risk in continuing to use a test about which he has no valid information. Better to spend a small amount of money consulting an attorney than to risk what could be a significant amount of money if his company is sued for discriminatory employment practices.

5. As the study guide points out, people make many assumptions about the law which turn out to be untrue altogether or at least highly misleading. Probably the *main* reason for these mistaken assumptions is that

a. attorneys and other representatives of the law have made the whole thing deliberately confusing.

b. when it comes right down to it, most laypeople simply lack the background and ability to clearly understand business law.

c. the law has been presented in such a distorted way in the media — especially on television and in films — that people no longer understand its purpose.

d. most people have limited personal experience with the law and often base what they know on hearsay. (*)

(Level 5, Study Guide) Questions at this level require you to demonstrate skill in evaluating and assessing the information presented. You may even be required to synthesize some new information based on what you've learned. For example, to answer this question, you must not only take note of the fact that we all make assumptions about the law, but must ask, "What do these various assumptions have in common?" Nothing in the study guide suggests that Option A, B, or C would necessarily be true and, in fact, all are exaggerations. We hope you recognize them as such — though, admittedly, any one of these statements might be deemed *partially* correct in some situations and to some extent. What's really important about the assumptions presented in the study guide, however, is that all rely on very limited information, information that is not gathered through firsthand experience. Therefore, Option D is the most likely answer of the four.

These few examples should give you a good idea of the kinds of questions to expect on the self-tests and exams associated with the course. If you read the study guide overview and key terms, study the textbook assignment carefully, watch the assigned video for the lesson, pay close attention to the key terms, test your understanding of the lesson's concepts with the self-test questions, and respond thoughtfully to the *Your Opinion, Please* scenarios, you should be very well prepared for the exams.

YOUR OPINION, PLEASE

Just a brief note before you begin this section: As mentioned earlier, each of the study guide lessons contains a set of hypothetical scenarios designed to illustrate both the key points of the legal concepts you've just studied and to show you how the law is rarely applied in a black-and-white manner. As you consider each of the legal problems presented throughout the course, we suggest that you focus less on determining the correct outcome of the dispute and more on the different principles that affect the situation. These problems are purposely difficult and are intentionally designed to prevent you from finding a single, indisputably correct answer.

Now, read each of the following scenarios and answer the questions about the decisions you would make in each situation. Give these questions some serious thought; they may be used as the basis for the development of a more complex essay. You should base your decisions on what you've learned from this lesson, though you may incorporate outside readings or information gained through your own experience if it is relevant.

Scenario I

MacIntyre has recently decided to start his own company. He and a team of craftsmen intend to do specialized remodeling of both residential and commercial buildings. He is wondering about the advisability of consulting an attorney, but it seems very early in his new company's career to be worrying about such things. The company is very small, after all, and includes only himself and three employees.

MacIntyre is advised by his father-in-law, Edmonds, to consult—for now—with the attorney who has handled the family's financial affairs, including real estate transactions and wills. "He's a friend," Edmonds points out. "We've known him for years, he's familiar with our affairs, and we all trust him. You couldn't get better legal advice anywhere."

What's your opinion? Based on what you know of the situation, do you think MacIntyre would be hasty in seeking the counsel of an attorney at this point, so early in the development of his business? Or would it be a sound idea? If he does decide to see an attorney, should he accept the advice of his father-in-law as to which attorney to consult?

- Do you think MacIntyre should visit with an attorney at this point? Why or why not?

- If he does see an attorney, should he follow his father-in-law's advice and work with the family attorney?
- What advantages might there be in the approach you suggest?
- What disadvantages might there be?

Scenario 2

Hilary has just been offered a position with Western Star Manufacturing. She is satisfied with her employment agreement as it's written — except for one clause, which stipulates that she may not work for any other employers or companies while employed by Western Star, and that she can be terminated without notice if she is caught violating this agreement. Since the job at Western Star is only part-time — three days a week — Hilary is not sure she can afford to limit her opportunities this way. Still, she has no full-time employment prospects. She's also afraid that if she doesn't sign the contract without raising any objections, she'll lose the chance for this job.

A friend, Ludwell, who has studied some business law, assures her that there is nothing to worry about since "no court would ever enforce such an unfair agreement." Further, he tells her, she might as well go ahead and sign because if she has second thoughts, "there is always a loophole — a way out."

What's your opinion? Based on what you know of the situation, do you think Hilary should sign the employment agreement as it's written? Why or why not? Is Ludwell's advice sound? How would you advise Hilary at this point?

- Should Hilary sign the employment agreement?
- What are the potential ramifications if she *does* sign?
- What are the potential ramifications if she *does not* sign?
- What general advice would you give Hilary at this point? In other words, what steps should she take in resolving her situation and making a sound decision?

2

Law and the Legal System

LEARNING OBJECTIVES

Upon completing your study of this lesson, you should be able to

- Identify and discuss the elements that are incorporated in the definition of *law*.
- Identify six components that a legal system needs, from the perspective of the society it serves.
- List and discuss the purposes of a legal system.
- Identify and explain the eight elements (sources of law) which, taken together, comprise the entire body of law in the American legal system.
- Describe and give examples of each of the four classifications of law in the American legal system: *federal v. state* law, *common v. statutory* law, *civil v. criminal* law, and *substantive v. procedural* law.
- Explain the role and importance of the U.S. Constitution in the American legal system.
- Distinguish between the federal and state court systems and identify the types of courts which make up each system.
- State the stages or steps through which a lawsuit passes from when a person first visits a lawyer to when a final decision is made in court.

Virtually every society on earth has laws: rules set forth and enforced by someone in authority for the purpose of keeping order within the society. Even in primitive societies that may not have written laws, the rules that govern the way people in that society interact or conduct their daily affairs are likely to be well known to everyone. Chances are, of course, that in a society where law is a matter of tradition and not part of a written system, the law is relatively simple. In our society, by contrast, things are quite different.

For one thing, our law exists in writing. This apparently modest distinction has profound and far-reaching implications for the ways in which law is used and interpreted. To begin with, our legal system is anything but simple; it's extraordinarily complex. So much so, in fact, that we must often rely on specialists — judges and attorneys who have devoted their professional lives to its study — to interpret the law for us.

On the other hand, though, our legal system has one important factor in common with that of the primitive society: it is *not imposed from without*, but has evolved to reflect the values of society and to promote the general social welfare. As much as anything, this single factor greatly affects our whole attitude toward the legal system and toward those who maintain and enforce that system.

Consider, for instance, the businessperson who is sued. For the time being, it may seem to this person that the law is very unfriendly — a forbidding, threatening sort of entity, a trap for the unwary. The whole business of appearing in court, being represented by an attorney, and having others — to some extent — control one's fate may seem intimidating, even frightening. Appearing before a judge or jury isn't something most of us do routinely, after all.

But to an objective observer who comprehends the rationale behind the whole legal system, it is clear that the underlying purpose of the law is simply to threaten potential violators. The law attempts to protect those who wish to conduct their business in a safe and sane environment where systematic, consistent rules maintain the general order. And the courts exist to provide a forum for those who feel their rights have been infringed upon. In other words, lawsuits, hearings, and trial proceedings have evolved as a logical means of getting at the "truth" of a given situation, sorting out the facts, and providing a reasonably fair resolution to both sides.

OVERVIEW

As we've noted already, every society on earth has laws in some form. In a more primitive society, where change happens slowly, the "legal system" may remain relatively constant over long periods of time — even for centuries. A society that changes very little hasn't much need for new laws or for new interpretations of existing laws. Law in such societies is largely a matter of tradition and custom.

That is true to some extent in our society as well, since much of our legal heritage is based on the English laws in place during colonial days. However, our legal system has changed markedly throughout our country's history, growing in complexity to match the needs of a changing society. Our culture isn't simple anymore; neither is our economy. As our lifestyles shift and new products and ways of doing business expand our marketplace, our legal system must evolve to answer questions no one would have thought to pose a few years ago: What are the appropriate procedures when the increased debt incurred during a corporate buyout lowers the value of investors' bonds? What code of ethics must a Wall Street stockbroker uphold? How much information can a developer of computer programs "borrow" from another before it's *too* much? Still, while the system undergoes continual revision and expansion, its ultimate purpose must remain constant: to preserve the welfare of the society it exists to serve.

Law: A Definition

The *law*, as it's generally presented in the textbook, consists of *rules that must be obeyed*. That's a simple definition. Here's one that expands this basic definition just a bit: *The law is a set of principles, rules, and standards of conduct that*

- *has general application in the society,*
- *has been developed by an authority for that society, and,*
- *when violated, results in the imposition of a penalty by society.*

The term *law* also has a more limited definition: *a rule declared by a legislature*. As used in our discussion, however, the term *law* will encompass not only federal law and state statutes, but also local ordinances and city and county regulations. It will also encompass court decisions, which interpret or apply the law to a particular set of facts or circumstances and thus themselves become part of the law on which future decisions are based. Law, in short, includes any rules that are enforceable by the courts.

The concept of enforceability is crucial to our discussion. It is this distinction that separates *rules* from laws. All laws are rules, but not all rules are laws. Sometimes there's a big difference. For instance, a local library may have a rule stipulating that patrons must speak quietly. But a person who shouts in a library won't be arrested and taken to jail. She may incur the wrath of the librarian, but the law will not bother with enforcing the rule of silence.

Similarly, a school may have a rule specifying that children must wear rubber-soled shoes on the gym floor. If a child wears hard-soled shoes to gym class, the school may not allow her to participate in sports activities that day, but her parents will not be fined or imprisoned. It's up to the persons or agencies who make these rules to enforce them as best they can; the law will not intervene to enforce this type of rule. Therefore, we say that rules are not *legally enforceable*.

On the other hand, persons who exceed the speed limit, violate copyright laws, embezzle funds, or otherwise act in a manner that is contrary to the written law of our society are subject to legal sanctions. They may be required to pay money damages, they may be subject to a court order—or injunction—which directs them to do or not do something, or they may wind up in prison. It is sometimes said that the law operates like the policies and procedures of a corporation. The law sets standards of behavior and principles of action. Citizens, like employees in a company, are asked to meet these standards, and when they are not met, appropriate steps are taken to ensure compliance and restore the status quo.

We wouldn't need a legal system, of course, if we could absolutely count on everyone to behave in the same "fair" way all the time. But that is not the way of things. In the first place, some members of society will inevitably place a higher priority on their own personal welfare than on the greater social good. So laws exist, in part, to hold the behavior of such persons in check. In addition, however, not everyone holds the same view of "fairness." In the absence of any written definitions for acceptable behavior, therefore, we would likely find ourselves mired in endless theoretical debates about what was right or not right. We might get little else done, and our whole business system would collapse around us as the debates raged on. Law maintains a sense of order in our society. It simplifies our lives to know that the rules are the same for everyone, that they are more or less constant day to day, and that they exist in writing and are therefore verifiable. Most of us would be very uncomfortable with a legal system that existed only in the hearts and minds of judges and attorneys, however trustworthy they might be.

One way of looking at the law is to say that it is an endless search for justice— fairness, that is—given the values of society at any one time. If one interest or "side" is favored in the law, it is usually because the values or perspectives of that interest are more accepted by society at that time. But societal values change over time— and thus are reflected in new legislation and new court decisions that try to strike a different balance between competing factors or that introduce new factors, as appropriate, to consider in the decisionmaking process. In fact, matters such as regulation against excessive interest rates, recognition of minimum wage laws, rules against child labor, restrictions against air and water pollution, and any number of matters that we now accept as appropriate for consideration were all at one time not even allowed to enter into the process of deciding what was a "fair" resolution to a dispute.

Within this context, laws exist not only to promote the general social welfare, but also to maintain a critical balance between two sides on any issue: between employer and employee, for example, or salesperson and customer. True, those who break the law may be fined or jailed. But the law's intent in imposing these sanctions is not primarily to seek revenge. It is to restore a sense of order and balance to the situation. Further, any time the law seems to consistently favor one side over another—to give employers greater rights and privileges than employees, for instance—the law is likely to evolve to place matters back in balance.

Of course, perfect justice isn't always achievable. A man whose money is stolen and then returned when the thief is captured may feel that justice has been well served. But a parent who loses a child in a traffic accident may feel very poorly compensated when the driver is fined or jailed for a short period. Again, however, we must remember that the law does not exist to avenge all injustices. It provides a vehicle for reflecting our values and forming a society responsive to changing values—and that allows us to treat *all* citizens equally in light of those values.

Remember, too, that the law is grounded on the concept of *practicability*. In other words, while great emphasis is placed on the need to search for justice, there is recognition of the need to make the search as practical and expedient as possible. For instance, if Gray is caught walking against the traffic signal, she may simply be given a citation on the spot—which she can contest, of course. But the court will not spend its time tracking down witnesses to verify whether the light actually was red when Gray entered the intersection, or whether the arresting officer was positioned at a good angle to render a fair judgment. All of this might seem at first glance to be in the interest of fairness, but in the end, it would benefit society little. Further, the cost of such investigations would be prohibitive, and would be disproportionate to the tiny increment of additional "justice" achieved. The law must put its energies into achieving the greatest good for the greatest numbers—at the lowest reasonable cost. After all, any legal system must be financed by the society it serves.

The Six Needs of a Legal System

In the preceding paragraphs, we talked about fairness—fairness to both sides of a controversy, and fairness, in a larger sense, to society as a whole. How is this fairness achieved? Well, as you might expect, great care is given to the way in which laws are written. It is expected that our laws will meet several important criteria.

First, laws must be *based on reason*. That is, there must be some demonstrable reason for a law to exist. Sometimes, we can use our own experience or intuitive sense of right and wrong to comprehend the reasons for a law. It is obviously not in the interests of society to allow citizens to discharge firearms in the middle of a busy city street, for example. Similarly, no reasonable person questions laws governing homicide, robbery, rape, or other serious crimes. But suppose the law suddenly required all persons to wear yellow socks. Most of us would want to know the reason behind this new ruling, and we would be quite within our rights to question it.

Second, laws must be *definite*, not vague. For instance, a law stating that *an automobile's driver must wear a safety belt while operating a motor vehicle* would be enforceable because it's specific and clear. A driver at any given time is either wearing a safety belt or not; it is not a matter of opinion. By contrast, a law requiring persons to *be considerate when operating a motor vehicle* would not be enforceable. It's too open to subjective interpretation. It is one thing to prove that a driver has exceeded the speed limit or run a red light or driven the wrong way on a one-way street. Such allegations are observable and provable, given sufficient fact-based evidence. But there is no ready way to prove that someone has behaved in an inconsiderate manner; that is a matter of judgment and opinion. And few of us would like the notion of being subjected to fines or other sanctions on the basis of someone's opinion. We want laws we can understand, laws that are likely to be interpreted and enforced with consistency over time and from one situation to the next.

Third, the law must be *flexible*. Wait a moment, you say. Haven't we just made the point that it's desirable to have consistency in the way the law is applied? Certainly. But the courts recognize that individual situations are different. In fact, one important reason our legal system changes over time is that judges and others who deal with the law are constantly seeking more perceptive, more accurate, and more fair ways of interpreting and applying laws in diverse situations. It is extraordinarily difficult, if not impossible, to devise any written rule that will apply equitably to all situations. Sometimes the law must flex and stretch a bit. For instance, consider a speeder who is out joyriding, perhaps drinking as he drives. He is caught exceeding the speed limit by 20 mph. Is his offense the same as that of a woman, also exceeding the speed limit by 20 mph, who is rushing her injured husband to the hospital? In a factual sense, yes. But in a more personal assessment of the situation, most of us are likely to say no. The events may be similar, but the circumstances are not. The law will allow for some consideration of circumstances as long as the rules do not become *so* flexible as to be meaningless. Thus, the law values consistency, but consistency applied within the context of intelligence and wisdom.

Fourth, the law must be *practical* in its orientation. It can go just so far in providing justice or resolving problems. If an innocent bystander is shot in the knee during an armed robbery and, as a result, loses the proper use of his right leg, the law can do only so much to compensate for this unfortunate situation. There is no legal remedy that will restore to this citizen the use of his leg. But a practical solution might be to allow suit for damages, so that the injured victim receives some monetary compensation for his discomfort, medical expense, and disability. This isn't a perfect solution. But it's a practical one.

Fifth, the law must be *published*. In other words, it must exist in writing and be accessible to every citizen. We tend to take this for granted, but think if it were otherwise. Suppose you are arrested one day, not really understanding why, and taken to court to appear before the judge. When you ask for some explanation as to how you have broken the law, the judge says, "Well, I can't actually point to any *written* law. But believe me, I've seen many criminals come and go in my time, and your behavior *is* criminal. I just sense it." This scenario may seem a little extreme. But it isn't far removed from how things might operate if our legal system existed only in the heads—or even in the private notebooks—of those who enforced it. We have a right to demand that the standards for which we're held accountable be spelled out in writing.

Of course, this doesn't mean that the courts will go to great lengths to interpret laws to citizens on a one-to-one basis, or even to make sure that every citizen is aware of the law. Knowing and understanding the law is each individual's responsibility. The court *assumes* that every person *does* know the law, whether that is in fact the case or not. This may seem like a big assumption—and it is—given that there is an overwhelming amount to know. But common sense tells us it cannot be otherwise. If ignorance were a defense for breaking the law, then it would be extremely hard to prosecute any lawbreaker ever. Everyone from shoplifter to bank robber would have only to say, "Sorry! I just didn't realize that was the law!" And soon our society would dissolve into chaos.

Sixth, the law must be *final*. That is, there must be a point at which any situation is fully resolved. This doesn't rule out the possibility that some cases tried in court will be appealed and reconsidered. A prosecutor in a criminal case usually does not have the right to appeal if the court finds in favor of the defendant; but a defendant often has the right to appeal to a higher court. Eventually, however, the chain of appeals is exhausted, and one way or another, the case is resolved. Once this happens, it's over. The decision is made, and both sides must live with it. Again—consider the alternative. Were this not the way of things, there would be no point in taking a case to court. If citizens went about saying, "Well, I don't think I'll accept *that* verdict," soon no one would respect the authority of the law.

The Eight Purposes of a Legal System

Let's take a moment here to distinguish between *needs* and *purposes*. We've discussed the six needs in the sense of criteria that a good legal system must meet. In other words, there are certain things we expect of our laws if they are to work well for us. Purposes are a little different. Here, we consider the overriding goals of the legal system as a whole—not so much the qualities or characteristics of individual laws, but what our legal system is attempting to achieve.

First, our legal system seeks to *achieve justice*. If a certain manufacturer misrepresents goods in its advertising or fails to live up to its warranties, society now believes that such behavior is unfair. Through the legal system, it will provide support to the consumer who is wronged as a result of the unfairness.

Second, the legal system *provides police power*. We generally think of police power as being exemplified by officers in uniform. But the real emphasis here is on enforceability. There is little point in having laws that can be broken or disregarded without consequence. We derive our feelings of safety and security from the knowledge that the laws we create as a society will be systematically upheld.

Third, the legal system *maintains the peace and, generally, the status quo*. Laws are not intended to make life difficult or complicated for businesspeople and other citizens. They're designed to further our society's view of what will make our life more livable. Further, they tend to ensure that change does not occur without a good reason. If a new tax is imposed, it's because Congress saw some justification for it. If no justification can be provided for an idea, the law takes the position that it is better to keep things as they are. Should pollution laws be liberalized? Not without a sound reason; that's the law's position. The law is not inflexible. But it is firm, and, generally, can be modified only with sound reasoning based on evidence.

Fourth, the legal system *provides answers*—answers in disputes between individuals, between corporations, between the state or other governing body and its citizens. Eventually, in any dispute, the law will take a side and, in doing so, will further our already vast definition of right and wrong. Of course, we may not always like or agree with the answers the law provides. And it is our privilege to disagree, so long as that disagreement doesn't provoke a violation of the law. But think how frustrating it would be if the law did *not* answer our legal questions in definite terms. Suppose Tudor sues Sidney for assault and battery. We would not expect the court to say, "Well, this case is a toughie, all right. There's really no way to tell who's in the right." No matter how difficult the issue, no matter how sensitive the question, the law cannot skirt issues; it must take a position.

Fifth, the law *provides protection*. For example, every person in the United States has civil rights guaranteed under the country's Constitution and Bill of Rights. The law protects these rights and ensures that in the event they are violated, the person who suffers as a result of the violation will have legal recourse. In addition, the law protects each person's individual rights. Few of us find the world a totally safe place to be all the time, but we do have the comfort of knowing that if we should be assaulted, robbed, or otherwise personally abused, the law is on our side and wants to hold the violators accountable for their actions. Also, the law provides protection for property rights. Neither real property nor personal property can be taken from us legally without due process of law. A person who does not make scheduled mortgage payments can lose her house, but explicit legal procedures must be followed in securing the debtor's property. The law will not allow her creditor to remove her at gunpoint or, for example, even allow the mortgage holder to confiscate the house without notifying the homeowner of its intentions.

Sixth, the law *provides rehabilitation*. While not everyone agrees on how prisons should be run, it is generally agreed that rehabilitating criminals is, in the long run, more in society's interests that merely punishing them. Prisons are expensive to maintain. If, when a person leaves prison, there is a high probability that he will commit another crime and so be required to serve another prison sentence, then nothing has been accomplished, and much has been lost. Similarly, the law takes the position that a person hopelessly in debt should be given an opportunity, by declaring bankruptcy, to begin fresh. On the one hand, this may seem a bit unfair to those of us who have kept our financial situations under control and so must go on paying our bills. But the rationale here is that *overwhelming* debt from which there is little hope of escape is likely to destroy incentive and potential productivity. And that could mean a serious loss to society, which benefits when each citizen produces in accordance with his or her potential.

Seventh, the law *enforces intent*. One point here which is of particular importance to the businessperson is the law's position on contracts. To a large extent, the law permits citizens to create their own "laws" within the context of a contract agreement—so long as there is nothing within the contract that violates contract law, and so long as the agreement is not *unconscionable* in nature. For example, Willis can contract with Murphy to purchase a piano, and the law will not intervene to ensure that the price is fair or that Murphy agrees to polish the piano before delivery, and so forth. These details are left to the contracting parties to work out. However, if Murphy does not legally own the piano, he cannot legally contract to sell it—and if he attempts to do so, the law will step in.

Eighth, the law *facilitates commercial transactions*. The law doesn't require people to buy and sell, but it does attempt to make it easier for them to do so. For example, the law provides for the use of checks and credit cards so that buyers need not always pay cash for their purchases. The law also makes provisions for extending credit, and it allows consumers to use their personal and real property as collateral to encourage the extension of credit. Few of us really like the idea of being in debt, of course. But without credit, our commercial world would be very different. How many of us, without credit, could afford to buy houses, cars, or other expensive items? The fact is, we simply wouldn't—as a society—be buying nearly as much. Those who feel our society is too materialistic might see that as a benefit. But the ramifications would extend far beyond the philosophical level. Businesses, stripped of a sound financial base, would cease to expand, and many would shrink to a minimally functional level or disband altogether. Commerce would become slower and less reliable. Fewer goods would be produced, services would be cut, and innovations would become rare and precious. And the effect on employees—and their families—would be disastrous, with wholesale lay-offs and severe cuts in hours, salaries, and benefits for those who still worked. Thus, in a very real sense, the law protects the financial welfare—and ultimately the existence—of the business world—and society—as we know it.

Sources of the American Legal System

Where do laws come from? From a wide range of interconnected sources—some historical, some not. On the one hand, law is ever evolving; as we've noted already, it must change and expand even as the society it serves changes and expands. Laws relating to such social issues as pornography and abortion, for example, are relatively "young," and are likely to undergo much debate and modification as they mature. On the other hand, law is not without a traditional base. As we shall see, much of our modern legal system springs from the U.S. Constitution, although its roots go back centuries to the development of the English legal system and even to the ideas and practices of early Greek and Roman civilizations.

A constitution is the *fundamental law of a nation*. Part rules, part philosophy, the United States Constitution sets forth the powers of government and, in addition, imposes definite limits on those powers. (More on this later.) The U.S. Constitution is *written*, though this is not the case with those of some other nations. The federal Constitution is the supreme legal document in the U.S., but states also have constitutions, and each serves as the fundamental law for its particular jurisdiction. However, in a conflict between the state and federal constitutions, the federal document will take precedence.

With but one exception (treaties), all elements of our legal system are derived from the federal Constitution. In other words, they are an extension of the legal philosophy embodied in that document. (*Treaties*, or *formal agreements between two or more nations*, are the only source of law that does not derive authority from the Constitution itself, but rather, from the sovereign power of the United States. Once established, treaties—like the Constitution itself—become the supreme law of the land. That is, their authority cannot be overridden, even by Congress.)

Statutes are the *acts of legislative bodies*. In other words, they are laws enacted through legislative debate and agreement. Statutes are created by Congress at the federal level and by each state's legislature at the state level. The Uniform Commercial Code (UCC), which governs most business transactions, including sales, use of checks and other commercial paper, bank deposits, investments, and so forth, is perhaps the most important example of statutory law. The UCC, with some relatively minor modifications by each state, is accepted by all fifty states.

Ordinances are *laws passed by municipal bodies* such as counties, cities, towns, or villages. Like statutes, ordinances are intended to serve the public welfare. Note, however, that they are not created through legislative action, nor is their influence particularly widespread. A town ordinance, for example, is only enforceable within the boundaries of the town that enacted it.

Administrative regulations are *rules created by governmental bodies created by the legislative branch of government*. These rules serve to "flesh out" the details of the statutes passed by a legislative or municipal body. In the business context, detailed regulations govern real estate, insurance, securities, investments, pollution control, incorporation, mergers, and a host of other business concerns.

Common law consists of *those principles and rules of action which derive their authority from usage and custom, or from court judgment based on such custom*. In the course of hearing a case, judges sometimes have the opportunity to "make law" when the law as it exists does not fully satisfy a given situation. In other words, common law comes into being when one or more preceding cases relate to the case at hand, but no existing law is sufficiently clear or detailed to meet all the specifics of that case. Judges in the U.S. and some other countries have authority to extend common law through their interpretations and applications of existing law. In doing so, of course, they create new precedents on which other judges hearing other cases will rely.

The *law merchant* consists of the *body of rules traditionally employed by merchants*. In short, it's similar to the concept of common law, but with a definite business theme.

Case law is *the law as pronounced by judges*. In other words, it consists of the interpretations judges provide in explaining how existing law applies to each given case. Notice that no new law is created here; unlike common law, case law is simply a matter of thoughtfully applying appropriate *existing* law to the case at hand.

Equity is defined as a *body of rules applied to legal controversies when there is no adequate remedy at law*. Recall that earlier we made the point that the law must provide answers. The court cannot simply say, "We're stumped—you figure it out." And this holds true, *even if* there are seemingly no written laws to cover the situation at hand. For example, suppose Kirby lives in an area with no animal control laws. His neighbor's goats are devouring the shrubbery and most of the produce from his garden. Must Kirby put up with this nuisance simply because there is no current remedy at law? No. He can request that the court issue an injunction requiring the neighbor to keep her goats at home. And if the court agrees that Kirby has a just grievance, and that there is no suitable remedy at law, they may well issue the injunction based on equity.

Remember that despite the diversity of sources from which the U.S. legal system is derived, virtually every component—with the single exception of treaties—harkens back to the supreme authority of the Constitution. This is another way of saying that all these various sources seek not to create a new body of law, but to build upon the foundation that the Constitution provides. Each new legislative act, in fact, builds on those which have gone before, and it is this interconnectedness that gives our legal system its strength. Let's take a closer look now at the role and scope of the Constitution.

The Federal Constitution

Two things make the United States Constitution unique. First, it is the oldest written national constitution. And second, it was the first constitution designed specifically to ensure a *separation of powers* among the main branches of government. Let's take a moment to consider why this separation of powers is so significant.

First, the U.S. federal government is separated into three branches: the legislative, the executive, and the judicial. The legislative branch is composed of the Congress which, in turn, includes the Senate and the House of Representatives. Congress has the power to levy and collect taxes, to pay national debts, to create laws affecting national defense and welfare, to regulate commerce, to coin money, and to create courts inferior to the Supreme Court.

The executive branch includes the offices of president and vice president and the various departments and agencies created to help the president administer the laws of the country. The president, as commander-in-chief of the armed forces, controls most military operations, though Congress has retained the right to declare war. The president also has the power to make treaties and to nominate ambassadors, judges, and high-ranking officers — the military chief of staff, cabinet positions (such as the secretaries of state, defense, and education), and so on.

The judicial branch includes the Supreme Court and whatever other inferior courts might be created by Congress. Federal court judges are all nominated by the president and, if confirmed by the Senate, serve until their death or retirement, unless impeached by Congress.

Effective federal government requires a smooth interaction among these three branches, each of which is granted its power through the Constitution. Note that the three branches are interdependent; none can function fully without cooperation from the others. Yet, each has its own distinct responsibilities. This is precisely what the authors of the Constitution had in mind.

Much of the day-to-day power of government is vested in the first two branches — the legislative and the executive. The legislative branch, with its power to levy and collect taxes, retains primary fiscal power. The executive branch, with its control over the armed forces, retains primary military power. In the minds of the Constitution's creators, were these two powers to fall under common control, the potential for tyrannical domination would be extreme. Imagine, for instance, a government — and there have been and still are many in the world — in which a single person or small group of persons has the right to declare war, deploy military troops, and raise funds (through taxes) to finance the effort. Such systems can be — and often are — highly repressive, and pose a grave threat to both social welfare and national resources. The Constitution, through its checks-and-balances approach, spreads the power around, ensuring that decisions made by any one branch will be carefully reviewed by the others.

In fact, it is the primary responsibility of the judicial branch—wherein the Supreme Court resides—to resolve disagreements with and challenges to the initiatives of the other two branches, and to determine whether their various activities are constitutional. This review serves as a kind of final check over both executive and legislative powers. The Supreme Court reserves the right, for example, to declare unconstitutional administrative rules made by the executive branch or statutes passed by Congress. Thus, neither the president nor the Congress has ultimate power. Nevertheless, the principal duty of the Supreme Court—its only justification, in fact—is to uphold the Constitution, the basis of all U.S. law. In other words, the Supreme Court is not entitled to override the Congress just for the sake of argument; as the guardians, as it were, of Constitutional law, Supreme Court justices must base their objections to legislative or executive action on the words and interpretations of other statutes, court cases, and, above all, the Constitution.

Remember, the Supreme Court is a judicial body, not a philosophical one. Its purpose is to uphold, defend, and interpret the Constitution, not to tell citizens how to think. In this country, there is a vast difference between the kinds of political questions deemed suitable for public debate and those issues deemed appropriate for court hearing. A citizen who opposed a national policy of placing U.S. military personnel in another country, for example, could not take the issue to court on the basis of his or her own moral beliefs. Such a topic is viewed as a political controversy. It is not readily or appropriately resolvable within the judicial system, both because the issue is not related to existing laws and because it is not clear who has damaged whom and to what extent. If an existing law regulated the use of U.S. military personnel abroad, however, and someone felt that troops were being used in violation of that law, this type of "real" controversy could be decided by the courts.

Under the concept of *judicial restraint*, courts refuse to devote their time and resources to considering political questions which have a largely philosophical— as opposed to legal—base. The courts exist to resolve legal questions through the enforcement and interpretation of the law. Contrast the military personnel example with one in which a plaintiff sues a company for discriminatory hiring practices. Clearly, this issue has a philosophical side to it. But it's also a legal question, and as such, it can be resolved. The company is either guilty of discrimination *under the law* or it is not. Presentation of appropriate evidence and testimony will resolve the issue in relatively short order. But moral arguments over troops in foriegn countries may go on for decades and are not allowed to dominate the resources of the courts.

Federal and State Court Systems

As you are likely aware, there are many different kinds of courts, operating at different levels. When a certain court case arises, then, which court will hear it, and how is this determined? Generally, the primary consideration here is one of *jurisdiction*. In simple terms, jurisdiction is defined as *the legal power of a court to decide a particular matter*. The legal grounds of jurisdiction are defined according to several components. The first of these is *subject matter*. A state juvenile court, for example, is limited to hearing cases solely concerning children, just as a federal bankruptcy court may not decide a criminal case since its jurisdiction is limited to bankruptcy matters.

Another component of jurisdiction concerns *the person whose rights, duties, and obligations will be decided in court*. This jurisdiction is concerned with residence of the individual involved in a given matter. For example, if both the plaintiff and the defendant are residents of California, then California has jurisdiction over them. But if only one of the parties is a resident of California, it is possible that California will not have proper jurisdiction over the nonresident party.

A third component of jurisdiction concerns whether the federal and state courts have either *concurrent* or *exclusive jurisdiction*. In some cases, federal courts will have jurisdiction; in others, state courts will. Occasionally, the two may share jurisdiction, and this is called *concurrent jurisdiction*. Certain kinds of cases, however, may be heard only in federal court—usually because of the nature of the issue. Federal courts have *exclusive jurisdiction* in cases involving treason, for instance—where the United States itself is a party to the action. Any violation of federal law prompts a case which can be heard in federal court.

Jurisdiction is also dependent on *venue*, or *the proper geographical area or district where a suit may be brought*. The appropriate venue may depend in part on where the incident at issue occurred (e.g., the site of the robbery, embezzlement, assault, or whatever), or upon the residence of the plaintiff and/or defendant. Appropriate venue must be determined on a case-by-case basis.

In addition to the general guidelines associated with jurisdiction, there are two specific grounds for federal jurisdiction: (1) federal question (or issue) and (2) diversity of citizenship and the amount in dispute. Federal questions are *questions that pertain to the federal Constitution, statutes of the United States, and treaties of the United States*. As we already noted, a case involving treason would automatically fall under federal jurisdiction because treason is a violation of federal law. So is copyright infringement. So is discrimination in employment practices.

If there is no violation of federal law, the federal courts will nevertheless retain jurisdiction if there is diversity of citizenship and if the amount involved is sufficiently high. Diversity of citizenship exists when the person bringing the suit (the plaintiff) and the person being sued (the defendant) are residents of different states, or when one is a U.S. citizen and one is not. Because there are so many cases involving diversity of citizenship, however, the courts impose another requirement for federal jurisdiction: the amount involved in the case must exceed $50,000. This requirement is designed to prevent federal courts from having to deal with trivial matters. Thus, if Barker sues Winston for $2,000, the case will not fall under federal jurisdiction even if they live in different states.

Federal courts include a number of *specialized courts* created to hear cases involving bankruptcy, international trade, taxation, and other specific issues. In addition, Congress has created *federal district courts* in each state. These district

courts are the trial courts, where the case is first filed and where the facts and testimony come out. The district courts are grouped into thirteen circuits nationwide,
each with a *circuit court of appeals*. The Court of Appeals in a circuit hears appeals from cases first decided in the district courts of the circuit. The decisions of
this court are generally final although, in a very few instances, cases may be appealed to the U.S. Supreme Court. Conditions for appeal to the Supreme Court
are rigorous, and relatively few cases each year are accepted by the Supreme Court
for review.

Cases which are not heard by a federal court will be heard in a *state court*, most
of which are categorized by the type of case or by venue. The states' court systems
are similar to the federal system, in that there are lower-level trial courts and then
a series of appellate courts which can be asked to review the decisions of the trial
courts. In most states, cases are assigned to a level of trial court by the type of case
which is heard (domestic relations, probate — for settling estates of dead people —
or juvenile, for example) or by the relative "seriousness" of the case based on the
amount of money involved or the length of jail time which an alleged criminal might
be sentenced to serve. (The names and responsibilities for the different trial courts
vary from state to state).

It is not crucial that you memorize these individual classifications. What is more
important for purposes of this discussion is that you realize that a system exists of
lower-level trial courts (where the judge and jury listen to the witnesses, parties,
and attorneys and then decide the case) and upper-division appeals courts that can
review the decisions of the trial courts. And while some courts limit their cases to
certain topics, this is more a reflection of the enormous complexity of our legal system than of the conceptual framework of the courts. Notice, however, that the
different courts are all interrelated in the sense that each derives its authority from
the Supreme Court and the Congress (or state legislatures for state courts), and the
laws that each interprets and upholds have their common origins in the federal
Constitution or in the applicable state constitution.

The Four Classifications of Law

So far in our discussion, we've classified needs, purposes, sources of law, and courts
themselves. As you might suspect, laws are also subject to classification. Our purpose here is not to present a detailed review of that classification, but only to provide, in brief, another structured way of looking at a system that, without these
various classifications, would be rather unwieldy and difficult to conceptualize.
This particular classification is crucial because when a law is violated, the classification of that law often determines how and where the violator will be prosecuted,
and what sorts of sanctions will be provided under the law. Also, as we shall see,
the U.S. legal system — which includes common law — differs from many others.

In this section, we'll draw four distinctions. The first involves *federal law* and
state law. As mentioned, federal law includes Constitutional law and any laws
passed by the Congress. State laws are passed by state legislatures and govern be-

havior within that state. While the details of the laws of two different states on any particular topic may well be different, frequently there will be general rules that the majority of the states will follow. This general position—or majority rule—can provide some comfort to the businessperson as a guideline that will more likely than not be applied in a jurisdiction. In law school, prospective attorneys generally are taught the law of the federal courts and the majority rule, with exceptions applicable to their own state occasionally highlighted.

Our system also distinguishes between *common law* and *statutory law*. Statutory law is written law enacted by a legislative body. Such law is common to other nations, too; all European nations, for instance, have statutory law. By contrast, common law—law which evolves from the decisions of the judges and which can be applied in future cases—is relatively uncommon. As discussed above, both the English and U.S. legal systems include common law. But under some European legal systems, the decisions a judge makes in a particular case apply only to that case—they do *not* become "law" that a judge can use as the basis for a decision in a later case. In these countries without common law, a decision must be based solely on a judge's interpretation of the applicable statutes and rules—and will not have any effect beyond the particular case in which it was made.

The third dichotomy is between *civil law* and *criminal law*. Civil law covers private disputes between individuals. If Harrington's dog bites Mitchell, Mitchell may sue Harrington for monetary damages under civil law. Criminal law is *public law* in which society as "The People" or "The State" sues a person. If Harrington, angered over the dog incident, shoots and kills Mitchell, the state quite certainly will arrest and *prosecute* (the criminal law terminology for "sue") Harrington under criminal law. If Harrington is convicted, he is likely to face a prison sentence. It's also possible that a particular action may give rise to both a civil and a criminal case. If in Harrington's town, the city council had earlier passed an ordinance against allowing vicious dogs to run loose, Mitchell could have complained to the police and city attorney about the dog bite. If they decided that the case was appropriate, the city attorney, on behalf of "The People of the City of Willow Bank" could have filed a criminal action against Harrington, seeking whatever penalties the city ordinance provided. This case would follow its own path, separate from Mitchell's civil action against Harrington for medical expenses and associated damages.

Finally, we also distinguish between *substantive law* and *procedural law*. Substantive law is what most of us mean when we use the term *law*. Substantive law concerns the *rights and duties given or imposed by the legal system*. Laws which forbid persons to discriminate on the basis of race, run red lights, disturb the peace, keep livestock in the city limits, rob banks, and so forth are substantive. They're the do's and don'ts of the legal system. Procedural law specifies *how those rights and duties are enforced*. In other words, when Mitchell, the dog-bite victim in our preceding scenario, sues dog owner Harrington, the law sets forth specific procedures governing how all this takes place. Mitchell cannot simply seize Harrington by the lapels and drag him before the nearest judge—however upset he may feel. He must follow the procedures set forth by law. A brief review of these procedures provides the topic for our final discussion in this overview—the steps in bringing a civil lawsuit.

Methodology of a Civil Lawsuit

Virtually every aspect of a civil suit is governed by law, beginning with the attorney–client relationship. Both plaintiff and defendant in a lawsuit are generally represented and counseled by their own attorneys. The relationship between attorney and client is a formal one, governed by contract law. The attorney plays one of two roles, depending on the situation. As an *independent contractor*, the attorney seeks to meet the objectives of the client, but uses her own strategies and means to accomplish this end. As an *agent* of the client, however, the attorney acts under the direction of the client (the *principal*), subject to the absolute authority of the client.

The attorney may place herself in this role, for example, when she presents the client with two options and asks the client to make a decision. Remember Mitchell, who was bitten by the dog? Let's say his attorney confers with Harrington's attorney, and Harrington offers to settle the matter out of court by paying all of Mitchell's medical expenses but nothing more. Mitchell must then make a decision about whether to accept that settlement or sue for further damages. The decision will *not* be made by Mitchell's attorney. In her role as Mitchell's agent, she will apprise him of all the facts, including the expenses or hassles involved in pursuing the case further. But Mitchell must decide what to do and direct his attorney to proceed accordingly—to either file suit or proceed in negotiating the settlement.

Our legal system is based on an *adversarial process* that requires each side *to present its case in its most favorable light*. Neither side is required to present the whole truth. Though deliberate distortion or deceit are of course in conflict with the Code of Professional Responsibility to which each attorney must adhere, neither side is required to emphasize, or even present, facts that may weigh favorably for the other side. Each side is permitted—encouraged, in fact—to present its own perspective, its own way of looking at the events of the case. And it is presumed that out of these diverse perspectives, the "truth" will emerge.

In our ongoing scenario, for instance, Mitchell's attorney might try to characterize Harrington's dog as unusually vicious, present evidence of previous attacks, or bring out the fact that Harrington had taken his dog for specialized training as a guard dog. Harrington's attorney, in turn, might try to show that Mitchell had antagonized or teased the animal, thereby provoking the attack. Both sides might be quite truthful within the limits of the information presented. But it's up to the judge or jury to carefully consider *all* evidence and allegations and decide what they believe—and the law will then say—happened.

The role of the judge in our system is obviously important; the judge is the representative of the unbiased law seeking the truth. Unlike the prosecutor or the plaintiff's attorney, the judge does not seek to prove the wrongdoing of the defendant. And unlike the defendant's attorney, the judge does not seek to prove a client's innocence or lack of guilt. And judges generally refrain from directing the proceedings by, for instance, instructing the attorneys to summon additional witnesses or outlining the kinds of evidence that should be presented. For the most part, then, the substance and content of the trial are left to the attorneys themselves. However, a judge may intervene if he or she believes further clarification is required (a judge may, for instance, ask additional questions of a witness). A judge is charged with keeping order in the courtroom. If one attorney objects to the procedures of the other, the judge will rule on this objection. And perhaps most important, the judge tells the jury what laws they are to consider in reaching their decision on the case.

Proponents of the adversarial system strongly believe that only by allowing each side to present the strongest possible case can all relevant evidence be uncovered. Critics, however, charge that the approach favors the more skilled or articulate attorney, who may win for the client through a more adept presentation of a potentially weaker case. To the extent this criticism is true, some allege, the system favors the wealthy, who can afford to hire the most skilled and experienced attorneys.

At this point, let's use our example with Harrington, Mitchell, and Harrington's dog to review — very briefly — the steps involved in a civil suit.

1. Identification of a problem. Not all grievances provide grounds for suit. For example, Mitchell might dislike Harrington's dog intensely, and wish that Harrington would get rid of the animal. He might even be fearful that Harrington's dog might someday bite him. But fear and loathing are not grounds for suit. A dog bite, however, presents a different picture. Thus, the first step for Mitchell to take is an interview with an attorney to determine whether grounds for suit exist and, if so, what procedures to follow. In this case, we'll suppose that Mitchell's attorney, Long, says that yes, Mitchell definitely has grounds for suit. Once that is determined, Mitchell and Long can set up a contract to determine how much and under what circumstances Long will be paid for her future services.

2. Investigation of the facts. Much of the work of an attorney takes place not in court, but behind the scenes, gathering information with which to build a case. Attorney Long will likely begin her investigation by thoroughly interviewing Mitchell to determine, from his point of view, all the details of the incident. Later, she may talk with neighbors to find out whether anyone witnessed the biting incident or simply to discover whether anyone else has had problems with Harrington's dog. If Harrington did have the dog trained as a guard dog, Long may interview the dog trainer. Long also will continue her research of the law and see whether and how the newly discovered facts can be presented to strengthen the legal claims of her client.

3. Settlement. At this point, Long may contact Harrington — or Harrington's attorney, if he has one — to present Mitchell's grievance and demands and to see whether an out-of-court settlement can be reached. Many cases never come to court at all, but are instead settled through some negotiated compromise. Harrington may agree to pay for Mitchell's medical treatment, for instance, and perhaps cover the cost of time missed from work. Let's suppose that Mitchell doesn't feel the proposed compensation is adequate, however, and determines to go ahead with the demands.

4. Filing the suit. The filing of a lawsuit begins with the filing of a formal *complaint* or *petition* — the required legal papers that set out the claims, demands, and legal theory to support the claims — with the court. The complaint gets officially delivered to the defendant along with the court *summons*. The summons is the official order and notice of the court advising a defendant that a lawsuit has been filed against him or her. It tells the defendant that if he or she does not file proper papers with the court within a specified time period, the plaintiff will win the lawsuit automatically. The purpose of the defendant's *answer* or *response* is to further ascertain the appropriateness of the complaint, and to begin outlining the important facts and issues of the case that are in dispute.

The complaint itself summarizes the main allegations of the plaintiff—Mitchell, in this case. The defendant, Harrington, must respond to each point within the complaint. For instance, Mitchell might allege that on the day of the incident Harrington had left his dog untied, and that the animal attacked him (Mitchell) without provocation. Harrington might counter that the animal was untied because Mitchell himself freed the dog or because the dog's collar broke. Further, he might admit that yes, Mitchell was bitten, but deny that the attack was unprovoked since Mitchell shouted at and kicked the dog prior to the incident. These claims and responses—along with any counterclaims Harrington may have against Mitchell (for veterinarian bills from kicking the dog unnecessarily, for example)—will then provide the basic outline for the investigation and testimony to follow.

5. Pretrial proceedings. Pretrial proceedings provide a series of rules governing *discovery*—that is, the process for gathering evidence. During this time, Long continues her investigation of the facts. She may again interview the dog trainer, for example. And if that person's testimony seems relevant, she may request a deposition—a sworn statement based on questioning by both sides' attorneys—which may be presented later in court. She may seek documents or other forms of relevant evidence for later presentation in court—a signed certificate from the local veterinarian stating that Harrington's dog has had rabies and distemper shots, for instance. The defendant's attorney also continues his or her investigation. And most likely each party will take the formal deposition of the other party to see what that person thinks happened and would testify to if the case goes to trial.

6. The result of discovery. As a result of the discovery process, each party's attorney now has a clear picture of what the other side would say in court—and what evidence each side has available to bring to court to support their side. Each attorney will now re-evaluate the strength of each side's position and advise their own client "how it looks." Based on this information, Harrington may or may not make further attempts to settle the matter out of court, and Mitchell may or may not be more inclined to accept the original or another settlement offer.

7. The trial. In our scenario, we'll suppose that Harrington and Mitchell are unable to settle. In that event, the case will go to trial. Again, the law is very specific in laying out procedures for all stages of the trial, beginning with jury selection. Both sides have the right to reject jurors whom they feel cannot be objective in their appraisal of the facts. For example, Harrington's attorney would probably not be happy having friends or relatives of the plaintiff Mitchell on the jury. He might be equally unhappy with the local dog catcher, who might seem to be prejudiced against dogs. Mitchell's attorney, on the other hand, might not wish to see a dog breeder or a member of the local humane society on the jury.

The trial begins with an opening statement from each side, and proceeds through examination and cross-examination of each witness. Again, note that the emphasis, in keeping with the general adversarial approach, is on revealing as much as possible of *both* sides to the issue. Following the closing arguments of each attorney, the judge "charges the jury" by explaining the points of law that are relevant to the case. In this case, for instance, the judge would probably direct the jury to consider any relevant dog control ordinances and the standard of due care required of a dog owner. The jury then withdraws from the courtroom to review the evidence and arguments and law and to reach their verdict. If the jury in this case finds in favor of the plaintiff Mitchell, part of their responsibility will be to determine the amount of damages to be awarded, within the bounds of what Mitchell asked for in his complaint.

If either Harrington or Mitchell believes the evidence has not been properly considered, or that some pertinent laws were not followed in the case, he may file an appeal. The appeals court will re-examine what happened at trial in light of the issues the person appealing believes are important. If the appeals court disagrees with the *appellant* and believes everything in the trial was proper, the verdict of the jury will be upheld. If the state has another level of appeals court, the losing party can try to get that appeals court to review the earlier decisions. But if the court won't hear the case, the decision of the first appeals court is final, and both sides must abide by it.

SOME PRACTICAL ADVICE

In the United States, where personal rights are taken so much as a matter of course, surprising numbers of people are quite unfamiliar with the content of the Constitution and its amendments. For the businessperson who has not thoroughly reviewed these documents, that might be a good place to start a business-oriented investigation of law. This is not to say that acquaintance with these documents will provide a sufficient legal education for a businessperson. But it's an important beginning since our entire legal system—with extremely few exceptions—rests on the precepts of these documents.

Second, in a time when the lawsuit seems such a commonplace part of conducting business, it is well to understand that not every business problem provides—nor should provide—grounds for legal action. The businessperson who has difficulties dealing with employees or contractors, for instance, or who feels he or she has suffered unfairly at the hands of competitors may or may not have grounds for suit. Many types of business-related problems are more appropriately dealt with in very different ways—through informal negotiations, or through the intervention of nonlegal specialists such as business consultants. Remember, the courts only deal with cases involving violations of the law. Lawsuits are a serious matter—and society does not view them as an appropriate outlet for everyday anger and frustration. Moreover, bringing suit can be expensive. The time spent in court is usually a small fraction of the time required for an attorney to put together a case. And attorney's fees must be paid even when cases are lost. In short, court is no place to resolve trivial disagreements.

Third, though no one likes to contemplate the prospect of being sued, it is well for any businessperson to recognize this as a real possibility. Persons who are sued are not all evil-minded culprits. Many are thoughtful, well-intentioned persons who simply find themselves in the midst of a legal dispute that cannot be resolved without the help of the court. In short, it is a good idea for any businessperson to become familiar with the general procedures involved in a lawsuit so that if he or she is served with a summons, the whole procedure seems more familiar, less intimidating. Naturally, it is absolutely critical to seek the advice and help of an attorney under such circumstances. Nevertheless, just knowing what to expect can help a great deal.

Finally, attitude is crucial—as we noted at the outset. Lawsuits are unpleasant events, to be sure. But the intent of this lesson is not to suggest how threatening the legal system can be, but rather to show how *supportive* the law can be in guarding the rights of all businesspeople and other citizens. Those who know the law and who take every reasonable step to abide by the law are unlikely to find themselves in trouble. Of course, keep in mind that ignorance is not an excuse. The employer who is discriminatory in his hiring practices, for instance, cannot use ignorance of discrimination laws as a proper defense. And here's where the regular counsel of an attorney who specializes in business law can be invaluable. At the same time, however, good intentions often do count, for the underlying purpose of the law is to provide just resolutions for both sides in any disagreement.

ASSIGNMENTS

- Before you watch the video program, be sure you've read through the preceding overview, familiarized yourself with the learning objectives for this lesson, and looked at the key terms below. Then, read Chapters 1 and 2, Chapter 5, and the introduction to Chapter 6 (pages 92-95) of Davidson et al., *Business Law*.

- After completing these tasks, view the video program for Lesson 2.

- After watching the program, take time to review what you've learned. First, evaluate your learning with the self-test which follows the key terms. Then, apply and evaluate what you've learned with the "Your Opinion, Please" scenarios at the end of this telecourse study guide lesson.

KEY TERMS

Before you read through the textbook assignment and watch the video program, take a minute to look at the key terms associated with this lesson. When you encounter them in the textbook and video program, pay careful attention to their meaning.

Administrative regulations	Jurisdiction
Adversarial process	Law
Appeal	Law merchant
Case law	Legislative power
Civil law	Ordinance
Common law	Plaintiff
Court of appeals	Pretrial proceedings
Criminal law	Procedural law
Deposition	State courts
Discovery	Statute
Diversity of citizenship	Suit
Federal courts	Summons
Federal law	Subject matter jurisdiction
Judicial power	Treaty
Judicial restraint	Venue
Judicial review	

SELF-TEST

The questions below will help you evaluate how well you've learned the material in this lesson. Read each one carefully, and select the letter of the option that best answers the question. You'll find the correct answer, along with a reference to the page number(s) where the topic is discussed, in the back of this telecourse study guide.

1. The term *law*, as it's presented in the lesson, is probably *best* defined as

    a. a system of sanctions.
    b. rules that must be obeyed.
    c. social control.
    d. the collective traditions of a society.

2. The lesson suggests that, in some ways, law enforcement is like the policies and procedures of businesses. This most likely means that

    a. citizens, like company employees, are expected to meet a certain standard of conduct.

    b. in business as in law, one person or group tends to make most of the decisions.

    c. in both business and law, there must be serious sanctions for those who break the rules.

    d. the primary purpose of law is to control citizens.

3. Which of the following *best* distinguishes between *rule* and *law* as introduced in the lesson?

    a. There is no real difference. The terms are synonymous.

    b. Laws are made by courts, while rules are voted in by the public.

    c. Laws are legislative statutes; rules are essentially a system of procedures by which laws are enforced.

    d. Laws are legally enforceable, while rules are not.

4. This lesson defines six needs of a legal system. One of these, the *need to be published*, refers to the fact that

    a. some instruction in law is now a required component of public education.

    b. all laws need to be available to the public in written form.

    c. all laws must be written in language understandable to the average layperson.

    d. the courts have a responsibility to ensure that all citizens have at least a basic understanding of the law.

5. Which of the following is *not* a major purpose of our legal system?

    a. Achieving fairness for both sides

    b. Guarding civil rights

    c. Equitably redistributing access to power in government

    d. Facilitating commercial transactions

6. Stillwell and McCary have an unusual business arrangement. According to the terms of their contract, Stillwell, a professional musician, has agreed to provide ten piano lessons to McCary. In exchange for this instruction, McCary, an electrician, has agreed to do all the wiring in Stillwell's new office building. Is the court likely to look on this arrangement as *legal*?

    a. Yes—assuming there is no violation of contract law.

    b. No; it's simply too big a departure from more traditional work arrangements.

    c. We cannot say without knowing more about the relative value of each person's services.

7. The Uniform Commercial Code, which has (with modification) been adopted by legislatures in all fifty states, provides much of the legal framework within which U.S. business operates. This law is *best* described as

   a. a constitutional amendment.
   b. a statute.
   c. common law.
   d. a rule.

8. McDuff, a judge, discovers that her law books contain conflicting legal opinions relating to the primary issues involved in a current case being heard within her court. After much research and debate, McDuff issues a ruling which draws heavily on these precedents but offers a new interpretation to guide future similar cases. This new ruling is an example of

   a. equity.
   b. procedural law.
   c. a constitutional amendment.
   d. common law.

9. Under the adversarial system, the role of the judge is primarily viewed as

   a. passive, though the judge does facilitate proceedings, issue rulings at the request of the attorneys, and help interpret the law to the jury.
   b. moderately active, since it is the judge who usually determines what evidence will be collected and presented.
   c. aggressive, since the judge directs most of the trial proceedings and also determines the verdict in many cases.
   d. *None* of the above; the judge plays almost no role at all until it is time to determine the outcome of the case.

10. The Supreme Court has the power to do all of the following *except one*. The Supreme Court does *not* have the power to

    a. appoint judges to serve on the Supreme Court.
    b. order the Executive Branch to reverse an administrative action.
    c. declare an act of Congress unconstitutional.
    d. invalidate state legislation.

YOUR OPINION, PLEASE

Read each of the following scenarios and answer the questions about the decisions you would make in each situation. Give these questions some serious thought; they may be used as the basis for the development of a more complex essay. You should base your decisions on what you've learned from this lesson, though you may incorporate outside readings or information gained through your own experience if it is relevant.

Scenario 1

Jarlstaadt lives in a heavily forested rural area where forest fires have posed a severe threat to the community for the past several years. His farm is situated two miles outside the city limits of tiny Fern Ridge on a 40-acre property adjoining government-owned land. He heats his home with a wood stove and has no other source of heat.

This year, for the first time, the City of Fern Ridge (population 512) has passed a city ordinance stating that "no person may, for any reason, ignite a fireplace fire or woodstove fire within the city limits of Fern Ridge, nor within a four-mile radius extending in all directions from the city limits." The law is entered in writing in the record books of the city council, and the results of the council's decision are published in the Fern Ridge *Gazette*, which Jarlstaadt does not read. The new ordinance is also announced on the radio and on the local television news, but Jarlstaadt does not own a television or radio, so he does not hear the announcement.

A few days following passage of the new ordinance, Jarlstaadt is reported by one of his neighbors for keeping a woodstove fire burning and is subsequently cited for violation of the ordinance. If convicted, he faces a potential fine of up to $1,000 and/or imprisonment in the county jail for up to three months. Jarlstaadt vehemently and vocally protests the arrest as a direct violation of his civil rights, asserting that there was no way for him to know anything of the law, and that in any event, it is an unfair and biased law that creates a personal hardship for him.

What's your opinion? Based on what you know of the situation, do you think Jarlstaadt can successfully defend his actions? Is the court in fact violating his civil rights, or must Jarlstaadt abide by the new ordinance? Do you think the ordinance is enforceable?

- Is Jarlstaadt likely to defend his position successfully? If so, on what grounds?
- What factors support your answer?
- What factors might a prosecuting attorney cite in arguing against your view?
- What steps, if any, might Jarlstaadt have taken to prevent prosecution in this situation?
- What steps, if any, should the city council have taken to help citizens avoid the kind of situation Jarlstaadt now faces? (Or, to put it another way, is this a fair law? Is the manner in which it is being enforced fair? Give your reasons.)

Scenario 2

Two companies, Meyer Computers and Zenith Desktop Publishing, share a common parking area. Each company pays 50% of the monthly rental fee, which goes to the building's owner. Meyer, a retail outlet, needs every available parking space for customers, especially since nearby street parking is severely restricted due to heavy traffic.

Zenith, which works with its customers primarily at the customers' offices, is not much concerned about parking, except for its employees. Unfortunately, Zenith has marked off half of the parking spaces as "Reserved for Zenith" and has placed signs warning that the cars of others will be towed away. Meyer, therefore, must either require its employees to park a very inconvenient distance from the business, or else leave no parking area whatever for its customers.

Discussions between the two companies have resolved nothing. Zenith takes the position that since they pay half the rental fee on the parking lot, they are entitled to use it as they see fit. Meyer counters that their right to conduct their business is being interfered with, that they are losing countless customers because of the inconveniences created by Zenith's unreasonable attitude and behavior. They determine to bring suit against Zenith, but are advised by their corporate attorney that, so far as she can determine, Zenith is not technically violating any current law.

What's your opinion? Based on what you know of the situation, what options are open to Meyer at this point? If Zenith is not breaking any current law, must Meyer simply make the best of the situation? What would be your advice to Meyer (and Zenith) about resolving this situation?

- If Zenith is not in violation of any current law, does Meyer have any legal options for resolving the problem?
- What factors support your position?
- What factors might an attorney representing Zenith cite in arguing against your view?
- What steps, if any, might Meyer take to avoid similar situations in the future?
- What steps, if any, might Zenith take to avoid similar situations in the future?

3

Business Crimes and Business Torts

LEARNING OBJECTIVES

Upon completing your study of this lesson, you should be able to

- Distinguish between torts and crimes and provide an example of each.
- Discuss the nature of crime in the world of business and provide specific examples.
- Identify the two necessary components of criminal liability and give an example of each.
- Identify seven crimes that can occur in the business marketplace.
- Discuss the nature of torts in a business context and give three examples of conduct in a business setting that would give rise to tort liability.
- Define *intentional tort* and give business-related examples of actions that would give rise to intentional tort liability.
- Define what is meant by *negligence* in tort liability and give two business-related examples of actions that would give rise to liability based on negligence.
- Define *strict liability* in torts and give business-related examples of situations in which strict liability might apply.

Every society on earth has certain standards of conduct to which its citizens are expected to adhere — and about which laws are made. Ours is no exception.

At first, it might seem that the laws governing right and wrong behavior would be largely a matter of common sense, for doesn't everyone have a general idea about what is acceptable and unacceptable, what is legal or illegal? In part, yes. Most of us recognize that we could get ourselves into serious legal difficulties by shooting another person or taking another's property for our own use. So common sense and experience *do* play a part in our understanding of the law. However, they're not always sufficient to provide us with the kind of knowledge and insight needed to ensure that our business and personal conduct will always be free of legal liability. Among those persons who have only a passing or casual acquaintance with the law, for instance, how many would likely know all five of the elements necessary to support a charge of fraud? How many could accurately define terms like *negligence* or *defamation*?

Of course, one reason we have attorneys is to help us answer questions like these. Not everyone can become a legal expert. Extensive expertise is not required, however, to distinguish between torts and crimes, to understand the kinds of behavior that our society generally defines as tortious or criminal, or to gain some insight about the key elements that figure in a court's determination of criminal or tortious liability.

As we explore the issues relating to business crimes and business torts, it is likely to occur to you that the law has much flexibility. This doesn't mean that the lines of legality are fuzzy and uncertain; anyone who commits a crime believing this to be the case is likely in for some rude enlightenment. However, it is true that laws change over time, usually as society's view of what is acceptable changes. Further, each situation that prompts legal action is likely to be unique in some respects. Thus, if the law as it's currently written does not seem capable of restoring some measure of fairness to a given situation, society may feel it's time to change or expand the law. And as this occurs, the process of identifying and interpreting appropriate conduct grows ever more complicated. Still, there are threads of consistency that run through the law, many of which have existed for centuries. Unraveling some of the broader threads is the focus of this lesson.

OVERVIEW

We've already noted that the law is an attempt to synthesize and reflect — in a systematic and structured way — the moral precepts of a given society. Definitions under the law must be precise to allow for consistency in interpretation, while still allowing some flexibility to accommodate new situations, unforeseen events.

Of course, any accurate reflection of how society measures human conduct must go beyond a mere distinction between right and wrong. Society's reasoning is not that simplistic, and neither is the law. For example, there are levels of unacceptability; stealing a grapefruit isn't equated with armed robbery or murder. Further, the law distinguishes between so-called *public* wrongs, and civil or *personal* wrongs — and this distinction marks the beginning of our discussion.

Torts and Crimes

Tort law is concerned with *private* wrongs — those perpetrated against an individual. Defaming someone's character or misrepresenting the condition of goods being sold are examples of intentional torts. *Crimes* involve *public* wrongs — wrongs which Congress, state legislatures, and other legislative bodies view as sufficiently serious to pose a threat to the public good as a whole. A crime is defined legally as *an act or conduct against society or the state that is subject to penal sanctions.*

For purposes of understanding the difference between a tort and a crime, it's important to note that for a crime to have occurred, there must be a law which makes the conduct a criminal offense. For this reason, then, although the criminal act or conduct itself happens to an individual — an individual is murdered or a home is robbed — it is society as a whole that is the legally injured party and that reaches out against the wrongdoer.

Crimes may be classed as *felonies* or *misdemeanors*, depending on the seriousness of the crime. Rape, murder, and armed robbery are examples of felonies. Traffic offenses, simple assault, stealing goods of relatively small value, and disturbing the peace are examples of misdemeanors.

Crimes — together with the elements necessary to establish proof and the proposed punishments in the event guilt is established — are defined under Congressional (federal) law or by state statute. In other words, a federal or state legislature has passed a law to define each criminal action.

Society has also developed a system of tort law to resolve those situations in which a person *breaches* a civil duty or fails to exercise due care — yet does not commit a crime. For example, a person who operates a business is expected to exercise certain care in making the place of business safe for customers to enter. Let's say that Blake operates a corner grocery in a Midwest town with severe winters. During the wintertime, if Blake fails to shovel his front walkway, customers must brave the snow and ice to enter his front door. If one falls and breaks a leg, Blake may find himself involved in a lawsuit. He has probably not committed a crime. Nevertheless, society will look on his failure to shovel the sidewalk as an example of tortious conduct, and he may well be liable under the tort of negligence (which we'll discuss more fully later).

Persons who commit crimes and are subsequently arrested and charged are sued by *the state* in which the crime is committed or by *the people* of that state as a body politic. Crimes may be punishable by fine, imprisonment, or loss of privilege — such as loss of the opportunity to vote. Indeed, death by hanging, firing squad, electrocution, lethal injection, or poisionous gas have, at different places and times, all been deemed suitable punishments for extremely reprehensible crimes. But persons who commit torts may be sued by an individual who suffers some harm as a result of the violation; that plaintiff will generally be seeking *monetary damages* — an award of money paid by the defendant to help compensate for the harm.

The proof demanded in each case is a little different. In a criminal trial, guilt must be established *beyond a reasonable doubt*, which leaves little room for speculation. In the case of a civil trial, the court is more lenient in its demands. Once all the available evidence has been presented, the court must decide in favor of one party or the other — defendant or plaintiff — and so will simply weigh the evidence to determine which position is better supported — that is, which side has the *preponderance of evidence* to support their side. A defendant's position might not be undisputably correct, but if it appears after presentation of all evidence to be nevertheless stronger than the plaintiff's case, the defendant will win — even if there are "reasonable doubts" on both sides.

Keep in mind that our definitions of what is criminal do change over time. Some acts, such as blasphemy, which were once defined as criminal, are not likely to still be on the statute books as a crime. On the other hand, other actions once considered acceptable may now be classified as criminal. Consider, for instance, how attitudes toward electronic eavesdropping and invasions of computer files have changed over the past few years — and how laws have changed to treat that behavior.

Business Crimes

Embezzlement, insider trading, forgery, and computer crimes — the sort of things we've tended to label *white-collar crimes* because they're usually committed by professional businesspeople — have, in recent years, aroused far more public wrath than in the past. While such activities were never viewed as respectable or desirable, there was a general tendency to take a more lenient attitude toward, say, a theft of computer data than toward theft of an automobile. This may have been, in part, because white-collar crimes generally involve little or no force or violence. Computer hackers are not typically labeled "armed and dangerous." Whatever the reason, there was a tendency to look aside, and to focus primarily on what seemed to be more tangible crimes. Now, however, there is increasing public demand to take such activity seriously, with appeals for more consistent enforcement of the law and clear standards for businesspeople.

It is a rare business these days that is not affected by crime in some way. If you are a businessperson, the odds of your being touched by crime, either as a victim or even an unwitting accomplice, are greater today than ever before.

Potential Business-Related Crimes

In this section of the lesson, we'll review a few of the more common forms of crime that affect the business sector. Throughout this discussion, it may be helpful to consider some ways in which business crime might be prevented, or the ways in which its ramifications could be lessened.

Arson.   Arson is the *intentional burning of any property by fire or explosion*. Today, the definition has been expanded to include any real property and most personal property. Thus, setting fire to a woodpile or stand of trees will be considered arson, as will setting off fire-causing explosives in a house, business, or public building. The burning of valuable papers—a will or contract, for example—could also be considered arson.

Burglary.   Burglary is the *breaking and entering of a structure with the intent to commit a felony*. Let's say the Hamiltons are on vacation. If neighbor Crosby breaks into their house to steal money or snatch the television, he is guilty of burglary—even if he is unarmed during the break-in. But suppose Crosby discovers as he's mowing the lawn that the Hamiltons have left their kitchen faucet running and the overflowing sink is doing considerable damage to the floor. If he breaks into the house to repair the situation, he is not guilty of burglary because, in getting into the house, he didn't intend to commit a felony.

Embezzlement.   Embezzlement is the *taking of money or other property by an employee who has been entrusted with the money or property by his or her employer*. It is among the most common of white-collar crimes.

Forgery.   Forgery is the *making or altering of a negotiable instrument or credit card invoice in order to create or to shift legal liability for the instrument*. In other words, forgery is a form of fraud. To win a case of forgery, the state must show that the accused acted with the intent to defraud. Suppose, for instance, that Anderson, Inc., uses a company stamp to sign checks. Fentley, a company employee, is normally in charge of issuing the checks. If she deliberately signs over an unauthorized check to herself, stamping it with the company signature, or if she alters the amount on one of the corporate checks, she is guilty of fraud. But suppose she issues a check which she believes is fully authorized, only to have her employer state later that no, he did *not* intend to authorize the check. Is Fentley guilty of forgery? Because the state would have to prove that she acted with deliberate intent to defraud in order to make its charge stick, Fentley will almost certainly be found not guilty.

Fraud.   Fraud—which typically is a tort but can be defined by the legislature as also a crime—is very complex. In general, it is the *misrepresentation of a material fact made with the intention to deceive*, and in the criminal context can be viewed as theft by deception. In order to successfully sue for criminal fraud, the state must show not only that there was factual misrepresentation and intent to deceive, but also that the injured party relied upon the deception and was damaged as a result. For example, suppose Flurry Chemical deliberately misrepresents the purity of one of its products to Millstone Medical Laboratory in order to boost its own profits by selling the chemical at a higher price because of its misrepresented purity. Millstone relies on the information and uses the product in manufacturing a vaccine for cats. Several cats die as a result of the vaccine, and Millstone's reputation is damaged. Here we have all five of the basic elements of fraud:

1. A material fact (not an opinion) was given: *A chemical was identified and labeled as having certain purity*.

2. The fact was misrepresented: *The labeling and identification were incorrect*.

3. The misrepresentation was deliberate, made with the intention to deceive: *Flurry Chemical intended to deceive Millstone*.

4. The injured party relied on the misrepresentation: *Millstone depended on Flurry's information and used the chemical in one of its products*.

5. Some injury resulted because of the reliance: *Animals injected with the chemical substance died; and Millstone's reputation suffered*.

One might well question the thoroughness with which Millstone tests its own products, of course. But ignoring this and other issues, unless Flurry can show that Millstone should have known of the deception, or that Millstone's own internal negligence or carelessness contributed to the deception, Flurry may well be prosecuted by the government and found guilty of fraud. And Flurry most likely will also face a civil suit by Millstone for the tort of fraud.

Larceny. Larceny is the *wrongful taking and carrying away of the personal property of another without the owner's consent and with the intent to deprive the owner of the property permanently*. Shoplifting and pickpocketing are the most common forms of larceny. Note that larceny *per se* does not involve any force or violence.

Robbery. Robbery is *larceny combined with the threat to use violence or force*. A person who surreptitiously sneaks a diamond ring into her pocket and walks out of the store is guilty of larceny. A person who holds a gun on a jeweler and demands that the contents of the display case be turned over to her is guilty of robbery.

Requirements for Criminal Liability

The basis for criminal liability consists of two elements: a criminal act and an appropriate mental state. If either of these elements is missing, no crime has been committed. For instance, suppose Harris becomes so violently angry with Ford he decides to kill Ford. He even goes so far as to load his gun, put it into the glove compartment of his car, and drive to Ford's house. At the last minute, though, he has a change of heart and goes home, leaving Ford to enjoy a quiet night by the fire, unmindful of his near escape. Has Harris committed the crime of murder? No. He has—or had—intent, but there's no action. Can he be charged with attempted murder? No; there was still no action—no actual attempt to kill. It doesn't matter *why* Harris changed his mind; it makes no difference whether he saw the error of his ways or simply noticed Ford's vicious guard dog. (Note, however, that Harris may well have committed the crime of carrying a loaded, concealed weapon—and could be found guilty of, and punished for, that crime.)

On the other hand, action without the necessary intent doesn't constitute crime either. Suppose Willoughby is riding the subway and has the misfortune to sit near a bank robber. Eager to divest himself of incriminating evidence, the robber slips his gun into Willoughby's coat pocket while she's engrossed in the evening paper, and then leaves the subway. Is Willoughby guilty of being an accomplice to the robbery or of hiding or withholding evidence? Not at all. She may have "assisted" the robber, but she did so totally unwittingly.

Various terms have been used to describe the mental state in which one deliberately commits an act. These terms include *consciously*, *intentionally*, *maliciously*, *unlawfully*, and *willfully*. Each of these terms, of course, is highly subjective and therefore difficult to define with much precision. Recently, there has been an effort to pinpoint the *degree* of intent with a series of carefully defined terms, any one of which can suggest deliberate intent. These are

1. *Purpose*: A person is said to act with purpose if it is his or her conscious objective to commit the act. Willoughby, with the hidden gun in her pocket, wouldn't qualify.

2. *Knowledge*: A person acts with knowledge if she is aware of what she is doing. An intoxicated person, for instance, might not have knowledge of her actions.

3. *Recklessness*: A person acts with recklessness if he disregards an evident and substantial risk that criminal harm or injury might result from his actions. For example, a person who was demonstrating a shotgun to friends when the gun went off and injured someone might be charged with criminal liability on grounds of recklessness.

4. *Negligence*: A person is criminally negligent if she fails to foresee the substantial and unreasonable risk resulting from her actions—when a reasonable and prudent person would have foreseen such risk (more on this hypothetical person later). For instance, a person driving without headlights at night might be considered criminally negligent.

5. *Strict liability*: A person can be held strictly liable if he acts in a manner that the law considers criminal *even if* none of the first four degrees of intent are present. Violation of a public health law is a case in point. Let's say a restaurant manager serves contaminated tuna. Even if she did not deliberately endanger the public health, had no knowledge of the situation, and was not guilty of either recklessness or negligence, she can still be held strictly liable under the law. The purpose of strict liability, from the court's point of view, is to protect the public welfare without the expense or time required to prove intent. It is the court's way of saying, in effect, a violation is a violation, period—regardless of intent.

Criminal action also requires not only that an action be deliberate, but that it be voluntary. If Albert steals the marketing plan for his company's new product because Clive is holding his wife hostage and will not release her until Albert delivers the documents, Albert's attorney will certainly argue that he cannot be held criminally liable, despite his actions and *apparent* intent. If it's proven to the court's satisfaction that Albert is acting against his will, true intent cannot be established and Albert will be found not guilty.

Business Torts

Tort law, remember, covers private—that is, civil—wrongs against persons or property. A kind of perpetual balancing act is required here to protect citizens' rights on the one hand, while also expecting them to fulfill certain social duties in the public interest. The question is, What should be expected? What is acceptable behavior, and to what extent should the law allow someone to seek compensation or redress when the boundaries of acceptability are overstepped? Further, how much does society have a right to expect?

For instance, citizens in one location may feel quite comfortable having pets roam freely without the owners' supervision and feel that it was their bad luck—not the pet owner's responsibility—if property were damaged or someone were injured by another's loose pet. In this instance, the law of the society probably would not allow someone to sue the pet owner for damage to property or person. In another location, that behavior could be considered quite unthinkable. It might seem quite reasonable to expect that a person who owns pets would have a duty to control and supervise them at all times—and to compensate someone whose property or person was damaged by the pet owner's animals. In this situation, society might well recognize a private duty to control animals—and a private right to sue for damages they cause. In that case, a person whose dog bit another could well be liable under *tort* law.

Suppose, though, that some time later, dog attacks rose dramatically, dogs became increasingly vicious, or dogs were shown to be the reason a life-threatening disease was spreading rapidly through the population. The legislature might well establish a law that would make it a crime to let pets wander the neighborhood unsupervised. Thus, through heightened public awareness and substantial public pressure, actions that were subject to tort law may become subject to criminal law.

These days, there are three ways to establish tort liability: (1) the defendant committed an *intentional* tort, (2) the defendant was negligent, and (3) the defendant—though not necessarily negligent or wishing to harm anyone—is guilty under the doctrine of *strict liability*. Let's consider each of these in turn, with some examples.

Intentional Torts

Intentional torts occur when the person at fault either wanted to harm someone or knew that what she did could result in harm. For instance, if Eichert becomes irritated on an overcrowded bus and pushes Ringold onto the floor, Eichert has committed the intentional tort of battery. She either intended to harm Ringold or—

at the very least—knew that the act of pushing someone onto the floor of a bus was very likely to result in that person's injury.

Examples of Intentional Torts

There are a number of intentional torts—and the list of what actions or behaviors are intentional torts is one area of law in which many changes are occurring. We'll very briefly define here a few of the more established and common intentional torts.

Assault. Assault is the *threat or reasonable apprehension that one person will strike another*. Verbal threats are not assaults. But raising an arm as if to strike someone, brandishing a weapon, or even moving toward another person in a menacing or hostile manner could be interpreted as assault.

Battery. Battery is sometimes defined as *consummated assault*. It is not just the threat of attack, but the attack itself. Battery need not involve shooting, stabbing, or beating. It can be as minor as intentionally bumping another person. The law views the individual's dignity as sacrosanct; it must not be violated. And if the person is harmed as a result of the battery—no matter how nonviolent the original "attack" may have seemed—the assailant can be held liable.

Defamation. Defamation takes two forms: libel and slander. *Libel* is any written communication that causes a person to suffer a loss of reputation. *Slander* is any spoken communication that causes a person to suffer a loss of reputation. The best defense to a charge of defamation is truth. For instance, if Carson alleges on a radio broadcast that Wharton is a thief, Wharton may sue for defamation on grounds of slander. But suppose it turns out that Carson has proof that Wharton is indeed a thief. Under such circumstances, Wharton has not been slandered. On the other hand, if the charge is false, Carson is likely to face a judgment for money to compensate Wharton's loss of reputation.

False imprisonment. False imprisonment is the *detention of one person by another against the former's will and without just cause*. The last point—*without just cause*—is particularly important. For example, if a store detective stops a customer *believing* (even mistakenly) that the customer is guilty of shoplifting, there are no grounds for false imprisonment. On the other hand, suppose a car salesperson were to high-pressure a customer by locking the salesroom door and implying that the customer was not free to leave until the salesperson had completed his pitch. That would definitely be a case of false imprisonment—the salesperson had no "just cause" for detaining the customer; he was doing it for his own selfish interests. "Just cause" means, usually, grounds for believing that another person has committed a crime or tort.

Mental distress. Mental distress implies a *serious indignity that causes emotional distress*. This might occur, for instance, if a salesperson were unusually abusive to a customer, particularly if the incident occurred in front of other customers. An employer who choses to openly criticize an employee's behavior in front of other employees might also be liable, depending on the nature and severity of the criticism.

At one time, under the law, it was necessary for the plaintiff to show some physical symptoms of the alleged distress—sleeplessness, headaches, high blood pressure, and that sort of thing. This is no longer the case in many states. Nevertheless, society—and the law—is not willing to give relief to everyone who has been treated rudely or to punish everyone who is rude. Mental distress—not discomfort—must occur, and trivial complaints won't get much of a hearing. On the other hand, an incident that violates the bounds of what our hypothetical "reasonable and prudent person" would consider to be part of what we just have to tolerate as social interaction may well provide grounds for liability.

Invasion of privacy. Invasion of privacy occurs when *an individual's personal life is opened to unwarranted public scrutiny without that individual's permission*. Again, the term *unwarranted* is crucial. If a person were an accused murderer, let's say, it would not constitute invasion of privacy for the local television station to cover the story. But, the station might want to rethink the matter before deciding to do a story on "A Day in the Life of Mildred Crooner." If Crooner were not a public figure (even given a fairly broad reading of that term) and had no reason for being in the public eye, dogging her around all day, video camera in hand, could lead to some legitimate threats of legal action—unless she agreed to the project, of course.

Trespass. Trespass occurs when *one person ventures onto the land of another without permission*. It is still trespass even if no damage is done to the real property and even if the property owner has *not* posted a "No Trespassing" sign. Of course, sometimes the trespasser may not know that the land is owned privately or may believe herself to be on someone else's property. In such instances, proving intent to trespass may be difficult—if the owner decides to pursue the issue at all. But if the trespasser has been warned and quite clearly did intend to trespass, damages could be sought. (Exactly how much damages would be awarded are another matter, especially if no physical harm happened to the property.) By the way, a tenant who remains on the property of another after a lease has expired is guilty of trespass. And leaving one's personal possessions on another's property is also a form of trespass. For example, a person who parked her car on the property of her neighbor without that neighbor's permission would be trespassing.

Conversion. Conversion occurs when *a person intentionally exercises exclusive control over the personal property of another without permission*. Let's say Barker borrows an electric typewriter from Hicks. Barker is supposed to return the typewriter within a few days, but when Barker's neighbor Croft comes by and offers to buy it for $500, Barker takes the money and gives the typewriter to Croft. Since Barker does not have the right to sell Hicks's property without Hicks's express permission, Barker is liable under the tort of conversion and will have to pay damages. Note, by the way, that Barker does *not* use any unlawful means to gain possession of the property in this scenario. The problem comes when Barker takes advantage of that situation to exercise control over the property, which she has no right to do.

Fraud. Fraud, as we've noted earlier, can be a crime as well as a tort, depending on the circumstances and whether the legislature has defined the act as criminal. Since we discussed fraud in that earlier section, we won't repeat all the details here, except for a brief reminder that fraud does include five distinct elements, and that all five must be present. Fraud—unfortunately—is far from rare, so examples are not difficult to construct. Here are just a few: A jeweler sells a "gold" ring, knowing it is not really gold; a businessman borrows money to begin a new business using false credit information in order to qualify for the loan; a landowner sells a tract of land representing that a mobile trailer home is included in the purchase, then removes the trailer before the new owner takes possession.

Disparagement. Disparagement is a *false statement about the products or services of a person in business*. For example, suppose that Fuller tells everyone that Bloomington Restaurant, which claims to serve "the juiciest prime all-beef steaks in town," is really serving horsemeat, not beef at all. Fuller might well be liable in this case under the tort of disparagement—if his statement is indeed false and *if*—this is key—Bloomington can show it suffered some loss of business as a result of Fuller's publicity. If, for instance, everyone in town decides that eating horsemeat might be more healthful than eating beef or, more likely, that Fuller's statement is untrue, Bloomington's business might not drop. In this case, it would have no damages to sue for—even if it didn't much like Fuller's disparaging statement.

Defenses to Intentional Torts

The key element in establishing liability for an intentional tort is to show *intended harm*—that the person committed the act with the intent of harming another or with the knowledge that harm was likely to occur. As a result, demonstrating that there was no intent to harm is an effective defense to an intentional tort.

In addition to absence of intent, there are four other defenses to intentional torts: consent, privilege, necessity, and truth. A defendant who can prove an appropriate defense will be able to defeat the plaintiff's lawsuit. Let's touch briefly on each of these, with some examples.

Actions that could constitute a tort in one circumstance will provide no grounds for liability in another context if the actions occur *with the consent* of the "injured" party. For example, a boxer could not sue another boxer under the tort of battery. That would be ludicrous since battery is the essence of boxing; boxers enter the ring expecting to be hit, and by entering the ring are effectively granting the other person permission to batter them. People do not, however, walk down the street expecting to be hit about the head and body. As you can see, then, context, circumstance, and normal expectations are crucial in establishing liability or in alleging the defense of consent.

The law grants a defendant the *privilege* of defending him- or herself under certain circumstances. For example, if a person makes a move to strike another, the defendant need not sit passively by and take it without trying to defend herself. She may strike her assailant or do whatever is necessary and reasonable for her own self-defense. Similarly, if your neighbor should make off with your tennis racquet, you would have the right to retrieve it. Retail businesspeople have the right to detain customers whom they suspect of shoplifting. And persons engaged in public debate—politicians, for instance—have the right to make statements that might be construed as slanderous in other situations.

The defense of *necessity* is allowed when someone enters the property of another in order to protect him- or herself from some harm. For instance, let's say Fisher, a hiker, is caught in a raging blizzard and takes shelter in the barn of Cooper, a farmer. Fisher is not guilty of trespass, even if he did not have Cooper's permission to be on the land, since the "necessity" of protecting oneself from a storm and sickness overrides this property owner's interest.

And as mentioned earlier, *truth* is the best defense to the tort of defamation. If sued under the tort of defamation, the defendant will win if he or she can show that the claims and statements made were accurate.

Negligence as a Basis for Tort Liability

In addition to intentional tort, a person may also have tort liability under the concept of negligence. The basic idea here is that each member of society has a duty to conduct his or her life in a way that avoids injury to others—exercising *due care* in the conduct of his or her affairs. It is not reasonable, for instance, to block a public sidewalk with unshoveled snow or to bury drums of toxic chemicals in one's back yard. Such things might not be done with a conscious, willful desire to injure another person, but they certainly would create potentially hazardous situations that could result in harm to others. And that's the key here.

Negligence exists when four conditions are met:

1. The defendant must have owed the plaintiff a duty.
2. The defendant must have breached that duty.
3. The breach must be the actual and legal cause of the plaintiff's injury.
4. The injury must be one that the law recognizes and one for which monetary damages may be recovered.

In determining duty, the law considers—once again—what would be expected of a reasonable and prudent person under the same circumstances. While this is sometimes difficult to sort out, an example may help.

Let's say that Tyler, a guest at a resort, is standing on the dock when he sees that Niles is in trouble and may be about to drown. Does Tyler have a duty to try to rescue Niles? Our natural inclination, probably, is to say yes; and most people would likely try to do *something*—even if only to yell for help. But from a strictly legal standpoint, Tyler has no obligation to help Niles. He did nothing to create the situation, and so has no duty to Niles in this situation. Moreover, the law will ask what Tyler might be giving up in attempting a rescue. Would he be jeopardizing his own life, for instance? Civil duty does not extend that far; there's a limit to what the law expects. Thus, while we might wish for Tyler to attempt a rescue, and applaud his courage and his efforts if he does so, the point is, he is not legally *obligated* to do anything and cannot be held liable if he does nothing.

On the other hand, let's change our scenario a bit and make Tyler the lifeguard and swimming instructor at the resort. Let's suppose that Niles, a mediocre swimmer at best, is instructed by Tyler to swim 100 yards into the lake in water over Niles's head. He is nervous, but Tyler is insistent, so Niles plunges in and does his best. About fifteen yards out from the dock, Niles gets into trouble. Does Tyler have a duty to rescue him? In this instance, yes. He is responsible for creating the hazard. Further, as a lifeguard and swimming instructor, Tyler has a duty to keep Niles safe and rescue him from danger. He has breached that duty by putting Niles in danger, and will breach that duty again if he does not now try to rescue him.

What about the issues of *actual cause* and *proximate cause*? Well, in determining actual cause, the law applies the *but-for* test. In other words, the court will say, in effect, "If X had not occurred, Y would not have occurred either." And this test fits our scenario well. If Tyler had not ordered Niles to swim in water over his head, Niles would not have gotten into trouble. Tyler's instructional approach is indeed the actual cause of the harm.

What about proximate cause? In this case, the law asks

1. What is the likelihood that this conduct will injure others?

2. What would likely be the *seriousness* of the injury?

3. What must the defendant sacrifice to avoid the risk of causing injury?

Let's consider the previous scenario in light of these questions. To begin with, the likelihood of injuring others would appear to be fairly great. If Tyler is in the habit of putting inexperienced swimmers in water out of their depth, he must expect some problems. What would be the seriousness if injury did result? Fairly grave; Niles could drown. But what must the defendant sacrifice to avoid the risk? Very little. Tyler can change his instructional approach, or enter the water himself and thereby be ready to rescue any swimmers who get into trouble. In other words, the law will likely conclude that it won't cost Tyler much to reduce or eliminate the risk, and that the risk itself is extreme and unjustified under the circumstances. In short, if Niles *should* drown or suffer some emotional or physical trauma as the result of a near-drowning, Tyler would most likely be held liable under the tort of negligence.

One more point before we consider defenses to negligence. In considering what a hypothetical reasonable person might do in a given situation, the law looks at three elements: knowledge, investigation, and judgment. Let's see how these apply in our scenario with Niles and Tyler, and whether this perspective will help or hurt Tyler's case.

First, some knowledge of the law is presumed in order to keep our legal system functioning. In other words, the court will not allow as a defense simple ignorance. It will not help Tyler's case for him to say, "Sorry—I didn't know that I had responsibility for the safety of my students." In placing himself in a position of responsibility, Tyler is expected to *know* what the law requires of him; and if he does not know, *he* must take responsibility for finding out. Explaining the law to Tyler after the fact is not the duty of the court.

Second, the law expects each responsible member of society to investigate a given situation as appropriate to ensure that it is reasonably free from unwarranted hazards. If Tyler instructed students to dive into the water, for instance, when he had no idea how deep the lake was at that point or whether there were sharp rocks or logs on the bottom, he would surely be negligent. Under the circumstances, he would have a duty to investigate the area and to know it well.

Third, the law expects each individual to exercise judgment—not unprecedented insight and intuition, mind you, but some significant combination of reason and common sense. For instance, in our current scenario, the court is likely to pose the question, "Should it be considered good judgment for a swimming instructor to engage students in activities in which their personal safety cannot be assured?" *Most* people are likely to say no. The conclusion: Tyler has not behaved as most members of society would expect a reasonable and prudent person to behave in the same situation.

Defenses to Negligence

Since negligence does not require any intent to damage, you might think that it would be difficult *not* to be negligent in the course of normal life. There is some truth to that observation, but there are three defenses to negligence that reduce the number of times negligent behavior can be proven:

1. The plaintiff assumed the risk voluntarily.
2. The plaintiff's actions accounted for the injury.
3. The plaintiff's actions in part accounted for the injury.

Let's look at some examples to see how each of these defenses might apply in real life.

First, there is no negligence in a case where the defendant assumes the risk voluntarily. For instance, a manufacturer of a household cleaning product might inscribe on the container a warning that the product must not be consumed or inhaled because "serious illness could result." If the defendant were to *drink* this product or deliberately inhale the fumes and then become gravely ill as a result, the manufacturer could not be held liable. The consumer was warned, yet assumed the risk by behaving in a way that was unreasonable—drinking a cleaning product—and contrary to the manufacturer's recommendations.

Let's return for a moment to our scenario with Tyler and Niles. Did Niles assume the risk voluntarily? That is a little trickier to sort out here. We can assume that Niles is voluntarily taking the class, but it's also reasonable to assume that Niles had no intention of placing his life in danger by taking the class. And recall that he was apprehensive about jumping into the deep water. Reasonably, therefore, we have to conclude that Niles didn't volunteer to swim in deep water and run the risk of drowning.

Second, in those states that follow the doctrine of contributory negligence, if the plaintiff's actions at all contributed to the injury, the defendant will not be liable. In our scenario, for instance, this might have been the case if Tyler asked all the students to wear lifejackets during this particular exercise, but Niles took his off at the last minute when Tyler wasn't watching and then swam away out of Tyler's field of vision. In this case, the defendant's own *contributory* negligence might well bar recovery (the awarding of money, or damages) should he or his family choose to sue Tyler. The tricky part here is determining whether the defendant's behavior — as opposed to the plaintiff's — contributes to the harm or injury. If it did, then the defendant is not at all liable.

The third "defense" in negligence is really an alternative form of the second. States are now reevaluating their laws on contributory negligence — where the defendant escapes all liability if the plaintiff's actions at all contributed to the injury — and increasingly replacing them with the theory of *comparative negligence*. Under comparative negligence, the *relative* responsibilities of the plaintiff and defendant are assessed — and each then assumes responsibility for a percentage of the damages coextensive with their relative responsibility for the injury. For instance, suppose that Mendoza is injured in a collision caused by Sphinks. Suppose, too, that Mendoza was not wearing a safety belt and that testimony makes it clear that the injuries would have been much less severe had a safety belt been worn. In some jurisdictions, a court *might* then determine that Mendoza's failure to wear a safety belt accounted for, say, 35% of the problem — leaving Sphinks with 65% of the blame. If Mendoza were injured to the extent of $100,000, Sphinks would then be liable for $65,000, not for the full $100,000. (Note, however, that if the plaintiff accounts for 50% or more of his or her own injury, the defendant will not be held liable at all.)

Strict Liability as a Basis for Tort Liability

Some situations are so inherently dangerous that the law does not bother looking to see who — defendant or plaintiff — was more at fault in the situation. Society has instead decided that if you are doing X and damages result, you *will* be responsible for those damages, regardless. Firing a loaded pistol at a target in the backyard, for example, would probably place the defendant in a position of strict liability. It would be useless for the defendant to argue, for instance, that the plaintiff contributed to the harm by being in the area "during target practice." Similarly, a person who carried volatile explosives on a crowded bus could not argue sensibly that "such explosives usually don't explode accidentally." Strict liability is pretty much established by the legislature, and those people engaged in these ultrahazardous activities do so knowing the risk they run.

Regardless of the situation, *foreseeability* is a crucial consideration underlying the determination of liability in tort law. That is, the court will always ask, *could* the defendant — *should* the defendant — have foreseen the consequences of his or her actions in this situation? A person who rides a bus while carrying explosives would be expected to foresee the probable harm that would result should something go wrong. A person who drives at night without her headlights on would be expected to foresee the dangers such conduct could present. Perhaps a simple way of looking at it is to say that the court expects each person to exercise the same care and wisdom in protecting others' safety that he or she would want others to exercise.

SOME PRACTICAL ADVICE

The first and most obvious point, of course, is to know the law. Often, this may mean seeking the advice of an attorney, particularly before embarking on any new business venture which could pose a hazard or threat to any of the persons involved. Remember, the law will not tolerate ignorance as an excuse. You must know your duties and potential liabilities.

Second, it is wise to investigate any situation thoroughly and to ask whether there is any risk of harm—however remote. For instance, could employees suffer any injury or loss of health because of new products or procedures? Could competitors suffer loss of reputation through a new advertising campaign? Better to pose the questions before taking action. Sometimes, the barely plausible becomes reality.

Third, it's often a good idea to ask what others in the industry are doing, how they're conducting their business, what steps they're taking to ensure the safety of consumers and employees. Let's say you're the manager of a white-water rafting company that takes customers on river excursions. Should you expect customers to sign a release, freeing you from liability in the event of an accident? Probably so. Indeed, it's standard practice in the industry. Should you insist that all customers wear lifejackets—or that they be experienced swimmers? And even with the customers' releases, what standards should you have for those who guide the tours, who are directly responsible for the safety of others? Again, you can begin by asking what others in the industry are doing. But in addition, you'll also want to ask yourself what risks you, as a businessperson, might be taking if you do otherwise.

Fourth, realize that a company can be held liable for the actions of its officers or other employees in decisionmaking positions. Thus, an employee who commits a crime or tort may be personally liable, but may likely create corporate liability as well. No wonder so many companies are particular about which employees represent them to the public and how such representation is handled.

Finally, it's a good idea to measure the wisdom of any option by asking what the reasonably prudent person would do when faced with the same circumstances. The key here is due care—an appropriate social-minded concern for the welfare of others. This does not presume a selfless devotion to making the world a better place. It does, however, presume a sense of responsibility to society as a whole, and a willingness to forego shortcuts—and even profits—if these things spell potential harm to others.

ASSIGNMENTS

- Before you watch the video program, be sure you've read through the preceding overview, familiarized yourself with the learning objectives for this lesson, and looked at the key terms below. Then, read Chapters 3 and 4 of Davidson et al., *Business Law*.
- After completing these tasks, view the video program for Lesson 3.
- After watching the program, take time to review what you've learned. First, evaluate your learning with the self-test that follows the key terms. Then, apply and evaluate what you've learned with the "Your Opinion, Please" scenarios at the end of this telecourse study guide lesson.

KEY TERMS

Before you read through the textbook assignment and watch the video program, take a minute to look at the key terms associated with this lesson. When you encounter them in the textbook and video program, pay careful attention to their meaning.

Actual cause	False imprisonment
Arson	Felony
Assault	Forgery
Assumption of risk	Foreseeability
Battery	Fraud
Beyond a reasonable doubt	Harm
Breach of duty	Insanity
Burglary	Intentional tort
Civil duty	Invasion of privacy
Comparative negligence	Larceny
Consent	Libel
Contributory negligence	Mental distress
Conversion	Misdemeanor
Crime	Negligence
Defamation	Proximate cause
Defense	Robbery
Disparagement	Slander
Due care	Strict liability
Duress	Tort
Duty	Trespass
Embezzlement	White-collar crime

SELF-TEST

The questions below will help you evaluate how well you've learned the material in this lesson. Read each one carefully, and select the letter of the option that best answers the question. You'll find the correct answer, along with a reference to the page number(s) where the topic is discussed, in the back of this telecourse study guide.

1. A public wrong that violates federal or state law and is punishable by imprisonment is *best* described as

    a. a tort.
    b. a crime.
    c. negligence.
    d. strict liability.

2. Whether a crime is classed as a *felony* or *misdemeanor* depends *primarily* on

    a. the state in which the crime is committed.
    b. the attitude of the jury.
    c. whether the defendant committed the crime *deliberately*.
    d. the seriousness of the crime.

3. Donahue, who is short of cash, decides to hold up the all-night grocery to get some money for unpaid bills. When he gets inside, however, he loses his courage, walks out, and goes straight home. Based on the facts in this scenario, is Donahue guilty of any crime or tort?

    a. Yes, he is guilty of the crime of robbery.
    b. Yes, he is guilty of the tort of assault.
    c. Yes, he is guilty of the tort of trespass.
    d. No, he is not guilty of any crime or tort.

4. The breaking and entering of a structure with the intent to commit a felony is known as

    a. burglary.
    b. trespass.
    c. robbery.
    d. larceny.

5. Peterson is arrested for criminal assault and battery when he fires a loaded pistol and seriously wounds his neighbor, Flores. Peterson can use the defense of *justification* if

    a. Flores was trespassing.
    b. Peterson believed Flores intended to seriously harm him or his family.
    c. Peterson was intoxicated at the time of the shooting.
    d. *None* of the above; justification will not provide a defense in this case.

6. A tort committed by someone who either *wanted* to harm another or knew that his or her actions would most probably result in harm falls under the general category of

    a. negligence.
    b. strict liability.
    c. intentional torts.
    d. crimes.

7. In which of the following situations is the defendant *most likely* to be found liable under the theory of strict tort liability?

    a. Freemont's attack dog jumps the fence and mauls the mailman.
    b. Morris fails to park his car correctly and it rolls over the curb, injuring two pedestrians.
    c. After drinking several beers, Cartwright drives his speedboat into a rock ledge, killing a passenger.
    d. Angered by the behavior of a colleague at work, Hathaway shoves him into the water cooler.

8. There are two types of defamation: slander and libel. Which of the following *best* explains the primary difference between the two?

    a. There is no difference; the terms are synonymous.
    b. Unlike slander, libel involves violation of a written contract.
    c. Libel involves a serious moral accusation, while slander—much less serious—is often considered mere "gossip."
    d. Libel is written defamation of character; slander is oral defamation.

9. Kincaid likes to fire his pistol at rabbits that wander near his home. This action is *likely* to be

    a. perfectly legal, assuming no human being is affected.
    b. a tort.
    c. a crime.
    d. viewed differently depending on the laws of the jurisdiction he lives in.

10. In determining negligence, the courts will generally ask

    a. what a reasonable and prudent person would do in the same circumstances.
    b. whether the defendant *intended* to cause harm to another.
    c. whether there was any possible way for the defendant to have prevented the situation.
    d. whether the defendant knew in advance that harm would come to the plaintiff personally.

YOUR OPINION, PLEASE

Read each of the following scenarios and answer the questions about the decisions you would make in each situation. Give these questions some serious thought; they may be used as the basis for the development of a more complex essay. You should base your decisions on what you've learned from this lesson, though you may incorporate outside readings or information gained through your own experience if it is relevant.

Scenario I

Late Halloween night, Oster is walking home from a Halloween party along a road that is poorly lighted. She is still wearing her Halloween witch's costume—a black dress and cape, black hat, black shoes, and black mask. She has no light clothing, no flashlight, nothing that would help make her visible to a driver.

Worley is driving home from another party along the same road. He has just discovered, upon leaving the party, that one of his headlights is burned out. He feels uncomfortable about driving that way, but reasons that since it is only a short way to his house, nothing is likely to happen. In any case, at 11 p.m., there do not seem to be many alternatives.

Despite the problems he has seeing with only one headlight, Worley drives about five miles an hour over the speed limit. He isn't intending to speed, really, and in fact doesn't even know what the speed limit is along this road; he's just driving at a pace that feels comfortable. Oster hears Worley's car coming and tries to stay to the side of the road. She has a difficult time telling just where that is, but believes she is well to the edge. Nevertheless, as Worley rounds a corner, he is unable to take the curve quite sharply enough, sees Oster only at the last second (she is on the darker side, where the light is out), and cannot avoid her altogether. Upon impact, Oster is thrown ten feet and suffers a broken shoulder and two broken legs. She sues for damages, accusing Worley of negligence. Worley counters that Oster is also responsible for the accident—perhaps even more responsible than he.

What's your opinion? Based on what you know of the situation, do you think Oster is likely to be successful in her suit? Why or why not? Can Worley successfully invoke the defense of contributory negligence? To what extent do you believe Worley is responsible for the accident? To what extent, if at all, is Oster responsible? How will these determinations affect the outcome of the case?

- Is Oster likely to win her suit? If so, on what grounds?
- What factors support your answer?
- What factors might an attorney cite in arguing against your case? Specifically, what defenses, if any, are open to Worley?
- What steps, if any, might Worley have taken to prevent a lawsuit in this case?

- What steps, if any, might Oster have taken to prevent a lawsuit in this case?

Scenario 2

Muldoon has spent more than four months developing a special computer program designed to train engineering technicians. The program is still in the development stage, and Muldoon knows it is important to field test the program. A colleague and fellow programmer, Fitzer, who works in another department, offers to review the program just for the privilege of becoming more familiar with it. Muldoon reluctantly agrees, with the stipulation that Fitzer return the program to her the next day. Fitzer promises that he will.

Once the program is in his hands, however, Fitzer becomes fascinated. He asks Muldoon if he may keep it longer than the one day. She declines, saying she needs to work on it further, and besides, she is afraid an unauthorized person may get it. Fitzer thinks Muldoon is just being paranoid, and he decides to keep the program for a while. Though Muldoon has other copies of the program, she is very concerned about protecting her work and ensuring that no one else will copy it. So, she becomes anxious when Fitzer no longer returns her calls.

Since Fitzer's work area is "off limits" to employees in general and cannot be entered without special permission, Muldoon waits till the noon hour, when many employees — including Fitzer — are out. She manages to slip past the receptionist and enters Fitzer's office, which is unlocked. Sure enough, he has the program loaded up on his computer. Furious, Muldoon sets about to remove the program, but in the course of doing so — because she is generally unfamiliar with the organization of Fitzer's computer files — she also erases valuable data. There is no damage to the computer itself, but the data loss costs Fitzer ten workdays and untold grief. Muldoon says it serves him right for refusing to return her property. Fitzer, however, is unwilling to let things go so easily. He sues Muldoon for trespass.

What's your opinion? Based on what you know of the situation, do you think Fitzer can build a case for trespass? Do you think Muldoon was within her rights, or should she have acted differently in trying to reclaim the computer program? How would you sort out the liability in this case?

- Is Fitzer likely to win a suit on grounds of trespass?
- What factors support your answer?
- What factors might an attorney cite in arguing against your view? Specifically, what defenses, if any, are open to Muldoon?
- What steps, if any, might Muldoon have taken to prevent a lawsuit in this situation?
- What steps, if any, might Fitzer have taken to prevent a lawsuit in this situation?

4

The Nature of Contract Law

LEARNING OBJECTIVES

Upon completing your study of this lesson, you should be able to:

- Define the meaning of the term *contract*.
- Discuss the importance of contracts in the business world.
- Identify six elements of a contract.
- Identify and discuss the types of classifications of contracts.

Lesson 4 is an introduction to contract law. Through the course of this lesson, you'll have a chance to learn what a contract is, how contract law has evolved over time, what elements are essential in a valid contract, and how contracts can be classified.

OVERVIEW

Virtually every phase of our lives is governed in one way or another by contracts. This is true of our private lives and our business lives as well. When we marry, buy or rent a home, purchase a car, use a credit card, send children to private school or college, or purchase insurance of any kind, our obligations and rights within the context of each action are covered in some way by contract law. Similarly, such commonplace business activities as employing other workers, agreeing to serve as someone else's employee, renting space, leasing equipment, and purchasing supplies are normally governed by contracts as well. The influence of contract law is so pervasive, in fact, that few of us can go through a day without somehow fulfilling the requirements of some contract or other—even if we're not really conscious all of the time of doing so.

It wasn't always like that, however. Most of the early laws enforced by governments dealt only with property rights—who owned what tract of land, what responsibilities adjoining landowners had to each other, who was liable if someone else's herd of cattle got loose and trampled down the wheat crop of another landowner, and so on. Governments paid little attention to what we now consider "contract" law—either between individuals or in a commercial setting.

The Development of Contract Law

Commercial contract law originated in the customs of the early merchants and traders; its roots go back all the way to Phoenician businessmen trading around the Mediterranean Sea. Their trade customs, and those of the businesspeople who followed, came to be seen as "rules" for the behavior of merchants. These rules were enforced not in government courts, but in separate mercantile courts run by the merchants' trade organizations.

As trade continued to expand, government courts also began to decide disputes between individuals, between individuals and the government, and between individuals and merchants. From these courts, separate from mercantile courts, came what we now call "common law" contract law—law which was molded and modified by the court judges as new circumstances came before the courts in different cases. Then, as the Western world became ever more commercial, governments started to restrict the powers of the merchant guilds and the mercantile courts. As they did so, the rules of commerce were folded into the common law of the government courts. At the same time, governments began to use their legislatures to pass laws—that is, to make statutes—which governed commercial transactions. These statutes, logically enough, were interpreted by government courts whenever disputes arose.

In the United States, the principal power to establish laws and rules governing business — that is, commercial — transactions rested with the individual state governments. Unfortunately, this resulted in wide variations as to how a given type of commercial transaction should be governed. Imagine the difficulties of doing business when the rights and responsibilities of the different parties to the transaction vary dramatically from state to state. By the 1940s, commerce had expanded so much that the situation was intolerable. Businesspeople in New York who conducted business in California wanted and needed rules and laws for doing business in California that were generally similar to the laws and rules they were used to dealing with in their own state.

Since these commercial laws were not the province of the federal government, a standardized set of laws needed to be adopted by the states themselves. To aid this process, the American Law Institute and the National Commission on Uniform State Laws provided state legislatures with model (that is, uniform) statutes for governing business transactions. And since the standardization of business laws across states was perceived as a worthwhile objective, state legislatures adopted the statutes — which today are known as the Uniform Commercial Code — with only minor tinkering.

Widespread adoption of the Uniform Commercial Code (UCC) revolutionized commercial law. Henceforth, all commercial transactions had certain common elements and could, therefore, be treated somewhat the same under law. At the same time, the UCC clarified and simplified laws governing commercial transactions and, of particular importance, provided a basis for more uniform interpretation of commercial law by the courts of the different states. What's more, all contracts — regardless of content or circumstance — now had to meet certain basic criteria considered essential to sound business practice.

But given how rapidly the business world is changing, not every circumstance can be foreseen. Nor, for that matter, would we probably want our legislatures attempting to legislate every possible situation that would need legal resolution. But doesn't this approach leave a gap where no applicable law exists?

Generally not. As noted above, there was a time when regular government courts were deciding cases of contract disputes alongside the guild mercantile courts. The "judge-made" — that is, common — law and the code explicitly state that the code must be supplemented by common law. As you can well imagine, it didn't occur to the framers of the UCC to include regulations covering software copyrights, satellite transmissions, genetic engineering, and so on. But changes in the business world aren't just technologically related. Employee rights and benefits are expanding in new directions, consumers are gaining new protections, rules about accounting and taxation change constantly.

So keep in mind that what is commonplace for one generation may be difficult for preceding generations even to envision, that not every commercial situation can be anticipated. The concept of absolute uniformity in contract law is appealing, but impractical. Laws cannot be written once and for all; they must allow for some change, some flexibility. And while it's extremely valuable to have a standardized body of commercial law like the UCC as a starting point, the law is best viewed as constantly evolving, changing to suit the times as a result of careful and prudent judgment.

The Six Elements of a Contract

Just what is a contract? A contract is *any legally binding and legally enforceable promise or set of promises between two or more competent parties*. Most of us probably picture a written document, but while most contracts are written, they do not have to be. For example, suppose Joe tells an old classmate, Ed, "If you're ever in Philadelphia, stop by the office—we could use a bright person like you in our firm." The implication here is that Joe will give Ed a job with his firm if Ed ever decides to move to Philadelphia. But if Ed begins packing in the belief that he has a firm contract, he will be in for an unpleasant surprise. A court is not likely to look on Joe's statement as a legally enforceable contract—even if Joe acknowledges his remark. To understand why, let's explore the six elements that are required in any legal contract.

First, *there must be agreement*—an offer by one party and acceptance of the offer by the other. The question to be asked here is, Would any reasonably prudent person believe that an offer had actually been made and accepted?

Suppose, for instance, that in our preceding example, Ed sells his home in Detroit, quits his old job, and moves his wife and three children to Philadelphia, intending to go to work for Joe. When Ed drops in to learn where his parking space is, Joe is totally surprised. Joe tells Ed that he's sorry about the misunderstanding, but he has no present openings suited to Ed's qualifications, and doesn't anticipate any in the future. Ed believes he was offered a job, which he's moved a long way to accept. But Joe's position is that he merely noted how rewarding it would be to have an employee of Ed's caliber and talent.

Does an agreement exist? Look to see whether an offer for a job was made *and* whether an acceptance of the offer occurred. Would a reasonably prudent person have taken Joe's statement as a firm job offer? Think about it: What was said about salary? Starting time? Job responsibilities? Benefits? Without discussing these details, would you think that a job offer had been extended? And how did Ed accept this possible offer? Did he say "Gee, thanks, Joe. I'll see you in Philadelphia bright and early on the 18th. I'm happy to be working with you"? Did he write to Joe's office saying that he and his wife had thought about the offer and decided to take the new job? Would a reasonably prudent person think Ed had accepted an "offer" of a job? Based on this first requirement of a contract—offer and acceptance— you'd probably agree that Ed's chances of demonstrating the existence of a bona fide agreement are probably remote.

Second, *the contract must be supported by consideration*. That is, something must be bargained for and given in exchange for the promises expressed in the offer and acceptance. Suppose Jones offers to sell Smith a chainsaw, and Smith says, "OK, I'll buy it." In determining whether this agreement has the elements of a legal contract, the court will want to know what Smith is providing in exchange for the chainsaw. In other words, simple acceptance of an offer is not enough. A legal contract must specify clearly what each side is giving and what each expects in return. Regardless of whether Jones wants fifty dollars, tickets to a football game, or Smith's new Mercedes in exchange for his chainsaw, each party must receive consideration.

Third, *each side must have the capacity or legal ability to contract*. Suppose overworked dentist Brown hires Anderson to help reduce his patient load—not knowing that Anderson's licensing credentials are forged. If Brown subsequently discovers that Anderson cannot legally practice dentistry and fires her, Anderson would have a hard time getting a court to "enforce" her employment agreement. A court could rule that Anderson did not have the legal capacity to agree to practice dentistry. And since a contract must be made by parties who have the legal capacity to contract, the court would refuse to enforce the employment agreement.

Fourth, *a valid contract must be based on the genuine assent of both parties*. If the contract is obtained by fraud or duress, it may be set aside by the court. Perhaps Wilson contracts to purchase a tract of land in another state on the basis of a photograph supplied by Quagmire Realty. Now suppose Wilson later learns that the photograph really showed the much nicer parcel of land next to the parcel he actually bought. If Slick sues Wilson for the money when Wilson refuses to make his payments, the court may well not enforce the sales contract. If Wilson can show that he was deliberately misled by Slick and was reasonable in believing what Slick said to and showed him, his assent to the contract would not be genuine.

Similarly, let's say that the White Company pressures Simmons to sign a contract to sell it goods from her store at a price below what she paid for them. Since White Company threatens to buy up the building housing her store and throw her out if she doesn't agree to the contract, Simmons signs. If Simmons later decides not to sell the agreed-upon goods and White Company were to sue for delivery, a court could find that Simmons did not freely (that is, genuinely) agree to the terms of the contract. It would then rule that the contract was not enforceable, since both parties to any contract must genuinely and freely agree to the contract.

Fifth, *the terms of the contract must be legal*. Courts will not, for example, uphold contracts to import illegal drugs, steal, embezzle, defraud the public, misappropriate or misuse funds, and so forth. In such cases, it is of no consequence how well-written or sound the contract might be in other respects. The requirements of both parties must be totally legal. If one party refuses to go through with the contract and the other party were to try and sue to force the illegal actions, a court would not enforce the contract.

Sixth, *the contract must be in proper form* before it is legally binding. As you might imagine, the most common element of proper form is that some contracts have to be in writing. Each state has its own laws about what particular types of contracts must be in writing before the court will enforce them. In most states, for example, any contract to sell real estate must be in writing in order to be enforced by the court. And in many states, contracts for purchases over a certain dollar figure must be written.

But whenever a contract is not required by state law to be in a certain form or meet certain prerequisites, the contract could be in most any form and still be enforceable—if it's a verbal agreement. Courts will uphold oral contracts, but entering into an oral contract is particularly risky. Proving the terms of the contract—even if there were witnesses to the conversation—is usually very difficult, especially if your witnesses remember differently than those of your opponent. This is one reason that business owners usually insist on written contracts governing agreements with colleagues, even those whom they also consider to be close friends. Sound business practice suggests that it is only sensible to clarify in writing all expectations on both sides in order to minimize the chances of later misunderstandings.

Classifications of Contracts

Contracts can be classified in a number of different ways, and the various classifications are not mutually exclusive. In other words, any given contract can be, and usually is, classified in more than one category.

First, contracts can be *formal* or *informal*. A formal contract is one in which some ceremony or formality must be carried out to make the contract valid. Five hundred years ago, for example, certain types of contracts would not be valid until sealed with wax and marked with the kin's signet ring. Today, a few states still require that some contracts be "under seal." Contracts of record—agreements that have been recorded by a court—are another example of a formal contract, as is a special type of commercial contract called a "negotiable instrument." All in all, though, very few types of contracts require a special formality to be valid.

An informal contract is any contract which does not by law require a formality for the contract to be valid. An oral contract is one fairly obvious example of an informal contract. But written contracts—even those drawn up by lawyers—are also informal contracts unless some special formality is required by law. Informal contracts are also known as simple contracts, and they are by far the more common form of contract in the Western business world.

A second classification divides contracts into *unilateral* and *bilateral*. The distinguishing feature for this classification is the manner in which the offer of the potential contract is accepted. If the offer is accepted by performing the act requested in the offer, the contract becomes unilateral. However, if the offer is accepted by promising to later perform the act requested in the offer, a bilateral contract is created. In a bilateral contract, it's the promise to perform—not the actual performance—that accepts the offer and that creates the contract.

An example will help clarify the difference. Let's suppose that Mr. Thomas offers to pay Johnny, his neighbor's son, $3 if Johnny will wash the Thomas family car. If Johnny responds by getting out the hose and soaping up the car, he accepted Mr. Thomas's offer of $3 and created a unilateral contract. On the other hand, what if Johnny agrees but, instead of washing the car, promises he will wash the car the next evening? He has accepted Mr. Thomas's offer of $3 by promising to wash the car. He and Mr. Thomas now have a bilateral contract.

A third classification categorizes contracts on the basis of what would or could happen to the contract in a court of law if one of the parties wanted to cancel the contract and the other wanted to enforce it. A *valid* contract is one that is legally binding and with which a court would require the parties to comply, regardless of which party tried to cancel the contract. On the other hand, there are three other types of contract—*void, voidable,* and *enforceable*—that have some defect that might keep the court from insisting that their terms be performed.

Voidable contracts are those that may be accepted (even though they have a defect) or rejected at the option of one party. Let's say that 17-year-old Manny Perez buys a Mercedes from Capitol Motors. Because of his age, Manny can't be compelled to follow through on his end of the contract. He could, if he wanted, have the contract voided because of that defect. On the other hand, he may want to keep the car and follow through with the contract conditions. So even though the contract is defective (because of Manny's age), it will stand unless Manny takes action to void it.

This is different from a void contract. A void contract is one that has no lawful purpose. An agreement between an arsonist and a retailer who wants his competitor's store burned down is void. The agreement has no lawful purpose and neither party has the right to ask the court to enforce it. But it's not only illegal activities that lead to void contracts. Suppose Helen is deeply in love with Troy, so they get married. Unfortunately, Helen is still married to Ron and, generally, a marriage between two people when one of the people is still married is a void marriage. Whether or not the parties want the marriage to be legal, the law says it is not and will not give to either of the parties the legal rights which the husband and wife relationship normally has.

An unenforceable contract is one that would have been valid had it been made with attention to all the details required by law. For example, it is almost always necessary to have contracts for the sale of real estate in written form. Suppose the owner of Dewdrop Inn contracts to sell the vacant lot behind the inn to Schemdley Parking for $2,000. Let's further say that all of the other necessary elements of the contract are in place and that both parties are initially pleased with the agreement, which was made orally. If a dispute arises and the matter goes to court, the Dewdrop Inn will come out the owner of the lot. The court would say that without a written contract, the agreement to sell is unenforceable.

A fourth categorization separates contracts into *express* and *implied*. An express contract—the more common form—is one in which both parties know that they are making a contract. An implied contract is one in which the existence of the contract is inferred from the conduct of the parties over time. Suppose, for instance, that Goodie's Restaurant is directly adjacent to Low Risk Insurance. Low Risk normally uses only a quarter of its allotted parking space, and rents the remainder to Goodie's for a fee. Though no written contract exists regarding the parking lot rental, Goodie's has been renting the space for several years now, reimbursing Low Risk regularly on a semiannual basis. If Low Risk suddenly blocked off its parking spaces and refused to let Goodie's use the spaces for its customers, Goodie's could sue Low Risk to force access to the parking spaces. A court would probably rule that an implied contract existed between Low Risk and Goodie's that allowed

Goodie's to rent the spaces for six months at a time. Although the court would likely support Low Risk's right to refuse to "re-rent" the spaces to Goodie's, Low Risk would most likely be forced to allow access by Goodie's customers for the time remaining on the implied six-month "lease."

Finally, contracts may be *executory* or *executed*. An executory contract is one for which some condition or promise remains to be completed by one or both parties. An executed contract, on the other hand, is one that has been fulfilled totally — all conditions have been fully met by both parties. Obviously, all bilateral contracts change from executory to executed once the contract has been completed.

In addition to these categories, sometimes a situation arises in which someone stands to unfairly benefit from a relationship. This benefit would come from their own underhanded dealings or from their own or other people's innocent actions. But often no crimes have been committed and no other legal remedies exist to prevent the injustice and the receipt of unwarranted or unearned benefits. Can anything be done to prevent the unjust enrichment?

Where it is possible and practical to remedy the situation, the court may step in and create a quasi contract. Although both parties admit that no real contract exists and at least one of the parties does not want a contract to exist, this artificial contract is created to preclude the receipt of the unjust enrichment. Suppose that Cushy Company has a contract to deliver new office furniture to Herbert Browne and Associates on March 1. The furniture arrives on time but is delivered by mistake to Lester Brown, one floor up. Lester accepts the furniture without protest, as if it were a gift. Now, of course, this situation could be easily corrected if it were discovered soon enough. But suppose Lester keeps the new furniture for a month, during which time some snags, scratches, and coffee stains accumulate. Now Cushy can't simply transfer the furniture to Herbert Browne; it's used furniture, and Herbert paid for new furniture. Is Cushy simply out the value of the furniture it delivered by mistake to Lester Brown?

Not necessarily. The court can create a quasi contract between Cushy and Lester Brown, requiring Lester to pay for the furniture that he's implicitly accepted through his conduct. Creation of the quasi contract ensures that Lester Brown is not unjustly enriched by receiving a new set of furniture without having to pay for it. And even though the error in delivery was Cushy's, the quasi contract will keep Cushy from being out the cost of the furniture Lester has kept.

Not every case of unjust benefit is as straightforward, however. Note that in the preceding example, Lester Brown accepts the furniture when clearly he had not ordered it; there was more than simple error involved. But suppose that the crew from E-Z-Rid Exterminators contracts to spray the Herbert Browne and Associates offices. They, too, go to the wrong offices — to those of Lester Brown, Consultant, which are closed for remodeling. The remodeling crew, thinking they are doing Lester a big favor, let the exterminators in and even agree to leave early so the place can air out before the next workday. Later, E-Z-Rid bills Lester Brown for a pest spraying that was never requested. Will the court create a quasi contract to cover E-Z-Rid's loses?

That's more difficult to say. In this case, it's hard to hold Lester morally responsible for the debt because it was incurred through no fault of his. He did not request the service, neither he nor his staff were present when it was performed, and there's no way for him to return "the benefit" to E-Z-Rid. But just as clearly, Lester received a benefit for which he thus far has not paid. And even though the facts place responsibility for the mix-up in offices on E-Z-Rid staff, E-Z-Rid still is out the cost of chemicals and staff salaries.

If the court were to create a quasi contract, it would undoubtedly try to strike a balance that attempted to make the situation equitable. If Lester's offices had never had pests, if Lester had never sprayed and had no intention of ever spraying, and if spraying for pests was the exception rather than the rule in his area, the "unjust benefit" to Lester is sufficiently small that he might not be required to pay for the spraying. But if it turned out that Lester himself had contracted with another company for a similar spraying for two weeks hence, the court would likely rule that the benefit to Lester was considerable and that he should pay a substantial amount of E-Z-Rid's costs.

SOME PRACTICAL ADVICE

What are, from the businessperson's perspective, the most significant elements of contract law to keep in mind? Well, first, that a contract is more than an agreement. Taking someone's word as binding may be a fine basis for friendship, but it is a poor—and sometimes unacceptable—basis for business contracting. Written contracts define exceptions for both sides and minimize opportunities for misunderstanding later. And if misunderstandings do occur, the written contract provides a better basis for the courts to resolve the problem.

Remember, too, that certain elements are required for a contract to be legally binding and enforceable. This does not mean that the contract must be couched in difficult-to-decipher legal jargon, nor even that it must be drawn up by an attorney (though that is often a good idea). It does mean, however, that every contract must have these six elements:

- agreement,
- consideration,
- capacity (the legal ability of both sides to contract),
- genuine assent of both parties to the terms,
- a legal purpose, and, if required,
- proper form.

As we've seen, there are times when an agreement that the parties entered into will not be recognized as a contract; when a dispute arises and one of the parties turns to a court for help, the court may not enforce the contract. The prudent business perspective, however, is to presume that any contract will be enforced. The majority are, and it is a very poor practice to enter into any contract with the assumption that the contract can simply be set aside if things don't work out as expected. Similarly, if the contract is advantageous to your company — as it presumably is — you want to make certain that the other party can be forced to live up to its obligations.

In other words, a businessperson must have a sense of what makes a good contract. The soundness of the business dealings are a matter for another course, but from a legal viewpoint, it's necessary to

- understand the terms of the offer and acceptance,
- assure that the agreement has consideration,
- enter into contracts only with parties legally capable of making them,
- assure that both parties genuinely agree to the terms of the contract,
- contract only for legal purposes and not against public policy, and, where necessary,
- have the contract be in proper legal form.

The courts do consider the fairness of the agreement to both sides, but relying on the courts to protect you against unwise business actions is an expensive, troublesome, and often ineffective tactic. It is much more practical to develop the understanding of basic contract law necessary to evaluate the implications of any contract before signing. The financial success — and sometimes the very survival — of a business may hang in the balance.

ASSIGNMENTS

- Before you watch the video program, be sure you've read through the preceding overview, familiarized yourself with the learning objectives for this lesson, and looked at the key terms below. Then, read Chapter 8 of Davidson et al., *Business Law*.
- After completing these tasks, view the video program for Lesson 4
- After watching the program, take time to review what you've learned. First, evaluate your learning with the self-test which follows the key terms. Then, apply and evaluate what you've learned with the "Your Opinion, Please" scenarios at the end of this telecourse study guide lesson.

KEY TERMS

Before you read through the textbook assignment and watch the video program, take a minute to look at the key terms associated with this lesson. When you encounter them in the textbook and video program, pay careful attention to their meaning.

Agreement
Bilateral contract
Capacity
Common law
Consideration
Contract
Detriment
Economic obligation
Executed
Executory
Express contract
Formal contract
Free enterprise
Genuine assent
Implied contract
Implied in fact
Implied in law
Informal contract

Mercantile
Offeree
Offeror
Proper form
Public policy
Quasi contract
Secured transactions
Security interest
Simple contract
Social obligation
Status
Unenforceable
Uniform Commercial Code (UCC)
Unilateral contract
Unjust enrichment
Valid
Void
Voidable

SELF-TEST

The questions below will help you evaluate how well you've learned the material in this lesson. Read each one carefully, and select the letter of the option that best answers the question. You'll find the correct answer, along with a reference to the page number(s) where the topic is discussed, in the back of this telecourse study guide.

1. How likely is it that the average person will, at some point, be involved in transactions governed by contract law?

   a. Extremely likely—in fact it's almost inevitable for nearly every adult person.
   b. Quite likely for those persons who own or operate businesses, but far less likely for others.
   c. Rather unlikely since even in business settings, only a handful of persons have reason to actually sign contracts.
   d. Extremely unlikely since only those with formal training and proper authorization are even allowed to sign contracts.

2. Which of the following *best* sums up the goal or purpose of the Uniform Commercial Code (UCC)?

   a. To ensure that all proper contracts are legally enforceable.

b. To bring consistency to the laws that regulate and govern commercial transactions.

c. To protect the security interests of sellers in business transactions.

d. To assist each state in creating a set of statutes that reflects its own regional needs.

3. The term "judge-made" law refers to laws that

a. are part of the Uniform Commercial Code.

b. were written by specially appointed panels of judges at the time the guild courts were disbanded.

c. originated in the seventeenth century English parliament.

d. developed from precedents derived from disputes previously settled in court.

4. Historically, the term "contract" has been defined in various ways. According to the textbook, which of the following is the *best* business definition?

a. Any legally binding and legally enforceable promise, or set of promises, between two or more competent parties.

b. Any agreement between two or more competent parties that exists in written form.

c. Any bona fide promise or set of promises, given and accepted — whether expressed in written form or not — by which one or both parties stand to benefit economically.

d. Any document drawn up by an attorney or other appropriate legal representative, where the document's contents relate to a legal issue.

5. Jones's landlord threatens eviction when Jones will not get rid of his pet boa constrictor. Upset by these threats, Jones hires Blunt to kill his landlord. This agreement will be viewed by a court of law as a valid, enforceable contract *only if*

a. it is documented in writing.

b. Blunt actually carries out his part of the agreement and does, in fact, kill the landlord.

c. Jones can demonstrate that Blunt entered into the contract willingly and with no coercion.

d. *None* of the above; under no circumstances will the court recognize this agreement as a valid contract.

6. Smith writes out an agreement in which she states that "Riles will be duly compensated for services rendered." Both parties sign the statement willingly. Is such an agreement likely to be upheld as a legal, enforceable contract in a court of law?

a. Yes, absolutely; it's a written agreement, willingly entered into and signed by both parties.

b. Not unless Smith and Riles have further clarified and agreed to the terms of performance and compensation.

c. Not unless the signing of the agreement is witnessed by a third party.

d. It would depend entirely on whether Smith's compensation to Riles is indeed just and sufficient.

7. It is usually recommended that contracts be in written form. The *main* reason for this is that

a. unwritten contracts are difficult to "prove" the terms of and difficult for a court to enforce or uphold should a dispute occur.

b. only written contracts are legal; thus, courts will not even attempt to enforce an oral contract in the event of a dispute.

c. courts require ongoing records of all legal contracts, and such records can only be maintained with written documentation.

d. written contracts are much simpler to renegotiate should that prove necessary at some point.

8. According to the textbook, contract law was rather slow to develop in Europe. One of the *main* reasons cited for this was that

a. European society didn't have an established legal system until well into the twentieth century.

b. the rise of capitalistic ethics suppressed attempts to create a system of contract law.

c. increasing emphasis on individual rights made many persons rebel at the restrictions imposed by contract law.

d. in socially stratified European society, rights were pretty much determined by one's class and status, rather than egalitarian laws.

9. Through the doctrine of unconscionability, the courts seek to protect persons who

a. are pressured into agreeing to unfavorable contracts by someone with superior bargaining power.

b. regret having signed a contract and now consider it a hardship to have to follow through with its performance.

c. have agreed to contracts that—though they didn't know it at the time—somehow violate public policy.

d. according to the best judgment of the court, are not receiving fair compensation according to the terms of the contract.

10. Johnson wants to hire Murray as a security guard for the next nine months. Johnson draws up a written agreement defining the terms of employment and outlining all details of compensation, including salary, benefits, and so forth. If Murray accepts the job offer, he and Johnson have created a contract. Three of the four options below describe the type of contract that exists. Which one of the following does *not* describe the type of contract between Johnson and Murray?

a. A unilateral contract

b. A quasi contract

c. An informal contract

d. An executory contract

YOUR OPINION, PLEASE

Read each of the following scenarios and answer the questions about the decision you would make in each situation. Give these questions some serious thought; they may be used as the basis for the development of a more complex essay. You should base your decisions on what you've learned from this lesson, though you may incorporate outside readings or information gained through your own experience if it is relevant.

Scenario I

For about fourteen months now, Green Grass Feedstore has had a contract with Goodgrain Suppliers for a weekly shipment of oats in 100 twenty-five-pound sacks. The Goodgrain driver—through a simple paperwork error—has regularly been delivering five extra sacks, for which Green Grass has not been billed. Goodgrain inventory managers have noted the missing sacks, but felt that these had, perhaps, been included to make up for potential damage in shipment. In any event, it didn't look like an error; the shipments always contained 105 bags.

One day, a Goodgrain auditor discovers the paperwork error—and the Goodgrain accountant promptly takes steps to correct it. Among other things, he notifies the accounts receivable department that Green Grass can be billed for the extra grain. Green Grass, however, refuses to pay, stating that they cannot be held accountable for Goodgrain's accounting errors.

Goodgrain thereupon threatens to sue on grounds of unjust enrichment, pointing out that its loss over a fourteen-month period has been substantial and cannot be tolerated. Green Grass counters that given the length of time over which Goodgrain has been delivering the extra oats, an implicit contract exists. Under this contract, Green Grass was entitled to buy the 105-bag shipment of grain at the 100-bag price. But Goodgrain management is not convinced. They contend that the extra grain deliveries constituted a mistake, pure and simple—a mistake they've now taken steps to correct, but one that Green Grass was well aware of and had the responsibility to point out in the first place. Green Grass, meanwhile, holds firm, contending that responsibility for the mistake belongs to Goodgrain, especially since it was their paperwork which contained the error—and continued to contain it for an extended period.

What's your opinion? Based on what you know of the situation, do you think a court will uphold Goodgrain's suit on the grounds of unjust enrichment? Which side—Green Grass or Goodgrain—is responsible for the mistake? Does the fact that the shipments continued over an extended period justify Green Grass's contention that an "implicit" contract exists entitling them to the larger shipment of oats at the same price?

- Is Goodgrain's suit likely to be upheld in court? Why or why not?
- What factors support your answer?
- What factors might an attorney cite in arguing against your view?
- What steps, if any, might Green Grass have taken to prevent a lawsuit in this situation?
- What steps, if any, might Goodgrain have taken to protect their rights in this situation?

Scenario 2

The Johnsons, who have been car hunting for several months, are delighted to come upon a car they consider perfect in all respects—a used four-wheel-drive vehicle with low mileage and great maintenance. Sharp, the owner, is asking $10,000. The Johnsons offer $8,000. Sharp doesn't really want to come down, but he's had the car on the market for some time. What's more, he's in a hurry to close the deal since he's planning to move out of state. Somewhat reluctantly he agrees orally to the Johnsons' offer, provided they give him a check for the full amount during the next three days. They tell him it will be no problem whatever since they have a sizeable savings account and excellent credit.

Upon completing the necessary arrangements at the bank, the Johnsons arrive back at Sharp's door the very next afternoon, check in hand, prepared to close the sale. They're dismayed and angered when Sharp tells them sorry, but he's had an offer of $9,000 and cannot afford to turn that down. He adds, however, that he will reconsider their offer if they care to raise the price to something over $9,000. The Johnsons argue that they already have an oral contract for the sale of the car at the agreed-upon price of $8,000, and that they have no intention of paying more. Sharp, they contend further, will have to stand by his agreement since legally he has no alternative. If he does not, the Johnsons maintain, they will sue for violation of contract. Sharp argues, however, that no contract exists, and that he cannot legally be required to do anything.

What's your opinion? Based on what you know of the situation, do you think Sharp and the Johnsons have a contract? If so, is it legally enforceable? Can Sharp legally refuse to sell the vehicle to the Johnsons at the agreed-upon $8,000 price?

- Is a court likely to view the agreement between Sharp and the Johnsons as a legally enforceable contract? Why or why not?
- What factors support your answer?
- What factors might an attorney cite in arguing against your view?
- What steps, if any, might Sharp have taken to prevent a lawsuit in this situation?

- What steps, if any, might the Johnsons have taken to protect their interests in this situation?

5

Contract Requirement: The Agreement

LEARNING OBJECTIVES

Upon completing your study of this lesson, you should be able to:

- Define the term *mutual assent* and relate mutual assent to contract formation.
- Explain the three basic elements of an offer.
- Describe some special problems involved in viewing advertisements, auctions, rewards, and bids as offers, and explain how the court tends to look on each special case.
- Identify and describe four methods by which an offer can be terminated.
- Relate the concept of *acceptance* to developing mutual assent.
- Describe the means by which acceptance may be communicated under various circumstances.
- Explain how acceptance differs in bilateral and unilateral contracts.

The purpose of this lesson is to examine the basic foundation for any contract: agreement. In the course of this lesson, you will have an opportunity to consider the importance of mutual assent, explore the relationship between offer and acceptance, and learn several ways in which offers may be terminated. And, as you'll see, if there is no agreement (mutual assent, that is), there will be no contract.

OVERVIEW

Agreement is the basis of any contract. Or, to put it another way, without agreement, there can be no contract. Perhaps this seems rather obvious. Yet disputes often arise because two parties believe they have agreed to very different things. A knowledge of the basic nature of mutual assent can help prevent such misunderstandings.

Mutual Assent

The term *mutual assent*—which essentially means agreement—has two parts. First, it requires that both parties agree to the terms of a contract. When the terms are satisfactory to only one party, a contract cannot be formed. Second, it requires that both parties agree to the *same* terms. In short, the two parties must show that they intend to be bound by the terms of the contract, that the terms are mutually agreeable, and that they are fully understood by both.

Suppose, for example, that McKluskey leases an apartment unit from Wright. Wright demands a one-time $500 fee, which he looks on as a sort of cover charge for potential damage or any necessary redecorating that must be done when McKluskey leaves. McKluskey, however, views the $500 as an advance toward her first month's rent of $1,000. Both parties believe they have a contract because Wright has agreed to lease the apartment to McKluskey. In fact, however, the court is not likely to view this agreement as a bona fide contract because Wright and McKluskey have not agreed to the same terms. In other words, no mutual assent exists here.

It is also important to keep in mind that from the court's perspective, whether a valid offer exists will be judged by an *objective standard*, that is, by whether there is some observable, verifiable means of demonstrating that a bona fide offer was made.

For instance, say that Bayliss raises champion hunting dogs. One day, Wilson, who is visiting the kennel, remarks on what a fine dog the grand champion Flash is. "Yes," laughs Bayliss, in a moment of levity. "Why don't you buy one of the others and I'll just toss this one in for free." Bayliss doesn't for a moment mean what he's saying; he's just joking. However, if Wilson decides to take him up on his offer, a court *may* view the offer as valid. In taking a position, the court will ask whether a reasonable person, putting herself in the offeree's position, would be likely to look upon the offer as genuine. In matters of contract law, the court holds, it is impossible to read minds. Though circumstances will be considered, it isn't always possible to tell when someone else is joking or speaking out of impulse. While the proverb suggests that actions speak louder than words, the law generally holds that words speak louder than intentions.

The Requirements of an Offer

An offer is defined as *an indication — by promise or other commitment — of willingness to do or refrain from doing something in the future*. In order to be valid, an offer must have three elements: First, there must be a clear intent to contract. Second, the offer must be definite in all respects. And third, the offer must be communicated by the offeror to the offeree. Let's consider each of these elements in turn.

First — clear intent. Let's return for a moment to Wilson and Bayliss at the kennel. Suppose that Bayliss has had, through the years, hundreds of offers to buy his champion dog, Flash. He's attached to Flash, however, and has never seriously considered selling. Still, he begins to wonder if he's being sensible to totally disregard all offers. So one day, he mentions to Wilson that in fact he might consider selling Flash "sometime later if I get a great offer." Is this sufficient evidence of "clear intent?" Probably not. It's ambiguous enough that we can't say for certain that Bayliss is inviting an offer; it's more likely that he's just thinking out loud and hasn't really made up his mind yet about selling Flash. It would be quite different if he were to say, for instance, "Do you still want Flash? I've decided that I'll sell him to you, though I haven't decided how much I'd like to get."

And that brings us to the second element — the definite terms of the offer. A statement that one might be willing to sell something at a "fair price" or "at the right price" is not the same thing as an offer. Instead, such a statement is really an *invitation* to the other person (or persons) to *make an offer*. A valid offer specifies terms. For instance, in our current scenario, Bayliss might say to Wilson, "I'd be willing to sell Flash if I could get $600 for him. Are you interested?" This is a valid offer. It shows clear intent to contract and it specifies terms.

It also meets the third requirement — clear communication from offeror to offeree. In most cases, there's nothing very tricky about the communication between offeror and offeree. Certainly Wilson has every opportunity to act on Bayliss's offer to sell Flash, given that he's standing right there when Bayliss makes it. But suppose Wilson has taken the train back to Chicago when Bayliss suddenly makes up his mind to sell the dog. Bayliss writes to Wilson, stating that he will sell the dog for $600 — but the letter is addressed incorrectly and never arrives. So despite Bayliss's intentions, no offer has actually been made. Thus far the situation isn't too serious, though. The worst that can happen here is probably that Bayliss will wonder why Wilson doesn't bother to answer his letter.

But let's complicate things a little by supposing that Bayliss assumes Wilson (who always seemed to want to own Flash) will accept the offer. Maybe Wilson has already told Bayliss that if he could buy Flash, he — Wilson — would pay all shipping expenses. Bayliss, planning to surprise Wilson, crates up old Flash and puts him aboard the next plane to Chicago. Where do things stand now? No matter how eager Wilson may have seemed during their earlier discussions, the court would likely hold that since the offer to sell Flash was not communicated to Wilson, no real offer has been made. Wilson is under no obligation to accept the dog at this point, and if he decides he doesn't want Flash after all, responsibility for paying the costs associated with Flash's tour of the country falls to Bayliss.

Special Issues

Under contract law principles, not everything that looks like an offer can be legally construed as an offer. Take advertisements; contrary to what one might wish, they are generally *not* viewed by the court as valid offers. Rather, an advertisement is looked on only as an invitation to deal or as a statement of intention to sell merchandise. There are at least two reasons for the court's position on this matter.

First, most ads lack specificity. Remember, we've already noted the importance of including definite terms within an offer. An ad for "the city's largest collection of fine women's fashions," for instance, is much too vague to be viewed as an offer. It is impossible to say precisely what merchandise is being offered or under what terms. Occasionally, an ad—say, one printed in a mail-order catalog—may be so explicit and detailed as to be considered a valid offer, but that would be a rare exception to the rule.

Second, merchants do not stock most goods in infinite supply forever. Viewing an ad as a bona fide offer would put the merchant in the highly awkward position of having to follow through on the offer with every potential customer who ever took him up on it. Your local Ford dealer may have advertised a new Ford for $2,000 thirty years ago, but it would be unreasonable to expect that offer to be valid today. No merchant is in the position of contracting with every potential buyer. The intent of an ad—as the court views it—is to invite some prospective buyers to make offers to the merchant.

On the other hand, when a merchant imposes certain limitations on an ad, it may be viewed as an offer. For example, a clothing merchant may state that men's sport coats will go for the rate of $40 "while supplies last." Or a tanning salon may state that "for one day only" customers' names will be entered into a drawing for a free trip to Bermuda. The court views these prescribed conditions as having the elements of an offer and will hold the merchants responsible for fulfilling the terms of each offer, under contract law. Thus, for example, if Stardust Jewelers runs an ad stating that "All gold jewelry in stock will be on sale for half price for two days— April 1 and 2," the store is obliged to live up to those terms. The Stardust manager cannot suddenly determine on the evening of April 1, for example, that the store has sold enough jewelry at half price and will cancel the sale for April 2. Nor can she decide arbitrarily that gold rings will not be included in the sale merchandise. The terms of the offer specify "*all* gold jewelry in stock," and those terms must be honored.

(This would be a good time to point out that this lesson—including the preceding analysis—looks at advertisements and business practices under principles of contract law. However, many state legislatures have passed special statutes that also regulate what businesses can say and do in conducting their trade. These statutes—often called truth in advertising, unlawful trade practices, or deceptive advertising statutes—give consumers another legal basis for evaluating the actions of businesses. Intended to help consumers with problems that general contract law cannot remedy, such statutes sometimes take precedence over what was previously an established contract law principle.)

Auctions also constitute a special case. It might seem logical to suppose that whoever is selling merchandise at an auction is the one making the offer, but in fact that is not the case. Remember, contract law views an advertisement as an *invitation* to make an offer. It views putting merchandise up for auction in much the same way. The person auctioning merchandise is not making an offer, but inviting others to do so. Further, unless an auction is conducted "without reserve," the seller may refuse any bid; the phrase "with reserve" implies that the seller "reserves" the right to refuse any bid he or she deems unsatisfactory. But in an auction conducted "without reserve," the seller must allow the merchandise to go to the highest bidder—even if the seller feels that the bid is too low.

Like the merchant or the seller at auction, a person who requests a bid on a project is not making an offer but inviting others to make offers. For example, a housing contractor may invite subcontractors to bid on the brick work for several houses within a development. Let's suppose three subcontractors bid and that their bids differ greatly, the second bidder being about $25,000 over the first, and the third about $10,000 over that. The contractor may accept any one of these three bids—or none of them. He's under no obligation whatever because he has not made an offer. He's merely invited others to make offers, which he is then free to accept or reject.

Sometimes circumstances arise that call for a *general offer*. Perhaps the most common example is the reward offered for some service or the return of some merchandise. Let's say that Schmitt loses an heirloom ring worth thousands of dollars and posts a reward stating that he will pay $250 for the recovery of the ring. The court views Schmitt's promise of reward as a valid offer for a unilateral contract—one in which a promise is made on one side. In order to accept the offer and thereby form a valid contract, an offeree would have to provide two remaining elements: first, to produce the ring; and second, to reveal awareness of Schmitt's offer. Without that awareness, no contract is formed.

For instance, suppose that an early-morning jogger one day passes Schmitt's house, notices something shining under the shrubbery, produces a ring, and asks Schmitt whether it belongs to him. The jogger has no apparent knowledge that a reward has been offered for recovery of the ring. Is Schmitt legally obligated to pay the reward? No. We might think less of him for not giving the reward, but the fact remains, he technically owes the jogger nothing. She was not responding to Schmitt's offer, and so did not create a contract—her admirable behavior notwithstanding.

Duration of Offers

Sometimes, an offeror sets forth at the outset the duration of an offer. For instance, let's say a well-known author visits town for five days. For public relations purposes, the author offers to address any group of 500 persons or more free of charge, provided arrangements can be made within the first three days of her visit. After that time, the offer is said to *lapse*. In other words, it's no longer valid. The author may, however, renew the offer if she decides speaking is more interesting than sightseeing, or she may extend the same offer to her fans in another city.

If no time is specified within the terms of an offer, the court holds that the offeree must respond within a "reasonable" time. What's reasonable? That's for the court—judge and jury—to determine. Generally speaking, an offer may be terminated in any of four ways: it may lapse, be revoked (by the offeror), be rejected (by the offeree), or be accepted (by the offeree). Let's look more closely at each possibility.

Termination by Lapse

In the preceding example, the offer extended by the author lapses after three days simply because the time specified in the offer runs out at that point. Lapse can occur in other ways, too.

For instance, an offer will lapse if either the offeror or offeree dies or is declared insane prior to acceptance. It will also lapse if there is a *supervening illegality*—in other words, if some condition within the intended contract becomes illegal during the course of negotiations. Suppose, for example, that Lane tells Frost that he wants to start a small dairy on his land, and Frost offers to sell Lane five head from his own dairy herd. While they're dickering over price, the city council is busy passing an ordinance that now makes it illegal for anyone to keep livestock on less than twenty acres of land. Since Lane has only ten acres, he can't legally own the cows, and the offer lapses.

A lapse also occurs in the case of damage to or destruction of the subject matter. Let's say Green offers to sell Gray a motorcycle for $900, but during the night, someone breaks into Green's garage, takes the motorcycle joyriding, and returns it in badly damaged condition. The offer automatically lapses.

Termination by Revocation

Now let's consider the second way in which an offer may be terminated—revocation. Under common law, the offeror may revoke an offer at any time prior to acceptance of that offer by another party. For instance, if White offers to pay $5,000 to anyone who will fly him to New Zealand, he can revoke the offer at any time and without advance notice—provided no one has yet accepted the offer. But a revocation does not become effective until it is either directly or indirectly communicated to the offeree. In the case of White's New Zealand trip, the communication might take the form of phone calls to charter services, or White might simply take down the notice of the offer he put on the supermarket bulletin board and allow prospective offerees to draw their own conclusions.

Normally, when a general offer is made (for instance, the posting of a reward or White's solicitation for New Zealand flights), the revocation may take the same form as the general offer. It wouldn't be reasonable — or even feasible — for instance, to ask White to personally contact each person who had read the notice in the supermarket and considered flying him to New Zealand.

However, let's consider a somewhat different example. Suppose that Wheeler, a freelance gardener, offers to do yard maintenance for Dunlap at the rate of $150 per month. Dunlap says he will think it over. The offer remains open for a "reasonable" period unless Wheeler revokes the offer. She might just phone Dunlap and say that she's thought it over, the arthritis in her knees is too bad to allow her to do much gardening after all, and she wishes to revoke her offer. Since Dunlap has not yet accepted, Wheeler is fully within her rights and the matter is closed.

Termination by Rejection

Rejection is the third manner in which offers are terminated. In the example of Dunlap and Wheeler, Dunlap (the offeree) can reject the offer — either directly or implicitly. Dunlap might, for instance, phone Wheeler and say that he's decided to do his own gardening. Or Wheeler might just come by one day to find that Dunlap has already hired Quigley to trim his trees. Either way, the offer has been rejected.

Take care not to confuse rejection and revocation. Keep in mind that only the offeror can revoke an offer — take it back, that is. Only an offeree can reject — or turn down — an offer.

Termination by Acceptance

The fourth way in which an offer can be terminated is through acceptance by the offeree. Acceptance, in fact, is the simplest and most common means by which offers are terminated. (Rejection, of course, also happens a lot; lapse and revocation are much less common.)

Do you recall that rejection only becomes effective when communicated to the offeror? Well, unless otherwise stipulated in the offer, acceptance becomes effective upon *dispatch* to the offeror — at least in most states. Keep in mind, too, that if an offeree accepts an offer, the *offer itself* is terminated. That's not to say that the *business dealings* between the two parties are terminated; they're not. Rather, the offer is replaced by formation of a contract, which occurs at the time of acceptance. In other words, there's not really such a thing as an "accepted offer"; as soon as an offer is accepted, it is terminated and replaced by a contract.

If an offeree decides that he or she wants to accept an offer after it has been terminated by lapse or revocation — or even after the offeree earlier rejected the offer — the offeror is under no legal obligation to go through with the contract, because the offer *was* terminated. Of course, what the offeree had intended to be the acceptance may result in new negotiations and, ultimately, a contract. There is, however, no legal duty on the part of the offeror to reinitiate negotiations, let alone to reinitiate negotiations on the same terms as earlier extended. Once an offer is terminated, the offeror alone decides whether to enter into talks with a person who now—too late—would like to accept the offer.

Acceptance

Acceptance involves the offeree's assent to all terms of an offer. Under common law, acceptance of an offer must be clear and unconditional. Further, the acceptance must precisely match—or mirror—the language of the offer, term for term, word for word. Any deviation, however slight, changes the acceptance to a *qualified acceptance* or *counteroffer*. And under common law, a counteroffer automatically terminates the original offer; that is, it operates as a rejection.

Keep in mind that the Uniform Commercial Code takes a more pragmatic view of offers and acceptances than does contract common law. Under the UCC, an offer remains in force even if the offeree proposes new terms. The UCC position is designed to reflect the realities of the modern business world where negotiations may proceed for weeks or months and entail much give and take on both sides. It would hardly be practical or efficient for businesses to look on offers as being terminated every time a slight adjustment were made. Further, the UCC recognizes that many businesses have standard forms that they use in establishing contracts, and the language in one party's form may not match that in another's precisely—even though both parties agree on the intent of a contract.

Suppose millet buyer Watkins Feed sends a standardized purchase order to millet seller Crawford Grain ordering one ton of millet. The Watkins Feed purchase order is filled with a multitude of clauses generally favorable to them; the Crawford Grain order acceptance form is filled with an equal number of clauses generally written in their favor. Under common law, the offer from Watkins to purchase the millet would, as a result of the mirror-image rule, be terminated by the "counteroffer" contained on the Crawford acceptance form. But the two parties are basically in agreement. Since they agree on amount, price, delivery date, quality, and several other factors, it would waste everyone's time and good will if the offer were terminated under common law. Under the UCC, however, the offer stands if the two parties are basically in agreement.

There is, to be sure, still concern about the differing terms, and sometimes problems arise. But because of the provisions of the UCC, the problems aren't as frequent as you might think. According to UCC law, the *new* terms (that is, the terms contained in the buyer's "counteroffer") normally become part of a contract, superseding the terms of the original offer whenever they conflict. There are, however, three conditions under which this provision doesn't apply: (1) when the original offer requires the offeree to accept the terms of the offer in entirety, without modification; (2) when the additional terms alter the offer in such a way as to make it oppressive or grossly unfair to the offeror; or (3) when the original offeror notifies the offeree outright that the new terms are unacceptable.

Communication of Acceptance

You might think that simply stating your acceptance of an offer would be sufficient. Often it is — but sometimes not. The law requires that an offer be accepted in the *mode* — manner or means, that is — specified by the offeror or, if none was specified, in the same manner in which it was presented. Thus, if the offer is presented in writing, a phone call accepting the offer probably won't do unless the offeror has specified that a phone call will be sufficient.

Now, in most cases, if the offeror doesn't specify how the acceptance must be given, then anything reasonable — phone call, letter, wire — will do. However, the offeree is still required to act within a "reasonable" (as defined by the court) time. If Bailey offers to sell Ross a used typewriter, Ross cannot "think things over" for months on end; some reasonable dispatch is required.

Most states will also uphold a *mailbox* or *implied agency* rule. According to this rule, acceptance by mail or wire becomes effective at the time it's sent — not when it's received by the offeror. In other words, if Fitz accepts an offer from Waldo, and her letter of acceptance is postmarked 10:30 a.m., March 1, then that is the official time of acceptance. If Waldo has insisted upon a reply no later than noon of March 1, Fitz has still met the deadline, even though Waldo may not have the news in his hands till a day or two later. Meanwhile, if Waldo extends the offer to someone else, thinking that Fitz has not accepted, and the third party accepts the offer, Fitz may have grounds to sue. Waldo could, however, avoid the problem by stating that acceptance must be *"received at the offices* of Waldo and Sons no later than noon, March 1."* If the acceptance is not at the Waldo offices by noon, Waldo is free to immediately extend the offer to another party.

Perhaps no news is good news in some circles. But in the world of contract law, silence doesn't count for much; it certainly doesn't count as acceptance. Since an offeree is generally under no obligation to reply to an offer, silence or inaction is generally not an acceptance. As with most rules governing contracts, though, there are exceptions. Suppose Joseph and Smythe — who have dealt with one another hundreds of times over a period of years — have an agreement that whenever Joseph sends a contract to Smythe through the mail, Joseph may assume agreement to all terms of the contract unless Smythe notifies him otherwise. In that case, Joseph might be safe in interpreting Smythe's silence as implicit agreement. Of course, since there's always the risk that Smythe has died, moved to Australia, or retired to the mountains, problems could arise. In most instances, an offeror would be well advised *not* to assume acceptance until the acceptance has been made explicit.

Bilateral versus Unilateral Agreements

For an offer that will result in a *unilateral* contract, the offeree communicates acceptance merely by fulfilling the terms of the contract. Say Warren offers Bates $20 if Bates will pull Warren's car out of the ditch, where it has inconveniently become stuck. Merely by pulling the car out, Bates accepts the offer, and the result is a unilateral contract. Bates needn't orally agree, shake hands, or sign anything.

An offer for a *bilateral* agreement, on the other hand, is accepted by direct communication or a counterpromise. Let's say Erskine offers Whitford $500 a month to do some modest bookkeeping for Erskine. Whitford says that yes, he will do it, and that he can begin the following Monday. Thus far, Whitford hasn't performed any bookkeeping for Erskine; nevertheless, they have a bilateral contract by virtue of Whitford's acceptance.

Courts disfavor unilateral contracts because often the offeree—unlike Bates in our earlier example—doesn't act immediately. If much time goes by, it may become unclear whether a contract exists, or whether even the intent to contract still exists. Bilateral contracts are more readily enforced because the promises given on both sides make the intent to contract clear. And in the acceptance of a bilateral contract, the details of the agreement tend to be more explicitly stated. Explicit details make it easier for the court to interpret and enforce the contract if called upon to do so.

SOME PRACTICAL ADVICE

Most people—both in their business and in their private lives—make agreements with the best of intentions. Yet misunderstandings frequently occur. What practical advice can we take from this lesson to help prevent such misunderstandings?

First, beware of making any offer you do not mean, even as a joke. There is always the chance that someone will take you seriously. True enough, if your feelings—humor, anger, or whatever—are very clear and if you have witnesses to back your story, the court may uphold your position that no valid offer was intended. However, there is always the risk that the court, applying the objective standard, will hold that a reasonable person would have taken the offer seriously—and will therefore hold you to the terms of that offer, however unfair and unintended those terms may seem to you.

Second, be cautious about accepting or fulfilling the requirements of any offer until you're sure an offer exists. It could be that you have misunderstood some terms of the offer, or that your acceptance is unclear or unknown to the offeror; in either case, the offer may already have been revoked or accepted by someone else. You could easily be out time, money, and effort if you take it upon yourself to agree to or fulfill what you thought was your part of the bargain before knowing that a bargain was in fact proposed. Remember, too, that while completing the act called for is sufficient to create a unilateral contract, it is always advisable to inform the offeror of your acceptance and to specify a date on which performance will begin. Taking these simple steps protects interests on both sides.

Finally, be sure that all offers made or accepted are explicit and detailed. To the extent it is practical, the nature of performance on both sides—along with fees, dates, and so forth—should all be specified as precisely as possible. Do not rely on "understandings." Even a signed "contract" may be set aside by the court if it can be conclusively shown that both sides did not agree to the same terms. In other words, the more explicit the contract, the less likely it is that such a misunderstanding will arise. Clearly, of course, oral contracts have an inherent risk of misunderstanding. Thus, it is wise, whenever practical and possible, to extend offers in writing and to request that acceptance take the same form.

ASSIGNMENTS

- Before you watch the video program, be sure you've read through the preceding overview, familiarized yourself with the learning objectives for this lesson, and looked at the key terms below. Then, read Chapter 9 of Davidson et al., *Business Law*.
- After completing these tasks, view the video program for Lesson 5.
- After watching the program, take time to review what you've learned. First, evaluate your learning with the self-test which follows the key terms. Then, apply and evaluate what you've learned with the "Your Opinion, Please" scenarios at the end of this telecourse study guide lesson.

KEY TERMS

Before you read through the textbook assignment and watch the video program, take a minute to look at the key terms associated with this lesson. When you encounter them in the textbook and video program, pay careful attention to their meaning.

Acceptance	Objective standard
Bilateral contract	Rejection
Bona fide	Revocation
Counteroffer	Subjective standard
General offer	Supervening
Lapse	Unilateral contract
Mailbox (implied agency) rule	Valid acceptance
Mirror image rule	Valid offer
Mutual assent	

SELF-TEST

The questions below will help you evaluate how well you've learned the material in this lesson. Read each one carefully, and select the letter of the option that best answers the question. You'll find the correct answer, along with a reference to the page number(s) where the topic is discussed, in the back of this telecourse study guide.

1. According to the textbook, once there has been a *valid* offer by the offeror and a *valid* acceptance by the offeree,

   a. an agreement exists.
   b. the offeree and offeror have reached agreement—assuming there are no problems with the legality of that agreement.
   c. *one* element of a proper agreement—though by no means the most important element—is in place.
   d. state law must be consulted to determine whether an agreement exists; state laws vary dramatically on the significance of offer and acceptance.

2. The *objective theory of contracts* refers to the fact that in determining whether a valid offer exists, the court will *mainly* consider whether

   a. the offeror and offeree were acting in a calm, reasonable, unemotional manner.
   b. the intentions—both obvious and unobserved—of the offeror and offeree match their actions.
   c. the offer would seem fair from the perspective of a prudent and reasonable person.
   d. a reasonable person, observing the situation, would believe a genuine offer had been made.

3. Bayliss tells Smith that she (Smith) will get a raise if she improves her attitude. Would a court *likely* look on this promise as a bona fide common law offer?

   a. Yes, definitely. It's a clear commitment on Bayliss' part.
   b. Only if Smith immediately agrees to Bayliss' conditions and makes a conscious effort to improve.
   c. No. Bayliss' remark lacks definiteness and is only a statement of general intention.

4. Twinkly Jewelers has a sign in its front window that reads, "We'll sell you the diamond ring that will win her heart." Is the court likely to look on Twinkly's claim about the effects of its diamond rings as a bona fide offer?

   a. Yes, because it's both definite and clear in intent.
   b. No; ads are rarely looked on as offers.
   c. We cannot say without knowing more about Twinkly's merchandise.

5. Larson returns Ruckles's stray cat, Pogo, not knowing Ruckles has posted a $50 reward. Is Ruckles legally, as opposed to morally, obliged to pay Larson the $50 for finding Pogo?

   a. Yes; even though Larson didn't know of the reward, he fulfilled the terms of the offer.
   b. Yes; since a reward is an established exception to the need to have both offer and acceptance in a transaction.
   c. No; since Larson didn't know, he wasn't really responding to the offer.

6. In Question 5, Larson and Ruckles could be said to have

   a. a unilateral contract.
   b. a bilateral contract.
   c. no contract at all.

7. Casper promises to sell Hershey his 1957 Chevrolet Bel Air convertible. But before they conclude their negotiations, Casper dies. Which of the following becomes true upon Casper's death?

   a. Casper's heirs must honor his promise and sell the car to Hershey.
   b. The heirs need not sell the car, but they are obliged to inform Hershey of Casper's death.
   c. Casper's offer automatically lapses, and there is no obligation of any kind to Hershey.

8. Which of the following *best* describes a situation in which an offer expires because too much time has gone by?

   a. Lapse
   b. Revocation
   c. Rejection
   d. Promissory estoppel

9. At lunch with Beverly and Joyce one day, Samantha said that if either wanted to buy her very expensive sewing machine, she would sell it for $200. Beverly and Joyce, who both knew that sewing was Samantha's principal hobby and talent, laughed and told her that she was working too much. Two days later, Samantha told Joyce she was just as happy no one had bought the machine; she had thought it over and was determined to make time for her sewing. The next day, however, Beverly came by Samantha's office with a check for $200. Joyce *had* told her about Samantha's change of heart, but since Samantha hadn't told her, Beverly figured the offer was still open for her. Why isn't Samantha's conversation with Joyce a valid revocation of the offer?

   a. The attempted revocation came too close to the time Samantha originally made the offer.
   b. Although Joyce had told Beverly about the conversation, Samantha herself has to personally revoke the offer with all potential buyers.
   c. Samantha was too vague in her talk with Joyce; she didn't specifically use the word "revoke."

d. Samantha's second conversation *is* a valid revocation, for both Joyce and Beverly.

10. Of the options below, the *most common* way an offer is terminated is

a. revocation.
b. acceptance.
c. forebearance.
d. lapse.

YOUR OPINION, PLEASE

Read each of the following scenarios and answer the questions about the decisions you would make in each situation. Give these questions some serious thought; they may be used as the basis for the development of a more complex essay. You should base your decisions on what you've learned from this lesson, though you may incorporate outside readings or information gained through your own experience if it is relevant.

Scenario I

One day, Witt and Quimby are walking around Quimby's newly purchased home. Quimby is complaining roundly of the builder's pathetic landscaping, which has left him with weedy grass and dying shrubbery. It's the one thing about his new home he's unhappy with. But, as he explains to Witt, since the builder threw the landscaping in for free, he—Quimby—will have to pay to replace it. Witt, seizing her opportunity, remarks that she has some experience in landscape design and believes she knows just what Quimby's property needs.

Quimby didn't know Witt was a landscaping professional and, in fact, doesn't quite believe she can do the job. Nevertheless, Quimby doesn't want to hurt Witt's feelings, so he says he'll be glad to listen to any ideas she comes up with. In fact, he tells her, if she can come up with a good-looking design that solves the erosion problems in the back yard, he'll gladly pay her the going rate for landscape work, based on an hourly rate. Witt says she'll see what she can do and, without Quimby's knowledge, goes to work on a complex design. She puts many hours into research and sketching, hoping to surprise Quimby with the quality of her work.

Quimby, meanwhile, decides to do the landscaping work himself. About four weeks after their original discussion, Witt stops by to show Quimby what she hopes will be a satisfactory design, and finds Quimby busily planting trees and moving rocks about. He tells her that he's sorry about the misunderstanding, but he didn't take her seriously and in any case, he couldn't wait any longer. Witt is rather put out and tells Quimby that in her mind they had a contract; Quimby made an offer that she accepted—and she has the landscape design to prove it. As far as she's concerned, they have a unilateral contract, and she feels she must be paid at least for the time she's invested thus far. Quimby says that while he'd like to accommodate Witt, he has revoked his offer—and that the revocation should be obvious from the fact he's doing his own work. Witt threatens to sue for breach of contract, but Quimby holds to his position that no contract exists.

What's your opinion? Based on what you know of the situation, do you think Witt and Quimby have a contract? Will a court likely support Witt's position in a lawsuit? Was Quimby's original offer to Witt genuine?

- Is Witt likely to win a lawsuit against Quimby? Why or why not?
- What factors support your answer?
- What factors might an attorney cite in arguing against your view?
- What steps, if any, might Quimby have taken to prevent a lawsuit?
- What steps, if any, might Witt have taken to prevent a lawsuit?

Scenario 2

Henry has inherited a dilapidated 1850s farmhouse, which he sells at a closed (that is, secret bid) auction. Balboni, the highest bidder, is delighted to purchase the farmhouse for "a measly $5,000!" Henry is equally delighted to be rid of the property—that is, until it's discovered that the attic is full of valuable antiques, worth many times what Balboni has paid for the property. Balboni is overjoyed, feeling particularly pleased with himself even if his good fortune was largely a matter of luck.

Henry claims that the antiques were not included with the farmhouse, and that since Balboni didn't know they were there, he could not have been making an offer on both the antiques and the house. Balboni counters that he made the $5,000 offer on the house as it was—and the fact that it happened to include the antiques was just lucky for him. Henry threatens to sue unless Balboni returns the antiques, but Balboni stands firm, maintaining that the antiques were certainly included in the price of the farmhouse, even if Henry didn't realize what he was selling. Henry counters that the original agreement would have had to specify the presence of the antiques and that since it did not, he has more right to them than Balboni.

What's your opinion? Based on what you know of the situation, do you think a court would likely support Henry's lawsuit? Or would the court consider that Balboni was entitled to the antiques together with the purchase of the house?

- Is the court likely to uphold Henry's position in a suit against Balboni? Why or why not?
- What factors support your answer?
- What factors might an attorney cite in arguing against your view?
- What steps, if any, might Henry have taken to prevent a lawsuit in this situation?

- What steps, if any, might Balboni have taken to prevent a lawsuit in this situation?

6

Contract Requirement: Consideration

LEARNING OBJECTIVES

Upon completing your study of this lesson, you should be able to

- Define the term *consideration*.
- Discuss the concept of *adequacy of consideration*.
- Relate the concept of consideration to several special contexts, including contracts for the sale of goods, surety contracts, *liquidated* and *unliquidated debts*, and composition agreements.
- Identify and discuss several circumstances under which a court will find total absence of consideration, and thus will not enforce an agreement between two parties.
- Identify and discuss several circumstances under which a court will enforce an agreement despite absence of consideration.

The purpose of this lesson is to introduce you to the concept of consideration — the "exchange of value" portion of a contract. In this lesson, you'll have an opportunity to look carefully at the various forms consideration can take, and to appreciate the importance of consideration from both the offeror's and offeree's perspective.

OVERVIEW

The notion of getting something for nothing intrigues most of us, yet we tend to not quite believe in it. Courts don't believe in it much either — in the sense that the law nearly always requires that any valid contract be supported by consideration, that is, something of value bargained for and exchanged by the contracting parties. The "something of value" can take many forms. Often, consideration is money. But it doesn't have to be money. It can be whatever the offeror is satisfied to receive from the offeree: a service, a promise, an action, or a forbearance from some action. Let's look at a more formal definition, followed by some examples.

Definition of Consideration

According to one of the most common definitions, a consideration is a *waiver, or promised waiver, of rights bargained for in exchange for a promise*. Clearly, this definition could encompass a great many things other than money, though money is the most common form of consideration. Another way to look at it is to say that the consideration consists of some benefit to the *promisor* (the one who makes a promise) or some detriment to the *promisee* (the one to whom the promise is made) — in exchange for whatever the promisor promises to do. Don't look on "detriment" too negatively in this context; it merely refers to the fact that the promisee is giving something up. Perhaps money. Perhaps time. Perhaps some other opportunity that might have been realized had the contract or agreement not intervened.

Uncle Milton tells his niece Louise that he will give her the family farm if she gives him $100,000. In this case, money is the consideration. Or, perhaps Uncle Milton says Louise can have the farm if she promises to convert to Hinduism — or, if she declines to marry for at least twenty years. In the last two examples, Louise's conversion and her forbearance from marriage are the respective considerations. Contrast these examples with the case in which Uncle Milton, always generous of spirit, says, "Louise, I want you to have the farm." In this case, no contract exists. There is no consideration. The farm is a gift.

Keep in mind that consideration is *whatever the offeror wants enough to bargain for*. It may or may not be something that benefits the offeror directly. Suppose Roth tells Smith that she'll pay him $20 if he will trim her shrubbery on a Saturday afternoon. Smith agrees to trim the shrubbery, but says he'll have to have

$40 rather than $20 because he will have to miss his team's basketball game in order to do the shrubbery, and $20 won't make missing the game worth his while. Roth agrees to the $40. In this scenario, Roth is both the offeror (the one who originally suggests entering into a contract) and the promisor (the one who promises the $40 in exchange for the trimming). Smith is both the offeree (the one to whom the original offer to contract is made) and the promisee (the one who must give up something to the promissor). Smith gives up his time on Saturday, the energy and expertise needed to trim the shrubbery, and the opportunity to attend the concert.

These things together make up the consideration in the contract. Notice that only the trimming of the shrubbery benefits Roth directly. Were her own shrubs not involved, the issue of whether Smith trims shrubs or attends concerts on Saturdays is—we assume—of little inherent interest to Roth. But this is not the point. The point is, Roth got what she wanted—trimmed shrubs—from the bargain. Roth might hire Smith to trim her mother's shrubbery on the other side of town, and the terms of consideration could be the same. In that case, Roth wouldn't even benefit directly from the trimming of the shrubbery; but again, she would have gotten what she wanted from the contract. Either way, there is a detriment to Smith, who has given up time he might have used doing something else. Notice that he does so willingly, and that he is compensated for the time. From a legal perspective, though, compensation does not *remove* the detriment; it simply makes it worth putting up with.

Let's consider one more example. Black, an ace medical student, is contemplating dropping out of medical school to marry one of the several men who have been courting her. Her parents, distressed at this notion, promise Black that they'll send her on a round-the-world cruise when she successfully completes medical school—following which she may marry anyone of her choice with their best wishes. Black, who dislikes the idea of spending several more years of intensive study, strongly prefers to be married. But the cruise tempts her sufficiently that she agrees. They write up a contract which both Black and her parents sign.

In this scenario, Black's parents are the promisors, Black the promisee. Black's agreement to continue medical school is the consideration. It doesn't directly benefit Black's parents, though they have the satisfaction of seeing their daughter achieve an important goal; nevertheless, it is consideration in support of the contract because they're receiving what they asked for. Should they decide later to revoke their promise and not send Black on the cruise, would she have grounds for a lawsuit? Very likely. She has a bona fide contract, with a definite promise from her parents. The consideration she provides—continuing in and finishing medical school—makes the contract enforceable, provided it is valid in other respects.

Consideration Must Be Real

For consideration to create a valid contract, however, it's critical that the promise for which the consideration is given be a real, and not an illusory, promise. An *illusory promise* is one that really does not commit the promisor to anything. It sounds like a real promise, but close analysis of the wording shows that it is not. For example, if Black's father says to Black, "The summer after you graduate from medical school, we will send you on a cruise around the world on the *Queen Elizabeth II*," that is a real promise, definite and straightforward. Contrast that statement with this one: "If you graduate from medical school, we might consider rewarding you in some way — perhaps with a cruise around the world." The second statement seems to imply the promise of a cruise, but there is nothing definite. Black's father has left himself open to change his mind or to substitute some other form of "reward," one Black may find much less appealing. So before Black gives up her marriage plans and continues her medical schooling, she should make sure that the promise for which she is exchanging consideration is a real — not an illusory — promise.

Unilateral versus Bilateral Contracts

The nature of consideration can differ slightly depending on whether the contract is unilateral or bilateral in nature. In our preceding example, Black and her parents have a unilateral contract — one in which only one side extends a promise. In a unilateral contract, the consideration consists of the act or forbearance to act required of the promisee. (As it so happens, in this scenario we have examples of both types of consideration. The act her parents require is completing medical school; the forbearance to act that her parents want is Black's declining to marry until she's completed medical school. The act and the forbearance to act together make up the consideration in this contract.)

Let's shift the scenario a bit to explore the nature of a bilateral contract, one in which promises are made on both sides. Suppose that Black herself is the offeror. She goes to her parents one evening and tells them that she's very much in love and would like to marry and drop out of medical school. She will promise not to do this, however, if they in turn will promise to send her on an expensive cruise around the world. Though the two situations are similar in outcome, the circumstances under which the agreements are struck differ. In the second case, promises are made on both sides; thus, this is a bilateral contract. In a bilateral contract, consideration consists not of actions themselves, but rather of *promises* to act or to forbear from taking some action. In our scenario, consideration is given on both sides — by Black in the form of a promise to complete medical school and not to marry, by her parents in the form of a promise to provide a cruise. Assuming promises on both sides are real and not illusory, a valid bilateral contract now exists between Black and her parents.

Adequacy of Consideration

Generally, the court's position is that it is up to individuals to determine the adequacy of any consideration claimed to support a contract. Let's say Brock owns a small mercantile store in a rural town. Above the store is an attic, packed with odds and ends. Wilson, a struggling freelance writer who doesn't have sufficient income to rent office space, offers to clean out the attic and dispose of all the debris if Brock will let him use half of the space as an office without charge for one year. Brock agrees. But later, he has second thoughts. While it's nice to have the attic cleared and to have some extra storage space (in the half Wilson doesn't use), he dislikes his loss of privacy and resents having Wilson get by rent-free. Suppose he takes the dispute to court and tries to argue that Wilson really isn't suffering any detriment; in fact, he's benefitting unfairly from the bargain. Will the court support Brock's position? Not likely. The court will usually take the view that it was up to Brock and Wilson to strike a bargain both were happy with at the time they made the contract. If Brock wanted a fee for the space, he should have spoken up at the time the promise was made.

Consideration in Special Contexts

Thus far we've talked in generalities about the concept of consideration. Let's see how it operates in several specific contexts, beginning with contracts for the sale of goods.

In many cases, as we've seen from our earlier examples, the courts will not uphold or enforce promises that are not supported by consideration. In order to simplify everyday business dealings, however, the Uniform Commercial Code states that a *merchant's* offer to buy or sell goods — backed by assurances in writing that the offer will be held open — is irrevocable for periods of up to three months without any consideration. It's important to note that this special provision applies to merchants — commercial buyers and sellers of goods — and not to personal consumers.

For example, suppose Green Garden, Inc., asks Tom's Nursery to stock a new hand trowel that Green Garden has just developed. Green Garden thinks that gardeners will love this trowel. It offers Tom's a price just above manufacturing costs as an incentive to stock the tool and thus get buyers to purchase it. Tom's owner is interested and asks for a firm offer in writing because he wants to think about the size of the order. Assuming that the paperwork meets the UCC requirements of a firm offer, Tom can withhold his order for up to three months and still get the price in the firm offer quote. He can do this even if in the two months he takes to decide he learns that the tool has become the talk of the town and that Green Garden now sells it to other customers for much more. As a merchant, Green Garden is bound by the UCC rules on firm offer.

On the other hand, consideration is an absolute requirement in suretyship contracts — those in which a third person (the surety) agrees to be responsible to a creditor for a loan in the event that the principle debtor fails to pay off the loan. In business, it is common practice for creditors to decrease the risk of default (failure to pay) by requiring a surety (that is, a guarantor) to give the creditor assurance that the loan will be repaid. In return for that assurance, though, the law requires that some consideration be given. Let's see how this works.

Suppose, for example, that the Johnsons are remodeling their home and have approached the credit union for a loan. The credit union agrees, but requires that Mrs. Johnson's parents, the Stones, act as sureties for the loan. In other words, the credit union wants the Stones to take responsibility for the debt in case the Johnsons cannot pay. The Johnsons and their in-laws visit the credit union on the same day and simultaneously agree to take responsibility for the debt. In this case, the credit union need only give the money to the Johnsons, and it has provided consideration to both parties for the promises they made to repay the loan. Notice that while this transaction does not benefit the Stones directly, it still provides consideration because it satisfies their request: that is, that the Johnsons get their loan.

Let's suppose, however, that the credit union first agrees to provide the loan without requiring a surety. But suppose, too, that in the original agreement, the credit union retains the right to later ask for a surety if it seems that the Johnsons are no longer a good credit risk. When Mr. Johnson's work hours are cut by 40%, the credit union, feeling at risk, asks for a surety to guarantee the repayment of the loan. Again, the Stones are asked to sign. But where will the consideration come from? The money has already been lent. That cannot be used as consideration for the Stones' promise in this case. So, perhaps, the credit union will make another concession. They may, for instance, allow the Johnsons to extend their repayment period over an additional six months. And that concession provides the consideration for the Stones' promise to guarantee the loan.

Now let's see how differently the concept of consideration applies in cases of liquidated versus nonliquidated debts. *Liquidated debts* are those which are *not* in dispute. Let's say you owe your insurance company $100. You knew what the fee would be, you are satisfied with the service, and you don't question that you actually do owe the money. That's a liquidated debt. On the other hand, suppose your auto mechanic bills you for $50 for mounting your snow tires and, further, that one of the wheel rims is damaged in the process. As you think about it, you consider the $50 an exorbitant rate for a very simple task you now wish you'd done yourself. In that case, you might well dispute the fairness of the debt. The debt to the garage is now *unliquidated* — in dispute, that is.

When a debt is liquidated — not in dispute — partial payment of the debt cannot be given as consideration for full discharge of the debt. In other words, you can't say to your insurance agent, "Look, I'll give you $80 of the $100 I owe, and you agree to call us even." And no wonder. Who would ever pay the full amount owed if it were possible to create a new, enforceable contract simply by turning over partial payment? On the other hand, when a debt is unliquidated — in dispute, that is — a partial payment may well be given in consideration for waiving the right to full payment. For instance, you might call your mechanic at the garage and say, "You damaged my wheel rim which will cost me $25 to replace, so I'll pay you $25 of the $50 you billed me if you'll agree that's fair payment for the services rendered." In this case, the garage waives right to full payment in exchange for a partially paid debt. Both sides benefit — you by not having to pay so much, and the garage by getting part of the money owed. And both sides suffer some detriment — you by paying more than you think is a fair price for a simple service, and the garage by sacrificing whatever time, effort, and expense went into installing the faulty wheel.

Unliquidated debt forms the basis for enforcement of a *composition agreement*, a sort of compromise in which debtor and creditor negotiate and agree that some smaller sum will be accepted in payment for a larger debt. Creditors often make such concessions if, for instance, the debtor is close to bankruptcy. After all, a creditor may well decide that a fixed and certain partial payment is better than the even smaller sum the creditor is likely to realize if bankruptcy is declared. In such cases, the sum paid to the creditor is the consideration—in return for which the creditor promises to waive right to full payment of the debt.

Absence of Consideration Resulting in Nonenforcement of Contracts

What happens when the court finds no evidence of consideration in an agreement between two parties? Well, in some circumstances that means that the agreement will not be enforced—but that's not always the case. Let's consider several examples of each, beginning with circumstances in which the agreement is *not* enforced.

We've already mentioned illusory promises—those which seem to offer something to the promisee, but which are really nothing more than statements of elusive possibilities. The manager of Pete's Doughnuts may tell the bothersome Fluffy Flour sales representative that "You don't need to call any more; we'll be ordering whatever supplies we need from you over the next six months." That might sound like a promise of considerable business, but the manager may just be trying to get rid of the pesky and persistent Fluffy rep. When Pete's fails to place any orders over the coming months, can Fluffy sue for breach of promise? Not really; there was no consideration from Fluffy given in exchange for Pete's "promise." This contract fails because there was an absence of consideration. In the absence of consideration, no real agreement exists.

Let's also consider the circumstance of *preexisting duty*, in which a person is already obligated to perform a certain act or acts. Suppose Haines works in a large office building downtown and parks in an attended underground garage. A series of petty thefts have left Haines uneasy, and knowing this, the garage attendant tells Haines he'll keep an eye on his car for a fee of $5 per day. Haines agrees at first, but later, when no one else in his office seems to be having trouble, he feels he's being used—and he promptly stops the $5 fee. Could the attendant successfully sue Haines for breach of promise? Probably not. The court would likely hold that the attendant suffered no detriment since he was only doing what he'd already been hired to do—namely, patrol the parking area—and did not supply Haines with any new consideration in return for the $5 payments.

Preexisting duty often stems from the nature of one's job, but it can also stem from a contractual agreement specifying what that duty will be. For example, suppose Schwartz agrees to mow Brent's lawn for $10. Halfway through, with the back lawn left untouched, Schwartz says he's too tired, it's too hot, and he will not finish the job unless Brent pays an additional $10. Is Brent obliged to pay the extra fee? No. According to the original agreement, Schwartz is obligated to fulfill his part of the bargain for the agreed upon fee. Brent may be a compassionate sort who decides that yes, on a hot day, Schwartz has earned the extra $10—but he is under no obligation to pay it. On the other hand, suppose Schwartz discovers that the back lawn is filled with small rocks and thus cannot be mowed till these rocks are removed. This changes the nature of the agreement, and the court would be more inclined to uphold Schwartz's claim that he is entitled to more money, assuming that Schwartz could not reasonably have known about the rocks. He might get $10 for the mowing job but also $10 for the task of moving the rocks—a task not stated as part of the original agreement but required in order to complete the original agreement.

Similarly, because the courts do not consider a moral obligation as adequate consideration, and promises made as a result of moral obligation are not normally enforced. Suppose that Flint is driving down the road when Kelley's dog dashes out in pursuit of a ball. Flint deftly swerves to miss the dog, but smashes into a fence that leaves his car badly dented and his head badly bruised. Overcome with gratitude that Flint missed his dog, Kelley says he will "cover all expenses—mechanical and medical." However, when he learns how much it will cost to repair both Flint's car and head, Kelley's enthusiasm wanes considerably. Will the court enforce Kelley's agreement with Flint? No. The court will likely view Flint's nifty (and perhaps automatic) gesture as a "gift." No bargaining occurred prior to the accident; Kelley did not say, "If you promise you'll never hit my dog with your car, I'll promise to cover any expenses you incur in swerving to avoid him." But Kelley's promise after the accident is not adequate consideration to create a contract at that point.

Consider, too, that in the eyes of the court, past consideration is the equivalent of no consideration. In other words, once consideration has been rendered, there is nothing more to exchange; agreements based on past consideration are generally not enforceable. For example, let's say that Coach Reynolds is very proud of his all-star football team; so proud, in fact, that when they win the state championship, he says he'll pay all expenses for an overnight trip to the mountains. Perhaps, however, Reynolds never makes his promise good. While we might find such behavior reprehensible from a social or ethical standpoint, Reynolds cannot be legally taken to task. The champs have already won the football games; thus, his consideration is past. Had Reynolds said months prior, "If you guys win the championship, I'll pay all expenses for a trip to the mountains," that would have been another story.

Situations in Which Courts Will Enforce Agreements Despite Absence of Consideration

From the above examples, you should have the idea that consideration is a key component of most contracts. As we noted earlier, there are, however, situations in which the courts will enforce agreements despite an absence of consideration. Let's consider four such situations.

First, *a promisee might use promissory estoppel in place of consideration to force a promisor to keep his or her word.* Promissory estoppel is only applicable in cases where the court determines that injustice will result if a promise is not fulfilled. The promisee must show that a promise was made, that he or she reasonably relied on that promise, that the promisee suffered as a result of the promise not being fulfilled, and that justice can only be served if indeed the promise is fulfilled.

Let's look at two brothers, George and Fred. George owns a highly successful textile business in which he encourages Fred, a baker, to invest. Fred feels he might be better off putting his money in the bank, but he succumbs to George's urgings. For many years George's advice appears sound as the textile company continues to grow. When the textile business suffers a major setback, just about the time of Fred's retirement, George isn't much affected; he has numerous other successful investments. Fred, however, has a serious financial problem, having invested all his savings in George's company. Fred takes his situation to George and seeks his advice on whether to retire as planned and scrape by on very little income or to continue working several years past when he had hoped to retire. George, feeling responsible for the textile investment that had been critical to Fred's retirement plans, tells Fred not to worry, that he'll provide a monthly stipend to see Fred and his family through.

If George does not fulfill this promise, Fred might well use promissory estoppel to force George to keep his part of the bargain. He would not sue for breach of contract because he would need to show consideration to establish a contract; since there wasn't consideration for George's promise, a contract probably didn't exist. Note that consideration would have existed here had the agreement between Fred and George been worked out differently. For instance, when he needed cash in the early stages of the textile business, George might have said, "Listen, Fred—you invest all your extra cash with my company, and in return I'll promise you that if everything goes awry, I'll support you after retirement." In that case—assuming Fred agreed—Fred's investment would have constituted consideration for George's promise to support Fred. And that contract would have been enforceable.

Second, *the courts normally do not require consideration in the case of charitable subscriptions.* The theory here is that charitable institutions rely on the pledges—promises—of donors. And unless those promises are honored, the institutions cannot survive. If you sense the doctrine of promissory estoppel is operating here, you're right. The court holds that charitable institutions are usually worthy, and that serious detriment could result if the work such institutions perform were thwarted when pledges were allowed to go unpaid. Let's consider an example. Successful software developer Yu pledges all the royalties from the sale of her programs to the local symphony's first European tour. As the trip planning is underway, Yu decides the money would be better spent buying out another software company. If the symphony, which has gone to considerable expense setting up the tour, were to sue to enforce Yu's pledge, the court may well choose to enforce the pledge and require Yu to pay. The argument will be that the charity in question has relied on Yu's promise, and that under the doctrine of promissory estoppel, she must make it good.

Third, *some promises to pay debts may be enforced by the courts even when they can no longer be legally collected.* You may have wondered at some point whether uncollected debts can be allowed to go on forever, compounding interest charges over the years until astronomical sums of money are owed to the creditor. The answer is no. States have *statutes of limitations* which restrict the amount of time a creditor has to sue for payment of a debt. Normally, this period runs from two to six years; after that time, the court will not recognize grounds for suit. However, if a debtor, for whatever reason, promises to pay the debt after the allotted period, a court may well require the debtor to make good on this new promise, even though the debtor received no consideration from the creditor for this new promise.

Finally, *a debtor may choose to pay a debt after being discharged from that debt through bankruptcy.* Note that no consideration exists for this new promise to pay. The creditor could offer some consideration, of course, such as an extension of the payment period, or an offer to accept smaller installments. But in open bankruptcy court, if a debtor freely and with understanding of the consequences decides to continue paying on a bill, a creditor can hold the debtor to that promise to pay.

SOME PRACTICAL ADVICE

Perhaps the most important concept in what we've discussed is that valid, enforceable contracts virtually always demand the presence of consideration. As we've seen, there are exceptions to this rule, but they're few. And even when the court recognizes an exception in general terms, that in itself is no guarantee that a particular agreement will be upheld.

How will you know whether consideration is present? If you've followed this discussion closely, you've probably recognized that consideration is not the simplest of terms to define. After all, the nature of consideration can shift from one agreement to the next. The test is this: The terms within any agreement should be definite and precise, and it should be clear that the offeror is receiving, in exchange for a promise, *something of value.* That something, as we've noted, is most often money. But it need not be money. It can be anything the offeror finds worth bargaining for—anything valuable enough to the offeror to bind him or her to a contract. The courts will just as readily enforce agreements wherein the consideration is some action—say, keeping one's guard dog locked up—or some forbearance to act—say, not driving one's car on weekends so that someone else may use it. The point here is that if you learn to recognize consideration, you stand a better chance of knowing whether a contract actually exists.

On the other hand, don't look to the courts to help you settle issues of unequal compensation. That is, if you come to feel that the consideration you've received for a promise made is inadequate, the court is likely to view that as your problem. Cases of fraud notwithstanding, it is up to contracting parties to ensure that each side feels comfortable with the bargain. Finally, be cautious about offering promises you do not intend to keep—even when no consideration is present. In the case of a charitable pledge, for example, or any instance in which the promisee can show cause for applying promissory estoppel, it's possible that you can be held to your promise, whether consideration is present or not.

As we've constantly pointed out, legal issues are subject to interpretation. As a businessperson, however, you don't want matters left to a court's interpretation, an expensive and lengthy process. Therefore, as a promisee, you are well advised to ensure the presence of consideration as a means of increasing the likelihood that any contract will be enforceable. As a promisor, on the other hand, you want to ensure that you can fulfill any promise made, regardless of whether consideration exists.

ASSIGNMENTS

- Before you watch the video program, be sure you've read through the preceding overview, familiarized yourself with the learning objectives for this lesson, and looked at the key terms below. Then, read Chapter 10 of Davidson et al., *Business Law*.

- After completing these tasks, view the video program for Lesson 6.

- After watching the program, take time to review what you've learned. First, evaluate your learning with the self-test which follows the key terms. Then, read and evaluate what you've learned with the "Your Opinion, Please" scenarios at the end of this telecourse study guide lesson.

KEY TERMS

Before you read through the textbook assignment and watch the video program, take a minute to look at the key terms associated with this lesson. When you encounter them in the textbook and video program, pay careful attention to their meaning.

Accord	Compromise
Adequacy of consideration	Consideration
Bankruptcy	Creditor
Cancellation	Debtor
Charitable subscription	Default
Composition agreement	Forbearance

Illusory promise
Liquidated debt
Moral obligation
Past consideration
Preexisting duty
Promisee

Promisor
Promissory estoppel
Satisfaction
Statute of limitations
Unliquidated debt
Waiver

SELF-TEST

The questions below will help you evaluate how well you've learned the material in this lesson. Read each one carefully, and select the letter of the option that best answers the question. You'll find the correct answer, along with a reference to the page number(s) where the topic is discussed, in the back of this telecourse study guide.

1. According to the textbook, how important is consideration in determining the validity of a contract? Generally speaking, consideration is

   a. not only unimportant, but often detrimental since it can get in the way of smooth negotiations for everyday business contracts.
   b. not really important—though from the offeror's perspective, it's always valuable.
   c. quite important as one way of demonstrating validity, but certainly not essential.
   d. essential—with a few special-case exceptions—to the validity of an agreement.

2. There are several different ways to define *consideration*. Which of the following is probably the *best* and *most useful* definition? Consideration is *best* defined as

   a. money.
   b. something of value the offeror bargains for.
   c. something detrimental to the offeree.
   d. something which benefits the offeror.

3. Henry Knott tells Sam Wilson that Wilson may use Knott's swimming pool on weekends if Wilson will keep his dog tied up so that it doesn't dig up Knott's flowers. Does consideration exist in this agreement?

   a. No; no money is exchanging hands here.
   b. No; the dog should be tied up anyway, so a promise to keep the dog tied up is irrelevant.
   c. Yes; Wilson's keeping the dog tied is the consideration.
   d. Yes; Knott's offering the use of his pool is the consideration.

4. Miles offers Beale a flat fee of $100, paid in advance, to wash the Miles's family station wagon every Saturday for six months. Beale accepts, but after two months decides it isn't worth it—he feels he's earned the $100 already and quits. The court's position in this case would *most likely* be that

  a. Beale has a legitimate complaint; $100 isn't realistic for such a task, and Miles will have to pay more if he wants the full six months' worth of washes.
  b. fairness aside, Beale agreed to the $100, and is legally obligated to fulfill his side of the bargain.
  c. we cannot say without knowing whether Miles feels he's getting his money's worth from the kind of job Beale is doing.

5. Frank wishes to buy a car, but since he's only 18 and has only a part-time job, the bank will not loan him the $800 he needs unless he can get another person to guarantee the loan. Frank's father agrees. In this scenario, Frank's father would be termed

  a. a promisor.
  b. a promisee.
  c. a surety.
  d. an offeree.

6. Langley calls Ready Repairs to fix her refrigerator, after which they submit a bill for $80. Later, Langley discovers that while the refrigerator now operates at the correct temperature, it also makes a drumming sound that keeps the household awake at night. Dissatisfied, Langley tells Ready she's unwilling to pay the full $80. Langley's debt in this scenario is *best* described as

  a. a liquidated debt.
  b. an unliquidated debt.
  c. a default.
  d. a cancellation.

7. Ready Repair (Question 6) is totally baffled over the noisy refrigerator, but they agree to accept $50 from Langley—rather than the original $80 she owed—and call it even. In this case, the $50 is *best* described as

  a. a liquidated debt.
  b. a composition agreement.
  c. surety.
  d. consideration.

8. Reese, a salesman with a large territory in the Northwest, finds himself behind schedule and charters a private plane to fly him to his next destination. The weather is extremely stormy, but at a particularly rough part of the ride the pilot says he's willing to detour around the storm if Reese will provide an extra $200 over and above the transportation cost. Reese agrees, but upon arriving at his destination, changes his mind. Would the court *likely* support the pilot's position if he decides to sue Reese for breach of promise?

  a. No; the pilot has suffered no detriment, so there is no consideration.

b. Yes, definitely; the $200 is the consideration.

c. Yes; the promise of the safe trip is the consideration.

9. Several months before Evans retires from Blackwell and Associates, Blackwell agrees to pay her a small monthly stipend in recognition of her past exceptional service—and feels especially obliged to do so since Evans did not qualify to receive a pension under company regulations. If, a month later, Blackwell changes his mind about paying the stipend, will the court force him to pay?

a. Yes; the good service provided by Evans provides the consideration that makes this agreement enforceable.

b. Yes; promises made out of "moral obligation" are always enforceable, regardless of whether consideration is present.

c. No; there really is no consideration here, so the agreement is not enforceable.

10. Suppose Blackwell (Question 9) paid the stipend for five years and then changed his mind. If Evans wanted to contest Blackwell's refusal to continue the stipend, which of the following would probably afford her the *best* argument?

a. The doctrine of past consideration

b. The doctrine of moral obligation

c. The doctrine of promissory estoppel

d. The doctrine of preexisting duty

YOUR OPINION, PLEASE

Read each of the following scenarios and answer the questions about the decisions you would make in each situation. Give these questions some serious thought; they may be used as the basis for the development of a more complex essay. You should base your decisions on what you've learned from this lesson, though you may incorporate outside readings or information gained through your own experience if it is relevant.

Scenario I

Brinkley, a copy editor for a big-city newspaper, spots what she fears may be a serious error in the banner headline of the paper's front-page news story. Brinkley checks out the facts and, sure enough, the headline—which now reads "Senator Condones New Tax Legislation"—should read "Senator Condemns New Tax Legislation." Brinkley makes the change just in time—the paper is about to go to press—and points out her discovery to the chief editor, Casey. Casey is delighted that the paper has been saved serious embarrassment and offers Brinkley a $500 bonus on the spot—payable with her next check.

Brinkley is delighted, but other copy editors are grumbling. They tell Casey he's showing favoritism, that it isn't fair for one copy editor to receive a bonus—especially one so large. Casey points out that if the paper had gone out with the mistaken headline, they would all be in trouble. At the least, they'd lose credibility, and they might have been sued. Avoidance of that kind of trouble, he maintains, is worth $500—and then some. At length, however, Casey fears he'll have major rebellion among the staff unless he takes back his promise. Reluctantly, he does so.

Upon learning that Casey has changed his mind, Brinkley threatens to sue. She claims she earned the money, that Casey promised it, and that since she has already performed the service, there is no way he can go back on the agreement.

What's your opinion? Based on what you know of the situation, do you think Brinkley can successfully build a case against Casey? Do they have a valid agreement supported by consideration?

- Is the court likely to support Brinkley if she sues Casey for breach of contract? Why or why not?
- What factors support your answer?
- What factors might an attorney cite in arguing against your view?
- What steps, if any, might Casey have taken to prevent a lawsuit?
- What steps, if any, might Brinkley have taken to prevent a lawsuit?

Scenario 2

Dudley has spent the whole weekend watching a telethon presentation—dozens of stars performing and seeking donations, personal stories from children and adults who've overcome dramatic odds to lead successful lives. At times, Dudley finds himself moved almost to tears, and finally, on Sunday evening—alone in the house—he rushes to the phone and impulsively pledges $500, much more than he can afford. The next day, his wife is appalled to learn of his gesture and asks why he did not pledge a more reasonable amount.

Reacting to her remarks, Dudley decides to withdraw his pledge. He's dismayed to find, however, that the charity to whom he pledged the $500 will not accept his withdrawal. They point out again how desperately needed the money is and how much they're counting on it. And, they add, they're sorry that Dudley is now having second thoughts, but he will need to live up to his commitment.

Dudley points out that there is no real commitment because there is no consideration—and in the absence of consideration, the agreement cannot be valid, despite the phone pledge (which he fully admits to making). The charity—with some regrets—takes the position that unless Dudley provides the money, they will sue, and they add that the doctrine of promissory estoppel will enable them to win their case.

What's your opinion? Based on what you know of the situation, do you think a court would likely support the charity's position in a lawsuit against Dudley? Or is Dudley justified in stating that the agreement is not enforceable in the absence of consideration?

- If the charity sues Dudley, is the court likely to support their case on the theory of promissory estoppel? Why or why not?
- What factors support your answer?
- What factors might an attorney cite in arguing against your view?
- What steps, if any, might the charity have taken to preclude a lawsuit in this situation?
- What steps, if any, might Dudley have taken to preclude a lawsuit in this situation?

7

Contract Requirement: Contractual Capacity

LEARNING OBJECTIVES

Upon completing your study of this lesson, you should be able to

- Define the term *capacity*.
- Relate the contractual concept of legal capacity to the rights of minors.
- Relate the concept of contractual capacity to the rights of insane persons, intoxicated persons, aliens, and convicts.

Most discussions of contract law tend to focus on the agreement: the nature and terms of the agreement, or the circumstances under which agreement came about. In this lesson, however, we take a close look at the parties who enter into the agreement. Our primary question will be, "Under what circumstances do persons have the legal capacity to contract?" For while most contracts, as we shall see, are ultimately honored, certain persons—minors, aliens, convicts, and others—are restricted in their capacity to contract. When such persons attempt to enter into contractual agreements, the consequences can be very serious, both for them and for the parties with whom they contract. To understand why, we'll look closely at the meaning of legal capacity in a variety of contexts, with some hypothetical examples based in real life.

OVERVIEW

In order for a contract to be legally enforceable, both parties must understand what the contract requires—in other words, must agree to the same terms. In addition, they must enter the contract willingly. And they must demonstrate some evidence of their commitment through the presence of consideration—money, or something else of value bargained for.

But even if these elements are present, there is no valid contract without legal capacity, *the legal ability of the contracting parties to bind themselves to the contract and to enforce any promises made to them.* It is, of course, quite possible that the party lacking the legal capacity to contract will nevertheless fulfill his or her side of the agreement, in which case the other party may never even know that legal capacity was lacking. However, should a dispute arise, the absence of legal capacity on either side will usually render the contract voidable.

Because absence of legal capacity is the exception and not the rule, the courts take the position that most contracts will wind up being enforced. This means that in the event of any dispute, it will be up to the party that first raises the question of incapacity to prove that incapacity exists. Say, for example, that Barnes signs a contract to lease an apartment for the next twelve months. It turns out, however, that Barnes was a minor at the time of contract signing. If Barnes wants to get out of the contract on the basis of incapacity, he must demonstrate that he was below majority age (eighteen in most states) when the contract was signed—which probably won't be very difficult to do, assuming the contract is dated.

Let's consider a somewhat trickier example. Hayes signs a contract entitling Wiggs to a 30% share of company profits, a whopping 25% increase over what Wiggs was previously receiving. Later, Hayes sues for *rescission* (that is, annulment or cancellation) of the contract, arguing that because he was intoxicated at the time, he did not have the legal capacity to contract. Hayes has raised the issue of lack of legal capacity, so the burden of proof is on him. And since incapacity on the basis of intoxication is not as straightforward an issue as age, Hayes may have a difficult time winning his suit, even if he has witnesses to his alleged intoxication.

Why are certain persons designated as lacking legal capacity to contract? In making this determination, the law looks at the relative bargaining power of each side. Children, for example, usually lack the experience and insight to bargain equitably with adults. To ensure that adults will not take advantage of minors in contractual agreements, the law, therefore, decrees that minors lack the legal capacity to contract. Similarly, the law tends to regard insane persons, intoxicated persons, convicts, and aliens as being at a potential bargaining disadvantage. Accordingly, the law in many states has *circumscribed* — or limited — their legal rights to contract.

The Contractual Capacity of Minors

The earlier common law rule held that any person of either sex under twenty-one years of age would be considered a *minor* or *infant*. In most states, majority status now comes about at eighteen years of age, at least for most legal purposes. In some states, minority status ends with marriage, even if the marriage occurs prior to the age of eighteen. Likewise, if the minor is *emancipated* — legally independent of parental influence and control — some states give adult status to that minor.

In its tradition of protecting children in their dealings with adults, the law stipulates that minors may *disaffirm* (simply walk away from) contracts with adults in all but a few specialized situations. In other words, a contract between an adult and a minor is not legally enforceable by the adult. The minor may choose to uphold the contract, but in most cases, there is no legal obligation on the minor's part to do so. Thus the contract may be voided at any time. On the other hand, the contract *cannot* be disaffirmed by the adult; he or she is required to uphold the bargain, even though the minor could disaffirm the agreement at any time.

Needless to say, such a situation can leave an adult businessperson in a precarious position. And for that reason, many prudent businesses require that a minor signing a contract also have an adult cosigner. In this case, the adult cosigner will be liable for the terms of the contract even if the minor disaffirms it.

The fact that one contracting party may not be aware of another's capacity to legally contract certainly complicates the issue from the businessperson's perspective. Consider for a moment just the problems with minors, who may appear older than they are, may claim to be older, and may even have forged identification to back that false claim: What then?

Well, suppose for example that Wilson, age sixteen, contracts with Soundwaves, Inc., to purchase expensive stereo components, which Wilson agrees to pay for over a period of two years. But after a few months, Wilson — who is unemployed and a full-time high school student — cannot make the payments. She elects to disaffirm the contract and tells Soundwaves that she will no longer make payments on the contract. What options are open to Soundwaves at this point? That depends a lot on state statutes. But in many instances, Wilson may simply walk away from the situation without having to make any sort of payment or concession to Soundwaves.

As we shall see, many variables influence a court's decision in such situations. One consideration, which we'll discuss more later, is whether the subject matter of the contract can be classified as a *necessary* — something directly important to Wilson's well-being. But it is well to keep in mind that while the court will carefully consider the full range of circumstances of any specific case, most interpretations will lean heavily toward the "protection" of minors.

On the other hand, there is also concern that businesses that act in good faith not find themselves repeatedly deprived of goods and services simply because they've contracted with minors. Let's return for a moment to our scenario. Let's suppose that Wilson looks older than she is, that she used a forged driver's license to show that she was over eighteen, that she told Soundwaves she was over eighteen, and that the Soundwaves sales rep had no reasonable cause to doubt her word. In that case, some states will allow rescission of the contract, but, under a rule known as *duty of restoration*, will require that Wilson return the stereo.

Requiring the return of the goods is the court's way of ensuring that, in the course of protecting the rights of a minor, it is not excessively unfair to the rights of a property owner with whom a minor might contract. After all, things would soon grow rather chaotic in the business world if young people could go around regularly contracting for the purchase of various goods, disaffirm the contracts, and then keep the goods anyway. If this were the norm, it would undoubtedly become very difficult for minors to make even the simplest purchases, since businesses could never be sure of getting either their money or their property.

What would happen if, in our scenario, Wilson had sold the various stereo components at an impromptu garage sale and had no reasonable means of recovering them? In many states, she might be required — under the *duty of restitution* — to restore Soundwaves to the same economic status it enjoyed prior to contracting with her. In short, since she couldn't return the stereo itself, she would have to pay some reasonable amount for the stereo. That "reasonable amount" might be the purchase price, or it might be the wholesale cost of the stereo; that would be up to the court to determine. Courts do not always, however, impose the duty of restitution on minors — particularly if the minor's status was well known to the other contracting party.

There are many ways for a minor to disaffirm a contract. In our scenario, for example, Wilson might disaffirm her contract with Soundwaves through a formal lawsuit. But that wouldn't be likely since formalities aren't required. She could just as well disaffirm the contract through a letter or phone call or by stopping payment on the contract. Suppose that Wilson had the stereo half paid for when she reached her eighteenth birthday, but then decided she could not pay for the remainder. Could she still disaffirm the contract? Yes — for a time. A minor's power of disaffirmance extends up until the minor reaches majority age (which we're supposing in Wilson's state is eighteen), and for a "reasonable time" thereafter. What's reasonable? That is for a court to determine. If Wilson kept the stereo until she were twenty and then tried to disaffirm the contract, it's unlikely any court would support her effort.

Ratification of Contracts

Ratification is the opposite of disaffirmance. In other words, it's a clear declaration of intent to be bound to the terms of a contract. A minor can ratify a contract by expressly stating that he or she will fulfill the obligations of the contract, or simply by acting in a manner that implies ratification—such as making payments on a purchase, for instance.

The point to keep in mind here is that even with express ratification *in writing*—which some states insist on—ratification cannot take effect until a minor reaches majority. Suppose Duff, a minor, contracts with McGee to perform some light maintenance work at McGee's place of business. Recognizing that he's contracting with a minor, McGee asks for ratification of their contract in writing—which Duff cheerfully provides. Is the contract now enforceable? No—not yet. If Duff chooses to disaffirm it, McGee has little recourse. However, once Duff reaches his majority, the ratification will go into effect—and he will no longer have the privilege of disaffirming the contract. Similarly, in our earlier example of Wilson and the stereo, if Wilson makes payments on the purchase contract after her eighteenth birthday, many states will conclude that she reaffirmed the contract by making of those payments. The payments made after her eighteenth birthday will be seen as the necessary expression of intent required to reaffirm the contract. At that point, any later attempt to disaffirm the contract would probably be unsuccessful, and Wilson would be bound to complete the contract as originally made.

Necessaries

Under certain circumstances, a minor's normal power to disaffirm a contract is lessened. For example, in the case of a contract for necessaries, the lack of legal capacity will void the contract, but the court will create a *quasi contract*—an artificial contract, so to speak—under which the minor will still be liable for the cost of the necessaries. As a practical matter, in most of these cases, the liability falls to the minor's parent or guardian. But if the parent or guardian is unable to pay, the minor will be held responsible.

The term *necessaries* originally comprised the basics of life: food, clothing, and shelter. In recent years, the meaning of this term has been expanded. It is now somewhat more open to interpretation. In general, it's taken to mean anything *that directly fosters the minor's well-being.* But that broad definition may cover different things in different situations. For example, a bicycle might be classed as a necessary in one situation, particularly if the minor used it for a paper route that helped earn money her family needed to buy school books or school clothes for the children. But in another situation—say, where a minor purchased it as an extravagant gift for a friend—it probably would not be looked on as a necessary. Such items as loans for college tuition or for medical or dental services are likely to be looked on as necessaries. But the definition will differ, depending on the circumstances, the minor's social status, and the laws of the state in which the minor lives or contracted.

Special Statutes Governing Contracts with Minors

Most states have special statutes under which minors will be liable for contract-related costs in special circumstances. Typically, such statutes cover things like medical and dental costs, insurance policies, educational loans, airline tickets, and so forth. Such statutes are designed to keep certain kinds of desirable business transactions from bogging down due to fear that contracts will not be honored. For example, if students could not be held liable for student tuition loans, then those making the loans would be unlikely to grant them—and both sides would suffer.

Adults' interests are also protected in cases where the adult suffers a loss resulting from a *tort*—a violation of civil responsibility—or crime committed by the minor. However, minors will not be held liable if they are considered by the court to be too young to understand the consequences of their actions.

Contractual Capacity of Insane Persons, Intoxicated Persons, Aliens, and Convicts

We've devoted most of our discussion to cases involving minors because these are the most common cases involving questions of capacity to contract. Other persons, however, may also lack full capacity to contract. Remember that in establishing categories of people who lack full capacity to contract, the law looks primarily at the relative ability to understand the terms of the contract and the bargaining power of the two parties.

For example, contracts with persons judged insane are not normally enforceable. To be insane from the perspective of contract law, a person must be *so mentally infirm or deranged as to be unable to understand what he or she is agreeing to or the consequences attendant upon that agreement*. The causes of such "insanity"—senility, drug abuse, mental stress—are not relevant, only the inability to understand. The tricky part here is that insanity, quite unlike minority, is rarely a clearcut either/or condition. In other words, while it is relatively easy to demonstrate that a person was a minor at the time of signing a contract, it is more difficult to demonstrate that someone was "insane" at the time of signing a contract. And even if a person can be judged insane at the time a suit is brought, if it can be shown that he or she was lucid—capable of understanding the terms and consequences of the contract—at the time of signing, the contract will still be enforceable. Conversely, a person who signs a contract while insane may ratify that contract upon regaining sanity, thereby making it enforceable.

A person too intoxicated to understand the nature or consequences of a contract he or she signs may also disaffirm (or ratify, for that matter) that contract upon regaining sobriety. As you might suppose, in order to disaffirm such a contract, the formerly intoxicated person must act within a reasonable period of time. Failure to promptly disaffirm is viewed by the court as an implied ratification. Further, the extent of intoxication will usually have a bearing on the case. A person who signs a contract over a "social" glass of wine, for instance, will be hard-pressed to disaffirm that contract on the basis of intoxication. On the other hand, if it can be shown that one party was in fact so intoxicated as to be unaware of what has happening, a claim of intoxication may well be sufficient to disaffirm the contract.

The contractual rights of *aliens* — citizens of foreign countries — have expanded somewhat in recent years, but still vary state to state. Under most state statutes, legal aliens have the same basic contractual rights as U.S. citizens, though their rights to own, sell, or inherit real property may be somewhat restricted. This is also generally true for "illegal" aliens, aliens who are in the United States without proper immigration papers. Enemy aliens, on the other hand, or residents of countries with whom the U.S. is formally at war, cannot enforce contracts during the period of hostility.

The contractual rights of convicts are also governed by state law, and in some states are restricted — but only during imprisonment. Upon release from prison, a convict regains all common law contractual rights, although state or federal statutes may make the results of some contracts illegal. For example, where felons are prohibited from owning a gun, a felon's capacity to contract to purchase a gun might be in question.

SOME PRACTICAL ADVICE

While most contracts are ultimately upheld, contracts are clearly not guarantees of a satisfactory result. The lack of legal capacity is one element which could transform a transaction from routine to nettlesome. What advice, then, can a prudent businessperson take from this lesson to help ensure that contracts will be enforceable?

First, be wary of contracting with minors. Although, as we've seen, the law makes some provisions for protecting the rights of adults who contract with minors, it is ultimately the minors' rights of which the court is most protective. And this perspective often holds true even when the adults who contract with minors suffer significant loss or inconvenience. Remember that most contracts with a minor (usually defined in state law as someone under eighteen) are voidable at that person's option throughout the period of minority, and sometimes even for a time after the person reaches majority. Often, the most that a contracting adult can hope for when a minor disaffirms a contract is restoration of property or restitution — consideration sufficient to return the adult to original economic status. But even these options are not consistently available in all states, and different courts may take quite different positions in interpreting contractual rights where minors are involved.

Whenever contracting with a minor seems, for whatever reason, necessary or desirable, it's wise to have a cosigner — a parent or legal guardian or other adult who will assume liability under the terms of the contract even if the minor disaffirms that contract. It may also be advisable to ask the minor to ratify the contract *in writing*. However, keep in mind that such ratification does not take effect until the minor reaches majority. Even a ratified contract may be disaffirmed by a minor up until the time he or she reaches majority.

Because minors can be held liable for any "necessaries" they've contracted for, it often makes sense to consider whether the basis of the contract might be classified as a necessary. Here a knowledge of state statutes—perhaps summarized or interpreted with the help of an attorney—can be useful. It's important to keep in mind that the definition of "necessary" is subjective and variable, both from state to state and from case to case. Therefore, simply assuming that a minor will be held liable for a contract because *you* think it concerns "a necessary" is risky at best.

And finally—though it seems obvious to state it—it is imperative to ensure that the other party has the legal capacity to contract prior to signing that contract. Remember, it isn't only minors who lack such capacity; aliens, intoxicated persons, and those who have been declared insane may lack the capacity under your state's laws to sign legally binding agreements—even when the circumstances appear otherwise to you. After all, should the court take the position that the contracting party lacked the capacity to contract, the contract you signed may be worthless, perhaps at great expense and difficulty to you.

ASSIGNMENTS

- Before you watch the video program, be sure you've read through the preceding overview, familiarized yourself with the learning objectives for this lesson, and looked at the key terms below. Then, read Chapter 11 of Davidson et al., *Business Law*.

- After completing these tasks, view the video program for Lesson 7.

- After watching the program, take time to review what you've learned. First, evaluate your learning with the self-test which follows the key terms. Then, apply and evaluate what you've learned with the "Your Opinion, Please" scenarios at the end of this telecourse study guide lesson.

KEY TERMS

Before you read through the textbook assignment and watch the video program, take a minute to look at the key terms associated with this lesson. When you encounter them in the textbook and video program, pay careful attention to their meaning.

Alien
Circumscribe
Disaffirmance
Duty of restitution
Duty of restoration
Emancipation
Enemy alien
Infant
Insane

Legal capacity
Majority status
Minor
Necessaries
Quasi contract
Ratification
Rescission
Tort

SELF-TEST

The questions below will help you evaluate how well you've learned the material in this lesson. Read each one carefully, and select the letter of the option that best answers the question. You'll find the correct answer, along with a reference to the page number(s) where the topic is discussed, in the back of this telecourse study guide.

1. In determining categories of persons who lack contractual capacity, the law looks *mainly* at the

   a. ages of the contracting parties.
   b. relative bargaining power of the contracting parties.
   c. terms of the contract itself.
   d. evidence that each contracting party is willing to be bound to the terms of the contract.

2. Hart is very upset when his father signs a contract giving a movie company "un-limited rights" to use the family ranch as a location for filmmaking. He later asks that the contract be declared void on the grounds that his father was in-sane at the time the contract was signed. Given what we know from this scenario, which of the following is true?

   a. Hart raised the issue of insanity, so the burden of proving incapacity falls to him.
   b. In this case, it is up to Hart's father to demonstrate that he was legally sane at the time of contract signing.
   c. The insanity charge need not be proven or disproven; the accusation will be sufficient to void the contract automatically.
   d. *None* of the above; legal insanity is not sufficient grounds in itself for void-ing a contract.

3. Under which of the following circumstances would a minor probably *not* be allowed to disaffirm a contract which he or she had signed?

   a. If the minor has received necessaries under the terms of the contract.
   b. If disaffirmance will create serious financial loss for the other party.
   c. If there is also a cosigner.
   d. *None* of the above; there are no circumstances under which a minor can be refused the right to disaffirm a contract.

4. Normally, a minor's power of disaffirmance extends

   a. until the age at which the minor reaches majority—but no further.
   b. until the age of majority and for some "reasonable" period beyond.
   c. for any period of time to which the other contracting party is willing to agree.
   d. indefinitely; a contract signed while one is a minor can be disaffirmed at any time thereafter.

5. Marlys, a minor, signs a contract to purchase expensive camping equipment using a payment plan, telling the department store that she is twenty-one. When the camping equipment is badly damaged in a fire a month later, Marlys disaffirms the contract. Can she legally do this?

   a. No; now that her purchase is damaged, Marlys forfeits her right to disaffirm the contract.
   b. No; but only because she misrepresented her age.
   c. Yes; despite the circumstances, Marlys can still disaffirm the contract.

6. Under most states' laws, if a court imposed a *duty of restoration* on Marlys (Question 5), she could fulfill her duty by

   a. simply returning the camping gear—even though it's damaged.
   b. paying the department store enough money to return them to their economic status prior to the contract.
   c. returning the camping gear *and* continuing to make payments until the debt is gone.
   d. *None* of the above; under the circumstances, Marlys has no way to fulfill her duty of restoration.

7. In general, laws governing contractual capacity tend to

   a. protect adults—sometimes at the expense of minors.
   b. protect adults and minors about equally.
   c. be overwhelmingly protective of minors, even at the expense of adults.
   d. protect those persons who have acted most fairly, regardless of age.

8. Brad, a seventeen-year-old college student, buys an expensive painting on the recommendation of a friend. Brad has little knowledge of art and has never owned a painting; he is interested in the painting only as an investment. Based

on the information in this scenario, would a court *likely* look on the painting as a necessary?

a. Yes, definitely, given its high monetary value.

b. No, because though valuable, the painting is not "essential" to Brad's welfare.

c. It is impossible to say without knowing more about Brad's economic and social status; interpretation of the term *necessary* is highly subjective.

9. Strong, who has been appointed Miller's legal guardian, signs a contract on behalf of Miller during a period when Miller has been judged legally insane. Later, upon regaining her sanity, Miller wishes to disaffirm the contract. Does she have the legal right to do so?

a. No; Strong had the right, as Miller's guardian, to sign the contract—regardless of Miller's own mental state now and at the time of contract signing.

b. Yes, definitely; even a contract signed by a guardian can be disaffirmed if Miller herself was insane at the time of signing.

c. Only if Miller was also under legal age; insanity in itself is not sufficient grounds for disaffirmance in most states.

d. Miller's insanity is irrelevant, since a contract signed by one person on behalf of another is automatically void anyway.

10. Bloom is contemplating signing a contract with a minor for the sale of a used car. Which of the following would be the *most effective* way for Bloom to protect his rights as an adult under this contract?

a. Ask the minor to ratify the contract in writing.

b. Insist that the minor have an adult cosigner who will assume liability with the minor.

c. Ask for an oral promise of restoration—which in most states is legally binding.

d. Include within the contract a clause defining the car as a necessary.

YOUR OPINION, PLEASE

Read each of the following scenarios and answer the questions about the decisions you would make in each situation. Give these questions some serious thought; they may be used as the basis for the development of a more complex essay. You should base your decisions on what you've learned from this lesson, though you may incorporate outside readings or information gained through your own experience if it is relevant.

Scenario 1

Helen Muckler, a seventeen-year-old who works part-time, has her own apartment in Tranquility Villa. Normally, Tranquility is very careful about requiring a cosigner with any minor renting an apartment, but the regular manager was out of town the day Helen moved, and the assistant took Helen's word for it that she was over twenty-one, particularly when she talked about her work at the local department store. She provided names of three references as required—her father, employer, and an older friend in the same apartment complex.

During the next several months, Helen made regular rent payments and did nothing to attract attention from the manager who, upon his return, took brief note of the fact that another unit had been rented, but did not check into the details or bother to meet Helen personally.

When the department store was forced to make some cutbacks due to financial difficulties, Helen lost her job. When she couldn't find another, she decided she would have to move back in with her parents and informed the Tranquility manager that she would be moving out. Under the terms of the lease, Tranquility reserved the right to inspect apartments upon renters' departure and to hold renters responsible for any serious damages noted. The inspection of Helen's apartment revealed a fair amount of damage. The carpeting had a number of pet stains from Helen's cat. Kitchen countertops were scratched beyond repair. The wallpaper in one bedroom was shredded, and the kitchen walls, coated with grease and dirt, required repainting. Helen had hung numerous pictures and shelves on the walls, and when these were removed, the wallboard was badly damaged. In all, the manager determined that overall costs of making the apartment rentable again would total about $1,500.

When Helen learned of the cost, she promptly disaffirmed the contract, thereby also leaving her last month's rent unpaid. The apartment manager argued that he had a right to sue Helen (or her parents) for restitution.

What's your opinion? Based on what you know of the situation, do you think the apartment manager can successfully sue Helen for the amount of the damages? Or does Helen's disaffirmance of the contract free her (and her parents) of all liability in this situation?

- Is the manager likely to win a case for restitution? Why or why not?
- What factors support your answer?
- What factors might an attorney cite in arguing against your view?
- What steps, if any, might Helen have taken to prevent a lawsuit in this situation?
- What steps, if any, might the apartment manager have taken to prevent a lawsuit in this situation?

Scenario 2

Ted D., seventeen, surprises his parents with a new color television for their twenty-fifth wedding anniversary. The store manager at Colberg Appliances is aware that Ted is a minor and that it is against store policy to contract with minors. However, he knows Ted personally (although not well), knows the reason for the purchase, and feels comfortable about making an exception in this case.

Seeing how thrilled his parents are with such a generous gift, Ted is very pleased by his decision. He's worked out the costs carefully, and determined that given the down payment he made out of savings, he can just manage to keep up with the monthly payments out of his earnings from various odd jobs. He has no regular employment.

About a year later, just a month or so after Ted's eighteenth birthday, the television's tuner goes bad. An estimate indicates that the cost of fixing it will run several hundred dollars — much more than Ted wants his parents to pay, but he cannot afford to cover the cost himself. Since it is only a few days past the expiration date on the warranty, Ted decides to see whether Colberg Appliances will pay all or part of the cost. When they refuse, Ted becomes angry. He goes to the store with the TV in his truck and demands his money back.

Again, Colberg refuses. They claim they will accept the television without demanding further payments, but they will not return any of the money Ted has already paid. Further, they argue, Ted cannot disaffirm the contract since it is past his eighteenth birthday, and his regular payments on the TV over the past year are sufficient to imply ratification. And, they add, if Ted does not leave the television with them, they will sue for the remainder of the money owed.

What do you think? Based on what you know of the situation, is Ted legally able to disaffirm the contract? Is the return of the television sufficient to meet any duty of restoration? Is he entitled to any or all of the money he's already paid, provided the store accepts the television?

- Can Ted legally disaffirm the contract? Why or why not? If Colberg sues Ted for the remaining payments, is the court likely to support their case? Why or why not?

- What factors support your answer?

- What factors might an attorney cite in arguing against your view?

- What steps, if any, might Colberg Appliances have taken to prevent a lawsuit in this situation?

- What steps, if any, might Ted have taken to prevent a lawsuit in this situation?

8

Contract Requirement: Legal Purpose

LEARNING OBJECTIVES

Upon completing your study of this lesson, you should be able to

- Define *legality* as it relates to contract law, and discuss the explicit conditions under which a contractual agreement might be regarded as illegal.
- Describe and discuss several types of agreements that would be considered illegal — e.g., agreements to commit a crime, agreements to commit a tort, agreements violating statutes, agreements violating public policy — and provide at least one hypothetical example of each.
- Discuss the special circumstances under which an illegal agreement will be upheld, and provide at least one hypothetical example illustrating such circumstances.

This lesson focuses on one of the primary requirements of any contract: the fact that it must be created for a legal purpose. In exploring the implications of legality, we'll consider what the term *legal* really means as it applies to contracts, look at several situations in which contracts that do not meet the criteria for legality would not be enforceable, and also consider those special situations in which a court might choose to uphold a contract despite some elements of illegality.

OVERVIEW

We usually tend to think of contracts as affecting those persons who actually sign the contract and who agree to be bound by its requirements. The courts recognize, however, that many contracts have potential influence extending far beyond the lives or behaviors of the original contractors. Sometimes, in fact, contracts may influence public welfare in general. To ensure, therefore, that the public—when it is somehow influenced—derives the greatest possible benefit and escapes any unnecessary detriment, the law requires that the subject matter and purpose of any agreement be legal before that agreement can be granted the status of a contract. You may at some point hear the expression "illegal contract." That's a contradiction in terms. In fact, if an agreement is illegal it cannot be a contract—even though it may well give every appearance of being one.

Imagine, for example, a hypothetical corporation—Zaplee Chemicals—working on the development of a new plastic, and in the process polluting the adjacent river with waste products from the plastic manufacturing process. Suppose that Zaplee could—legally—strike a bargain with the local bureau of waterways management under which the bureau would overlook the pollution problem in exchange for a percentage of the profits from the sale of Zaplee's new plastics products. This, of course, is a fairly simplified and obvious example. But it helps illustrate the importance of ensuring that contracts are legal in substance and intent. Obviously, many persons other than the corporate heads of Zaplee and the water bureau would be affected in our little scenario. The health and welfare of the entire population in the town where Zaplee operates might be endangered, and there could be long-term implications for the ecology of both the immediate and extended geographic areas, to say nothing of the fact that permitting such an agreement would set a dangerous precedent for others to follow.

Sometimes the legality of an issue is pretty obvious. A "contract" to have someone killed or kidnapped, for instance, could never be legal. But sometimes legality is not so obvious. In cases where the application of the law is not readily apparent and where there may be no precedents to guide a decision, the court must call upon all of its interpretive powers, always looking to see how the public welfare will best be served by a given decision. As you go through this lesson, you may find it helpful to keep in mind the court's perspective in considering the ramifications of enforcing or voiding a contract. In making its final determination, the court will ask, under which circumstances will the general good best be served?

Components of Illegality

Before going further, we need to define what we mean by *illegality*. For purposes of contract law, a bargain is illegal *if its performance is criminal, tortious, or otherwise opposed to public policy*. Further, in order for an agreement to be legal, *both* the subject matter of the bargain and the means by which its objectives will be realized must be legal. For instance, suppose that Goodwall Builders contracts to put up a new office complex. So far, so good. However, in order to save money, Goodwall chooses to ignore the city's ordinance prohibiting the use of unlicensed electricians and hires nonlicensed electricians to do the wiring. In this instance, the subject matter of the contract—erecting the office complex—is perfectly legal, but Goodwall's means of fulfilling the requirements of the contract—by using nonlicensed electricians—is not. The types of agreements or contracts which are considered illegal include agreements to commit a crime, agreements to commit a tort, agreements violating statutes, and agreements violating public policy.

Agreements to Commit a Crime

An agreement is illegal—and automatically void—if it calls for the commission of a crime. A crime, for purposes of this discussion, may be defined as an act (or sometimes a failure to act) which has been officially defined through legislative action as a punishable offense. In other words, a crime is something for which one could be officially charged or arrested. The seriousness of the offense may vary widely. Murder is a crime. In some places, allowing one's dog to wander about unleashed is also a crime. While no reasonable person could look upon these two crimes as comparable, the point here is that neither could form the basis for a legal, enforceable contract.

Let's return for a moment to our earlier example with Goodwall Construction. Suppose that Swift Productions, owners of the new office complex, discover that Goodwall is using nonlicensed electricians and thus refuses to pay for the wiring costs on the new building. Could Goodwall successfully sue Swift to recover those costs? Probably not. Although—as we shall see later in this lesson—the court is often reluctant to declare an entire contract void, it might well rule that Goodwall was not entitled to recover any costs for wiring done in violation of local building codes although they should get paid for the rest of the contract. Now obviously, two contractors can strike an illegal bargain that both will agree to uphold with no one else the wiser. If, however, either decides not to carry out the terms of the agreement, the other party cannot successfully sue for breach of contract since the court will not uphold an illegal bargain.

Agreements to Commit a Tort

An agreement to commit a tort is also illegal and void. A tort is a breach of a civil duty or a failure to exercise due care that results in harm to some person or property. The offense, while not necessarily in violation of any law, may provide grounds for a civil suit. For example, suppose that three publishing companies—Writewell, Writemore, and Swelldraft—are competing for a fairly limited market in one portion of the country. Writewell and Writemore, in order to gain a disproportionate share of the market for themselves, agree that they'll spread rumors questioning the solvency of Swelldraft, hinting that the company is close to bankruptcy, that future contracts with Swelldraft may not be honored, that lawsuits relating to former publications are pending, and that the company may go down within a year. Such an agreement, to damage the good name of a competitor, is automatically illegal and void; it cannot gain the status of a bona fide contract.

Agreements Violating Public Policy

Any agreement that is held to be in violation of public policy is unenforceable. Public policy is interpreted somewhat differently by different courts, depending on local standards and expectations as well as the prevailing moral climate of the times. In general, public policy may be thought of as the overall attitude of the public toward certain behavior—in other words, the public sense of what is right or wrong. For example, an airline may have a policy stating that it will "do everything possible" to reclaim lost luggage but that it will ultimately not bear responsibility for any items that are checked rather than brought on board by passengers. While such behavior might not be regarded as criminal or even tortious, and while we might even appreciate the rationale underlying it, it is still difficult to justify such treatment of airline patrons who have—our sense of public policy tells us—a right to expect that their goods will be handled with reasonable care.

Public policy evolves over time as attitudes shift. What was considered appropriate in 1800 might or might not be considered appropriate now—and vice versa. Similarly, public policy will undoubtedly be quite different in the year 2050 from what it is now. And it can even vary with geographic location, since what's acceptable in a suburban West Coast community may be frowned on in a small town in the Midwest. A violation of public policy does not provide grounds for arrest since there has been no official legislative decision relating to the conduct involved. Nor does it generally provide grounds for suit—as a tort might—since there is usually no precedent for such action (though certain violations of public policy may, in time, come to be recognized as torts—which may, in turn, become violations of the law if the legislature examines and rules on such actions). Because no law has been broken in an agreement violating public policy, the court must consider—in determining whether to uphold such an agreement—how the public interests will best be served. Two sorts of examples help illustrate the kind of thinking that generally characterizes current decisions in this still rather gray area.

Noncompete Clauses

First, let's consider so-called noncompete clauses, agreements that the seller of a business or an employee who leaves a business *will not engage in the same or a similar business or occupation for a period of time in a certain geographic area.* Such agreements may or may not be considered legal by the court, and the decision usually rests on the intent of the agreement and the degree of restrictiveness sought by the contract. In general, the court will take the position that clauses that prevent another person from making a living are unreasonable and unenforceable. Further, a clause that, in effect, isolates a business from outside competition will also be regarded as unreasonable and unenforceable.

On the other hand, a clause that prevents a former employee from using what he or she has learned at one company's expense in beginning a new business or promoting the welfare of a competing business may well be upheld. For instance, suppose that Jones works for Bit-By-Bit Computers, specialists in computerized accounting. Jones comes to the company a true novice, with no experience in working with computers whatever, but he has a natural talent and lots of interest, and within a year he's vice president — with a goal of beginning his own firm. Fine. Nothing wrong with that. Yet it seems a little unfair to allow Jones, who has clearly gained most of his computer-related expertise at Bit-By-Bit's expense, to set up shop three blocks down the road and — potentially at least — steal some of Bit's business. A noncompete clause in Jones's original employment contract might require Jones to wait for a period of time — say, six months — before launching any competitive enterprise, and perhaps to locate his business some reasonable geographic distance from Bit. The court would probably regard such a clause as reasonable and enforceable.

By contrast, suppose Jones was a well-recognized specialist in computerized accounting when he was hired by Bit. If Bit demanded that Jones sign a noncompete clause stating that for a year after leaving Bit he would not work for any other company as a computerized accounting specialist, would the court uphold that clause? Probably not. They might view it as unreasonably restrictive since it could well keep Jones from making a living during the year-long period. What the court will sometimes do in such situations is effect a compromise by rewriting the clause so it's less restrictive. This process is called *blue pencilling.* For instance, they might decrease the time limit, stating that Jones could work for someone else in three months — or they might allow Jones to work for a competitor outside Bit's immediate geographic area. Blue pencilling is not, however, the most common solution. Far more commonly, the court will simply void the restrictive clause altogether while upholding the remainder of the contract between Jones and Bit. Why? Because it is not viewed as being in the public interest either to keep persons from making a living or to insulate companies from fair competition.

Exculpatory Clauses

Let's consider now exculpatory clauses, *attempts to avoid liability by disclaiming liability in advance.* If you've ever seen a posted sign that says "Not responsible

for lost or stolen goods," then you already have a good notion of what an exculpatory clause is about. Courts will judge the legality of such clauses on a case-by-
case basis, and again, the question here is, "What will serve the public interest best?"
In making a determination, the court will generally ask whether the party "agreeing" to assume a risk for the other's potential negligence has done so voluntarily.
A written agreement might be one indication that one has assumed a risk at least
knowing that the risk existed. Yet the court might also wish to know whether there
was any choice about the matter. If the court has reason to suppose that an *adhesion contract* exists — a contract drafted by the stronger party, the one in the better
bargaining position, in order to force unreasonable terms from the weaker party —
then the court may well rule that such an agreement violates public policy.

For instance, suppose that Torres arrives home from work to find a city maintenance department notice that the condition of the sidewalk in front of Torres's
home has fallen below city standards and must be repaired. Torres calls the city
and learns that while city work crews or a private certified contractor can do the repair, he must bear the cost. Much to his chagrin, Torres learns that the city, as well
as all the certified contractors, will require that he sign a contract holding them
blameless for any damage that might occur to trees or underground sprinkler systems in the course of the sidewalk repair. Because he must get the sidewalk done
or face an immediate city fine, Torres reluctantly signs on with a company to do the
work. On the day scheduled for the repair work, Torres meets the crew at his home.
He talks to the foreman about the underground sprinkler system and gives him the
plan showing where the pipes are located, hoping that his precautions will prevent
any damage to his system. Nevertheless, the sprinkler system is damaged, turning
Torres's lawn into a swamp.

Will a court uphold the clause freeing the repair company from liability? Very
likely not. Though Torres has agreed not to hold the contractor liable, he didn't
have much choice in the matter. All approved contractors, including the city crews,
required the same clause in their contracts, and Torres was faced with signing a contract or being fined for a dangerous sidewalk. The court may determine that it
would not be in the public interest to establish a precedent whereby a company,
with apparent city approval, could virtually "insist" that it be freed of responsibility
for damages caused by its work. After all, if he chose not to repair his sidewalk in
light of waiving his ability to recover for damages to his property, Torres not only
would face the likelihood of a city fine but also the possibility of liability if someone
fell on his poorly maintained sidewalk. The court might well consider this risk unreasonable, both for Torres and for the public in general, which expects sidewalks
to be maintained within reasonable standards.

In examining this type of case, the court will also look at the ages of the parties
involved, their relative expertise (Is one more knowledgeable and therefore more
capable of bargaining than the other?), their mental condition at the time of signing a contract with an exculpatory clause, and other such factors. Remember, the
primary questions here are, "Did the party who signed or agreed to the clause know
of the risk?" and, "Did the party have a choice?"

Agreements Violating Statutes

Ordinarily, courts will not uphold agreements that are in violation of state statutes. But it is important to keep in mind that such statutes are not consistent from state to state, so, from a business perspective, awareness of what is allowable in one's own area is critical. Let's consider several examples of actions normally held to be in violation of state statutes.

Price-Fixing Agreements

Price-fixing agreements are generally held to be illegal. The rationale here is that price fixing restricts competition, and that is viewed by the courts as being in violation of the public's best interests. Further, federal legislation—namely, the Sherman Antitrust Act, the Clayton Act, and the Federal Trade Commission Act—prohibit price fixing explicitly. Such agreements, therefore, which run afoul of federal legislation, state statutes, and public policy alike, stand virtually no chance of being upheld by any court.

Performance of Services Without a License

Agreements to perform services without a license may violate state statutes, depending on the nature of such services. All states require licensing of some professionals—doctors and dentists, for example. With other professions, licensing requirements may vary from state to state. If a nonlicensed person contracts to perform a service for which the other party later refuses to pay, can the nonlicensed party sue for payment and recover it? That depends. In making this decision, the court will generally consider the purpose of the licensing requirement. If it is simply a revenue-collecting device—in other words, the fee for the licensing is merely a formality, a way for the state to collect money—then the service-provider (although potentially subject to fines for not being licensed) will usually be able to collect. As the court sees it, one person would be as likely as another to hold a license since all that's required is to pay a fee.

However, if the licensing is done for regulatory purposes and the licensed person must pass a test or demonstrate competence in some way in order to obtain a license, then the nonlicensed party will usually *not* be able to collect. One reason for this is to uphold the regulatory purpose of the license—to assure that only those qualified to act would be able to hold themselves out as practitioners and to legally collect fees. If people could, for example, practice medicine without a license, there would be little assurance that those holding themselves out as skilled resources actually had the knowledge they represented themselves as having. Preventing the recovery of fees is also a way to "punish" those trying to avoid the regulatory process.

But there are exceptions to this concept. Remember our early example in which Goodwall Construction was building an office complex for Swift Productions? As you'll recall, Goodwall had hired nonlicensed electricians to do the wiring in order to lower Goodwall's costs. As we've just noted, the odds are that if Swift refused to pay, Goodwall could not collect. On the other hand, though, suppose Goodwall could show that Swift *knew* about the use of unlicensed electricians and agreed to the work in order to save themselves — as well as Goodwall — money. Suppose, too, that it were further determined that the electricians would suffer substantial loss of income as a result of not collecting the fee. Under such circumstances, the court might uphold their right to recover the fee — or at least some of it. But suppose further that Goodwall botched the wiring job. Could Swift then sue for damages given that the Goodwall electricians were not licensed? Yes. The absence of a license does *not* preclude the other contracting party's right to sue for any damages resulting from negligence or faulty workmanship.

Sunday Laws

If you live in a state where certain businesses are required to remain closed on Sunday or where the sale of liquor is prohibited on Sunday, then you're familiar with the effects of Sunday Laws — laws that *prohibit the formation or performance of contracts on Sundays*. Such laws vary widely from state to state and may have overwhelming impact on business negotiations in one state, but little or none in another. Violation of a Sunday statute may void a contract altogether unless it can be shown that one party or the other had no knowledge that the contract was executed on Sunday, or alternatively, that although the contract was *initiated* on Sunday, it was not accepted until later. Post-dated sales receipts or checks might, for instance, be used to advance such an argument — which might or might not be accepted by the court.

Wagering Statutes

Many states have statutes that prohibit wagering, gambling, and lotteries in order to protect the public from what some believe is the associated crime and family discord. In order to be illegal, wagering must require a person to pay some consideration or value — usually money — in the hope of receiving a prize or reward. Further, the wager must involve artificial risk — odds which are controlled, in other words. Some persons might say that investing money in the stock market is gambling. Certainly there's risk involved. But the point is, the risk is not controlled and manipulated in secret by the stockbroker who invests your money. To the lawmakers of the states were wagering or gambling is illegal, investing in the stock market is quite different from, say, playing the lottery or putting money in a slot machine.

Usury Statutes

Agreements that violate usury statutes are also illegal, but determining usury can be complex. Three elements are involved: (1) a loan of money, (2) the agreement of the debtor to pay higher than the current legal rate of interest, and (3) the *intention* of the lender to violate usury laws. If all three elements are present, the contract will be void. Keep in mind, however, that usury laws are highly variable from state to state. Further, interpretation of such laws is complicated by the many exceptions. For instance, acceleration clauses and prepayment clauses are not considered usurious, nor are conditional sales contracts. The court's position is that the relative risks of both buyer and seller must be considered, and thus a higher than usual rate of interest may be viewed as compensation for additional risk on the part of the seller, rather than as usury. Further, it's important to recognize that the general trend today is for courts to allow exceptions to usury laws.

Enforcement of Illegal Agreements

As we noted earlier, there are certain rare situations in which an illegal agreement will be enforced. Keep in mind that such agreements are the exception.

First, if one party is less "guilty" than the other in establishing the illegal agreement, the law holds that the parties are not *in pari delicto* — that is, they are not equally at fault. In that case, the *less* guilty party may sue for recovery if that recovery would somehow serve the public interest. For instance, suppose that Winston is not licensed to sell securities, but sets up a rather successful business in the basement of his home. If Johnson, for whom Winston invests a substantial amount of money, chooses to sue Winston for recovery of that money, the court is likely to uphold Johnson's right to sue on the grounds that such action helps, in the long run, to protect the public from unknowingly dealing with unlicensed tradespeople.

Second, even if the parties are equally guilty — or *in pari delicto* — the law allows recovery by the person who shows repentance by rescinding the illegal contract before it is executed, or completed. For instance, in our running scenario involving Swift Productions and Goodwall Construction, let's suppose that Swift knows perfectly well that Goodwall plans to use nonlicensed electricians to wire the office building, and agrees in order to save money. Before Goodwall begins the wiring, however, Swift's manager, Clark, has second thoughts. He worries that the wiring will not be up to code, and that a fire would more likely break out. If someone were to be injured, Clark would never forgive himself. Repentant, Clark seeks to undo the bargain, but Goodwall refuses either to return the down payment Swift has already made or to use licensed electricians. Can Clark sue for recovery? In all likelihood, yes. The court's rationale here is that Clark's recovery of the money paid to Goodwall furthers the public interest in deterring illegal agreements.

Third, many contracts are complex and consist of not just one agreement, but several or many. What happens if just one agreement within the lot is held to be illegal? In that case, only the clause involving the illegal agreement may be voided while the rest of the contract would be upheld. This is often the case with restrictive or noncompete clauses, for instance. The court may determine that the noncompete clause itself is unenforceable, but may still uphold the remainder of the contract.

SOME PRACTICAL ADVICE

It seems rather obvious to advise extreme care in ensuring that the substance of any contract is legal—yet, this is not always so simple as it sounds. While such acts as arson and murder are universally recognized as illegal, the complexities of state statutes almost guarantee that many persons will, at some point, have reason to question the legality of certain actions or intentions. Therefore, if there is any question whatever, it is wise to seek the advice of an attorney who can review a contract for you before you sign it or give it to someone else to sign. Remember, even if you are unaware that what you're agreeing to (or asking someone else to agree to) is illegal, the court may still void the contract.

Keep in mind, too, that state statutes differ widely. What is quite acceptable in one location may be unacceptable in another. This has special implications for businesses that operate in more than one state.

Be wary of dealing with unlicensed persons. Some knowledge of state licensing requirements is valuable, keeping in mind the distinction that the court is likely to make between licensing as a revenue-raising device and licensing that in fact is designed to ensure that those practicing a profession have the qualifications to do so. If you contract with a nonlicensed professional, however, believing that later you'll have the option to pay or not, you may be in for a surprise. The court may consider your contract void, or it may uphold the nonlicensed party's right to collect the money owed. Such decisions are rarely clearcut and depend, as we've noted, on how the court considers that the public good will best be served.

Similarly, noncompete clauses may or may not be upheld, depending on which outcome the court considers will serve the public interest. As an employer, you should not hope to protect yourself from outside competition merely by imposing restrictive clauses on employees; attempts to avoid all competition are not likely to be upheld. On the other hand, as an employee, don't make the mistake of agreeing to a noncompete clause under the assumption that it will never be enforced. It might be. If the court determines that the clause is not unreasonably restrictive and that it merely protects the company from unfair competition, it's likely to be upheld.

Finally, remember that the law itself does not define the boundaries of all that is acceptable or unacceptable in contracts. Any contract that involves committing a tort or that violates public policy—even though it may not call for the breaking of any law—will normally be considered void. For instance, a contract that is deliberately contrived to free a business from the responsibility of serving the public interest or exercising reasonable care for its customers and their property is not likely to be upheld, even if no violation of the law is intended. Invariably, the court will consider how the public welfare will be affected by any contract. Therefore, in signing or drafting any contract for any business purpose, it is always wise to ask, "What will be the ramifications for the public as a whole if all elements within this contract are enforced as intended?" In order to gain the court's perspective on the legality of an agreement, it is necessary to look beyond the welfare of the contracting parties.

ASSIGNMENTS

- Before you watch the video program, be sure you've read through the preceding overview, familiarized yourself with the learning objectives for this lesson, and looked at the key terms below. Then, read Chapter 12 of Davidson et al., *Business Law*.
- After completing these tasks, view the video program for Lesson 8.
- After watching the program, take time to review what you've learned. First, evaluate your learning with the self-test which follows the key terms. Then, apply and evaluate what you've learned with the "Your Opinion, Please" scenarios at the end of this telecourse study guide lesson.

KEY TERMS

Before you read through the textbook assignment and watch the video program, take a minute to look at the key terms associated with this lesson. When you encounter them in the textbook and video program, pay careful attention to their meaning.

Contract of adhesion	Partial illegality
Covenants not to compete	Public policy
Exculpatory clause	Restrictive covenant
Illegality	Sunday laws
In pari delicto	Tortious conduct
Mala in se	Usury statutes
Mala prohibita	Wagering statutes
Not *in pari delicto*	

SELF-TEST

The questions below will help you evaluate how well you've learned the material in this lesson. Read each one carefully, and select the letter of the option that best answers the question. You'll find the correct answer, along with a reference to the page number(s) where the topic is discussed, in the back of this telecourse study guide.

1. It's sometimes said that the term "illegal contract" is a misnomer—a misleading or mistaken term. This most likely refers to the fact that

   a. an illegal agreement can never gain the status of a contract in the first place.
   b. a contract can never really be illegal—only unenforceable.
   c. a contract cannot be judged legal or illegal until a court has made an official ruling.
   d. contracts containing illegal components are properly termed "tortious."

2. Which of the following is the *best* example of an exculpatory clause?

   a. A private game reserve has signs posted all around the perimeter that say "No Trespassing."
   b. A motel posts a sign next to its swimming pool saying "Not responsible for patrons' safety—swim at your own risk."
   c. A school posts a sign by the front entrance requiring all visitors to check in and show identification at the office.
   d. A parking lot posts a sign indicating that the lot will not be patrolled or supervised after 10 p.m.

3. A bargain that violates public policy but that contains no elements that are either tortious or criminal may *best* be regarded as

   a. illegal and unenforceable.
   b. legal, but not always enforceable should suit be brought.
   c. both legal and enforceable.
   d. illegal, but possibly enforceable just the same.

4. An agreement to commit a crime *may* be upheld by the courts *if* it can be shown that

   a. in the long run, the greater public good will be served if the contract is enforced.
   b. neither party knew at the time of contract signing that the contract called for the commission of a crime.
   c. one party was more "guilty" than the other of intent to commit a crime.
   d. *None* of the above; agreements to commit a crime are never upheld, regardless of circumstance.

5. Hart and Riley, friendly competitors, privately agree that they will conspire to "make life difficult" for a third competitor, Fitch, in hopes of getting Fitch to relocate so they can claim his share of the market. They have several ideas for making Fitch's life stressful—delaying shipments, trying to hire Fitch's most valuable employees, spreading rumors about suppliers going out of business, and so forth. Nothing they plan violates the law, however. The behavior of Hart and Riley in this scenario could *best* be described as

   a. a violation of state statutes.
   b. tortious conduct.
   c. *mala in se.*
   d. criminal.

6. Wells, new to the area, selects a dentist from the telephone book and visits that dentist to have a tooth pulled. Unbeknownst to Wells, the dentist has never passed state licensing exams. Later, when Wells discovers the truth, he refuses to pay his bill. If the dentist sues for recovery of the tooth extraction fee, will the court *most likely* support the dentist's claim?

   a. Yes, probably; it was up to Wells to verify the dentist's qualifications prior to having the tooth pulled.

   b. No, probably not; the court is likely to take the position that it is in the public interest to offer protection from unlicensed "dentists."

   c. We cannot say without knowing whether Wells suffered any injury as a result of the dental work.

7. Upon going to work for Acme, Black signed a noncompete agreement, which she has since violated. Now Acme is suing her. In reviewing the agreement, the court concludes that it is unreasonably restrictive and designed only to protect Acme from normal competition. Based on what we know from this lesson about how courts usually respond in such situations, we can predict that the court will *most likely*

   a. blue-pencil the clause so that it is less restrictive.

   b. void the restrictive clause altogether while upholding the remainder of the contract.

   c. void the entire contract automatically.

   d. uphold the contract, including the restrictive clause, despite its apparent unfairness.

8. In judging the relative legality of an exculpatory clause when there is no statute or clear precedent covering the case, the *main* issue the court will usually consider is whether

   a. the party agreeing to assume the risk of negligence without recovery entered the agreement voluntarily.

   b. the party agreeing to assume the risk of negligence without recovery made that intention clear in writing.

   c. the party initiating the exculpatory clause made a deliberate and conscious effort to ensure that the agreeing party understood all elements of the agreement.

   d. there exists—all things considered—any true risk of damage to people or property.

9. Martha has worked for six months as a receptionist in the office of a doctor who is not licensed to practice medicine in the state where he works. Martha is, however, unaware of that fact. If the doctor refuses to pay Martha's wages, is she likely to win a suit against him for those wages, even though the doctor's office was operating in violation of state statues?

   a. No; in the court's view, Martha has also violated the state statute, even though she did not initiate the violation.

b. Yes; since she did not know the doctor was unlicensed, she is not considered equally guilty in the eyes of the law.

c. We cannot say until we know more about Martha's performance as an employee.

10. West and Fraser, joint owners of an apartment building, agree to bribe an appraiser in order to receive a more favorable report about the building's condition and thus command a higher sales price. Shortly before forwarding a large sum of money to the appraiser, West decides not to go through with the bribe. This act is known as

a. *in pari delicto.*
b. partial illegality.
c. adhesion.
d. repentance.

YOUR OPINION, PLEASE

Read each of the following scenarios and answer the questions about the decisions you would make in each situation. Give these questions some serious thought; they may be used as the basis for the development of a more complex essay. You should base your decisions on what you've learned from this lesson, though you may incorporate outside readings or information gained through your own experience if it is relevant.

Scenario 1

Collins is a rancher with a degree in biology. He had intended to become a veterinarian at one time, but never completed his medical studies and is not licensed to practice veterinary medicine. Nevertheless, having grown up working with animals, and having had some college training in diagnosing and treating various ailments, he is widely recognized in his community as exceptionally qualified to treat many common ailments. The members of Collins's community are aware that he is unlicensed, but they trust him in treating their animals and commonly refer to him as the "local vet." There is no licensed veterinarian available within a hundred miles.

When Rockne's prize brood mare, T.J., suffers a serious infection in her leg, Rockne does not hesitate to bring her to Collins for treatment. He's been to Collins before, knows of his qualifications, and trusts him implicitly. However, things do not go well this time. For whatever reason, Collins is unable to treat the infection successfully. The infection grows worse, and T.J. is left slightly, but permanently, lame. Collins assures Rockne that he can still use T.J. as a brood mare, but Rockne isn't so sure about that. Further, he feels that Collins has taken far too long to treat the situation and now wishes he'd gone elsewhere—"to a real veterinarian." He refuses to pay the bill, which now amounts to a total of well over $1,500, medicines included. Collins tells Rockne that if he does not pay, he (Collins) will be forced to sue for the amount of the bill since he cannot afford to lose such a substantial sum of money. Rockne argues that since Collins is not a licensed veterinarian, he will not be able to collect and will only cause problems for himself.

What's your opinion? Based on what you know of the situation, do you think Collins can successfully sue for recovery of the money owed to him by Rockne? Or will the court uphold Rockne's refusal to pay?

- Is Collins likely to win a suit for recovery of the money owed him? If so, on what grounds? If not, why not?
- What factors support your answer?
- What factors might an attorney cite in arguing against your view?
- What steps, if any, might Collins have taken to preclude a lawsuit in this situation?
- What steps, if any, might Rockne have taken to preclude a lawsuit in this situation?

Scenario 2

Jenkins is a very talented and successful marketing specialist who has worked for AdCraft Advertising for over two years. Upon going to work for AdCraft, Jenkins signed a restrictive covenant agreeing that if she left AdCraft for any reason she would not go to work for a competitor anywhere in AdCraft's "territory" for a period of six months. At that time, AdCraft's marketing area did not extend beyond the city where the home office is based, but now—largely due to Jenkins's own efforts—that territory has expanded to a three-state area. Jenkins acknowledges that she did not take the clause too seriously, having been under the impression that such clauses are seldom enforceable.

During the twenty-four months, AdCraft spared no expense to provide Jenkins with the extra training and education they felt a person of her caliber deserved. She was sent, at AdCraft's expense, to several night courses at the local university and to half a dozen seminars providing training in the latest product marketing techniques. Jenkins admits to having benefitted personally and professionally from this training, but points out that AdCraft has also benefitted since she's brought in a number of new clients whose fees will more than offset the training expense—substantial though that may have been.

Recently, Jenkins has made the decision to work for a competing agency in a neighboring state. This agency now competes directly with AdCraft for clients; thus, AdCraft feels Jenkins's decision is in direct violation of the noncompete clause to which she agreed. Jenkins, however, argues that the new company, Trendy and Associates, is well outside the boundaries of what could have been construed as AdCraft's marketing territory at the time the agreement was signed. Further, she argues that an agreement that prevents her from earning a living for a period of six months is unreasonable and unenforceable. AdCraft disagrees, and tells Jenkins that if she signs an employment agreement with Trendy, they will sue for violation of contract.

What's your opinion? Based on what you know of the situation, do you think AdCraft can successfully sue Jenkins for violating her noncompete clause? Or is the court likely to look on that clause as unreasonably restrictive in this case?

- Is AdCraft likely to win a suit against Jenkins for violation of contract? If so, on what grounds? If not, why?
- What factors support your answer?
- What factors might an attorney cite in arguing against your view?
- What steps, if any, might Jenkins have taken to preclude a lawsuit in this situation?
- What steps, if any, might AdCraft have taken to preclude a lawsuit in this situation?

9

Contract Requirement: Genuineness of Assent

LEARNING OBJECTIVES

Upon completing your study of this lesson, you should be able to

- Define *reality of consent* and explain how it relates to the validity of a contract.
- List and describe the six integral components of fraud and explain the affect of fraud on reality of assent.
- Distinguish between fraud and misrepresentation and explain the affect of misrepresentation on reality of consent.
- Define the legal doctrine of mistake and distinguish between unilateral and bilateral mistakes through the use of examples.
- Define duress and explain how it affects reality of consent.
- Define undue influence and explain how it affects reality of consent.
- Provide at least one example of a situation in which unconscionability undermines reality of consent.

We tend to think of an agreement as legally binding so long as there's a contract—especially a written contract—involved. As it turns out, this is not necessarily so. It takes more than written words to make a contract. It takes mutual understanding, openness, and something called assent—meaning, willing agreement to the terms of the contract. Whether you're the one proposing or the one agreeing to a contract, it's important to understand the situations under which the nature of assent, or agreement, can affect whether that contract will be legally binding—or whether it's likely to be rescinded in a court of law. Knowing these conditions in advance, and preparing to avoid them, can save a businessperson a great deal of grief and expense.

OVERVIEW

In order for a contract to be legal, it must be entered into willingly by both parties. This is another way of saying that assent must be *genuine*—which is to say, real. Appearances can, at times, be deceiving and may ultimately mean little. It's what the two parties understand the contract to say, and what their *genuine* intent is upon signing, that ultimately counts. Of course, such things can be difficult to sort out, so be warned: If you sign a contract with the belief that later you can extricate yourself from a commitment on the grounds of misunderstanding, you are probably mistaken. Contracts are generally upheld. On the other hand, if you should sign a contract thinking you were signing something else—a receipt for delivered goods, let's say—or you signed a contract because you feared some consequences if you did not sign—legal prosecution, for instance—the contract would stand a good chance of being declared legally void.

To understand just why a contract might be declared void in one situation but not in another, we need to get a little more specific. The particular circumstances which could preclude mutual assent are *fraud, misrepresentation, mistake, duress, undue influence,* and *unconscionability.*

Let's consider each of these in turn, together with some realistic hypothetical examples drawn from the business world. As we consider each example, ask yourself, "What steps can a prudent businessperson take to ensure that a contract will be legally binding?" And, from the other perspective, "What steps can a prudent businessperson take to ensure that any contract governs the parties' actions as they intended?" These are not questions to be asked or answered lightly. In the business world, most relationships are governed by contractual arrangements. Whether a business builds a reputation as fair, open, and honest will have much to do with the nature of the contracts that structure or define the business's dealings.

Fraud

Let's begin with fraud—a term most of us use in our everyday language, but one that few of us may understand in the strictly legal sense. Most of us think of fraud as synonymous with deception, and that's not a bad starting point for our legal definition. From the legal perspective, fraud begins when there is a *deliberate* misrepresentation of a material fact with the intent of inducing another person to enter into a contract that will become injurious to that person. If that other person reasonably relies on, and is damaged by, the misrepresentation, the contract may be voided due to fraud.

For example, let's say that Jones is the owner and proprietor of a used-car dealership, Acme Motors, Inc. Every time a person buys a car from Jones—or sells or trades a used car—that transaction will be handled by written contract. Obviously, Jones has a stake in representing his merchandise in its best light—so long as he can manage to do so without misrepresenting it or giving false information. Legally, he's allowed to engage in some *puffing*—which is to say, sales talk. Prospective buyers must interpret his less-than-accurate statements in light of their own knowledge and experience, distinguishing fact from opinion as best you can.

One day, in comes Smith, looking for a good used car. Jones shows Smith a car he's eager to sell, and tells Smith, "This is the best car for you." If, in fact, the car isn't all Smith ever dreamed of, is Jones guilty of fraud? No. The car may or may not be the "best one" for Smith, but this really makes no difference. The point is, Jones is just giving his opinion or, more likely, just engaging in some "dealer talk," and it's up to Smith to recognize Jones's statement as opinion and to deal with it accordingly. Suppose, on the other hand, Jones tells Smith, "This car gets an average of twenty-five miles to the gallon, and has been driven only ten thousand miles." Later, Smith discovers—to her great dismay—that the car gets less than 10 mpg, and that it has probably been driven in excess of fifty thousand miles.

Is Jones guilty of fraud in this case? Perhaps. The big difference between this situation and the preceding example is that Jones is no longer providing opinions; he's dealing with facts. And the facts as he's presented them to Smith are incorrect—substantially so. That makes for the beginnings of a fraud case. But there's a little more to it than this. In fact, there are *six* elements to fraud. Let's consider them one by one.

The Six Elements of Fraud

First, as we've indicated, *the information in question must be a matter of fact, not opinion*. The age of the car, mileage thus far, repair record, place of manufacture, and so forth would all be matters of fact. The relative value of the car or how easily it handles or its potential resale value are all by and large matters of opinion. They generally cannot be proven one way or the other, nor would we expect all persons to agree about them. There can be no disagreement about factual matters, however; a car was either manufactured in 1983, for instance, or it was not. So far, so good.

The second element is *materiality* — or the importance of the fact to the potential plaintiff (in this case, Smith). Suppose Smith tells Jones, "Look, I couldn't care less about what gas mileage a car gets. What matters to me is what it looks like and how comfortable it is." In that case, even if Jones misrepresents the gas mileage, Smith would be hard pressed to justify an allegation of fraud, since it wasn't material to Smith's decision to buy the car.

The third element is the *knowledge that the information one is presenting is false*. Let's say that, unbeknownst to Jones, the odometer of the car he was selling had been tampered with; Jones *believed* that the car had only ten thousand miles on it, even though that was not the case. Or let's say that most cars like the one Jones was trying to sell Smith *did* in fact get about twenty-five miles to the gallon. This particular one, however, happened to have engine troubles that made its gas mileage terrible. But Jones didn't know that at the time of the transaction, nor did Jones have any reason to suppose that *this* particular car would be the exception to the rule. In this situation, Jones could not be said to have known that what he was saying was false, and there is no guilty knowledge.

In fact, not only did Jones not know the true facts, but he had no intention to mislead Smith. Therefore, this example also does not contain the fourth element of fraud — *intent to deceive*. On the other hand, let's say that this car originally belonged to Jones's brother, and he was well aware that its performance and record were not as he presented them. This presents a different situation. Even if *most* cars of the same type get excellent mileage, if Jones just happens to know that this particular one is a gas guzzler, he needs to respond truthfully to Smith's questions about this car's gas mileage. If he does not respond truthfully because he wants her to buy the car and suspects she won't if she knows of its poor gas mileage, he will be guilty of intent to deceive. (Smith's practical problem, of course, will be to "prove" that Jones knew the truth and intended to deceive her. Given that this one car is exceptional — the one lemon out of the bunch — Smith may have a difficult time actually winning her claim, especially if Jones's merchandise and business conduct have previously been acceptable.)

According to the fifth element of fraud, a plaintiff must prove that he or she justifiably *relied on the deception*. The issue here is, could a reasonable person have justifiably relied on the statements of Jones? For instance, let's say Jones tries to tell Smith that he's selling her a "brand new" car, but the fenders and hood are rusted, the door locks stick, the windshield is cracked, and the upholstery is torn. The court will not uphold a charge of fraud in this case, no matter what Jones tells Smith, because it's obvious from the car's appearance that it is not new, and a reasonable person would not have been taken in by such a claim. But, let's say that the issue is faulty electrical wiring. Less obvious. You can't tell the internal wiring is faulty just by looking at the car. Of course, Smith could examine the service record, test drive the car, ask about the electrical system, and take other steps to ensure that the electrical wiring was in good condition. In fact, the court is likely to suggest that Smith is obliged to do these things. But if the car had a wiring problem that would still not be detectable and Jones knew about it, Smith's reliance on a statement by Jones that "the electrical system is fine" would likely be found justifiable.

What if Jones makes it difficult for Smith to act reasonably? He pressures Smith. He tells her that yes, everything has been checked, that she can examine the service record another time, but there's really no reason to do so—she can trust him. He further claims that he has a buyer waiting impatiently for this particular automobile, and that if she wants it at the current low price, she'll have to act today, right now, not a moment to lose. Now Smith is in the position of taking Jones's word for something that she cannot objectively judge without more time and further examination. Jones is saying not to worry, that it's all right to rely on him. And that's the key. In ruling on the degree to which it was reasonable for the plaintiff to have relied on the deception, the court will look at whether the defect—in this case, the faulty wiring—was patent (readily determinable) or latent (not readily determinable). Given a patent defect—a sagging roof on a house, or a visibly cracked foundation—fraud will be extremely difficult to prove. Given a latent defect, however—a section of plumbing that the seller knows has deteriorated, for example—building a case for fraud becomes more plausible.

Which brings us to the sixth element of proof for fraud, *detriment*. Detriment is the damage and discomfort incurred by the plaintiff as a result of the transaction. This is not a world of perfection, and few things are totally as they're represented. If every slight defect or flaw were to constitute the basis for a case of fraud, the courts would have little time to deal with anything else. So fraud cases require the plaintiff to show some serious injury, damage, or inconvenience. For instance, let's say that Jones sells Smith a used car that he claims gets 25 mpg, and it turns out to get about 23 mpg. That's hardly a substantial difference—not enough actual "damages" to make a case for Smith. No substantial injury or inconvenience has occurred—and in any case, it may be Smith's sporty driving that is making the difference. But let's say that Jones sells Smith a car that supposedly is fresh from the overhaul shop with "new" brakes but that, as Jones knows, really has a marginal braking system. A few miles out of town, the brakes fail, Smith has an accident, the car must be towed, and Smith winds up in the hospital with moderate injuries—and possible loss of employment.

Jones is now in trouble. There's no doubt about serious injury and inconvenience. Provided Smith can also show (1) misrepresentation of facts, (2) materiality of the facts so represented, (3) Jones's knowledge that the claims were false, (4) Jones's intent to deceive, and (5) her own reasonable reliance on the deception, she's got the makings of a case—a good case—against Jones, based on the charge of fraud. But to be successful, Smith will have to show that all six of these elements are present. Proving four or five elements may serve to demonstrate that Jones is not a pinnacle of ethical business practices, but it will never substantiate a charge of fraud.

Silence and Fiduciary Responsibility

We've all heard the expression, "Let the buyer beware." If Jones just kept quiet and let Smith take her chances on picking the best car, that would absolve him of all responsibility, right? Perhaps not. Though the courts are not consistent in their rulings on silence, many courts have ruled that a person in Jones's position has an *obligation* to share any information on defects, problems, hazards, or other conditions that may cause later damage or inconvenience. For example, if Jones knew the brakes were faulty, he may well have an obligation to provide such information, *regardless* of whether Smith asked about the brakes. Other courts interpret this point of law somewhat differently, saying that Jones is only required to answer what Smith asks. But aside from the traditional contract law precepts that we've just discussed here, many states have special laws prohibiting certain "unlawful trade practices." These statutes make the old "let the buyer beware" adage even more outdated.

There is, however, *always* a duty to speak up in situations involving *fiduciary responsibility*—which is to say, a situation of *special trust*. No such relationship exists between Smith and Jones, obviously, nor is such a relationship normally present in strict buy–sell arrangements. It often occurs, however, in an instance where one of the parties is an expert in a particular field or holds specialized information not readily obtainable except through an expert. In such a situation, the court will presume a client's reliance on and tendency to heed another's advice. For instance, a doctor–patient relationship would have a fiduciary element, as would a lawyer–client relationship.

Let's look at a specific example. Green, an investor, wants to purchase a racehorse. Knowing little of horses himself, Green hires White, a licensed veterinarian, to inspect the horse he's considering buying and to tell him whether the animal is sound and worthy of his investment. Here, White is hired expressly to render an expert opinion on a very definite matter, and the fiduciary relationship between Green and White *demands* that White disclose any information that will be helpful to Green in making his decision. White should not, for instance, fail to mention that he believes the horse is diseased or that it has unsound bone structure or that it is older than the seller claimed. Regardless of whether Green specifically requested such information, White is obligated to share whatever he can about the horse's condition.

The concept of fiduciary responsibility doesn't just apply to fraud, however. While fraud—one of the more difficult-to-prove situations under which a legal contract may be voided—may hinge on issues of fiduciary responsibility, fiduciary responsibility can play a role in any "genuineness of assent" situation. Indeed, there are four other similar kinds of circumstances businesspeople need to understand, the first of them very much like fraud—with one notable exception.

Misrepresentation

Misrepresentation is similar to fraud with two very significant differences: First, it is *missing* the element of scienter (that is, guilty knowledge—the realization that one is providing false information), and second, there is no intent to deceive. Because it is, therefore, less obviously malicious than fraud, it is often called "innocent misrepresentation." This situation still involves a misstatement of material fact and still involves injury to the party who relied on the misstatement, but the deception is not deliberate or intentional in any sense.

For example, let's say Edgars, a real estate agent, sells McBride a house that seems perfectly sound and is much to McBride's liking. McBride specifically asks Edgars whether the house has any structural damage, and Edgars—relying on a statement in the multiple listing book that an inspection was performed—states that it does not, and even goes so far as to certify that in writing. Notice that Edgars has not personally inspected the house; she is telling the truth as she knows it. As it turns out, however, underground springs have damaged the foundation—a fact that comes to light shortly after McBride purchases the house and heavy rains cause a flooded basement. This looks like a case of misrepresentation. Edgars did misstate a material fact, McBride did rely on that fact, and McBride has been injured. However, since Edgars did not know she was providing false information and did not intend to deceive McBride, no fraud took place.

Remember, too, that a party seeking to rescind a contract should, upon learning of the misrepresentation, act promptly to disavow the contract. Suppose McBride lives in the house for a couple of years—thinking at first that the problem is not too bad, then trying to repair the damage. Perhaps it's two years after the problem surfaces that he decides he just cannot live with the problem. If so, he's not in a very strong position; a court is likely to decide that he has accepted the condition of the house, and it will probably not rescind the contract so long after the problem arose.

Plaintiffs who have been given misinformation often sue simultaneously on grounds of both misrepresentation and fraud. It's desirable to prove fraud, from the plaintiff's perspective, since not only would the contract generally be voided, but proving fraud allows the court to award extra, punitive damages. On the other hand, even if fraud cannot be proven—and it is certainly the tougher case of the two—misrepresentation will often be sufficient to cancel the contract.

Mistake

Mistake occurs when one or both parties believe differently or incorrectly about some fact central to the transaction. If both parties are in error, the mistake is considered a *bilateral mistake*; if just one party is in error, the mistake is considered a unilateral mistake.

Misrepresentation and mistake may, to the casual observer, seem hard to distinguish. After all, in both cases, some critical element of the agreement is in error. True, but the difference is in *how* the error comes into the contract process. If, as in the previous example, an incorrect statement of fact is made by one party, and the other party depends and relies on that statement in deciding how or whether to contract, that's misrepresentation. But if the parties to the agreement each *assume* or *believe* the status of some central fact—as opposed to relying on an assertion by the other party—then mistake is more likely to be the basis for invalidating the contract if damages result. Let's look at an historic example of mistake to help clarify the situation.

Well over a hundred years ago, a contract was drawn up to purchase 125 bales of cotton being delivered to England from Bombay on the ship *Peerless*. Pretty straightforward, right? Unfortunately, there were *two* ships named *Peerless* and both were sailing from Bombay, one in October and the other in December. The buyer of the cotton had in mind the ship sailing in October; the seller intended to use the ship sailing in December. Neither party knew that there were two ships named *Peerless* or had any reason to think that the other party was thinking of a different ship. In short, neither party was "to blame." The court held that no contract existed, that you can't have genuine assent when each party—without influence from and unknown to the other—has attached a different meaning to some central element of the contract.

Suppose the seller believes and says to the buyer, "The *Peerless* sails from Bombay in October and it will be carrying your cotton." When they find out that the cotton actually is being carried on the December *Peerless*, it is likely that the contract could be set aside for misrepresentation. The seller made an incorrect statement of fact on which the buyer relied. But if both parties have made different assumptions about some central fact and neither knows of the inconsistency, there has been a bilateral (or mutual) mistake.

Let's look at another example. Suppose Bligh and Duff have negotiated the purchase of an "antique" necklace by Bligh. Seller Duff uses the term "antique" loosely to mean anything over twenty-five years old that has fallen into general disuse. So she had attached a placard to the necklace stating "Antique Necklace." To Bligh, however, "antique" has a more rigorous definition: a hundred or more years old and held as having considerable monetary value in its own right. And because that doesn't happen to be true of this particular necklace, Duff's labeling leads to a *mistake through ambiguity*. To Duff, "antique" was a correct label for the necklace. To Bligh, the label was totally inappropriate. Because they were defining "antique" differently, a serious misunderstanding arose and rescission of the contract for bilateral mistake is possible.

As with fraud and misrepresentation, the mistake has to be substantial to cancel the contract; you can't build a case for mistake based on trivia. For example, Murphy signs a contract with Gordon Furniture to purchase office furniture, deliverable to her office in fourteen days. As it turns out, Murphy wanted the furniture delivered within fourteen calendar days, while Gordon Furniture understood delivery to be required within fourteen working days. The misunderstanding resulted in the furniture being delivered two days later than Murphy had wanted. There is a mistake here, yes, but it's a minor one, and Murphy would be hard put to show sufficient grounds on which to win a suit.

It's also the case that if only one party has made the mistake, a *unilateral mistake*, the contract generally remains in force. A buyer who finds that the truckload of "grade 2 or better two-by-fours" he purchased isn't of adequate quality for the project at hand will have no recourse if the load meets that grading standard. The buyer's mistaken assumption that "grade 2 or better" lumber must be pretty good stuff is neither shared by, nor any fault of, the seller; the contract would probably stand. (Note, however, that if the seller had reason to believe that the buyer was mistaken about the adequacy of "grade 2 or better" lumber, there *might*—it is by no means certain—be reason to void the contract.)

Duress

Another reason that a contract to which there is apparent assent will be set aside is duress. At one level, duress is fairly simple to visualize: When Hollywood tough guys point their .45-caliber pistols and tell the bad guys, "Make my day," they are using duress in its extreme form. However, few of us have to sign contracts with guns aimed at our heads, nor are we likely ever to coerce others in this manner. In the business world, duress is generally more subtle—but it can, nevertheless, be cause for cancelling a contract. In essence, duress is anything that forces a person to sign a contract against his or her will. It could be a physical threat (real or implied) or some other sort of threat—say, a withholding of desired privileges or income, or disclosure of information that could cause stress or mental anguish for the party involved.

Let's say Buildmore Construction wishes to purchase some valuable property east of town in order to erect luxury condominiums. Thus far, property owner Hayes has refused to sell. Hayes owns a chain of hardware stores in town, and is looking at opening another in the new westside shopping center. Unfortunately, heading the committee that approves new tenants for the shopping center is M. Steele, who is the brother of the president of Buildmore Construction, D. Steele. In several preliminary meetings, D. Steele makes it clear to Hayes that a place in the new shopping center will be easier to secure if Buildmore gets title to that eastside property for its condominiums. While Hayes is considering this predicament, another representative of Buildmore asks Hayes whether he's ever been concerned about the threat of fire in his oldest store—"the downtown building being so old and all." Here are two implied threats, neither direct, but both coercive, both directed at forcing Hayes to sign a contract he doesn't wish to sign.

Now, let's complicate our scenario by including an element of economic duress. Suppose Buildmore, while continuing to pressure Hayes to sell, buys the property on which Hayes's highest grossing store is located and threatens to raise the rent by one-third. Now Hayes is in a double bind; not only is duress being applied by Buildmore's threats, but economic duress is present in Buildmore's threatened rent increase. Contracts signed under such duress might well be voided.

The preceding example shows economic duress being imposed by the prospective buyer. A seller can also cause economic duress and is, in fact, more frequently found to do so. Remember, economic duress is usually defined as forcing one party to agree to additional demands in order to receive services or goods to which the party is already entitled by contract. Let's look at an example to illustrate how it more commonly works.

Suppose, for instance, that Saunders and Saunders Insurance Company buys a new computer system from Digits, Inc. During contract negotiations, it's implied that Digits will not only design a system to meet S&S specifications, but will install the equipment and provide S&S employees with special training in operating the system to maximum benefit. Subsequently, though, S&S learns that Digits has no intention of providing such services for free. They will impose an extra charge for system delivery, another for hardware installation, another for program installation, and still another for provision of training—all of which the parties had agreed were to be included within the original agreement under the topic "related services." Because Saunders and Saunders has already invested weeks of time in working out its needs with Digits, whose staff are intimately familiar with the layout of the S&S office as well as with the informational needs of staff, S&S will lose considerably more time and money than the "extra" costs Digits is charging if they go elsewhere—much as they'd like to do so. Digits has S&S over the economic duress barrel.

Contracts signed under duress—whether physical, economic, mental, or any other sort—are normally voidable, except in the case where the injured party gives in for an unreasonably long period of time. Suppose, for example, that Witt and Sons are building an office complex. The contractor, Tuffwall Corporation, is being paid a percentage of the total building cost. Not the most ethical of businesses, Tuffwall takes every opportunity to delay construction; by doing so, they will then need expensive overtime work to complete construction on time (thus letting them bill a percentage of a large total cost). Indeed, the construction costs keep going up incrementally, until the sum threatens to bankrupt Witt, but what to do? He cannot afford to call in a new contractor or halt construction, so he goes along with the increases, borrowing the money to stay afloat. After a couple of years in the new office, with business down and bills hard to meet, Witt decides to bring suit. Can he muster a case? Unlikely; he did not act promptly against Tuffwall.

There is an exception to the requirement to act promptly, however—and it involves the situation in which one party is acting to protect another. Suppose a landlord, Blackmore, owns both the office where Wilson pays rent and the apartment building where Wilson's aging mother lives—and from which it would be extremely difficult for her to move. Blackmore threatens to evict Wilson's mother—along with a number of other tenants—unless Wilson agrees to exorbitant increases in office rent. Wilson goes along with the increases to protect his mother. But legally, Wilson has an out. He could sue Blackmore on grounds of duress. And the time element would not work against Wilson, no matter how long he'd agreed to the higher rent, *because he was acting to protect a threatened third person*—in this case, his mother.

Undue Influence

Undue influence is closely related to duress. It involves using a relationship of trust and confidence to gain contractual advantages or, in other words, using one's special relationship with another person to undue advantage, even to the point of undermining that person's free will.

Such a situation might occur, for instance, if physician Purvis finds that his patient Harris owns a valuable Ferrari automobile. Purvis's brother-in-law sells rare automobiles and knows that Harris's Ferrari is very valuable. Now suppose that Purvis tells Harris that "with an illness like yours, you could die at any time. You'd do best to start making plans right away for the financial security of your family." Purvis's brother-in-law calls shortly thereafter and offers an understandably frantic Harris $100,000 for the Ferrari. Harris accepts, but a few months later (and very much alive), he finds that Ferraris have gained in value so much that $400,000 would have been a much fairer price. Aside from any claims he might have against Purvis for unprofessional conduct, if Harris did indeed sell the car quickly because of Purvis's dire warnings and undue influence, the sale might be cancelled. The definite possibility exists that Purvis's warning constituted unfair use of a special relationship.

Unconscionability

The existence of unconscionability can also render a contract invalid. This situation is defined, for legal purposes, as total lack of equality in bargaining power such that meaningful assent is virtually impossible to attain. In other words, it's a way of saying that the parties were not in an equal position to bargain in the first place; thus, it was all but inevitable that one would take undue advantage of the other.

For instance, suppose Brown knows that Ames is of limited mental ability, has no formal education, and cannot read. Brown has a contract for services drawn up, "explains the important points of the contract" to Ames (leaving out "a few technicalities"), and persuades Ames to sign. Trusting Brown, Ames signs without worry, only to learn afterward that he has agreed to much more than he bargained for. In the absence of an attorney or some other representative, there was no way Ames could have fairly negotiated his own position. Brown and Ames were not equals in the bargaining process, and Ames could sue to cancel the contract, raising allegations of unconscionability.

SOME PRACTICAL ADVICE

Maybe this whole contract business seems a little intimidating. Does a businessperson dare take a step without an attorney along for advice? Will you get into trouble signing or drawing up a contract so long as you act in good faith? Well, let's start by saying that if a business is not out to deceive or coerce anyone, it's much less likely to get into trouble. But good intentions, while admirable, make for a less than seaworthy legal liferaft.

In our scenarios, we've seen some rather unscrupulous behavior; you might well say that these people deserve whatever the court can manage to throw at them. But some pretty forthright businesspeople have been sued because the other party was claiming lack of genuine assent in entering into a contract. In these cases, being a nice person isn't a suitable or safe defense. Caution, combined with a solid knowledge of the applicable laws, is necessary to ensure protection.

In the case of fraud, for example, how might a businessperson realistically go about minimizing the chances of a fraud allegation? First, knowing one's merchandise is important. It's easy to fall into the trap of misrepresenting the facts if one doesn't know the facts very well. And pleading ignorance later on may not help if your position is one where you're expected to have a certain level of knowledge or where you have ready access to pertinent information. Second, it's wise not to make claims that cannot be substantiated or backed with evidence. Don't, for instance, providing information about product performance, costs, or warranties unless that information is accurate and supportable. Third, it's always wise to take a position of acting in the client's best interests — imagining the questions the customer might have and truthfully providing the necessary information.

To reduce the possibility of ambiguity causing allegations of mistake, there are certain other steps that a businessperson might wish to take. First, work to eliminate all possible sources of ambiguity. Second, see that all terms in contract negotiations are commonly defined and understood by those involved in the negotiations. Third, ensure that all contracts are drafted in the clearest, simplest language possible. Complex syntax and overly sophisticated or technical language are likely to create more problems than they'll solve. Fourth, ensure that all parties involved thoroughly read any contract before signing. Never rush anyone into signing a contract before he or she has had an opportunity to completely read through it; don't allow yourself to be rushed, either. Remember, if anything seems unclear, it is best to clarify terms of the agreement prior to signing and encourage open discussion of any terms that may create misunderstanding or ambiguity.

Remember, one important reason for a contract is to clarify an agreement, thus improving communications by decreasing the chance for misunderstanding. Still, written words — even carefully constructed written words — can only do so much. Anything in writing is subject to interpretation — including, for example, the information provided in this book. That's why courts exist in the first place — to interpret the law. Therefore, before signing a contract, whether it's one you've had drawn up yourself or one you've been asked to sign, see that everyone's expectations are fully clarified. Verify that all terms have been defined thoroughly and explicitly and that whatever the contract requires of you is something with which you're willing and able to comply. A contract should not signal the end of communication between negotiating parties, but a structure around which meaningful business communications can be built. You cannot willingly enter into an agreement you do not fully understand; such an understanding is the basis for genuine assent.

In the final analysis, it's simply good business practice to ensure the best possible match between a customer's needs and the services or goods provided — regardless of the possibility of legal action. A businessperson interested in making money by using any tactic available is likely to face not only legal problems but serious business problems as well. The businessperson trying to sell a product or service that really does fulfill the customer's needs and wants is likely to fare better from *both* a business and a legal perspective.

ASSIGNMENTS

- Before you watch the video program, be sure you've read through the preceding overview, familiarized yourself with the learning objectives for this lesson, and looked at the key terms below. Then, read Chapter 13 of Davidson et al., *Business Law*.
- After completing these tasks, view the video program for Lesson 9.
- After watching the program, take time to review what you've learned. First, evaluate your learning with the self-test which follows the key terms. Then, apply and evaluate what you've learned with the "Your Opinion, Please" scenarios at the end of this telecourse study guide lesson.

KEY TERMS

Before you read through the textbook assignment and watch the video program, take a minute to look at the key terms associated with this lesson. When you encounter them in the textbook and video program, pay careful attention to their meaning.

Ambiguities	Patent defect
Assent	Puffs/puffing
Bilateral mistake	Reality of consent
Detriment	Rescission
Duress	Reformation
Economic duress	Scienter
Fiduciary	Silence
Fraud	Status quo
Latent defect	Unconscionability
Misrepresentation	Undue influence
Mistake	Unilateral mistake

SELF-TEST

The questions below will help you evaluate how well you've learned the material in this lesson. Read each one carefully, and select the letter of the option that best answers the question. You'll find the correct answer, along with a reference to the page number(s) where the topic is discussed, in the back of this telecourse study guide.

1. According to the textbook, in order for a contract to be legally enforceable, it is necessary that

   a. the contract be in writing.
   b. the consent between the two parties be real.
   c. most, if not all, of the contract be drawn up by an attorney.
   d. the signing of the contract be witnessed by a third party.

2. A deliberate misrepresentation of a material fact with intent to induce another person to enter into a contract—and on which the person reasonably relies and does enter into a contract that is injurious to that person—is defined in the legal community as

   a. fraud.
   b. misrepresentation.
   c. materiality.
   d. "puffery."

3. Blackman wants to purchase a car. The salesperson, Murphy, shows Blackman a 1965 model and tells him, "This car is speedy, economical—just a good all-around car." After purchasing the car and driving it for a month, Blackman feels the mileage is exceptionally poor and that the car has little power or maneuverability. Is Murphy liable to a charge of fraud?

   a. Yes; the information he provided was clearly false and misleading.
   b. No; Murphy was only offering an opinion, which Blackman was free to accept or reject.
   c. No; but Murphy is liable for misrepresentation.
   d. The answer cannot be determined from the information given.

4. In an allegation of fraud, a fact is considered *material* if

   a. it is mixed with opinion.
   b. it can be shown to be accurate.
   c. it has some direct bearing on the case at hand.
   d. it was of significant importance to the decision to enter into the contract.

5. Brown sells Kilbeck a house. When they go together to inspect it, the small—and hard to get to—basement is flooded, but Kilbeck doesn't learn this. The inspection trip was short, and she and Brown decide to skip the basement inspection. Later, Kilbeck sues Brown for fraud, claiming that Brown had an obligation to inform her fully about the leaky basement. Is Brown liable to a charge of fraud?

   a. No, probably not, since the defect would have been obvious to Kilbeck had she taken time for a thorough inspection.
   b. Yes; Brown, who clearly knew the property best, should have made a special point of informing Kilbeck about the defective plumbing.
   c. We cannot say without first learning whether Brown knew about the leaky basement prior to the close of the sale.

6. Toffel is in the process of selling a vacant restaurant to Riles. The building, though suitable in most respects, has a serious ventilation problem — of which Toffel is well aware. But Riles does not ask about the ventilation, and Toffel declines to mention it. Could Toffel be liable to a charge of fraud?

   a. Quite possibly; most courts will uphold a plaintiff's right to full disclosure of information that could prevent subsequent detriment or injury.
   b. Not likely; most courts would only require Toffel to answer specific questions posed by Riles.
   c. No, because a ventilation problem is an obvious defect of which a prospective buyer is required to be aware.

7. All *fiduciary* relationships involve

   a. money.
   b. special trust.
   c. contract obligations.
   d. active lawsuits.

8. Miller sells Brisbee a ten-acre property that supposedly includes a creek and a pond. Subsequent surveying of the property reveals — to the surprise of both Miller and Brisbee — that the pond and much of the creek are actually outside the property boundaries. This is a case of

   a. bilateral mistake.
   b. unilateral mistake.
   c. fraud.
   d. misrepresentation.

9. Rickles delivers some merchandise to Adams Publishing. The receptionist, Fields, signs what she believes to be a receipt acknowledging delivery. Later examination of the fine print reveals that Fields has actually signed a contract agreeing that Adams will purchase additional goods from the same company at a higher price. Is this contract legally enforceable?

   a. Yes; although Fields was remiss in not reading what she signed more closely, the point is, she *did* sign the contract.
   b. No; Fields clearly had no reason to suppose that she was signing a contract, and a court will likely declare the contract void.
   c. Yes; but only if Fields has authorization from Acme to sign contracts.

10. Misusing a relationship of trust in order to gain unfair advantage over another person in a contractual relationship is known as

    a. unconscionability.
    b. undue influence.
    c. fiduciary fraud.
    d. contract rescission.

YOUR OPINION, PLEASE

Review each of the following scenarios and answer the questions about the decisions you would make in each situation. Give these questions some serious thought; they may be used as the basis for the development of a more complex essay. You should base your decisions on what you've learned from this lesson, though you may incorporate outside readings or information gained through your own experience if it is relevant.

Scenario I

Phelps has just purchased from Unger a registered thoroughbred horse for the price of $10,000. It is Phelps's intention to race the horse, though he did not disclose this intention to Unger at the time of the sale. Phelps understands the term "registered" to imply that the horse is a purebred thoroughbred, and is later dismayed to learn from Unger that in fact the horse is only three-fourths thoroughbred and one-fourth quarterhorse, despite the registry. Unger maintains that he believed Phelps understood the term "registered" at the time of the sale and saw no reason to define it specifically.

Following the sale, Phelps calls in a veterinarian and a trainer to inspect the horse. The veterinarian pronounces the horse sound, but informs Phelps that he is approximately eight years old—too old to race. Similarly, the trainer assures Phelps that the horse is an excellent and sound animal and well trained, but estimates the approximate market value at somewhere between $2,000 and $3,000—well short of the price Phelps has paid. Phelps feels cheated and sues Unger for fraud. Unger, for his part, maintains that Phelps should have been more clear about his intentions to race the horse and should have asked about the registry of the animal. Further, Unger maintains that he still believes the horse to be worth the selling price, regardless of others' opinions.

What's your opinion? Based on what you know of the situation, do you think Phelps can successfully build a case to rescind the contract? Or should the contract stand?

- Is Phelps likely to win a case for rescission? If so, on what grounds? If not, why?
- What factors support your answer?
- What factors might an attorney cite in arguing against your view?
- What steps, if any, might Unger have taken to prevent a lawsuit in this situation?
- What steps, if any, might Phelps have taken to prevent a lawsuit in this situation?

Scenario 2

Fielding has just purchased a country home in southwest Connecticut; it's an older house which he intends to renovate. He's delighted to discover that the attic is crammed full of miscellaneous "treasures," an odd assortment of tools, furniture, kitchenware, clothing, and decorative items. Among the collection is a carefully wrapped and crated old painting of flowers by a pond in an ornate frame. The style is distinctive, but it doesn't appeal to Fielding. He decides to put the painting—along with various other odds and ends from his treasure hunting—in a weekend estate sale. Since he has no sense of what the painting is worth and does not recognize the artist's signature, he simply marks it "Rare Old Painting—Best Offer."

Higgins, an antique collector, spends some time browsing through the items at the sale. He is struck by the painting and asks Fielding about it. Fielding tells Higgins he believes the painting is probably quite rare and valuable, given the careful way in which it was wrapped; further, the previous owners of the country house were, in fact, art collectors, so there is no telling what they might have hidden and forgotten in the attic. Higgins, who likes the painting anyway and who finds himself impressed by Fielding's story, offers Fielding $3,000—expecting that this "modest" offer for such a valuable painting will be rejected. Fielding is thunderstruck by the offer and, doing his best to appear calm, promptly accepts Higgins's check, scarcely able to believe his good fortune.

Later, Higgins has the painting appraised and learns that the value is quite low—somewhere between $200 and $300. Higgins, infuriated, attempts to return the painting to Fielding. Fielding, however, refuses; he tells Higgins he's sorry, but Higgins, after all, made the offer. Since he (Fielding) has already cashed the check and spent the money, he doesn't see that there's much to be done. Higgins thereupon sues Fielding for both fraud and misrepresentation.

What's your opinion? Based on what you know of the situation, do you think Higgins can build a case for fraud? For misrepresentation? Which of the necessary elements for each are present in this situation?

- Do you think Higgins is likely to win a suit for misrepresentation? For fraud? Why or why not?
- What factors support your answer?
- What factors might an attorney cite in arguing against your view?
- What steps, if any, might Higgins have taken to avoid a lawsuit in this situation?
- What steps, if any, might Fielding have taken to avoid a lawsuit in this situation?

10

Contract Requirement: Proper Form

LEARNING OBJECTIVES

Upon completing your study of this lesson, you should be able to

- Discuss the rationale for putting certain contracts in writing.
- Explain how state statutes regarding fraud evolved from and were influenced by early English parliamentary law.
- List several types of contracts that *must* be in writing to be enforceable.
- Describe, in general terms, the required basic elements of a written contract.
- Define, for purposes of contract law, what may be interpreted as a "signature."

As you are already aware, contracts — in most circumstances — may be either oral or written. In certain situations, however, the law requires that contracts exist in writing if they are to be enforceable. The purpose of this lesson is to explore various circumstances under which contracts must be in writing, and also to begin defining what is meant by a "written contract."

OVERVIEW

If you enter into a contract for any purpose whatever, you may feel — almost instinctively — that it would be better to have that contract expressed in writing. Usually, that is the case. Oral agreements are an imprecise and ambiguous form of communication at best. Even with the noblest of intentions, two contractors may discover that they have very different perspectives on precisely what it is they've agreed to within the terms of a contract. And the potential for imprecision and ambiguity increases dramatically when a contract does not exist in writing. Without a written document, not only must the two parties agree on the meaning of the words used to describe the terms of the contract, but they must *recall* just what those words and terms were. And relying on memory — yours or that of a party with whom you contract — is almost always risky.

The law requires that certain types of contracts (which we'll list in a moment) be in writing in order to be enforceable. The writing is taken as proof of the parties' intent to actually contract and to include certain specifications or terms within the scope of the contract. The existence of a written contract reduces the possibility of perjury (lying under oath) by one party or the other, in the event of any dispute. And it helps clarify the original terms of the agreement — and that's critical. For as we've indicated, disagreements can arise even when both sides are doing their best to tell the truth about the circumstances surrounding the agreement.

What happens if the contract is not in writing? Assuming that no dispute arises, nothing. An oral contract is perfectly acceptable. And some oral contracts are enforceable in court as well. Not all, however — and that's the point. The real purpose of putting a contract into writing is to protect both sides in the event that any dispute about that contract arises. Often, because of the conduct or behavior of the two parties, it is quite a simple matter for the court to infer that an oral contract does, in fact, exist. But figuring out the exact terms of the contract may be quite another matter.

For example, suppose Jones and Brown have an oral contract specifying that Jones will provide childcare for Brown's three children for a period of one year at a rate of $25 per day. Even though Jones and Brown have not put their agreement in writing, the existence of a contract will be pretty easy to infer from the fact that Brown's children spend their days at Jones's house and that Jones receives monthly checks from Brown for the sum of approximately $500. What is not so simple to piece together, however, is the precise terms of the agreement — and that is where some dispute is likely to occur. For example, Brown may say that Jones is obligated to care for the children for eight hours a day, while Jones may claim that the $25 fee covers only five hours' worth of childcare. Or, Jones may say that their agreement includes an understanding that she is free to transport Brown's children in her own automobile while running personal errands; but Brown may claim that the agreement specifies Jones would keep the children at her home and would, under no circumstances, transport them anywhere in an automobile.

The Statute of Frauds

Obviously, one could construct dozens of similar hypothetical disputes that could arise out of this seemingly simple agreement between Jones and Brown. No wonder the courts prefer to deal with agreements specified in writing. From the court's perspective, having to reconstruct agreements out of scattered bits and pieces of evidence is simply too time-consuming and difficult. Further, there is no way ever to be certain that the reconstructed agreement will match the original intentions of the contractors. Therefore, the court insists that certain types of agreements be specified in writing if either side wishes to reserve the right — at some future date — to call upon the court to enforce the contract. This is another way of saying that the court will not, in most cases, accept responsibility for constructing contracts; that responsibility rightly falls, say the courts, to the contracting parties. Once the terms of a contract can be specified — and often that means it must be in writing — the court will accept responsibility for enforcing the contract.

How did this requirement of writing come about? It's a combination of tradition and practicality, really. Historically, perjury was extremely widespread in lawsuits arising out of oral contracts. In order to stop this practice of trying to deceive or defraud the court, the English Parliament decreed in 1677 that certain contracts would no longer be enforceable unless they existed in writing. This statute to prevent frauds — now generally referred to as the *Statute of Frauds* — wasn't designed to prevent attempts to deceive another party or to coerce someone into signing a contract against his or her will. Rather, it was to prevent the court from being tricked into enforcing a contract that did not exist. Today, each state's Statute of Frauds identifies the categories of contract that in that state must be in writing to be able to be enforced in court.

Contracts that Must Be in Writing

What sorts of agreements should be in writing? Well, from a prudent business perspective, it is wise to put anything in writing that is so important you would not want to take the chance that the other party might not live up to the terms of the contract and there would be nothing you could do about it. Take our case of Brown and Jones. If Jones decides one day that she does not want to provide childcare for Brown anymore, despite their oral agreement, she might just stop doing so. What impact will this decision have on Brown? Well, if there are lots of competent, trustworthy people in Brown's community seeking employment as childcare givers, it probably won't be much of a problem. But suppose that Brown and Jones live in a rural community where neighbors are far apart. If Jones doesn't care for Brown's children, Brown may be forced to either quit her job or drive her children seventy-five miles a day to provide them with comparable childcare. In that case, the importance of the agreement to Brown, and the seriousness of the consequences if the agreement is broken, suggest that putting the terms in writing would have been a prudent idea.

That basic consideration aside, there are six types of contracts that the Statute of Frauds in most states insists *must* exist in writing to be enforceable. Briefly, these are

1. contracts to answer for the debt of another person;
2. contracts covering interests in land;
3. contracts not to be performed (concluded, that is) within one year of their making;
4. contracts for the sale of goods priced at $500 or more;
5. promises of executors and administrators of estates; and
6. contracts made in consideration of marriage.

Let's examine each of these situations in turn.

Contracts to Answer for the Debt of Another Person

Oral contracts in which one directly incurs a personal debt are usually enforceable in court. For example, White agrees to buy a rug from Green for $300. When Green orally agrees to sell the rug and White orally agrees to pay the $300, White and Green have a contract. Both have made what are known legally as *original* promises, meaning essentially that they take personal responsibility for upholding their parts in the contract. In this case, White is responsible for his own debt — the $300. Green is responsible for providing the rug. If either defaults, there is no third party agreeing to make things right.

In a *collateral* contract, by contrast, one person agrees to be responsible for the debt of another, should that person default. In a collateral contract, three parties are involved. And there are two promises: an original promise made by the debtor to the creditor, and a collateral promise made by a third party to the creditor. This secondary promise comes into effect if — and only if — the original promise from the debtor to the creditor is not kept. In our example, for instance, suppose that a week or so goes by and White still hasn't paid Green for the rug. Green agrees to give White another month to come up with the money, provided that White's brother will be responsible for the $300 in the event that White does not pay. If White's brother agrees to this, White's brother would be assuming secondary liability. Under these circumstances, Green could not hold White's brother responsible for the $300, however, until it became clear that White could not or would not pay the debt. Further, because this is a case of secondary responsibility, the collateral contract among White, Green, and White's brother would only be enforceable if it existed in writing.

Incidentally, notice that in our example, White agreed to be the original responsible person on the rug contract; his brother did not enter the picture until the question of White's ability to pay arose. If, on the other hand, White and his brother had *together* contracted with Green, agreeing to be jointly and originally responsible for the debt, that agreement would *not* be recognized as a collateral contract. Rather, such an agreement would be viewed by the court as an original three-party contract and would therefore not have to be in writing to be enforceable. Lawsuits involving secondary liability can be very complex. But keep in mind that ordinarily, in the event of default, the creditor must sue the primary debtor before the secondary debtor can be held liable.

There is one important exception to the rule that a collateral contract must be in writing before it is enforceable. This rule is known as the *leading-object*, or *main-purpose*, exception. It has to do with the motivation of the third party in agreeing to the secondary liability. If it can be shown that the third party is motivated by desire for personal economic gain, then from the court's perspective, that motivation is equivalent to making an original promise to assume the debt, and the promise will be enforced even if it does not exist in writing. For instance, suppose that Bates applies for a loan to buy an valuable old car that he intends to fix up and resell. Waldo agrees to assume secondary responsibility for the loan, which is then granted to Bates. If Bates defaults, the bank must ordinarily sue Bates unsuccessfully before it can hold Waldo liable; and further, such liability will require that Waldo's promise be in writing.

However, suppose it can be demonstrated that Waldo agreed to assume secondary responsibility only because Bates promised him 60% of the profits on the resale of the restored automobile—for whom they already have a buyer. In that case, it can be argued that Waldo was only furthering his own economic situation by agreeing to the secondary liability. Thus, the bank can allege that Waldo is the equivalent of an original promisor, and as such has primary responsibility (right along with Bates) for the loan. In this instance, some courts are likely to allow the bank to act directly against Waldo—without first suing Banks—and, further, not require that the contract be in writing.

Contracts for Interests in Land

Agreements that involve buying, selling, or transferring interests in land must be in writing if they are to be enforceable. These agreements include contracts involving mineral rights, leasing of property, timber harvesting, and so forth, as well as the actual transfer of property ownership. For example, suppose you are driving through the country one day, spot a tract of land that catches your eye, and impulsively offer to buy the land for some reasonable price. If the owner agrees, do you have an enforceable contract? Not yet. Not without a written agreement.

Sometimes, however, the court will make an exception to this rule under the *doctrine of part performance*. According to this doctrine, if the purchaser pays part of the selling price, moves onto the land (with the owner's permission), and makes some improvements on the property, the court will normally enforce the sale contract even if it does not exist in writing. For instance, suppose Miller owns an older home which Rasp offers to buy for $50,000. Miller orally agrees and promptly leaves for a three-month trip to Europe. Rasp, meanwhile, pays the $5,000 down that Miller asked for, moves into the old house, and proceeds to make a number of repairs, including installing new plumbing, painting the exterior and interior, and putting in new carpeting. Upon returning from Europe, can Miller simply claim that no contract exists, evict Rasp, and move into his remodeled home, $5,000 richer? Not likely. The court will take the position that Rasp's conduct can *only* be explained — from the perspective of any reasonable person — by the existence of a contract to purchase the house. In other words, it isn't plausible that Rasp simply moves into other persons' houses and fixes them up for the fun of it, without compensation. Any reasonable person would conclude, viewing the situation, that Miller intended to sell Rasp the house; and the court will almost surely hold him to that agreement.

Contracts Not to Be Performed Within One Year

A promise within a contract that *cannot possibly* be performed within one year of contract initiation must be in writing to be enforceable. Most employment contracts fall into this category, unless of course they involve short-term agreements to complete specific tasks.

For instance, let's say Haley hires Peterson to remove three diseased elm trees from her back yard. Assuming that Peterson intends to begin work on this project in the near future, an oral contract will probably cover this sort of employment agreement perfectly well. The task is specified and limited, and it is perfectly conceivable — probable, in fact — that Peterson will complete it within one year of the date on which the agreement is first made.

On the other hand, if Forest hires Wilkes as a confidential assistant and is intent upon her working for him for two years, an oral agreement will not provide Forest with any recourse if Wilkes leaves before the two years are completed. Typical employment agreements involving permanent full-time or part-time positions are open-ended and assumed to be at the pleasure of the two parties involved. If either party wants the employment to be for a specific period of time and wants to be able to recover damages for early termination or get a court to order that the employment continue for the specific duration of the employment agreement, the employment agreement must be in writing and specify the time period involved to be enforceable in court.

It is the general policy of the court to seek a way to uphold most contracts. Thus, some courts will stretch reality a bit in determining which promises can be performed or upheld within a year. For instance, suppose that in our earlier example with the elm trees, Haley owned hundreds of acres of land, not just a city lot. And suppose she contracted with Peterson to remove not just three diseased trees but "all diseased trees on the property." Is that a task Peterson could complete within a year? We can't say. If there weren't any diseased trees, Peterson wouldn't have much to do. If half the trees were diseased, the task might take a considerable amount of time for one person. Thus, the court is likely to take the position that *conceivably*—since no one knows the real scope of the task—Peterson *could* fulfill the contract within a year. This interpretation—based on what *could* be true under certain conditions—makes the contract enforceable even if it doesn't exist in writing. In short, an oral contract involving any promise which could possibly be fulfilled within a year—even under the remotest of circumstances—will often be enforced by the court. In our example, the court could conclude that if Peterson merely hired enough helpers, the job could easily be done within one year and was therefore enforceable, even though when Peterson signed the contract he didn't have any assistants.

Contracts for the Sale of Goods Priced at $500 or More

Under most circumstances, contracts for the sale of goods priced at $500 or more must be in writing to be enforceable. Thus, if Johnson decides to sell her used car, she need not have a written contract to validate the agreement if she sells the car for $450. But if she sells it for $550, the agreement will not be enforceable unless it is in writing. Later in this lesson we'll learn about what "writing" is required.

Again—as we've seen with the other situations—there are some exceptions. First, if the goods involved are to be specially manufactured for the buyer and are not suitable for sale to others, the contract will usually be enforceable even if it isn't in writing. Notice that in this case, the intent of the buyer would likely be easy to demonstrate precisely because of the special nature of the goods. If George, a carpenter, designs cabinets for Murphy's kitchen, they may not be saleable to anyone else. Second, the court will normally uphold the contract if the buyer makes a partial payment or a partial acceptance, though the contract will only be enforced for that portion of goods paid for or accepted. Again, the emphasis is on the intent of the parties involved, as demonstrated through their actions. And third, the contract will be enforced if the party being sued admits in court that a contract was made for a certain quantity of goods.

The Uniform Commercial Code makes one important exception to this provision of the Statute of Frauds as far as businesspeople are concerned. It states that a merchant who receives a signed written confirmation for the sale of goods is bound to the contract governing that sale unless the merchant makes a formal written protest within ten days after receiving the confirmation. For instance, suppose that Fleming—a building supply wholesaler—sends Ramirez, owner of Ramirez Plumbing, the following confirmation notice: "This is to confirm the sale of 1,000 lineal feet of 1-1/4" diameter pressure-rated polyethylene pipe at the price of $600, to be delivered June 5. /signed/ George Fleming." Ramirez may feel there's been some mistake. Ramirez may not even have that pipe available to sell to Fleming; perhaps he had just given Fleming a ballpark figure of what that much pipe *might* cost. But Fleming has decided he wants a thousand feet of pipe and thinks that he has an agreement whereby Ramirez will sell it to him for $600. At this point, from the court's perspective, he does have an agreement—unless Ramirez objects, and quickly. Ramirez has ten days to object, in writing, or he has—in the court's eyes—contracted with Fleming for an order of pipe.

Promises of Executors or Administrators of Estates

The promises of executors or administrators of estates to pay estate claims out of their own personal funds must be in writing to be enforceable. The court holds that such promises are fairly unusual — somewhat in the nature of an agreement to assume another person's debt in the event that person defaults. Insisting upon a written agreement is the court's way of saying, "This isn't the sort of thing one usually agrees to do; therefore, we'd like to see some evidence that the agreement is real."

Contracts Made in Consideration of Marriage

As with promises of executors to pay estate claims, unilateral promises to pay money or transfer property in consideration of marriage are uncommon and must therefore be in writing to be enforceable. For instance, Johnson may agree to marry Wolfe if Wolfe will pay for the college education of Johnson's two sons. Such an agreement will not be upheld by the court unless it exists in writing.

The Required Basic Elements of a Written Contract

We've talked so much about the importance of having agreements in writing in this lesson, perhaps we should consider what is meant by a written agreement. You may be thinking that contracts will only be enforceable if they are formal documents drawn up by attorneys and expressed in legal jargon. Nothing could be further from the truth. Actually, the writing required to satisfy the Statute of Frauds may take the form of a letter or note, a telegram, or any sort of memoranda. Further, various bits of writing may be pieced together to create a larger "contract." What is more, a written signature isn't always required to confirm one party's agreement to the contract. Courts will sometimes look upon stamped signatures or even stationery letterheads as "signatures" for the purposes of enforcing contracts. Also, the signature of the party's authorized agent will normally be acceptable. It is imperative, however, that, at a minimum, the "writing" identifies the contracting parties, the basic substance of the agreement, and the major terms and conditions to which each party will be held. Such information can, as we've indicated, be scattered across several documents; it need not be contained neatly in one document (though that's certainly handier).

SOME PRACTICAL ADVICE

It will come as no surprise that the most important caution to come out of this lesson is that, whenever possible, contracts — especially business contracts — should be in writing. Or to put it another way, in deciding whether to put a contract in writing, the prudent businessperson should ask what the consequences would be if the other party should default on the contract or should dispute the terms of the contract. Even when the other party's intentions are the best, misunderstandings or disagreements about dates, technical terms, or responsibilities can lead to serious problems. Thus, it is wise to put contracts in writing even when the law does not require a written document in order to make the contract enforceable. Remember, even in circumstances where the court upholds the existence of the contract, there is no guarantee that an unwritten contract will be enforced according to the parties' original intentions. Recreating those intentions can be very difficult in the absence of written documentation.

That general premise aside, businesspeople should take care that, at a minimum, written contracts are created to govern all transactions involving

- the assumption of another's debt,
- interests in land,
- tasks or promises not to be fulfilled within a year,
- sales of goods priced at $500 or more,
- promises of executors or administrators of estates, and
- promises made in consideration of marriage.

Also, the prudent businessperson should be especially careful to attend to any signed, written confirmations of contracts to purchase goods that were never ordered. You may think it's rather unreasonable that someone could be held responsible for covering the cost of unordered merchandise. But were that not the case, it might become necessary to restrict the common business practice of making purchase orders by phone, in order to protect merchants who send products to other merchants in good faith. So, the practice of sending out a confirmation notice makes things more convenient for everyone and gives the businessperson, as a potential buyer, a last chance to say no. The businessperson who fails to read his or her mail carefully, however, could wind up in the awkward position of having to purchase something no one in the company wants or needs.

Consider, too, that alluding to any business transactions in writing—even in letters or notes—can provide the basis for what may later be viewed as a "contract." Remember that the court's position is to uphold contracts whenever possible. If you agree to something orally, feeling that the Statute of Frauds will save you should you later want out of the agreement, you're taking a big risk. And the risk is heightened if the other party can produce written documents relating to the agreement. You might not think of a letter discussing the terms of a long-range sales agreement as committing you to anything. But in attempting to determine your intentions, especially if you are backing out of something "after the fact," the court might very well view that letter as sufficient to satisfy the Statute of Frauds requirement. And even if you didn't sign the letter, your business letterhead or your stamped signature could be sufficient to bind you to the agreement.

Finally, remember that the requirement involving writing is not intended to complicate life for contracting parties. Quite the opposite, in fact. It is intended to help ensure that ultimately, to the extent possible, contracts will be enforced according to the contracting parties' original intentions. Therefore, a written agreement is, in the simplest of terms, a practical way of protecting everyone's business interests.

ASSIGNMENTS

- Before you watch the video program, be sure you've read through the preceding overview, familiarized yourself with the learning objectives for this lesson, and looked at the key terms below. Then, read Chapter 14 (pages 241–251) of Davidson et al., *Business Law*.
- After completing these tasks, view the video program for Lesson 10.
- After watching the program, take time to review what you've learned. First, evaluate your learning with the self-test which follows the key terms. Then, apply and evaluate what you've learned with the "Your Opinion, Please" scenarios at the end of this telecourse study guide lesson.

KEY TERMS

Before you read through the textbook assignment and watch the video program, take a minute to look at the key terms associated with this lesson. When you encounter them in the textbook and video program, pay careful attention to their meaning.

Doctrine of part performance	Original contract
Guarantor	Primarily liable
Intent of the parties	Secondarily liable
Leading-object (main-purpose) exception	"Signature"
	Statute of Frauds
Lease	Surety
Mortgage	"Writing"
Novation	

SELF-TEST

The questions below will help you evaluate how well you've learned the material in this lesson. Read each one carefully and select the letter of the option that best answers the question. You'll find the correct answer, along with a reference to the page number(s) where the topic is discussed, in the back of this telecourse study guide.

1. The Statute of Frauds was created by the English Parliament *primarily* to

   a. protect each party in a contract from deliberate deceit by the other.
   b. cut down on the amount of perjury in lawsuits involving oral contracts.
   c. bring some consistency to the way in which contracts were interpreted by the courts.
   d. ensure that the substance of all contracts would be legal.

2. Which of the following contracts would have to be written in order to be enforceable? A contract under which

   a. White agrees to sell Bailey a used accordion for $150.
   b. Grant and Wright agree to take joint responsibility for repaying a loan made to Grant.
   c. Fleming agrees to lease Rich a horse pasture for six months at a rate of $100 a month.
   d. Arnold agrees to care for the Rolfs' dog for three months, while they are vacationing, for $100 a month.

3. Clark Stationery receives in the mail a notice that reads as follows: "This is to confirm our sale to you of 2,000 units of Handywrite Notepads at $5.95 per unit. /signed/ F. S. Harlow, Manager, Handywrite, Inc." Since he doesn't recall ordering anything of the sort, Clark phones Handywrite to say he doesn't want the pads. Two weeks pass. Handywrite delivers the pads and demands payment. At this point, which of the following positions is the court *most likely* to take?

   a. Like it or not, Clark has agreed to purchase the notepads at the given price.
   b. No enforceable contract exists between Clark and Handywrite — they'll have to take the pads back.
   c. We cannot say without knowing whether some previous oral agreement existed between Clark and Harlow, Inc.

4. Anderson says she will marry Flint if he will agree to give her sole title to his Ferrari automobile. Flint agrees orally. Is this promise enforceable?

   a. Yes, because Anderson is not paying any money for the Ferrari.
   b. No, because a promise given in consideration of marriage must be in writing to be enforceable.
   c. There is no way to say; it depends entirely on how the judge chooses to view the case.

5. Hawkins applies for a loan, which the bank grants. When Hawkins has difficulty repaying the loan, the bank grants an extension, provided Larson will

agree to assume the debt if Hawkins defaults. In this scenario, Larson is *best* described as

a. a promisee.
b. a primary contractor.
c. a novation.
d. a surety.

6. Suppose that Hawkins (Question 5) defaults on the loan. Can the bank then sue Larson for recovery of the money?

a. Yes, definitely; Larson has agreed to be responsible.
b. Yes, probably—but only after suing Hawkins unsuccessfully.
c. No, definitely not; despite Larson's agreement, there is no way to force a secondary debtor to repay a loan.
d. We cannot say without knowing whether Larson agreed in writing to assume the debt.

7. The so-called *leading-object* or *main-purpose* exception comes into play when it can be shown that a third party agrees to be liable on a loan *chiefly*

a. to protect the second party.
b. to protect the creditor.
c. to further his or her own economic interest.
d. to further the general public interest.

8. Henley makes an oral offer to buy a small house on land owned by Rogers. Rogers accepts orally and cashes Henley's check for 20% of the purchase price. Henley promptly moves into the house, repaints it, and plants a garden. Is this contract enforceable?

a. Yes, definitely; the contract doesn't need to be written in this case because Henley immediately paid 20% of the purchase price.
b. No, definitely not; contracts involving land must be in writing or they are never upheld by the court.
c. We cannot say for sure without knowing whether the court will interpret Henley's and Rogers's conduct as implying the existence of a contract.

9. On January 1, Wilson, a restauranteur, and Frank, a supplier, make an oral agreement that beginning on February 1 and for one year thereafter, Wilson will not order any supplies that Frank carries from anyone other than Frank. Is this contract enforceable?

a. Yes, because it does not extend beyond one year.
b. No, because it extends for thirteen months beyond the date of the agreement.
c. We cannot say without knowing more about the price of the supplies involved.

10. In considering what sort of writing will satisfy legal requirements, which of the following will the court normally view as a "signature"?

a. *Any* of the following *could*, under some conditions, be viewed as a signature.

b. A company's letterhead

c. A stamped signature

d. A company's printed order confirmation form

YOUR OPINION, PLEASE

Read each of the following scenarios and answer the questions about the decisions you would make in each situation. Give these questions some serious thought; they may be used as the basis for the development of a more complex essay. You should base your decisions on what you've learned from this lesson, though you may incorporate outside readings or information gained through your own experience if it is relevant.

Scenario 1

Ames applies for a loan from the local credit union to build a small bed-and-breakfast inn on a bluff overlooking the river just outside town. Because Ames already owns the land free and clear and has a good business standing in the community, the credit union agrees to the loan provided Ames can find someone to assume secondary liability. Ames asks his friend and business associate, Littlefield, if he will agree to be secondarily liable, but Littlefield is uneasy about the matter. To make the deal more appealing, Ames offers Littlefield a position as general manager of the inn once it is built—at a salary to be determined later. "It all depends on how successful we are," he tells Littlefield, "and as manager, a lot of that success will depend on you." After signing a provisional contract as manager (meaning he will take the position upon completion of construction), Littlefield agrees to assume secondary liability; the note is drawn up accordingly and signed by both Ames and Littlefield.

The first year of the inn's business is a rousing success. They're booked to capacity every night and able to charge higher prices than they'd predicted. Littlefield makes a salary of $40,000, and Ames agrees to give Littlefield a percentage of the profits for the following year.

But the next year, things do not go so well. A new freeway bypass takes traffic away from the site, minor flooding problems necessitate a temporary closure and costly repairs, and supplies rise sufficiently in price to make profits less easily come by. With all things taken together, Ames is unable to make his loan payments, or even to pay Littlefield his salary.

The credit union eventually files suit against Ames and threatens suit against Littlefield as well. Littlefield counters that since he has only secondary liability—and the written note to prove it—there is no basis for a lawsuit against him unless the suit against Ames proves unsuccessful. But the credit union replies that under the leading-purpose exception they can easily make a case against Littlefield. Can they?

What's your opinion? Based on what you know of the situation, do you think the credit union can successfully bring suit against Littlefield? Or is he correct in stating that he has only secondary liability and cannot be sued unless the suit against Ames is unsuccessful?

- Is the credit union likely to succeed in bringing suit against Littlefield? Why or why not?
- What factors support your answer?
- What factors might an attorney cite in arguing against your view?
- What steps, if any, might Littlefield have taken to prevent a lawsuit in this situation?
- What steps, if any, might the credit union have taken to prevent a lawsuit in this situation?

Scenario 2

Meeker is a computer components broker who travels around the world looking for bargains in various markets. He does most of his business by telephone, contacting clients in the U.S., who tend to trust Meeker's professional judgment and allow him to place orders to meet their needs. Just before Meeker leaves on an extended buying trip, he receives a letter from a business associate, Wiley, who owns a computer business in New York. The letter instructs Meeker to provide Wiley with prices on various components, which Wiley lists specifically in his letter.

Meeker does so, and phones Wiley's office from overseas with the results. Soon after, Meeker receives another letter from Wiley, forwarded to him by his (Meeker's) office. The letter says, in effect, "I'm very interested in the components we discussed and I think we can do business. Send more details as soon as possible, and we'll make final arrangements for shipment." This letter, like the first, is written on Wiley's business stationery, with letterhead at the top. It is "signed" with a stamped signature of Wiley's name.

Meeker sends the requested information, then phones Wiley's office to see whether he should arrange for shipment. Wiley is out, however. Fearful that he will miss out on current low market prices if he waits any longer, and feeling confident that Wiley is about to place the order anyway, Meeker makes the purchase and arranges for shipment to Wiley. He also forwards a confirmation notice that lists all components mentioned by Wiley in his first letter to Meeker, along with current market prices. The shipment totals $35,000 worth of merchandise.

Upon receipt of the confirmation notice, Wiley takes the position that Meeker is being highly presumptuous, and sends back a letter objecting to the terms of the confirmation and stating explicitly his unwillingness to accept any portion of the shipment. Meeker, in turn, points out that this particular order of components was assembled expressly to meet the needs of Wiley's company and that remarketing the components will cause great difficulty and inconvenience. Wiley tells Meeker that although he regrets the inconvenience, he doesn't see it as his problem. Meeker thereupon decides to sue Wiley for breach of contract. Wiley claims that no contract exists—just an oral understanding. They were, he tells Meeker, still in the negotiation stage, and Meeker acted without authorization. Meeker counters that Wiley's correspondence shows otherwise. Who is right?

What's your opinion? Based on what you know of the situation, do you think Meeker can successfully sue Wiley for breach of contract? Or is Wiley correct in asserting that no contract exists?

- Is Meeker likely to make a successful case against Wiley for breach of contract? Why or why not?
- What factors support your answer?
- What factors might an attorney cite in arguing against your view?
- What steps, if any, might Meeker have taken to prevent a lawsuit in this situation?
- What steps, if any, might Wiley have taken to prevent a lawsuit in this situation?

11

Interpretation of Contracts

LEARNING OBJECTIVES

Upon completing your study of this lesson, you should be able to

- Define the concept of *judicial interpretation* and discuss its implications for the enforcement of contracts.

- List and discuss the various guidelines or "tools" that courts are likely to use in their interpretation of contracts; e.g., standards of interpretation, rules of interpretation, conduct of the parties involved, integration, and usages of trade.

- Distinguish between a *condition* and a *promise*, and discuss the implications of this distinction for interpreting a contract.

- Explain the intent of the parol evidence (oral statement) rule, and explain the circumstances under which parol evidence is or is not admissible in interpreting a contract.

The purpose of this lesson is to explore the role that judicial interpretation plays in enforcing contracts. No matter how carefully two contracting parties think they have prepared or worded a contract, questions may arise about what that contract really says or what responsibilities each party has in fulfilling the contract. Sometimes, the contracting parties are able to resolve these questions on their own. Other times, however, they need the help of the court in interpreting what the document really says or requires. In this lesson, we'll look at some tools and guidelines courts use to make that job easier.

OVERVIEW

Regardless of whether two parties contract orally or in writing, they must rely on words to convey their intentions. Unfortunately, words—no matter how carefully chosen—can sometimes be ambiguous. Thus it sometimes happens that one party interprets a contract to mean one thing, while the other has conflicting ideas. Often, these conflicts revolve around issues that are basic to the performance of a contract, and unless they can be resolved, the contract itself becomes all but meaningless.

For example, suppose homebuilder Ames contracts with Greenwood Timber to purchase $20,000 worth of "lumber." Ames thinks he is purchasing finished lumber direct from the sawmill, but Greenwood commonly uses the term "lumber" to refer to uncut logs—which Ames would have to process himself before they would be usable in construction. Unless Ames and Greenwood are able to settle this disagreement, they cannot very well continue to do business with each other. And it may be they will not be able to settle it without the intervention of the court.

How will the court go about this task? First, it's important to understand that the contract between Ames and Greenwood—or any other contract, for that matter—will not be judicially interpreted according to one judge's whims or perspectives. Rather, the court has a number of standards and tools it can apply to assist in the process of interpretation. But before exploring these in detail, let's consider what interpretation means in a legal sense.

Concept of Judicial Interpretation

Interpretation, for our purposes in this discussion, is defined as *the process of determining the meaning of the words and other manifestations of intent that the parties have used in forging their agreement when the language of the agreement is not clear.* What are "other manifestations"? Mostly, the actions people take regarding the matter at hand. For instance, in our example, if Ames accepts uncut timber from Greenwood, processes it himself, and *then* decides to challenge the contract, that behavior is likely to "manifest" itself differently than if Ames had challenged the contract immediately following the first delivery. In other words, how people act can affect an understanding or an agreement, no matter what their words say.

Two important guidelines underlie any court's interpretation of a contract. First, it is not the court's job to *create* contracts, though it may assist in interpreting contracts that already exist. This means that the court will assume—since a contract in some form must exist before any dispute about it can arise—that at some point the contracting parties had or thought they had a *meeting of the minds*. Thus, the court will try, to the extent possible, to enforce any contract according to the original intentions of the contracting parties. This is another way of saying that the court tries not to violate the original intentions, or to introduce any new interpretations that would change the spirit or essence of the original contract. Second, in deciding between two opposing views, the court will ask how the situation would seem to a "reasonable person," an outsider viewing the situation from an objective perspective. This reasonable person perspective has been adopted over the years to result in the fairest, most sensible possible interpretation.

Interpretation of Contracts

Because interpretation involves comparing the parties' words and conduct from a more objective perspective, certain guidelines or tools have evolved over the years to aid the court in interpreting contracts. These guidelines include: standards of interpretation (general usage and limited usage), integration, rules of interpretation, conduct of the parties involved, and usages of trade.

Standards of Interpretation

The most common standard of interpretation is the standard of *general usage*, which refers to the meaning that a reasonably prudent person familiar with the circumstances surrounding an agreement would attach to certain words or terms. In the case of Ames and Greenwood, for example, the court will look to see whether a reasonable person, contracting with Greenwood Lumber, would have expected to receive uncut or processed logs. And the answer to that question, in turn, probably depends a lot on how Ames and Greenwood and other people buying and selling wood usually do business. If it's usual practice to quote prices on unprocessed lumber, that is likely to lead to one interpretation of what the term "lumber" meant in the context of their contract. If, however, Greenwood's practice is considered quite unusual, then the standard of general usage suggests that Ames has every right to protest; Greenwood isn't using the term "lumber" the way most people in the industry have come to expect.

The court may also apply the standard of *limited usage* in interpreting contracts. This standard refers to the way that words or terms are interpreted *in a specific locale*. For example, let's say that it's common throughout most of the wood products industry to use the term "lumber" to refer to processed, cut, ready-to-use wood. However, in the particular region where Greenwood does business, the term isn't used in this way at all. Rather, it refers to rough lumber—unprocessed, uncut logs. Even though Greenwood's use of the term may not conform to common use elsewhere, it does reflect the way people use the term locally. The court may, therefore, hold that a reasonable person doing business with Greenwood would also take the term "lumber" to mean unprocessed wood.

Total and Partial Integration

The standards used by the court in interpreting a contract may depend on whether that contract is perceived as being totally integrated or partially integrated. A *totally integrated* contract is one that represents the parties' final and complete statement of their agreement. A *partially integrated* contract, by contrast, is one that is *intended* to be the final statement, but is incomplete. How will the court judge the difference? Well, in general, the more formal and complete a document appears, the more likely the court is to view it as being totally integrated. Thus, a "contract" which is pieced together from various bits of correspondence that the two parties have had over a period of some months is much less likely to be considered fully integrated than a single twenty-page document detailing all specifics of the agreement. This is because, from the court's perspective, there is no way to be sure that these various bits of correspondence really represent the parties' final intentions regarding their agreement or were merely negotiations leading up to some final agreement.

Why does it matter whether a contract is judged to be fully or partially integrated? A court will view a fully integrated contract as the sum total of the relevant documentation. Oral discussions, isolated correspondence, and other potentially relevant information may not be considered in interpreting a fully integrated contract. The court does not allow any other evidence to be presented that would show a difference from what the writing itself says. If Benson and Rafferty hammer out a contract of impressive detail and length, Rafferty's subsequent claim that he telephoned Benson to change one of the conditions will not carry much weight if the court is called upon to interpret the contract elements. However, if the parties' agreement is constructed from portions of different letters, memorandums, and notes (a partially integrated contract), it's much more likely that other information and negotiations between the parties will be considered when interpreting the contract. This will be done to "fill in the blanks" in a contract.

Rules of Interpretation

The standards of interpretation are a crucial, but not the complete, set of guidelines the courts use for contract interpretation. Several *rules of interpretation* supplement the various standards. And although these rules are applied with some variability from court to court, it is well to be aware of them nonetheless. The following four rules are the most commonly applied.

First, *the courts will attempt to enforce the intentions of the contracting parties.* As we've already noted, it is not the court's responsibility (or intention, under most circumstances) to either create a new contract or change in any substantive way the conditions of an original contract.

Second, *the courts will examine the contract as a whole in determining the intentions of the contracting parties.* In other words, a review of the contract as a whole may shed some light on how one provision or clause within that contract should best be interpreted. Suppose in our Ames–Greenwood example, for instance, that homebuilder Ames regularly buys finished wood flooring and trim from Greenwood, and this time, as part of a larger contract, Ames is also purchasing "lumber" to be used in framing the house. If the contract as a whole covers ready-to-use wood products, that would tend to suggest that ready-to-use is what Ames is probably expecting in the way of framing, too.

Third, *ordinary words will be given their ordinary meanings, and technical words will be given their technical meanings, unless the circumstances indicate otherwise.* For instance, the word *lesion* may mean one thing to a surgeon, another to a layperson; but in a technical document, the technical meaning should be upheld. Similarly, a word like *irrigation* may be used somewhat differently by a civil engineer, a farmer, and a doctor. Words are usually interpreted by the court according to context and intent.

Finally, *all circumstances surrounding a transaction should be taken into account.* In other words, the court tries to get as complete a picture of the situation as possible before making any final interpretations. (This rule is, however, subject to the requirements of the parol evidence rule—which limits the types of evidence that can influence contract interpretation. We'll learn more about the parol evidence rule later in this lesson.)

There are other, less important rules of interpretation. For example, courts give precedence to handwritten words over printed words where part of a contract is handwritten. They will favor the most reasonable of available alternatives for resolving disputes. They will enforce the contract most strictly against the party that drafted the contract. And, whenever the public welfare is involved, the courts will ensure that contracts will be interpreted in ways that promote rather than hinder public welfare.

Conditions Within Contracts

A single condition within a contract can often influence interpretation—and sometimes make interpretation more difficult. Conditions are not the same as promises. A *promise* is an agreement to do—or refrain from doing—something. A *condition*, on the other hand, is an act or event that limits or qualifies a promise. For instance, suppose Rose offers to buy a house from Beale for $50,000 *on the condition* that Beale sell the draperies with the house. If Beale decides to take the draperies with her to her new home, then Rose is no longer under any obligation to fulfill his promise to buy the house. The condition has, in other words, qualified Rose's promise to buy the house, and if the condition is not met, the promise is off.

There are two different ways to classify conditions. The first has to do with the manner in which the condition comes into being. *Express conditions* are those imposed by the contracting parties themselves, *either explicitly or impliedly*, within the contract. The condition set up by Rose in the preceding example, for instance, is an express condition.

On the other hand, a *constructive condition* is one that is not expressed or imposed by the parties but *read into the contract in order to serve justice*. For example, suppose that our building contractor from the earlier example, Ames, contracts to buy a large amount of premixed concrete from Goodfellow Sand and Gravel. Perhaps the contract says nothing about the delivery of the concrete to the building site, but such a *constructive condition* may well be imposed by the court in the interest of fairness. A large amount of premixed concrete is not the sort of thing one can normally deliver oneself. It is not reasonable to suppose that Ames will come and pick up his own concrete; thus, the court is likely to hold that delivery is a part of the contract agreement, even if it isn't explicitly noted.

The other manner of categorizing conditions has to do with the timing of the condition relative to performance of some action within the contract. Conditions classified in this manner fall into one of three categories: conditions precedent, concurrent conditions, and conditions subsequent. The names probably give you a good clue as to the meanings.

Conditions precedent are those which must occur before the other party has a duty to perform or before a contract exists. The preceding example, in which Rose offered to buy the house *provided* Beale included the draperies involves a condition precedent; unless Beale includes the draperies, no contract will be formed.

A *concurrent condition* obligates both parties to perform at the same time. Sales agreements are often of this type. For instance, Henry offers to buy a television set from Bright Electronics for $1,000. Bright agrees to the sale. According to the concurrent conditions of the sale, Bright will deliver the television set to Henry's residence on June 1 in exchange for payment upon delivery of the total purchase price. Because the payment and delivery occur at the same time, these are concurrent conditions.

A *condition subsequent* is any occurrence that the parties have agreed will cut off an existing legal duty. In other words, if a condition subsequent occurs, all or part of an existing contract will become ineffective. For instance, suppose Petrie offer his goods with a thirty-day "no questions asked" guarantee of satisfaction. Suppose Markov purchases, on Petrie's credit plan, a washing machine that does not satisfy him. The *condition subsequent*—Markov's lack of satisfaction and return of the washer—allows Markov to escape his previous duty to pay Petrie for the washing machine. And at that point, Markov and Petrie would no longer have a contract.

Sometimes conditions that appear to be conditions subsequent are really looked on by the courts as conditions precedent. For example, suppose the contract between Acme Motors and Nelson states that Acme will replace the engine on the used car Nelson purchased if it fails during the first year of Nelson's ownership. The contract also says, however, that this replacement offer is not valid unless Nelson brings the car to Acme's mechanics for a checkup after he's driven it for a month. This is, a court might decide, another way of saying that Acme *will* be responsible for engine replacement *if* Nelson brings his car in for the required checkup. Notice how casting the engine replacement offer in this light turns it into a condition precedent (if Nelson comes in for the checkup, Acme takes responsibility for replacement), and that is how the court is likely to view it.

Conduct of the Parties

Another means of interpretation is known as the *course of conduct* or the *conduct of the parties*. This means that the court will look at how the parties to the contract have structured and interpreted previous contracts. If the parties have agreed in previous contracts that all payments will be made by the tenth of the month, then a disagreement over the time of payment will most likely be interpreted as "payment by the tenth."

Usages of Trade

Similar to conduct of the parties is another standard of interpretation — *usages of trade*. This refers to the generally accepted practice of an industry. For instance, in a dispute between two parties involving the grade of lettuce to be supplied to fill a contract, if the industry practice is to accept a mixture of 80% Grade A and 20% Grade B, then a dispute involving 60% Grade A and 40% Grade B lettuce would be objectively resolved.

The Parol Evidence Rule

The *parol evidence rule* is based on the belief that oral evidence should not be admissible to alter, add to, or vary the terms of an integrated, written contract. It's fairly simple to see why the law upholds this point of view; were it otherwise, one contracting party or the other would only have to say, "No, that wasn't what I intended," and the contract could be changed or become unenforceable. In time, written contracts would come to have little or no meaning, and the business world as we know it would dissolve into chaos. Thus, the court holds that once a contract is *integrated* — that is, accepted as the final agreement between two parties — it cannot be undone merely by conflicting oral statements.

There are, however, certain circumstances under which parol evidence — oral statements, that is — will be admissible in interpreting contracts. First, the parol evidence rule is applied less rigorously when interpreting partially integrated contracts — those that are not complete. Oral statements cannot be used to overturn the intent of such a contract, but they can *add to* that contract. For example, say Henderson and Phlug create an employment agreement under which Phlug will work for Henderson; Henderson and Phlug have extensively discussed an arrangement whereby Phlug will manage the branch office in Dallas. Suppose, too, that the contract neglects to clearly state that Phlug will move to Dallas. If Phlug refuses to move to Dallas to assume the position Henderson hired her for, the oral discussions wherein they discussed the Dallas move could be introduced as evidence at court, since they involve an addition to or explanation of the existing contract.

On the other hand, suppose that Phlug maintained that in a discussion held at the time of contract signing, Henderson offered a salary $10,000 higher than that reflected in the contract—an oversight Phlug says she failed to notice before signing. Would the court admit such evidence? Probably not, because it contradicts the existing contract.

Parol evidence is also admissible to show mistake, fraud, duress, or failure of consideration. Such situations cast doubt on the validity of the contract itself, and thus the court finds no compelling reason to justify the exclusion of such evidence. For instance, let's say Murphy signs a contract with Reynolds in which Murphy agrees not to impose any rent increase on Reynolds for the next five years. However, as it turns out, Murphy agreed to this arrangement only because Reynolds said that Murphy's son Bob would lose his job at Reynold's company if the elder Murphy did not agree to the rent freeze. It appears that Murphy signed the contract under duress, and the court may well allow him to testify about those conversations when asking the court to cancel the contract.

In addition, parol evidence is admissible to clear up ambiguities or to show that an agreement was not intended to become binding until some condition precedent was met—such as the approval of the contract by one party's attorney. One caution, however: The court will not admit evidence about a condition precedent if it contradicts the current written terms of the contract. For instance, let's say Holmes and Grant have a contract by which Holmes will purchase a small office building from Grant. The contract explicitly states that Holmes will bear all expenses relating to required county and state inspections prior to the finalization of the sale. However, Holmes contends that the sale was contingent on the orally stated condition precedent that Grant, not he, would cover the cost of the final building inspection by the county officials. Holmes would not be allowed to introduce such evidence in a court dispute, because it directly contradicts the terms of the written agreement.

Remember, the overriding goal of the court is to uphold the original terms and intentions of the contracting parties. And from the court's point of view, introducing evidence that is contradictory to the written terms only undermines that goal. Be aware, too, that the UCC recognizes the parol evidence rule but modifies its impact by allowing oral evidence relating to normal industry customs or practices. The rationale here is that such evidence is more likely to clarify meaning than to contradict existing agreements.

SOME PRACTICAL ADVICE

From a prudent business perspective, what is to be learned from this lesson? First, and most basically, a written contract is no guarantee that misunderstandings will not occur. Even the most carefully constructed documents can turn out to be ambiguous—either because of the words it uses or because it did not anticipate and cover a problem which later occurs. On the other hand, though, realizing that misunderstandings are a fairly common occurrence should encourage the careful businessperson to be particularly careful. Take some time when constructing or reading any contract to clarify as much as possible the meanings of any terms used — even if they seem to be common terms. A few minutes spent "belaboring the obvious" can save much time and clarification later — and may eliminate the need for involvement by the court.

Second, recognize that a totally integrated contract is less subject to later change than a partially integrated contract. While neither can be contradicted or overruled by new agreements, a partially integrated contract can be supplemented by later agreements — including those introduced by oral evidence. Strive to produce a document that the court will consider fully integrated.

Third, take care to distinguish between promises and conditions. A condition — while not a promise to do (or not to do) something — may nevertheless affect the way in which a promise is carried out or the circumstances under which a party is no longer obligated to fulfill the promise as originally intended. When the contract is being drawn up, conditions can seem minor, unimportant, scarcely worth noticing. Yet they frequently affect contract performance in major ways.

Finally, the prudent businessperson must be aware of the various circumstances in which the parol evidence rule will — or will not — be enforced. As a person signing a contract, don't assume that you will later be able to introduce oral evidence contradicting the terms of that contract. In most circumstances, you cannot. While parol evidence may be allowed to explain some of the terms, it is really only in cases of partially integrated contracts (unless there is reason to suspect fraud, duress, mistake, and so forth) that oral evidence will be admitted to establish terms of the contract.

Above all, keep in mind that the court's purpose in interpreting contracts is not to create new and better documents. It is to help contracting parties in clarifying and fulfilling the terms of their original agreement. Therefore, the more accurately and thoroughly any contract you sign reflects your intentions in contracting, the happier you are likely to be with any subsequent "interpretation" imposed by a court — should that become necessary.

ASSIGNMENTS

- Before you watch the video program, be sure you've read through the preceding overview, familiarized yourself with the learning objectives for this lesson, and looked at the key terms below. Then, read Chapter 14 (pages 234–243) of Davidson et al., *Business Law*.

- After completing these tasks, view the video program for Lesson 11.

- After watching the program, take time to review what you've learned. First, evaluate your learning with the self-test which follows the key terms. Then, apply and evaluate what you've learned with the "Your Opinion, Please" scenarios at the end of this telecourse study guide lesson.

KEY TERMS

Before you read through the textbook assignment and watch the video program, take a minute to look at the key terms associated with this lesson. When you encounter them in the textbook and video program, pay careful attention to their meaning.

Concurrent condition
Condition precedent
Condition subsequent
Constructive condition
Express condition
General usage
Interpretation

Limited usage
Parol evidence
Partial integration
Rules of interpretation
Standards
Total integration

SELF-TEST

The questions below will help you evaluate how well you've learned the material in this lesson. Read each one carefully, and select the letter of the option that best answers the question. You'll find the correct answer, along with a reference to the page number(s) where the topic is discussed, in the back of this telecourse study guide.

1. According to the textbook, which of the following is usually adequate to guarantee that there will never be any question about what a contract "really says"?

   a. Put the contract in writing.
   b. Define all terms within the contract.
   c. Have the contract reviewed by an attorney.
   d. *None* of the above provides a guarantee; there is no single way to make sure that problems won't arise.

2. In general, the *parol evidence rule* states that

   a. a contract may never be altered in any way, under any conditions.
   b. oral evidence will not be admissible to add to or change a contract.
   c. oral evidence relating to a contract will not be admissible under any circumstances whatsoever.
   d. only partially integrated contracts will be open to interpretation by the court.

3. Hemming has a contract under which he leases land from Girdler. The contract includes a clause stating that Hemming will not use the land "for any purpose detrimental to the community." In interpreting this clause, the court would be *most likely* to

   a. ask Hemming for his definition of the term "detrimental."
   b. ask Girdler for his definition of the term.
   c. ask what a "reasonably prudent person" would consider detrimental to the local community.
   d. rely on the unique opinion of the presiding judge to interpret this term.

4. A totally integrated contract is one that

   a. represents the parties' final, complete agreement.
   b. has been pieced together from various other documents, including correspondence.
   c. is intended to be final, but which has been amended in some way.
   d. contains no ambiguous terms.

5. In interpreting contracts, courts will generally

   a. focus on each clause independently, rather than view the contract as a whole.
   b. make every attempt to uphold the original intentions of the contracting parties.
   c. impose the most precise existing legal or technical definition on most words—even if that definition was not originally intended.
   d. restrict all interpretation to the contract document itself, regarding other circumstances as irrelevant.

6. In looking over a long-term sales agreement with Newsome, Inc., Wiles determined she did not like the way one clause within that document was worded. It was, however, unhandy to take the contract back to the office to have it redone, so she crossed out the clause, initialed it, and rewrote it in her own handwriting. Black, president of Newsome, initialed Wiles's handwritten clause and signed the contract. Later, if some dispute arises over the handwritten clause, which of the following positions is the court *most likely* to take?

   a. The handwritten clause will take precedence over the printed portion.
   b. The original printed clause will take precedence, even though the contracting parties initialed the handwritten version.
   c. The court will tend to uphold whichever clause the judge deems more fair.
   d. Both clauses are likely to be ignored since there is a contradiction between them.

7. Which of the options most accurately completes this sentence? Courts tend to apply the rules of interpretation

   a. very rarely; in fact, they're not of much importance.
   b. somewhat arbitrarily, according to the inclinations of the presiding judge.
   c. only when dealing with partially integrated contracts.

d. whenever such rules are useful in determining how to interpret a contract.

8. A *condition* is *best* defined as

   a. a promise to do something.
   b. a promise to refrain from doing something.
   c. a limitation or qualification imposed on a promise.
   d. any occurrence which cuts off a legal duty.

9. Brown has contracted with RidPest Termite Control for termite control services. RidPest's five-year guarantee against termite damage states that they "will not fulfill the terms of the warranty" if Brown "fails to have RidPest conduct yearly inspections of her dwelling." In interpreting the terms of this contract, the court is *most likely* to view this specification as

   a. a condition precedent.
   b. a concurrent condition.
   c. a constructive condition.
   d. a condition subsequent.

10. Under which of the following circumstances would a court be *most likely* to admit parol evidence?

    a. *None* of the following; parol evidence is never admitted under any circumstances in contract interpretation.
    b. Where there is reason to suspect a contract was signed under duress.
    c. Where one party alleges that a contract is incomplete, though the court has ruled otherwise.
    d. Where one party disputes the agreed-to price within a sales contract.

YOUR OPINION, PLEASE

Read each of the following scenarios and answer the questions about the decisions you would make in each situation. Give these questions some serious thought; they may be used as the basis for the development of a more complex essay. You should base your decisions on what you've learned from this lesson, though you may incorporate outside readings or information gained through your own experience if it is relevant.

Scenario I

Willard has been touring a display of model homes built by Knothole, Inc. He likes one model very much and decides to buy it. In the final contract, written by Knothole, the house is described as "finished," a word which Willard interprets to mean the house will include carpeting, draperies, and appliances. But later, when inquiring about selecting his carpeting, Knothole says no, that is not their custom. They will make carpeting available at a discount price for Willard to pay, and they will cover the cost of installation, but the cost of providing draperies and appliances will fall entirely to Willard.

Willard is quite upset. He does some research and discovers that it is common throughout the building industry to use the term "finished" to reference a house with builder-supplied carpeting, draperies, and appliances (except for a refrigerator). That may be, Knothole replies, but that is not their custom and never has been. Further, most other builders in their immediate area do not use the term "finished" in the way Willard is suggesting.

Outraged, Willard counters that any reasonable, thinking person would expect the term "finished" to imply that the house was ready to move into. Knothole counters that the term "finished" means only that construction on the house is concluded, and that no reasonable, thinking person could imagine otherwise. Willard sues Knothole to obtain the "missing" carpeting, drapes, and appliances.

What's your opinion? Based on what you know of the situation, do you think a court would interpret this contract in favor of Knothole or in favor of Willard — and on what grounds?

- Is Willard's interpretation of "finished" likely to be supported by the court? Why or why not?
- What factors support your answer?
- What factors might an attorney cite in arguing against your view?
- What steps, if any, might Willard have taken to eliminate the court's involvement in interpreting this contract?
- What steps, if any, might Knothole, Inc., have taken to eliminate the court's involvement in interpreting this contract?

Scenario 2

The City of Liverton has a long-term contract with Greenleaf Landscapers to provide landscaping for city-owned areas adjacent to apartment complexes, condominiums, office buildings, and shopping areas, including a new downtown mall area. During negotiations, at a meeting of the city council, Liverton representatives ask Greenleaf if they will take responsibility for replacing any shrubbery or trees that die within six months following planting. Fearful of losing the contract, the Greenleaf representative orally agrees to the six-month replacement term.

The previously submitted written contract, however, reads differently. It stipulates explicitly that Greenleaf will be responsible for replacing shrubbery at no cost for a period of *one* month following planting, but will replace shrubbery and trees at wholesale price, with a "reasonable" labor charge, for up to six months following planting. The inconsistency is not noticed by council members, and they approve the contract. The next day, city officials sign the document — as do Greenleaf representatives.

Two months following planting, disease wipes out two dozen large maple trees planted in the new downtown mall. Not replacing them in such a high-visibility area is unthinkable — but Greenleaf refuses to replace the trees free of charge, noting that the contract requires the city to cover the wholesale and labor costs. At this point, the city wants to amend the written contract to hold Greenleaf to their original oral agreement. Greenleaf says no.

The city claims that the written contract does not accurately reflect the true terms of the original agreement, that the "one month" should have read "six months." After all, they point out, they have the minutes from the city council meeting to prove their point. Greenleaf counters by referencing similar city contracts with other landscaping companies reflecting wording identical to that in the Liverton contract. The one-month full-replacement agreement is the standard way of doing business, Greenleaf maintains, and their oral agreement to extend that period to six months was just a spur-of-the-moment response under the duress of the council meeting and is not binding. Who is right?

What's your opinion? Based on what you know of the situation, if this contract is interpreted by the court, is the interpretation likely to favor Greenleaf's position or that of the City of Liverton?

- Is the court's interpretation likely to uphold Greenleaf's position that the written contract should stand without any amendments or additions? Why?

- What factors support your answer?

- What factors might an attorney cite in arguing against your view?

- What steps, if any, might Greenleaf have taken to avoid the court's involvement in interpreting this contract?

- What steps, if any, might the City of Liverton have taken to avoid the court's involvement in interpreting this contract?

12

Rights of Third Parties

LEARNING OBJECTIVES

Upon completing your study of this lesson, you should be able to

- Describe several situations in which persons who were not originally parties to a contract may nevertheless sue to enforce their rights under that contract.

- Define the term *third-party beneficiary*.

- Distinguish between an *intended beneficiary* and an *incidental beneficiary* and discuss the impact of this distinction in determining the rights of a third-party beneficiary to a contract.

- Define the terms *donee beneficiary* and *creditor beneficiary* and explain the circumstances under which these persons become third-party beneficiaries to a contract.

- Explain how the assignment of rights within a contract is created, give several examples of such "rights," and list the conditions affecting the legal assignment of rights within a contract.

- Distinguish between the assignment of a contractual right and the delegation of a contractual duty, and provide a hypothetical example to illustrate that distinction.

Any contract influences the legal rights of the two parties who enter it. Sometimes, however, a contract also influences the rights of third parties—persons or agencies who were not directly involved in and did not sign the original contract but whose welfare, financial or otherwise, is affected by the way the contract is enforced or interpreted. In some cases, if third parties feel their interests are not being served by the way in which a contract is carried out, they may sue to protect those interests. The purpose of this lesson is twofold—to examine the circumstances under which the court will or will not enforce the rights of these third persons and to examine the criteria a court uses in determining those rights in the first place.

OVERVIEW

Persons or agencies that receive benefits under a contract they have not signed are called *third-party beneficiaries*. Some people think the term third-*person* beneficiaries would be more appropriate than third-*party* beneficiaries, given that these third persons were *not* necessarily parties to the contract negotiation or signing. But the more important point here is that such persons may, under some circumstances, have legal rights granted by the nature or circumstances of the contract— and may be able to sue to protect those rights. This situation could arise through creation of a third-party beneficiary contract, for example, or the assignment of contract rights or benefits, or through the delegation of contract duties. We'll discuss each of these in turn, with some hypothetical examples from the business world.

Throughout this discussion, you'll find it helpful to keep in mind the distinction between *promisor* and *promisee*. The promisor is the party within a contract who promises to perform; the promisee is the party to whom that promise is made. For example, Scott promises to walk Nelson's Great Dane every Sunday for a month for a weekly fee (or consideration) of $5. Scott is the promisor, Nelson the promisee.

Third-Party Beneficiary

In some contracts, the promise involves a third party who benefits directly from the contract even though he or she may know nothing of the contract when it is formed. For example, Wilson contracts with Whirlwind Tours for a month-long holiday in Nepal, which he orders presented to his daughter and new son-in-law, the Whites, as a wedding gift. The Whites in this example are third party beneficiaries, and they have a legal right to what's promised in the contract—namely, the month-long holiday.

The term *beneficiary* can be misleading. The Whites, for example, may feel anything but delighted to be the recipients of this gift. They may wish they could have gone to Hawaii or had the money to use as a down payment on a new house instead. But from a legal perspective, all that is irrelevant. The beneficiary need not know about the contract in order for it to be valid. Nor is it necessary that the beneficiary approve of or be at all pleased by the contract. In fact—as with the Whites—the beneficiary may be displeased. What *does* matter, however, is that at least one of the contracting parties (usually, as in this case, the promisee) *intended* for the third-party beneficiary to receive the goods or services promised in the contract. That intention is key in determining the rights of the third party.

Intended and Incidental Beneficiaries

When at least one of the original contracting parties intends for the goods or services or activities specified within a contract to benefit a third party, the noncontracting party is known as an *intended beneficiary*. When the benefit or action is not intended, the noncontracting party is known as an *incidental beneficiary*. This distinction is important because intended beneficiaries have legal rights, whereas incidental beneficiaries do not. To help clarify the distinction, let's consider an example.

Miller owns a vacant lot just on the outskirts of town adjacent to a new motel owned by Reeves. Miller sells the land to Flint, who builds a large family restaurant complete with a playground. The restaurant benefits Reeves enormously because families are more eager to stay in a motel that has nearby eating facilities. However, Miller and Flint did not intend this benefit; they didn't build the restaurant to boost Reeves's motel business. It just turned out that way. In this case, Reeves is an incidental beneficiary. If Flint decided to close down the restaurant or turn it into a dress shop, Reeves couldn't sue for violation of his rights. He has no legal rights under the Miller–Flint contract to have the restaurant remain in operation.

An intended beneficiary *does* have legal rights. Further, the beneficiary need not be mentioned by name in order to claim legal rights under a contract. Clear intent to give the beneficiary rights under the agreement is sufficient. For example, suppose a two-story school contracts to build a ramp to make it easier for handicapped students to get from one level to the other. These students would almost certainly not be mentioned by name in the contract, but it would be clear from the nature of the contract that the ramp was designed for their direct benefit. Thus, the school's handicapped students as a group would be intended beneficiaries of the contract, even though they were not named in the contract. Also, the school's future handicapped students, once at the school, would become intended beneficiaries (and, obviously, they couldn't have been named in the original contract).

Donee and Creditor Beneficiaries

Third-party beneficiaries of goods and services can be classified as either donee or creditor beneficiaries. If the promisee means to make a gift to the third party, then the third party is a *donee beneficiary*. Recall our earlier example with the trip to Nepal; the Whites, to whom the trip was given, would be considered donee beneficiaries. A person named as the beneficiary in a life insurance policy (or any similar contract) would also be considered a donee beneficiary if the policy or contract were taken out voluntarily by the promisee (as opposed to under some legal duty).

In some states, the law provides that a donee beneficiary's rights cannot be terminated after a contract is made. In other states, though, the rules protecting donee beneficiaries apply only when the beneficiary knows about the contract and either accepts it verbally or can show that he or she has relied on its terms. Such reliance or acceptance is considered a *vested interest* in the contract. Once it's established that such a vested interest exists, the contract may not be altered without the donee beneficiary's consent.

Suppose Wiley takes out a life insurance policy on himself and names his wife as beneficiary. In some states, he retains the right to change the beneficiary as he pleases. In a state that protects donee beneficiaries, however, Wiley may not be able to readily change the beneficiary. Suppose his wife knew about the policy and had contributed to the payments for the policy, or she had given up certain rights or otherwise relied on the policy. Depending on the rules in Wiley's state, she might have to agree to the change of beneficiary. (Interestingly, though, if Wiley were intent on not letting his wife be the beneficiary of his insurance policy, he could fail to perform the contract — that is, fail to pay his premium. If the policy were then cancelled, the donee beneficiary — his wife — would be left without recourse under most states' beneficiary laws.)

As we've seen, a donee beneficiary is the recipient of a gift. By contrast, a *creditor beneficiary* benefits from the performance of a legal duty. In the preceding example, Wiley's wife could not be considered a creditor beneficiary because Wiley had no legal duty to purchase insurance and to name his wife as the beneficiary of that insurance. If he were obliged by law to do so (perhaps as a result of a pre-marital agreement), then the insurance benefits would not be considered a "gift."

But let's look at a different sort of situation. Suppose that a famous actor has received an advance payment for work to be performed on a movie. Further suppose that this actor does a lot of his own stuntwork in films. The movie studio requires the actor by contract to take out a life insurance policy on himself, naming the film studio as a beneficiary. In this case, the actor is not purchasing the policy out of a sense of moral obligation or as an affectionate gesture; he is doing it because he is contractually obligated to do it. If he does not, the studio won't hire him. The policy is merely their way of protecting the money they're investing in the actor and in making the film. If their star breaks his neck jumping off a cliff, they might not be able to complete or release the film, and the money spent in making it would be lost. The insurance benefits would help them recover that loss and the lost salary advance. Thus, in this case, the studio would be considered a creditor beneficiary.

As such, what rights would they have? Unlike a donee beneficiary, the studio could — in any state — sue to force the actor to reinstate them as beneficiary. Or, if the actor were dead, it could sue his estate for recovery of benefits to which they were legally entitled. And if the actor cancelled the policy in order to escape having to pay the premiums, the studio could sue him to force him to maintain the insurance.

It is principally in the area of enforcement that the rights of donee and creditor beneficiaries are different. In other respects, they are much the same; neither, for example, will be able to intervene in or regulate the original contract. And depending upon the nature of the contract, both donee and creditor beneficiaries may forfeit their rights if the promisee fails to fulfill his or her contractual obligations.

In determining the potential rights of any third-party beneficiary, three important questions must be answered. First, was the third party involved from the beginning, or did that party enter the picture some time following creation of the original contract? Note that an intended beneficiary—one who has unquestionable legal rights—must in some manner be thought of in connection with the contract from the beginning, even if not *named* in the contract. Second, did the promisee intend to benefit the third party, or was it accidental? Keep in mind that intended beneficiaries have legal rights, whereas incidental beneficiaries do not. And, finally, was the promisee making a gift to the third party or fulfilling a contract obligation to the third party? (As noted, there is sometimes a distinction between the rights of a donee beneficiary and the rights of a creditor beneficiary, though these distinctions are becoming smaller and less significant.)

Assignment of Rights

A third person who becomes involved *after* initial contract formation is not a third-party beneficiary. However, that person may have certain defensible rights transferred or assigned by someone else. To understand how this works, we must first distinguish between *assignments* and *delegations*. This distinction, in turn, rests on the difference between *contractual rights* and *contractual duties*. Contractual rights are those things within a contract that a person is entitled to receive—such as payment for the performance of some work. Contractual duties are those things within a contract that a person is obligated to give or perform—such as the work done in exchange for payment. When Moore contracts with Freeman to dig a well for $1,500, Moore has a *duty* to dig the well; he has a *right* to receive payment of $1,500, provided he fulfills that duty.

Rights can be assigned; duties cannot. Thus, if Moore owes the bank $1,500 on an unpaid loan for drilling equipment, he can give the bank his right to the money Freeman would normally pay to him and have the money paid directly to the bank. In that case, Moore has transferred—or assigned—his contractual right (that of being paid) to the bank. Moore is the assignor, the bank the assignee. When Moore takes this step, he forfeits his original right to the money; that right now belongs solely and entirely to the bank. Moore cannot reclaim it. And if Freeman doesn't pay, it's the bank, not Moore, who has the right to sue Freeman.

An assignment of rights may seem rather official—and sometimes it is—but it doesn't have to follow any special format or use any special wording. Thus, Moore might simply write telling Valley View Bank that it has his rights to the money Freeman owes him. This expression by Moore of his intent to assign his rights to Valley View should be sufficient for the court.

The relationship between assignor and assignee can involve either a contract or a gift. This is another way of saying that consideration need not be part of an assignment—though in a business context it usually is. In our scenario, for example, Moore isn't offering the bank a gift of his hard-earned money. He's getting some consideration from the bank—in this case, cancellation of the debt owed. Contrast this with a situation in which Simpson received a cash award of, say, $500 and asked that it be donated to the local university library. In that case, Simpson would not expect or receive any consideration from the library; thus, the $500 would be a gift. Either way, though, Simpson would be transferring his rights to the money.

Should you ever find yourself the recipient of transferred contractual rights—the assignee, that is—it's excellent practice to let the promisor know of the situation. This practice of *giving notice* to the promisor can go a long way toward protecting your rights in the event that the assignor should be unethical or dishonest. Consider our example with Moore, the well digger. Suppose that Valley View Bank isn't Moore's only creditor. Perhaps he also owes money to Sharkley Loan Agency. Moore tells both Valley View and Sharkley that he is assigning money from the Freeman job to them. Moore can, if he chooses, divide the money from the Freeman contract equally among his creditors. But maybe that isn't what Moore has in mind at all. Instead, he leads both creditors to believe that they will receive *all* the money from the contract. If neither assignee notifies Freeman of this situation, however, they cannot take legal action against him if Moore fails to follow through on the assignments. They *can* sue Moore—but he may have left town with the money by that time.

Suppose both give Freeman notice. Then who has the stronger claim? That depends. In deciding between the rights of assignees with conflicting claims, some courts will apply the *first-in-time approach*, also known as the *American Rule*. Under this approach, the first assignee to receive assignment automatically receives all rights—the theory being that once the assignor assigned the rights there was nothing more to be transferred and so all subsequent assignments were invalid. If it could be shown that Moore transferred rights to Sharkley on June 1 and to Valley View on June 3, this approach would work well. But if the dates of assignment could not be conclusively determined, the first-in-time approach would obviously be less satisfactory.

Some courts apply instead the *first-to-give-notice* rule, also known as the *English Rule*. According to this approach, the assignee who first gives notice to the promisor of his or her status is the one to receive full rights. This rule is intended to encourage assignees to give notice, thus protecting themselves and simplifying the determination of legal rights. Let's say Moore transferred rights to Sharkley on June 1, but Sharkley did not notify Freeman of that fact. Moore then transferred rights to Valley View on June 3, and they immediately notified Freeman. According to the first-to-give-notice rule, Valley View would be entitled to the money; Sharkley would not. Moreover, since Valley View had notified Freeman of the situation, they could—if Moore failed to pay—take legal action against Freeman.

It might occur to you that this situation could put Freeman in a very awkward and undesirable position. Here he is, merely contracting to have a new well dug, and suddenly he finds himself in the middle of a hassle over his well digger's debts.

Is the court likely to view this situation as reasonable? Perhaps not, in this particular case. In many situations, however, rights are assignable even if the promisor (Freeman, in our scenario) objects. Let's take a closer look at how this works.

Assignable and Nonassignable Rights

The assignment of rights is very common practice in the business world. Most of us, however, are quite unaware of it, even though we may often be in a position parallel to that of the promisor Freeman in the preceding example. For instance, retailers who sell expensive goods on time often assign monthly payments to a credit corporation in exchange for cash. The courts are generally very supportive of this process because it's good for business all around. The retailer gets cash with which to buy new products and meet consumers' demands. Consumers are happy because they can get the products they want and can buy them on time instead of deferring their purchases until they have all the cash at once.

It wouldn't occur to most of us, probably, when we pay our monthly bill to the local retail store to attach a note saying, "By the way, don't transfer this money to a credit corporation." All that's behind the scenes. We don't think to question it because we trust most businesses to be forthright in their dealings with us. So all we care about is getting good value on the merchandise we buy. In a more personal context, like that between Freeman and Moore, it is not unusual for the promisor to protest any transfer of contract rights to an assignee. In most cases, however, the court will allow assignment, *even if the promisor protests*.

In seeking to prevent the assignment, the promisor must demonstrate to the court that at least one of the following three conditions exists:

1. The assignment would *materially* change the duty of the promisor.

2. The assignment would *materially* impair the chance of return performance.

3. The assignment would *materially* increase the burden or risk imposed by the contract.

In other words, the promisor must show the court that he or she would be in a substantially worse position if the assignment were allowed.

For instance, suppose CarpetClean—as a promotional gimmick—phones Smith at home and agrees to steam clean all the carpeting in any room of her choice for $25. They back their promise with a written agreement, which Smith signs. Later, she assigns her right to her husband, who decides to have CarpetClean do the 2,000-square-foot boardroom of his company's headquarters. Clearly, this was not what CarpetClean had in mind. The extent of the task has altered considerably, and CarpetClean is likely to have a fairly easy time convincing the court that the assignment "would materially change the duty of the promisor." Thus, the court is likely *not* to allow the assignment in this case.

Let's return for a moment to our example with Freeman and Moore, the well digger. Freeman might argue that if Moore were to spend all his money paying creditors, he (Moore) might have to accept another job in order to make enough money to live on; thus, the construction of Freeman's well would be delayed. This is another way of saying that the assignment "would materially impair the chance of return performance." Or, Freeman could argue that since Moore wasn't receiving any money directly for his work, he might be less committed to doing a high-quality job; in other words, the assignment would "materially increase the burden or risk imposed by the contract." And under either argument, the court might support Freeman's right to protest assignment in this case.

It's important to keep in mind, however, that in most cases, courts do support assignments of rights. In fact, even if a contract includes a statement to the effect that "there shall be no assignment without the prior consent of the promisor," most courts will allow assignment of rights. Where such a clause exists, however, the assignor will be held legally liable for any loss that the promisor endures as a result of the assignment. In order to ensure that such a transfer of rights will not be allowed by the court, the promisor can include in a contract a stronger statement, e.g., "Any attempt at assignment shall be null and void." Most courts will support such a statement.

Delegations

While delegations and assignments often occur simultaneously, they are not the same thing. Rights within a contract are assigned. Duties within a contract—those things that someone is obligated to do—are delegated. When the original promisor wishes to delegate a duty and finds someone willing to do the duty, the original promisor is called the *delegant*; the "new" promisor—the one to whom is delegated the duty—is called the *delegatee*.

The delegation of duties usually occurs because a promisor is unable to fulfill a contract in accordance with the original agreement. For instance, suppose that our favorite well digger Moore breaks a leg on a weekend ski trip and is unable to operate his machinery. He might then delegate the digging to a colleague, Grey. The relationship between Moore and Grey could involve a contract or be a gift, depending, as always, on whether there is consideration. If Moore pays Grey to do the well digging work, then there is consideration, and Grey and Moore have a contract.

Suppose, however, that Grey is an old friend who says, "Look, you're in a tough situation. I'll help you out here while you're looking for a replacement. Maybe you'll do me a favor someday." In that case, the work performed by Grey (the new promisor and the delegatee) is a gift from Grey to Moore (the original promisor and the delegant). This distinction becomes critical in the event that Grey fails to fulfill the promise or does inferior work, thereby not living up to the specifications of the contract between Moore and Freeman. If there is a contract relationship between Moore and Grey, Moore can sue him if Grey does not fulfill his promise. But if there is no consideration, the court holds that Grey merely made a promise to perform sometime in the future, and since future promises are not ordinarily enforceable, Moore cannot sue for Grey's failure to come through.

Courts tend not to look nearly so favorably on delegations as they do on assignments. And it is fairly easy to understand why. Most businesspeople sign contracts because they respect and desire the particular services of the party with whom they're contracting. If contractual duties could be arbitrarily transferred at a contracting party's whim, contracts would be less reliable and have less value. Of course, in a case where a contracting party is clearly unable to fulfill the terms of the contract—because of disability, for instance—the delegation of duties may seem a logical solution. Usually, however, courts will disallow delegation of duties if a original contracting party objects, particularly if a contract contains a clause stating "there shall be no delegations" or words to that effect.

SOME PRACTICAL ADVICE

It is quite likely that at some point in your business career—or your personal life, for that matter—you will find yourself either the third-party beneficiary of a contract or one of the original parties to a contract that has a third-party beneficiary. If you are an original party to any contract, it is important to be aware of all parties whom that contract directly or indirectly benefits or affects. After all, if a clear relationship can be established, it may be that the third party will have legal rights under the contract. And if it is your intention to grant those rights, why not make that intention explicit? While an intended beneficiary may have a relatively easy time obtaining his or her rights through legal channels, there is always the chance for confusion or misunderstanding when such a beneficiary is not named directly as a party to the contract.

If you are a potential third-party beneficiary, it is well to be aware of your legal rights. Recognize, however, that in order to claim rights under a contract, you will have to demonstrate that you are an intended beneficiary of that contract, or that contract rights have been assigned to you by the previous beneficiary.

Assignments and delegations can complicate contractual relationships immensely. Including in contracts clauses that forbid either or both of these transactions may gain you the support of the court. However, it's well to be aware that assignments—unlike delegations—will normally be allowed by the court even when expressly forbidden within the contract. But, such a provision will at least guarantee you, as an original contracting party, the assurance that the assignor will be held liable for any loss you incur as a result of the transfer. Since there's nothing especially complex about assignments—no special language is required, no forms, no consideration even—there's little practical guarantee that the rights within a contract will not be assigned to someone else.

Keep in mind, though, that this practice of assigning rights often works to your benefit. In a person-to-person contract, such a transfer might cause considerable inconvenience. But when a person is dealing with a corporation, he or she is unlikely even to be aware of the assignment of rights to another party—or to be much affected by it. In short, there's nothing inherently problematic about the assignment of contract rights. However, if you can demonstrate to a court's satisfaction that assignment will compromise your contractual rights, the assignment may not be allowed. Nevertheless, if you're involved in a contract where you anticipate problems with a transfer of rights, it may be wise to seek legal advice to determine what can be done to prevent the transfer before it occurs.

If you're contracting for the performance of a service or activity or the delivery of some goods, you can take comfort in knowing that the duties outlined within a contract cannot readily be delegated to someone else; courts tend to be somewhat hostile to that practice. If you are the person obligated to perform under the contract, it's also wise to be aware that if you try to delegate your duties to another party without the approval of the other original contracting party, you are not likely to win the court's support for that action. In summary, courts readily approve the transfer of contractual rights, but rarely support the transfer of contractual obligations.

ASSIGNMENTS

- Before you watch the video program, be sure you've read through the preceding overview, familiarized yourself with the learning objectives for this lesson, and looked at the key terms below. Then, read Chapter 15 of Davidson et al., *Business Law*.
- After completing these tasks, view the video program for Lesson 12.
- After watching the program, take time to review what you've learned. First, evaluate your learning with the self-test which follows the key terms. Then, apply and evaluate what you've learned with the "Your Opinion, Please" scenarios at the end of this telecourse study guide lesson.

KEY TERMS

Before you read through the textbook assignment and watch the video program, take a minute to look at the key terms associated with this lesson. When you encounter them in the textbook and video program, pay careful attention to their meaning.

Assignee	Contractual rights
Assignment	Creditor beneficiary
Assignor	Delegation
Beneficiaries	Delegant
Consideration	Delegatee
Contractual duties	Donee beneficiary

First-in-time approach (American Rule)

Intended beneficiary

First-to-give-notice rule (English Rule)

Promisee

Incidental beneficiary

Promisor

Third-party beneficiary

SELF-TEST

The questions below will help you evaluate how well you've learned the material in this lesson. Read each one carefully, and select the letter of the option that best answers the question. You'll find the correct answer, along with a reference to the page number(s) where the topic is discussed, in the back of this telecourse study guide.

1. Persons or corporations that receive rights through a contract they have never signed are known as third-party

   a. beneficiaries.
   b. delegants.
   c. assignors.
   d. promisees.

2. The city contracts with Laidlow Paving to construct sidewalks throughout a residential area. In relation to the city's contract with Laidlow, the residents of the area are

   a. intended beneficiaries.
   b. incidental beneficiaries.
   c. donee beneficiaries.
   d. *None* of the above; the residents are not beneficiaries at all.

3. Jones purchases life insurance on his own life, naming his daughter as beneficiary. In this example, who is the promisor?

   a. Jones
   b. Jones's daughter
   c. The life insurance company
   d. *None* of the above; there is no promisor in this example.

4. Menefee and her housemate Nettles decide Menefee should purchase an insurance policy on her life as part of their joint household's investment plan. Nettles is named as beneficiary. If Menefee suddenly decides she will no longer pay the premiums, what might Nettles, as a third-party beneficiary, reasonably do?

   a. She can sue Menefee for breach of contract.
   b. She can sue the insurance company for breach of contract.

   c. She can sue Menefee and the insurance company simultaneously, thus doubling the value of the original contract.

   d. *None* of the above are likely to be successful for her.

5. In the preceding example (Question 4), Menefee's housemate is a

   a. creditor beneficiary.

   b. donee beneficiary.

   c. incidental beneficiary.

   d. assignee.

6. In most ways, in comparison to a donee beneficiary, a creditor beneficiary has

   a. about the same legal rights.

   b. substantially greater legal rights.

   c. substantially fewer legal rights.

   d. virtually no legal rights whatever.

7. When judging whether someone or some group is a third-party beneficiary, which one of these criteria has to be met?

   a. The third party has knowledge of the contract.

   b. The third party is affected by the contract.

   c. The third party approves of the contract terms.

   d. The third party actually signs the contract.

8. Jensen works for a company whose policy is to give a year-end bonus, based on sales production. Jensen asked the company to donate his bonus every year to Pickwick Players, a local theater organization. In this scenario, Pickwick is

   a. a creditor beneficiary.

   b. an assignor.

   c. an assignee.

   d. a donee beneficiary.

9. In the preceding scenario (Question 8), the relationship between Jensen and Pickwick involves

   a. a gift.

   b. a contract.

   c. an obligation.

   d. We cannot say without knowing whether Jensen receives any consideration for the money.

10. Suppose that Jensen (Questions 8 and 9) told Pickwick on December 1 that he would send them the bonus money. On December 5, he informed Platt School that they would receive the money. Only Platt School informed Jensen's employer of Jensen's intention. According to the first-in-time approach, also known as the American Rule, the money would *probably* go to

   a. Pickwick.

   b. Platt.

    c. both Pickwick and Platt, being evenly divided between them.

    d. neither Pickwick nor Platt; under this rule, such a conflict prevents a gift from going to either party.

YOUR OPINION, PLEASE

Read each of the following scenarios and answer the questions about the decisions you would make in each situation. Give these questions some serious thought; they may be used as the basis for the development of a more complex essay. You should base your decisions on what you've learned from this lesson, though you may incorporate outside readings or information gained through your own experience if it is relevant.

Scenario I

Oletzke stipulates in his will that his house and the surrounding ten-acre property will go to his sister, Ruth Hemby, upon his death. Since he is twelve years older than Ruth, he has good reason to suppose that she will outlive him. Further, he feels a certain obligation to provide for his sister since she is a widow who has never been employed and has only limited sources of income. Hemby's daughter, Helen, who has always lived with and cared for her mother, assumes the house will one day be hers (Helen's). Oletzke is fully aware of Helen's assumption and has never said anything to discourage it or suggest it was in any way unreasonable. He often expresses his gratitude to Helen for caring for his sister, and Helen assumes that Oletzke means for her to have the house as a means of repaying her for that dedication. Oletzke never says this directly, however, nor is Helen Hemby's name mentioned in the will.

    Helen Hemby has never been married. Though employed, she does not earn sufficient income to support a household on her own. She and her mother are dependent on their combined incomes to meet their daily living expenses.

    When Ruth Hemby unexpectedly dies in an automobile accident, Oletzke changes his will and leaves his house to a charitable organization with the stipulation that upon his death the house will be sold at auction and the proceeds given to the charity. Upon learning of the change, Helen Hemby immediately protests, claiming that she had rights as an intended beneficiary of the original will. She alleges that Oletzke always meant for the house to belong to her ultimately, and that she relied upon that promise. Oletzke tells Hemby he is sorry, but that his sense of obligation extended only to her mother. At that point, Helen Hemby determines to sue Oletzke to have her named as his beneficiary.

    What's your opinion? Based on what you know of the situation, do you think Hemby can successfully sue Oletzke? Or is Oletzke quite within his rights to exclude Hemby at this point from the will?

- Is Hemby likely to be successful in her lawsuit? Why or why not?
- What factors support your answer?
- What factors might an attorney cite in arguing against your view?
- What steps, if any, might Oletzke have taken to prevent a lawsuit in this situation?
- What steps, if any, might Hemby have taken to prevent a lawsuit in this situation?

Scenario 2

Rainey contracts with Gunderson, a master carpenter, for the construction of a rosewood desk for Rainey's new office. The contract specifically names Paul R. Rainey and Gunderson Carpentry as the contracting parties. The cost of the rosewood desk is $6,000. Rainey feels this price is high, but agrees to it because he has seen and admired Gunderson's work.

Before he is able to do more than cut the wood for the desk, Gunderson finds himself falling behind on his projects. He has taken on more work than he can reasonably hope to complete, and none of his clients, including Rainey, are open to granting him extensions. Not wishing to default on the contract with Rainey—which specifies that the desk will be completed by July 1—Gunderson contracts with a fellow craftsman, Whitcombe, to finish the desk. He does not tell Rainey of this decision at the time. Whitcombe does a reasonably good job, Gunderson feels, though perhaps not quite up to his own standards. He believes that the differences are visible only to a trained eye and that no one who is not familiar with carpentry is likely to spot them.

Rainey himself likes the desk very much until he discovers that Gunderson has not personally done the work. At that point, he is very unhappy. He contends that he would not have contracted with Gunderson Carpentry except with the implied understanding that Gunderson himself would build the desk. Gunderson points out that Rainey contracted with the company, not with him individually, and that the contract did not expressly forbid delegations. He further points out that since the desk was expressly built for Rainey, according to his specifications, he (Gunderson) cannot as readily sell it to someone else, even though it is a fine piece of furniture. Rainey, however, refuses to pay for the desk, arguing that it is not what he contracted for. Gunderson, who cannot afford a $6,000 loss, sues Rainey for breach of contract.

What's your opinion? Based on what you know of the situation, was Gunderson within his rights to delegate the work to Whitcombe? Or was he obligated to build the desk himself?

- Is the court likely to support Gunderson in his claim against Rainey?
- What factors support your answer?
- What factors might an attorney cite in arguing against your view?

- What steps, if any, might Gunderson have taken to prevent a lawsuit in this situation?
- What steps, if any, might Rainey have taken to prevent a lawsuit in this situation?

13

Performance and Discharge

LEARNING OBJECTIVES

Upon completing your study of this lesson, you should be able to

- Define the term *discharge of a contract*.
- Identify and describe the four ways in which a contract is normally discharged.
- Distinguish between *complete performance* and *substantial performance*, and discuss the implications of this distinction for discharge of a contract.
- Identify and discuss four methods by which the contracting parties themselves can agree to discharge the contract (e.g., release, rescission, accord and satisfaction, novation).
- Discuss several circumstances where a contract may be discharged by operation of the law.
- Identify and discuss the four circumstances under which a contract can be discharged by nonperformance (e.g., impossibility, commercial frustration, breach, and conditions).

We usually think of contracts as ending when both parties have completed their sides of the bargain in accordance with contract specifications. But in fact, that is only one means of discharging a contract. It sometimes happens, for instance, that one or both parties will reconsider the situation and want out of the contract, or, for whatever reason, fulfillment of contract terms becomes extraordinarily difficult—or even impossible. As we'll see in this lesson, there are, fortunately, several means of discharging contracts to handle these and various other circumstances.

OVERVIEW

Parties don't generally—and shouldn't—enter into a contract with the idea that one or the other will get tired of the situation and want out of the contract. Nor should they expect that some unforeseen circumstance will probably make completion of the contract difficult or impossible. Were this the way of things, contracts would command little respect or attention. And the fact is, contracting parties usually enter the contract with good faith, intending to fulfill their obligations. Moreover, that is most often precisely what happens.

When both parties do whatever it is the contract calls for, that is another way of saying that their duties under that contract have been *discharged*. The discharge of a contract represents *the legally valid termination of a contract duty*.

Note that termination, however, is not necessarily the same thing as completion. Under some circumstances, a contract may be terminated (that is, ended) legally before the duties outlined in that contract have been totally, or even partially, concluded. This is fairly rare, but it happens. In fact, there are four means by which a contract duty can be legally discharged:

- by performance (the most common means),
- by agreement of the parties,
- by operation of law, and
- by nonperformance.

We'll take a closer look at each of these in the discussion that follows.

Discharge by Performance

When the parties do whatever the contract calls for, their actions constitute performance. Under the law, there are two degrees of performance: *complete performance* and *substantial performance*. Complete performance, as its name suggests, constitutes the parties' *exact fulfillment of the terms of the contract* in a manner that satisfies the intent of the contract. In other words, the parties have done what they set out to do; they have lived up to their original reason for contracting. For instance, say Hemming contracts with North for the delivery of eight truckloads of hay at $6 a bale; North delivers the eight truckloads of hay and Hemming pays the specified price upon delivery. At that point, the contract between North and Hemming is discharged by complete performance.

Substantial performance occurs when one party makes a good faith effort to live up to the terms of the contract, but there are some *minor deviations* from contract specifications. In many cases, the law will view substantial performance as sufficient even though, technically, it involves a breach of contract. Whether the performance will be considered sufficient depends on two factors: (1) the seriousness of the breach itself, and (2) whether the breach was willful.

For example, let's say Johnson contracts to typeset a company newsletter for Frost. According to the contract, the final copy will be "camera-ready, error-free" copy. When proofreading the final printed edition, Frost notices a typographical error toward the bottom of the last page; it's the only error in the entire newsletter. Has Johnson breached the contract? Technically, yes. The copy is not "error-free." However, the error is not particularly serious. Further, given that the rest of the copy is in fact error-free, there is substantial evidence to suggest that Johnson acted in good faith in attempting to live up to a very demanding contract—and nearly succeeded.

On the other hand, suppose Johnson is merrily handing out copies of his new corporate newsletter and notices to his horror that several article headlines on the front page are incorrect. Misspellings abound, words have been omitted, and entire paragraphs of stories have been printed out of order. Here we have a very different situation. The breach here is such that it undermines the very purpose of the contract itself; no one would willingly contract with a printer who did such work. Further, the number and seriousness of the errors suggest negligence on Johnson's part; he'll have a hard time demonstrating that he acted in good faith. In this case, a court would likely hold that Johnson had not substantially performed the duties required under the contract and would likely rule for Frost in a suit for damages.

Notice that the two cases we've presented here are extremes: one tiny error versus an abundance of relatively serious errors. Just where does the court draw the line in determining whether the performance is substantial performance, sufficient to discharge the responsibilities of the performing party? Frequently, it's a matter of judgment. And the court will generally ask, "What would be the response of a reasonably prudent person under similar circumstances?" In our preceding examples, for instance, no reasonably prudent person would likely make much fuss over one unimportant typographical error in an otherwise perfect multi-page document; a document riddled with errors, however, would be expected to raise the blood pressure of even the most forgiving among our population of hypothetical "reasonably prudent persons."

One particularly sticky situation involves contracts that require one party to perform "to the satisfaction" of the other. In such cases, the court will usually apply the reasonable-person approach *if* the judgment to be made is relatively objective, rather than a matter of personal taste. It helps, of course, if the contracting parties have included precise specifications within the contract. For instance, suppose Huber contracts with Brumbley to build a house and specifies within the contract that the floors will be level to "within 1/16 of an inch." In that case, it's fairly simple to determine just how good performance has to be to meet expectations.

In other cases, the court will use marketability or mechanical performance as a guide to "satisfaction." For example, suppose Martin contracts with Ace Motors to service her car "to the owner's satisfaction." Despite this wording, Martin cannot reasonably expect to keep Ace working round the clock indefinitely simply by saying she isn't happy yet. The court is more likely to take the position that once the car is operating as well as could be expected, given its age, condition, or other relevant factors, Ace has done enough to satisfy the "reasonably prudent person."

Courts will *sometimes* take the reasonable person perspective where personal taste is involved—but often not. It frequently depends on the recourse open to the dissatisfied party. For example, suppose Brown purchases a sport coat from Wellner's Clothiers, but it requires extensive alteration. Brown pays for the coat. The contract specifies that the alterations "will be done to the customer's complete satisfaction." When Brown tries on the altered coat, the tailor and salesman think it looks wonderful, but Brown is unhappy. Has Wellner breached the contract? The courts will often say yes, and require that Wellner fulfill Brown's expectations in order to discharge the contract—even if those expectations would seem unreasonable to an outsider. (However, Brown, as a dissatisfied customer, probably has a duty to return merchandise he's unhappy with.)

Contrast this situation with one in which Brown contracts with Stonehenge Builders for construction of a house. After moving in, Brown decides the house is not to his satisfaction after all. He cannot simply return it for a refund, however. In this case, the court might be more likely to apply the doctrine of substantial performance. In other words, the court will hold that Stonehenge has substantially fulfilled the contract. That puts Brown in the position of having to pay for the house in accordance with the contract terms while being free to sue for damages (which he'll collect if he can show that the deviation from the contract warrants them). For example, if Stonehenge has used substandard plumbing pipe, Brown will have little difficulty showing that he is entitled to damages. If his primary complaint is that the fireplace "just doesn't look the way I'd pictured it," he'll understandably have a more difficult time.

Discharge by Agreement of the Parties

As mentioned above, contracts are most often discharged by performance. But the parties themselves can also agree to discharge the contract in one of several other ways: release, rescission, accord and satisfaction, or novation. Let's consider each of these in turn.

Release

A *release*, in effect, is an agreement to give up enforcing the original agreement. One party releases the other from the terms of the contract—usually because something or other has gone awry. The something may or may not be sufficiently serious to provide grounds for a lawsuit, but in either case, one party or the other may be particularly eager to terminate the contract. And in terminating a contract by release, there is usually some consideration involved.

For instance, let's say that Green has also contracted with Stonehenge Builders to build a house. One day, he's having lunch with Brown, who brings up the matter of the substandard piping. Now Green is uneasy; he no longer trusts Stonehenge and would like to end the contract with Stonehenge. Stonehenge, however, may already have completed some preliminary planning and may not want to give up the profit it will eventually make on completing the house. Thus, Green likely will need to provide Stonehenge with some consideration—say an appropriate fee to cover these early expenses and inconvenience—in exchange for which Stonehenge will release Green from the contract.

Rescission

Rescission is a little different. For one thing, it's a mutual agreement rather than one which comes about primarily because one party wants the contract discharged (as with release). Further, it is less likely to involve consideration. In legal terms, rescission is defined as a *voluntary, mutual surrender and discharge of contractual rights and duties whereby the parties are returned to the original status quo*. In other words, rescission leaves the situation as if the parties had never contracted. To illustrate, let's reconstruct our example with Green and Stonehenge Builders, varying the circumstances a little. This time, let's suppose Stonehenge is about to go out of business. Green is their only customer—and they'd just as soon get out of the contract with him. When Stonehenge begins the discussions with Green, Green tells them he feels he acted hastily, that he doesn't feel ready to build a house just now. Stonehenge replies that that's a happy coincidence indeed because they're about to be out of the building business altogether. *Mutually*, without consideration on either side, both parties agree to terminate the contract.

Rescissions may be written or oral; either way they're legally binding. It may occur to you, of course, that the oral rescission of a written contract could be risky. If Stonehenge later decides to remain in the building business, they may wish to carry out the contract with Green. And while an oral rescission is legally binding, Green might have a difficult time convincing the court that he and Stonehenge Builders in fact mutually agreed *not* to build the house for which Green contracted in writing.

Accord and Satisfaction

Sometimes contracting parties do not wish to end a contract; they just want to modify it. An agreement to accept performance different from that required by the original bargain is known as an *accord*. And when the parties *comply with the accord, satisfaction* occurs. To illustrate, let's go back to our earlier Stonehenge customer, Brown. Recall that he was unhappy, in our example, with the look of his fireplace. Let's suppose that early in construction, before the fireplace was completed, Brown decided that instead of a small corner fireplace made of metal he wanted a see-through fireplace of natural stone, two stories high.

Obviously, such a change would materially alter the contract—but it could be done, if both parties were willing. And that's the key. An accord is only binding if there is evidence of agreement on both sides—and that usually means a written agreement. Further, the accord becomes legally binding only when the required performance—the satisfaction—is given. In this case, Brown and Stonehenge would have to modify or amend the original contract to reflect the addition of the new fireplace, and the agreement would become binding upon the completion of that fireplace.

Novation

In the case of Brown and the fireplace, the substitution involves the performance of the parties—a different fireplace built by Stonehenge, more money (we presume) paid by Brown. Under certain conditions, the substitution might involve different parties; in these instances, the modification is known as a *novation*. A novation involves the substitution of a party who was *neither owed a duty nor obligated to perform in the original contract*.

A novation differs from an accord in two important respects. First, recall that an accord is not legally binding—does not change the parties' rights and obligations—until the substituted performance (the building of the new fireplace, in the preceding example) is concluded. A novation, however, *immediately discharges* the previously existing contractual obligation. Second, a novation *must* be supported by consideration.

For example, suppose that during negotiations about Brown's massive fireplace, Stonehenge explains that their crews have no experience working with stone; thus, they would rather help Brown get in touch with an experienced stonemason with whom Brown would contract directly. Brown will agree to the substitution for a consideration: Stonehenge must reduce the cost of the house by $1,000, about what the metal fireplace originally specified would have cost. As soon as Brown agrees to the novation, Stonehenge is released from their original obligation to install *any* fireplace.

Discharge by Operation of Law

In some cases, the law can mandate the discharge of certain contracts. This occurs, for instance, where one party files for bankruptcy. A final order of bankruptcy automatically discharges that party's contractual obligations—and covered creditors may not sue to recover money previously owed. (In some states, however, those obligations may be revived at a later time, if the *debtor* so desires.)

Certain classes of statutes can cause the discharge of a contract. Statutes of limitations, for example, set limits on the length of time a contracting party may wait to bring suit. For example, when one party fails to pay for goods purchased from the other, the seller must usually file suit within the time set by the applicable law for raising the legal problem. Suits begun after that time will not be allowed to continue. (Usually, however, it is up to the defendant to raise the statute of limitations issue, and if the defendant doesn't object, the suit can go ahead.) The time allowed by the statute of limitations for any particular problem varies depending on state law, federal law, the nature of the transaction, and the legal theory under which the plaintiff is seeking relief.

The law will also discharge any contract that has been materially altered by one party without the express consent of the other. For example — to return for a moment to Brown and Stonehenge — suppose that Brown was quite happy with his plans for the original metal corner fireplace. However, the Stonehenge architect concluded that a see-through stone fireplace piercing through a seventeen-foot cathedral ceiling would be far more dramatic. The change would be worth doing, Stonehenge decided, even at no charge to Brown, because it would help attract customers. Unfortunately for Stonehenge, however, even if they are truly providing something of greater value with no increase in cost to Brown, they could not make that substitution without Brown's consent. Such a substantial substitution would constitute a material alteration of the contract and, without the other party's express consent, a discharge of the contract.

Discharge by Nonperformance

We've already seen that performance of a contract will discharge the obligations of that contract. In some cases, nonperformance will have the same effect. There are four circumstances under which this may occur: impossibility, commercial frustration (or commercial impracticability), breach, and failure to meet conditions. Let's consider each of these in turn.

Impossibility

Impossibility refers to an unforeseen event or condition that precludes the possibility of the party's performing as promised. For example, Wilson contracts with Stonehenge to buy a particular house Stonehenge built. However, the day after the contract is signed, the house is struck by lightning and destroyed in the ensuing fire. There is no way for the contract to be fulfilled; since Stonehenge can't provide the house, it's impossible for Wilson to buy it.

Similarly, an intervening law will sometimes result in discharge by nonperformance. Suppose a local rancher, Murdock, contracts with an Australian rancher, Thomas, to import sheep. Before Thomas can ship the sheep, a law is passed forbidding the importation of sheep. Again, there is no way that Thomas — or anyone else — can fulfill the contract, can get the sheep to Murdock.

Sometimes, the conduct of one party makes fulfillment of the contract by the other impossible. Let's say a local producer contracts with a touring theater company to stage a special benefit performance. Later it's discovered that he's already booked the theater for another purpose on the night of the benefit. In this example, one contracting party—the local producer—has taken action that makes performance by the other contracting party—the touring company—impossible.

Notice that in each of these examples, nonperformance is unavoidable; there is simply no way out. No amount of good will or effort on the part of the contracting parties could change the circumstances. In the court's eyes, this situation is viewed as *objective impossibility*—the sort of situation in which you simply cannot force the performance called for in the contract.

Some courts have held, however, that *subjective impossibility*—that is, nonperformance owing to a difficult personal situation—will not discharge contractual obligations. For example, if our Australian rancher, Thomas, simply had a bad year and didn't have as many lambs to export as he'd anticipated, the court would likely take the position that as a professional rancher and exporter, he should have anticipated this difficulty and made allowances for it prior to contracting. In other words, his personal difficulties would not absolve him of his contractual obligation. Similarly, if the members of the touring theater company had problems making their engagement because the truck carrying the stage sets broke down, the court would probably take the position that, as professionals, they could be expected to have reliable transportation and now should have to compensate for the difficulties they "caused."

Commercial Frustration

Note that the circumstances of objective impossibility tend to be quite rigid. In fact, the courts rarely discharge contracts on this basis. (In personal services contracts, death and disability of one party are usually the only situations in which a court will discharge a contract for impossibility.) Because this rule is so rigid, the *doctrine of commercial frustration* has recently emerged as a basis for nonperformance. This doctrine excuses performance in cases where *the essential purpose and value of the contract have been frustrated*. Even so, if the event causing this frustration could have been anticipated, the court will not allow the discharge of the contract.

Suppose that the herd that rancher Murdock purchased from Australian Thomas was halfway across the Pacific when the sheep contracted a rare virus brought on board from another source. There was no way Thomas could have foreseen this difficulty, and the doctrine of commercial frustration might be used in any lawsuit arising out of this situation. On the other hand, if the infection was a common one and could have been prevented if Thomas had taken the time and trouble to vaccinate his stock, the court would be very unlikely to accept the doctrine of commercial frustration if offered as a defense by Thomas. In other words, a court would likely enforce the contract as written.

Breach

Breach of contract occurs when one or more contracting parties fails to perform according to the terms set forth in the contract. A *complete* breach (also called an *actual* breach) involves nonperformance of some duty so *material* to the agreement that in its absence the contract has little or no purpose. For instance, Riles signs an employment agreement with Millford Hardware but—without a word—never shows up for work. Not showing up for work is a pretty material breach of an employment agreement, so Millford has every reason to consider the agreement terminated.

Anticipatory Breach

Anticipatory breach is different in that it involves giving advance notice, either through words or conduct, that one does not intend to fulfill a contract as written. Let's turn the preceding example around a bit. Suppose Millford and Riles contract for Riles to serve as store manager. But the day before Riles is supposed to report for work, Millford phones him to say they've hired someone else and do not intend to honor the employment agreement. Or, suppose that a week before his new job is scheduled to begin, Riles wanders by the hardware store and discovers, to his surprise and consternation, that Sawyer's Wrecking is demolishing the building because Millford has gone out of business. In either case, Millford's actions—which clearly indicate it doesn't intend to fulfill its contract with Riles—constitute an anticipatory breach of contract. After acting reasonably to check with Millford, Riles is within his legal rights to discharge the contract. (Riles, of course, may well have other remedies to pursue as well.)

Contracting parties sometimes set forth certain conditions within a contract that must be met in order for the contract to be discharged by performance. If these conditions are not met, the contract is automatically discharged by nonperformance. For instance, in our earlier example, the American rancher Murdock might stipulate in his contract with the Australian rancher Thomas that he would accept the sheep *only* on condition that they arrived in excellent health. If they did not, the contract would be discharged through nonperformance—since the stipulated condition of arrival in excellent health was not met.

SOME PRACTICAL ADVICE

What advice can we offer the prudent businessperson based upon this lesson? First, never assume that a contract will be carried out precisely as written. That's often the case, but it's far from inevitable. After signing a contract, for instance, you—or the party with whom you contract—may come to view your situation differently, and want to either rescind or change the contract in some way. Similarly, there's always the chance that one or more terms within the contract will become difficult or impossible to meet, for whatever reason. Therefore, the wise and cautious businessperson will prepare for eventualities. Ask some "What if?" questions to anticipate the consequences of potential obstacles and "disasters"—including the other party's failure to fulfill the contract terms as you see them. And to the extent possible, attempt to cover these eventualities in the contract.

Second, don't ever expect the courts to bail you out of a bad bargain. Keep in mind that most contracts are upheld. In the eyes of the court, difficult circumstances do not constitute impossibility of performance. From a legal perspective, the professional businessperson is expected to anticipate—and prepare for—diverse twists of fate. Thus, running out of time, money, or resources will not normally win you the sympathy of the court or free you from contractual obligations.

Third, if your contractual requirements are precise, be sure they're reflected accurately and totally within the contract. In many cases, substantial performance is regarded as sufficient to discharge contractual duties (though as the party providing the performance, you should not count on it!). Even if you suffer as the result of the other party's failure at complete performance, you'll have to prove material damages in order to sue successfully if the performance can be viewed as substantial.

Finally, beware of clauses requiring performance "to the satisfaction" of the contracting party. Such subjective interpretations are frequently tricky to handle. If you are the party responsible for the performance, you may have a difficult time indeed living up to someone else's expectations. And if you're the party holding the high expectations, realize that while some courts will enforce your right to be as particular as you wish, you'll often be required to settle for the more down-to-earth standards that a reasonably prudent person would apply.

ASSIGNMENTS

- Before you watch the video program, be sure you've read through the preceding overview, familiarized yourself with the learning objectives for this lesson, and looked at the key terms below. Then, read Chapter 16 of Davidson et al., *Business Law.*

- After completing these tasks, view the video program for Lesson 13.

- After watching the program, take time to review what you've learned. First, evaluate your learning with the self-test which follows the key terms. Then, apply and evaluate what you've learned with the "Your Opinion, Please" scenarios at the end of this telecourse study guide lesson.

KEY TERMS

Before you read through the textbook assignment and watch the video program, take a minute to look at the key terms associated with this lesson. When you encounter them in the textbook and video program, pay careful attention to their meaning.

Accord and satisfaction	Express conditions
Actual breach	Express rescission
Anticipatory breach	Implied conditions
Commercial frustration	Implied rescission
Commercially impracticable	Impossibility
Complete performance	Material duty
Conditions (limitations, qualifications)	Nonperformance
Degrees of performance	Novation
Discharge	Performance
Discharge by agreement	Release
Discharge by operation of law	Rescission
Discharge by performance	Substantial performance

SELF-TEST

The questions below will help you evaluate how well you've learned the material in this lesson. Read each one carefully, and select the letter of the option that best answers the question. You'll find the correct answer, along with a reference to the page number(s) where the topic is discussed, in the back of this telecourse study guide.

1. According to the text, the legally valid termination of a contractual duty is known as
   a. discharge of the contract.
   b. substantial performance.
   c. contractual release.
   d. rescission.

2. The doctrine of substantial performance can be applied to discharge the duties of the performing party *only* where
   a. there is no breach of contract.
   b. any breach of contract is both material and willful.
   c. any breach of contract is material but not willful.
   d. any breach of contract is neither material nor willful.

3. Sullivan signs an employment agreement with Keller Construction. Two days after signing, Sullivan receives a job offer from Big Sky Construction for considerably more money. He explains the situation and asks to be released from the Keller contract. Keller agrees orally, provided Sullivan will help them find a replacement. Is this release valid?
   a. No, because it is not supported by consideration.
   b. No, because a release must be in writing to be valid.

    c. Yes; it meets the requirements for a valid release.

    d. We cannot say without knowing whether Sullivan has yet done any work for Keller.

4. A rescission usually occurs when

    a. one party wants out of the contract but the other does not.

    b. neither party wants out, but it is clear that one party cannot fulfill the terms of the agreement.

    c. each party commits a serious breach of contract that undermines the value of the contract to the other party.

    d. both parties want to terminate the contract.

5. Clark contracts to deliver two tons of chicken feed to Whitney's chicken ranch. Upon reflection, Whitney decides he needs another half-ton of feed, and Clark agrees to deliver it. This new agreement is *best* defined as

    a. express rescission.

    b. implied rescission.

    c. release.

    d. accord and satisfaction.

6. Which of the following is the *most common* means of discharging a contract?

    a. Discharge by operation of the law

    b. Discharge by nonperformance

    c. Discharge by performance

    d. Discharge by agreement of the parties

7. Ely Enterprises rents a convention hall from VastVision for a series of workshops for business managers. Because of poor advance enrollment, Ely wants out of the contract. VastVision agrees when they learn that Mindset, Inc., Ely's major rival, is willing to assume the contract and rent the convention center for the same dates. The transaction described in this scenario is known as

    a. novation.

    b. accord and satisfaction.

    c. discharge by operation of law.

    d. release.

8. The transaction described in Question 7 will become legally binding *only when*

    a. Ely Enterprises agrees to let Mindset rent the hall.

    b. some consideration is provided to VastVision.

    c. consideration is provided to Mindset, Inc.

    d. satisfaction occurs.

9. The court would be *most likely* to support discharge by nonperformance in a case where

    a. a foreseeable shortage of materials made it difficult for one party to fulfill contract obligations.

    b. insolvency left one party unable to complete the contract as written.

    c. the passage of a new law made the terms of the original contract illegal.

    d. price increases made the terms of the contract far less profitable to one or both contracting parties.

10. Hanes tells Miller that he will purchase an automobile from Miller for $12,000—on condition that Miller will fully service the car and deliver it to Hanes by February 1. If Miller fails to meet these conditions, which one of the following will be true?

    a. Hanes is free of any obligation to purchase the car.

    b. Hanes is still obligated to buy the car, but he can deduct the cost of having the service done (and, perhaps, renting a car) from the amount he owes Miller.

    c. Hanes's obligation to buy the car can be discharged, but only if he can get Miller's written admission that Miller failed to meet the conditions.

    d. Hanes is still obligated to buy the car, but at a lower cost that the court will determine.

YOUR OPINION, PLEASE

Read each of the following scenarios and answer the questions about the decisions you would make in each situation. Give these questions some serious thought; they may be used as the basis for the development of a more complex essay. You should base your decisions on what you've learned from this lesson, though you may incorporate outside readings or information gained through your own experience if it is relevant.

Scenario 1

Steele contracts with Evergood Builders to build a house. Steele makes it clear, both orally and in writing, that he wants the house to have a prefinished metal roof in a color that blends in with the exterior of the house—a natural, unstained cedar. In fact, the manufacturer's product number and color code for the metal roofing are written into the contract. Some unforeseeable problems with the foundation delay the construction by approximately six weeks. When the time comes to install the roof, Evergood is unable to get hold of the precise roofing Steele has ordered. A call to the roofing supplier reveals that that particular color has all been sold; the manufacturer tells Evergood that they can provide more, but there will be a four- to six-month wait before they run that color again.

    Delaying completion of the roof is not a good option, especially with winter weather approaching. Evergood thus takes what they consider to be the most prudent course: they substitute roofing of a very similar color from another manufacturer. They feel it's a good compromise, but Steele is unhappy. He claims that Evergood has breached the contract by failing to provide the materials specified (by product number and color code, no less) in the contract; he refuses to pay the amount of the construction cost attributable to the roof. Evergood counters that they have come as close as possible, under the circumstances, to fulfilling the terms of the bargain, and they sue for recovery of the contract price of the roof.

What's your opinion? Based on what you know of the situation, do you think Evergood can successfully sue for recovery of the roofing costs? Is Steele right in alleging that Evergood has breached the contract?

- Is Evergood likely to win a suit for recovery of the roofing costs?
- What factors support your answer?
- What factors might an attorney cite in arguing against your view?
- What steps, if any, might Evergood have taken to prevent a lawsuit in this situation?
- What steps, if any, might Steele have taken to prevent a lawsuit in this situation?

Scenario 2

Edison Computers contracts with Top Bill, an advertising agency, to promote its new pocket-size personal computer. The contract calls for Top Bill to write and produce a series of radio commercials that, subject to approval by Edison, Top Bill will distribute nationally. The contract specifies that the "content and wording of all promotional materials must meet Edison's normal high standards of professionalism and quality in every respect."

During a preliminary review of early scripts, Edison managers become very unhappy. They claim the commercials are entirely "too gimmicky," and that they are "not in keeping with the company's professional, executive-oriented image." In fact, Edison claims, the commercials are nothing like what they intended to receive when they wrote the original contract.

Top Bill suggests that perhaps Edison would be happier with a TV promotional campaign, and that the radio scripts might be rewritten slightly to accommodate that approach. Edison agrees that this sounds like a good compromise, and signs a written amendment to the first contract specifying that the radio scripts will be revised for television production. Meanwhile, Top Bill wants to be paid for development of the original radio scripts. Edison says no; the scripts were not written to their satisfaction, and in any case, the contract specifies that the radio scripts will be replaced with the television scripts; under the doctrine of accord and satisfaction, Edison argues, that is all they need to pay for. Top Bill counters that this will not be a satisfactory solution, since the fee for the television scripts does not cover the original development costs. They intend to sue for recovery of the $20,000 they have invested in development of the original radio commercials.

What's your opinion? Based on what you know of the situation, do you think Top Bill can successfully sue for recovery of the original $20,000 investment? Or is Edison right in alleging that under the doctrine of accord and satisfaction, they can only be held responsible for the $50,000 required to revise the scripts for television?

- Is Top Bill likely to be successful in their suit for recovery of the $20,000?
- What factors support your answer?
- What factors might an attorney cite in arguing against your view?
- What steps, if any, might Top Bill have taken to prevent a lawsuit in this situation?
- What steps, if any, might Edison have taken to prevent a lawsuit in this situation?

14

Contractual Remedies

LEARNING OBJECTIVES

Upon completing your study of this lesson, you should be able to

- Define the term *contractual remedy*, describe its purpose, and distinguish between *legal remedies* and *equitable remedies*.

- Define the term *damages* and explain how damages are assessed in bringing about contractual remedies.

- Distinguish among *compensatory*, *consequential*, *punitive*, *liquidated*, and *nominal* damages.

- Discuss the concept of *equitable remedies* and explain the circumstances under which a court might award equitable remedies, using a hypothetical example to illustrate your explanation.

- List and discuss five specific types of equitable relief (e.g., rescission, restitution), explaining the requirements imposed by the court under each circumstance.

What happens when one party or the other fails to live up to the obligations set forth in a contract? Answering that question is what this lesson is all about. As we shall see, several courses of action, known generally as *remedies*, are open to the "injured" party—that is, the party who does not receive the performance he or she deserves according to the contract. Most of us tend to think of contractual remedies as involving damages—money paid by one party to the other—and, often, damages of one kind or another are awarded. Sometimes, however, the court finds other ways of helping the contracting parties fulfill the original intent of the contract. In this lesson, we'll examine both *legal remedies*, which usually involve money damages, and *equitable remedies*, which usually involve finding a way to set things right without the payment of money damages.

OVERVIEW

When contracting parties have done whatever the contract requires them to do, we say that their duties under the contract are discharged. Sometimes, however, one party or the other—for whatever reason—fails to live up to these obligations. This nonperformance constitutes a *breach* of contract, a failure to perform as required; a breach entitles the injured party to certain remedies. A *remedy* is a *cause of action resulting from breach of contract*. In other words, it's a way of attempting to fulfill the contracting parties' expectations at the time the original contract was drawn up, an effort to make things all right again.

Remedies generally fall into two broad categories: *legal* remedies and *equitable* remedies. In general, *legal remedies involve a suit for damages*—an amount of money that would return the injured party to the same economic position that that person would have enjoyed had the other party performed as expected. Legal remedies are, not surprisingly, administered by a court of law.

When such remedies are not well suited to the case at hand—for instance, if it is impossible to determine what the appropriate damages are, or if money alone will not solve the problem—a court may impose equitable remedies. *Equitable remedies are simply efforts to ensure fairness between the contracting parties* and, as we shall see later in this discussion, usually do not involve the exchange of money as damages. Let's start by taking a closer look at legal remedies and the nature of damages.

Damages

As we've noted, a breach of contract entitles the injured party to sue for damages. The law recognizes five different classes or types of damages which can be claimed and awarded in court: compensatory, consequential, punitive, liquidated, and nominal. One or more of these classes of damages may be sought in any one lawsuit, but regardless of the type(s) of damages sought, a court will first look to see whether the injured party attempted to *mitigate* — or minimize — the damages. That is, did the plaintiff take steps to avoid or work around the expected injury of the breach? If the injured party took reasonable steps to mitigate the anticipated damages, then those damages which nevertheless occurred are more likely to be recovered in court.

Compensatory Damages

The most common type of damages is *compensatory damages* — the sum of money that will place the party in the same economic position that would have been enjoyed had the contract been performed. Sometimes that sum is readily determined, sometimes not. It is not, however, required that the injured party be able to compute this sum precisely; the court will make that determination. The injured party must, however, show that a loss of economic position did in fact result directly from the breach of contract. The court will also ask whether a reasonable person would have predicted at the time of contracting that the losses claimed to have been suffered would have resulted from a breach of the contract. If the breaching party should have foreseen such consequences, the court will usually award compensatory damages to cover those consequences.

For example, let's say that Niles is a bookseller with his own shop. He contracts with Snelling for the purchase of a computer system that will manage his inventory (over 40,000 volumes) and also handle billing and other accounting functions. The contract calls for Snelling to evaluate Niles's needs and then supply the appropriate computer equipment and software to handle the task by a certain date. Unfortunately, Snelling delivers the equipment ten weeks late, and Niles — having counted on the computer — is unable to carry out his monthly billings on time. His records show that this delay cost the business a great deal of money. Without this income, Niles cannot purchase new inventory, nor can he meet all of his own business expenses, such as rent, utility bills, advertising expenditures, and so forth.

Clearly, Snelling has breached the contract and Niles has suffered some damages. In determining the nature and extent of the damages it will require Snelling to pay, however, the court will ask what the precise costs were to Niles in doing without the computer services for an additional ten weeks and whether Snelling should have foreseen that his failure to deliver the computer system on time would "create" such costs for Niles and his business. And, because Niles does have a duty to mitigate damages, the court will also look to see what Niles did to avoid or reduce the losses caused by the delay in getting the computer.

Consequential Damages

In addition to compensatory damages, courts will sometimes award *consequential damages* — indirect or special damages resulting from the consequences of the breach. For instance, suppose that as a result of not having a computerized billing system, Niles loses a contract to supply textbooks to a local university. Had the system been installed and operating on the day the university contacted him, he would have surely gotten the contract. In determining whether to award consequential damages, the court will consider two important factors: first, whether the breaching party could have reasonably foreseen the indirect damages, and second, whether the injured party took any steps to *mitigate*, or minimize, the loss. Let's consider these one at a time, using our Snelling–Niles example.

First, could Snelling have foreseen Niles's loss of the university contract? Perhaps—but the court will not merely take Niles's word for this. If Niles could show that he specifically told Snelling he wanted the computer system in time to be able to secure an upcoming university contract, that would be one thing; Niles would have the beginnings of a strong claim for consequential damages. On the other hand, if he told Snelling simply that he "wanted to make the business a little more efficient," his case for consequential damages would be much weaker.

Second, as with a decision to award compensatory damages, the court will want to know whether Niles took any steps to mitigate the damages—in other words, did he do his best to minimize the damages to his book company? Did Niles phone Snelling, for instance, to say that he was in a hurry to get the computer installed and that the delay was very detrimental to his business? Did he attempt to acquire a computer system from another source, or see if a computer service could handle the university contract requirements while he was waiting for his own equipment? If Niles took no steps on his own to remedy the situation, his case against Snelling will be much weaker.

Punitive Damages

A third class of damages, *punitive damages*, are those awarded not to compensate the injured party but rather to punish or make an example of the wrongdoer. This "punishment" is handed out in the interest of discouraging the wrongdoer and others from similar behavior in the future. While in most cases, courts will not award punitive damages in breach-of-contract suits, there are some exceptions. These exceptions usually occur when the breaching party not only acts willfully in avoiding contractual obligations, but also engages in behavior that, if not "punished," will set a bad precedent in the business community.

For example, if an insurance company neglected to pay benefits rightfully owed to a client, the court might take the position that discouraging such conduct—through the awarding of punitive damages—was important to the general public welfare. Simply ordering the company to pay the required benefits—ordering compensatory damages—would not deter the company from avoiding paying other claims. On the other hand, if the insurance company could show they had acted in good faith, that they had reason to doubt the benefits were owed, the court would not award punitive damages. The court would, however, still order payment of the benefit amount—the compensatory damages.

Keep in mind that punitive damages (or exemplary damages, as they're sometimes called) are intended—as the name suggests—to impose punishment. Therefore, they're usually reserved for the few cases in which the court determines that the wrongdoing is so serious and flagrant that society demands such conduct be punished. In our insurance example, the company had the contractual duty to pay benefits under the terms of the policy. When it refused to pay benefits—regardless of whether its decision was made in good faith—it breached its insurance contract. This breach allows the injured party to claim compensatory damages. But if the company's bad-faith refusal to pay benefits was sufficiently outrageous, then the injured party might well be able to convince a court to award punitive damages.

Liquidated Damages

Liquidated damages—a sum of money agreed upon in advance by the parties as damages in the event of a breach—are a fourth type of damages. Necessarily, the sum of money—or formula for calculating it—will be specified in the original contract. But even if both parties agree to liquidated damages, the court will not grant them if the amount appears to be a penalty. Two conditions must be met for a court to award liquidated damages and not see the contract clause as a penalty clause. First, the amount agreed to must be reasonable in light of the actual damage to the injured party. Second, it must be difficult or impossible to calculate the actual amount of the damage. In other words, if liquidated damages are so preposterously high that they're out of all proportion to the actual damage, the court will view them as penalties and will not uphold the contract clause that provided for them.

For instance, suppose that our two friends Snelling and Niles had an agreement that for each day Snelling was late delivering the computer system, Niles would owe $50 less on the total contract amount. The court might well view that agreement as just. The amount isn't burdensome and it helps compensate Niles for the inconvenience of not having the computer installed on time. Additionally, it saves the extreme difficulty of having to calculate the real cost created by the late billing problem. All in all, it offers a simple, reasonable means of remedying the problem.

On the other hand, suppose the contract required Snelling (who is confident of his ability to deliver the system on time) to pay Niles $20,000 if the system were even one day late. Given what we know about the transaction and the nature of Niles's business, it's unlikely the court would enforce such an agreement. The amount of liquidated damages called for in the contract is unfairly advantageous to Niles and appears unrelated to any actual loss the parties would reasonably anticipate.

A contract clause covering liquidated damages should not be whimsically inserted into any contract, even as an expression of confidence in performance. It is probably *most* useful in a situation where the contracting parties clearly know their own situation best. Providing for reasonable liquidated damages avoids relying on the future judgment of the court in determining appropriate damages should one or the other party default. For example, such clauses are common in contracts involving construction, where the real "damage" of a delay can be extraordinarily complex to calculate.

Nominal Damages

As we've noted already, *any* breach of contract entitles the injured party to sue for damages. Sometimes, however, the economic damages are so slight that even though technically a breach of contract has occurred, the court is reluctant to do much more than simply acknowledge that breach. For instance, suppose that Snelling was required by contract to deliver the computer system by noon on June 1, and actually delivered the system around 2 p.m. on that date. Technically, Snelling breached the contract. And while he may have caused Niles some slight inconvenience, chances are Niles will have a hard time showing that his whole billing system was thrown into chaos due to the brief delay. In that case, assuming Niles perversely took the trouble to sue, the court might award *nominal damages* — a small amount of compensation given primarily for the principle of the matter.

An award of nominal damages — our fifth type of damages — is the court's way of saying, "Yes, a breach occurred, and we don't condone this sort of thing. But on the other hand, no one really suffered economically, so we're not going to award much compensation." Nominal damages keep things in perspective. Where no real economic injury has occurred, awarding nominal damages underscores the court's perspective that, even though there was no economic loss to recover or pay for, parties should still live up to the terms of the contracts they sign.

Equitable Remedies

When the "legal" remedy of damages is unavailable, indeterminable, or inadequate, *equitable remedies* may be sought by the injured party. This generally occurs, for example, when money really won't remedy the situation, when it is extremely difficult to determine what is owed, or when some other type of action or behavior needs to be ordered. We'll discuss fives different types of equitable remedies: rescission and restitution, specific performance, quasi contract, reformation, and injunction.

Rescision and Restitution

As you may know, contracting parties may voluntarily agree to *rescind* or set aside a contract before either has performed the duties specified by that contract. Their circumstances may have changed, or they may decide mutually that they acted in haste and would simply like to undo the contract. *Rescission* may also be sought in court by one party to a contract when the other party has breached the contract. In this context, rescission refers to a *cancellation or termination of the contract through the restoration of the parties to the status quo*. And as part of a claim for rescission, the injured party may also seek *restitution* — the return of any goods, money, or property involved in the contract. Sometimes restitution also includes claims for the reasonable value of services rendered.

For instance, suppose that in our case of computer seller Snelling and bookstore owner Niles, Niles hasn't suffered anything other than inconvenience due to Snelling's delay. However, Niles has come to think that Snelling has neither the skills nor the time to complete the contract. In that case, Niles really doesn't want to enforce the contract by forcing Snelling to install the system and pay damages. What he wants is to terminate the agreement and contract with a different computer seller. However, Niles also wants the return of his down payment to Snelling. In that case, Niles needs to sue for breach of contract, seeking return of the down payment. Note, however, that technically, Niles and Snelling no longer have a contract once rescission has occurred. What then is the basis of the suit? When the suit is brought, the court will create a quasi contract, an agreement imposed or presumed by the court for a particular purpose. The newly created quasi contract will serve as the basis for the suit.

This brings us to another important point. In most jurisdictions, Niles cannot sue Snelling for *both* rescission and damages. The court will require him to make a choice. After all, suing for damages requires the existence of a contract—which rescission automatically voids. Thus, Niles will have to decide whether to keep the contract and sue for damages or to sue for rescission of the contract and simply end the agreement.

Specific Performance

Sometimes, neither ending the contract nor collecting damages is a particularly satisfactory solution. It may be that *only* fulfillment of the specific terms of the contract will satisfy the injured party. In such cases, that party may then elect to sue for *specific performance*. Under the doctrine of specific performance, the court compels the breaching party to perform according to the exact terms of the agreement. Specific performance is commonly applied in real estate transactions or to other contracts involving unique commodities—paintings, for instance, or other works of art—that are not replaceable.

Let's say Bell contracts with Whitney to purchase a castle home located on a mountain overlooking the Pacific Ocean—clearly an unusual piece of property. (Keep in mind, though, that *all* real estate by definition is unique; no two pieces of property are exactly alike, though two condominiums in the same development are likely to be *more* alike than two mountain chalets.) The point here is that if Whitney breaches the contract, Bell is not likely to be satisfied either with rescission of the contract or with the collection of damages. Even if the court awarded her sufficient damages to purchase another mountaintop castle with a sweeping ocean view, Bell may argue that she wants this particular property, not something "comparable." If she wins her suit for specific performance, the court will require Whitney to sell the property to Bell as promised.

Courts tend not to grant specific performance in cases involving personal services contracts. From the court's perspective, it is in no one's best interests to force one party to work for another. Thus, if Lopez, an actor, signs a contract to perform for three months with a touring theater ensemble of Shakespearean actors and then defaults on her contract, the court is not likely to uphold a suit for specific performance. The court's position will be that little is to be gained from forcing Lopez to perform onstage if she doesn't want to; Lopez won't be happy, and, probably, her audiences won't either. The court might, however, award damages to the theater company if, for instance, the company could show that it lost revenue as a result of no longer having the benefits of Lopez's recognized talents. Again, keep in mind that the court views these two approaches—specific performance and damages—

as conflicting. The theater company could not sue for both specific performance and damages; they would have to make a choice. Moreover, this is a case where legal remedies (that is, damages) are applicable; thus, the court is unlikely to consider equitable remedies (that is, specific performance).

Reformation

Another equitable remedy is available when a contract does not reflect the true intentions of the contracting parties. It may be a case of simple error or some ambiguity in the language that creates misunderstanding. In such situations, the court may call for *reformation* of the contract—rewriting the contract to make it conform more closely to the parties' original intentions.

Injunction

Occasionally, a court will issue an *injunction*, a court order directing a person to do or refrain from doing some particular act. For example, in 1931, the heavyweight boxing champion was Louie Carnera. Carnera agreed with Madison Square Garden to fight the winner of the Schmeling–Stribling fight in Madison Square Garden; the Carnera fight would be for the heavyweight title of the world. Because the Garden management wanted to make sure that the fight to be held at the Garden would, in fact, determine the heavyweight champion, Carnera's contract prohibited him from fighting anyone else prior to that bout. However, in violation of the contract, Carnera agreed to fight Jack Sharkey before he fought the Garden bout with the winner of the Schmeling–Stribling fight. Prior to the planned Carnera–Sharkey fight, Madison Square Garden brought suit against Carnera. The Garden was worried that Carnera might be injured in the bout with Sharkey and that, should Carnera lose to Sharkey, its originally valuable contract for a world heavyweight fight would suddenly be worth very little.

What did the Garden sue for? Not for damages, since the actual amount of their loss would be very difficult to determine. And not for rescission; they *wanted* the Carnera title bout to take place. The only remedy that made sense was to ask for an injunction to prohibit Carnera from fighting Sharkey prior to the title fight at Madison Square Garden. And, since Carnera clearly breached the Garden contract when he signed for the Sharkey fight, the injunction was granted. If, despite the injunction, Carnera had fought Sharkey, he would have been held in contempt of court—and likely fined or imprisoned.

As with other equitable remedies, the injunction is an attempt to impose fairness. It is a sensible alternative to damages where, as in the Carnera–Madison Square Garden case, the wronged party might have unreasonable difficulty determining and proving just how extensive their "injuries" would be if the other party acted in violation of their contract. And, as with the other equitable remedies, an injunction is likely to be granted only where legal remedies do not afford satisfactory solutions.

Waiver of Breach

You may get the idea from this lesson that every time contracting parties commit the slightest default, they wind up in a legal battle. Obviously, that's untrue. In some cases—especially if the breach is not particularly serious or is seen as the result of a temporary situation—the injured party may be willing to *waive* the right to the complete performance set forth in the contract.

Remember computer seller Snelling and bookstore owner Niles? Suppose that Snelling, acting in good faith, delivered the computer system on time. Unfortunately, he forgot to include the software, which created a delay for Niles's business. Technically, Snelling has breached the contract, but if no major economic injury has occurred as a result of the delay, Niles isn't likely to accomplish much by suing him. While he could sue for nominal damages, as discussed earlier, Niles will instead probably waive the breach—give up his right to perfect performance, that is—but insist on the quickest possible delivery of the software.

Reaffirming the need for compliance, even while waiving one breach, is particularly significant in the event of a long-term contract where performance is not limited to one act or one date. For instance, suppose Stormproof Roofing has an ongoing contract with Flint Construction to deliver roofing materials to a number of construction sites over an extended period of time. Delays may be costly and may also result in damage to other materials that cannot be properly protected if a roof is not completed when planned. If, after several months of timely performance, Stormproof defaults once, Flint is likely to waive the breach. Flint would, however, be wise to make it perfectly clear that it will not tolerate this sort of behavior in the future. Otherwise, if a serious problem does arise, Stormproof may argue that waivers of breach were commonly granted by Flint and that Stormproof had no reason to suppose they would be strictly held to the delivery dates specified. Remember that, from the court's perspective, the behavior of the contracting parties is sometimes more telling than their words—either written or oral.

SOME PRACTICAL ADVICE

First, and perhaps most obvious, any prudent businessperson will think long and carefully before violating a contract in any way. Sometimes, of course, breach of contract is all but inevitable—illness, disability, or some unforeseen turn of events may render performance very difficult or impossible. When you cause a breach, it is best to contact the other contracting party to see whether some renegotiation can resolve the situation without a lawsuit. Remember, though, that any willful breach or any breach occurring through negligence is likely to leave you open to considerable troubles. As we've seen in this lesson, many remedies are open to the injured party in such situations. In other words, breach of contract can be costly, in terms of time, money, or performance.

Second, remember that there are a number of options open to the businessperson who's the injured party—the one who's been wronged by the breach. We've covered a number in this lesson, but keep in mind that, with the assistance of an attorney, you will generally need to choose between two broad alternatives: legal remedies and equitable remedies. From the court's perspective, the important issue is to uphold the original intent of the contract. A secondary issue is to enforce the original contract as simply as possible.

Thus, wherever legal remedies (damages to compensate the injured party) are suitable, they will usually be more readily granted. When legal remedies do not apply well, however, the court will look to impose equitable remedies. Don't view this as an automatic process, however; it's anything but. A plaintiff seeking equitable remedies will need to clearly demonstrate that legal remedies will not solve the problem. The plaintiff will also have to show that he or she has acted in good faith. The court insists that fairness go both ways—even when a plaintiff has ample grounds for suit.

Third, if you find yourself seeking legal damages, it's well to keep in mind that what you perceive as fair and just may or may not correspond with the perspective of the court. Numerous factors enter into the court's determination of what damages should be awarded, including (but not limited to) the extent of direct costs incurred by the plaintiff, the defendant's knowledge of the plaintiff's situation, and the plaintiff's efforts to mitigate or minimize the damages. In other words, if you do not take steps to minimize your own losses, the court is likely to be much less sympathetic toward your situation.

Overall, keep in mind that—with a few rare exceptions—courts do not award damages in order to punish or make examples of contracting parties. The court's primary objective is to aid the parties in fulfilling the terms of the original contract. Thus, whatever remedy the court supports—whether legal or equitable—is likely to work toward that end. This is another way of saying that, as a businessperson, you would want to be careful that any contract you signed reflected your true intentions and worked toward your interests; always assume that—whether voluntarily or through legal intervention—you will be held to that contract.

ASSIGNMENTS

- Before you watch the video program, be sure you've read through the preceding overview, familiarized yourself with the learning objectives for this lesson, and looked at the key terms below. Then, read Chapter 17 of Davidson et al., *Business Law*.

- After completing these tasks, view the video program for Lesson 14.

- After watching the program, take time to review what you've learned. First, evaluate your learning with the self-test which follows the key terms. Then, apply and evaluate what you've learned with the "Your Opinion, Please" scenarios at the end of this telecourse study guide lesson.

KEY TERMS

Before you read through the textbook assignment and watch the video program, take a minute to look at the key terms associated with this lesson. When you encounter them in the textbook and video program, pay careful attention to their meaning.

Compensatory damages	Nominal damages
Consequential damages	Punitive damages
Damages	Reformation
Equitable remedies	Rescission
Injunction	Restitution
Legal remedies	Specific performance
Liquidated damages	Quasi contract
Mitigate	Waiver of breach

SELF-TEST

The questions below will help you evaluate how well you've learned the material in this lesson. Read each one carefully, and select the letter of the option that best answers the question. You'll find the correct answer, along with a reference to the page number(s) where the topic is discussed, in the back of this telecourse study guide.

1. A cause of action resulting from a breach of contract is *best* termed

   a. a waiver.
   b. a remedy.
   c. damages.
   d. specific performance.

2. Legal remedies most commonly involve

   a. damages.
   b. waivers.
   c. rescission and restitution.
   d. injunctions.

3. According to the text, the court's powers to grant equitable remedies are *discretionary*. This basically means that

   a. the court has the power to decide whether equitable remedies are appropriate.
   b. the court's powers are virtually limitless.

c. equitable remedies are virtually automatic in certain situations.

d. very few people are aware of the court's powers.

4. Collins, a business manager, hires a consultant to provide training in computerized data management to three of her staff members. When the trainer cancels out two days prior to the session, Collins sues for the consultant's fee plus
the cost of setting up the training. If she wins the suit, the court will *most
likely* award

a. nominal damages.

b. punitive damages.

c. liquidated damages.

d. compensatory damages.

5. Collins (Question 4) might also sue for consequential damages if she feels she
can show that

a. the contract required her to pay the consultant in advance.

b. she had contracted for the consultant's services far in advance of the training date.

c. the consultant knew Collins's staff would lose an important contract if they
did not get this training at this time.

d. scheduling a training session that never occurred caused Collins great inconvenience.

6. In suing for consequential damages, Collins (Questions 4 and 5) would have
a much stronger case against the training consultant if she could show that

a. the consultant's fee was unreasonably high.

b. she had cancelled an important meeting in order to schedule the training.

c. the consultant had agreed in the contract to refund half the training fee if
the training had to be rescheduled.

d. she took some action to lessen her own costs and lost opportunities.

7. Punitive damages are awarded in breach-of-contract situations where

a. compensatory and consequential damages are insufficient to cover the injured party's costs.

b. the court wishes to deter others from conduct similar to that of the breaching party.

c. the breach was the result of error rather than a willful refusal to perform
under the contract.

d. *None* of the above; punitive damages are never awarded in breach-of-contract suits.

8. In a case where money will not appropriately compensate a plaintiff for loss
resulting from breach-of-contract, the court will usually turn to

a. punitive damages.

b. treble damages.

c. equitable remedies.

d. a waiver of breach.

9. Brown sues Green for breach of contract. Upon reviewing the case, the court determines that, while Green technically has breached the contract, no real injury has resulted. In such a case, the court is *most likely* to

a. award nominal damages.
b. insist upon a waiver of breach.
c. grant rescission of the contract.
d. grant Brown an injunction.

10. An injunction is *best* defined as

a. the voluntary, intentional surrender of one's legal rights to the performance outlined in a contract.
b. a court order requiring a person to do or refrain from doing something.
c. a court order requiring a person to perform according to the *exact* terms of a contract.
d. an agreement written into a contract specifying that an injured party will receive a certain sum of money if a breach of the contract occurs.

YOUR OPINION, PLEASE

Read each of the following scenarios and answer the questions about the decisions you would make in each situation. Give these questions some serious thought; they may be used as the basis for the development of a more complex essay. You should base your decisions on what you've learned from this lesson, though you may incorporate outside readings or information gained through your own experience if it is relevant.

Scenario I

Barnes manages a forest-products company. In the course of her work, she contracts with Pioneer Construction for the lease of road equipment to build a roadway through a heavily forested area. The road construction is scheduled to begin July 10.

On July 1, Pioneer informs Barnes that due to extremely heavy commitments to other projects, they cannot provide the equipment Barnes has requested until July 12; they ask whether that two-day delay will create serious problems. Barnes is not pleased, but she tells Pioneer that the delay will not be a problem, provided they *absolutely* assure her they will indeed come through on July 12. She explains that she has a customer waiting for timber and she cannot honor that contract unless she is able to have the roadway usable by August 1. Pioneer assures Barnes there will be no problem, though they admit this is their busiest season.

On July 11, Pioneer contacts Barnes to say they cannot have the equipment on-site the next day after all. Unforeseeable delays with other projects have made delivery impossible. The earliest date on which they can now provide the equipment will be July 20. They do, however, offer to append to the contract a liquidated damages clause. Under the terms of the clause, they will pay Barnes a compensatory fee of $500 per day for each day after July 20 that they are unable to deliver the road equipment.

Barnes, however, is unmoved by this gesture; she is out of patience. She informs Pioneer that as a result of their persistent delays, she has not only jeopardized a current lumber contract (the one about which she had informed Pioneer earlier), but also has lost opportunities for future work with the same customer. She plans to sue Pioneer for breach of contract and seek compensatory, consequential, and punitive damages based on her own losses and on what she terms Pioneer's "unconscionable conduct."

What's your opinion? Based on what you know of the situation, do you think Barnes can successfully sue for breach of contract? If she wins, what remedy (or remedies) do you think the court is *most likely* to grant?

- Is Barnes likely to win her suit for breach of contract? If so, what remedy or remedies will the court grant?

- What factors support your answer?

- What factors might an attorney cite in arguing against your view?

- What steps, if any, might Barnes have taken to prevent a lawsuit in this situation?

- What steps, if any, might Pioneer have taken to prevent a lawsuit in this situation?

Scenario 2

Finley operates a resort in northern Wisconsin. Most of the cabins and other buildings in the resort are over twenty years old, and Finley has determined he must perform some extensive maintenance to stay competitive with other resorts in the area. As a result, he contracts with Felson, Inc., to clean the wooden roofs of the cabins and apply a chemical treatment. The chemical is designed to destroy moss and fungus, prevent invasion by insects, and generally provide weatherproofing. The product description, which is made an attachment to the contract, specifies that the chemical will extend the life of the roofs by 50% but will not substantially alter the appearance of the wood in any way whatsoever except to give the roofs a "newer, cleaner look." The contract price, which includes the cleaning and treatment of twelve cabins, a private residence, the main lodge, the store, and the boathouse, totals $20,000.

When the work is first performed, Finley is very satisfied. The appearance of the cabins is much improved and there is no sign of insects, moss, or other potentially damaging agents. All the roofs seem fully water-repellent as well. Satisfied, he pays

Felson's invoice in full. Within a few weeks, however, the chemical reacts with the wood in an unanticipated manner, turning them a very dark and blotchy orange. While there is no apparent damage to the wood itself, the appearance is anything but attractive. When Finley questions Felson about this, they admit that such a re-action does occur on very infrequent occasions — so infrequently, however, that they do not take the trouble to worry customers unnecessarily about this potential side effect. They assure Finley that the orange coloration will fade over time and will not affect the weatherproofing of the wood.

Finley, however, is unsatisfied with this response. He sues for breach of con-tract. He points out that the cabins no longer have much aesthetic appeal; far from blending into the woodsy background, they now stand out "like so many wooden fire hydrants." He also cites the fact that reservations at the resort have declined since the roof cleaning, and that he's had to cancel printing of a new advertising brochure since he doesn't want the cabins photographed in their current state. His business, he claims, will not return to normal until the cabins regain their previous color — which Felson estimates will occur in about a year. Felson counters that re-gardless of the appearance of the roofs, Finley is better off than before since he now has cabin roofs that are solid, longer-lasting, and much more weatherproof; thus, Felson argues, they have fulfilled the primary intent of the contract.

What's your opinion? Based on what you know of the situation, do you think Finley can successfully sue Felson for breach of contract? If he wins, what remedy (or remedies) do you think the court is *most likely* to grant?

- Is Finley likely to win his suit for breach of contract? If so, what remedy or remedies do you think the court is likely to grant?

- What factors support your answer?

- What factors might an attorney cite in arguing against your view?

- What steps, if any, might Finley have taken to prevent a lawsuit in this sit-uation?

- What steps, if any, might Felson have taken to prevent a lawsuit in this sit-uation?

15

Sales and Sales Contracts

LEARNING OBJECTIVES

Upon completing your study of this lesson, you should be able to

- Explain how and why sales contracts differ from contracts created under common law.

- Explain how and under what circumstances Article 2 of the Uniform Commercial Code applies to sales contracts.

- Distinguish between Article 2 and the common law of contracts by noting four observable differences in the ways each is applied in enforcing or interpreting commercial contracts.

- Describe the requirements for formation of a sales contract under Article 2.

- List and describe the requirements of buyer and seller under a sales contract, and explain the obligation of merchants to *act in a commercially reasonable manner*.

In this lesson we will talk about a special category of contracts — sales contracts. This is a topic to which virtually everyone can relate, perhaps as a seller operating a business, but if not, then certainly as a consumer. In fact, it's difficult to get through a single week without being affected in some way by a sales contract.

Consider your own situation for a moment. If, during the past week or so, you have bought or sold groceries, gasoline, clothing, furniture, sporting goods, household appliances, books, electronic equipment — or any of thousands of other goods you might think of — you have been a party in a sales contract. And each transaction in which you participated was — probably without your being aware of it — governed by rules and expectations set forth in the Uniform Commercial Code (UCC). As we shall see in this lesson, sales contracts are somewhat different from common law contracts — for a number of reasons. Knowing something about the laws regulating sales contracts should enable you to act with more confidence as a consumer or purchaser, and should give you greater awareness of your obligations as a seller or merchant, should you ever find yourself in that role.

OVERVIEW

If you are familiar with common law contracts, then you already know that they have six basic requirements:

- an agreement between two parties;
- some consideration (something bargained for and given in exchange for a promise);
- legal capacity to contract on both sides;
- the genuine assent of each contracting party;
- legality of the bargain; and
- proper form.

Fail to meet any one of these six requirements and, under common law, a contract is no longer valid. In fact, it's easy to see how contracting under common law could become quite complicated.

Now, of course, these requirements are anything but arbitrary. They're not designed to put obstacles in the way of the contracting parties; they're designed to protect the interests of both parties and to ensure, to the extent possible, that the purpose of the original agreement is fulfilled as intended. So far so good.

The problem with common law contracts, from the perspective of the business community, is that the very complexity and attention to detail so important to protecting both parties' interests could slow business negotiations to a crawl. Who would want to go to the grocery store, for instance, and have to go through the trouble of drawing up a contract defining obligations of buyer and seller, itemizing purchases, specifying conditions under which each item could or could not be returned, and so forth? While we were standing in line, perusing the fine print and deciding whether to sign, the next customer, ice cream melting, would undoubtedly grow very impatient. And this is only one small example.

The world runs on commerce. And it runs at a fast pace. Sales transactions at all levels must be conceived and concluded in short order if things are to keep humming. That means simplifying the means by which sales contracts are drawn up and enforced—while not losing sight of the need to protect contracting parties' rights. Article 2 of the Uniform Commercial Code, which governs the sale of goods, is designed to do just that. Let's take a closer look at what this means and how it affects our daily business lives.

The Nature of Sales Under Article 2

As we have noted, Article 2 of the UCC covers the sale of *goods*. According to the Code's definition, *goods* are *all things that are movable at the time they are identified to the contract*. In other words, anything tangible that can be physically delivered from seller to buyer would qualify.

Under this definition, groceries, clothing, furniture, automobiles, and products of all descriptions would be considered goods. The definition also extends to cover the unborn young of animals, growing crops (which can later be harvested and shipped), and anything attached to land which could be detached and sold apart from the land—a trailer home, for instance, or timber, minerals, or gravel. The land itself would not be included, however, since—though tangible—it cannot be moved from place to place. In fact, real estate in general is excluded for this reason. Similarly, services of all sorts are excluded. Certainly a person may "sell" his or her services, but contracts affecting employment are normally covered under common law, not under the UCC.

Sales Defined

A *sale*, in turn, is defined as *the passing of title from the seller to the buyer for a price*. A *contract for sale* can cover a sale that occurs at the time the contract is formed, or it can be an agreement to sell goods in the future. A *present sale* is a sale that occurs at the time the contract is formed. Most of what we purchase in our daily lives as consumers is covered by present-sale contracts. In the business world, however, it is common practice to buy goods in installments or over extended periods of time; under such circumstances, contracts for sale represent a real convenience.

As one would expect, every sale involves a *buyer*, the person who purchases or agrees to purchase the goods, and a *seller*, the person who provides or agrees to provide the goods identified in the contract. These persons need not be merchants in order for their transaction to be covered by the UCC. If they are merchants, however, the UCC has special rules for their transactions; further, the basic UCC regulations tend to be applied somewhat more stringently to merchants. Let's see why.

Merchants versus Nonmerchants

Under the Code, a *merchant* is defined as someone who deals in the sort of goods involved in the transaction, who claims to be an expert with relation to the goods, or who employs someone who is an expert. Determining who is or is not a merchant can sometimes be difficult enough that the decision rests on the judgment of the court. But let's start by considering a fairly straightforward example.

Let's say Babcock is a landholder who sells timber to a local lumber company. He knows nothing about timber per se; he's a rancher. He is selling the timber only because he's been approached by the lumber company, and they have made him a worthwhile offer. The representatives of the lumber company, on the other hand, know a great deal about the buying and selling of timber; that is, after all, their livelihood. In this scenario, the lumber company would be considered a merchant, but Babcock would not.

Now let's complicate our scenario a bit. Suppose Babcock makes so much money selling timber from his land that he decides ranching is, by comparison, far less rewarding. He takes the proceeds from his timber sales and invests in more land on which to grow more trees. Further, he takes a few courses in forest management, begins to ask questions of knowledgeable sources, and, in short, prepares himself to be a good negotiator in the timber industry. At some point during his education — the point at which Babcock should able to negotiate with other timber merchants on equal footing — Babcock himself attains the status of merchant. And that will affect, in turn, the behavior expected of him under UCC regulations.

According to the Code, a person who is *not* a merchant but who engages in buying or selling goods is simply required to *act in good faith*. In other words, the person must act in an honest manner, making a serious and sincere effort to live up to the terms of the contract. If the buyer or seller is a merchant, however, the Code requires not only that that person act in good faith, but also that he or she act in a *commercially reasonable manner*.

Under common law, the court will often apply the so-called "reasonable person" rule; in effect, the court will ask what a hypothetical reasonable person would do or think or conclude given the set of circumstances at hand. For example, if Rink hires Kirschen to "provide complete lawncare and maintenance" at her residence for a month, would a reasonable person assume that Rink meant for Kirschen to water the grass as needed — even if Rink didn't specify that in the contract? Since there is no absolute right or wrong answer to such a question, the court may rely on the judgment of the hypothetical "reasonable person" to interpret and apply contract law in the fairest possible manner. And chances are that our hypothetical reasonable person would say that, since the grass would die without water, yard-care certainly should include watering — and the court would rule on the Kirschen–Rink contract accordingly.

Reasonableness is an important component of UCC Article 2 as well; however, the term "reasonable" is applied somewhat differently. Keep in mind that the Code was designed to govern dealings in the business world. In defining what is "reasonable," then, the UCC looks not at hypothetical "reasonable person" examples, but rather at common practice within the relevant industry. Thus, the question is not so much "What *would* a reasonable person do?" but rather "What *do* reasonable and prudent businesspeople do every day in similar circumstances?" And the court will use the answer to that question in setting its parameters for *commercially reasonable* behavior.

The distinction the UCC makes between merchants and nonmerchants is well grounded in practical logic. The courts recognize that most nonmerchants must, of necessity, place a certain amount of trust in those with whom they do business. It is not possible for most of us to be experts in everything from automobiles to timber products, computer components to livestock. In order to keep the economic wheels turning, each businessperson must often rely on the expertise and judgment of others. Thus, the UCC demands a higher code of conduct from merchants—the experts in their fields. Under common law, as you may know, the court will normally presume that the two parties who enter a contract are equal in their ability to negotiate unless evidence or circumstance shows otherwise. With sales contracts, however, the court often does not make this assumption. In fact, if one party is a merchant and one is not, the court will presume *inequality* in the two parties' abilities to negotiate; the different standards for merchants and nonmerchants are the court's way of rebalancing the scales by demanding a little more of the "experts."

Forming the Contract and Differences from Common Law

The Code recognizes the existence of a contract whenever the parties act as if they have an agreement. Thus, if Cholick delivers a truckload of hay to Diller, and Diller gives Cholick $200 in cash, the UCC will regard them as having a sales contract—regardless of whether there is any paperwork relating to the sale.

Offer and Acceptance

Further, in comparison to common law, the UCC requirements are rather flexible and open. For example, the contract would not have to specify precisely how or when Cholick would deliver the hay, or whether Diller would pay in cash or by check. In fact, the agreement might not even specify precisely how much hay Cholick would deliver or how much Diller would pay. These terms might—if both parties felt comfortable with the arrangement—be negotiated later. It would be enough for the court to be able to say that if either Cholick or Diller were dissatisfied with the arrangements, some remedy *could* be found—in other words, the terms of the contract could be legally worked out. Note that contracts under common law are not granted this flexibility; under common law, the terms of the contract must usually be spelled out or the contract might fail owing to indefiniteness of the terms.

There are limits to this flexibility; UCC Section 2-206 does require that a sales contract have both a valid offer and acceptance. Unless the offer specifies otherwise, though, the acceptance can take any form that is reasonable. Take our example with Cholick and Diller. Cholick might call Diller one night to say that he has hay for sale, and Diller might offer to buy some "at a fair price." Cholick could accept Diller's offer verbally right then, or he could phone back later, or write Diller a note, or just stop by with the truckload of hay. Any of these responses would constitute a valid acceptance, unless, of course, Diller specified otherwise. For instance, Diller might say, "I can pay $4 a bale; if you agree to that price, write up a confirmation stating how much you'll sell at that rate and when you'll deliver it." In that case, Cholick could not validly accept the offer just by driving by with the hay. In most cases, however, offer and acceptance tend to be fairly casual and informal—primarily in the name of expedience. Again, remember that the overriding goals of the UCC are to ensure fairness to both sides while allowing sufficient flexibility to let business take its course.

One caution, though. When the offer to buy goods calls for prompt shipment, the seller can accept in one of two ways. The seller can promptly ship *conforming goods*—goods which correspond to whatever is called for in the contract—to the buyer or can notify the buyer that such goods *will be* shipped promptly. However, this arrangement can cause real problems—sometimes on both sides.

Suppose the seller misunderstands or is out of the merchandise requested, and so ships something different. In our example with Cholick and Diller, for instance, suppose Diller asks for top-grade alfalfa hay, and Cholick substitutes bedding straw. What then? From a legal perspective, Cholick has, by shipping goods, technically accepted the offer, even though the shipment was of *nonconforming goods*. True, he may have breached the contract by providing something other than what was called for—but that is a discussion for another lesson. The main point here is that regardless of whether Cholick ships conforming or nonconforming goods, his response to Diller's offer—the shipment—constitutes a form of acceptance. If Diller is unhappy with what is shipped, he will have to work that out with Cholick, either personally or through legal remedy. That can be time-consuming and inconvenient for both. In the scenario with Cholick and Diller, the risk is probably minimal. If Cholick delivers the hay in person, and Diller is right there to inspect and accept or reject it, most misunderstandings can probably be worked out on the spot.

Sometimes, it's the seller who encounters the greatest risk when an offer is accepted by shipment of goods. Let's say that Chatfield, who lives in New York, offers to purchase encyclopedias from bookseller Thorndike, who lives in Los Angeles. Thorndike accepts by promptly shipping the encyclopedias which, through a shipping foul-up, are mistakenly routed to Denver and left to sit in a warehouse for over a month before they're properly rerouted. Meanwhile, Chatfield, believing that Thorndike apparently wasn't interested in the offer after all, has purchased the needed encyclopedias from another source. When the misrouted books finally do arrive in New York, Chatfield has no legal obligation to pay for them and—unless the encyclopedia business is booming—is unlikely to do so. Thorndike thus finds himself in a very unenviable position: Not only has he lost a sale on which he may have counted, but he has now incurred the various expenses required to ship a couple of tons of encyclopedias across the country.

Clearly, acceptances that are written—or even oral—sometimes have great advantage over implied acceptances. On the other hand, from the court's viewpoint, actions often speak louder than words. Let's say that Thorndike's shipper is competent and the encyclopedias arrive at Chatfield's within a few days. Further, suppose that together with the encyclopedias, Thorndike mails a written form that Chatfield is to sign, thereby acknowledging his acceptance of the shipment. Only Chatfield doesn't sign the form; in fact, he throws it away with the rest of the packing materials. He does, however, put the encyclopedias in his warehouse and proceeds to market them, even selling one set to a local bookstore. Can Chatfield later argue, if he wishes, that he did not actually accept the offer? No. Even though he didn't sign the form, his actions clearly show that he intended to accept. He was behaving as though a contract existed; under the UCC, therefore, Chatfield and Thorndike do, in fact, have a sales contract.

Standard Forms and Proposed Additions

Most businesses have standard forms or preprinted contract forms that they use to simplify standard or frequent negotiations. Such forms outline the business's usual procedures or expectations, with blank spaces left for names, dates, descriptions of merchandise, prices, and other negotiable terms unique to each order. Obviously, such forms differ from one business to another. Under common law, this would create a real problem. For example, let's say Company X makes an offer using its "offer" form; Company Y accepts using its "acceptance" form. According to the common law perspective, Company Y's acceptance would actually constitute a counteroffer, even if it differed only slightly from the terms outlined in X's original offer. The Code, however, makes allowance for such differences in the interest of getting on with the business at hand.

If the proposed acceptance does, in fact, contain terms that expand or change those in the original agreement, the Code tends to view these terms simply as *proposed additions* which will automatically make them part of the contract *unless*

1. the original offer explicitly rules out acceptance of the new terms,
2. the new terms materially (substantially, that is) alter the contract, or
3. the offeror objects to the new terms within some reasonable period of time.

The third condition is particularly important to businesspeople who may feel they cannot take time to go through all the paperwork provided by another company with which they are doing business. Since silence can imply agreement, reading the fine print makes good business sense.

Firm Offers

Under common law, a firm offer can be revoked any time prior to acceptance unless the offeree has an option from the offeror—a promise (granted for consideration). Under the Code, however, a firm offer cannot be revoked until after a reasonable period. It is crucial to understand, however, what is implied by *firm offer*.

According to the Code definition, a firm offer exists when *a merchant* promises in writing to keep an offer open and unmodified for some specified period of time, and *signs the writing*. Remember our earlier example with Cholick and Diller? If Diller, a merchant, said casually to Cholick, "Sure, I'd like to buy some hay. Call me next week," that would not constitute a firm offer. It's not in writing nor does it specify a period of time.

It would be quite a different matter if Diller were to write up and sign an agreement specifying that he would buy a given amount of hay from Cholick at a given price, provided Cholick could deliver. In that case, Diller could not change his mind when Cholick drove up to unload the hay. The UCC would say that Diller had made a firm offer and that he would have to stand by it. For how long? According to the UCC, for a "reasonable period" not to exceed three months. The three-month cut-off will hold, by the way, even if Diller unthinkingly writes into the offer his willingness to hold the offer open for a year or more. The Code will not bind him to his own impulsive generosity.

The Statute of Frauds and Parol Evidence

As we have seen, the Code is designed to help enforce the original intentions of the two contracting parties without unproductive complexity. In some cases, however, there are rules that will override intent.

The Statute of Frauds, for example, specifies that contracts for the sale of goods totalling $500 or more must be in writing to be enforceable. Oral contracts for goods exceeding this amount are legal, of course. But parties enter such a contract at their own risk since, if a disagreement arises, the court will not normally enforce an oral contract for sales over $500.

There are three common exceptions to the Statute of Frauds requirement that sales contracts be in writing to be enforceable. First, according to the Code, no writing is needed if the goods are being *specially* manufactured for the buyer and cannot, given their nature, be readily resold to another buyer in the normal course of business. Second, and logically enough, no writing is needed if the party being sued admits in court or during other legal proceedings that a contract did in fact exist. Finally, no writing is needed to cover goods already delivered and accepted or already paid for and accepted.

Another rule applies to a sales contract between two merchants. If one sends a written *confirmation* (that is, a memorandum or notation of agreement), the merchant who receives that confirmation of the sale is bound by it unless he or she objects within ten days. The purpose of this rule is to ensure that merchants will attend to one another's forms with more than a passing glance. Suppose, for instance, that merchants Chan and Palmer are talking one day about Chan's paper-product business. Chan mistakenly believes that Palmer—who is really only asking for more information—is interested in purchasing a sizable quantity of merchandise from her store. Accordingly, Chan sends Palmer a confirmation notice to that effect. If Palmer does not object to that notice within ten days of receipt, he is bound to the sales agreement specified on the confirmation, like it or not. Note, however, that if Palmer were not also a merchant, the Code would not hold him to the same requirement.

Although the UCC makes several modifications to common law statutes, it does not modify the parole evidence rule; where a written agreement *does* exist, the parol evidence rule applies. This rule states that parol evidence — oral evidence, that is — cannot be introduced to contradict or overturn the terms of the written agreement. Oral statements an be introduced, however, to clarify what is in writing, to fill in informational gaps, or to explain any behavior that does not seem to be covered by the contract.

Obligations Under a Sales Contract

As we have already noted, the parties in a sales contract are required by the UCC to act in good faith. If they are merchants, they are also required to act in a commercially reasonable manner. Those contracting, be they merchants or not, have some other obligations as well. Let's consider them here.

The first is rather obvious: The seller must transfer and deliver conforming goods to the buyer; the buyer, in turn, must accept and pay for the goods delivered. This seems straightforward, but as we noted earlier, sales contracts are sometimes less than explicit with respect to some terms of the agreement. The law makes provision for this, however, and if certain terms are undefined by the contracting parties, the court can define them in ways set forth under the Code.

For instance, the Code specifies that unless the contract specifies otherwise, goods will be delivered in one complete shipment. In addition, the Code states that delivery will normally occur at the *seller's* place of business. This may seem confusing until you think about it for a moment. The word *delivery* may cause you to picture a delivery truck bringing goods to your residence or place of business. True, that often happens. In most business transactions, however, the buyer *takes* delivery of the merchandise from wherever it is sold or stored. And those are the terms the Code will impose unless a contract specifies otherwise.

What about time of delivery? If the contract makes no provisions for this, the Code simply requires that the delivery occur within a reasonable time, according to both clock and calendar. What is "reasonable" is, again, likely to be determined by typical business practice. If you order an expensive, handbuilt rosewood desk, for instance, delivery within thirty or sixty days may be deemed "reasonable," given the performance standards set by most furniture craftspeople. You might have trouble insisting upon delivery of your desk within two days; by the same token, the court would probably frown on a seller who still had not delivered after six months.

Price may be determined in much the same way if it has not been specified in the contract. This sounds a bit odd, perhaps, to most of us, who are accustomed to thinking of price as a central issue in any sales negotiations. Nevertheless, it sometimes happens that two parties will agree on a sale without agreeing on price. Again, the court will consider, under the rules of the Code, what price would be regarded as "reasonable" at the time of delivery, and a fair market value will be assigned to the goods. This price, of course, may not suit the contracting parties, who will then regret not having agreed on a price as part of the contract.

The Code also covers options—choices about certain terms left open in the contract. For example, if the contract calls for an unspecified assortment of goods, the option of defining that assortment falls to the buyer. On the other hand, if the method of shipment is left unspecified, the option of determining how goods will be shipped falls to the seller. Recognize, though, that if the party having the option fails to act on that option within a reasonable period, the other party may automatically have a say in how things are done.

Unconscionability

Section 2-302 of the Code also addresses *unconscionable* contracts, those that are so one-sided as to "shock the conscience" of the court. Normally, if the court determines that a contract is unconscionable, it will not uphold that contract; however, if just one clause within the contract is judged to be unconscionable, the court will normally uphold the contract and void only the offending clause.

For instance, remember Thorndike the encyclopedia seller, and Chatfield, the buyer from New York? Let's suppose for a moment that Chatfield is not a seasoned bookseller at all, but a college professor who has just inherited a bookstore from his wealthy uncle. He has never contracted to buy books in large volume before, and knows virtually nothing about it. Thorndike, seizing an opportunity, determines to rid himself of a truckload of outdated encyclopedias by shipping them to Chatfield. Chatfield, believing he has stumbled upon a bargain, accepts delivery; only later does he discover that he is being charged many times more than the market value for old encyclopedias. Further, he finds that Thorndike has appended rather high charges to cover administrative costs, order processing, handling, insurance during shipping, "extra-protective" packaging, and other assorted costs—bringing the total to more than he would have paid for new encyclopedias. If Chatfield objects, is the court likely to uphold such a contract? Probably not. In the court's eyes, Thorndike may have acted unconscionably by taking advantage of Chatfield's lack of experience.

Finally, the two contracting parties are expected to cooperate with each other in carrying out the contract. Failing to act in a cooperative manner or deliberately interfering with the performance of the other party can be considered a breach of contract.

SOME PRACTICAL ADVICE

What points in this lesson should the prudent businessperson particularly attend to? First, it's well to remember that contract formation under UCC rules is a little different from contract formation under common law. It is more open, less complex, more expedient. But expedience usually has a price. True, the UCC regulations allow businesspeople to proceed rapidly through most negotiations, but the other side to this is that sales contracts formed in haste may well be legally enforceable. Thus, it is imperative to ensure that the contract reflects terms that are agreeable, feasible in practice, and reasonably profitable to both sides.

Remember, too, that in determining whether a sales contract exists, the court will look primarily at the behavior of buyer and seller. If they behave as if they have a contract, the court will usually take the position that they do—and act accordingly.

What are the implications here? Under common law, most disputes can be settled by a review of the contract, which serves not only as a negotiating instrument to clarify the terms of the agreement, but also as a guideline that helps govern the conduct of the parties *after* the initial agreement. With a sales contract, things are not always that simple. There may not be any written document at all; or if there is one, it may not have all the terms specified. It's therefore important, from a business standpoint, to know how the UCC will "fill in" any missing terms. Of course, the court will not act arbitrarily in assigning the terms of an incomplete contract; it will follow certain rules laid out by the Code. But in so doing, it may impose terms that are less than satisfactory to one or both parties. In other words, the time to negotiate in one's own best interests is *prior* to forming the contract.

It is also useful to know what is expected of you as a party in a sales contract—and what sort of conduct you have a right to expect from a party with whom you contract. As a simple buyer or seller, you are expected to act in good faith—honestly, that is. Once considered a merchant, however, you are also expected to act in a commercially reasonable manner. Let's look at this from two perspectives.

First, suppose you are a consumer. If you deal with a merchant, you have a right to expect that the merchant will deal honestly with you, will not abuse your trust, will make every effort to represent his or her products fairly and honestly, and so forth. Keep in mind, however, that you do *not* have to the right to expect commercially reasonable treatment from someone who is not a merchant within the industry. For instance, you cannot expect the same standards of behavior from a neighbor who sells you a used car that you would expect from a used-car dealer whose profession it is to sell cars. In short, if you wish to demand the highest standards of professional conduct, you must deal with recognized professionals.

Second, from the other side of things, suppose you are a merchant yourself—the acknowledged "professional" or "expert" in your field. Whether buying or selling, you will, under the UCC, be expected to behave in a manner that is consistent with the standards of conduct established by others in the same field. Thus, it will be important for you to be aware of others' business practices and the way in which they commonly serve their clients or customers. Under the Code, you cannot do less without good justification. Be aware, too, that from the court's perspective, merchants have a decided bargaining edge in dealing with customers or clients who are not themselves merchants. Thus, if a sales contract is perceived as unfair or one-sided, it may be declared void on grounds of unconscionability.

Some practical points are worth noting, too. As a merchant, beware of accepting any offer by simply shipping the requested goods. If they do not arrive rapidly, or if their arrival is overlooked or not acknowledged, you may find yourself in the unhappy position of having encountered delays and shipping costs (both ways!) without receiving anything in return. On the other hand, if you find yourself the recipient of nonconforming goods — that is, something other than what you expected — be aware that the seller has, in fact, legally accepted your offer. A breach of contract may exist, true, and a remedy may be open to you. On the other hand, you're likely to justifiably feel that life would have been simpler without this problem to straighten out. In short, consider carefully at the outset how you would like to determine or acknowledge acceptance of an offer, and, if the means or time of acceptance is important, be sure to specify that in the contract.

Further, be sure to read any and all documents provided by other merchants. Preprinted contract forms may contain new terms that, if they do not materially alter the terms of your original contract, may become binding unless you object to them openly, rapidly, and directly. Similarly, a sales confirmation may bind you to an agreement you didn't even know you had made — unless you object within ten days of receipt. In the business world, reading the mail isn't just a good way of filling the mid-morning break; it's a vital business strategy.

Above all, remember that regardless of whether you are a merchant, any time you are involved in a sales contract, the law requires that you cooperate with the other party and make every effort to fulfill the contract in a fair manner. The simplifications allowed by the UCC are not to be interpreted as a relaxation of principles of fairness.

ASSIGNMENTS

- Before you watch the video program, be sure you've read through the preceding overview, familiarized yourself with the learning objectives for this lesson, and looked at the key terms below. Then, read Chapter 18 of Davidson et al., *Business Law*.

- After completing these tasks, view the video program for Lesson 15.

- After watching the program, take time to review what you've learned. First, evaluate your learning with the self-test which follows the key terms. Then, apply and evaluate what you've learned with the "Your Opinion, Please" scenarios at the end of this telecourse study guide lesson.

KEY TERMS

Before you read through the textbook assignment and watch the video program, take a minute to look at the key terms associated with this lesson. When you encounter them in the textbook and video program, pay careful attention to their meaning.

Buyer	Options
Commercially reasonable manner	Preprinted (or standard) contract form
Confirmation	"Reasonable"
Conforming goods	Remedy
Contract for sale	Sale
Delivery	Seller
Firm offer	Statute of Frauds
Good faith	Unconscionability
Goods	Uniform Commercial Code
Merchant	Usage of trade
Nonconforming goods	

SELF-TEST

The questions below will help you evaluate how well you've learned the material in this lesson. Read each one carefully, and select the letter of the option that best answers the question. You'll find the correct answer, along with a reference to the page number(s) where the topic is discussed, in the back of this telecourse study guide.

1. In legal terms, *goods* are *best* defined as

   a. marketable products for which there is public demand.
   b. anything that the seller is willing to trade for money.
   c. things that are movable at the time they are identified in the contract.
   d. anything that does not fall under the heading of "services."

2. According to the Uniform Commercial Code (UCC), which of the following persons would *most likely* be classified as a merchant?

   a. *All* of the following are merchants, according to the Code's definition.
   b. Wilkes, a dentist, who is selling used dental equipment.
   c. Nathan, a doctor, who is selling his used Chevrolet.
   d. Holly, a used-car dealer, who inherited a hardware store and is attempting to sell the inventory.

3. To all appearances, Avalon and Banasky would seem to have a contract. Each Saturday, Avalon delivers fruit to Banasky's grocery and Banasky pays. However, they have no written agreement, the time of delivery is variable, and they determine price on the spot. Under the Code, the court would most likely take the position that

   a. Avalon and Banasky don't have and never had a contract.
   b. while they have a contract of sorts, it is completely unenforceable due to the indefiniteness of the terms.

   c. while a contract originally existed between Avalon and Banasky, it has sub-sequently become void due to the vagueness of the terms.

   d. Avalon and Banasky definitely have a valid contract.

4. Googins orders twenty-five rolls of pink rose-patterned wallpaper from Mulberry Decorators, Inc. Mulberry promptly ships twenty-five rolls of lavender iris-patterned wallpaper. According to the UCC, which of the following is true?

   a. Mulberry has accepted the offer by shipping nonconforming goods.

   b. Mulberry has rejected the offer by shipping nonconforming goods.

   c. Technically, Mulberry has not yet responded to the offer.

   d. The lavender wallpaper constitutes a counteroffer that Googins is now free to accept or reject.

5. Malone orders sixty cases of computer diskettes from Garcia. Malone orders using his company's preprinted order form; Garcia sends his company's pre-printed contract form back to Malone with the shipment of diskettes. Unlike Malone's form, which specifies nothing whatever about shipment, Garcia's form specifies that the diskettes will be shipped at Malone's expense in three separate installments. Which of the following is true?

   a. Regardless of what Garcia's form says, the merchandise must all be shipped at one time.

   b. Garcia's "proposal" for shipping will hold unless Malone objects within a reasonable time.

   c. Garcia's proposal materially alters the contract, rendering it void.

   d. The UCC does not cover the shipping of merchandise; Garcia and Malone must work things out for themselves.

6. According to the Code, an oral contract for the sale of goods will not be en-forceable if the total value of those goods is

   a. more than $100.

   b. more than $500.

   c. *Neither* of the above; oral contracts for the sale of goods are *always* enforce-able.

   d. *None* of the above; oral contracts for the sale of goods are *never* enforce-able.

7. Under the parol evidence rule, oral evidence regarding a contract may

   a. never be introduced under any circumstances.

   b. not be used to explain or supplement the writing.

   c. not be used to fill apparent gaps in the writing.

   d. not be used to contradict the original writing.

8. In defining "commercially reasonable" behavior and conduct for merchants, the court will generally focus

   a. solely on whether the actions of the merchants are legal.

   b. solely on what behavior the court considers "fair."

    c. primarily on how a hypothetical "reasonable" person in the same situation would likely respond.

    d. primarily on how other merchants in the same circumstances normally conduct themselves.

9. Forkner (the seller) and Gluth have a contract for the sale of sports equipment. Since the goods would not be delivered for many months, they left the price open. Under the Code, which of the following would be true at the time of delivery?

    a. They will need to set a fair market price based on the value of goods at the time of delivery.

    b. They will need to set a reasonable price based on the value of goods at the time of original contract negotiations — regardless of shifts in market value.

    c. Forkner has the freedom to set any price he wishes; under the Code, Gluth — who has foolishly agreed to an open-price contract — must pay whatever is asked.

    d. *None* of the above; the contract is not valid since it does not include a price.

10. Foti contracts with King to purchase an unspecified assortment of machine screws for Foti's variety store. Since the contract does not specify, item by item, what size and quantity of screws will be shipped to Foti, who will make this determination?

    a. King; it's the seller's option

    b. Foti; it's the buyer's option

    c. Neither King nor Foti; under the UCC, buyer and seller alike give up their options when they do not specify a relevant term of the contract, and standard business practice would determine the common assortments usually shipped in such transactions.

YOUR OPINION, PLEASE

Read each of the following scenarios and answer the questions about the decisions you would make in each situation. Give these questions some serious thought; they may be used as the basis for the development of a more complex essay. You should base your decisions on what you've learned from this lesson, though you may incorporate outside readings or information gained through your own experience if it is relevant.

Scenario I

Ancell, a rancher, orders 5,000 yards of fencing material from Great Plains Fencing, Inc. GPF doesn't have the precise fencing Ancell wants in stock at the time of the order, but not wishing to lose the sale altogether, they ship what they consider to be an improved, more durable product—the cost of which is only slightly higher than what Ancell ordered. GPF also sends a letter explaining the reason for the substitution, and agreeing to let Ancell have the new fencing for the same price he would have paid for the original product he ordered. They request a prompt response from Ancell indicating whether the new fencing will be satisfactory. They also include with the shipment a contract form which requires Ancell's signature to acknowledge delivery and acceptance of the fencing.

Ancell receives the shipment promptly and in good order. He responds by sending GPF a brief letter stating only that "the fencing has arrived on time." He does not comment on the substitution or on his relative satisfaction with the product. Nor does he sign and return GPF's contract form.

When Ancell has installed approximately 20% of the fencing from GPF, he discovers he can obtain the product he originally wanted from another dealer at much lower cost than the GPF price for either fencing product. He thereupon notifies GPF that they do not in fact have a valid contract and asks that they reclaim the unused portion (80%) of their product. GPF responds that they certainly do have a contract, and they demand payment for the fencing in full, in accordance with the rate and schedule outlined on their contract form. Ancell points out that he has not signed the form and does not intend to. Further, he argues, he did not contract for this particular fencing and will not pay. GPF thereupon sues for breach of contract.

What's your opinion? Based on what you know of the situation, do you think GPF and Ancell have a valid contract? Has GPF acted in a commercially responsible manner throughout the negotiations? Has Ancell acted in good faith? Would Ancell be regarded as a merchant in the eyes of the court?

- Is the court likely to uphold GPF's position and enforce the contract between GPF and Ancell, or agree with Ancell that no contract exists?
- What factors support your answer?
- What factors might an attorney cite in arguing against your view?
- What steps, if any, might Ancell have taken to prevent a lawsuit in this situation?
- What steps, if any, might GPF have taken to prevent a lawsuit in this situation?

Scenario 2

Dadour has just moved to a new town, bought a small house barely within her budget, and accepted a position with very modest pay. She supports three children; thus, her childcare costs absorb a disproportionate amount of her very limited income. She has no savings and is having an extremely difficult time establishing credit.

Badly in need of furniture, she explores her options. They are not promising. All furniture dealers in town, with one exception, demand a down payment of 20% or more of the purchase price. The one exception, Wellbuilt Furniture, is willing to extend Dadour credit and to forego any down payment. However, their finance charges are more than 50% higher than those of any competitor, and unlike other furniture dealers, they will not extend the period of payment beyond six months. According to their proposal, they will allow Dadour to take possession of $1,300 worth of furniture, and pay nothing down. However, she will owe the full amount, including finance and delivery charges—$1,600 total—in three monthly installments, beginning two months after delivery, and continuing every other month for two more payments. According to the contract, if any payment is missed or late by more than five days, Wellbuilt reserves the right to reclaim all furniture.

Dadour manages to make the first payment of $534, but realizes that, unless she finds another source of income, the second and third payments will be beyond her budget. She notifies Wellbuilt of her concerns and requests an extension of the period to pay or some renegotiation of the contract agreement. Wellbuilt refuses. When Dadour is unable to make her second payment on time, Wellbuilt reclaims all the furniture Dadour has purchased and refuses to refund any of the money from the first payment. Dadour thereupon sues for recovery of either the furniture or the $534 she has already paid to Wellbuilt.

What's your opinion? Based on what you know of the situation and the principles of the UCC, do you think the court will support Dadour's position? Will the court likely find that Dadour acted in good faith? that Wellbuilt acted in good faith and in a commercially reasonable manner?

- Is Dadour likely to win a case for recovery of the furniture or the money she has paid thus far? Why or why not?
- What factors support your answer?
- What factors might an attorney cite in arguing against your view?
- What steps, if any, might Dadour have taken to prevent a lawsuit in this situation?
- What steps, if any, might Wellbuilt have taken to prevent a lawsuit in this situation?

16

Passage of Title and Risk of Loss

LEARNING OBJECTIVES

Upon completing your study of this lesson, you should be able to

- Define the concept of *insurable interest* and explain the circumstances under which either buyer or seller can be said to have an insurable interest.
- Explain the relationship between title to goods and one's rights under a sales contract.
- Define the concept *risk of loss* and relate this concept to that of insurable interest.
- Distinguish between risk of loss *with* breach of contract and risk of loss *without* breach of contract, using hypothetical examples to illustrate this distinction.
- Discuss the four steps buyer and seller are required to take as part of bulk sales or transfers, and explain the implications if these steps are not followed.

Most of the time, in the world of buying and selling, things go fairly smoothly. Buyer and seller negotiate a deal, and goods change hands at the agreed-on time for an agreed-on price. Occasionally, however, something goes awry. Before the transfer of ownership from seller to buyer can be completed, the goods may be lost, damaged, destroyed, or stolen. If some mishap occurs, who takes responsibility for replacing or repairing lost or damaged goods? Often, this is a more difficult question to answer than one might think.

In order to keep the wheels of commerce turning, to keep things from coming to a standstill while buyer and seller haggle over who will bear which costs, the Uniform Commercial Code has established definite guidelines for determining precisely when ownership changes hands and when responsibility for merchandise shifts from seller to buyer. Exploring those guidelines is what this lesson is all about.

OVERVIEW

Buyers and sellers of goods must have a way of protecting their interests in the event of fire, flood, theft, or other mishap. As you might guess, they secure this protection primarily through insurance. But in order to qualify for insurance, the law demands that buyers and sellers have what is known as *insurable interest* — the right to purchase insurance on goods to protect one's property rights and interest in the goods. Simply put, insurable interest means that the buyer or seller has something financial to lose — a vested interest in the goods, as it were.

Insurable Interest: Buyers and Sellers

The buyer gains an insurable interest when the goods in question are *identified to the contract*. This means they've been shipped, marked for shipment, or in some other way designated as the goods that conform to the specifications of the contract. Sometimes, of course, a buyer will contract for goods that are not yet in existence, goods that will be produced sometime in the future — say, a car to be manufactured to a customer's exact specifications. In that case, the buyer acquires an insurable interest when those goods come into existence, but not before.

The seller has an insurable interest for as long as he or she retains title to the goods or has — even in the absence of any title — any possibility of incurring a financial loss in the event something should happen to those goods. To understand this better, let's take a closer look, first, at what it means to have title, and then what it means to have an insurable interest.

Title to Goods in a Sales Contract

Title is the equivalent of *legal ownership*. Title passes from seller to buyer when goods are sold. Under common law, title had great significance, because risk of loss always fell upon the party holding title. Under the UCC, title and risk of loss do not always go hand in hand. In fact, a party may have an insurable interest in goods without holding title; however, title cannot pass from one party to another in the absence of insurable interest. Let's look now at the Code's particular provisions for the manner in which title is transferred from one party to another.

First, as a general rule, title passes from seller to buyer when the seller completes performance of *delivery*. This makes the type of delivery contract very important. In a *shipment contract*, title passes to the buyer at the time and place of shipment. For example, suppose Chaffin contracts with Brusseau to purchase 100 filing cabinets. If theirs is a shipment contract, title passes to Chaffin when and where Brusseau ships the cabinets. Keep this in mind, for it has implications regarding who is responsible should anything happen to the cabinets during shipment.

On the other hand, suppose Chaffin and Brusseau have a *destination contract*. In that case, title would pass to Chaffin only when the cabinets were delivered at the prescribed destination — Chaffin's warehouse or place of business, let's say. Notice that in the case of a destination contract, the goods are still the responsibility of the seller during shipment; in other words, if anything happens to the goods en route, it is the seller who will have to make things right.

Perhaps you've ordered lots of things, but never remember specifying whether you had a shipment or a destination contract. That's because the law treats any contract as a shipment contract unless it is specifically designated otherwise; in other words, a destination contract must be explicitly identified as such. This is another way of saying that the burden of responsibility — in most cases — falls automatically to the buyer.

Some goods, of course, are not shipped from one place to another at the time of sale. What then? Well, if a document of title is involved, title passes when and where that document is delivered to the buyer. If there is no document of title involved, title passes when and where the contract of sale itself is made. For example, suppose that Bixel contracts with Rice to purchase all the lodge-pole pine trees on a five-acre tract of Rice's land. Rice is not going to deliver the trees; Bixel will go and cut them as he needs them. Nor is there a document of title for the trees. In this case, therefore, title passes at the time and place where the contract for sale of the trees is made.

Now let's consider a similar, but slightly different, example. Suppose that Dietrich Drilling Company purchases the mineral rights on a twenty-acre piece of land owned by Starch. In this case, there *is* a document of title. Thus, the title of ownership to the mineral rights passes from Starch to Dietrich Drilling when that document is transferred to Dietrich.

What happens if the buyer rejects the goods? Suppose Chaffin, the cabinet buyer in our earlier example, discovers that the filing cabinets shipped by Brusseau do not meet the specifications of the contract; he wanted heavy-duty steel cabinets, and Brusseau has shipped cabinets made of wood. At the point when Chaffin rejects the cabinets, title automatically shifts back to Brusseau—or *revests* in Brusseau. And this is true even if Chaffin has made a down payment on the purchase of the cabinets. By the way, even if the cabinets *did* conform to the contract and *were* made of heavy steel, title would nevertheless revert to Brusseau if Chaffin rejected them. In short, title automatically revests in the seller when a buyer rejects goods, even if the rejection is improper.

Creditors' Rights

One reason the issue of title is so critical is that creditors of either buyer or seller may wish to *attach* the merchandise—that is, to seize the property under court order, or to place a claim upon it in order to satisfy a debt. Obviously, then, creditors are very eager to know just who has title to the merchandise in question.

A secured creditor, one whose financial rights are protected or covered by merchandise identified to the contract, has clear legal recourse for satisfying a debt. In other words, suppose Carter borrows money from LaMonte, a debt that is secured in writing with an interest in some of the expensive fixtures in the restaurant owned by Carter. If Carter does not repay the debt to LaMonte, but tries—in the course of closing his restaurant—to sell the fixtures to a third party, LaMonte can *attach* the restaurant fixtures. That is, LaMonte can put a claim on the fixtures to help satisfy the debt Carter owes him.

An unsecured creditor, however, one whose claim is not covered by specific collateral (such as Carter's restaurant fixtures), is in a much shakier position. Since there are no specific goods identified as security for the loan, the creditor has no right to stop the sale of any particular merchandise. Indeed, if LaMonte is an unsecured creditor, he'll simply has to wait in line with other unsecured creditors for his share of whatever assets are left after the entire restaurant is sold and the secured creditors are satisfied. As an unsecured creditor, LaMonte cannot tell Carter, "Your loan is due. If you don't have the money, I'm attaching your pastry cart." In fact, for all LaMonte knows, the pastry cart might be the security interest for someone else's loan to Carter. All in all, if LaMonte lent money to Carter but did not secure it with any sort of collateral, he would have limited recourse if Carter runs out of funds.

Let's look now at a very different kind of situation, but one that also involves creditors' rights. Suppose that a seller unscrupulously "sells" goods in order to avoid having them attached by creditors, but retains possession and control of those goods just as if no "sale" had occurred. For instance, in our previous example, Carter might "sell" his restaurant fixtures to his brother-in-law, Riles—with the implicit understanding that Carter would continue to use the equipment rent-free. Riles might be the owner of the fixtures on paper, but both Riles and Carter understand that Riles would have no real benefits from that ownership and would have no decision-making power over the restaurant.

Clearly, such an arrangement does *not* constitute a sale in the usual sense at all, since Carter really has no intention of transferring ownership of the restaurant fixtures; he's only seeking a way to insulate himself from creditors' threats. Though laws governing such situations differ somewhat state to state, Carter's "sale" really will not help him. Carter's creditors would, in fact, probably sue to set aside the sale as fraud. And if the sale were viewed by the court as fraudulent, creditors would have the right to regard the sale as void and to attach the fixtures in order to satisfy debts.

Risk of Loss

The term *risk of loss* refers to the financial responsibility between buyer and seller if the goods are lost, damaged, or destroyed before the buyer has accepted them. Notice that risk of loss covers the relationship between buyer and seller, but does not address the liability of any independent carrier or insurer of the goods. In fact, an independent carrier may ultimately be liable for damage or loss, if it can be shown that the carrier was negligent in handling or transporting the goods. But such liability would be assigned through a separate contract—between seller and carrier or buyer and carrier, for instance.

The nature of the contract between buyer and seller—shipment or destination—is the major factor in determining risk of loss. In a shipment contract, where title passes at time and place of shipment, the buyer is responsible for damage or loss during shipment, provided that the seller has shipped conforming goods. With a destination contract, however, in which title passes when the goods reach their destination, the seller bears the risk of loss during shipment. If something goes wrong, the seller must replace the goods or repair them or do whatever is necessary to make things right with the buyer.

As we noted earlier, destination contracts tend to be the exception. And simply specifying a point of delivery in a contract is not likely to be sufficient in the eyes of the court to make an agreement a destination contract. For example, suppose Harrison, while touring overseas, purchases an expensive camera from Jeska, Inc. The contract of sale specifies that the camera will be shipped to Harrison's residence in Newport Beach. Is that clause sufficient to make the agreement a destination contract? Not likely. In fact, if Harrison examines the fine print on the agreement, he is likely to find a statement specifying, in effect, that goods purchased at Jeska's will be shipped "at the purchaser's risk." If Harrison wishes to have a destination contract, he must specify that wish in writing in the contract; a direct statement making Jeska, Inc., liable for the safety of the goods up until the time of delivery is best.

Incidentally, when the buyer has risk of loss, the buyer must pay the seller for the goods even if loss or damage makes those goods worthless to the buyer. Even if the grand piano you bought from Aunt Agatha in Texas arrives at your house in a few hundred pieces, you probably still have to pay Agatha the agreed-on amount. And when risk of loss falls to the seller, the seller must replace or repair goods as required, at no expense to the buyer. Small wonder then that buyers and sellers are very concerned about insurable interests.

Loss with Breach of Contract

As we've mentioned, despite the fact that risk of loss falls either to buyer or seller, an independent carrier may sometimes be ultimately liable under separate contract if it can be shown that the carrier has not acted properly or with due care in transporting goods. And third-party carriers, of course, also have insurance to protect themselves against just such eventualities. But goods are not always transferred by an independent carrier. Often the buyer or seller takes responsibility for delivery. And when that's the case, risk of loss often depends on how adequately each of the two parties have performed. Let's first consider the case where some breach of contract occurs, then look at how risk of loss is determined where no breach occurs.

If the seller breaches the contract by shipping nonconforming goods, risk of loss remains with the seller until either (1) the seller makes things right by curing the defect or (2) the buyer accepts the goods even though they do not conform to the contract. But the seller will be held responsible only if the goods are sufficiently nonconforming that the buyer can properly reject them. In other words, nitpicking is frowned upon. Suppose Mitzel, a car dealer, has ordered fifty automobiles from a manufacturer in another city. If the manufacturer sends station wagons when Mitzel ordered sport coupes, the court is likely to view that as a breach of contract, support Mitzel's right to reject the order, and hold the seller responsible for the goods until the correction is made. On the other hand, if Mitzel requests that half the cars in the shipment be equipped with automatic sunroofs and the manufacturer ships only twenty-four cars (out of fifty) that are so equipped, the court is not likely to view such a slight deviation from the agreement as a breach—assuming the manufacturer has acted in good faith.

Depending on the sales agreement, buyers sometimes have a period of time during which to ensure that goods conform to the contract. This may be particularly important with unusually large or diverse shipments of goods that cannot reasonably be inspected thoroughly within moments of delivery. For example, a building contractor may order large volumes of lumber, shingles, and related building supplies from a supplier and accept the goods upon delivery—yet still need time to ensure that everything meets contract specifications. In order to provide optimum fairness to both buyer and seller, the UCC holds that, following acceptance, the buyer assumes the risk of loss, even though conformity may be impossible to determine in full. If nonconformity is later discovered, however, the buyer will be liable for any intervening damage to the goods only to the extent of his or her insurance; the seller will have to make up the difference if the buyer's insurance is insufficient to cover any loss or damage. Clearly, the buyer is assuming some risk in accepting the goods prior to verifying that the entire shipment conforms to the contract; still, there is often little choice if buyers and sellers want their negotiations to move along promptly.

Buyers may also breach a contract—by rejecting *conforming* goods after they are identified to the contract but before they can be delivered. Because risk of loss has not yet shifted from seller to buyer, the seller is liable for damage or loss during this interim period. But—as in the preceding example—the seller is liable only to the extent of coverage provided by his or her insurance. Losses in excess of the seller's insurance coverage must be covered by the buyer.

Loss Without Breach of Contract

Where no breach occurs, placing risk of loss is somewhat more difficult, and it rests on circumstances rather than performance. Five different situations are possible.

First, as we've mentioned, if the seller sends the goods via shipment contract by means of a carrier, risk of loss passes to the buyer at the moment the goods are delivered to the carrier. In the case of a destination contract, however, risk of loss does not pass to the buyer until the goods are turned over to the buyer at the point of destination.

Second, if the goods are held for a time by a bailee — a party appointed to hold the goods under direction of the seller until negotiations are concluded — risk of loss transfers with a document of title, contract of sale, or other nonnegotiable instrument, or at such time as the bailee recognizes the rights of the buyer to the goods in question. How might this situation arise? Suppose that motorcycles shipped from Japan are sold by the manufacturer to a local dealer, but the motorcycles are actually imported, received, and temporarily stored by the manufacturer's distributor. This distributor would be the bailee of the manufacturer, and thus the risk of loss would remain with the manufacturer until the titles to the motorcycles were transferred to the local dealer — even though the motorcycles are 7,000 miles closer to the buyer.

Third, if the goods are to remain in the hands of the seller until the buyer comes to take possession personally (that is, not via a carrier), then the status of the seller is the key to assigning risk of loss. If the seller is a merchant, risk of loss passes to the buyer only when the buyer takes actual delivery of the goods. But if the seller is *not* a merchant, risk of loss passes to the buyer upon *tender of delivery* — in other words, as soon as the seller tells the buyer how and when to take delivery. For instance, if Lewis buys a boat from Waterways, Inc., and is told to take delivery at the Waterways Marina, risk of loss passes to Lewis only when she picks up the boat at the marina. If the boat is stolen before Lewis can take delivery, Waterways, Inc., is responsible. On the other hand, if Lewis buys a boat from a neighbor, Claussen, and Claussen tells Lewis to pick up the boat from the marina at her convenience, risk of loss passes to Lewis at the moment Claussen tells her how and when to take delivery. If the boat is stolen before she can get to the marina, Lewis is just out of luck — she must pay Claussen for the boat even though she has nothing of value to show for her money.

Fourth, in the event of a *sale on approval*, the risk of loss remains with the seller until the buyer accepts the goods, either through direct acknowledgment or (more commonly) simply by not returning them within a specified time. Of course, this does not mean that the seller must be responsible for damage to the goods resulting from the buyer's negligence or deliberate mistreatment of merchandise. But if something outside the buyer's control goes wrong, the seller is responsible. For example, if Fensley buys a computer with the clear understanding that it is on approval for ten days and it is stolen the day it arrives, the risk of loss is with the dealer (assuming, of course, that Fensley was in no way negligent).

Fifth, the buyer and seller can agree between themselves how and when risk of loss will be transferred from one to the other; the court will honor any agreement regarding risk of loss that is spelled out explicitly in the contract. Remember, though, if there is any confusion or if no provisions are made, the rules set forth by the UCC will be applied automatically.

Bulk Sales or Transfers

Article 6 of the Code covers bulk sales or transfers of goods. Bulk sales are not—as the name might at first suggest—sales of ungainly quantities of merchandise. Rather, they are the "lock, stock, and barrel" sorts of sales that an owner may conduct to raise cash quickly or to dispose of a business that is not doing well. Under the UCC, a bulk transfer is defined as *any transfer in bulk and not in the ordinary course of the transferor's business of a major part of the materials, supplies, merchandise, or other inventory*. If such sale includes a *substantial* portion of the seller's equipment (e.g., tools, computers, typewriters, photocopiers, and so forth), such equipment is also covered by the rules of Article 6.

How much is a "major" portion? How much is a "substantial" portion? The Code is deliberately indefinite about these amounts; interpretation is left up to the court. In part, this is to prevent businesses from juggling their sales records or taking other actions specifically to avoid the requirements of Article 6. But, in general, a sale of over half of the materials, supplies, merchandise, or inventory would qualify as a sale of a "major part" of the business. (Note, however, that Article 6 is specifically written to cover those businesses that deal in the selling of goods, not services. Thus, a retail clothing store would be covered, but a quick-copy business probably would not.)

Essentially, Article 6 is designed to protect the interests of unsecured creditors from unscrupulous or financially distressed business owners who might sell all or most of a business, pocket the money, and leave the creditors to deal with the new business owner. The UCC does not say, of course, that owners cannot dispose of their businesses or merchandise through sale. Rather, it specifies that they cannot use such a strategy as a means of avoiding legitimate debts.

To protect unsecured creditors, the UCC sets up a procedure that enlists the buyer's help and speaks to the buyer's self-interest. In simplest terms, if the Code's four-step procedure for identifying and notifying creditors is followed, then the buyer's purchase will be *free and clear* of claims by creditors not identified (or who did not come forward) during the procedure. So, while this process imposes heavy responsibilities on the buyer—rather than on the seller, as might first be expected—both buyer and unsecured creditors benefit from the UCC procedure.

The first step requires the seller to list in writing and under oath all creditors to the business. The list must include each creditor's name and address and the amount owed. The seller is wholly responsible for the accuracy of this list unless the buyer knows of some inaccuracy (e.g., a creditor whose name has been omitted) and chooses to ignore it. However, the buyer is well advised to question the accuracy and completeness of the list as a means of showing good faith in responding to the claims of potential creditors.

The second step requires buyer and seller jointly to itemize all merchandise being transferred. The list must be complete, specific, and detailed enough to allow a third party to determine precisely what has changed hands. This list, together with the creditor list, must be retained by the buyer for a period of at least six months following the sale.

Third, the *buyer* must notify every creditor on the list of the sale and the date when it will occur, and must do so *at least* ten days in advance of the sale. A creditor who is not notified may claim against the goods just as if the sale had not occurred. (This rule does not apply, however, if the goods are sold through auction.)

Finally, the *buyer* must ensure that any payments made relating to the sale of the goods are applied to the seller's debts.

It may seem at first as if a large responsibility falls to the buyer rather than to the seller who, after all, incurred the debts in the first place. Is this really fair? The Code rules do place a heavy burden on the buyer, but in doing so, the Code is attempting to protect public interests, even when they are counter to the personal interests of the buyer. The law recognizes that creditors—particularly unsecured creditors—are often not in a good position to ensure payment of debts owed to them. Further, the seller—who may already be in financial difficulty—cannot always be counted on to take care of the debts either. How many sellers, if faced with financial difficulties, are likely to place creditors' interests above their own? Yet it is in the public interest to ensure that debts are paid. Thus, responsibility is given to the buyer because he or she is in the best position to see to it that the money goes where it belongs.

By the way, a buyer who follows all four steps in good faith will be free of any claims from other creditors of whom that buyer had no legitimate knowledge. But—and here's the key—the buyer must be able to show that the steps required by the Code were carefully followed and that every effort was made to determine the debts of the business.

SOME PRACTICAL ADVICE

As either a buyer or seller, it is important to recognize the circumstances under which you have an insurable interest in goods or merchandise that change hands. Because the rules governing risk of loss are fairly complex and because risk of loss does not always fall to the party holding title, insurance is vital in relation to any major purchase or sale.

As a seller, it will normally be in your best interest to sell merchandise through a shipment contract, in which title and risk of loss pass to the buyer at the time of shipment. Be advised, however, that failure to conform to the terms of the contract can place you at some risk should the buyer reject the goods.

As a buyer, it is usually in your best interest to negotiate a destination contract, which places the seller at risk of loss until such time as the goods are delivered to their intended destination. Such a contract must be explicitly identified as a destination contract, however, since in the absence of such designation the court will always assume a shipment contract — in which case, most liability will fall to you as the buyer. (Be aware, though, that you're likely to have limited success in insisting that routine transactions be changed to destination contracts. It's unlikely, for example, that the mail-order office-products dealer selling you a box of file folders is going to renegotiate their normal sales contract to accommodate your preferences.)

Perhaps most important, as either buyer or seller, you are well advised to know precisely when exchange of title occurs because your rights under the contract can be affected. In particular, title transfer has a great deal to do with risk of loss.

Just how important is risk of loss? It can be critical. As a buyer, if risk of loss falls to you, keep in mind that you may be required to pay a seller for goods *even if* they have been stolen, lost, damaged, or destroyed; you could, in fact, be forced to pay substantial sums for nothing more than thin air. As a seller, if risk of loss falls to you, you'll probably be required to repair or replace goods that are lost or damaged. Again, the importance of having insurance adequate to protect your financial interests as either buyer or seller cannot be overemphasized.

Entrusting goods to a third-party carrier entails risks of its own. Remember, risk of loss does *not* transfer to that third party; it remains with either buyer or seller, depending on the situation. Of course, if the third-party carrier does not perform in good faith in the course of delivering the goods, you may have legal recourse. But the third party's liability is defined under a separate contract — and may or may not be covered by sufficient insurance to replace or recover the goods in the event of a problem. In short, if a third-party carrier must be involved, it is best to depend on a trusted, experienced professional whose reputation and insured status are well known.

As a buyer, be wary of purchasing goods from a nonmerchant. You may feel it is in your best interests to buy goods from a trusted friend or business associate, but if that person is not a merchant, keep in mind that risk of loss falls to you from the moment delivery is tendered — that is, from the moment your friend or colleague explains how or when to take delivery. In other words, you may be responsible for the merchandise hours or even days before it is in your hands. Should it be lost, destroyed, or stolen, you would still — legally, at any rate — owe your friend or colleague the agreed-on price.

Professional merchants should be cautious about negotiating sales on approval. Such arrangements can be very effective from a public relations standpoint, but the risk of loss remains with the seller until such time as the buyer accepts the goods. For this reason, it is important to specify within the sales contract such details as the time limit for the period of approval, or any circumstances under which the seller will not be responsible for damages (e.g., negligent mishandling of merchandise by the buyer).

Finally, should you ever be involved as a buyer or seller in a bulk transfer sale, be prepared to show that you have taken the steps required by the Code to identify, list, and contact all creditors to the business in question. Only then can you be certain that the goods are transferred free and clear, that they cannot be attached by creditors. And should you find yourself in the position of being a creditor to a business, you are obviously well advised to keep close tabs on the status of that business. Should it change hands, or should a portion of the goods from that business be sold, you'll need to be certain that the new owner knew *prior to the transfer* of your status as a creditor. That is the only way to protect your rights—and even then, there are no guarantees that the rights of the new buyer will not take precedence.

ASSIGNMENTS

- Before you watch the video program, be sure you've read through the preceding overview, familiarized yourself with the learning objectives for this lesson, and looked at the key terms below. Then, read Chapter 20 of Davidson et al., *Business Law*.
- After completing these tasks, view the video program for Lesson 16.
- After watching the program, take time to review what you've learned. First, evaluate your learning with the self-test which follows the key terms. Then, apply and evaluate what you've learned with the "Your Opinion, Please" scenarios at the end of this telecourse study guide lesson.

KEY TERMS

Before you read through the textbook assignment and watch the video program, take a minute to look at the key terms associated with this lesson. When you encounter them in the textbook and video program, pay careful attention to their meaning.

Bulk transfer sale	Risk of loss
Creditor	Sale on approval
Delivery	Shipment contract
Destination contract	Title
Insurable interest	Unsecured creditor
Revest	

SELF-TEST

The questions below will help you evaluate how well you've learned the material in this lesson. Read each one carefully, and select the letter of the option that best answers the question. You'll find the correct answer, along with a reference to the page number(s) where the topic is discussed, in the back of this telecourse study guide.

1. The term *title* is most closely related to

   a. insurable interest.
   b. legal ownership.
   c. attachment of goods.
   d. freedom from risk of loss.

2. Under the Uniform Commercial Code, title passes from seller to buyer when

   a. the seller completes performance of delivery.
   b. goods are identified to the contract.
   c. the seller exercises reservation of title.
   d. the buyer is presented with a negotiable document.

3. Output, Inc., purchases 200 personal computers from an overseas manufacturer through a telephone transaction. The manufacturer, upon discovering that the model Output had requested is not in stock, substitutes a comparable but slightly different model computer at the same wholesale cost. At this point, given the substitution, does Output, Inc., have an insurable interest in the personal computers?

   a. Yes, definitely—even though, technically, they are nonconforming goods.
   b. No; given the substitution, Output has no insurable interest.
   c. We cannot say without knowing whether Output will eventually accept nonconforming goods.

4. The term *insurable interest* is *best* defined as

   a. ownership.
   b. free and clear title to goods.
   c. the right to purchase insurance on goods.
   d. possession of goods—even if one does not own them.

5. Blake takes an expensive grandfather clock to Harvey's Clock Shop to be refinished. Harvey's specializes in the repair and restoration of old clocks. If an uninformed sales clerk at Harvey's sells Blake's clock to Arnold before Blake can come to pick it up, which of the following is true?

   a. Arnold will be required to return the clock to Blake.
   b. Blake can sue Harvey's for fraud.

     c. Unfair as it may seem, Blake entrusted the clock to Harvey's and now can
do nothing.

     d. Though Arnold now has a legal right to the clock, Blake can sue Harvey's
for recovery of the value of the clock.

6. A contract specifying that "all merchandise is shipped at the purchaser's risk"
is *most likely* to be viewed by the court as

    a. a destination contract.

    b. a shipment contract.

    c. There is no way of predicting since courts make this determination on a case-
by-case basis.

7. When a contract does not involve the use of an independent carrier to transport goods, the courts will — if the goods are damaged in transit — usually assign risk of loss between buyer and seller by looking at

    a. who currently holds title to the goods.

    b. the relative insurable interest of the two parties.

    c. whether the contract is a destination or a shipment contract.

    d. the performance of buyer and seller.

8. When goods are being sold, during what period of time is a bailee *most likely*
to be held responsible for risk of loss?

    a. Never; risk of loss is *strictly* limited to the relationship between buyer and
seller.

    b. During the entire period of time that the goods are in the bailee's hands.

    c. Only until the bailee acknowledges the rights of the buyer in the goods.

    d. Until such time as the buyer has had ample opportunity to examine and
accept the goods.

9. How much of its material, supplies, or merchandise must a business plan to
sell in a transaction before the UCC will look on the sale as a bulk transfer?

    a. Any amount over 25%

    b. 50% or more

    c. No less than 90%

    d. No set amount; the definition of a bulk transfer sale is open to the inter-
pretation of the court

10. UCC laws governing bulk transfer sales are viewed by some as placing an unjustified burden on the buyer. Probably the *main* reason for the UCC's position on this matter is that

    a. past experience indicates that the buyer is more likely than the seller to be
guilty of misconduct.

    b. the buyer is seen as being in the best position to ensure that public policy
is upheld through payment of the seller's debts.

    c. by virtue of selling the business, the seller simply excuses himself from all
further responsibility for that business's debts.

d. *None* of the above; it is simply an extension of the general "let the buyer beware" philosophy common in modern business.

YOUR OPINION, PLEASE

Read each of the following scenarios and answer the questions about the decisions you would make in each situation. Give these questions some serious thought; they may be used as the basis for the development of a more complex essay. You should base your decisions on what you've learned from this lesson, though you may incorporate outside readings or information gained through your own experience if it is relevant.

Scenario 1

Volume Video orders twenty-five video cameras from Electronic Age, Inc., a manufacturing company. The contract specifies that the video cameras are to be delivered to Volume Video's retail outlet address, 732 West Main. On the day of delivery, however, the carrier's truck has engine trouble, and to simplify matters and avoid a delay in the time of delivery, the driver deposits the cameras at Volume Video's warehouse outside town, where delivery is acknowledged by a warehouse supervisor.

That evening, a warehouse fire damages the cameras (along with other merchandise). Volume Video subsequently refuses to pay Electronic Age for the cameras, stating that Electronic had risk of loss up until the time of delivery at the specified destination. Electronic, in turn, charges that the goods were not only delivered to, but actually accepted by, an authorized Volume representative; it insists there can be no doubt that the risk of loss was Volume's. The whole thing is ridiculous, claims Electronic; the cameras were destroyed in a fire at a Volume warehouse, so how could they not be Volume's responsibility?

And, Electronic contends, if all that weren't enough, the contract with Volume was a shipment contract anyway, and was thus fulfilled upon shipment of conforming goods. Risk of loss, according to Electronic, belonged to Volume Video from the time of shipment; therefore, they charge, Volume will have to pay, despite the loss, or Electronic will sue to recover the cost of the cameras.

What's your opinion? Based on what you know of the situation, do you think Electronic is right in stating that the risk of loss belonged to Volume Video at the time of delivery to the warehouse? Has Electronic fulfilled the contract, or are they in breach? And who should bear the risk of loss?

- Is a court likely to support Electronic's position and require that Volume Video pay for the cameras? If so, on what grounds? If not, why?

- What factors support your answer?

- What factors might an attorney cite in arguing against your view?

- What steps, if any, might Electronic Age have taken to avoid a lawsuit in this situation?

- What steps, if any, might Volume Video have taken to avoid a lawsuit in this situation?

Scenario 2

Yesteryears Retail has a contract with Citywide Antiques for the purchase and delivery of $90,000 worth of antique furniture and other home furnishings. According to the terms of the contract, Yesteryears has twenty-one days following delivery in which to inspect merchandise and ensure quality and genuineness before the contract becomes final.

Yesteryears accepts the goods upon delivery and pays Citywide half the purchase price plus all delivery costs, with the remainder to be paid in two installments, thirty and sixty days following delivery.

Several days following delivery, Yesteryears' resident expert on antiques, in the course of inspecting the merchandise from Citywide, determines that at least half of it consists of high-quality replications which, though admirable in detail, are not genuine antiques. Yesteryears thereupon rejects the goods on the grounds that they do not conform to the contract, and requests immediate replacement of all imitation "antique" merchandise. Citywide agrees. Yesteryears, eager now to conclude the transaction, crates the merchandise hastily for its trip back to Citywide. Unfortunately, much of it is badly damaged in the course of being returned to Citywide.

Citywide refuses to accept return of the damaged reproductions, claiming that the risk of loss at the time of the return shipment belonged to Yesteryears. Yesteryears disagrees, saying that the goods were clearly received "on approval" and they had, therefore, no responsibility; it's unfortunate that the goods were damaged, but it is no concern of theirs. Besides, they point out, their insurance will cover only a fraction of the loss, so Citywide is going to have to pay something. Citywide, meanwhile, argues that Yesteryears assumed risk of loss at the moment they accepted delivery—even though they later rejected the merchandise following the inspection. No matter how you look at it, Citywide contends, there's no way they should have to pay anything.

What's your opinion? Based on what you know of the situation, do you think Citywide is right in their view that risk of loss rests with Yesteryears? That is, is the court likely to agree with Citywide that the risk of loss belonged to Yesteryears at the time of the damage? Or is Citywide responsible for all or part of the loss incurred through damage to the goods?

- If Citywide sues Yesteryears for their loss, is the court likely to support their position?

- What factors support your answer?

- What factors might an attorney cite in arguing against your view?

- What steps, if any, might Citywide have taken to prevent a lawsuit in this situation?
- What steps, if any, might Yesteryears have taken to prevent a lawsuit in this situation?

17

Performance
of a Sales Contract

LEARNING OBJECTIVES

Upon completing your study of this lesson, you should be able to

- Discuss the nature of the duties of the buyer and seller in a contract for the sale of goods.

- Identify the seller's principal duty in a sales contract and list and discuss the five ways in which this duty may be fulfilled.

- List and define six common shipping terms (e.g., F.O.B.) and explain the implications of each for the performance of the seller's duties.

- Define the terms *inspection* and *cure* and explain how these relate to the UCC's provisions for determining adequacy of performance.

- Identify and discuss the two duties imposed on a buyer under a sales contract.

- Discuss the special conditions affecting sales contracts under four new forms of business dealings: sale on approval, sale or return, consignment, and auction.

We don't usually think of sales transactions as being especially complicated — and most of the time they're not. The buyer makes an offer to purchase goods, the seller accepts, goods and money change hands, and the bargain is concluded. This apparently straightforward exchange is somewhat more complex in the eyes of the courts, however. Both buyer and seller have specific duties that they are required to perform in the course of the sale. And each has intervening rights as well — rights that come into play after the seller's duties are completed but before the buyer's duties begin — to help ensure that everything goes as it should. The purpose of this lesson is to outline those basic duties and rights as well as to explore several different kinds of contracts, each defined according to the conditions under which goods are transferred from seller to buyer.

OVERVIEW

What are the duties of a buyer and seller under a sales contract? First, and most basically, buyer and seller have a duty to perform the contract according to the terms of the contract. The Uniform Commercial Code allows buyer and seller great flexibility in determining how that performance will be carried out. Though the Code does provide rules of conduct governing sales, those rules are not meant to box the buyer and seller in. On the contrary, they're intended to provide some direction for those areas of performance that buyer and seller may have overlooked or simply not bothered to spell out. In interpreting a contract or establishing rules of performance, the UCC will also consider how others within a given industry generally conduct their business; buyers and sellers are expected to uphold the broad code of ethics defined by the accepted customs and practices of the trade.

It's important to note that a sales agreement can be modified without consideration, so long as the modifications meet with the approval of buyer and seller. Again, in the case of disagreement, common industry practices are likely to set guidelines for what will be expected. In addition, parole evidence — oral testimony, that is — may be offered in court by buyer or seller to help clarify ambiguous terms or requirements. But note that such evidence may *only* be used for purposes of clarification, not to add or change contract terms.

It is important that both buyer and seller know their rights — as well as their duties — under a sales contract. In fact, failure to demand that the other party perform as agreed on may be viewed by the court as a waiver of rights. For example, if a seller fails to deliver goods on time but the buyer does not object, the lack of objection may be interpreted by the courts as meaning, in effect, that so far as the buyer is concerned, late delivery is no big deal. Such an attitude (even if the assumption is inaccurate) tends to establish a precedent by which future performance will be judged; in other words, once the buyer sets a pattern of failing to object to late delivery, subsequent objections become difficult and are less likely to gain support. A seller who does not object to late payment by the buyer faces the same sort of dilemma. In short, while it makes good business sense for buyers and sellers to be accommodating and reasonable, allowing too much deviation from the terms set forth in a contract can easily place one party or the other in a compromising position.

Overall, the UCC requires that both buyer and seller act in good faith—honestly and fairly, that is. Sellers are expected to represent their goods accurately, not to promise delivery if they lack the means to make good on that promise, and not to behave in any way that makes it difficult for the buyer to fulfill his or her side of the agreement. Buyers, in turn, are expected not to make offers on goods they're unwilling or unable to pay for, to conclude performance under the contract in a timely manner, and to avoid doing anything which makes it difficult for the seller to fulfill his or her side of the agreement.

Let's look more specifically now at the rights and duties of buyers and sellers, and at some of the shipping terms that help define the conditions under which delivery occurs.

The Seller's Duties

The basic duty of the seller is to *tender delivery of conforming goods according to the terms of the contract*. The means by which delivery occurs is less important than the fact that the seller *facilitates* delivery by ensuring that the goods are available to the buyer and that the buyer knows of their availability. In other words, a seller who sets unreasonable conditions for delivery, or who keeps goods locked in a warehouse where they are generally unavailable, or who repeatedly fails to deliver goods on time would not be acting in good faith.

Delivery of the goods may occur in any of one of five different, non-overlapping ways:

1. the buyer personally takes the goods *from* the seller;

2. the seller personally takes the goods *to* the buyer;

3. the seller ships the goods to the buyer via common carrier;

4. the goods are placed in the hands of a third person, or bailee, who later releases them to the buyer without any documents of title; or

5. the goods are placed in the hands of a third person, or bailee, who later releases them to the buyer upon transfer of a document of title from seller to buyer.

All methods are fairly straightforward, and none is necessarily fraught with problems. Understandably, though, methods 1 and 2 are the least complicated because they involve only two parties—buyer and seller. The fewer the number of players, the less complex the game and the fewer the opportunities for something to go wrong. Methods 3, 4, and 5 tend to complicate the picture simply by virtue of involving other parties. This is not to suggest that buyers and sellers should not, for example, make use of common carriers; often that's the only practical and sensible way to transport goods. It is vital, however, to ensure that the carrier is reputable and experienced, and that the role of each party is carefully defined in terms of how and when goods will change hands.

Shipping Terms

Every shipping contract is either a *shipment* contract or a *destination* contract. This distinction is important because it determines who—buyer or seller—has risk of loss, or financial responsibility, while the goods are in transit.

Shipment Contract

Under a shipment contract, once the seller has properly contracted with a carrier and turned the goods over to that carrier for shipment, the goods belong to the buyer. And with that ownership goes risk of loss, or financial responsibility, in the event of damage, loss, or destruction. The only way the seller could be held responsible at this point is if it could be shown that the seller deliberately shipped nonconforming goods or somehow caused damage or loss. For example, let's say Montgomery buys a load of furniture from Justin, who arranges for delivery through a common carrier. Under the rules governing shipment contracts, the furniture and all responsibility for it belong to Montgomery as soon as Justin has contracted with the common carrier and delivered the furniture to that carrier for loading. If the furniture were damaged en route, Montgomery would have to pay for the loss. But suppose Justin crated the furniture himself instead of entrusting that responsibility to the carrier. If it could be shown that the crating were improper or careless, Justin might still be responsible for all or some of the damage. In most cases, however, shipment contracts place risk of loss upon the buyer.

Destination Contract

Under a destination contract, by contrast, the seller retains title and all risk of loss until the goods are delivered to the destination specified by the contract. In our previous example, if Justin and Montgomery had a destination contract—which must, by the way, be specified as such—then Justin would be financially responsible for the furniture until the carrier delivered it to Montgomery. In short, destination contracts place most risk upon the seller, until such time as delivery is completed and title transfers to the buyer.

You may be thinking that the UCC goes to a great deal of trouble to specify just who has responsibility and when. After all, most shipments of furniture arrive at their destinations in reasonably good shape. But some shipments don't arrive that way. And when you're awash in broken chair legs and scratched table tops, it's not the best time to begin haggling over who will pay for damages. Yet experience shows that buyers and sellers are notoriously casual about defining responsibilities until faced with a loss—when it's often too late to negotiate sensibly. Hence the importance of the UCC regulations.

Standard Shipping Terms

Now let's look at a few terms that relate to the details of shipment and destination contracts. F.O.B., or *free on board*, contracts may be either shipment or destination contracts, depending on whether the place of shipment or the destination is specified. These contracts call for the seller to be responsible for the goods up to the point they are "on board" the carrier at the specified departure point. For example, suppose Hart of Boston, the seller, ships a load of coal to Whitmore of Kansas City. If the contract reads F.O.B. Kansas City (the buyer's location), Whitmore and Hart have a destination contract—meaning that the seller, Hart, will have responsibility for the coal until the goods arrive at Kansas City. But if the coal is shipped F.O.B. Boston (the seller's location), theirs is a shipment contract, one in which the seller, Hart, has financial responsibility for the goods only until they are loaded "on board" in Boston.

F.A.S., or *free along side*, is a shipping term that was previously used to define contracts in which the seller was required only to get the goods to the named vessel and shipping port—at which time the seller's performance was concluded. The buyer then had all risks during loading, transporting, and unloading. Under current popular usage, however, F.A.S. is interpreted much the same way as F.O.B., with the named port determining whether the contract is a shipment or destination contract.

Ex ship indicates transportation by sea. In an ex ship contract, the seller is responsible for getting the goods to the named vessel and port *and* later unloading them. In other words, the goods become the buyer's responsibility only when they're unloaded upon the destination dock.

C.I.F. stands for *cost-insurance-freight*. C&F stands for *cost and freight*. Under either type of contract, the seller quotes a total price to the buyer—a price that includes not only the cost of the goods themselves, but also the costs of shipping and insuring those goods. Financial responsibility, however, falls to the buyer during transportation.

In a *no arrival, no sale* contract, the seller assumes risk of loss during transit—but may not have to replace the goods if they are lost or damaged during transit. That is, if the seller acted in good faith, shipped conforming goods, and was in no way responsible for the loss, there is no obligation to further perform under the sales contract. In other words, the seller is out the goods that were lost, but need not replace them in order to conclude the contract with the buyer. However, if it can be shown that the seller did not ship conforming goods or that the seller was in any way responsible for the loss, the seller *must* complete performance—that is, must replace the goods and get them to the buyer. As you may have noted, while risk of loss technically falls to the seller under this sort of contract, the buyer is somewhat "at risk" as well—even though he or she does not stand to lose anything financially. After all, if the goods are lost, the buyer will likely have to renegotiate their purchase; this means that the buyer no longer has timely delivery of the needed merchandise—and may have to pay a higher price than previously agreed to.

C.O.D., or *collect on delivery*, is a term most consumers know well. Nearly everyone makes a C.O.D. purchase at some point. C.O.D. contracts are destination contracts, in which the risk during transit remains with the seller. On delivery, the buyer is obligated to pay for the purchase immediately, and *before* inspecting the merchandise. If the buyer cannot pay on delivery, or refuses to pay, title to the goods remains with the seller. Payment, by the way, is not considered acceptance in this case. In other words, the buyer still has the right to examine the goods later, to report or object to any defects or nonconformities, and to request that those defects be corrected or *cured*.

Intervening Rights of Buyer and Seller

Once delivery is completed, the seller's duty under the contract has been performed. Before it is time for the buyer to perform, however, both buyer and seller have intervening rights. And these concern the inspection of the goods to ensure conformity and the possible correction of any nonconformities. First, let's look at the intervening rights of the buyer.

Rights of the Buyer

Under the UCC, the buyer has the right to inspect any goods purchased in any reasonable manner and at any reasonable time and place. The buyer may even, if the situation warrants it, conduct laboratory tests or do whatever is necessary to make sure the goods conform to required specifications. The cost of any inspection must, however, be borne fully by the buyer. (The exception to this is in cases where the inspection reveals nonconformity and the buyer rejects the goods on the basis of that nonconformity; in such cases, the seller is obligated to pay for the inspection costs.)

It's fairly simple to understand this rationale. Let's say Gillespie purchases four tons of chemical fertilizer from Furber. Gillespie, being a particular sort, wants a certain percentage of the shipment analyzed to make certain it conforms precisely to his specifications. The laboratory tests—though important—may well be fairly costly and time-consuming, but since Gillespie is footing the bill himself, it's in his own interest to make sure those tests are as time- and cost-efficient as possible. At the same time, though, he is likely to make sure that the tests are thorough and revealing, worth the time and money invested. And he's unlikely to bother with tests that are unnecessary.

What happens if the buyer does not conduct an inspection or conducts only a hasty, cursory inspection? Such behavior is risky and may constitute a waiver of rights. Let's say Gillespie visits the freightyard on the day the fertilizer arrives, but he's in a hurry. He looks it over, examines it hastily, sees that all the paperwork is in order, and, based on the reputation of the seller's company, decides no further inspection is necessary. He notifies the seller that "Everything seems to be in order," saying, in effect, that he will accept the merchandise. Some weeks later, a routine chemical analysis reveals some irregularity that may cause damage to Gillespie's crops. Can he now raise an objection, so long after the fact? Probably not. Unless it can be shown that this irregularity was not likely to have shown up in a good, thorough inspection, or that the nature of the irregularity makes it highly questionable whether the seller acted in good faith, the court is likely to take the position that Gillespie should have been more conscientious in performing his inspection—and he's now just out of luck.

The buyer always has this right to inspect, but with that right goes an obligation to conduct a thorough inspection within a reasonable time. What's "reasonable" is likely to be a matter of interpretation. Certainly, buyers are not expected to visit shipyards in the middle of the night in order to review merchandise immediately upon delivery. But neither are they permitted to delay weeks before raising objections. Remember, most UCC regulations are designed, ultimately, to keep the world of commerce in motion.

What happens when inspection reveals that the goods do not conform? In that case, the buyer faces a choice. He or she may either decide that the nonconformity is not worth haggling over and just accept the goods anyway, or decide that the nonconformity makes the goods unacceptable. If the goods aren't acceptable, the buyer must promptly notify the seller that all is not well; at this point, the seller has an intervening right: the right to *cure* the defect—to put the goods into conformity with the contract—so as not to be held in breach.

Rights of the Seller

Note, however, that the seller must cure the problem *by the deadline* for performance set forth in the contract. Thus, sellers who procrastinate about shipping goods had better be quite certain that those goods do conform to contract specifications. For instance, let's say Feathersoft Furniture ships a brown leather couch which gets to Challinor on May 30, with a contract deadline of June 1. Unfortunately, Challinor had ordered purple velvet, not brown leather, and immediately phones Feathersoft about the mixup. Feathersoft now has only two days in which to deliver the correct couch or risk being held in breach of contract.

On the other hand, recall that the UCC places considerable importance on past history and performance in determining acceptable behavior between buyer and seller. For example, suppose that Partytime Glassware routinely orders crystal, stoneware, and chinaware from Choruby Importers. Choruby fills the orders as best it can, but it often makes substitutions when certain items are unavailable or out of stock—and this behavior has always been satisfactory to Partytime. What happens if Partytime suddenly—for the first time in ten years of business dealings—objects to an order they claim is nonconforming? Will the court uphold their right to make this objection? Yes; after all, the goods are nonconforming.

Choruby will, however, be given an extended period in which to conform to the contract. Based on past performance, the court will hold that Choruby was not being at all unreasonable in assuming that Partytime would overlook the substitutions. A contract will always be enforced precisely if the parties insist on it; that, after all, is the purpose of having a contract in the first place—to clarify expectations. But at the same time, where any elements are open to interpretation, past behavior invariably counts. And notoriously tolerant buyers who suddenly become sticklers for performance are likely to find themselves forced into continued patience, even though their demands may ultimately be met.

The Buyer's Duties

The buyer's duties arise *only* after the seller's duties are completed and after both parties have had an opportunity to exercise their intervening rights (notably, the buyer to inspect the goods, the seller to correct or cure any nonconformities). The buyer has two duties: acceptance and payment. Acceptance, which obligates the buyer to pay for the goods at the contract price, occurs after the buyer has had a reasonable time in which to inspect the goods.

Acceptance of goods can occur in any one of these four non-overlapping ways:

1. The buyer tells the seller that the goods conform to the contract.

2. The buyer tells the seller that although the goods do not precisely conform, they will be acceptable all the same.

3. The buyer notes upon inspection that the goods do not conform, but fails to properly reject them.

4. The buyer does something that is not consistent with the seller's ownership of the goods (e.g., misuses the goods or damages the goods before title has transferred).

Obviously, the first two situations are the least troublesome. Recognize, though, that once goods are accepted, the buyer cannot later reject them unless one of two situations occurs: (1) the buyer discovers a "hidden" defect that could not reasonably have been uncovered through a normal inspection, or (2) the buyer has accepted the goods with the understanding that the seller will cure some nonconformity which the seller then fails to cure.

Discovering hidden defects can be tricky business, and goods that are inconsistent in quality can create particular difficulties. For instance, suppose Denman orders feed for his livestock from Blewett Brothers Feedlot. Denman cannot reasonably inspect every bale of hay or every bushel of grain in a multi-ton load. He will have to inspect a sample of the order and trust that the quality of that sample reflects the quality of the lot. What if it doesn't, though? Well, under the Code, acceptance of one portion of a commercial unit—such as a ton of hay—is considered acceptance of the whole thing. So technically, if Denman inspects only a small portion of the feed and then accepts the load, he's accepted everything.

The validity of a later objection will probably rest on several factors: (1) the likelihood of Denman's discovering the problem had his inspection been a little more thorough; (2) the seriousness of the problem itself—that is, the extent of the nonconformity; (3) the usual course of performance for buyers and sellers in similar circumstances; and (4) the relative good faith in which the seller has acted. In other words, is it likely that the seller deliberately shipped nonconforming goods, hoping to sneak them by, or was the nonconformity largely outside the seller's control? In short, the buying and selling of large quantities of merchandise places heavy obligations on both the buyer — to ensure that acceptance is based on reasonable and thorough examination of the goods — and the seller — to ensure that the goods themselves are reasonably consistent in quality so that inspection is simplified and valid.

Once the buyer accepts goods (or fails to reject goods properly), the buyer has a second duty: to tender payment. The buyer may pay for goods in any manner that is consistent with the usual course of business in a given trade. For example, a car dealer cannot arbitrarily refuse to accept checks when checks are a common method of payment in the car dealing business. In many cases, however, while the seller has a right to demand cash, in doing so he or she must allow the buyer a reasonable period of time — usually one full business day — in which to obtain the cash.

Special Situations

Sellers eager for sales may create special contracts designed to appeal to buyers. But these contracts, while often enticing, may create some special problems.

Sale on Approval

For example, in a *sale on approval* the buyer purchases goods primarily for personal use, with the understanding that the goods can be returned within a specified time even if they conform fully to the contract. During the extended period of inspection, the buyer is free to use the goods in the manner intended, so long as he or she does not *misuse* the goods. For example, say Morris buys a stereo on a thirty-day sale-on-approval contract. She need not leave the stereo in the shipping box. She is quite free to hook it up and use it, provided she treats it with reasonable care. Setting it up outdoors in a rainstorm or letting her seven-year-old daughter take it to school would likely constitute an abuse of her contract privileges, however, and obligate her to pay for the stereo.

At the end of the thirty days, Morris could choose to keep the stereo and pay for it, or she could return it to the store without any obligation. Morris would be viewed as accepting the stereo if she did any of the following:

1. notified the store that she wanted the stereo and intended to keep it;

2. simply failed to return the stereo within the thirty days, even if she did not more directly indicate acceptance; or

3. subjected the stereo to any sort of abuse or mistreatment.

Sale or Return

A *sale or return* contract is quite common for merchant-to-merchant sales. It exists when a buyer purchases goods that he or she intends to turn around and sell. Under such a contract, title and risk go hand in hand with possession of the goods.

While the buyer is in possession, he or she has both title and risk of loss. So if something happens and the goods cannot be returned to the seller, the buyer has, in effect, "purchased" them, even though they may have been stolen or destroyed by fire rather than resold. The buyer reserves the right to return any undamaged goods to the seller, however, without obligation to pay. Suppose Jenkins, who runs a theater lobby concession stand, buys 1,000 packs of Caramel Chewies from Goody Foods on a sale-or-return contract. If Chewies aren't a hit with theater goers, Jenkins can simply return them to Goody and owe only for those Chewies that were bought. On the other hand, if someone breaks into the theater after hours and steals the Chewies, Jenkins owes Goody for whatever was stolen.

Consignment

Under a *consignment* contract, the owner of the goods — the consignor — allows a consignee to display and sell those goods for a percentage of the selling price. Because of problems in clarifying risk of loss in consignment contracts, the UCC states that consignment will be treated as a sale-or-return contract unless other specific arrangements are made. And when the consignment is a sale or return, risk of loss falls to the party currently in possession of the goods. In other words, under current practice, if Axtell accepts a gold watch on consignment from Dellwood and the watch is stolen before Axtell can sell it, Axtell is responsible. The watch was in his possession — even though he may have always thought of Dellwood as the "owner" of the watch — and the risk of loss became his when he took the watch on consignment.

Auction

In an *auction*, the auctioneer sells the goods to the highest bidder on behalf of the seller. Auctions are a little different from most sales transactions in that the auctioneer does not give the same warranties to a buyer that other sellers typically give. In an auction, the sale is complete when the auctioneer accepts the bid. But even in the course of accepting, an auctioneer may elect to reopen the bidding.

Goods at auction may be sold *with reserve* or *without reserve*. If the auction is held without reserve, the goods *must* be sold to the highest bidder; if it's held with reserve, the auctioneer (acting on behalf of the seller) may declare all the bids on an item too low and refuse to accept any of them. (Incidentally, sellers themselves sometimes bid on their own merchandise in an effort to drive the bidding up; this practice is not considered ethical, however. A bidder who is forced into a higher bid by such a practice may legally take the goods at the last bid before the seller entered the action, or may reject the sale altogether.)

SOME PRACTICAL ADVICE

As a buyer or seller, it's important to be aware that you have both specific rights and specific duties under the law, regardless of the form your sales contract may take. How much freedom you have in exercising those rights and duties is at least partly up to you, since you can always negotiate a sales contract to suit yourself and the other party, subject to the Code's mandate to act in good faith. Keep in mind, however, that any specifics of performance that are not spelled out in the contract will fall under the direction of the UCC, in accordance with recognized common business practices. With that in mind, it's wise to know what others in a given field are doing. Their performance is likely to influence what's legally expected of you and how your contract and business problems will be resolved.

Both buyer and seller are always smart to consider the most expedient possible means of delivery. Indeed, simplifying delivery is often critical to ensuring that a sales transaction is concluded smoothly. Where it is necessary to use a carrier, make sure that the carrier is reputable and experienced and that the roles of all parties are well defined. And it's certainly worth your while, as a buyer or seller, to become familiar with common shipping terms like F.O.B. and F.A.S.; if you're not, you may find yourself with unexpected costs for transportation and unforeseen responsibilities for the security of the goods. Knowing precisely when and how you take ownership of the goods in question, as well as when and under what circumstances you could be at financial risk for their damage or loss, can save much grief later. Remember, the time to negotiate is before the sales contract is signed; once you have entered into an agreement, your liability is largely determined by the UCC regulations governing your type of contract.

As we've noted, both buyer and seller are expected to act in good faith. What does this mean specifically? Let's consider things first from the seller's perspective, then from the buyer's. First, recall that the seller's basic duty is to tender delivery of the goods. Sounds simple enough, but it does involve some specific obligations. First, the seller has responsibility for ensuring that the goods conform to the contract; failure to do so can increase the seller's potential liability under most contracts. And obviously, a seller who attempts to hide defects, hoping that the buyer will overlook them or not discover them through inspection, risks becoming the target of legal action. Second, the seller must provide for reasonable packaging and transportation, taking into account the nature of the goods themselves and whether they're fragile, perishable, and so forth. Choosing to ship forty pounds of T-bone steaks by parcel post in an uninsulated cardboard box is likely to make the seller liable if the steaks don't survive the trip.

The buyer, as you'll recall, has two basic duties: to accept the goods, and then to pay for any goods that are accepted. This has several implications. First, buyers should be particularly conscientious about inspecting goods prior to acceptance. A cursory review is not in a buyer's interest and may waive a buyer's right to demand that the seller cure any defects that are later discovered. Thorough inspection is the buyer's best strategy in ensuring that responsibility for dealing with any nonconformities will fall to the seller. Second, the buyer must act in a prompt and reasonable manner, regardless of whether the goods are accepted or rejected. Failure to respond within a reasonable period is likely to be interpreted as acceptance, and may leave a buyer in the position of paying for goods he or she would not otherwise have purchased. Third—though it seems an obvious point—a buyer is wise to make sure of his or her own ability to pay for goods ordered.

A final caution: Sellers who create or use special contracts such as sale-on-approval contracts often find such arrangements to be effective marketing tools. But they can involve problems. Unscrupulous buyers can cause considerable inconvenience and expense for merchants who allow their goods to be used on a trial basis with little obligation to the buyer. On the other hand, a buyer who accepts merchandise on such a basis is under strict obligation to handle it with the utmost care, and any damage that occurs to the merchandise during the trial period—even if it's slight—may obligate the buyer to purchase an unwanted product. Perhaps the real lesson here is that buyers and sellers alike should be fully aware of all obligations and rights before entering any sales contract.

Above all, remember that if you don't like the way in which the terms of a contract are drafted, you have the right—before signing—to attempt to negotiate changes. Remember, the UCC will respect any arrangement between buyer and seller that does not violate the law or the general business ethics of the industry. Once a contract is signed, however, UCC regulations will have great influence over how any matters not addressed in the contract will be interpreted.

ASSIGNMENTS

- Before you watch the video program, be sure you've read through the preceding overview, familiarized yourself with the learning objectives for this lesson, and looked at the key terms below. Then, read Chapter 19 of Davidson et al., *Business Law*.
- After completing these tasks, view the video program for Lesson 17.
- After watching the program, take time to review what you've learned. First, evaluate your learning with the self-test which follows the key terms. Then, apply and evaluate what you've learned with the "Your Opinion, Please" scenarios at the end of this telecourse study guide lesson.

KEY TERMS

Before you read through the textbook assignment and watch the video program, take a minute to look at the key terms associated with this lesson. When you encounter them in the textbook and video program, pay careful attention to their meaning.

Auction	F.A.S.
Bailee	F.O.B.
C.I.F. and C&F	Intervening rights
C.O.D.	Negotiable document
Commercial unit	No arrival, no sale
Common carrier	Nonconforming goods
Conforming goods	Rejection
Consignment	Risk of loss
Cure	Sale on approval
Destination contract	Sale or return
Document of title	Shipment contract
Ex ship	Tender delivery

SELF-TEST

The questions below will help you evaluate how well you've learned the material in this lesson. Read each one carefully, and select the letter of the option that best answers the question. You'll find the correct answer, along with a reference to the page number(s) where the topic is discussed, in the back of this telecourse study guide.

1. The *basic* duty of a seller in a sales contract is to

   a. set a fair price.
   b. advertise the merchandise to attract as many buyers as possible.
   c. tender delivery of conforming goods.
   d. ensure that the buyer thoroughly inspects goods prior to acceptance.

2. Which of the following is a common, legally acceptable way for delivery to occur?

   a. All of the following are acceptable, common methods of delivery.
   b. The buyer personally picks up the goods from the seller
   c. The goods are placed in the hands of a bailee until the seller delivers a document of title to the buyer
   d. The seller ships the goods to the buyer via common carrier

3. Delivery of goods usually proceeds smoothly. But when problems *do* arise, it is, according to the lesson, most often because

   a. a third person is involved in the delivery, thereby complicating the situation.
   b. buyer and seller do not take time to negotiate a clear, unambiguous contract.
   c. either buyer or seller fails to act in good faith.
   d. the nature of the goods themselves makes delivery very difficult.

4. It is generally to the buyer's advantage, whenever possible, to negotiate a

    a. shipment contract.
    b. destination contract.
    c. *Either one*; both are advantageous to the buyer.
    d. *Neither*; both are advantageous to the seller.

5. Eber, an auto broker in New York, purchases ten cars from LaMontagne, a dealer in France. LaMontagne specifies one unit price which includes the cost of the cars, the cost of loading and shipment, insurance, and the cost of unloading and final transport to destination. This is an example of which kind of contract?

    a. C.O.D.
    b. C.I.F.
    c. Ex ship
    d. No arrival, no sale

6. Miller orders a pair of custom leather boots, C.O.D., from Happy Trails Boot Makers. When they arrive, Miller pays the carrier for the boots, then opens the package, only to discover that the boots are the wrong color and three sizes too small. Clearly, Happy Trails has shipped the wrong order. At this point, which of the following is true?

    a. In paying for the boots, Miller has accepted them; if he wants others, the only recourse now is to place a new order.
    b. If Miller contacts Happy Trails promptly, they will have to send the correct boots—at their expense.
    c. Unfortunately, Happy Trails can allege that Miller did not conduct a proper inspection; therefore, though Happy Trails must cure, Miller is obligated to pay for the return of the incorrect goods and the shipment of the new goods.

7. Which of the following is an intervening right of the buyer?

    a. The right to accept merchandise without paying for it
    b. The right to accept nonconforming merchandise
    c. The right to accept merchandise without inspection
    d. The right to inspect merchandise before accepting it

8. Car dealer Klein is selling Doig a car. At high speeds (60 mph or over), the steering of this car becomes erratic, making the car all but impossible to control. Doig test drives the car around the streets near Klein's dealership and discovers nothing wrong—but during the test drive, he never drives anywhere close to 60 mph. If Doig later discovers the defect, is Klein responsible for curing it?

    a. Yes, probably; Doig can argue that the steering problem is a hidden defect, unlikely to be discovered through the test-drive procedure.
    b. No, probably not; once Doig has accepted the car, nothing more can be done—even if the defect is difficult to detect.

c. We cannot say without knowing whether this was a shipment contract or delivery contract.

9. Williams purchases goods from Kelly Mercantile on a ten-day sale-on-approval contract. Williams will be viewed as accepting the goods and will be obligated to pay the full contract price *if*

a. she uses them.
b. she finds that the goods conform fully to the contract.
c. she keeps the goods for the full ten days without rejecting them.
d. she subjects the goods to unreasonable usage.

10. Rowan attends an auction held without reserve and bids $500 on an antique rocker. The owner, believing that the bid is way too low, bids $750 on her own rocker in the hope of getting a higher price. Not wishing to lose the rocker, Rowan raises her bid to $800, which the auctioneer accepts. Later, Rowan discovers that it was the seller who bid against her. Which of the following is true?

a. Rowan may, if she wishes, buy the rocker for $750, the seller's bid.
b. Because the auctioneer has accepted her bid, Rowan must pay the $800.
c. Because the auction was held without reserve, Rowan is free now to change her bid, and the auctioneer must accept any offer she makes.
d. Rowan may, if she wishes, buy the rocker for $500 — or she may void the sale altogether.

YOUR OPINION, PLEASE

Read each of the following scenarios and answer the questions about the decisions you would make in each situation. Give these questions some serious thought; they may be used as the basis for the development of a more complex essay. You should base your decisions on what you've learned from this lesson, though you may incorporate outside readings or information gained through your own experience if it is relevant.

Scenario 1

Bailey orders a compact disc player C.O.D. from Peachtree Audio, an established and apparently reputable mail-order dealer from whom she's purchased other stereo equipment in the past. When the player arrives, Bailey pays for it in full, then unboxes it to have a look. Everything appears fine; it is the model she ordered, and so far as she can tell, it's brand new and has never been out of the box.

Because she is about to leave on a two-week vacation, Bailey doesn't want to take time to set up the stereo right away. Further, she does not see any need to hurry. She sets the CD player to one side in the den and forgets about it for the time being.

On returning home two weeks later, Bailey tries to set up her new player, but some apparent flaw causes a distortion in the sound. Bailey carefully reads the owner's manual but can discover no reason for the problem, and concludes that it is some internal defect well beyond her capabilities to analyze or fix. But when she calls Peachtree's customer-service department, they tell Bailey that they're sorry, but her failure to inform them of the problem on receiving the product constitutes acceptance of the merchandise. They advise Bailey to send the CD player to the manufacturer's warranty repair facilities. Unfortunately, they admit, it could take as much as ten weeks for Bailey to get her player back.

Bailey charges that the flaw is, in effect, a hidden defect that she could not reasonably be expected to have discovered in her initial inspection of the unit; she wants either her money back or a new, working player sent immediately. Peachtree disagrees, saying that the obvious way to inspect a piece of stereo equipment is to plug it in and see that it works; the defect certainly wasn't hidden. The manufacturer's warranty will get Bailey a working CD player, but she can't expect Peachtree to take responsibility. But that's exactly what Bailey expects; she sues for recovery of the cost of the compact disk player.

What's your opinion? Based on what you know of the situation, do you think Bailey's suit is likely to be successful? Is she correct in alleging that the sound-distortion problem constitutes a hidden defect? Or is that something she should have discovered on inspection? Has Bailey lived up to her responsibilities as a buyer? Has Peachtree acted responsibly as a seller?

- Is Bailey likely to win her suit for recovery of cost? Why?
- What factors support your answer?
- What factors might an attorney cite in arguing against your view?
- What steps, if any, might Bailey have taken to prevent a lawsuit in this situation?
- What steps, if any, might Peachtree Audio have taken to prevent a lawsuit in this situation?

Scenario 2

Caputo Contractors has been ordering wood for many years from Woodsman Lumber Products, Inc. Woodsman, whose inventory varies from week to week, often substitutes a slightly higher or lower grade of lumber, with subsequent price adjustments, about which Caputo has always been very flexible.

When Caputo places an order for lumber that's to be used in the construction of a new restaurant, however, the Caputo foreman specifies in writing that the lumber must be top grade, deliverable by July 1 on a shipment contract. Woodsman agrees. However, inspection on delivery, about noon on June 30, reveals that despite the special request, Woodsman has again substituted a lower grade of lumber—not satisfactory for this particular job. The Caputo foreman immediately phones Woodsman to tell them that they are not in compliance and to say that Caputo—having its own deadlines to meet—will sue unless Woodsman completes performance by the July 1 deadline.

Woodsman counters that a single day is not sufficient to replace the order. They are willing to make things right, but they need more time—at least until noon of July 5. Caputo says that will not do. Woodsman, however, eager to set things right, makes an extra effort, and does manage to pull together the order by noon on July 3—earlier than they had promised, but later than Caputo had demanded. Caputo refuses to accept delivery, however; they've already bought the required lumber from a different supplier and have had their carpenters working on the installation.

Woodsman now has a load of lumber but no purchaser. They contend Caputo must pay for the lumber. Caputo disagrees, maintaining that the contract was breached. Not so, says Woodsman, since delivery was made on June 30, and even though nonconforming goods were shipped, that hadn't ever bothered Caputo before. Caputo responds that this is a special case and they had informed Woodsman in writing of that fact. That's irrelevant given their past performance, claims Woodsman; they file suit against Caputo for the cost of the lumber.

What's your opinion? Based on what you know of the situation, do you think Woodsman Lumber acted in good faith? Is Caputo acting in good faith in rejecting the lower-quality lumber? In demanding performance by July 1? In refusing the subsequent delivery of conforming lumber?

- Is Woodsman likely to win a suit asking for payment for the lumber? Why or why not?

- What factors support your answer?

- What factors might an attorney cite in arguing against your view?

- What steps, if any, might Caputo have taken to prevent a lawsuit in this situation?

- What steps, if any, might Woodsman have taken to prevent a lawsuit in this situation?

18

Warranties and Product Liability

LEARNING OBJECTIVES

Upon completing your study of this lesson, you should be able to

- Define the term *warranty* and discuss its implications for the duties of the seller under contract law.

- Distinguish among the three main types of warranty — express, implied, and statutory — and provide a hypothetical example illustrating each.

- Explain how a seller may modify or exclude express and implied warranties, and explain the implications of such exclusions.

- Define the concept of *product liability* and discuss the potential remedies available under tort law to a person who is injured by goods for which no warranty provisions are made.

As buyers of goods, all of us are concerned with getting our money's worth from a product. Many of us, in fact, are reluctant to purchase any major product that is not covered by a warranty. How much protection does a warranty really provide? What are the obligations of the seller in providing a warranty, and how does one sort of warranty differ from another? These are just a few of the questions we'll explore in this lesson.

In addition, we'll look at the remedies open to the buyer when no warranty is available. And, as we shall see, the requirements imposed on a seller or manufacturer for ensuring quality and safety are considerable. In many ways, ours is a marketplace geared to the needs of the buyer. On the other hand, there are limits to sellers' or manufacturers' liabilities, and the wise purchaser will be aware of those limits and knowledgeable about the extent of consumer protection offered through warranty.

OVERVIEW

Some observers have suggested that the old saying "Let the buyer beware" has now become outmoded. With greater attention to consumers' needs and more laws directed at protecting consumers' rights, it's been suggested that the modern American marketplace is better characterized by a "Let the seller beware" maxim. Perhaps. It's only fair to recognize, however, that the laws governing product quality and safety are not intended to take sides between buyer and seller, or to make life more difficult for one than for the other. Rather, such laws are designed to serve the public good by ensuring that sellers and manufacturers will, to the extent reasonable, take responsibility for the products they make or sell. Sellers, after all, are not sellers all the time—sometimes they're consumers, too.

The seller or manufacturer is not, of course, responsible for protecting the safety or welfare of consumers who flagrantly misuse products. A consumer who used a backyard barbecue as a central heating source, for instance, would be hard-pressed to sue the seller or manufacturer for negligence if his house burned down. Like sellers and manufacturers, consumers are expected to act in a responsible manner. At the same time, however, consumers have a right to expect that the goods they purchase will be all they are promised to be. Promises and expectations are at the heart of laws governing warranties.

What Is a Warranty?

A *warranty* is a *promise that a proposition of fact is true*. Because it is a kind of promise, it becomes part of the sales contract, and, as such, it can be critical to the consumer. It is based on the seller's assurance to the buyer that the goods will meet certain standards. Whatever is promised through warranty *must* be provided by the seller; otherwise, the seller may be held in breach of contract. What is not promised through warranty, however, usually cannot be enforced against the seller — even if the buyer finds that position unfair.

Types of Warranties

In general, there are three types of warranties: *express*, *implied*, and *statutory*. We'll examine each of these in some detail, with examples. For now, simply keep in mind that the presence of one type of warranty does not rule out the others. In other words, while some products may be covered by only one type of warranty, others may be covered by all three types. In fact, coverage by all three warranties is not at all uncommon.

Express Warranties

Let's look first at *express* warranties. An express warranty can be given *only* by the seller. Such a warranty is said by the UCC to be a part of "the basis of the bargain." It is created in one of three different ways:

1. The seller *affirms* a fact or promise relating to the goods, thereby creating an express warranty that the goods will live up to that fact or promise. (Example: Borok, a car dealer, affirms the manufacturer's promise that the engine will not need substantial repair during the first 50,000 miles.)

2. The seller *describes* the goods, thereby creating an express warranty that the goods will match that description. (Example: Cardley, a furniture salesman, describes the covering on a couch as being 100% nylon, specially treated to be stain- and water-repellant.)

3. The seller provides a sample or model of the goods, thereby creating an express warranty that the goods purchased by the buyer will match that model or sample. (Example: Compton, a dealer in leather goods, shows an expensive leather suitcase to a customer and agrees to ship the buyer one "just like it.")

Express warranties may be created orally; they do not have to be written. Further, there is no need for the seller to *intend* to create a warranty. Nor is there need for the buyer to show that he or she relied on the seller's promise. For instance, to use one of our preceding examples, it doesn't matter whether Borok, the car dealer, knows that he is creating an express warranty when he affirms the manufacturer's promise that the engine will last. Nor does the buyer have to show that she relied on this promise in purchasing the car. It is enough that Borok makes the promise. Notice, however, that all the promises in these examples have something in common: They are all founded on fact, not opinion.

Opinions, or relative statements of comparison, are not taken to be warranties. For example, the car dealer, Borok, might say to a prospective buyer, "This is a dandy car—one you'll enjoy for years." That's opinion. It's not based on fact; it's not provable one way or the other. Similarly, if Cardley, the furniture salesman, tells his customers, "You won't find a finer couch for the money anywhere in the city," he may seem to be making a factual comparison, but in reality he's just applying his own subjective standards. Such claims are typically referred to as "puffery," and they are not binding on the seller. The buyer who takes such claims at face value does so at his or her own risk.

On the other hand, Cardley cannot claim the couch fabric is nylon if it is really rayon or some other fabric; it is either nylon or it is not. Similarly, when Compton promises her buyer a suitcase "just like" the one on display, there must be a reasonably identical match. She cannot substitute a different model on the grounds that the substitute is "of comparable quality." The implication when a model is displayed is that the consumer will purchase a product that matches that model—unless, of course, the seller clearly states otherwise.

Note that the seller is not required by law to provide any express warranties. And the simplest way of excluding such warranties is simply to make no oral claims about the products. Obviously, this may limit the seller's ability to negotiate freely with the consumer or to effectively market the product. At the same time, it helps make sellers responsible for the claims they do make.

Implied Warranties

Implied warranties are *not* created by the seller. Rather, they are imposed by law, and they are present without any promise at all by the seller *unless* the buyer surrenders them. There are four types of implied warranty:

1. *warranty of title*, the assurance that the buyer is receiving good title to the goods being transferred, and that such goods are free of hidden security interests, liens, or other claims that might be imposed by third parties;

2. *warranty of infringement*, the protection against the rightful claim of any third person—one who might claim a patent on the product, for instance;

3. *warranty of merchantability*, the assurance that the goods are fit for the purpose intended. In order to be considered merchantable under law, goods must meet a number of explicit criteria, including these: They must be adequately and appropriately labeled and packaged, must be of consistent quality in comparison to other similar goods within the trade, must be of consistent quality within the sample, must be suitable for the intended use, and must conform to any claims or facts that appear on the label. A manufacturer of ballpoint pens, for instance, would be considered in violation of the implied warranty of merchantability if some of the pens operated well while others did not, or if the label promised that the pens would work for at least a year and few worked for more than a few months, or if the pens melted upon exposure to sunlight, or if the pens in some other way deviated significantly from what consumers or

manufacturers within the industry would normally — promises aside — expect of ballpoint pens (and if the goods are fungible goods — virtually identical and interchangable, like bales of hay — then the goods must be of *fair average quality*; that is, they must be representative of the entire lot); and

4. *warranty of fitness for a particular purpose*, or the promise that a product is well suited to the known special intended use of the buyer.

Clearly, warranty of fitness for a particular purpose extends a bit beyond merchantability and so requires a bit more explanation. Let's look first at a special application of merchantability, then look in more detail at warranty of fitness for a particular purpose.

The general laws governing merchantability are intended to cover all types of products. However, as it turns out, a large number of lawsuits have involved food and drink. Therefore, the courts have developed some special tests to determine merchantability in such cases. These are the *foreign–natural* test and the *reasonable-expectations* test. The foreign–natural test is applied whenever consumers discover some substance within food or drink that they feel should not be there — such as a mouse skeleton in a soda bottle. The rules of this test are simple: If the undesired substance is "foreign" to the product, the product doesn't pass the test; however, if the substance is "natural," even though it might be undesirable, the seller cannot be held in breach.

Clearly, mouse skeletons are foreign to soda; mice are not (one hopes) part of the recipe for soda, and there is no reason to suppose one should ever find a mouse in a soda bottle unless something went wrong in the manufacturing. On the other hand, suppose Ianesco buys a jar of pimento-stuffed olives, bites into an olive that still contains the pit, and chips a tooth. Can she sue? Probably not. If the court applies the foreign–natural test, it must conclude that although the goods did not precisely conform to the label (since one olive still had the pit in it), pits are not foreign to olives and thus, even when purchasing "pitted" olives, buyers must be on the lookout for them.

The reasonable-expectations test is the court's way of asking what a reasonable person would expect to find in food or drink — even if the substance is not foreign. In the previous example, for instance, the court might apply the reasonable-expectations test to the olive case and perhaps conclude that reasonable persons *will expect* to find an occasional pit even in so-called pitted olives. Would a reasonable person also then expect to find bone fragments in soup, or shells in scrambled eggs, or peach pits in fresh fruit pies? Perhaps. While such questions are likely to be answered on a case-by-case basis, keep in mind the word "reasonable." It's really the key here. Ordinarily, the court will take the position that the seller must exercise due care, but a single clam shell fragment reported among millions of cans of chowder will not necessarily render a seller liable. However, a single straight pin among the cans of chowder would likely (and understandably) leave the seller exposed to potential damages.

As we noted a moment ago, merchantability is intended to cover normal purpose or use. But what about those instances when the buyer has a special use in mind? In that case, the product may be covered by a warranty of fitness for a particular purpose if—and only if—certain conditions are met. First, the seller must be aware that the buyer is contemplating that particular use for the goods. The seller must also be aware that the buyer is relying on the seller's expertise in selecting the right goods for the purpose. And finally, the buyer must not restrict the seller's range of choices by imposing criteria that make the proper choice difficult or impossible—for example, by restricting the amount the buyer is willing to pay.

Let's consider an example. Amini wishes to buy a computer for recreational use—no serious word processing or data management, just some computer games with the family. She tells the seller what she has in mind and tells him further that since she knows little or nothing about computers, she will rely on his judgment in helping her select the best model. The seller, only half-attending to what Amini is telling him, sells her a basic computer designed primarily for word processing. The computer monitor, or screen, will display only text—letters and numbers. It will not display any of the cartoons, graphics, or pictures necessary for games. In short, it's entirely unsuited to the purpose Amini has described.

If the seller refuses to replace the computer with another model, is Amini within her rights to sue? Most likely, yes. She clearly informed the seller of her intended purpose and relied on the seller's judgment. Further, she did not impose any restrictions that would have made her needs difficult to fill. Notice, however, that Amini would *not* have grounds to sue for violation of merchantability. While the computer is obviously not suited to the purpose Amini has in mind, we have no reason to believe that it is not well suited to the purpose for which it was designed and manufactured.

Statutory Warranties

Statutory warranties—the third type—are those established by the Congress or state legislatures. They have tended to come about because of specific court cases that suggested the need for further consumer protection. For example, prior to 1975, a number of manufacturers simply disclaimed warranty protection or provided warranties inside sealed packages so that consumers were left wondering until after purchase just what sort of protection was available to them. Under current law, however, a manufacturer must provide the consumer with full warranty information *prior to any sale*. Further, the manufacturer must set up informal settlement procedures to benefit the customer; in other words, the manufacturer must assist the consumer in getting any problems resolved, wherever possible, without requiring the consumer to file suit.

Full and Limited Warranties

The seller who does give a warranty must designate that warranty as either *full* or *limited*. A full warranty must meet four requirements:

1. it must warrant that defects will be remedied within a reasonable time (the term *reasonable* being subject to interpretation, according to common practice within the industry);

2. it must conspicuously display any exclusions or limitations. For instance, if a car dealer's warranty does not extend to the upholstery or floor coverings, that exclusion must be specified;

3. an implied warranty—one imposed by law, that is—cannot be limited in time; and

4. if attempts by the seller to remedy any defects fail, the warranty must promise that the consumer will be allowed to select either a refund or a replacement of the product.

Any warranty that does not meet *all four* of these requirements will be considered a limited warranty.

Warranty Exclusions

What about exclusions? Can the seller modify or get out of providing an express warranty? Yes. As we've noted already, an express warranty does not exist automatically; it has to be created by the seller. Therefore, a seller who does not create an express warranty is, in effect, excluding it automatically.

Excluding an implied warranty is much more difficult, however, since such warranties are normally imposed by law. However, there are provisions for doing so for legitimate reasons—for instance, when a seller wishes to sell goods that he or she knows are damaged or flawed. Such goods might be marked "as is" or "with all faults," thereby excluding any implied warranties that might otherwise be given. Such language, in effect, puts the buyer on notice that the seller is avoiding the usual responsibility a seller has for the quality of the product.

A buyer who refuses to examine goods when given the opportunity, or who makes only a cursory examination, may—through such behavior—free the seller from responsibility for providing any implied warranty to cover defects that a thorough examination should have revealed. For example, suppose Blake, a business executive in a hurry, purchases a calculator in a box off the shelf. Ordinarily, the seller would be responsible under implied warranty for ensuring the merchantability of the calculator. But suppose the seller says, "Look, sometimes these are damaged in shipment—let's open it to make sure everything is working properly." Blake, eager to dash off to his morning meeting, refuses: "No—I don't want one that's been opened. I'm sure it's fine." By refusing to inspect the merchandise when given the opportunity, Blake waives his right to hold the seller responsible for potential defects under implied warranty.

Warranty Protection: How Far Does It Extend?

You might think that warranties protect only the consumer who actually buys and pays for the products in question—and under common law, that was exactly the case. But today, warranty protection is generally far more extensive than that. Each state has selected one of the following three alternatives:

1. Warranties extend to any member of the buyer's family or household, or to any guest in the buyer's home who might reasonably be expected to use or consume the goods. Thus, if Baird has an out-of-town guest who generously offers to mow the lawn and is then injured when the lawn-mower shifts suddenly into reverse, the guest may well be protected by the manufacturer's implied warranty.

2. Warranties extend to any natural person (a human being, that is) who could reasonably be expected to use or consume the goods. Under these circumstances, the warranty on Baird's lawnmower would extend to a neighbor who borrowed it or to the boy down the block whom Baird hired weekly to mow the lawn.

3. Warranties extend to any person (including both human beings and businesses) who could reasonably be expected to use or consume the goods. If Baird lent his lawnmower to members of the local Park Beautification Society, they would be protected under such a warranty.

The seller may not, by the way, exclude or modify the extension of warranties to third-party beneficiaries. In other words, the seller is bound under the laws of the particular state in which he or she resides, and cannot say, in effect, "See here— I'll extend this warranty to you, but not to other members of your household." Once the warranty is provided, the law determines how far it will extend and who will be protected.

Product Liability

As we've seen, products are often—but not always—covered by warranties. But what happens when a consumer is injured by goods that are not covered by warranty? Is there any remedy? The answer is often yes. The law provides potential remedies under tort law; the consumer may sue on grounds of negligence or strict tort liability. Let's explore, through some examples, the possible grounds for these assertions.

Negligence

Under common law, a consumer could only assert negligence if he or she had contracted directly with the negligent party or if the goods in question were imminently or inherently dangerous. If you think this presents a fairly significant roadblock to asserting negligence, you're right. Not many of us contract directly with the manufacturer for the purchase of goods—and it would certainly be complicated to have to do so in order to be guaranteed some protection against a manufacturer's negligence. Today, courts following the MacPherson rule (named for the landmark case which overturned the common-law practice) do not require that the injured person have direct contact with the negligent party in order to recover for negligence.

Remember Baird and the lawnmower? Suppose the lawnmower was a discontinued model, sold "as is" without warranty. Nevertheless, if Baird (or a member of his household) were injured while operating the lawnmower, he might successfully sue the manufacturer on grounds of negligence, alleging that the lawnmower in its present condition was dangerous to operate.

Strict Tort Liability

In some cases, a consumer can also allege strict tort liability. This is a little different from negligence. The assertion here is not that the manufacturer was careless in putting the product together, but, rather, that the product by virtue of its design — even if produced with due care — increased the potential of injury for the user. For example, in the case of Baird's lawnmower, an assertion of negligence suggests that the manufacturer had carelessly assembled the lawnmower, or had not bothered to inspect it properly and had therefore not discovered that it goes suddenly and unexpectedly into reverse when it is meant to do nothing of the kind.

Suppose, however, that the gear shift for reverse were mounted on the handle in such a way that a user who was not paying careful attention could shift the mower into reverse without realizing it. In that case, the problem would not be due to negligence in the manufacturing of the lawnmower since, in fact, it would conform exactly with the intended design. On the other hand, though, it could certainly be argued that the design itself increased the danger to the user, and under such circumstances, Baird might sue based on strict tort liability. If damages occur, this approach may be used against one who sells a defective product or a product that is unreasonably dangerous to a consumer. However, strict liability is an option only when (1) the seller is a merchant in the product and (2) the product is expected to and does reach the consumer without substantial change in the condition in which it is sold.

Strict liability will apply even if the buyer does not buy the product directly from the manufacturer, and even if the manufacturer can show that all due care was exercised in the manufacture of the product. In other words, there is no need to show negligence in order to assert strict tort liability.

Keep in mind the requirement that the buyer purchase the product from a seller who normally deals in such goods. If it turned out that Baird bought the lawnmower from his neighbor, Murphy, he could not sue Murphy since Murphy is not a merchant as regards lawnmowers. Note, too, that he may have trouble suing the manufacturer as well, since the manufacturer might argue that the performance of the lawnmower was due to the way in which it had been handled (or mishandled) by the previous owner, and that they could no longer be held responsible. In some cases, such an allegation, even if untrue, could be difficult to disprove.

SOME PRACTICAL ADVICE

With so much consumer-oriented protection available, it's easy to adopt the complacent attitude that there's little need for the traditional "let the buyer beware" approach. However, buyers who take an active role in protecting their own interests still stand the best chance of achieving true consumer satisfaction.

First, buyers should learn to distinguish between true express warranties and the simple puffery of sales talk. Not all promises are legally enforceable. The key question here is this: Is the statement quantifiable, and stated as a fact, or is it relative, a matter of opinion or purely subjective judgment? Promises that allege that products are the *best, finest, simplest to operate, most desirable,* and so on are not enforceable and will not be treated by the court as express warranties. However, promises that deal in facts and numbers — *fully waterproof, 100% steel, pure virgin wool, 300 horsepower, guaranteed to increase productivity by 15%* — are express warranties and are legally enforceable. They will be viewed by the court as the basis of the bargain, part of the sales contract, and the seller can be required to make such promises good or — possibly — be held in breach of contract.

Sellers, therefore, should be cautious about overly zealous sales pitches. It is one thing to present a product enthusiastically, but quite another to make specific claims that may be difficult to fulfill. From the seller's perspective, the wisest course is, when in doubt, to make no claims whatever. The prudent seller will be careful not to exaggerate a product's qualities or capabilities, even in advertising. And, if questioned by a consumer, a seller should not invent answers about which he or she is unsure. It's almost always better to lose a sale than to be held in breach of contract because of a promise that cannot be fulfilled.

From the buyer's perspective, the wisest course is usually one of caution. Knowing that he or she can sue for breach of express warranty may or may not be very comforting to the buyer who winds up with a product very different from what was promised. The sheer hassle and expense of suing to enforce a warranty should be sufficient reason to exercise care in making a purchase. After all, is it a sensible use of your time, money, and energy go to court to resolve a problem with your television set or coffee maker?

It is wise for both buyers and sellers to know precisely what sorts of things are covered by implied warranties. While buyers must, of course, be concerned with having clear title and protecting themselves against infringement, the greatest concern for most is ensuring the merchantability of goods. Buyers have a right to expect that the goods they buy will live up to normal expectations, that they will be of consistent quality, and so on. It would be very disconcerting to imagine that every time one purchased a pound of butter or a quart of milk, that product would be a little different in both quantity and quality from previous purchases, or that the label on a gallon of milk could read 2% fat content when the real content was 5%. We tend to take our expectations about such things for granted, but they are protected by laws governing implied warranty — and such expectations may not be legally violated.

This places a great responsibility on sellers to ensure that their products meet general industry standards, that they are consistent over time, and that, given the way they are packaged and presented, they're likely to meet consumers' general expectations. Labeling must be very accurate and appropriate — not misleading — and in many cases, government regulations specify the exact composition a product must have to be labeled a certain way. A manufacturer whose product is half butter and half vegetable oil cannot label such a product "butter." Similarly, a manufacturer who whimsically colors butter with red or blue food coloring is likely to be seen as violating consumers' rightful expectations; for better or worse, consumers — supported by government regulations — generally want their butter to be pale yellow.

Merchants who deal in food and drink need to be concerned with some special rules — the foreign–natural test and the reasonable-expectations test. Generally, the courts are likely to frown on the distribution or sale of any food or drink products that contain foreign substances — worms in salad, stones in sandwiches, and so forth. Courts may sometimes be more lenient in applying the reasonable-expectations rule. The court may rule, for instance, that a reasonable person eating fish chowder must expect to encounter some fish bones and therefore must be responsible for dealing with them when they're encountered. But courts will not always side with the seller in such instances. So merchants who deal in food and drink are well advised to take special precautions in preparing or serving food to ensure that products contain nothing that could endanger consumers.

Merchantability is guaranteed by law, but consumers should recognize that warranty of fitness for a particular purpose can be created only under certain circumstances. First, the buyer must make clear the intended purpose. Second, the buyer must ensure that the seller knows of the buyer's reliance on the seller's expertise in making a product selection. If the buyer is in fact relying on the seller but the seller doesn't know that, the warranty is not likely to hold. Finally, the buyer must take care not to impose any criteria on the selection that limit the seller's choice of products. A buyer who requests the car with the best fuel consumption but insists on a powerful engine violates the conditions for this type of warranty. Buyers should also keep in mind that a product that does not live up to expectations for a *particular* purpose won't necessarily violate the warranty of merchantability; that is, it may be well suited to other general purposes for which it was intended. Thus, a buyer who wishes to be protected under a warranty of fitness for a particular purpose must take care to meet all three criteria required for the creation of such a warranty.

Sellers may sometimes feel that there's a lot for them to live up to, that it would be nice to shrug off some of the responsibility imposed by all these warranties. Usually, though, that is not possible. The seller may avoid the creation of express warranties by simply not offering or making them, but implied and statutory warranties are a different story. A seller can, however, avoid implied warranties by labeling a product "as is" or "in present damaged condition" or "including all flaws." Buyers who purchase such products should be aware that the warranties covering them are very limited or nonexistent. If there is any doubt, it is best to question the seller prior to purchase, since following purchase—in the absence of a warranty—there may be no remedies open.

Even in the absence of warranties, sellers and manufacturers are responsible for ensuring the safety of the products they make or sell. Negligence in the manufacture of a product (even one not covered by warranty) or the production of a product which threatens consumer safety (even if no negligence is involved) is an invitation to trouble. Sellers should note that a product that leaves the manufacturer's hands in fine shape but that becomes defective or dangerous while in the seller's possession will usually be that seller's responsibility in the event of a lawsuit. In other words, the court will often require that responsibility for a defect be traced to the appropriate party—which may be the manufacturer or the seller or both.

A word of caution to buyers here, too: Sellers and manufacturers will generally not be held responsible for injuries that result strictly through users' own negligence or misuse of a product. Consumers are wise, therefore, to read all manufacturer's instructions, warnings, and disclaimers thoroughly, and to use products only in accordance with instructions. If a product is to be used for a purpose not recommended by the manufacturer, consumers are well advised to ensure that there is no warning against such use, and further, that such use is approved by someone—such as a seller or manufacturer's representative—whose expertise can be relied on.

ASSIGNMENTS

- Before you watch the video program, be sure you've read through the preceding overview, familiarized yourself with the learning objectives for this lesson, and looked at the key terms below. Then, read Chapter 21 of Davidson et al., *Business Law*.

- After completing these tasks, view the video program for Lesson 18.

- After watching the program, take time to review what you've learned. First, evaluate your learning with the self-test which follows the key terms. Then, apply and evaluate what you've learned with the "Your Opinion, Please" scenarios at the end of this telecourse study guide lesson.

KEY TERMS

Before you read through the textbook assignment and watch the video program, take a minute to look at the key terms associated with this lesson. When you encounter them in the textbook and video program, pay careful attention to their meaning.

Exclusion	Quantifiable
✓Express warranty	Remedy
✓Foreign–natural test	Statutory warranty
✓Full warranty	Strict tort liability
✓Implied warranty	Warranty against infringement
Limited warranty	Warranty of fitness for a particular
Natural person	purpose
Negligence	Warranty of merchantability
Product liability	Warranty of title

SELF-TEST

The questions below will help you evaluate how well you've learned the material in this lesson. Read each one carefully, and select the letter of the option that best answers the question. You'll find the correct answer, along with a reference to the page number(s) where the topic is discussed, in the back of this telecourse study guide.

1. A warranty is *best* defined as

   a. a promise that becomes part of a contract in the sale of goods.

   b. a guarantee of the quality of a given product.

   c. assurance that the manufacturer (and possibly the seller) has thoroughly examined goods and found them free of all flaws.

   d. an agreement between buyer and seller that defective goods will be replaced.

2. Which of the following statements is *most likely* to be treated as an express warranty?

   a. *Both* of the following statements (b and c) are express warranties.

   b. "This shoe is made of genuine alligator hide."

   c. "This is the most comfortable shoe of its kind on the market."

   d. *Neither* statement (b or c) is an express warranty.

3. Which of the following is *not* guaranteed under an implied warranty?

   a. The goods are free of hidden security interests or liens

   b. The goods are not subject to rightful claim by a third person

   c. The goods are merchantable, according to trade definition

   d. The goods may be returned for refund or replaced in the event of any defect

4. Richroast harvests and sells coffee beans. Studies reveal the beans are of highly variable quality, depending on the date and place of harvest. But Richroast makes no distinction in their labeling, packaging, or pricing and the package labels make no guarantees or claims regarding the quality of the beans. Based on this information, is Richroast likely in violation of the warranty of merchantability?

a. No, assuming the variability in the beans is indicative of industry standards.

b. Yes, because merchantability demands absolute consistency in goods packaged similarly.

c. We cannot say without knowing whether Richroast offers its customers a warranty of merchantability.

5. While dining at Grandma's Olde Time Restaurant, Fenster chokes on a fragment of chicken bone found in the chicken and dumplings. If the state in which Grandma's is located applies both the foreign–natural test and the reasonable-expectations test, which of the following is the *most likely* outcome?

a. Grandma's dish will not pass either test.

b. Grandma's dish will pass the reasonable-expectations test, but not the foreign–natural test.

c. Grandma's dish will pass the foreign–natural test, but results of the reasonable-expectations test is uncertain.

6. Helman buys a set of racing tires for his street rod from auto parts dealer Rodmann. The manufacturer's label attached to the tires reads: "Dry weather use only—not suitable for use on wet pavement." Rodmann, however, tells Helman to ignore the label; the tires are "ideal" for use in rain. Helman says he specifically wants a tire he can use in both wet and dry conditions, but will rely on Rodmann's judgment. The first time Helman drives on wet pavement, his car skids uncontrollably and he is injured in the resulting crash. Which of the following is *most likely* true, based on the information presented?

a. Rodmann has violated the warranty of fitness for a particular purpose.

b. Rodmann has violated the warranty of merchantability, but not fitness for a particular purpose.

c. Rodmann has violated no warranties; Rodmann's claim that the tires were "ideal" was just an opinion.

7. As a result of the Magnuson-Moss Warranty–Consumer Protection Warranty Act, manufacturers of goods produced after 1975 are required to do which of the following?

a. Repair or replace all defective items sold, regardless of who is ultimately responsible for the defect.

b. Provide consumers with warranty information *prior to a sale.*

c. Provide followup on all sales to ensure customer satisfaction.

d. Offer full and unlimited warranties on all products.

8. In order to *exclude* a warranty of fitness for a particular purpose, a merchant

a. need do nothing; such a warranty will not exist unless the merchant takes deliberate steps to create it.

b. must put the exclusion in writing and make it conspicuous.

c. must make the exclusion orally, and directly to the buyer.

d. *None* of the above; there is no way to exclude such a warranty.

9. The potential remedies of negligence or strict tort liability are intended *mainly* to protect the rights of

a. the consumer who is injured by unsafe and defective products.

b. the seller, in the event goods are mishandled by the consumer.

c. the manufacturer, who cannot guard against inappropriate handling or misrepresentation of goods.

10. Fisher Mining purchases a case of explosives from a local supplier, and although the explosives are appropriately packaged and not defective in any way, two miners are injured during their use. Based on this information, does Fisher have grounds to sue the explosives manufacturer on grounds of negligence?

a. Yes, because the injuries resulted from use of a product that is inherently dangerous.

b. We cannot say without knowing whether the miners who handled the explosives were qualified to do so.

c. No, because although the products were inherently dangerous, that danger did not result from the manufacturer's (or seller's) negligence.

YOUR OPINION, PLEASE

Read each of the following scenarios and answer the questions about the decisions you would make in each situation. Give these questions some serious thought; they may be used as the basis for the development of a more complex essay. You should base your decisions on what you've learned from this lesson, though you may incorporate outside readings or information gained through your own experience if it is relevant.

Scenario 1

Ferri, an amateur marathon runner, goes to Kessler Sports to buy running shoes for an upcoming track event. She tells the salesman that she wants "the best shoe available for $70 or less." He recommends the Trackeater model. He tells Ferri that the Trackeater is "one of the best all-around athletic shoes in the business." The label on the box reads "Trackeater—Shoe of the Track Star!"

Ferri notes that nothing in the manufacturer's literature says the shoes are designed specifically for serious marathon running, but the salesman says the Trackeater is an outstanding value, comparable in quality to shoes selling for twice the price. He says he has sold the shoes to many other runners and has never had a complaint. Ferri, convinced, buys the shoes.

During the later stages of her next marathon, the inner linings of both shoes loosen, causing severe blistering on both of Ferri's feet and finally forcing her out of the race altogether — just a mile short of the finish. Her injuries are severe enough that she is required to stay out of competition and off her feet totally for ten weeks, thereby making it necessary to cancel her participation in several other events. Ferri, dismayed by the whole situation, sues Kessler Sports for violation of two types of implied warranty: merchantability and fitness for a particular purpose.

What's your opinion? Based on what you know of the situation, do you think Ferri can successfully sue Kessler Sports? What sort of warranties exist between Ferri and Kessler Sports? Which of those warranties, if any, has Kessler Sports violated? Do you believe Kessler Sports has acted unethically? Illegally?

- Is Ferri likely to win a suit for violation of warranty? If so, on what grounds? If not, why?
- What factors support your answer?
- What factors might an attorney cite in arguing against your view?
- What steps, if any, might Ferri have taken to prevent a lawsuit in this situation?
- What steps, if any, might Kessler Sports have taken to prevent a lawsuit in this situation?

Scenario 2

Kleerguard, manufacturers of commercial "security" windows, runs a video advertisement at a trade show in which professional actors, posing as burglars, first throw a rock at the window of a department store, then attempt to smash the window with a small hammer. The window reveals only minor damages — no serious chips or cracks. During the advertisement, the following disclaimer runs at the bottom of the screen in small letters: "This is a dramatization."

Esparza, proprietor of Esparza Jewelers, is impressed by the ad, and on the strength of it, purchases a large window from Kleerguard and installs it in the front of his store to protect a display case. Eager to show off his purchase to a neighboring merchant, Esparza tosses a relatively small rock (smaller than the one used in the video advertisement) at the window, believing that no damage will result. To his horror, the entire window shatters into a thousand fragments, creating a torrent of debris and damaging some merchandise in the showcase. Esparza thereupon sues Kleerguard for violation of express warranty.

What's your opinion? Based on what you know of the situation, do you think Esparza has grounds to sue Kleerguard? Is he right in taking the television demonstration as a form of express warranty? Or is he reading too much in, taking too much for granted?

- Is Esparza likely to win a suit for violation of express warranty? Why?
- What factors support your answer?
- What factors might an attorney cite in arguing against your view?
- What steps, if any, might Esparza have taken to prevent a lawsuit in this situation?
- What steps, if any, might Kleerguard have taken to prevent a lawsuit in this situation?

19

Remedies for Breach

LEARNING OBJECTIVES

Upon completing your study of this lesson, you should be able to

- Discuss the rationale for providing legal remedies for breach of a sales contract.

- List and describe six preacceptance remedies and two postacceptance remedies available to the seller.

- List and describe six preacceptance remedies and three postacceptance remedies available to the buyer.

- Describe ways in which parties to the contract may tailor remedies to fit a particular contract.

- Discuss the ways in which *anticipatory repudiation, adequate assurance, excused performance,* or *duty to particularize* may influence the court's interpretation of whether, how, or when a breach of contract has occurred.

- Discuss the implications of the statute of limitations on any litigation involving a breach of sales contract.

Most sales contracts are performed by a buyer and a seller just as expected. And if little things do go wrong—the buyer gets home with the wrong size or color, let's say—these minor problems are often remedied informally between parties eager to maintain good will in anticipation of future contracts. Sometimes, however, something goes wrong that cannot be readily resolved through simple good will. The seller may not deliver the goods specified in the contract or may fail to deliver them on time. The buyer may refuse to pay or may be unable to pay.

When a problem arises, it's best if the buyer and seller have already established, as part of the contract, how the problem will be resolved. But if the contract does not specify a solution for the problem, the Uniform Commercial Code offers specific remedies—ways of setting things right. In fact, the UCC specifies which remedies may be applied both before and after acceptance. Keep this before-and-after distinction in mind as you go through this lesson, because when it comes to remedies for breach of a sales contract, timing is critical. In other words, *when* the breach occurs makes a substantial difference in *how* it is handled before the law.

OVERVIEW

As we've noted, the majority of sales contracts are performed as expected. The seller tenders conforming goods to the buyer at the time and place of delivery, and the buyer inspects the goods, accepts them, and pays the agreed-on price. Sometimes, however, things do not go so smoothly. The seller may breach the contract by never delivering the goods or by delivering nonconforming goods. Further, the seller may refuse to cure a defect or may simply lack the time to do so. Or the buyer may breach the contract by refusing to pay the agreed-on price or by lacking the means to do so. But regardless of whether the buyer is insolvent or simply uncooperative, the upshot is the same for the seller: no compensation for the goods.

What remedies are available in the event of a breach? Let's look at this question first from the seller's perspective, then from the buyer's.

Remedies Available to the Seller

The seller is entitled to remedies if the buyer wrongfully rejects conforming goods, refuses to pay for conforming goods, or otherwise breaches the contract. The remedies available depend on when the breach occurs; there are six possible remedies available if the buyer breaches *before* acceptance, and two available if the buyer breaches *after* acceptance. *Preacceptance remedies* include:

1. withholding delivery of goods,

2. stopping delivery in transit,

3. identifying goods to the contract in order to establish damages,

4. reselling those goods that are in the seller's possession,

5. suing the buyer for damages, lost profits, or the contract price, and

6. cancelling all future performance owed to the buyer under the contract.

The seller does not need to choose just one remedy, but can apply as many as are needed to return the seller to the position he or she would have been in had the contract been fulfilled.

Postacceptance remedies — available if the buyer breaches after acceptance — include:

1. suing the buyer for the price of the goods, and

2. attempting to reclaim the goods (if the buyer is insolvent).

Seller's Preacceptance Remedies

Let's look at each of these eight remedies a little more closely.

Withholding Goods. The first remedy is perhaps the simplest. The seller merely withholds any goods that have not already been delivered or shipped to the buyer. This remedy is often applied midway through a contract, when the buyer's unwillingness to perform properly becomes obvious. For example, let's say that Rush orders wallpaper from Bleeker for an ongoing construction job. Bleeker provides the wallpaper through weekly deliveries, according to the terms of the contract, but Rush does not provide weekly payments. Along about the third week, Bleeker may decide that no further deliveries will be made unless payment is forthcoming, and may notify Rush accordingly. Further, if Bleeker has reason to believe that Rush is insolvent, Bleeker may insist that Rush pay in advance and in cash for all further merchandise delivered, and that payment include the cost of delivery.

Stopping Delivery. The second remedy involves stopping delivery of the goods in transit. Unlike the first remedy, this one is subject to some limitations — most particularly, that the goods be in the possession of a common carrier in transit. In other words, a seller can halt delivery on a truckload of engine parts or a carload of grain, but not on a lamp or a calculator or a pair of shoes that are being sent by regular mail. The seller must notify the carrier (the person making the delivery) in sufficient time to make the stoppage practical; allowing the carrier to arrive at the delivery site before receiving the message could make for awkward negotiations all around. Further, the seller must indemnify, or protect, the carrier against any charges or damages suffered as a result of the stoppage. In short, if the buyer suffers inconvenience or financial loss because delivery is halted, the seller must ensure that the carrier — usually an uninvolved third person — will not bear the cost of any damages awarded a wronged buyer.

Identifying Goods to the Contract. Sometimes, problems arise while the goods to be delivered are still *unidentified* goods — goods that are not yet clearly the buyer's. It may be, for instance, that the goods are still part of a larger stock of the product, such as 500 gallons of gasoline in a 100,000 gallon storage tank. Or perhaps the goods are still in the process of being manufactured. In this case, the seller has the option of completing production and selling the completed goods to another buyer, or stopping production and making another use of the raw materials.

If a breach occurs, the seller may immediately wish to specify which goods are the goods involved in the breached contract. An example will help here. Let's say that Neller has ordered several thousand pocket calculators from Feldstein. Feldstein doesn't have these in stock, but he is in the process of manufacturing them and has doubled production output in order to meet Neller's request. Now suppose that Feldstein has completed production on the second thousand when it becomes clear that Neller is not going to pay in a timely manner. In order to establish damages resulting from the contract breach, it may be wise for Feldstein to identify those calculators as being part of the Feldstein–Neller contract. If he doesn't, Neller can charge that they were simply part of Feldstein's regular production output, and that their manufacture caused the company no particular inconvenience, nor did it generate any unusual expense. Once the calculators are identified to the contract, however, Feldstein can better make the case that he is losing money due to Neller's breach.

Reselling Goods. The fourth remedy—one we just touched upon—is the seller's right to resell goods that are still in his or her possession. As you might suspect, Feldstein would be quite within his rights to sell the calculators Neller did not pay for and keep the money. However, since the amount he receives will reduce the damages that Neller may owe, Feldstein would have to conduct such a sale in a commercially reasonable manner. While the sale can be either a public or a private sale, the seller will need to ensure that it is—in terms of procedures and pricing—a true sale.

For instance, suppose that after Neller breached the contract, Feldstein contacted another merchant in pocket calculators—Chase—who said yes, he would be delighted to buy the calculators at 10% off the original contract price. If Feldstein then notified Neller of the situation, Neller would have little grounds to object. Let's suppose, however, that the scenario were quite different. What if Feldstein privately contacted two business associates, offered them the calculators at one-tenth of the original contract price (hoping to sue Neller for the balance), sold the goods at his own home after regular business hours, and failed to notify Neller of the sale. Neller could claim in this case that Feldstein did not act in a commercially reasonable manner. In order for a sale to be commercially reasonable, the method, time, place, sale price, and terms must all be in keeping with established, acceptable business practice.

Another point is important here, too: The commercially reasonable sale is a crucial part of later collecting damages for the breach. The seller who resells goods in a commercially reasonable manner may well be able to collect damages—the difference between the contract price and the resale price—from the buyer. Thus, if Feldstein sold the calculators to Chase for 90% of the original contract price, he could sue Neller for the remaining 10%—the damages. In our second scenario, however, because Feldstein did *not* behave in a commercially reasonable manner, he would have little success in a suit against Neller for damages.

Suing the Buyer. The fifth remedy is for the seller to sue the buyer — for damages, lost profits, or the contract price. A seller who has not yet completed the manufacture or delivery of goods or identified them to the contract will normally sue for damages. As we've noted, damages are, in this case, basically the difference between contract price and the price the goods are sold for to a third party. To this basic figure are added *incidental damages* — the costs the seller incurs as a result of attempting to fulfill the contract, costs that would never have arisen had the contract not existed.

In our previous example, for instance, Feldstein could allege that because he needed to double production to meet the contract demands, he suffered incidental damages involved in hiring extra personnel, maintaining longer production hours, and so forth. Those costs could be added to the total for damages. Did Feldstein save any money because of the calculator project? Perhaps nothing immediately obvious. But say, for instance, that because of the high-volume production required for this project, Feldstein was able to order certain components in bulk that he would otherwise have ordered in smaller volume and consequently have had to pay higher prices for. Such savings would have to be deducted from the total for damages.

Sometimes a suit for damages is insufficient to place the seller in the position he or she would have enjoyed had the contract been performed. This is particularly true in a case where the goods are of little or no value to anyone other than the contracting party. Such goods cannot readily be resold and it's difficult to establish any market value. For instance, suppose a campaign manager contracts with Kroft Company, a local novelties manufacturer, for the design and production of several thousand t-shirts and campaign buttons supporting Ambercrombie for state senator. Just as Kroft is cranking out the last of the t-shirts and buttons, Ambercrombie backs out of the race and the campaign committee refuses to honor the contract. Where does this leave Kroft? Aside from a few diligent political-button collectors, not many consumers are likely to want campaign trivia promoting a candidate whose name will soon be a dim memory. There is, in effect, no market for the goods. Kroft can, however, sue for reimbursement of reasonable expenses incurred in the production of the goods, as well as for lost profits, basing the amount on what the company *would* have netted had all the "Go, Ambercrombie!" t-shirts and buttons sold.

Cancelling Future Performance. The sixth preacceptance remedy involves the seller's right to cancel all future performance defined under the contract once the buyer breaches the contract. Using our earlier example, calculator manufacturer Feldstein need not keep manufacturing the product once calculator buyer Neller fails to pay in the specified manner for the first batch. Note that while this cancellation wipes out all the seller's remaining obligations, it does not free the buyer from complying with his or her duties to that point. Neller, in other words, is still obligated to pay for those calculators Feldstein has produced. And even though Feldstein has cancelled future performance, he can still sue under the contract for lost profits and damages related to the entire contract.

Seller's Postacceptance Remedies

If the breach occurs *after* the buyer has accepted the goods, two remedies are available to the seller. First, the seller may sue for the price of the goods. Keep in mind that the act of acceptance in itself automatically obligates the buyer to pay—though there are circumstances under which acceptance can be revoked (more about this shortly). The point is, the seller may sue the buyer for the price of the accepted goods and will almost always win the case.

But there's a problem. Often, when a buyer does not pay for goods, it's because he or she is insolvent—without funds, that is. Suing such a buyer may give the seller the satisfaction of establishing certain legal rights, but will not usually net any money. So, a second option is often preferable: To attempt to reclaim the goods. This remedy, however, isn't so simple and straightforward as one might think; before reclaiming goods, the seller must prove two things:

1. that the buyer received the goods on credit *while insolvent*; and

2. that the seller demanded the return of the goods within ten days of delivery to the buyer.

The ten-day time limit is waived, however, if it can be shown that the buyer misrepresented his or her solvency in writing to the seller within three months prior to delivery. For instance, if a buyer filled out a credit application on which he lied about his outstanding debts, the seller would not be bound by the ten-day limit.

Practically, though, sellers are often proud of their policies of extending credit with few restrictions: "Never had credit? No problem!" and that sort of thing. This approach hardly suggests a rigorous determination of the buyer's solvency. Further, many merchants extend credit for periods of thirty days or even much longer before any payment is required. What's more, reclaimed goods—though better than nothing—may no longer be very marketable following use. All in all, the chances of a seller meeting the two legal requirements for reclaiming goods and not losing money on the sale of the goods are pretty small.

Remedies Available to the Buyer

Now let's look at things from the buyer's perspective. If the seller breaches the contract by not delivering the goods as prescribed or by delivering nonconforming goods, the buyer has six preacceptance and three postacceptance remedies available.

The preacceptance remedies are:

1. suing for damages;

2. covering, and suing for damages resulting from the cost of the cover;

3. seeking specific performance for unique goods, or replevin for goods that—though not unique—are not generally available on the open market;

4. claiming any identified goods still in the possession of the seller if the seller has become insolvent within ten days of receiving a payment from the buyer;

5. reselling any nonconforming goods in order to minimize losses; and

6. cancelling any future duties under the contract without surrendering rights under that contract.

The following postacceptance remedies apply if the seller delivers nonconforming goods in which the nonconformity is hidden, or if a seller promises to cure a nonconformity but fails to do so:

1. revoking the acceptance *if* the nonconformity substantially reduces the value of the goods to the buyer;

2. suing for damages if the nonconformity is not sufficient to permit revocation; and

3. seeking recoupment by deducting damages suffered from the amount owed to the seller under the contract.

Again, let's look at these options one by one, keeping in mind the buyer's right to choose more than one remedy, depending on the situation.

Buyer's Preacceptance Remedies

Suing for Damages. The first preacceptance remedy is to sue for damages. The buyer is allowed to recover any excess of market price *over* contract price at the time of the breach. (We'll see why in a moment.) Additional damages, or costs associated with anticipating goods that are never delivered, are added to this figure; costs saved are subtracted.

Notice that this general approach gives some flexibility to the buyer who must seek another source for the goods in question. For example, let's say Miller contracts with Fremont to purchase 4,000 square yards of quality carpeting at $15 per square yard. So far so good; because Miller has contracted in advance with Fremont, he does not expect to have to pay more than the $15 negotiated price. But if delivery is not scheduled to occur for six months, and if Fremont breaches the contract by not delivering, Miller may find himself in a difficult bind. Suppose that, during the six months while he awaited delivery, the market price of comparable carpeting has risen to $17 per yard—enough to make a substantial difference on such a large order. Under the Uniform Commercial Code, Miller is allowed to recover the $2-per-yard difference (the excess of market price over contract price) through a suit for damages. Notice that this allowance does not constitute any sort of bonus or reward for Miller; it merely puts him in a position where he can purchase the goods he was promised through the original contract.

Covering. The second remedy available to the buyer is that of *cover*, meaning the purchase of comparable goods from another source within a reasonable time. In our current example, for instance, if Fremont breaches the contract, Miller has every right at that point to purchase carpeting from another merchant. And if Miller is unable to obtain carpeting of comparable quality for the anticipated $15 per square yard, he can collect the difference from Fremont. He can also charge Fremont for any expenses incurred in tracking down another seller or putting up with the delay in having the carpet installed.

Replevin. The third remedy—available if goods cannot be obtained by cover—involves either *specific performance* or *replevin*. If the goods are unique—a sculpture or painting, for example—the court may order specific performance, which requires the seller to deliver the identified goods in accordance with the contract. If the goods are not unique but are not currently available on the market, the court will likely order replevin. These approaches are similar in that both require the seller to complete the contract. For instance, a buyer might contract with a seller for a shipment of integrated circuit chips generally available through other sources. If the seller defaults on the contract, the buyer should first attempt to obtain the goods through cover—by purchasing them from another source, that is. But if other sellers did not presently have the desired goods in stock, the court could order replevin, requiring the seller to make the chips available to the buyer.

Claiming Goods. The fourth remedy—a rarity in practice—is designed to protect the buyer against a seller who becomes insolvent within ten days of receiving payment. Under such circumstances, assuming the seller has identified the goods to the contract, the buyer can claim the identified goods, even if the buyer has not paid for them in full. In our preceding example, suppose the electronics merchant failed to deliver the chips not because they weren't available but because insolvency had left the company financially incapable of supporting delivery costs. The chips could be sitting on a shelf in the back room, but there is no one available to package them or take them to the buyer. If the buyer has paid all or some portion of the contract price within ten days of the seller's becoming insolvent, *and* if the seller has identified the parts to the contract, the buyer can claim the goods. However, since insolvency is rarely so clear-cut as to fit nicely in the ten-day period, buyers can't usually avail themselves of this remedy.

Reselling Nonconforming Goods. The fifth remedy involves reselling the goods, and it's largely a matter of expedience for both buyer and seller. Upon receipt of nonconforming goods, the buyer is required to notify the seller of the nonconformity. If the buyer is a merchant, the buyer must also request instructions regarding how to dispose of the goods. If the seller doesn't provide those instructions, the buyer may—strange as this requirement may seem—attempt to resell the goods for the seller. The buyer is required to act in a commercially reasonable fashion in conducting this sale. He or she may deduct an appropriate amount from the sales revenue to cover commissions and expenses related to the sale, but must then return the excess to the seller.

Cancellation. The final preacceptance remedy involves the right to cancel. On discovery of breach, the buyer may notify the seller that all future obligations of the buyer are thereby canceled. Note that such cancellation does not affect the rights of the buyer; it limits only the obligations. Nor does it limit the availability of other remedies the buyer may elect to pursue.

Buyer's Postacceptance Remedies

Once the buyer has accepted the goods, he or she cannot reject them. There are, however, still three remedies available.

Revocation and Suing for Damages. Under some circumstances, the buyer may be able to *revoke* the acceptance. Revocation is allowed in the case of a hidden defect significant enough to substantially limit the value of the goods to the buyer. Revocation is also available in the case where a seller promises to cure a defect but fails to do so. Revocation enables a buyer to use any of the preacceptance remedies; in other words, the court treats revocation just as if the buyer had never accepted the goods in the first place.

If the defect is not substantial enough to warrant revocation, the buyer may still elect to sue for damages. Suppose, for example, that Wiley purchases an automobile from Nash. Wiley inspects the automobile and accepts it. She cannot now reject it. But let's say she discovers a malfunction in the electrical system a week following acceptance. The malfunction was not obvious before acceptance and, since it makes the car unreliable, it reduces the value of the automobile to Wiley. In this situation, the defect could, therefore, provide grounds for revocation. Or, to alter the scenario a bit, let's say that Wiley is fortunate enough to spot the electrical problem before acceptance and that she promptly notifies Nash, who promises to fix it. As it turns out, though, Nash isn't very mechanical, and the pesky electrical problem continues to make driving the car an unpredictable event. Does Wiley have grounds to revoke the acceptance? Yes. She notified Nash promptly and he promised to fix the problem, but he did not deliver on that promise. Note that Nash's willingness to *try* to solve the problem, however commendable, is not sufficient to relieve him of his obligation as seller.

Note, too, that the circumstances under which revocation is allowed are narrowly defined. Certainly, any buyer who routinely accepts goods thinking it will be simple enough to revoke the acceptance later is misinformed. On the other hand, even when revocation isn't an option, a buyer may have recourse. Suppose, for example, that the defect is by no means serious enough to permit revocation. Let's say that Wiley accepts the automobile before noticing that the sound from the left stereo speaker is intermittently distorted. Even if Wiley could make a convincing case that this defect was not obvious prior to acceptance, it's not likely to be viewed as significant enough to warrant revocation since it would not affect the overall functioning of the car. Still, Wiley—a music lover—might not be happy with the situation. Is she out of luck? Not necessarily; if Nash were unwilling to fix the problem, Wiley could sue for damages and try to recover the cost of repairing or replacing the speaker.

Recoupment. The third postacceptance remedy available to the buyer is *recoupment*, which involves deducting damages from the price owed to the seller. In our previous example, for instance, Wiley might tell Nash that she would keep the car but would deduct from her payments the cost of repairing or replacing the malfunctioning left speaker. But if Nash objected to this arrangement, Wiley could not use this remedy; she would instead have to sue Nash for damages.

Remedies Tailored by the Contract

The rules we've covered thus far will apply any time that buyer and seller do not make other provisions within the scope of their contract. But parties to a contract may always tailor remedies to suit their own purposes. And when the parties make their own arrangements regarding how things will be handled, the court will respect those arrangements—unless circumstances change so that the remedy provided for in the contract is no longer adequate to cover the situation or unless enforcement of the remedy is held to be unconscionable.

For instance, the parties may decide that *consequential damages*—those that are not direct or immediate—will be excluded or limited. Or, they may decide that because the value of the goods in question may be difficult to determine later in the event of a breach, they will provide for *liquidated damages:* a pre-specified amount to cover damages in the event of a breach. The main thing to note here is that the Uniform Commercial Code is designed to cover as many contingencies as possible in the event that buyer and seller have *not* negotiated their own advance arrangements. But to the extent possible, the court will uphold any contract agreement the two parties find mutually acceptable.

Special Problems of Interpretation

It isn't always simple to determine how, when, or whether a breach has occurred. Four types of special situations are important in making these decisions.

Repudiation

First, one party or the other may *repudiate* obligations *before* performance is due. Technically, this is not quite the same thing as a breach—though the ultimate effect may be the same—because performance wasn't yet required. Repudiation, in effect, is like an anticipation of a breach and may be looked on as such by the other party. Then, the nonrepudiating party has three possible courses of action:

1. to continue awaiting performance for a commercially reasonable time, hoping the repudiating party will come through after all, despite the repudiation;

2. to treat the repudiation as an immediate breach and seek any available remedies; or

3. to suspend his or her own performance under the contract.

Circumstances are likely to suggest the best course of action. Under the law, a repudiating party may retract the repudiation up until the time performance is required—unless the other party objects; an objection rules out retraction. In other words, if Winslow repudiates her contract with Sampson, but later wants to retract that repudiation, it's up to Sampson whether to go back to the original contract.

Assurances

The second special situation involves requests for *assurances*. Often, parties that have not dealt with each other regularly may have some apprehension about the other's ability or willingness to perform. An uneasy buyer or seller may demand in writing an assurance that the other party will perform as required by the contract. The requesting party's performance is suspended until the assurance is provided. And if the assurance is not forthcoming within thirty days from the demand, the lack of response is treated as repudiation of the contract.

Excused Performance

Excused performance, the third special situation, occurs when a seller is forced to delay in making a delivery, or can make only a partial delivery due to some unforeseen circumstance. When such a situation occurs, the seller is required to notify the buyer *seasonably*—meaning in a timely manner, given the nature of the situation. For example, suppose Foulk were scheduled to deliver a load of produce to Gravell's Grocery on June 1, but flooded roads made the delivery impossible. Such a delay would not be treated as a normal breach because it occurred through no fault of the seller, nor could it have been anticipated at the time of the contract. Assuming that Foulk provided prompt notification of the delay, there is no breach. His failure to perform is *excused*.

Performance is also excused if the delay or failure to deliver is caused by the seller's need to comply with a government order or regulation. Suppose Foulk has to cross the state line to deliver his apples, for example, but the neighboring state has just prohibited the importation of all apples due to apple maggot problems. Foulk's lack of performance would likely be excused. Government regulations regarding the inspection or transport of produce state to state are subject to considerable variation, depending on disease problems and other factors. An unexpected change in such regulations could create a delay that Foulk might not anticipate. As a result, such a delay would be excused, not treated as a breach.

Of course, it may have occurred to you already that from the buyer's viewpoint, excused performance can still mean substantial inconvenience. Therefore, once the seller notifies the buyer of the excuse for less than full performance, the buyer may choose either to live with the contract as modified—taking a late delivery or partial delivery, for instance—or terminate the contract altogether. In other words, having performance excused does not mean that the buyer will honor the contract; he or she has the option not to do so. In other words, Foulk will not be held liable for damages resulting from the inadequate—but excused—performance, but he may not get Gravell to pay for his produce either.

Duty to Particularize

The fourth special situation influencing decisions about whether a breach has occurred is the *duty to particularize:* a buyer who rejects goods is required to specify why the rejection is taking place. In other words, when goods are rejected because of a *curable* defect, the buyer is required to state precisely what that defect is and what might be done to make the goods acceptable. Ambiguous statements like "These won't do" or "This doesn't seem to work properly" are not sufficient. Failure to describe the defect in detail precludes the use of that defect in court to prove breach, which in turn makes proof of breach all but impossible. Further, if the buyer cannot prove breach, the seller—in the eyes of the court—is deemed to have acted properly. In short, a buyer who fails to particularize any problems with delivered goods is likely to wind up living with those problems or absorbing the cost of resolving them.

Statute of Limitations

Finally, note that there is a statute of limitations that affects the remedies available to wronged parties. Any lawsuit for breach of a sales contract must be started within four years of the breach. Notice that this does *not* mean within four years of *discovery* of the breach, but within four years of the time when the breach itself occurs. After that time, the statute of limitations rules out the possibility of lawsuit as a means of resolving contract problems. Again, the responsibility for ensuring thorough inspection of goods falls to the buyer—who will often suffer the consequences if faults go undetected.

SOME PRACTICAL ADVICE

It's wise to know in advance both the duties and obligations imposed by a sales contract and the remedies available to a buyer or seller should breach occur. Dealing with a reputable party is one way to minimize chances of breach, of course, but realistically, the possibility is always there.

If you do not know the party with whom you are dealing, or if you have any reason to feel doubtful about whether the contract will be performed as stated, you should make a written demand for *assurances* that performance will be tendered as indicated. If such assurance is not provided, you can terminate the contract automatically without obligation.

As either buyer or seller, keep in mind that in the event of a breach, a wide range of remedies is available to you. Further, use of one remedy does not rule out others. In all cases, the intent of the remedies is to restore the injured party to the condition that party would have been in had the contract been performed. But this shouldn't suggest that legal remedies are a substitute for careful contracting and good-faith efforts to make things go smoothly; resorting to any of these legal remedies will undoubtedly cause some — frequently major — disruption to your business.

As a seller, beware of contracting with a buyer who is insolvent — or, for that matter, extending credit to a buyer whose solvency is questionable. Should breach occur, you will have remedies open to you, certainly; but the results of pursuing those remedies are not always very satisfactory. Even if you later sue the buyer for the price of the goods, you cannot hope to collect damages from someone who is without funds. Further, recovering the goods themselves can be difficult. As a seller, you will, for example, be obligated to show that the buyer was insolvent at the time credit was extended and that you demanded return of the goods within ten days. These conditions are difficult for most sellers to fulfill. Further, even if you do manage to recover your goods, what condition will they be in at the time of recovery? The lesson here is obvious: dealing with persons of dubious financial health involves considerable risk.

As a buyer, take time to *thoroughly* inspect goods as soon after delivery as possible; you may not have another opportunity to hold the seller responsible. Failure to ensure conformity prior to acceptance could severely limit the remedies available to you, or even make it impossible to prove breach in the event of a lawsuit. (Remember, if the buyer can't prove a breach, the seller is likely to be viewed as having performed correctly.) Also keep in mind that once goods are accepted, you will almost always be required to pay for them. Revocation is possible only under very special and limited circumstances involving defects that are both hidden and substantial, or when a seller defaults on a promise to cure a defect. In other words, most minor defects, unless discovered prior to acceptance, turn out to be something the buyer must simply live with.

Under some conditions, performance relating to delivery of goods may be excused. But as a seller, realize that while you may not be held in breach in the event of excused performance, delayed delivery could cost you a contract if an inconvenienced buyer decides to terminate. What's more, failure to notify the buyer in a timely manner could mean that you'll be held in breach.

Remember that the nature and extent of remedies open to you is most affected by *when* a breach occurs. More remedies are available prior to acceptance than after acceptance. Further, as a buyer or seller, your right to sue for breach of contract is governed by the statute of limitations. A suit must be filed within four years of breach — not discovery of the breach, but the breach itself. But this doesn't mean that innocent parties should feel they have all the time in the world to contemplate their response to a potential breach. Parties to a contract still have an obligation to act in good faith, and that includes pointing out problems when they're discovered. Besides, the longer parties wait to resolve a conflict, the more difficult the details of any situation will be to sort out.

Finally, remember that the Uniform Commercial Code will, in nearly all cases, uphold the elements of any contract between buyer and seller, even when they depart from the usual rules of the Code. In other words, the court will give precedence to any reasonable agreement, even when it's not in line with normal business conduct. (The court will not, however, uphold agreements deemed unconscionably unfair to one party or the other.)

ASSIGNMENTS

- Before you watch the video program, be sure you've read through the preceding overview, familiarized yourself with the learning objectives for this lesson, and looked at the key terms below. Then, read Chapter 22 of Davidson et al., *Business Law*.

- After completing these tasks, view the video program for Lesson 19.

- After watching the program, take time to review what you've learned. First, evaluate your learning with the self-test which follows the key terms. Then, apply and evaluate what you've learned with the "Your Opinion, Please" scenarios at the end of this telecourse study guide lesson.

KEY TERMS

Before you read through the textbook assignment and watch the video program, take a minute to look at the key terms associated with this lesson. When you encounter them in the textbook and video program, pay careful attention to their meaning.

Adequate assurances
Cancellation
Consequential damages
Curable defect
Duty to particularize
Excused performance
Insolvent
Liquidated damages
Nonconforming goods
Postacceptance
Preacceptance
Private sale
Public sale

Reclaim [goods]
Recoupment
Rejection
Replevin
Repudiate
Revocation
Seasonable notice
Specific performance
Substantial impairment [of the value of goods]
Substitute goods
Suspend performance

SELF-TEST

The questions below will help you evaluate how well you've learned the material in this lesson. Read each one carefully, and select the letter of the option that best answers the question. You'll find the correct answer, along with a reference to the page number(s) where the topic is discussed, in the back of this telecourse study guide.

1. According to the lesson, the vast majority of sales contracts

    a. are repudiated by one party or the other before performance is ever required.
    b. involve flaws in performance that buyer and seller manage to work out without legal assistance.
    c. involve flaws in performance that ultimately can only be settled through lawsuit.
    d. are performed by the parties as expected.

2. The nature of the remedies available to buyer or seller in the event of a breach is likely to be *most* affected by which of the following factors?

    a. The seriousness of the breach itself
    b. When the breach occurs
    c. The nature of the goods identified to the contract
    d. Local state laws

3. Arnold purchases a refrigerator from Handy Appliance. Prior to delivery, Handy discovers that Arnold is insolvent. Arnold, however, wins a long-shot bet at the race track and pays Handy the full price for the refrigerator in cash. At this point, which of the following is true?

    a. Handy must deliver the refrigerator as promised since Arnold has fulfilled his part of the sales contract.
    b. Since Arnold is insolvent, Handy has no obligation to complete the contract and may — if it wants -- stop delivery and refund Arnold's money.
    c. We cannot say what can happen without knowing whether Arnold misrepresented his financial position at the time of signing the contract.

4. A seller who resells goods following a breach of contract by the buyer is under legal obligation to do which of the following?

    a. Ensure that the sale is conducted in a commercially reasonable manner.
    b. Sell the goods *at or above* the original contract price.
    c. Sell the entire lot of goods as a unit, rather than selling the goods individually.
    d. Sell the goods in a public sale, not through private sale.

5. Under which of the following circumstances would a seller *most likely* sue for lost profits?

    a. Through a simple error, the seller ships the wrong computer and the buyer does not accept.
    b. The buyer discovers a serious defect in a whole shipment of television sets and notifies the seller at once.

    c. Several new buyers offer to purchase furniture that a previous buyer has improperly rejected.

    d. A buyer commissions an oil painting of himself done in the living room of his home, but decides he doesn't like the pose and rejects it.

6. The term "damages" (as related to contractual remedies) is best summed up as the difference between

    a. true market value and what the seller is charging, according to the contract.

    b. the original contract price and what the buyer is willing to pay at the time of delivery.

    c. the contract price and the market price of the goods at the time of the sale.

    d. the manufacturer's production cost and the sale price of the goods.

7. The *most common* remedy available to sellers in the event of a postacceptance breach by the buyer is

    a. attempting to reclaim the goods.

    b. suing the buyer for the price of the goods.

    c. suing the buyer for lost profits.

    d. stopping shipment in transit.

8. Under which of the following circumstances could a buyer legitimately revoke acceptance of goods?

    a. Following acceptance, the buyer discovered a hidden defect that seriously decreased the value of the goods.

    b. Following acceptance, the buyer discovered a hidden defect that, though annoying, has not really affected the value of the goods.

    c. The buyer could legitimately revoke acceptance in *either* circumstance (a or b).

    d. *Neither* of the above; the buyer *never* has the right to revoke acceptance once it becomes official.

9. Quigley (the buyer) and Schlotzke (the seller) have a sales contract. They are *most likely* to provide for liquidated damages *if*

    a. the value of the goods in question is very high.

    b. Quigley anticipates that Schlotzke is likely to deliver nonconforming goods.

    c. both feel that in the event of a breach, the value of the goods would be difficult to determine.

    d. Schlotzke suspects that Quigley may be insolvent and therefore incapable of paying for the goods.

10. Norwich takes delivery of an expensive chain saw that is badly scratched, though the defect does not affect the operation of the saw in any way. Norwich does not want to bother having the saw replaced, so he phones the store to say he will keep it, but is deducting $20 from the payment because of the

defect. If the store objects, which of the following is Norwich legally entitled to do?

a. Norwich can still deduct the money, regardless of the objection; the seller has clearly breached the contract.
b. Norwich cannot deduct the money if the seller objects, though he can sue for damages if the seller refuses to fix the problem.
c. Even if the seller refuses to cure the defect, Norwich has no real recourse open at this point; he can neither deduct the money nor sue.

YOUR OPINION, PLEASE

Read each of the following scenarios and answer the questions about the decisions you would make in each situation. Give these questions some serious thought; they may be used as the basis for the development of a more complex essay. You should base your decisions on what you've learned from this lesson, though you may incorporate outside readings or information gained through your own experience if it is relevant.

Scenario I

Brookhaven School District orders fifteen new schoolbuses from Fleet Transit, Inc. The agreement states that "all buses will be subject to proper inspection and testing under the direction and supervision of Fleet Transit prior to delivery."

One week before the agreed-on delivery date, Fleet notifies the district that a recent state requirement (enacted two months prior to the phone call) demands that buses used to transport minors be subject to a government safety inspection in addition to the inspection provided by the manufacturer. Because a shortage of inspectors will delay the government inspection, it will not be possible to deliver all the buses at one time, nor will it be possible to deliver more than one of the buses by the agreed-on delivery date. Others are expected to be provided to the district at two- or three-day intervals, as the government inspection of each bus is concluded.

The district staff are enraged. This situation will not do, they tell Fleet. The inconvenience of notifying parents, double-scheduling current buses, hiring additional transportation, and so forth is all but unthinkable — to say nothing of the expense they'll incur. Fleet apologizes for the inconvenience; they're sympathetic, but insist there is nothing they can do. Further, they point out, Brookhaven needs the inspections completed; they could not legally use buses that didn't meet government standards. District staff retort that Fleet is to blame for this problem since they should have arranged for the government inspection at an earlier date. Fleet's response is that they were unaware the inspection was more than a "routine walkthrough," and that they certainly have no control over the government's inability to cope with the number of inspections desired.

Brookhaven subsequently sues Fleet for breach and seeks consequential damages in the form of costs relating to the rescheduling and notification of parents throughout the district.

What's your opinion? Based on what you know of the situation, do you think Brookhaven can successfully build a case against Fleet? If so, are they seeking the most practical remedy under the circumstances? Are other remedies available or desirable in this case? Can Fleet argue that performance should be excused in this instance? Why or why not?

- Is Brookhaven likely to win their suit for consequential damages? Why or why not?

- What factors support your opinion?

- What factors might an attorney cite in arguing against your view?

- What steps, if any, might Brookhaven have taken to prevent a lawsuit in this situation?

- What steps, if any, might Fleet have taken to prevent a lawsuit in this situation?

Scenario 2

Clark, a teller at a local bank, contracts with Fairhome Furnishings to have new carpeting installed in her townhouse. At the time of the contract signing, Clark is under notice from the bank that due to budget cutbacks, her employment is likely to be terminated within two weeks. Clark, who has been exploring other job possibilities and who is a strong contender for a comparable position at another bank, feels confident that no matter what happens she will be able to make the payments for the carpet. When asked about her employment, Clark tells the sales representative that she is "in the process of changing jobs"; she does not, however, disclose all the details of her situation to Fairhome.

When Clark does, in fact, lose her job and the second job does not come through, she finds herself in a financial bind. She is able to make the first payment on the carpeting with no difficulty, and is also able to follow through on the second of twenty-four monthly installments — but as her savings account dwindles, she finds she is not able to make additional payments. Fairhome notifies Clark that if she does not pay at least a portion of the money owed, they will be forced to reclaim the carpet. Unable to comply, however, Clark lets another two months pass without paying anything further on the debt.

Fairhome thereupon threatens to sue Clark for recovery of the goods. Clark, after reading a section of a law textbook, argues that Fairhome has waited too long in demanding return of those goods. Goods must be reclaimed within ten days, Clark counters, unless there is evidence of misrepresentation of the buyer's financial position. Since she was employed at the time of the purchase, she acted in good faith. Fairhome disagrees and proceeds with the suit.

What's your opinion? Based on what you know of the situation, is Fairhome likely to be successful in their suit to reclaim the goods? Under the circumstances, are they seeking the best remedy available? Do you agree or disagree that Clark acted in good faith when signing the contract? Did Fairhome have enough information to go on in extending credit? Who should be held responsible for this situation?

- Is Fairhome likely to win their suit to reclaim the goods? Why or why not?
- What factors support your answer?
- What factors might an attorney cite in arguing against your view?
- What steps, if any, should Fairhome have taken to prevent a lawsuit in this situation?
- What steps, if any, should Clark have taken to prevent a lawsuit in this situation?

20

Functions and Forms of Commercial Paper

LEARNING OBJECTIVES

Upon completing your study of this lesson, you should be able to

- Define the concept *commercial paper* and identify several forms that commercial paper can take.

- Distinguish between the two basic classes of commercial paper—*promises* to pay money and *orders* to pay money—and provide an example of each.

- Describe the two major functions of commercial paper.

- List the four forms that a negotiable instrument may take.

- Distinguish between *order paper* and *promise paper*, using examples to illustrate the distinction.

- Describe four uses of negotiable instruments, using examples to illustrate each use.

A number of people in our society like to pay as they go—in cash. But think how it might be if we *had* to use cash all the time, whenever money changed hands.

For instance, suppose you have a job that pays $2,000 a month, and on the last day of each month, your employer hands you an envelope containing $2,000 in cash—fifties, twenties, tens, fives. Well, that doesn't sound too bad, you may say. Perhaps not. Remember, though, you must use that money to pay others. Will you send cash through the mail? That sounds risky. But if you don't like that idea, you'll need to spend a lot of time during the next several days visiting your various creditors—your landlord, the local utility company, the phone company, the bureau of water management, the garbage collector, the dentist, and so on—paying a little cash out of your envelope to each and hoping to have enough left over for groceries, a new coat, a night at the movies, or whatever.

How inconvenient all this sounds. How time consuming—and rather unsafe as well. No wonder virtually every society has developed a form of *commercial paper* as a way of making negotiations in the business world safer, faster, and above all, much more convenient for all concerned. The different types of commercial paper—checks, drafts, promissory notes, and certificates of deposit—serve us well and simplify life enormously. Still, we need to understand when and how to apply them and recognize that, in effect, they operate like contracts under the law, imposing certain duties on the parties involved. In this lesson, we'll examine the various forms of commercial paper, explore the situations in which each is most appropriate, and take a close look at the contractual relationships that each form of negotiable instrument creates.

OVERVIEW

Commercial paper is basically a contract for the payment of money. It is used, in the form of various *negotiable instruments*, as a substitute for money. Commercial paper can also be used to extend credit.

The oldest negotiable instrument is the *promissory note*, which dates back to the earliest days of commerce. Hundreds of years ago, merchants discovered how handy it was to have the option of promising to pay money owed at a later time. The recognition of the promissory note as a form of legal contract gave it weight and validity; merchants were willing to accept promissory notes in place of cash because they knew the promise to pay would be enforced unconditionally. And it is largely because negotiable instruments have been viewed as contracts that their use has persisted into the modern business world.

The most common negotiable instrument in our business life today is the *check*. Nearly every adult in our society has been issued a check at one time or another; most receive checks regularly. And most of us have frequent occasion to issue checks ourselves, since this is the most common manner in which debts are paid. Without doubt, if checks were not widely accepted, our business negotiations would be far less convenient, and certainly riskier.

For example, suppose Cartwright wishes to order an automobile from a dealer in another state. The dealer will not send the car without a down payment of $5,000. Cartwright *could* send cash, but if the money is lost he cannot prove it was his, nor can he prevent the finder from spending it. Moreover, what happens to the negotiations on the car? Well, unless Cartwright is willing to shrug off his loss and come up with another $5,000, the deal is likely to fall through right there. In contrast, if Cartwright sends the dealer a check, he can feel secure in knowing that even though the check is negotiable—like money—it's a bit stickier for a third person to appropriate. If the check is lost, Cartwright can stop payment on it and issue another. Negotiations are not likely to be delayed by more than a few days, and no one will be out any money.

It's pretty easy to see that without the existence of legally enforceable commercial paper, business life as we know it would slow to a boggy pace. Merchants, skeptical of receiving their money, would likely insist on cash before turning over their goods. Meanwhile, buyers, faced with the inconvenience of having to cart bundles of cash about to cover the simplest purchases, might well restrict their buying to necessities—finding most shopping too troublesome to bother with. But thanks to the use of commercial paper, this economic standoff isn't likely to occur.

Classes of Commercial Paper

Commercial paper can be placed in one of two categories. These two categories are *promises* to pay money (used to extend credit) and *orders* to pay money, which are, in effect, substitutes for money.

Promissory notes and certificates of deposit issued by banks are promises to pay someone a sum of money. Drafts and checks are orders to another person to pay a sum of money to a third person. The contractual relationships created by drafts and checks—which involve three persons—can seem a bit confusing at first. We'll shortly sort out these relationships, but first let's elaborate on the reasons for having commercial paper in the first place.

Functions of Commercial Paper

As we've noted, commercial paper has two major functions: to serve as a substitute for money and to serve as a credit instrument. For example, when Robbins writes a check for $500 to pay for a new washing machine at Arnie's Appliance Store, she is using the check as a substitute for $500 in cash. If Robbins doesn't have enough in her checking account to cover the washing machine right now, she may write her check for $100, and sign a promissory note for the remaining $400. On the basis of the promissory note, Arnie's extends credit to Robbins until she's able to pay the full debt owed. Both the promissory note and the check are *negotiable instruments*, though one involves a promise to pay and one an order to pay.

To be negotiable, an instrument must be both *current in trade* and *payable in money*. Current in trade simply requires that the instrument needs to be sufficiently current. For example, suppose Robbins attempted to pay for her washing machine with a payroll check that had been issued to her a year earlier but that she had for some reason or other neglected to cash. Arnie's might understandably be reluctant to accept such a check, wondering why Robbins had not cashed it for such a long time and whether it might still be valid. Some checks, in fact, bear a statement to the effect that the check must be cashed within a certain period—say, six months. When a check has not been cashed for a long while, the merchant has a right to question whether the account on which the check has been written is still in existence, whether the appropriate amount of money is still available through that account, and whether the bearer of the check has a valid reason for not cashing the check sooner. Arnie's would not, for example, wish to find itself in the position of accepting a check on which payment had been stopped.

Let's change our scenario a bit now to examine the second criterion for negotiability—namely, that the instrument be payable in money. Suppose that Robbins really wants that new washing machine, but she is very short of cash right now. She tells Arnie's that although she can't pay any money, she'll come every Saturday and wash windows till the debt is satisfied. True, most merchants would probably be very reluctant to accept such an offer, but let's say Arnie's agrees. In that case, Robbins and Arnie's would have a contract, under which Robbins would "pay" for her merchandise by providing a needed service. Such a contract, while perfectly sensible and legal, would *not* be a negotiable instrument, however, because it's not payable in money. Arnie's cannot redeem the window washing contract for cash; it's simply an agreement. Note that every negotiable instrument—check, draft, promissory note, or certificate of deposit—is a contract. But the reverse is *not* true. Not every contract is a negotiable instrument, as the example with Robbins and Arnie's Appliance illustrates.

Because each negotiable instrument is a contract, the parties involved have certain contractual duties and rights specified by law. But because negotiable instruments are such a special—and important—type of contract, special rules, duties, and rights beyond those of regular contract law have been developed. Understanding all those rules, rights, and duties requires understanding the relationships that various negotiable instruments create among the parties. Let's take a closer look at those relationships.

Order Paper and Promise Paper

Promissory notes and certificates of deposit are classed as *promises* to pay, while drafts and checks are *orders* to pay. These two classes of negotiable instruments differ in the kind of language involved and in the number of parties involved. To see how this works, let's begin with an examination of order paper, sometimes termed *three-party* paper.

Order Paper

Checks and drafts, both forms of order paper, are distinguished from other forms of negotiable instruments by two features: both contain an *order* to pay money, and both involve three parties rather than just two.

Checks and drafts both contain language that reads something like "Pay to the order of." Such language is viewed legally as an order to pay, or a *demand* that payment be made. It is not a request. A check, for instance, assumes a preexisting legal relationship between the person who writes or issues the check and the party who is being ordered to pay the money (most commonly a bank). In other words, if Grier writes a check on his account at Tidewater Bank, Tidewater is legally compelled to honor Grier's demand for money and must (unless Grier is out of funds) pay the amount ordered when the check is properly presented. A check, which is a special form of draft, is considered a *demand* instrument, meaning that the money specified on the check is payable *on demand* to the payee.

Let's say, for example, that Grier buys a jacket and writes a check on his Tidewater account to Marv's Mercantile. In this scenario, Grier is the drawer, the person who issues or writes the check. Tidewater Bank is the drawee, the person responsible for honoring or responding to the demand. And Marv's Mercantile is the third party—the payee—that will ultimately receive payment.

At the time the check is written, the law assumes a contractual relationship between Grier (the drawer) and Tidewater Bank (the drawee). This means that Tidewater cannot arbitrarily decide that since they've had quite a few withdrawals this month, they won't honor any more checks. So long as Grier has sufficient money in his account to cover the amount of the check, Tidewater must provide that money on demand; that is the nature of their agreement. Further, in writing his check, Grier is creating another contractual relationship, this one between himself and Marv's Mercantile. This makes sense from a legal perspective; after all, it seems reasonable to assume that Grier isn't writing checks to Marv's just to help boost profits. He is, in fact, receiving something of value in return for his money—in this case, the jacket. Thus, the check establishes a contractual relationship between Grier and Marv's.

There is, however, no contractual relationship between Tidewater (the drawee) and Marv's (the payee) until *after the check has been accepted* by Tidewater. Up until that time, the drawee (Tidewater) has only one duty: the duty to accept the instrument. And this duty must be fulfilled unless there is good reason to reject the check—such as Grier's not having any money in his account. Once Tidewater accepts the check, however, that acceptance creates a new contractual obligation, this one between itself and the presenter of the check (which in this case is Marv's Mercantile).

The payee, remember, is *not* the holder of the money but the person to whom the check is issued—the person whose name follows the words "Pay to the order of." The payee may be an individual or a company or any entity with the power and authority to cash a check. When Barclay writes a check to cover her federal income taxes, for example, the U.S. government is the payee.

The words "Pay to the order of" generally give the payee the right to determine how the check will be negotiated. In other words, the payee may take payment personally or may endorse the check and order that payment be given to another presenter. For instance, suppose Black writes a check—using his account at the First National Bank—to McCoy to cover a $50 debt. The check reads "Pay to the order of John McCoy the sum of $50." McCoy can endorse the check and turn it over to his daughter, who now has the legal right to the money upon presenting the check to the drawee—the First National Bank, that is.

Note that it is only the First National Bank that has the obligation to pay the presenter of the check. So while another bank *may* pay the check, it is not legally obligated to do so. And, as you might know from personal experience, if McCoy's daughter takes the check to the supermarket and tries to buy groceries with it, the store may be reluctant to accept it and has no legal obligation to do so.

When merchants post signs stating that they will not accept "two-party" checks, however, they are usually referring not only to endorsed checks that have been turned over to another person, but also to checks presented by the payee rather than the drawer. In other words, when McCoy pays for her groceries, she may have no difficulty getting the merchant to accept a check she writes personally on her own account. In that case, she is the drawer and the grocer is the payee. But, if McCoy tries to use a check that has been made out to her by someone else—a check on which *she* is the payee—she's likely to find it won't be accepted. Merchants like direct contact with the drawer since this makes it simpler to verify that a checking account is real and current. By the way, the term *two-party check*—though widely used by merchants—is a little misleading because, in reality, such a thing does not exist. All checks are three-party instruments—there's a drawer, a drawee, and a payee—and if they pass to other parties through endorsement, there may be quite a handful of "parties" involved before the check is finally paid.

How does a check differ from a draft? Sometimes, it doesn't. Remember, a check is one special form of a draft. There are, however, other types of drafts that are different from checks in small but important ways. First, the drawee on a check *must* be a bank. Anyone can be the drawee on a draft, though the drawee is likely to be some sort of financial entity such as a credit union or other similar institution. Second, a check is always a *demand instrument*, meaning that the money is payable to the payee on demand—when the check is presented, that is. A draft, by contrast, may be a demand instrument or a *time instrument*, meaning that it may be payable at some future, determinable date.

For instance, let's say that Palmer, who resides in San Francisco, orders some goods from Kahl in Chicago. Palmer wants time to inspect the goods following delivery to ensure that they are precisely up to her specifications. Kahl, meanwhile, wants assurance that the debt will be paid once the goods are accepted. A check will not satisfy the needs of both parties here very well since if it's issued at the time of shipment, Palmer is likely to feel she hasn't had sufficient time to inspect the goods before turning over her money. And if the check is delayed, Kahl is likely to feel uncomfortable about shipping the goods in the first place. One answer would be a draft, an instrument payable at some specified later date. Palmer could send Kahl a draft on June 1, but specify *June 15* as the due date, or the date on which the draft could be cashed. That would give her time for inspection, but provide Kahl with assurance that he would have his money if all is in order. (Thus, as you might deduce, a post-dated check is a kind of draft.)

Promise Paper

With two-party—or promise—paper, only two parties are needed to fill the legal roles involved. There are two types of promise paper: promissory notes and certificates of deposit. Let's consider these in turn.

A promissory note, the oldest form of negotiable instrument, is—as its name clearly suggests—a promise to pay. A person who buys a house on time, for example, signs a special form of promissory note known as a *mortgage*. This is a common and very important type of promissory note in our society since very few persons are able or willing to pay the full price of their homes in cash. Promissory notes of one type or another are used, in fact, for almost every type of major purchase involving payments over time. Buyers typically sign promissory notes when purchasing automobiles, for instance. Such documents are often referred to as *installment* notes. Banks and other lending institutions also issue promissory notes when customers borrow money.

A promissory note may be a very straightforward and simple sort of instrument: "Wilkes hereby promises to pay Lowery the sum of $500 in five monthly installments of $100 apiece, beginning on July 1, and concluding with the final payment on November 1." Such a document, signed by Wilkes, would qualify as a promissory note. Many promissory notes, however—particularly those used by businesses in everyday negotiations—specify a wide range of additional information. For instance, they may contain details relating to interest payments, prepayment penalties, late charges, default or acceleration payments, required collateral, security of the debt, and so forth. Such details are not mandatory components of a legal promissory note, but they may be important elements in a promissory note issued by a business. Businesses usually have well-established procedures under which they extend credit and require payment of debt, and these will be spelled out in writing on any promissory note that the customer signs.

A certificate of deposit, the other form of promise or two-party paper, is much like a promissory note. It too involves the promise to repay a debt. However, a certificate of deposit is issued by a bank to a customer to recognize money deposited in the bank. It is the bank's official promise to pay out a specified amount in accordance with the terms of the certificate. Depending on the nature of the certificate, the money may either be payable on demand or payable following some specified time period—say, six months.

Both certificates of deposit and promissory notes involve only two parties: the maker and the payee (also called the holder). Recall that a three-party instrument involves three roles: drawer, drawee, and payee. In the case of a two-party paper, the roles of drawer and drawee are combined, and the *maker* assumes responsibility for both. In other words, the maker is the one who makes the promise—whether via promissory note or certificate of deposit—and is also the party responsible for payment when that instrument is presented sometime later by the payee. Some examples should make this clear.

Longman buys a car from James, giving James a down payment of $1,000 on a $10,000 total debt. James thereupon asks Longman to sign a promissory note for the unpaid balance. In this instance, Longman is the maker, the party making the promise to pay. But notice that Longman also assumes the role of drawee, since he will have to pay James the money when James presents the note. James is the payee, the one who will be paid. Notice, too, that Longman the maker is liable to James the payee from the time the original note is issued. This, as you'll recall, is different from the situation involving demand paper, where the drawee is not liable to the payee until *after* acceptance of the paper.

Now let's suppose that Wilhelm deposits $12,000 in the Payson County Bank. Payson County then issues Wilhelm a certificate of deposit. Who is the maker here? Payson County. Payson County *makes the promise* to repay the money, as recorded on the certificate of deposit. Payson County also issues the instrument, and has liability to pay upon proper presentment of that instrument by Wilhelm, thus making it also the drawee. Wilhelm, in this case, is the payee.

The Need for Negotiable Instruments

The various uses of negotiable instruments are likely quite clear to you by now, but to summarize:

- We use checks to pay bills, as a substitute for cash.
- We use drafts to pay for merchandise ordered — often as a way of delaying payment for some valid reason.
- We use promissory notes as instruments of credit, and to provide evidence of a debt.
- We use certificates of deposit to record the borrowing of money from a depositor; the certificates serve as a way of extending credit to a bank and as an assurance that the bank is ready to pay the money to the certificate holder.

Just how important are these various uses? Well, we've talked about inconvenience and risk. But, if we were willing to put up with a little more of each, could we survive economically without negotiable instruments? In answering that question, consider what would happen to business as we know it if there were no way of extending credit and no way of paying for products or services except with cash. On the surface, that might seem a simpler way of doing business, but in fact, it could lead to major breakdowns in commerce.

Not many of us would be willing to deposit money in a bank if we received no certificate guaranteeing that the money would be repaid to us. Few of us would have sufficient purchasing power to satisfy our wants and needs in the absence of credit. And deprived of all credit customers, merchants would find their potential for business expansion severely curtailed.

Eliminate credit from our business negotiations, and what would we be left with? Warehouses crammed with merchandise no one could buy? Only for a little while. Storing goods costs money, too. And without the cash flow generated through credit, merchants and manufacturers would soon be forced to cut both production and inventory.

Indeed, paying cash for everything would be virtually unthinkable. We might spend almost as much time rushing about paying for things as we spent earning the money in the first place. For better or worse, ours is a society built on credit and commercial promises. Take these things away, and our lives might be arguably simpler, but many of the goods and services we've come to depend on would no longer be available to us.

SOME PRACTICAL ADVICE

The information contained in this lesson is intended to help you sort out the various relationships involved in the exchange of commercial paper, and to help you understand the function of negotiable instruments in our business world. Unlike many other business law concepts, you are not likely to get into serious legal hot water if you forget the distinction between a check and a draft. Nor are you likely to be sued if you cannot define the role of the maker in relation to promise paper.

On the other hand, though, knowing how negotiable instruments work and understanding the duties involved in various roles can be essential in everyday business life. Would you know, for instance, when to issue a check or when a bank draft might be a better choice? Would you know how to recognize a promissory note, and would you understand your contractual obligations if you signed such a note? A wise businessperson will take time to define and clarify the duties and responsibilities inherent in being a party to any negotiable instrument. Remember, such instruments are contracts and, as such, are legally enforceable.

Here are a few things to keep in mind. In three-party (or order) paper, remember that the drawee (often, a bank) has no obligation to the payee prior to acceptance. Acceptance is fairly automatic if everything is in order, but it is contingent upon *proper presentment*. In other words, banks and other drawees have a right to insist on timely cashing of checks, presentation of appropriate identification by the payee, and so forth. Prior to acceptance, there is no contractual relationship whatsoever between the payee and the drawee.

The words "Pay to the order of" give the payee the right to order the drawee to make payment to someone else. But this duty extends *only* to the drawee — not to anyone else. In other words, endorsing a check and turning it over to another party will not guarantee that that person will have a simple time getting the money. The drawee — the bank — must honor the endorsement and comply with the demands of the drawer. That is understood, given the nature of their contractual relationship. But others — merchants, for instance — need not do so, and often will not.

Checks are so convenient and commonplace that it's easy to overlook the ways in which drafts can simplify life in business negotiations. Keep in mind that drafts — unlike checks — allow the drawer to specify the time when the instrument will come due. This can be a real plus in a situation where the drawer wishes to show good faith by promising the money but does not wish the payee to actually *collect* that money until some future date. A check will not permit this sort of delay. The drawer might ask the payee to refrain from cashing the check immediately, but the payee is under no legal obligation to do so. A check by definition is a demand instrument — payable on demand, that is. The only safe legal means of inserting a delay in the collection of the money is to use a draft rather than a check.

Promissory notes, as we've noted, are commonplace in business, where many kinds of merchandise are bought on time. While some are straightforward and readily understandable, many are not. These documents can be extremely complex and detailed, with numerous provisions involving late payments, need for collateral, and so forth. Customers who sign promissory notes, therefore, should take time to read these documents very carefully and to request explanations for any terms that seem unclear. Usually a promissory note is more than a simple promise to repay money; it commonly involves a promise to repay in a particular manner, with specified penalties for failing to fulfill those duties.

Finally — though it's a point we've made already — never forget that any promise paper or demand paper constitutes a legal contract and can be enforced as such. Checks — once signed — cannot be unsigned. Duties specified within a promissory note cannot be ignored just because the maker skimmed hastily through the fine print before signing. Businesspeople should, therefore, use the same care in signing promise or demand paper that they use in entering any legal contract.

ASSIGNMENTS

- Before you watch the video program, be sure you've read through the preceding overview, familiarized yourself with the learning objectives for this lesson, and looked at the key terms below. Then, read Chapter 23 of Davidson et al., *Business Law*.

- After completing these tasks, view the video program for Lesson 20.

- After watching the program, take time to review what you've learned. First, evaluate your learning with the self-test which follows the key terms. Then, apply and evaluate what you've learned with the "Your Opinion, Please" scenarios at the end of this telecourse study guide lesson.

KEY TERMS

Before you read through the textbook assignment and watch the video program, take a minute to look at the key terms associated with this lesson. When you encounter them in the textbook and video program, pay careful attention to their meaning.

Acceptance	Installment note
Certificate of deposit	Issue
Check	Maker
Collateral	Mortgage note
Commercial paper	Negotiable instrument
Current in trade	Order paper
Demand instrument	Payee
Draft	Presentment
Drawee	Promise paper
Drawer	Promissory note
Holder	Time instrument

SELF-TEST

The questions below will help you evaluate how well you've learned the material in this lesson. Read each one carefully, and select the letter of the option that best answers the question. You'll find the correct answer, along with a reference to the page number(s) where the topic is discussed, in the back of this telecourse study guide.

1. Article 3 of the Uniform Commercial Code covers commercial paper. This means that this article deals specifically with

   a. *All* of the following are covered.
   b. money.
   c. stocks and deeds of title.
   d. order paper and promise paper.

2. A negotiable instrument is *best* defined as

   a. a form of money.
   b. a transferable contract for the payment of money.
   c. an extension of credit.
   d. a legal record of a debt.

3. Williams and Horton have a contract stating that Williams may graze his cattle on Horton's land in exchange for water rights. Is this contract a negotiable instrument?

   a. Yes; all legal contracts are negotiable instruments.
   b. No; since it is not payable in money.
   c. We cannot say without knowing whether Williams and Horton have specifically *designated* this contract to be a negotiable instrument.

4. Negotiable instruments may be of two types: promise paper and order paper. In which of the following options are *both* examples *order* paper?

   a. Drafts and promissory notes
   b. Drafts and certificates of deposit
   c. Checks and certificates of deposit
   d. Checks and drafts

5. Elridge owes Kilroy $5,000. To cover the debt, Elridge issues an order paper that reads "Pay to the order of Kilroy the sum of $5,000." However, since Elridge is currently short of cash, he postdates the instrument by one month so that Kilroy cannot present it for cash immediately. The instrument in this scenario is *best* termed a

   a. certificate of deposit.
   b. promissory note.
   c. check.
   d. draft.

6. Simmons is holding a check that reads "Pay to the order of Hubert Simmons the sum of $100." The words "Pay to the order of" give Simmons the right to

   a. increase the payment to *more* than $100.
   b. demand that anyone cash the check.
   c. request that the drawee provide interest if the check is not cashed immediately.
   d. order the drawee to make payment to another person.

7. Simpson writes a $20 check, payable to Loomis, on Simpson's account with First City Bank. In this scenario, which of the following *best* describes the roles of the three parties involved?

   a. First City is the drawer, Simpson the drawee, and Loomis the payee.
   b. Simpson is the drawer, First City the drawee, and Loomis the payee.
   c. Simpson is the maker, First City the drawer, and Loomis the payee.
   d. First City is the payee, Simpson the drawer, and Loomis the drawee.

8. Hendricks signs a negotiable instrument to cover the unpaid balance on his new freezer. The instrument specifies that if Hendricks pays the debt early he

will be charged a prepayment penalty of 10% on the total cost of the freezer. Can Hendricks legally be held to this commitment?

a. No; prepayment penalties are not legal in negotiable instruments of this type.

b. Yes; the instrument is a legal contract and, as such, agreements made therein are fully binding.

c. We cannot say without knowing whether Hendricks was aware of the penalty clause at the time of signing the instrument.

9. Kunderson buys a motorcycle for $4,000 and signs an installment note to pay for the purchase over a two-year period. Which of the following terms *best* defines Kunderson's role in this example?

a. Payee

b. Drawer

c. Drawee

d. Maker

10. According to the lesson, negotiable instruments are widely used in our society. Probably the *main* reason for this is that

a. the UCC demands use of negotiable instruments among merchants.

b. the recent need for credit among consumers makes them critical.

c. fewer and fewer businesses will accept cash.

d. they're convenient.

YOUR OPINION, PLEASE

Read each of the following scenarios and answer the questions about the decisions you would make in each situation. Give these questions some serious thought; they may be used as the basis for the development of a more complex essay. You should base your decisions on what you've learned from this lesson, though you may incorporate outside readings or information gained through your own experience if it is relevant.

Scenario I

Parker is owner–manager of a small firm, Aunt Bea's Cookie Company, that he started in the kitchen of his own home. The business has been moderately successful at the local level and has now expanded to occupy a small downtown store where products are made and sold. Parker deals with a host of vendors, but they're all local and individual purchases tend to be small. Thus, Parker prefers to pay cash for many of these purchases. Aunt Bea's does have a checking account with the local bank, but Parker prefers to use it "only as a last resort."

Parker's accountant, Fensley, suggests that Parker begin paying for all purchases, however small, with checks — as a way of simplifying bookkeeping, if nothing else. But Parker stubbornly refuses, seeing no real advantage.

"Look," he tells Fensley, "we're a small company. We're not an international conglomerate. Why be pretentious about things? I like the idea of paying cash. It lets me know where I stand at all times; I can see at a glance whether I'm about to run out of funds. And as a result, Aunt Bea's never overspends. Besides, checkbooks aren't safe. Checks can be used by anyone — forged. Then where are you? If it's a record we need, we've got that in the sales slips the vendors give us. We don't need anything more. I don't like the idea of living on credit — and checks encourage that. If we can't afford to pay cash for something, we can't afford it. Period."

What's your opinion? Based on what you know of the situation, do you think Parker's thinking is sound? Or are there some flaws in his arguments? What are the relative advantages and disadvantages in paying cash for various items?

- Is Parker's cash-only policy sound? Why or why not?
- If you were in Fensley's position, what would you say to persuade Parker to change his mind?
- What outcomes would likely occur if Parker followed your advice?
- What outcomes would likely occur if Parker did *not* follow your advice?
- What compromise in procedures might Parker and Fensley agree on that would best meet the concerns of both?

Scenario 2

Rapp, who is short of cash, wishes to invest $20,000 in Pet Tracks, a new business that specializes in recovering lost or stolen pets. Deniro feels he *might*, under certain conditions, be willing to lend Rapp the money. But since Rapp is a long-time friend, Deniro feels awkward about asking to have the agreement stated in writing. Friends and family pressure him to draw up a promissory note for Rapp's signature, but Deniro isn't sure he feels comfortable with that — nor is he sure it would afford him any additional security in the event Rapp defaulted on the debt.

As they're discussing the project, Deniro tells Rapp that he would be willing to lend him the money if he had some assurance that there were other investors interested in Pet Tracks; he would really prefer to hold off a bit in the meantime. Rapp assures Deniro that he will have more information about that within a few weeks, but in the meantime, he would like some indication that Deniro does, in fact, intend to lend him the money.

Since Rapp is being so insistent, Deniro decides to raise the issue of the promissory note. But Rapp balks at that. He tells Deniro that the cancelled check will serve as a sufficient contract; the note is unnecessary. Deniro isn't sure about that, but feels hesitant to press further.

What's your opinion? Based on what you know of the situation, do you think Deniro should insist on a promissory note, or would a check be sufficient to establish their contractual relationship? Are there other alternatives they are overlooking?

- Should Deniro insist upon a promissory note? Why or why not?

- Why might Rapp be reluctant to sign a promissory note?

- From Rapp's perpective, are there reasons that it would be better for him to sign a promissory note?

- What problems, if any, might arise if the parties follow Rapp's advice and don't execute a promissory note?

- Whose position—Rapp's or Deniro's—is least likely to lead to a dispute and a possible lawsuit?

21

Negotiability

LEARNING OBJECTIVES

Upon completing your study of this lesson, you should be able to

- Define the term *negotiability* and provide several examples of a negotiable instrument.
- List and discuss the seven requirements (e.g., it must be in writing) that make an instrument negotiable.
- For each of the seven requirements for negotiability, provide at least one hypothetical example illustrating how an instrument might meet that specific requirement.
- List and discuss three guidelines that courts can use when difficulties arise in determining whether the seven requirements for negotiability have been met.

One of the big advantages in money, if you think about it, is the ease with which we can get rid of it. In other words, we do not have to wonder from one time to the next whether the tens and twenties in our pockets are spendable or not. Wouldn't it be rather odd if we did? Imagine going into the grocery store, picking out a few items for dinner, and proceeding cheerfully through the checkout line only to have the clerk say, "I'm sorry—but this twenty-dollar bill isn't acceptable," or "Twenties? Let's see, here . . . those are worth ten dollars today." We *assume* that the cash we carry with us will be perfectly spendable—negotiable, that is—almost anywhere, anytime, and that it will have a definite value we can rely on.

   Negotiable documents—checks, drafts, promissory notes—exist to be used as money. But in order to be accepted as substitutes, they need the same kind of reliability *and* transferability that cash has. In other words, they have to be spendable in order to serve their purpose well. After all, if they did not function in this way, within a very short time businesspeople would refuse to accept them as substitutes for money—and that would be a blow to commerce as we know it.

   Money itself, of course—paper bills and coins—has very little intrinsic value. But its negotiable value is guaranteed by the U.S. government through the promises inherent in each bill or coin. It is somewhat the same with negotiable instruments, except that these instruments need not be preprinted, nor is their value established or guaranteed by a government. Instead, the value is determined by the maker or drawer, whose signature on the instrument affirms the promise or order to pay. Further, negotiable instruments, unlike one-dollar bills, do not all look alike. Nor do they need to. But that doesn't mean there are no rules governing how such instruments can be put together or what information they must contain. In fact, the UCC provides very specific requirements for negotiability, and examining those requirements in some detail is what this lesson is all about.

OVERVIEW

How is negotiability created? That is the key question for this lesson. To begin with, negotiability is largely a matter of form—of how an instrument is put together, that is. And the rules governing negotiability must be consistent across time and from instrument to instrument. In other words, a bank cannot look at a negotiable instrument—say a check—on Monday and decide that yes, it's negotiable, and then look at the same instrument on Tuesday and arbitrarily decide that no, it isn't negotiable after all. Negotiability cannot rest on opinion or preference or whim; in order to ensure that holders will have confidence in negotiable instruments and will continue to accept them in place of money, we need specific requirements governing negotiability. And these are provided by the Uniform Commercial Code—the UCC.

Negotiability Defined

Let's begin by defining what we mean by the term *negotiability*. Negotiability involves the transfer of a document by endorsement (signature, that is) or delivery to another person in lieu of money. The person who receives the document or negotiable instrument becomes a *holder*. In turn, this holder of a negotiable instrument can choose to give it to another person, who then becomes the legal holder, entitled to the monetary benefits described within the instrument. An instrument that cannot readily be transferred from one holder to another in lieu of money is *not* considered negotiable. To look at it another way, a negotiable instrument is one that will move readily through the business world as money, without holding up commerce.

The clarity of the instrument itself has a lot to do with its acceptance. With a negotiable instrument, the intent of the maker is clear and easily determined. There are no ambiguities. There is no need to spend hours tracking down additional information in order to properly interpret the instrument. Everything will be right there, contained within the instrument itself, and readily understandable to the holder. If examination of the instrument leaves the holder with unanswered questions—Did Uncle Ted *really* intend to pay the money? When? How much?—odds are very good that the instrument is not negotiable. Given this general definition, let's get specific.

The Seven Requirements for Negotiability

For a document to be considered negotiable, it must meet seven specific requirements; meeting five or six of the requirements—while admittedly useful for clarifying matters—is insufficient to make a piece of paper a negotiable instrument.

Seven requirements may sound like quite a few. Actually, though, each is relatively simple in itself, and some are interrelated in such a way that it would be difficult—or at any rate *unusual*—for a document to meet one requirement without meeting the other.

The seven requirements for negotiability are as follows. The instrument must

1. be *in writing*;
2. be *signed* by the maker or drawer;
3. contain an *unconditional* promise or order to pay;
4. call for the payment of a *sum certain*;
5. be payable in (that is, be interchangeable with) *money*;
6. be payable at a *determinable time* (either on demand or at some definite time); and
7. be made payable *to order* or *to bearer*.

Though negotiability is not difficult to achieve, the slightest deviation from the requirements listed here can affect negotiability. This does not mean, by the way, that a nonnegotiable instrument is worthless. On the contrary, it could well be a bona fide contract, fully enforceable under the law. However, it would not be readily transferable to another party, and so could *not* be used as a substitute for money. Keep in mind that negotiability does not refer to value per se, but only to the ease with which that value can be transferred from one holder to another.

It's worth repeating that if even *one* of the requirements for negotiability is not met, the instrument will not be negotiable. The bank, for example, will not say, "Well—pretty close. We'll call that negotiable." All seven requirements must be met in full. So let's look now at each of the individual requirements, with some examples to show the circumstances under which an instrument would be regarded as nonnegotiable.

Requirement 1: In Writing

As you may know already, most kinds of contracts can be oral and still be valid. An oral contract, however, though valid and legal, may be difficult to enforce. Why? Because it is hard to know for certain what the contracting parties intended. And that is precisely the rationale behind the requirement that a negotiable instrument be in writing.

Think how it would be if things were otherwise. Instead of issuing Mills a check, for example, suppose King sent her to the bank with oral instructions that she was to receive $50 in cash, payable from his account. If this scenario seems absurd, that's because we already understand the importance of clarifying intentions in writing. How can the bank know that King really intends to pay Mills if King does not commit that promise to writing? How can they be certain of the amount? Mills could very well decide, en route to the bank, to ask for $500 instead of $50. There is no need to belabor the countless difficulties oral agreements could create in the world of commerce. The main point is clear: A written document provides clarification and evidence of intent.

At the same time, though, the writing requirement does *not* imply that the document must be drafted on some preprinted form. Most checks are written this way because when a customer opens a checking account, he or she agrees to use the bank's preprinted, easy-to-process check forms. Such forms certainly simplify life. They have the right blanks in the right places so that all pertinent information can be readily provided. And the bank's data processing department can quickly process such standardized forms; it would be chaotic if everyone used whatever piece of paper was handy every time a check was written. But while preprinted instruments are obviously valuable, they are not mandatory.

In our previous example, for instance, King could make out a check or promissory note to Mills on the inside cover of a matchbook or any other reasonably permanent thing. So long as it met all other requirements for negotiability, that instrument would be negotiable—unconventional though it might be in appearance. Of course, scribbling promissory notes in crayon on the back of a napkin is not recommended business practice. But a document created in this manner—assuming all other requirements were met—would nonetheless still be valid. Matchbook covers, notepads, paper napkins, and such objects may be regarded as sufficient to create a "permanent" instrument—one that will not fall apart or be destroyed through normal business use. A promissory note written on the sand at the beach, however, would *not* be considered permanent.

Note also that there is no requirement that the document be typeset or typewritten. A handwritten document, as our preceding example suggests, will fully meet the "in writing" requirement.

Requirement 2: Signed by the Maker or Drawer

The maker's or drawer's signature is required in order to ensure authenticity. In other words, it provides some protection against fraud or trickery by giving some evidence of the maker's intent to create the instrument and to live up to the conditions it imposes.

Given that a signature is required primarily to show *intent*, the law does not demand a manual, handwritten signature of one's name—an autograph, in other words. That is one type of acceptable signature, but it is not the only type. A signature could also be a stamp, an X, a thumbprint, or any symbol put on the instrument to show the maker's approval of the instrument and intention to fulfill the conditions of the instrument.

Further, the signature can appear anywhere at all on the instrument and still comply with this requirement. Checks, for example, are traditionally signed in the lower righthand corner. But the drawer could sign a check at the top and it would still be negotiable. She could also stamp the check with a rubber stamp bearing her name, and that would be fine, too. This shortcut is particularly useful to large corporations that must authorize thousands of checks and would literally have to employ full-time check signers if each check had to be personally autographed before it could be cashed.

Requirement 3: Unconditional Promise or Order

If an instrument is to be negotiable—transferable from one party to another, that is—the promise or order to pay given within the instrument must be unconditional. That is, it must be an absolute promise or order, one that will hold up regardless of circumstance—not one that is tentative or conditional on something else.

Further, it must be something more than a statement. For example, if Hank Favor writes "I owe you, Ken Case, $100" and signs it, does Case have a negotiable instrument? No. Favor has acknowledged a debt, nothing more. He has not promised to pay the debt or ordered someone else to pay it on his behalf. IOUs like this may be contracts, but they are not negotiable instruments.

Several elements are at issue here. First, as we've implied, the language of the document is crucial. A promise or order to pay will be considered unconditional if the wording is as follows: "I, John Wilson, promise to pay to the order of," or "Please pay to the order of." Notice that the wording here is unflinching, straightforward, and not at all ambiguous. Contrast that wording with the wording in these examples: "I, John Wilson, upon his complying with our employment agreement, promise to pay to the order of," or "Pending the sale of Property #3021, please pay to the order of." Now, suddenly, conditions have been introduced. John Wilson will fulfill his promise to pay *only if* the employment agreement is worked out; the drawer in the second example orders the drawee to pay only upon the sale of Property #3021. Such conditions make a document nonnegotiable.

As we've stressed earlier, however, that doesn't mean the document isn't valid. In other words, John Wilson can probably be held to his promise to pay if the employment agreement is complied with; however, the document itself is not a negotiable instrument and is not transferable as such to someone else. Why? Because that someone else would have no way of knowing — without checking with Wilson and the employee to ascertain the status of compliance with the employment agreement — whether the instrument even had any monetary value.

This brings us to the second element of negotiability relating to an unconditional promise. Courts frequently rely on something called the *four-corner* rule to help determine negotiability. According to this rule, all information pertaining to negotiability must be contained within the four corners of the instrument. In other words, if a person must look outside the instrument itself for necessary information, the instrument is not negotiable. In the example with John Wilson, for instance, it would not be possible to determine by examining a promissory note whether the employment agreement to which Wilson had referred to had been satisfactorily concluded. And while the matter could perhaps be cleared up with some phone calls, letters, or whatever, such extra work is contrary to the concept of a negotiable instrument.

Third, a notation on the negotiable instrument may require that a certain fund or type of fund be debited in order to cover the instrument — and that's fine. But tying the instrument to a particular *source* of funds will make it nonnegotiable. This is a somewhat tricky distinction, so some examples may help here.

Let's suppose Slater is a consultant who does various types of work for a firm called New Century, Inc. New Century issues Slater checks periodically, usually at two-month intervals, that are drawn on different funds within the company — depending on the type of work Slater has performed during the preceding period. For example, let's say that Slater sometimes does staff inservice training for New Century; the check to cover that work comes from Account #11333. During another period, Slater helps develop a new software program for use by the company; the check to cover that work comes from Account #11444. Such designations are perfectly proper and do not affect negotiability. They're simply a way for the company to help keep track of how it is spending its money. In both instances, the checks are being posted to a specific account — an accounting notation.

On the other hand, suppose Slater has an agreement with New Century to develop the software program on a royalty basis; if the program does not sell well, the company won't owe Slater much money. In this situation, they might issue a draft payable to Slater at some later date *out of proceeds on the sale* of the program. Such an instrument would *not* be negotiable. From the UCC's perspective, tying the payment to a particular source — rather than to the general assets of the company — makes the matter too risky. Ask yourself, would you want to accept a payment tied to the success of a computer program you don't know anything about? Most businesspeople wouldn't, and since the universal acceptability of an instrument is a cornerstone of negotiability, this instrument is not negotiable.

Once again, we must stress that "negotiability" is not the same as "legally binding." While all negotiable instruments are legally binding, many legally binding instruments aren't negotiable. It is, for example, perfectly legal (and common) for author and publisher to create a contract saying that the author will be compensated from the proceeds from the sale of the work. Provided the two parties are happy with this arrangement, the law is equally happy to recognize it. But such a contract is not a negotiable instrument because there is no way to determine its monetary value; thus, it cannot serve as a substitute for money.

There are some cases where you might think that the wording of the instrument might fail to meet the four-corner rule, but it really doesn't. For example, note that negotiability is *not* affected by the following:

- the words "as per agreement" or any reference to consideration given in exchange for a promise to pay
- reference to a separate agreement — unless the promise or order to pay is *dependent on fulfillment* of that agreement
- reference to collateral, as a means of securing a loan.

The underlying question is this: Is the money payable as promised or ordered *no matter what*? Or, must some condition be met before the money would be payable? If the answer to the first question is *yes*, the instrument is negotiable; if there is a condition of any kind, the instrument is not negotiable. And this holds true even if fulfillment of the condition is virtually inevitable; it holds true, in fact, even if the condition has already been satisfied.

By the way, you may be wondering about the negotiability of a personal check, which seems to be drawn on a specific account — that of the drawer. Is such an instrument negotiable? Yes, at least in theory. Although it might seem that the bank debits only the account in question, in reality the bank pays the holder from all its available funds but *charges* the check to a specific account — that of the drawer. In other words, the funds to cover a given check are always theoretically available as long as the bank itself is solvent, since the bank may draw from its full set of resources. (Obviously though, the bank requires that the drawer must make appropriate "contributions" to the bank — or lose the right to tap into the bank's larger resources.)

Requirement 4: Sum Certain

The promise or order to pay within an instrument must refer to a sum certain. In other words, the person who receives the instrument must be able to know exactly how much money will be received when the instrument is turned in for payment.

This requirement, like that relating to an unconditional promise or order, relies on the four-corner rule. In other words, the exact amount must be determinable within the instrument itself. If it can only be determined by looking at other documents, the instrument is not negotiable. Let's consider some examples.

Suppose for instance, that Bea Small wishes to buy an antique rug belonging to Helen Bliss. Bliss likes the idea of selling the rug, but wishes to keep it for six more months until she moves to a new house. During that six months, Bliss believes the value of the rug will increase, so she's uncertain what to charge. Small suggests that they draw up a contract specifying that Small will pay Bliss the appraised value of the rug on January 1st, which happens to be six months after their initial negotiations. If Bliss agrees, will they have a negotiable instrument? No. There's no way to determine appraised value without looking outside the instrument, so a contract based on an appraised or market value cannot be negotiable.

It is not, however, essential that the total figure be printed within the instrument. It is, for example, quite in order for a negotiable instrument to include interest at a specified rate. This will still qualify as a sum certain, even though the holder may have to do some math to learn the exact value of the instrument. But specifying that interest will be charged at, say, the *current prime rate* makes the sum uncertain. Reference is made to a rate presently being charged by financial institutions — in other words, a market rate. And because this sum is variable, it would obviously be necessary to look outside the instrument to verify the amount — and that defeats negotiability.

Note, however, that the specific phrase "with interest" will *not* defeat negotiability. That's because this phrase is taken to imply interest at the *judgment rate*, or whatever is legally allowable under the laws of the state or county in which the instrument is to be paid. True, this rate might not be common knowledge. However, the court takes the position that it *could* be; and in any case, it is a constant figure set by law, as opposed to the current market rate of interest. Of course, the contractors are free to determine their *own* agreeable rate of interest so long as it's specified within the document. Black may agree to pay Horn a 20% rate of interest, and that rate will not affect negotiability as long as it's made clear. Further, the interest rate can vary. For instance, Horn might not want any interest for the first six months, but ask for 20% interest on the remaining debt after that time — perhaps as an incentive to get the debt cleared up quickly. The particulars of the arrangement are up to the parties themselves, but those particulars must be specified clearly within the instrument to meet the sum-certain requirement for negotiability.

There is, however, one important exception to the four-corners rule under the sum-certain requirement. A note may contain a clause that provides for the payment of collection fees or attorney's fees in the event of a default. Even though this amount would not be calculable except by going outside the note, the clause would not make the instrument nonnegotiable. This exception is viewed as important to upholding common business practice and it does not really conflict with the underlying principal that the instrument must specify a sum certain. (After all, if all goes according to plan, the uncertain value of the collection and attorney's fees will have no bearing.)

Requirement 5: Payable in Money

Remember, negotiable instruments are considered substitutes for money. Therefore, they must be payable in money. Money, in this context, is defined as a *medium of exchange, authorized or adopted by a domestic or foreign government as part of its currency*. Thus, gold and diamonds would not be money. We don't routinely carry gold nuggets to the shopping mall or use diamonds to pay for automobiles or refrigerators. These items certainly have value and they can be exchanged for money, but they are not themselves money. On the other hand, pounds sterling, francs, and drachmas are money because they are recognized by a government as a medium of exchange.

How does all this relate to negotiability? Well, let's suppose that Dell issues a note promising to pay Frost $250. Dell cannot pay Frost off in bushels of corn, or in gold, or in services—as by washing Frost's car or mowing his lawn. He *must* pay in money. If the promise specifies that Dell will pay in dollars *or* bushels of corn, according to his option, the note is nonnegotiable. This is because, by introducing an alternative form of payment that he—not the holder—can select, Dell makes the note less "marketable." After all, Frost might want to transfer the note to someone who has no desire to receive bushels of corn for payment. Everyone, however, is assumed to have a business interest in money as a *universal* form of exchange.

Suppose, though, that Dell were to issue a note promising to pay Frost $250 or eighty bushels of corn—at the *holder's* (Frost's) option. Now the note would be negotiable, despite the alternative form of payment. The difference here is that the holder of the note is the one to decide how payment will be made and, further, that there is no chance that the note would shrink. Notice, though, that Dell now must have *both* $250 and eighty bushels of corn available in order to pay the note, regardless of the form of payment that might eventually be chosen by the holder.

What about foreign currency? A negotiable instrument *can* be payable in any currency, but it is important to know whether the instrument must be paid in a specific currency or whether there is an option. If, for instance, Dell states that he will pay Frost an amount *equal to* fifty pounds sterling, the payment may be made either in pounds sterling or in U.S. dollars—at the exchange rate effective on the payable date (*not* the exchange rate on the date the note is issued). However, if Dell states that he will pay Frost fifty pounds sterling, then dollars will not suffice. Dell will have to pay in pounds.

Requirement 6: Payable on Demand or at Some Definite Time

For a document to be a negotiable instrument, the holder must know *precisely* when payment can be obtained. Two sorts of provisions are possible. Either the instrument may be payable on demand, or it may be payable at some definite, specified date.

Checks are by their nature demand instruments, meaning that they are payable on demand, assuming proper presentment. The date on a check simply identifies the date of issue; it does not constitute an order to cash the check on that specific date. This sounds like a minor distinction, but it can be important; even though checks, as demand instruments, happen to be negotiable from the date of issue, date of issue is *not* the same thing as date of payment. (A check *may*, of course, be postdated, if the drawer does not wish the holder to cash it right away. A postdated check, however, is technically not a check at all, but a draft. Remember, drafts, of which checks are a special form, are time instruments, payable at a specified future date, rather than on demand.)

Instruments other than checks may be demand instruments if they specifically state "payable on demand." Moreover, the drawer who fails to specify the date for payment automatically makes the instrument payable on demand. In most cases, however, instruments other than checks are payable at a definite time. Just how "definite" must the time be? Let's see.

Clearly, a specific date — month, day, and year — is the simplest way of specifying when payment will be due: e.g., payable September 1, 1998. The time for payment may also be specified as "thirty days following September 1, 1998," or "ninety days prior to September 1, 1998." Under the UCC, the date will also be considered specific if it is tied to the time of presentation: e.g., "payable ninety days after sight," meaning ninety days after presentation of the instrument. The time for payment cannot, however, be linked to some other event — even if that event is viewed as predictable — if the instrument is to remain negotiable.

For instance, suppose Howard wishes to reward his son for several years of hard work at college and writes a promissory note stating that he will pay his son $2,500 "ten days following graduation from Harvard University." Such a document would not be a negotiable instrument because the holder would need to go outside the instrument to determine the exact date for payment. Note, by the way, that it's not the mention of the son's graduation per se that defeats negotiability; the note will not, for example, become negotiable once the son graduates. The point is that the date for payment is imprecise and not determinable within the four corners of the document — which is enough to make the instrument nonnegotiable.

Requirement 7: Words of Negotiability

Even if every one of the other six requirements is met in full, a document will only be a negotiable instrument if it contains *words of negotiability* — that is, words that allow for transfer of the instrument from one person to another.

The words "Pay to Alice Farmer" would defeat negotiability because they suggest that the drawer wishes the money paid to Alice Farmer and to no one else. The whole point of negotiability, remember, is to give the holder the freedom to transfer the instrument to someone else. If Farmer lacks that freedom, the instrument she holds isn't negotiable; only Farmer herself can present it to the drawee for payment.

Negotiability can be created through the words "Pay to the order of" or "Pay to bearer." Either wording suggests that the drawer's intention is to permit transfer of the instrument from one party to the other, and either wording gives the payee (Farmer, in our example) the right to name the next holder — or to receive payment herself. For example, the words "Pay to the order of Alice Farmer" would enable Farmer to endorse the instrument and turn it over to her husband, parent, child, friend, business associate, or anyone else of her choosing. The drawee, through such language, is required to follow Farmer's instructions in making payment—that's what the words "Pay to the order of" mean. The wording "Pay to Alice Farmer" eliminates that crucial flexibility.

The payee, incidentally, need not be a person. It can be an office, agency, company or corporation, or any entity capable of providing an endorsement. If no payee is specified by name when the instrument is originally issued, the instrument must be payable "to bearer" in order to be negotiable. Usually, the words "to bearer" are used explicitly in such a case, but sometimes checks are made out to "Cash," which has the same effect.

Guidelines for Interpretation

You may be thinking that the UCC goes to extraordinary lengths to define negotiability, anticipating a wide range of hypothetical circumstances and trying hard to think of all the possible things that could create confusion. You're right; it does. Yet, despite the Code's efforts, problems arise. Several standards, which apply across the board to all types of negotiable instruments, are intended to help users sort through the problems that might arise.

First, if there is a reasonable doubt as to whether an instrument is a draft or note, the holder may treat it as either. Moreover, a draft that names the drawer as drawee is treated as a note. An example will clarify this. Suppose Forster orders Northwest Wood Products, Inc., to pay to the order of Sam Nellor the sum of $5,000. As it turns out, though, Forster is sole owner, manager, and proprietor of Northwest Wood Products, a company he operates out of his home and whose funds he controls exclusively. In effect, then, he's issuing an order to himself. And what appears to be a draft is really a promissory note since the drawer (writer of the draft) and drawee (person ordered to make payment) are the same; they're both Forster.

Second, in the case of contradictions, handwritten terms control typewritten or typeset terms. If the contradiction is between typeset and typewritten terms, typewritten terms control. Suppose, for instance, that Simpson types a note promising to pay Bagley $500 by May 1, then crosses out the date in pen and writes in June 1 above. The handwritten date, June 1, is the official payment date of the document. The UCC assumes—logically enough—that handwritten entries are the "final word." In other words, most people do not first handwrite notes and then typeset or typewrite over the handwriting. The most recent entries are taken to be the most up-to-date—and therefore most accurate—reflection of the writer or maker's true intentions.

If there is a confusion over words and numbers, words control *unless they are ambiguous*—in which case, numbers control. For instance, let's say Fremont makes out a check for $25.00, but writes the amount in words as "Twenty and 00/100 dollars." How much is the amount of the check? Twenty dollars. Because there was no ambiguity in the words Fremont used to indicate the dollar amount, words control. Now let's suppose that Fremont makes out a check for $25.00, then writes the dollar amount as "Two and twenty-five and 00/100 dollars." Now what is the value of the check? Twenty-five dollars. The words are ambiguous; therefore, numbers control.

Third — as we noted earlier — a provision for interest that simply reads "with interest" will be interpreted to mean interest at the judgment rate for the jurisdiction where the instrument is to be paid. In addition, note that unless some other date is specified, interest runs from the date the instrument is created. Keep in mind that the UCC provisions relating to interest are not intended to suggest what sort of interest rates should be proposed or accepted. They're simply intended to simplify interpretation in cases where the maker of the instrument is not fully specific about rates or dates.

SOME PRACTICAL ADVICE

Intentions are key when dealing with negotiable instruments. Whether you're the one who writes the instrument up or the one who will receive the money, it's important to ask yourself what you intend to have happen. Do you wish the instrument to be negotiable? Is there a reason it might be transferred to another holder? Or to put it another way, do you intend it to be used like money, or is the document to represent a contractual agreement, payment for which you have no intention of ever transferring to someone else?

If negotiability is to be achieved, then certain conditions will have to be met. We won't review the conditions individually here, but will simply remind you that meeting *most* of the requirements for negotiability will not be sufficient. Negotiability isn't achieved by degrees. An instrument is either negotiable or it is not.

Why bother worrying about these conditions? What is the advantage of negotiability? Freedom, essentially. Flexibility. Remember, a negotiable instrument is like money; it's spendable. It can be used in business dealings as a substitute for money. A nonnegotiable instrument, by contrast, may serve as a perfectly valid contract, but it cannot be transferred as money to anyone else. And since it cannot serve as a substitute for money, it has value outside itself only through fulfillment (or anticipated fulfillment) of the conditions it specifies.

In negotiability, as with so many things in life, it's the little things that can hurt you. Here's a quick reminder about a few common pitfalls to watch out for when you're creating what you intend to be a negotiable document:

1. Avoid contingencies of any kind. An instrument that seems to relate payment to another event or contract is not likely to be viewed as an unconditional promise or order to pay. *Unconditional* means just that — no if's, how's, when's, or whether's about it. Payable, period.

2. Remember that a *sum certain* must be calculable, using information contained within the instrument itself. It cannot rest on future values that no one can foresee. Notes can include interest, but unless the amount

is stated specifically, the interest will be calculated at the judgment rate, and will be effective from the date the instrument is issued.

3. An instrument that doesn't specify a date of payment will automatically be payable on demand, like a check. This could come as quite a surprise to a drawer who merely forgot to postdate a check or date a draft they wanted payable in six months. Remember, as in this case, the UCC often makes provisions for handling oversights—and those provisions may not always agree with what the drawer originally had in mind.

4. Keep in mind the importance of wording. The difference between "Pay to Pete Ross" and "Pay to the order of Pete Ross" is the difference between nonnegotiability and negotiability. When Pete endorses the first check to Judy Gonzalas and she takes it to the bank, they may not honor it. Remember, a contract between you and Pete Ross is binding only on the two of you, and banks are not duty-bound to cash nonnegotiable instruments.

5. Watch out for little internal inconsistencies. If your words say one thing and your numbers another, the UCC has definite rules for determining meaning—and you'll have to trust to luck that you made your error in such a way that interpretation of the instrument won't cost you money.

A word of caution should be added: Negotiability can sneak up on you. Whimsically write a business associate a check on the back of a cocktail napkin, and you could find your checking account debited accordingly. Negotiability, for all the rules surrounding it, is sometimes achieved when we least expect it.

Finally, if you find yourself the holder of an instrument that is determined to be nonnegotiable, don't despair. Remember, negotiability is not all that makes a document valuable. Negotiability is, in fact, related to convenience more than anything else. Contractual rights are not lost just because an instrument you thought was negotiable turns out to be nonnegotiable. Your rights are still fully enforceable under the law, and all terms of the agreement are likely to be upheld. True, you will not be able to transfer the instrument to another holder as money, but perhaps that was never your intention.

ASSIGNMENTS

- Before you watch the video program, be sure you've read through the preceding overview, familiarized yourself with the learning objectives for this lesson, and looked at the key terms below. Then, read Chapter 24 of Davidson et al., *Business Law*.

- After completing these tasks, view the video program for Lesson 21.

- After watching the program, take time to review what you've learned. First, evaluate your learning with the self-test which follows the key terms. Then, apply and evaluate what you've learned with the "Your Opinion, Please" scenarios at the end of this telecourse study guide lesson.

KEY TERMS

Before you read through the textbook assignment and watch the video program, take a minute to look at the key terms associated with this lesson. When you encounter them in the textbook and video program, pay careful attention to their meaning.

Determinable time requirement
Four-corner rule
Judgment rate
Money requirement
Negotiable
Payable in money requirement
Postdated check

Signature requirement
Sum certain
Unconditional promise or order to
  pay
Words of negotiability requirement
Writing requirement

SELF-TEST

The questions below will help you evaluate how well you've learned the material in this lesson. Read each one carefully, and select the letter of the option that best answers the question. You'll find the correct answer, along with a reference to the page number(s) where the topic is discussed, in the back of this telecourse study guide.

1. According to the lesson, there are seven individual elements that define negotiability. An instrument would be considered negotiable if it had

   a. even one of these seven elements.
   b. two or more elements.
   c. a preponderance of the seven elements.
   d. *all* seven elements, with no exceptions whatever.

2. Under UCC regulations, a signature is best defined as

   a. a handwritten autograph that spells the person's name out in full.
   b. any handwritten mark—even an X.
   c. an official, authorized corporate or personal symbol, whether handwritten or typed.
   d. any mark or symbol *intended* as an authorized signature.

3. UCC regulations require that promises put forth in negotiable instruments be unconditional. The *main* reason for this is most likely that

   a. conditional promises slow down business negotiations.
   b. conditional promises can be too ambiguous and hard to interpret.
   c. only unconditional promises are allowable in any legal contract.
   d. forceful language is a matter of tradition and the precedent has been accepted.

4. Robert Reynolds makes out a draft to his son that reads "Pay to the order of Ted Reynolds the sum of $1,000, payable on the date Ted Reynolds reaches age 21." Is this a negotiable instrument?

   a. Yes, because the date is definite.
   b. No, because it would be necessary to look outside the document to determine the date of payment.
   c. We cannot say without knowing the period of time between the date of issue and the date on which the instrument becomes payable.

5. Tri-City Furniture issues a check to Luxury Leathers, Inc., drawn against Supplies Account #0204. Does this affect negotiability?

   a. Yes; in fact, the document is negotiable only *because of* this.
   b. Yes; because this restricts the source of the money, the document is *not* negotiable.
   c. No; it does not affect negotiability one way or the other.

6. Hamilton owes a debt to Fry that he can pay only if he manages to sell a tract of land valued at $10,000. He issues a draft to Fry that reads "Pay to the order of Jane Fry the sum of $2,500, subject to the sale of Tract B for the sum of $10,000 or more." Is this document negotiable?

   a. Assuming Hamilton signs the draft to show his acceptance, yes.
   b. It *would* have been negotiable if Hamilton had named the date on which he expected to sell the property.
   c. It is not negotiable because the promise to pay is conditional.

7. Which of the following would be *most likely* to make an instrument nonnegotiable? A document would be nonnegotiable if it contained a statement specifying that

   a. the payment would be secured with collateral.
   b. payment would occur in installments.
   c. the interest rate would increase after a certain date.
   d. the instrument would be subject to completion of a related contract.

8. Chicago commodities broker McPhee, who is short of cash, signs an instrument agreeing to pay his debt to LaRose in bushels of grain. Is this instrument negotiable?

   a. Only if the contract specifies the current market value of the grain.

b. Definitely not; grain is not recognized by the U.S. government as a medium of exchange.

c. Yes, absolutely; the grain serves as a medium of exchange in this situation.

9. Robbins signs an instrument agreeing to repay a $5,000 debt "with interest." Assuming that the document is otherwise negotiable, the interest rate in this case would be

a. set at the rate legally prescribed by the state or jurisdiction in which the instrument would be payable.

b. set according to the current rate charged by financial institutions where the instrument would be payable.

c. set at a fixed rate of 10%, the most common rate for negotiable instruments.

d. *None* of the above; the phrase "with interest" would automatically make the document nonnegotiable.

10. In a check or draft, which of these wordings would make the instrument non-negotiable?

a. "Pay to Pete French"

b. "Pay to the order of Pete French"

c. "Pay to Pete French or bearer"

d. *None* of the above; they would *all* be fully negotiable.

YOUR OPINION, PLEASE

Read each of the following scenarios and answer the questions about the decisions you would make in each situation. Give these questions some serious thought; they may be used as the basis for the development of a more complex essay. You should base your decisions on what you've learned from this lesson, though you may incorporate outside readings or information gained through your own experience if it is relevant.

Scenario 1

Quimby, who hasn't been happy at his job for months, works late one night, remaining at the office long after everyone else has departed. He discovers the door to the owner's office has been left open and the company checkbook is on a desk. Without taking time to think of the consequences, Quimby makes out a check that reads "Pay to the order of bearer." He does not fill in the date of issue. He enters the amount as "$5,000.00, Five thousand and 00/100 dollars." He signs the check using a company-issued stamp with his employer's name, Jonathan Edwards, imprinted on it.

The next morning, Quimby (rather nervously) presents the check at the bank. They do not ask him to endorse it, and they pay him $5,000 in $100 bills. Quimby promptly leaves town without a trace.

Throughout the remainder of that day and for several days to come, Edwards and other employees within the firm spend considerable time wondering what has become of Quimby. When the cancelled check is returned without other explanation, Edwards begins to put things together and certainly suspects Quimby—but cannot really establish much of a link without any endorsement on the check. Nevertheless, he feels enraged by the situation, which has apparently cost him $5,000.

He accuses the bank of cashing a nonnegotiable instrument, and threatens to sue for recovery of the $5,000. The bank counters that it was Edwards who negligently left the checkbook where Quimby could get it. Regardless, the check was perfectly negotiable, and they were well within their rights to accept and cash it.

What's your opinion? Based on what you know of the situation, do you think the check was a negotiable instrument? Must Edwards simply stand the loss, or is he within his rights to sue the bank?

- Is Edwards likely to win a suit for recovery of the $5,000?
- What factors support your answer?
- What factors might an attorney cite in arguing against your view?
- What steps, if any, might Edwards have taken to avoid this situation?
- What steps, if any, might the bank have taken to avoid this situation?

Scenario 2

Williams owes colleague Kittridge a debt of $1,000—which thus far, he has found numerous excuses not to pay. During a company retreat at a beach resort, Williams and Kittridge have an opportunity to discuss the matter while strolling along the beach. Kittridge is clearly put out, impatient, angry over the situation. Hoping to restore some humor and good will to the relationship, Williams rather whimsically writes a promissory note in the sand, complete with all pertinent information. The note reads, "I, Fred Williams, promise to pay to the order of Woodrow Kittridge the sum of $1,000, One thousand and 00/100 dollars." Williams signs the note.

Kittridge surprises Williams by taking out a 35-mm camera and taking several closeup snapshots of the note. He fully intends, he tells Williams, to use the best of the snapshots in cashing the note. Williams laughs, and tells him to go ahead and try.

A few days later, Kittridge phones Williams to tell him the pictures have come out extraordinarily well. He sends Williams a copy to verify this claim, and it's true. Every word is crystal clear, fully readable. Williams still thinks of the whole thing as a sort of joke—but he is beginning to get a little nervous. He tells Kittridge that if anyone attempts to cash the instrument, he will sue to obtain a court ruling on negotiability.

What's your opinion? Based on what you know of the situation, do you think the instrument is negotiable? What elements contribute to its negotiability? What elements could be questioned?

- If Williams does sue to obtain a ruling, how is the court likely to interpret the negotiability of this instrument?
- What factors support your answer?
- What factors might an attorney cite in arguing against your view?
- What steps, if any, might Kittridge have taken to avoid this situation?
- What steps, if any, might Williams have taken to avoid this situation?

22

Negotiations and Holders in Due Course

LEARNING OBJECTIVES

Upon completing your study of this lesson, you should be able to

- Define *negotiation* and explain the specific requirements of a negotiation.
- Define *endorsement* and explain the effects of endorsement on negotiation and liability.
- Distinguish among *special*, *blank*, *restrictive*, *unqualified*, and *qualified* endorsements.
- Define the terms *holder* and *holder in due course* and explain the circumstances under which a holder becomes a holder in due course.
- Explain the legal advantages inherent in the status of *holder in due course*.
- Distinguish between the *personal* and *real* defenses for a holder in due course, using hypothetical examples to illustrate the distinction.
- Define the term *liability* as it relates to commercial paper, and explain the circumstances under which such liability may come about.
- Using hypothetical examples, explain five ways in which the liability or potential liability on a negotiable instrument may be discharged (or removed).

In our business world, negotiable instruments are used as a substitute for money. In order for this substitution to work effectively, users must have confidence that negotiable instruments will be treated like cash, not just sometimes, or at the whim of the person who is offered the instrument, but all the time. Such confidence doesn't just happen. It comes as the result of having definite rules that govern the form negotiable instruments will take, the way in which they'll be handled, and the rights and responsibilities of the parties involved.

The Uniform Commercial Code has, in fact, set forth very specific rules detailing precisely the rights of the *holder* (the one in possession of the instrument) and the liabilities of the *maker* (the one who issues the instrument) in a wide range of circumstances. UCC regulations are intended to answer questions like these: When and to what extent are the rights of a holder protected? What happens when the maker who writes a check refuses to honor it or is short of funds? Who has the right to transfer a negotiable instrument to another person? Are there circumstances under which the maker of an instrument has good reason *not* to honor that instrument? What kinds of contractual relationships are created through negotiable instruments—or, in other words, who is obligated to whom? When a person signs or endorses a check or other negotiable instrument, to what—precisely—is he or she agreeing?

Answering these and related questions is most of what this lesson is about. But underlying these individual questions is a broader issue: the role of the negotiable instrument in keeping business on the move. Remember, a prudent businessperson will accept a negotiable instrument, such as a check, only so long as he or she has full faith that the instrument can be converted to cash—without any serious hassle. Undermine that confidence, and soon you'd have a cash-only business policy that would quickly erode both business volume and efficiency. On the other hand, too much attention to caution means untenable delays for everyone involved—and that isn't good for business either. So, the question becomes, how do UCC rules enable the businessperson to walk the fine line between careful judgment and immobilizing caution? Let's take a look.

OVERVIEW

A negotiable instrument, which—as we've noted already—takes the place of money in business transactions, is presumed to support some underlying contract between the parties. After all, people in the business world generally do not give each other money for no reason; there must be some compensation, something of value, some consideration given in exchange. In addition, the instrument itself creates a kind of contract between the parties involved, as we shall see shortly. Keep these two contract levels in mind, for they help define the kinds of defenses available to the drawer or maker—the person who issues the instrument—in the event he or she chooses not to honor that instrument (not to pay it, that is).

A negotiable instrument is put into circulation by the maker or drawer, the person who writes it up and *issues* it, or transfers it to a *holder*. From that point forward, unless it is declared legally void, the instrument serves as a substitute for money until such time as it is cashed or redeemed—which is one form of *discharge* (more about forms of discharge later). Once it's turned in for cash, that negotiable instrument's business life is over. (Note the difference here between a negotiable instrument and real money, which has an indeterminate life that lasts until the paper bill or coin wears out.)

The Meaning of Negotiation

The term *negotiable* refers to the fact that the instrument can be transferred from one person to another as money. *Negotiation* is the transfer of an instrument in such a manner that the person who receives it becomes a holder. A check is issued by the drawer, for instance, to a payee. If the payee transfers the instrument through negotiation to another person, that person (or business) becomes a holder. This holder, in turn may transfer it to another holder. This chain can continue indefinitely until one holder eventually presents the check to the drawer bank for payment in cash. As we shall see, however, should there be any difficulty in cashing the instrument somewhere along the line, such difficulty is greatly compounded when the chain of holders is very long. But let's keep things simple for now.

Suppose Monroe issues a check that reads "Pay to the order of Tom Devane the sum of $50." Monroe then delivers the check to Devane. Monroe is the drawer, Devane the payee and also, for now, the holder. The holder is a *person in possession of a negotiable instrument drawn, issued, or endorsed to him, to his order, to bearer, or in blank*. In this instance, the holder received the instrument directly from the drawer; but in some cases, the holder receives the instrument from another holder. Let's suppose now that Devane wishes to negotiate this instrument—to transfer it to another holder, such as his bank. How would he go about it? In other words, what constitutes a proper negotiation?

Form of the Instrument

In answering this question, we must consider the form of the instrument. If—as in this case—the instrument is payable *to order*, then it must be properly endorsed and delivered to be achieved. In other words, if Devane wishes to give his bank the check in exchange for cash, he must first endorse the check with his signature on the back, then deliver it to the bank and properly present it. He does not have to deliver it personally; he could, for example, ask his wife or brother to take it. But because the check reads "Pay to the order of Tom Devane," it must be endorsed with the signature of Tom Devane before it can be negotiated. Let's say Devane endorses the check and presents it at his bank to be cashed. If the bank accepts the check, the bank then becomes the holder. They, in turn, must endorse the check (which they will normally do with a stamp bearing the name and perhaps the address of the bank). From there, the check will go to the *drawee*, or the bank where Monroe (the drawer) maintains his account. Note that the drawee is the bank holding the money against which the check is written—*not* the bank where Devane takes the check to cash it. Keep these roles in mind because they will be important to our upcoming discussion of liability.

But let's suppose now that instead of making the check directly payable to Devane, Monroe wrote "Pay to the order of bearer." In that case, neither Devane nor any other person in possession of the check would need to endorse the check in order to cash it. Simply delivering—bearing—it to the bank would be enough to complete the negotiation.

What if the check read "Pay to the order of Tom Devane," but instead of taking the check to the bank, Devane—without endorsing the check—gave it to an associate, Will Friendly, in payment of a debt. Would this make Friendly a holder? No. He has possession of the check, but it is not endorsed to him or to his order, nor is it *bearer paper*—which it would be had Devane endorsed it with the words "pay to bearer" above his signature. While the very fact that Friendly has the check suggests that Devane wants Friendly to have the money it represents, that is not substantiated through endorsement; Friendly does not, at the moment, have a legal right to the money.

In this scenario, Friendly has the status of an *assignee*, one to whom an instrument has been delivered but not negotiated. Transferring less than the full balance of the instrument (say, $25 out of the total $50) is also treated legally as an assignment. This distinction between assignee and holder is significant primarily because the rights of an assignee are considerably less than those of a holder, and much less than those of a *holder in due course*. This becomes important if, upon presenting the instrument for payment, the drawee or drawer has decided *not* to pay out on the instrument.

An endorsement on an instrument creates a contract between the endorser and the transferee. In our example, Devane's endorsement of the check creates a contract between Devane and the bank to which he transferred the check. This is one reason that transferees—and banks especially—will often demand an endorsement even on an instrument that reads "Pay to the order of bearer." By the way, any signature on a negotiable instrument is presumed to be an endorsement unless it is specifically stipulated to be something other than an endorsement.

What are the implications of endorsing an instrument? That depends a great deal on the form of the endorsement. Let's look at some examples.

Endorsements: Forms and Effects

An endorsement affects two aspects of using a negotiable instrument: negotiation and liability. Let's consider liability first.

Qualified and Unqualified Endorsements

Every endorsement is either qualified or unqualified, and it is through these two types of endorsements that *liability* on the instrument is determined. Through these types of endorsements, an individual holding a negotiable instrument can control the degree to which she or he will be *liable on the instrument* to a subsequent holder if the instrument is dishonored upon presentment for payment. And by knowing whether prior endorsements are qualified or unqualified, a holder can also tell the degree to which prior endorsers are resources for collection on the instrument. An unqualified endorsement is one in which the endorser agrees to honor the contract of endorsement; a qualified endorsement is one in which the endorser denies any endorsement contract liability.

An unqualified endorsement contains no special wording. The simple signature "Tom Devane" would constitute one form of an unqualified endorsement. So would these: "Pay to the order of Harold Brown, Tom Devane" or "For deposit only, Tom Devane." There is nothing in the wording of any of these to suggest that Devane is denying liability on the contract.

Now contrast those examples with these endorsements: "Without recourse, Tom Devane" or "Pay to the order of Harold Brown, without recourse, Tom Devane" or "Without liability, Tom Devane." In each case here, Devane is explicitly denying liability. In other words, he is saying that if the maker defaults on the check and cannot or will not pay, he — Devane — will not be responsible. He will not cash the instrument. When Brown accepts a check endorsed by Devane with a qualified endorsement, he does so — in the law's eyes — with the understanding that if the check is dishonored or rejected, Brown cannot turn to Devane to recover the money. The qualified endorsement completely relieves Devane of this endorsement contract responsibility.

An *unqualified* endorsement has the opposite effect. In other words, it commits the endorser contractually to the next holder for the amount of the check. When Devane signs Monroe's check with an unqualified endorsement and then presents that check to the bank, he is creating a contract with the bank that states in effect that Devane will be responsible for providing the money to the bank if the bank cannot get the money from Monroe's bank. Now of course, if the drawer defaults and does not pay, Devane also has recourse; he, in turn, can try to recover the money from Monroe. Meanwhile, however, he is still responsible to the next holder — the bank. It may occur to you that people regularly endorse checks without realizing the nature of the contracts they're creating with the parties to whom they transfer those checks. That's true. Fortunately for us all, makers do not generally default.

Special, Blank, and Restrictive Endorsements

We've mentioned that all endorsements are either qualified or unqualified, and whether an endorsement is qualified or unqualified determines an endorser's *liability* on the instrument. In addition, each endorsement is either special, blank, or restrictive in nature. And it is the nature of an endorsement that affects the *negotiation* of the instrument—a difference best sorted out with examples.

Let's begin with the blank endorsement, since that's probably the most common. Such an endorsement is simply a signature—or it could be a company stamp—on the back of the instrument. "Tom Devane" is an example of a blank endorsement. So is "First City Bank, 222 Elm Street, Worthington." Note that a blank endorsement does not specify the party to whom the instrument is to be paid—and it is this aspect of the endorsement that affects negotiation. A blank endorsement converts the instrument to bearer paper, and this lets the instrument be cashed by anyone. In other words, once an instrument has a blank endorsement, it can be cashed by anyone. When Tom Devane has endorsed the check from Monroe, he has allowed it to be cashed by a friend, spouse, or colleague—without question. And if he loses the check, anyone who picks it up can cash it. In short, it is wise to cash such an instrument quickly before it becomes misplaced. Carrying it around or leaving it on an office desktop could be risky.

Unlike a blank endorsement, a special endorsement clearly states the name of the party to whom the instrument is to be paid or to whose order it is to be paid. By specifying who has the right to the instrument, the endorser is affecting its negotiation. Only the specified party now has the legal right to direct the future negotiation of the instrument. These are examples of special endorsements: "Pay to Sam Glick, Tom Devane" or "Pay to the order of Sue Rochester, Tom Devane."

A restrictive endorsement is a little different. As its label suggests, it attempts to restrict or limit further negotiation. These are examples of restrictive endorsements: "For deposit only, Tom Devane" or "For collection only, Ruth Wiser." As you can see, such endorsements attempt to say, "This is it. This instrument cannot be transferred further." In fact, though, once an instrument that meets all the requirements for negotiability is issued, no endorsement can remove its negotiable status. What a restrictive endorsement really does is indicate the *wishes* of the endorser—stating the terms under which that endorser is transferring the instrument. But nothing can legally prevent the next holder from transferring the instrument to another holder—despite the previous holder's apparent restriction.

Holders and Holders in Due Course

Let's look now at the various roles that can be assumed by the receiver, or the person to whom the negotiable instrument is transferred.

First, remember that if the instrument does *not* meet all the rules for negotiability, then the transfer is an assignment and the receiver an assignee. A holder, as noted earlier, is a person who is in possession of a negotiable instrument that is endorsed to him or her, or that is made out *to bearer*. The holder may receive the instrument from the original maker or from a previous holder. A holder has the right to transfer, negotiate, discharge, or enforce the instrument in his or her own name. In other words, as a holder, Tom Devane can transfer the check he got from Monroe to another holder (including Devane's own bank), can present it to

Monroe's bank, or can even try to obtain the money from Monroe directly by selling him back his check. At the same time, supposing that Monroe has some reason for not honoring the check, Devane — as a holder — is subject to any defenses that Monroe, as drawer, can assert.

The concept of a defense will become more clear in our upcoming discussion of real and personal defenses. For now, simply keep in mind that the position of *holder* is not as legally favorable or beneficial as the position of *holder in due course*. A holder in due course is a holder who takes an instrument *for value, in good faith, and without notice of any defenses or defects affecting the instrument*. Holder in due course status is important to a holder of a negotiable instrument, since with this status there are very few reasons for which the maker or drawer of the instrument can legally refuse to honor the instrument when it is presented for payment. But this status is not presumed; it must be claimed and proved by the party claiming holder in due course status.

An example here will help clarify the concept of holder in due course status. Devane Office Supply specializes in office supplies for small business. It has just received an order from Monroe and Monroe, a new firm in the area. As is its practice, Devane asked for partial payment to accompany the Monroe order. Monroe complied, sending Devane a check for $250, which Devane endorsed and deposited in the Devane account at Larchwood National Bank.

Remember, we noted earlier that negotiable instruments typically support some underlying contract. In other words, when one businessperson issues or negotiates a negotiable instrument to another, it is in relation to some other contract or agreement — some provision of goods or services by one to the other. In our example, Monroe issued a check to partially pay for the goods it ordered from Devane — and this contract for goods was the underlying contract represented by the negotiable instrument. Similarly, when Devane transferred (or negotiated) Monroe's check to Larchwood National, it did so in exchange for credit to its (Devane's) account at the bank. When Larchwood National credited Devane's account with $250, it in turn received the right to collect $250 from Monroe's account at its bank. Crediting the Devane account with $250 was the *value* Larchwood National gave in exchange for the $250 check.

The UCC specifies the types of activities that will meet the "for value" requirement of holder in due course status, but the most important of the points to remember is that the value must in fact *be given*. A promise to give value at a future date, for example, will not be sufficient for the person receiving the negotiable instrument to meet the "for value" requirement of holder in due course status. But assuming that value in fact is given, two other criteria must be met before Larchwood National becomes a holder in due course of the negotiable instrument Devane endorsed over to it.

The second criterion for holder in due course status is that the holder must accept the check in good faith. This means, in simple terms, that it was acting in an honest, straightforward manner. Let's examine Devane's bank, Larchwood National, as the receiver of the check Devane got from Monroe. Accepting the check in good faith means that Larchwood had no reason to suppose Monroe was insolvent, for example, or that the person endorsing the check was someone other than

Devane or someone not authorized to issue such a check. Good faith is presumed unless there is evidence of bad faith. Thus, usually all a holder need do to establish good faith is to claim that he or she so acted. This claim may, however, be challenged by the drawer or maker, if he or she has reason to think the holder did not in fact act in good faith. So far, Larchwood National has met two of the three criteria for holder in due course status.

Finally, it must be shown that the receiver (Larchwood National, in this case) accepted the check *without notice*. This means that there was no evidence of a defect or flaw in the check. No important information—such as the amount or name of the payee—was missing; there was no evidence the instrument had been tampered with or altered; there were no official notices stamped on the front of the instrument, such as "insufficient funds" or "payment stopped" or "void" or "paid," and all prior endorsements looked correct. Nor was the instrument *overdue*. An instrument is considered overdue if the holder has reason to know that any payment is overdue or in default.

Alternately, in the case of a demand instrument like a check, the instrument is considered overdue if payment does not occur within a "reasonable time" following issue. For a check, such time is interpreted as about thirty days. This may not seem like a lot, but the UCC recognizes that in the business world, much can change within thirty days. Accounts can be drained or closed out altogether or the drawer whose check goes uncashed may presume the check was lost or stolen and may stop payment. Remember, the overriding goal of UCC regulations, other than guaranteeing the rights of holders, is to see to it that business is kept in motion. Delays are to be avoided. (Somewhat longer time limits are allowed for drafts and bank notes, however.) Our scenario doesn't specify whether the check was without notice or overdue, but assuming it was not, Larchwood National has holder in due course status.

Where holder in due course status is established, it gives the holder a special "super" status beyond that of a simple holder. While a holder in due course is still subject to any real defenses that may be asserted on an instrument, a holder in due course is *not* subject to any personal defenses. What does that mean, and what are the implications? Let's take a closer look at the nature of personal and real defenses to find out.

Personal and Real Defenses

Keep in mind during this discussion our earlier distinction between the contract created by the instrument itself and the underlying contract or agreement that that instrument supports. That distinction should help you sort out the differences between real defenses and personal defenses. First of all, the term "defense," as used in this discussion, refers to a reason, justification, or excuse for not honoring the instrument. *Real defenses* challenge the validity of the instrument itself. *Personal defenses* have nothing to do with the validity of the instrument, but rather question the validity of the underlying contract. Remember, only real, not personal, defenses may be asserted against a holder in due course.

Personal Defenses

Personal defenses, because they relate to the underlying agreement, are those available on any simple contract. They include such things as fraud, duress, lack of consideration, or breach of warranty. Also included are nondelivery, theft, payment, or other cancellation. It is not critical to this discussion that you understand the nature of these defenses in detail, but only that you keep in mind that personal defenses relate to the underlying contract.

For example, in our ongoing scenario with Monroe, Devane, and Larchwood National Bank, suppose that Devane sold Monroe some electric staplers that he knew to be defective but that he represented as top quality. If Monroe felt that Devane was guilty of fraud through this deliberate deception, he might feel justified in stopping payment on his check. However, if Larchwood National held the status of holder in due course—rather than just holder—Monroe could *not* use the fraud of Devane (a personal defense) as a reason for not paying on the check now in the hands of Larchwood National.

Let's consider one more example of a personal defense. It works like this. Let's say Ray promises to deliver a used car to Bell. Bell issues Ray a check for $700—*with* the provision that the check may be cashed only following delivery of the car. If Ray doesn't deliver the car, technically Bell has never "delivered" the check either—even though Ray had the check in his possession. If Ray transferred the check to another person who is only a holder, rather than a holder in due course, Bell may assert the personal defense of nondelivery to justify a stop-payment order on the check.

Real Defenses

On the other hand, a *real* defense, sometimes called a universal defense, challenges the validity of the instrument itself. And even a holder in due course has no protection against such a defense. When a real defense is established, the instrument in question is voided by operation of law and the maker or drawer does not have to pay out on the instrument.

There are five types of real defenses that, if established, legally allow the maker or drawer of a negotiable instrument to avoid paying out on the instrument when it is presented for payment by either a holder or a holder in due course. Each category of real defense has certain exceptions and special conditions, but in general, the following five situations raise the likelihood of a real defense and of the maker or drawer avoiding liability on the instrument—even if the instrument is held by a holder in due course.

1. *Infancy*. An example would be issuing a check in payment for a car to a minor who is not of legal age to dispose of his or her property through sale.

2. *Incapacity, duress, or illegality*. Examples would be issuing a check to pay a gambling debt in a state where gambling is illegal and noting on the check that it is for a gambling debt; issuing a check for the purchase of chemicals banned for public or private use; issuing a promissory note in response to a threat of blackmail.

3. *Fraud in the execution*. Examples would be issuing a promissory note, check, or other instrument while *believing* one is really creating or signing some other sort of document, such as a receipt acknowledging delivery; unknowingly authorizing a check or other instrument to pay for goods or services never really received.

4. *Discharge in insolvency*. An example would involve filing for bankruptcy; the bankruptcy, if approved, automatically cancels all debts existing through negotiable instruments.

5. *Other discharges*. This involves issuing an instrument that is defective in some way—say, one on which the name of the payee or the amount is missing—but that is accepted by the holder despite its faults. (Notice, incidentally, that a holder who accepted such an instrument could *not* claim holder in due course status in any case since a holder in due course *must* accept the instrument without notice—that is, without awareness of any defects or problems.) It is difficult to imagine a flaw significant enough to constitute a real defense but not significant enough to be noticed by the holder. But if such a problem did occur, the holder will definitely lose to such a defense.

In addition to these five real defenses, a drawer or maker can avoid liability on an instrument in two additional ways: (1) if the signature on the instrument is a forgery or is otherwise unauthorized, the maker may avoid liability altogether; and (2) if the instrument is materially altered without the knowledge or consent of the maker, liability may be totally or partially altered. In the second case, the original version of the instrument—prior to alteration—may be enforced by a holder in due course. In other words, if Valenti issues a check to Lorenzo for $100, and Lorenzo proceeds to alter the check in order to give himself an extra $1,000, Valenti cannot be held liable for paying the full $1,100. But for any subsequent holder who is a holder in due course, Valenti can be held liable for paying the original $100.

Primary and Secondary Liability

We've talked enough about liability so that you have likely concluded that liability in this context refers to the *obligation to pay a negotiable instrument*. But there are two types of liability: primary and secondary.

The primary party—the party with primary liability—is the party to whom a holder would look first for payment. Secondary parties, logically enough, are those who agree to assume liability if the primary party and subsequent secondary parties default. In other words, secondary parties have *potential* liability. Remember, we noted earlier that an endorsement creates a contract between the endorser and the person to whom the instrument is transferred. That contract, in fact, commits the endorser to liability on the instrument.

In general, roles and status determine liability. For example, the maker of a note has primary liability on that note. This is because it is the maker to whom the payee will look for payment. If Vance issues a promissory note to Hawthorne, Hawthorne will not take the note to the bank to cash it. Vance is not only the drawer here, but also the drawee—the person with the funds to cover the note. As such, Vance has primary liability.

With a check or draft, it's a little different. At the time of issue, there is no primary liability. The drawer, and any subsequent endorsers, assume secondary liability—or potential liability. If Wertz issues a check to Clark, and Clark endorses the check to his bank, Wertz, Clark, and Clark's bank all have secondary liability. But once the drawee—Wertz's bank—accepts the check, that bank assumes primary liability; it becomes the party to whom Clark looks for payment.

To summarize, the drawer on a check or draft—and all endorsers of any negotiable instrument—are secondary parties on that instrument. A secondary party faces *potential* liability on the instrument, which becomes a real liability if three conditions are met:

1. *presentment* of the instrument is properly made;

2. the primary party dishonors the instrument—refuses to pay, that is; and

3. notice of the dishonor is properly given to the secondary party.

Let's look at an example. Suppose Williams issues a check to Worth for $5,000 to cover the cost of a used sailboat. At this point, there is no primary liability on the check; there is only an expectation that primary liability will exist sometime in the future. In order for such liability to exist, the drawee (Williams's bank) must accept the check, and that has not happened yet. Worth has secondary liability from the time the check is issued, and under most circumstances will retain that liability throughout the life of the instrument. Let's say now that Worth endorses the check and presents it to his bank. They accept it, endorse it, and forward it to Williams's bank, where it is properly presented and accepted. At this point, Williams's bank—the drawee—becomes the primary party; it is this bank that now must pay out on the check and to whom Worth ultimately looks for payment. Worth and Williams both have secondary liability now—to Worth's bank, in case Williams's bank does not pay.

To better see the implications of such liability, let's alter our scenario a bit—first, by bringing in a new character, Graffy. Suppose that, instead of taking Williams's check to the bank, Worth endorses it to Graffy to cover a personal debt, and Graffy takes it to her bank. They accept the check, give her the money, then endorse the check and forward it to Williams's bank, which is the drawee—the party holding the money. Unfortunately, this time around, Williams does not have enough money in his account to cover the $5,000 check. Thus, the bank refuses to honor the check. Where does this leave everyone? Well, notice that the first two conditions for secondary liability have been met: First, proper presentment of the instrument was made, and second, the drawee refused to accept the instrument. Only one condition remains: The secondary parties must be notified of the failure in payment; once this happens, they can be held liable on the check. Graffy's banker, as the only person in the scenario right now who knows what's going on, is the logical one to give such notice, though any party involved may give notice. But what is meant by notice, anyway?

Well, the banker could telephone the parties involved, or send letters or telegrams, or visit them in person, or use any other reasonable means of informing them about the situation. Notice must be given within a reasonable time—which is subject to interpretation. But common sense tells us that if the bank waits several months before notifying the secondary parties, it will be more difficult to establish liability than if they are contacted immediately. Failure to give what the court views as timely notice will effectively release all secondary parties from liability with the exception of the drawer. Not even improper notice will release the drawer—Williams, in this case—from having to pay on the instrument.

Notice must identify the instrument in question and must state that it was dishonored. The description of the instrument must be sufficiently precise to permit its identification, but minor flaws in the description are allowable if they are not misleading. For instance, if the bank phones Graffy to say that check #4204 from Ted Williams for $5,000 was dishonored, and it turns out that it was *really* check #4240, Graffy cannot reasonably claim that the bank did not give her proper notice.

Should the bank simply phone Graffy, the person who presented the check to them, or should they phone all the secondary parties? Because it may happen that one secondary party can't locate the previous holder, it is good procedure for the last holder to give notice to as many secondary parties as possible, including the drawer. Doing so increases the chances of eventually receiving payment on the check. According to the chain of liability, by the way, Graffy is liable to her bank (because they have paid her), Worth is liable to Graffy, and Williams is liable to Worth. This chain of liability may be altered, however, through cancellation—about which we will learn more in a moment.

Imposters

Under the so-called *imposter rule*, the drawer may be held liable for a check issued to someone posing as the true payee. For instance, suppose Sanchez owes Kurtz $200. One of Kurtz's assistants, Fraback—who knows of the debt—approaches Sanchez, presents himself as Kurtz, and requests payment. Sanchez thereupon makes out the check to Kurtz and gives it to Fraback—thinking he is giving it to Kurtz. Fraback takes the check to the bank, endorses it as "Ronald Kurtz," and cashes it. Has Sanchez discharged his debt to Kurtz? No—because Kurtz has yet to be paid. Is Sanchez liable on the check? Yes.

The court reasons this way: Someone must be responsible for the check, even though it was issued to an imposter. Both the bank, which cashed Fraback's falsely endorsed check, and Sanchez, who issued the check in the first place, are innocent parties here. The question is, which party was in the better position to have prevented this situation? And the answer, arguably perhaps, is Sanchez. True, it is difficult to know firsthand every person with whom one does business, but from the court's perspective, Sanchez has a responsibility to ensure that persons to whom he issues checks are who they purport to be. Thus, in issuing a check, Sanchez—or any businessperson—is taking a risk. The degree of risk, however, is usually not great and can be reduced if the businessperson insists on knowing his or her vendors and associates.

Discharge of Liability

The term *discharge* refers to the removal of liability or potential liability on a negotiable instrument. There are four primary ways in which discharge can occur: payment or satisfaction, tender of payment, cancellation and renunciation, and impairment. Let's look at each.

Payment is by far the most common way in which discharge occurs. Once payment is made or other satisfaction is given, all liability on the instrument is cancelled and it is taken out of circulation. Its life as a negotiable instrument is over.

Payment will not operate as a discharge, however, if it is made to a thief. Remember Fraback, alias Kurtz? He collected a $200 check from Sanchez in the name of Kurtz for a debt owed to Kurtz. Despite the unfortunate consequences for Sanchez, who has already paid $200, the check to Fraback posing as Kurtz does not discharge the debt to the real Kurtz. Of course, we should point out that Sanchez does have available legal remedies here. It is illegal to pose as someone else, and Sanchez can sue Fraback in civil court for recovery on the bad check. Sanchez can also go to the police and ask them to bring a criminal case against Fraback, in the hope that the judge will also order Fraback to pay restitution in the amount of the check to Sanchez. Meanwhile, however, he will still owe the real Kurtz the $200.

Tender of payment is an offer to pay. If a party tenders payment in full to a holder when an instrument is due (or later) and the holder refuses payment, discharge occurs. Let's say Wainright holds a note in which Gritch has promised to pay $4,000 at an annual interest rate of 5%. When the note comes due, Gritch offers to pay, but Wainright, hoping to collect more interest, refuses to accept the payment, saying he would prefer to wait a while longer. The UCC will not allow Wainright to play this waiting game, however. He must either accept Gritch's payment or discharge liability on the note, thereby freeing Gritch from all obligation to pay.

A holder may discharge liability by *cancellation* of a party's signature on a note or by cancellation of the instrument altogether. Suppose Wainwright isn't so unreasonable a character as we made him out to be in the preceding paragraph. Let's say he knows that Gritch has fallen on hard times and is unable to pay the debt on the note. He can cancel the note altogether, or if Gritch is but one party on the note, he could cancel Gritch's obligation by crossing out his name. Cancellation is only effective when done deliberately and, of course, it would be necessary to show that the cancellation was performed by someone to whom the cancelled party was obligated.

Renunciation operates much like cancellation, but works outside the instrument. Renunciation takes the form of a written, signed statement that discharges another party from all obligation on an instrument.

The word *impairment* refers to an interference with a legal right or remedy. As we've just noted, a holder may elect to release another party from obligation on an instrument—or for that matter, may release some collateral that is being used to secure a loan on a note. In so doing, however, the holder could make it hard for that secondary party to collect the money should anyone come to that secondary party looking for payment. Thus, the UCC deems it fair that, because of this impairment, secondary parties should also (under some conditions) be released from liability. In other words, in releasing one party from obligation, a holder could be releasing *all* parties from liability.

Let's say Farrell writes a check to Duffy, who endorses it to Wilson. If Wilson releases Farrell from all obligations, Duffy is automatically released. Why? Because his recourse in the event of default has been impaired; he can no longer look to Farrell for payment. There are some exceptions here, though. If Duffy *agreed* to the release, then he's not off the hook. Or, if Wilson expressly *reserves rights* against Duffy, then Duffy cannot be released.

SOME PRACTICAL ADVICE

Obviously, as a drawer or maker on a negotiable instrument, you should know the extent of your liability. Remember that on a note, you will have primary liability from the moment of issue. On a check or draft, you will have secondary liability and—except in the case of forgery or other unusual circumstance—you are not likely to be discharged from this liability until the check or draft is converted to money.

It is also wise to know the parties to whom you are issuing negotiable instruments. In the unlikely—but nonetheless plausible—event that you were to issue an instrument to an imposter, your "payment" to the imposter would not discharge your real debt. In other words, by paying the wrong person, you could double your liability—and incur a lot of time and expense in trying to recover the payment made to the imposter.

Endorsements, which we tend to look on as a very routine part of everyday business life, entail the creation of a contract and should be respected accordingly. Any time you endorse an instrument, realize that if the endorsement is unqualified, it constitutes a commitment between yourself and the party to whom you transfer the instrument—a commitment that states that under certain circumstances, you agree to assume liability on the instrument. If that agreement makes you uneasy, a qualified endorsement or nonacceptance of the instrument may be in order.

As a holder, you have certain rights, but they'll be affected by your status. Don't assume you'll be given the status of holder in due course. You need to demonstrate your right to that position, and it isn't always easy. For one thing, you'll need to show that you've given real value in exchange for the instrument; a promise to per-form sometime in the future isn't enough. And if there were any flaws in the instru-ment and you overlooked them, the court is likely to take the position that you ac-cepted the instrument *with notice* — flaws and all, that is. That leaves you in the position of holder, subject to both personal and real defenses — a position which makes enforcement of an instrument far more uncertain.

Finally, it may occur to you that certain UCC regulations can leave the parties on a negotiable instrument in what look to be very uncomfortable — if not downright unfair — positions. Suppose you do issue a check to an imposter. Is it right that you should be responsible for paying on that check once it's presented and accepted by the bank? Is it right that you should assume responsibility on a check you've en-dorsed if the drawer defaults on the check? Perhaps not. But keep in mind, the UCC regulations are designed to expedite resolution of the immediate problem, to keep things moving, to keep negotiable instruments in process so that lengthy hassles over responsibility do not impede the flow of everyday business. This does not mean that parties who are required to take temporary responsibility for a debt will not have recourse sometime in the future. Often they will. The person who writes a check to an imposter can sue that imposter for recovery, for instance. But solving sticky legal problems takes time. Meanwhile, the business world will not stand by, patiently awaiting the results. It will crunch on — with the UCC regula-tions on negotiable instruments helping to set the direction and the pace.

ASSIGNMENTS

- Before you watch the video program, be sure you've read through the preceding overview, familiarized yourself with the learning objectives for this lesson, and looked at the key terms below. Then, read Chapter 25 (pages 419–434) and Chap-ter 26 of Davidson et al., *Business Law*.

- After completing these tasks, view the video program for Lesson 22.

- After watching the program, take time to review what you've learned. First, evaluate your learning with the self-test which follows the key terms. Then, apply and evaluate what you've learned with the "Your Opinion, Please" scenarios at the end of this telecourse study guide lesson.

KEY TERMS

Before you read through the textbook assignment and watch the video program, take a minute to look at the key terms associated with this lesson. When you en-counter them in the textbook and video program, pay careful attention to their meaning.

Assignee	Personal defenses
Bearer paper	Primary liability
Blank endorsement	Primary party
Cancellation	Qualified/unqualified endorsements
Discharge	Real defenses
Dishonor	Renunciation
Endorse	Restrictive/nonrestrictive
Holder	endorsements
Holder in due course	Secondary liability
Impairment	Secondary party
Imposter	Special endorsement
Overdue	Tender of payment

SELF-TEST

The questions below will help you evaluate how well you've learned the material in this lesson. Read each one carefully, and select the letter of the option that best answers the question. You'll find the correct answer, along with a reference to the page number(s) where the topic is discussed, in the back of this telecourse study guide.

1. Lewis has possession of a check that reads "Pay to the order of R. L. Lewis." Without endorsing the check, Lewis gives it to Fremont to cover a debt. What is Fremont's status?

   a. Assignee
   b. Holder
   c. Holder in due course
   d. We cannot say without knowing whether Fremont accepts the check without notice

2. Wheeler has a check drawn on Downtown Bank that reads "Pay to the order of Sam Wheeler." He endorses the check simply with his signature—"Sam Wheeler"—and presents it at his bank, First City Bank. By endorsing the check, Wheeler is

   a. demanding payment on the check.
   b. retaining title to the check.
   c. denying liability on the check.
   d. transferring his rights to First City Bank.

3. Which of the following is the *best* example of a blank endorsement?

   a. "Pay to Will Speers, Charlie Ray"
   b. "Pay to Will Speers or order, Charlie Ray"

c. "For deposit only, Charlie Ray"
d. "Charlie Ray"

4. The primary purpose of a restrictive endorsement is to

   a. reduce the liability of the endorser.
   b. impose some conditions on negotiability.
   c. provide notice to the drawer.
   d. alter the instrument in some material way.

5. A check that reads "Pay to the order of Arthur Mills" is signed by Robert Wood, who has his checking account at InterCity Bank. Mills endorses the check and presents it at First State Bank for payment. By endorsing the check, Mills creates a contract between

   a. himself and First State.
   b. himself and InterCity.
   c. himself and Wood.
   d. First State and Wood.

6. A qualified endorsement is one that

   a. restricts negotiability.
   b. specifies the payee.
   c. establishes warranty rights.
   d. denies contractual liability.

7. Which of the following would *most likely* be considered notice sufficient enough to defeat holder in due course status?

   a. *Any of the following* three circumstances would be enough to defeat holder in due course status
   b. The issue date on a check is missing
   c. The instrument is postdated
   d. The amount on the instrument has been erased, then rewritten

8. In payment for an oak table, Forbest issues a check payable to Millstone for $200, with an attached written provision stating that Millstone must deliver the table prior to cashing the check. Assuming the check itself is valid, what defense — if any — may Forbest assert if Millstone endorses the check to another party but does not deliver the table?

   a. None; there are no personal or real defenses open, based on the information given.
   b. Nondelivery; technically, the check was never delivered to Millstone.
   c. Theft, since Millstone has no legal right to the check before delivering the table.
   d. Fraud in the execution, since Millstone misled Forbest.

9. In order to hold a secondary party liable on an instrument, the holder must show all of the following *but one*. Which of the following is the holder *not* required to show?

    a. The instrument was issued for value
    b. Proper presentment was made
    c. The primary party dishonored the instrument
    d. Notice of dishonor was properly given to the secondary party

10. The most common type of discharge of a negotiable instrument is

    a. impairment.
    b. cancellation.
    c. tender of payment.
    d. full payment or satisfaction.

YOUR OPINION, PLEASE

Read each of the following scenarios and answer the questions about the decisions you would make in each situation. Give these questions some serious thought; they may be used as the basis for the development of a more complex essay. You should base your decisions on what you've learned from this lesson, though you may incorporate outside readings or information gained through your own experience if it is relevant.

Scenario 1

Favor, who operates a horse ranch, buys a horse from Kupik for $600. Favor writes Kupik a check to cover the total amount of the purchase. Kupik knows at the time of the sale that the horse is intermittently lame, but he says nothing, hoping the defect will not be apparent until after he's had an opportunity to receive payment on the check.

Kupik endorses the check to the local vet, McRae, with this endorsement: "Pay to the order of Archie McRae, Gus Kupik." The amount of the check is just about what Kupik needs to cover his existing veterinary bills.

McRae, who has treated the horse in question and knows of his condition, is surprised to learn that Favor has purchased the horse, but he says nothing, feeling it is Favor's own business. McRae accepts the check in payment of Kupik's existing bill.

Within a day or so, the horse begins noticeably limping. Concerned, Favor takes the horse to the vet, McRae, where he discovers that the limp is the result of a long-standing injury, of which Kupik had knowledge. Favor asks Kupik to take the horse back and return the check, but Kupik refuses. Favor thereupon stops payment on the check. Thus, when McRae presents it at his own bank, they phone Favor's bank, learn of the stop-payment order, and refuse to accept the check. McRae thereupon notifies Kupik and Favor, both of whom refuse to honor the check.

What's your opinion? Based on what you know of the situation, how would you sort out the various rights and responsibilities related to this instrument?

- If neither Kupik nor Favor will honor the check, what options are available to McRae?
- What defenses are open to Favor in refusing to honor the check?
- What counter-arguments, if any, might an attorney present on behalf of McRae in asserting Favor's liability?
- Who, if anyone, has primary liability here?
- Is there a chain of secondary liability? If so, how would you describe it?
- What steps should the parties take to resolve this problem? What steps, if any, might Favor or McRae have taken to prevent this situation?

Scenario 2

Grunfield provides childcare services to Davis, who pays her on a monthly basis. Davis, who is in a hurry one evening when she picks up her children, gives Grunfield a signed check on which she has filled in the date of issue, but neither the payee's name nor the amount. She tells Grunfield to "fill in the check as appropriate — I don't have time to wait."

That night, Grunfield, who still has the incomplete check in her wallet, attends an auction. Intrigued by an antique stained-glass window, she bids $600 and the item is sold to her. Greenfield pays for the window with Davis's check, filling in the amount and the name of the payee, Valley View Auction. She later tells Davis she has lost the check and will need a new one to cover the childcare. Davis gives Grunfield a new check and also stops payment on the previous check. A week or so later, Davis receives notice from Valley View Auction that her check #3404 for $600 has not been honored and that Valley View is asking her to assume liability. Davis refuses, claiming she has never heard of Valley View Auction and certainly has not made a purchase from them. Valley View counters that they have her signed check and want to know when they may expect payment.

What's your opinion here? Based on what you know of the situation, how would you sort out the various rights and responsibilities?

- If Davis refuses to honor the check, what options are available to Valley View? Is Valley View an assignee? Holder? Holder in due course? How do you know?
- What defense(s), if any, might Davis assert in refusing to honor the check?
- What counter-arguments, if any, might an attorney present on behalf of Valley View in asserting Davis's liability?

- Who, if anyone, has primary liability here?
- Is there a chain of secondary liability? If so, how would you describe it?
- What steps should the parties take to resolve this situation? What steps, if any, might Davis or Valley View have followed to prevent this situation?

23

Bank–Customer Relations

LEARNING OBJECTIVES

Upon completing your study of this lesson, you should be able to

- List and describe several legal relationships that are created when a customer establishes an account with a bank.
- List and describe the rights and duties of the customer in a banking relationship.
- List and describe the rights and duties of the bank in a banking relationship.
- Explain how situations involving certified checks and unauthorized signatures may affect the rights and duties of the bank or customer in a banking relationship.

As an adult in the United States, if you do not have a checking account, you are in a small minority. In our society, checks are a way of life. Most of us receive our income through checks. And we use checks to cover a wide range of personal and business expenses, including rent and utilities, insurance, medical payments, groceries, childcare — the list is endless. We seem to love checks — so much so that we often resent merchants who won't accept them. We may think they're old-fashioned, or unreasonably cautious. After all, aren't checks a form of money?

The use of checks is so routine that we tend to take it for granted. So we give little thought to what goes on behind the scenes. In reality, though, the banks who handle much of the management side of things — with our support and cooperation — have to be extremely rigorous. To open a checking account is to set up a contractual relationship with the bank that handles that account, a relationship that involves well-defined rights and duties on both sides. And if something goes wrong, the extent to which each side has fulfilled its duties will determine, to a large extent, rights and liabilities. For example, if someone steals your checkbook, writes several checks on your account, and wipes you out, will the bank cover your losses, or will you be left to make them up as best you can? Answering such questions is what this lesson is about.

OVERVIEW

Typically, the new checking-account customer isn't thinking very much about rights and duties. She may be wondering whether the account pays interest and, if so, how much; whether she'll be able to get the kind of check blanks she finds attractive; and whether she has to maintain a minimum balance in the account in order to avoid monthly charges. But if she's like most customers, she isn't thinking much about duties to reconcile monthly statements or her right to stop payment on a check. Understanding the rights and duties of both customer and bank is crucial, though, especially for a businessperson. Lack of knowledge could be costly if some problem with the account arises later. To better understand the rights and duties on both sides, let's first examine the nature of the legal relationship a checking account creates between bank and customer.

Basic Legal Relationships

In opening checking accounts, customers create several legal relationships between themselves and the banks — often without being fully aware of the implications of any of them. First, the bank asks a new customer to sign a signature card, which is then kept on file so that the bank has some record of what the customer's authorized signature looks like. This signature card is, in fact, a *contract* that the customer accepts by signing. The nature of the contract depends somewhat on what's customary with each particular bank, but in general, it spells out such things as service charges, minimum balance, interest rates, and the mandatory rights and duties of each party.

In addition, the signature card creates an *agency* relationship. An *agent* is a person authorized to act on behalf of another, called the *principal*. When Delmar opens a checking account at First State, Delmar is the principal; he authorizes the bank — the agent — to act on his behalf at his direction. This means that when Delmar writes a check, he does not need to run down to the bank personally and take money out of the account to cover the check; that would defeat the whole purpose of having a checking account in the first place. Instead, Delmar authorizes the bank to act at his direction. The direction comes from the language of the check itself: "Pay to the order of." Such language is deliberately direct and forceful. It constitutes an order to the bank that the bank *must* obey — or face potential liability. In fact, the agent (the bank) is required to obey any lawful order of the principal (the depositor) covered by their agency agreement.

The third relationship is that of *debtor* and *creditor*. Assuming the customer or depositor has a positive balance in the checking account, the customer is a creditor of the bank, and the bank is a debtor of the customer. In other words, the bank in a sense "owes" the money in the account to the depositor and must pay it on demand. On the other hand, if the account has a negative balance, the depositor or customer becomes the debtor, the bank the creditor. This situation occurs when the customer is overdrawn because the bank honored an *overdraft* — a check for an amount larger than that held within the account. Banks sometimes honor overdrafts as a courtesy to a good customer or as the result of a special arrangement with a customer who is expected to repay the account quickly. UCC regulations do not, however, demand that banks honor overdrafts. And since banks are not in the habit of extending credit whimsically, they will usually do so only when they have good reason to suppose that the debt will be rapidly repaid. Further, the bank will often, depending on its contract with the depositor, impose a substantial overdraft charge for having "loaned" money to the depositor's account.

Rights and Duties of the Customer

As stressed above, the bank and the checking account customer have a contractual relationship that, as with any contractual relationship, creates a set of rights and duties. Let's look at these from the viewpoint of the customer.

Duties of the Customer

The customer has two primary duties: first and foremost, to act with care and diligence; and second, to examine and reconcile bank statements. These duties are interrelated, as we'll discover, and both are crucial since they have direct bearing on the customer's rights. Let's see how.

First, the customer is required to act in a careful and diligent manner, whether writing a check, balancing the monthly statement, or endorsing a check. A customer who routinely misspells payees' names, omits dates, or is otherwise careless about getting the right information on each check is not fulfilling this duty—and could be limiting the bank's liability should a costly mistake occur. From the UCC's perspective—as well as the bank's—checks are money; they are, in fact, a legal substitute for money and should be handled with the same care. Customers who are careless with checks are, in essence, being careless with their money.

Second, the customer has a duty to examine and reconcile bank statements in a timely manner—which generally means within fourteen days of receipt. The bank provides each customer a regular statement (usually monthly) summarizing all transactions that have occurred in relation to the account since the last statement. Cancelled checks are generally included with this summary so that the customer can look them over firsthand. The bank statement is compared to the parallel record the customer is obligated to keep in his or her checkbook. In reconciling the two, the customer looks to see whether the bank's record matches his or her own—and if not, tries to trace the source of the problem.

Usually, when things do not match up, the problem is a simple arithmetic error. But not always. A check may have been lost and forged. Or a payee may have altered the amount on a check, causing the bank to make a larger deduction than the drawer (the writer of the check) has noted in her checkbook. Or the bank may have made the error, perhaps failing to credit a deposit or subtracting a check written by someone else. Whatever the case, the customer has a duty to review both the final balance and the cancelled checks themselves and report any irregularities promptly—which, as mentioned, the UCC defines in this context as fourteen calendar days. The customer who complies with this fourteen-day limit can generally recover *all* the money lost through checks that were materially altered or forged.

For example, suppose Miller issues a check to Kendrick for $20, but Kendrick changes the amount so that it reads $120. Suppose, too, that the bank does not examine the check carefully enough to notice the alteration, thus giving Kendrick $120. If Miller does not examine her bank statement carefully, she might overlook the problem and thereby increase her own liability—responsibility to pay, that is. But if she reviews the statement carefully and reports the problem to the bank within fourteen days, she probably retains her right to "reclaim" from the bank the overpayment resulting from the alteration.

Suppose Miller does not discover the problem within fourteen days? What then? Does she give up all right ever to raise the issue? Well, not in this case because there's only one check involved. But what if there were several forgeries or alterations? What then? By not completing her reconciliation promptly—within fourteen days—Miller *would* waive some rights in favor of the bank and her ability to recover would be limited. Let's change our scenario just a bit to see how this works.

This time, suppose Miller issues three checks to Kendrick at weekly intervals, each check for $20. Kendrick alters all three checks, so that the amount of each is changed to $120. Miller, short of time, decides that reconciling her checkbook can wait until next month, so she throws the statement into a desk drawer. On the next month's statement, however, she notices the discrepancy between what her checkbook says and the amount the bank claims she still has in her account. What could have caused the $300 difference? Miller's search for the answer leads her back to the preceding month's statement, where a closer look at the cancelled checks makes Kendrick's trickery apparent. Miller notifies the bank at once—but is it too late?

Yes and no. Miller has up to a year to report an unauthorized signature or (as in this case) material alteration of a check, but—here's the catch—she is unlikely to recover the *full amount* if more than one check is involved. The UCC states that when notice is given to the bank after the fourteen-day period but within one year, the customer may recover the amount of the first *signature* (if there are several forgeries by different persons) or first *alteration* by the same person. In other words, Miller can recover the amount on the first $120 check to Kendrick, but cannot now recover from the bank on the second and third checks because she waited too long to give notice. Had each of those checks been issued to a *different* person, and each had been materially altered, Miller *could* collect on all three. As it is, however, Miller is left with taking action against Kendrick as the only alternative.

What if the alteration was an unauthorized endorsement? Say that Kendrick's brother Elmer sees the check on Amos Kendrick's desk, takes it, endorses it with his own name, and pursuades Miller's bank to cash the check. When Amos Kendrick keeps asking Miller for the money she's already paid him, she goes back to her old cancelled checks and finds the unauthorized endorsement. How long does she have to recover the money? In this case, the unauthorized endorsement must be reported to the bank within three years. More time is allowed in this situation because it sometimes happens that a check is endorsed to a series of persons. Thus, some additional time may be required to retrace the chain of liability and figure out just where and when the improper endorsement occurred.

Rights of the Customer

The rights of the customer include (1) the right to collect damages from the bank if the bank errs in the handling of the customer's account, and (2) the right to stop payment on a check. Let's look at the details of each of these two rights.

First, the customer can collect damages for injury or loss resulting from the bank's carelessness or negligence. In order to do so, however, the customer will have to show that he or she suffered a loss and that the bank's wrongful conduct was the *proximate cause* of that loss—meaning that had the bank's conduct been different, the loss or injury would not have occurred in the first place.

For instance, suppose that Revere deposits $2,000 in his checking account, using one of his own precoded deposit slips. The bank—through no fault of Revere's—credits another customer's account, leaving Revere's account showing a balance of $40. Revere, thinking himself considerably wealthier than that, purchases new tires for $400, and pays for them with a check that promptly bounces—is dishonored, that is. Now, it's likely that a few phone calls might straighten out this unfortunate situation; perhaps the people at the tire company are an understanding lot who don't mind waiting a few extra days for their money. But in the interest of figuring out who has what rights, let's create the worst-case scenario.

The tire company, impatient for the $400 and uninterested in excuses, sues Revere for recovery and also files criminal charges against Revere for passing bad checks. Revere is subsequently arrested, misses work, has to pay court costs and attorney's fees, and still — the unkindest cut of all — cannot cover the cost of his tires. If he can show that this unpleasant turn of events is all the bank's doing — *that they are the proximate cause of his misery* — he can collect damages to cover the costs of arrest, prosecution, and any other consequential damages (e.g., loss of compensation because he's missed work) that can be proved. Plus, of course, his account will be credited with the correct amount.

On the other hand, if Revere's own negligence contributed to the problem — perhaps not using his precoded deposit slip and then transposing the numbers in his account number when using the bank's general-purpose deposit slip — he would have a difficult time holding the bank responsible. In short, the customer's "right" to collect damages from a bank will be upheld only when it can be shown for certain that the bank's negligence — and not the customer's — created the problem.

Second, the customer has the right to stop payment on a check. The customer may issue a stop-payment order orally or in writing, but writing is both safer and more effective. An oral stop-payment order is only in force for fourteen days; after that, it expires unless it's put in writing. A written order is good for six months, and can be renewed for another six months.

Stop-payment orders must include a complete description of the check, including the check number, name of the payee, date of issue, and reason for stopping payment. The last is particularly important because whimsically stopping payment on a check for no very good reason is likely to lead the drawer into difficulty.

Normally, the bank is required because of the agency relationship to follow a customer's stop-payment order or face possible liability. If the bank overrides the order and cashes a check anyway, the customer may be able to collect damages, but she will have to show that she suffered damages when the check was paid. Or, to put it another way, she will have to show that if the bank had not paid, the holder of the check would not have been able to collect the money.

For example, suppose Proodian issues a $500 check to Wiley Watersports to pay for some scuba diving gear. The gear is perfectly fine, but on thinking things over, Proodian decides he's been self-indulgent to spend so much money on a purchase of this sort. In a fit of fiscal remorse, he issues a stop-payment order on the check. Normally the bank would follow the depositor's order and not honor the check. In this instance, however, let's suppose that because of some internal mistake, the bank honors the check, giving Wiley five hundred-dollar bills. Can Proodian successfully sue to recover the money?

Not likely. Wiley accepted the check in good faith and gave Proodian the goods he wanted in exchange. The goods were not damaged nor were they something other than what Proodian expected. They have a contract, and Wiley has provided consideration — the diving equipment. In short, Proodian's stop-payment order isn't based on a good legal reason for not paying. Thus, Proodian will not be able to show that if the bank hadn't paid the money, the holder of the check would not have collected. On the contrary, all the evidence we have suggests that Proodian would have had to pay Wiley.

Rights and Duties of the Bank

Now let's examine the rights and duties that the bank encounters from its side of the agency relationship.

Duties of the Bank

The bank has three duties: (1) to honor the terms and conditions of its contract with the customer, (2) to obey the rules of agency, and (3) to act in good faith in a commercially reasonable manner.

This means, first, that the bank must live up to the terms of its written contract. The bank cannot promise 4% interest on a checking account and then pay 3%. Nor can the bank promise free check-writing with a minimum balance of $1,000 and then levy a fee for checks written on an account that maintains that balance. Thus, when the customer signs that signature card, he or she is entering into a written contract that is enforceable and that both sides are obliged to uphold.

Second, in virtually all circumstances, the bank must honor the agency relationship by obeying all legal orders issued by the principal — the customer, that is. When the bank cashes a check, it is not simply performing a courtesy. It is honoring a legal agreement. The bank, by entering into the checking account contract with the customer, agrees to act as that customer's legal agent.

And third, the bank agrees to act in good faith — in an honest, forthright manner, that is — and in a commercially reasonable manner. In other words, the bank's conduct, overall, must be in keeping with what one would expect of an agency in that position. This means, among other things, that the bank will exercise the same due caution and care it expects of its customers. For example, the bank will request identification from persons cashing checks, verify that the account on which the money is drawn in fact exists, and verify that there is enough money in the account to cover the check. In short, the bank will behave responsibly.

Further, the bank must not act in an arbitrary fashion, cashing certain types of checks one day, but not the next. Nor could Great Eastern Federal, for example, decide to accept checks from all local banks *except* those drawn on the Hillside National Bank just because the Great Eastern board of directors perceives Hillside as too successful. Clearly, such actions could lead to chaos. Similarly, while a bank can and will delay in crediting a depositor's account until the deposited check clears, it cannot wait, say, three weeks if checks clear in five days; such an approach would be arbitrary and contrary to the bank's duty to act in a commercially reasonable manner.

Rights of the Bank

The bank has seven rights. Let's examine them one by one. First, the bank can charge to the customer's account any item properly payable from that account. In other words, the bank's duty to follow the orders of the principal entail a corresponding right—the right to debit the principal's account for any authorized amount.

Second, the bank can pay a check even if it creates an overdraft. That is, the bank can pay even if the amount of the check is more than the customer currently has credited to his or her account. As noted earlier, the bank is not required to honor an overdraft, but it may—as a courtesy to a customer. For example, suppose Ives, a customer of long standing with Greenway Bank, has $40,000 in certificates of deposit with the bank. Unfortunately, because a payment due Ives didn't arrive because the client forgot to put a stamp on the envelope, Ives's checking account balance is much lower than expected and there's not enough money to cover a check written for office supplies. The bank recognizes this as a temporary situation, and on the strength of Ives's exemplary credit rating and the deposits he has in other accounts, is willing to honor this overdraft. The bank is not obligated to give Ives this special attention, but may do so to create good customer relations with someone whose previous business is appreciated and whose future business they would like to have.

Third, the bank can pay a check that was incomplete when issued, even if it was completed by a later holder. For instance, suppose Mulligan issues a check to Stevens to cover the cost of some water pipe. Uncertain of the amount, but trusting Stevens not to cheat him, Mulligan fills out the date of issue and the name of the payee (Ray G. Stevens), and signs the check with his own name, Stan Mulligan. Stevens delivers the pipes, figures out the total cost following delivery, and fills in the amount—$62.50—on the way to the bank, in his own handwriting. This is not the way most businesspeople conduct their business; it certainly implies a great deal of trust between the two parties. Nevertheless, should the holder of the check fill in any portion of the check other than the authorized signature itself, it is quite legal for the bank to cash it. After all, were this not the case, typewritten or printed checks would also have to be illegal, since there is no way to be certain that the person who has a check typed or printed is also the person who signs it. The point here is that, from the bank's position, the signature on the check implies agreement to the terms of the check—even if those terms were filled in *after* the signature was present.

Fourth, the bank has the right to refuse to honor any *stale* checks—that is, checks more than six months old that are not certified. A certified check—as we'll see in a moment—has already been accepted, so it cannot be subsequently dishonored. In most cases, though, the bank need not accept checks that have been around for a long time—and will often refuse to do so. A lot can happen within six months—an account may be closed, or its funds depleted. Further, the bank is likely to ask, Why did the payee wait so long? Sometimes the reason is perfectly innocent—a check was tucked in a wallet or coat pocket and forgotten. But if the check is for a significant amount of money, the bank is likely to be skeptical of forgetfulness as an excuse, and to wonder—quite rightly—whether there wasn't at some point a stop-payment order that prevented the holder from presenting the check earlier.

Fifth, the bank is fully authorized to perform its normal banking functions on the account of a customer who has died or become incompetent until the bank knows of the occurrence and has had time to act—a length of time generally accepted to be ten days. In other words, the bank may continue to charge checks against the account of a person who has died for up to ten days after the death—unless an interested party puts a stop-payment order on the account. This regulation protects the interests of businesspeople who otherwise would have no recourse. Say, for instance, that Reed buys a stereo from Oliver, pays for it with a $500 check, then dies two days later. The chances of Oliver being able to recover the stereo under the circumstances may be small indeed. But if he presents the check within ten days of Reed's death, the bank will likely honor it provided no stop-payment has been placed on the account. This helps ensure that the contract between Reed and Oliver is properly concluded. If the bank did not honor the check, Oliver could still try to recover from Reed's estate, of course, but having to do so would certainly complicate his life.

Sixth, if a bank makes a mistake—say, honors a check that has a stop-payment order against it—the bank is entitled to *subrogation*. Subrogation means, essentially, the substitution of one person in place of another. For purposes of this discussion, we do not need to explore what all these substitutions might be. That would introduce a great deal more complexity than we need to make the central point, which is this: Whatever defenses would be open to *any* of the involved parties if the bank did not cash the check will be open to the bank if it *does cash the check*.

In other words, in trying to recover money wrongfully paid out, the bank does not need to limit itself to just one role (e.g., holder in due course, drawer, drawee). It can assume whatever role will place it in the best position—the position with the strongest defenses. If you're getting the idea that banks can sometimes turn out to be "right" even when they're wrong, you're correct. This doesn't mean that banks are not held accountable for their actions under the UCC, or that banks will never be liable for the mistakes they make. They are and they will. It does suggest, however, that proving a bank's liability requires a strong case—a case strengthened by proof of impeccable conduct on the part of the customer.

Seventh—and finally—the bank has the right to enforce the terms of its contract with the customer. This may mean, for instance, that a customer may be charged a fee for overdrafts or for such services as a stop-payment order. The customer may also be assessed a per-check fee either across the board or when the account falls below a certain minimum balance. The bank provides each customer with a written contract spelling out these terms, and it is a wise customer who takes the time and trouble to become thoroughly familiar with the terms of the contract.

Special Situations

Two other situations require special mention since each can influence the way in which bank and customer rights or duties are sorted out.

Certified Checks

A certified check is *one that has already been accepted by the drawee bank*. In other words, the bank has examined the check, determined that everything is in order, and agreed to accept it on later presentment. The check is marked by the bank in a way that indicates its status as a certified check, and once it is so marked, it cannot later be rejected or dishonored. In fact, on acceptance of the certified check, the bank debits the account of the drawer for the correct amount and credits its own certified-check account. This account will be debited later, when the check is presented to be cashed. Note that the drawer—whose account the bank has debited—has now "paid" the check, even though the holder may not exchange it for money for some time.

When the drawee bank accepts the check and certifies it, it assumes primary liability on the check from that moment forward. Remember, primary liability is fixed from the time of acceptance, not from the moment the check is cashed. If it is the drawer who seeks and receives certification, the drawer remains secondarily liable until final payment. But if it is the holder who seeks and receives certification, the drawer and all prior endorsers are discharged from liability at that moment.

Normally, a bank is not required to certify a check, so the bank *voluntarily* assumes liability on the check when giving this certification. In exchange for that liability, though, the bank normally charges a fee to the person requesting the certified check.

Unauthorized Signatures

An unauthorized signature is *one made without any express or implied authority*. The most well known form of an unauthorized signature is a forgery.

Normally, as you may know, a customer may recover a loss caused by an unauthorized signature if that loss is promptly reported to the bank. For instance, if Flowers promptly examines her monthly bank statement, finds that it includes a check for $100 signed by someone who forged her name, and reports that finding to the bank, she will not be held liable for the $100. However, if the bank can show that Flowers contributed to the unauthorized signing through her own negligence, she will often not have a case.

Why not? Keep in mind that the customer has a duty to act with due care and diligence. This means, among other things, keeping track of a checkbook, knowing where it is at all times, knowing who has access to it, and making sure that it is unlikely that blank checks or partially completed checks will fall into the wrong hands. If Flowers can show she is careful with her checkbook and checking account, she'll have a much stronger case than if it turns out she never reconciles her statements or routinely keeps her checkbook in plain sight on her office desktop where countless people walk by and see it.

Many businesses routinely sign checks with a stamp. That's fine; stamped signatures are perfectly legal. But such businesses have a duty—so far as the bank is concerned—to keep both checks and stamps out of unauthorized hands. A business that left its checks or its stamp in a place where they were readily accessible to unauthorized persons could be charged with negligence. The business's carelessness is, literally, a violation of the principal's duty in the contractual relationship between customer and bank. And it means, in practical terms, that if the company's checks are forged and then presented by a *good-faith* holder, the bank is unlikely to be liable. After all, the customer's own negligence contributed to the problem. And besides, the bank is doing nothing wrong in accepting a forged check *if* there is no reason to suspect forgery. When a bank accepts such an instrument from a good-faith holder, the bank is also acting in good faith, and—as the principal's agent—merely following orders. All in all, the customer whose own negligence contributes to his or her losses will generally bear the liability of those losses and will need to recover directly from the forger.

SOME PRACTICAL ADVICE

Checking accounts are convenient and save time. In fact, for today's businessperson, they're a virtual necessity. That doesn't mean, however, that the obligations that go along with maintaining a checking account can be taken lightly. Ignoring these rights and duties could result in serious liability.

First, it's wise to be thoroughly familiar with the contractual relationship established by opening a checking account. While all banks are required under the Uniform Commercial Code to behave in a commercially reasonable manner, they are not required to—and do not—have the same specific rules regarding fees, service charges, and so forth. Remember, in establishing a checking account, you are setting up a contractual relationship. If you were buying a house or loaning someone money, you'd carefully consider the terms of the contract, wouldn't you? The contractual relationship underlying your checking account deserves the same attention.

Second, it is a good idea to reconcile bank statements as quickly as possible, and to do so with the utmost care. This doesn't mean glancing at the statement to verify that there's still some money in it. Rather, it means reviewing each transaction, matching the bank's record against your own personal record, and examining every cancelled draft to make sure it has not been altered, that the signature on it is your own or another authorized signature, and that there are no unauthorized endorsements. Failure to report any problems quickly could seriously increase your liability. Rapid reporting of problems, by contrast, often means that the bank will have to assume responsibility for the problem.

Third, as we've attempted to show throughout this lesson, banks conduct their business with the utmost care. Mistakes are fairly rare. They do occur, of course, but in order for a bank to be held liable, the customer will need to show first that he or she suffered damages or loss; second, that the bank's conduct was indeed the proximate cause of any loss or injury; and third, that the customer's own conduct in no way contributed to the loss. Thus, a customer who behaves in a generally careless or casual fashion is unlikely to be able to win a suit for damages against a bank if the bank does make an error. Banks mean it when they say they demand care and diligence from their customers. When checks are dishonored, stolen, forged, or altered, someone must bear the loss while attempts are made to identify the actual wrongdoer and collect the misappropriated funds. Customers who are too free and easy with checking account responsibilities are likely to find themselves in that role.

ASSIGNMENTS

- Before you watch the video program, be sure you've read through the preceding overview, familiarized yourself with the learning objectives for this lesson, and looked at the key terms below. Then, read Chapter 27 of Davidson et al., *Business Law*.
- After completing these tasks, view the video program for Lesson 23.
- After watching the program, take time to review what you've learned. First, evaluate your learning with the self-test which follows the key terms. Then, apply and evaluate what you've learned with the "Your Opinion, Please" scenarios at the end of this telecourse study guide lesson.

KEY TERMS

Before you read through the textbook assignment and watch the video program, take a minute to look at the key terms associated with this lesson. When you encounter them in the textbook and video program, pay careful attention to their meaning.

Agent	Service charge
Certified check	Signature card
Negligence	Stale check
Overdraft	Statement
Principal	Stop payment
Proximate cause	Subrogation
Reconcile	Unauthorized signature

SELF-TEST

The questions below will help you evaluate how well you've learned the material in this lesson. Read each one carefully, and select the letter of the option that best answers the question. You'll find the correct answer, along with a reference to the page number(s) where the topic is discussed, in the back of this telecourse study guide.

1. In the U.S. today, checking accounts are

   a. commonplace among both individuals and businesses.
   b. common among individuals, but rarely held by businesses.
   c. popular with businesses, but on the decline among individuals because of the high risks and liabilities involved.
   d. far less popular in general than they once were because managing such an account has become highly technical.

2. Schultz issues a check for $50, then issues a stop-payment order before the payee, Winkler, can present the check. When Winkler presents the check eight days later, the bank will

   a. pay Winkler $50.
   b. not pay Winkler $50.
   c. pay Winkler $50 if the stop-payment order was oral; not pay Winkler if the stop-payment order was written.
   d. not pay Winkler if the bank thought Schultz had a good reason for the stop-payment order; pay Winkler if the bank thought the reason wasn't very good.

3. Wicke opens a new checking account at Trusty Bank and signs a signature card to complete the transaction. In signing this card, Wicke is doing which of the following?

   a. *All* of the following—b, c, and d—are accomplished.
   b. Authorizing the bank to act as her agent
   c. Creating a legal contract between herself and the bank
   d. Creating a debtor–creditor relationship with the bank

4. The *first and main* duty of a bank customer is to

   a. ensure that no overdrafts are ever written.
   b. act as the authorized agent of the bank.
   c. protect the bank against any potential liability.
   d. act with due care and diligence in managing a checking account.

5. A written summary of all activities relating to a person's account during a given period is referred to as a

   a. statement.
   b. service summary.

c. subrogation form.

d. contract.

6. Which of the following is *not* a right of the customer who has established a checking account at a bank?

   a. To stop payment on a check

   b. To require obedience of any lawful order

   c. To collect damages that result directly from the bank's mishandling of an account

   d. To demand that the bank honor an overdraft

7. A stop-payment order should include which of the following?

   a. The number of the check

   b. The name of the payee

   c. The amount for which the check was written

   d. *All* of the above—a, b, and c—*must be included* in a stop-payment order.

8. A customer has a duty to *reconcile* his or her checking account on a periodic basis. This means, in effect, that the customer must

   a. make sure his or her personal record of transactions matches that of the bank.

   b. ensure there is enough money in the account to cover all drafts.

   c. reimburse the bank for overdrafts.

   d. send the bank a monthly written summary of all transactions.

9. Under UCC regulations, the principal–agent relationship between a customer and the bank normally

   a. terminates at the moment of the customer's death.

   b. extends for a year beyond the customer's death.

   c. extends for ten days beyond the customer's death.

   d. never ends, even if the customer dies.

10. Seventeen-year-old Loretta opened a checking account last year with part of the money she had saved from her after-school job. She has always kept a healthy balance in the account, but today in the mail she received three checks that the bank had refused to cash as well as a notice cancelling her account. The enclosed letter reported that bank officials had discovered that when Loretta—a minor—had opened the account, the bank had forgotten to demand an adult co-signer. In closing Loretta's account in this fashion, did the bank breach any of the duties it owed to Loretta?

    a. No; since the bank acts as Loretta's principal, it can set the conditions of the agreement.

    b. No; the agency agreement was never valid in the first place.

    c. No; Loretta cannot prove that she has been damaged by the cancellation.

    d. Yes; the bank has breached several duties it owed Loretta.

YOUR OPINION, PLEASE

Read each of the following scenarios and answer the questions about the decisions you would make in each situation. Give these questions some serious thought; they may be used as the basis for the development of a more complex essay. You should base your decisions on what you've learned from this lesson, though you may incorporate outside readings or information gained through your own experience if it is relevant.

Scenario 1

Through a bank error, an additional $500 is added to Fields's account at Main Street Bank in early January. Main Street does not discover the error right away. Nor does Fields, who normally keeps a balance of several thousand dollars in his checking account and is not in the habit of keeping close tabs on his spending. Fields glances quickly through his monthly bank statement for January, but when the figures do not reconcile with his own estimates, he assumes the error must be his—"Banks don't make errors about this stuff"—and revises his checkbook accordingly without looking into the matter further.

In early March, Fields writes a $2,000 check to Eurosport Motors to cover extensive engine repairs to his car. Shortly after issuing this check, Fields receives notice regarding the bank error, together with a form letter of apology from Main Street Bank and a corrected statement. Meanwhile, Eurosport presents the check and it is dishonored. Having lost several thousand dollars earlier in the month when they accepted a bad check, Eurosport is incensed at Fields; they file suit to recover the $2,000, and also file criminal charges against Fields for passing bad checks.

Enraged at what he considers a humiliating—and costly, given the attorney's fees he incurs—experience resulting from the bank's carelessness, Fields sues the bank to collect damages. Main Street Bank readily acknowledges that the original error was indeed theirs, but maintains it was Fields's responsibility to discover it.

What's your opinion? Did Fields have a responsibility to discover the error, or should that responsibility rightly have been the bank's?

- Is Fields likely to win his suit against the bank for damages? If so, on what grounds?
- What factors support your answer?
- What factors might an attorney cite in arguing against your case?
- What steps, if any, might Fields have taken to preclude a lawsuit in this situation?
- What steps, if any, might the bank have taken to preclude a lawsuit in this situation?

Scenario 2

Higgins wishes to buy an antique desk from Ruff. The two agree that it will be sold for the average of two appraisals, but since the appraisals haven't been done yet, both are uncertain of the sale price. Higgins, believing the price will not exceed $2,000, issues a check made out to Ruff, and dated and signed by Higgins, but with the amount left blank. He tells Ruff to fill it in with the proper amount following the appraisals, and that he will pick up the desk the following Saturday. The next day, Ruff has the desk appraised; it is clearly more valuable than either thought— the average of the appraisals is $3,200.

Ruff fills in the check with the correct amount and presents it for payment on Friday. The unexpectedly high amount slightly exceeds what Higgins has in his checking account, but because he is a customer of many years' standing, the bank honors the overdraft and cashes the check, giving $3,200 to Ruff.

Higgins picks up the desk on Saturday from the warehouse where it was stored, and on Monday receives notice from the bank regarding the overdraft. Higgins is very upset at having paid so much for the desk, and contacts Ruff—who is not very sympathetic. The purchase price was clearly the average of the two appraisals, Ruff says, and he will neither return the money nor reclaim the desk.

Higgins thereupon sues the bank for recovery of the money, claiming they violated the basic agent–principal relationship by honoring an overdraft without Higgins's authorization. What do you think? Has the bank failed to act in a commercially responsible manner in this instance? Did they go too far in honoring the overdraft? Or is Higgins stuck with his expensive purchase?

- Is Higgins likely to win his suit against the bank?
- What factors support your answer?
- What factors might an attorney cite in arguing against your view?
- What steps, if any, might Higgins have taken to prevent a lawsuit in this situation?
- What steps, if any, might the bank have taken to prevent a lawsuit in this situation?

24

Creation and Termination of Agency

LEARNING OBJECTIVES

Upon completing your study of this lesson, you should be able to

- Define the terms *agency* and *agency relationship*.
- Explain, using examples, the circumstances under which an agency relationship might arise in both a business and nonbusiness context.
- Discuss the restrictions on agency relationships, and explain why such restrictions tend to be limited.
- List and discuss, using hypothetical examples, three types of agency relationships.
- Explain how the definition of employees as agents influences an employer's rights and liabilities.
- Describe the circumstances under which an independent contractor is defined as an agent, and discuss the implications of this definition for an employer's rights and liabilities.
- List and describe seven duties owed by an agent to the principal.
- List and describe two duties owed by a principal to the agent.
- Discuss six ways in which an agency relationship can be legally terminated.

Lesson 24 deals with the creation and termination of agency. During your study of this lesson, you'll be introduced to agency law, which deals with *agency relationships* — the relations of agents to the principals whose interests they represent. You will also learn about the duties and responsibilities each owes the other.

OVERVIEW

At one time or another each of us has acted as an agent for someone else. And each of us has had others act as our agents. When we were children and went to the store for our parents, we acted as their agents. When we ask a friend to drop a book off at the library or do a similar favor for us, we ask the friend to be our agent. In some cases we are paid as agents; in others, we aren't; one doesn't have to be paid to be an agent.

Agency and the Agency Relationship

Agency is simply a relationship in which one person acts for or represents the best interests of another person, and consents to do it under that other person's guidance or direction. The representative is called the *agent* and the person he or she represents is called the *principal*.

An agent can act in a business relationship or a nonbusiness one, paid or unpaid in either case. But in all cases, the agent *consents* to act on behalf of the principal. Therefore, the agreement between a principal and an agent is a *consensual* one. And, because it is a voluntary agreement, it can be broken off by either party. Also, in every case, the agent is subject to the guidance and control of the principal. The agent must always do the principal's bidding, or an agency relationship does not exist.

Agency law is that body of law that governs the relationships among principals, agents, and third parties. It grew out of the laws that governed relationships between masters and servants in times past. Some of the earliest agents of which we are aware were servants in royal households. They worked for kings and other nobles. They were among the most trusted servants and, as such, they acted as agents for the households in dealing with the public. For example, they may have purchased or sold goods for the household. In doing so they were acting as agents for their masters. The laws governing those transactions grew out of negotiations in court. They were court-made laws that have now come to be called common law. As in the days of masters and servants, agency law is usually concerned with the relationships of the agents to the third parties to whom the agents represent their principals. After all, by offering that principal's goods or services, the agent is attempting to contract with a third party; that sale then becomes, in effect, a contract between the principal and the buyer.

Restrictions on Creating an Agency Relationship

There are very few restrictions on who can become involved in such relationships or what such relationships may be formed to do. All persons except incompetents (persons the courts have judged incapable of handling their own affairs) and some minors can legally appoint agents to act on their behalf. Because the agency relationship is a consensual one, the principal must be legally capable of giving *operative consent* — that is, capable of making a legally binding agreement.

Generally, anyone who is legally capable of entering into a contract is capable of hiring agents. In some states for some purposes, this includes minors. In other states, minors may be principals but their agreements may be voidable. There are even fewer restrictions on who can be an agent than there are on who can be a principal. In particular, even minors and incompetents can be agents since the principal is the one responsible for them. The legal capacity of the principal controls the agency relationship; in other words, the principal is responsible for the work of the agent. Agents hired by principals may be employees or nonemployees — a distinction governed mainly by the amount of control the principal maintains over the agents hired to do the work.

Generally, principals can assign almost any task to an agent. There are, however, some tasks that are *nondelegable*. Here are some examples of nondelegable duties; different states may classify other duties as nondelegable duties. Nondelegable duties include

- an employer's duty to provide safe working conditions,
- a person's duty under specific contract terms,
- a landlord's duty to tenants,
- a common carrier's duty to passengers,
- a person's duty under a license issued to him or her, and
- the duty of a person engaged in inherently dangerous work to take precautions to prevent harm.

The term "nondelegable duty" is misleading. A duty itself *can* actually be delegated, but the *responsibility* for its successful completion may not be. This means that the principal may delegate the "nondelegable" duty to an agent but, if anything goes wrong, it is the principal who has the final responsibility. For example, though an architect will hire a construction company to actually build the building, the responsibility for the successful completion of the work remains with the architect.

Three Types of Agency Relationships

There are three types of agents. Two types — *general* and *special* — are agents for hire. The third type, a *gratuitous agent*, is one who volunteers his or her services. Suppose Patti had been hired to clean Mrs. Frickson's gutters, and Jean volunteered to help her so they could take off for the beach sooner. Jean would be acting as a gratuitous agent, helping her friend without pay.

A *general agent* is a person hired to do a number of tasks. Often, a general agent is one delegated a number of related tasks as part of a position of employment. For example, if Owens were hired by Meyer to run Meyer's grocery on the evening shift, Owens would be a general agent, perhaps responsible for everything from stocking shelves and selling merchandise to cleaning and closing up at night.

On the other hand, if Billy were hired by Meyer to deliver one package to a customer in exchange for a week's worth of ice cream bars, then Billy would be a *special agent*, an agent hired to perform a one-time special task. If Meyer hired Kowolski Paints to paint a sign for him, Kowolski Paints would also be a special agent, its responsibility limited to its single delegated task of painting the sign. That paint job might involve a number of related tasks such as scraping and sandblasting the old sign, but those are usually considered *closely related transactions* that are parts of the single assignment.

Courts treat the three kinds of agents—general, special, and gratuitous—differently. Obviously, a general agent has been delegated more authority than a special agent, and the courts will consider that if litigation arises because of an agent's actions. But the amount of *discretion* of the agent—the degree of judgment the agent is allowed to exercise—does *not* influence a court in deciding whether an agent is a general agent or a special one. Usually the court will consider these three factors in making that decision:

- the number of acts that will be completed to achieve the authorized results,
- the number of people dealt with in achieving the desired result, and
- the length of time necessary to achieve the desired result.

In general, the greater the number of acts to be completed, the more people to be dealt with, and the longer the time necessary to achieve the desired the result, the more likely it is that a court would find an agent to be a general (rather than a special) agent. But once the court has decided whether the agent is a general or a special one, the principal may be held responsible for the actions of the agent that are within the agent's range of responsibility.

In the case of the gutter cleaning mentioned above, suppose Jean, the gratuitous agent, had knocked a gutter off while moving her ladder. If the owner sued, who would be responsible? Probably Patti, since the court would probably find that Jean was acting on Patti's behalf for this task and thus hold Patti responsible for the damages. Obviously, though, Patti has no responsibility if Jean ruins Frickson's lawn mower while helping another friend do Frickson's yard work. Jean was an agent of Patti's *only* for the gutter cleaning; she is *not* Patti's general agent.

Employees and Independent Contractors

The distinction between an employee and an independent contractor is an important, though sometimes difficult, one to make. An *employee* is more like the servant of past times. In fact, the court often considers the terms employee and servant synonymous. The employer has greater rights to control when and where the employee works and, especially, *how* the employee works.

The employer exerts much less control on the *independent contractor*. In fact, the contractor is not always the agent of the employer. For example, if an employer hires an independent contractor to complete a job—but does not specify how the job is to be completed—the contractor is probably not an agent of the employer. Suppose Rand were hired to write a technical paper for the Bonanza Group. Suppose, too, that Bonanza controlled only the content of the finished paper, not how Rand produced it, what hours he worked, what equipment he used. Under these conditions, Rand, an independent contractor, was probably not Bonanza's agent. He owed no fiduciary duty to Bonanza — that is, Bonanza had placed no special trust in him, and Rand owed Bonanza only the completed technical paper.

On the other hand, if Melville were retained as Bonanza's attorney, responsible for handling all their legal matters, then she would have a fiduciary duty to Bonanza even though she was not their direct employee. She would be in a position of trust as an agent with the fiduciary duty to act in Bonanza's best interest in all legal matters. Though Melville was still an independent contractor who—just like Rand in the previous example—is not generally subject to Bonanza's control over where, when, or how she conducted her assignments, she would still be regarded as Bonanza's agent because of the extent of the trust delegated to her. It must be emphasized, however, that Melville's agency would extend only to those legal duties specifically delegated to her by Bonanza.

A firm or person who hires an independent contractor is usually not responsible for that person's wrongdoings. There are exceptions, however, the two major ones being (1) if the independent contractor were hired to commit a crime, and (2) if the work for which the independent contractor were hired was *ultrahazardous*. For instance, in our previous example of Melville and Bonanza, if Melville were convicted of accepting cocaine from one of her other clients in lieu of other payment, Bonanza would, sensibly enough, bear no responsibility for Melville's illegal action. But if Bonanza had asked Melville to draw up some papers that hid part of Bonanza's income from the Internal Revenue Service, and Melville did so, then Melville's employers at Bonanza would be as responsible for Melville's illegal actions as she herself would be.

But suppose Melville took the actions to hide Bonanza income without instructions from anyone at Bonanza to do so. Would Bonanza then be held responsible for Melville's criminal actions or would the normal rule of not being liable for the actions of an independent contractor apply to Bonanza? That's not totally clear—for recent court decisions have held that hiring parties must adequately supervise some actions of their independent contractors. It's likely that the question of how its tax matters are handled would be something a court would expect Bonanza to supervise carefully, and therefore hold Bonanza responsible for not having caught and corrected Melville's actions.

In the case of hiring an independent contractor to perform ultrahazardous activities, or an "inherently dangerous task," and a serious mishap occurs, the courts may well decide that the principal is responsible for the wrongs of the independent contractor. The principal can often remove this responsibility, however, by having its contract with the contractor include specific terms about taking precautions against that which is inherently dangerous in the job. But in the absence of such terms, if something goes wrong, the principal usually will be held responsible.

Duties of Agents and Principals

Agents are entrusted by principals to act in the principal's best interests. The law recognizes the following seven duties an agent owes his or her principal:

- First, every agent is obligated to provide faithful service to the principal, to *act in good faith*. This is the agent's fiduciary duty to the principal. The agent must reveal crucial facts about business operations, avoid skimming off profits, and generally avoid benefitting personally at the expense of the principal.

- Second, every agent has the *duty of loyalty* to the principal, the obligation to look out for the principal's best interests.

- Third, an agent must *follow lawful instructions*, so long as they do not subject the agent to the risk of injury. In fact, an agent is liable for any damages resulting from his or her failure to follow lawful instructions.

- Fourth, an agent must *act with reasonable care* on the principal's behalf. Any loss caused by failure to act carefully is the agent's responsibility.

- Fifth, an agent is *obligated to segregate funds* of the principal from other funds the agent controls, whether they are the agent's personal funds or those of other clients.

- Sixth, an agent has the duty to *account for money* received and turn it over to the principal.

- Finally, an agent has a duty to *give notice*, that is, to keep the principal aware of any information that may be crucial to the principal's best interests.

An agency relationship conveys all seven of these requirements to the agent; it's not possible to be an agent and decide to meet only four or five of these duties. Any agent must fulfill all seven of these duties.

Does the principal have any duties to the agent? Yes, two. First, the principal must compensate the agent according to the terms of the agreement. Second, the principal must provide a safe place and safe equipment for the agent's work, if the agent does not on his or her own provide the work place and equipment.

Termination of Agency

Obviously, agency relationships don't go on forever. People change jobs, take up different careers, and so on. And principals rarely need the services of even a general agent forever. After all, you wouldn't want the carpenter building your fence or the attorney drawing up your will to be your agent forever. An agency relationship, however, cannot be terminated haphazardly. In fact, there are six different ways that agency relationships may be legally terminated.

The first is *agreement*; an agency relationship may be terminated by the agreement of the parties. Often, the agreement to create an agency relationship will also set the time or cause for its termination. For example, if a real estate company is given a listing to sell a house, that listing makes the company the seller's agent for a set period of time. At the end of that period, both parties may agree to extend or end the agreement for the agency relationship.

The second is *termination at will* — if the agreement setting up the agency relationship does not specify a set date, period, or occurrence for the agency to end. With such an *agency at will* relationship, the agency relationship may be terminated by notice at the will of either party. Suppose Dell is employed by Fletcher as a truck driver, a situation that makes Dell the agent of Fletcher. Typically, either Fletcher or Dell can end this agency relationship (the employment agreement) by notifying the other of his desire to do so.

The traditional termination-at-will concept, however, is undergoing much change. Courts have begun to hold that loyal, long-term employees may *not* always be discharged at will. In several cases, courts have ruled that an employee's relationship with his or her employer may not be terminated unless the employer has a "good cause" reason. Exactly what reasons are good causes is becoming clearer as the courts further decide to what degree and in what circumstances they will overrule the termination-at-will rights normally accorded to employers. (Other accepted — and well-recognized — exceptions to an employer's rights to terminate at will have to do with firings based on race, age, sex, religion, national origin, and other equal-rights protections.)

The third way to terminate an agency relationship is *fulfillment*; an agency relationship will terminate when the purpose for which it was created has been fulfilled or no longer exists. If Ramos hires Baxter to paint his house, the agency relationship ends, logically enough, when the house is painted.

The fourth is *revocation*; an agent's responsibility may be revoked by proper notice by the principal. Lewis might be the attorney for Nelson Clothing, but this is an agency relationship that Nelson can revoke by notifying Lewis. However, if the revocation is a breach of contract on the principal's part, the principal may be liable for damages incurred by the agent.

The fifth is *renunciation*; an agent may renounce his or her service to the principal. This is the opposite of revocation; here it is the agent seeking to terminate the relationship. And, as you might guess, if such renunciation is a breach of contract, the agent may be liable for damages to the principal.

The final way to terminate an agency relationship is *operation of law*; an agency relationship may be terminated by events outside the abilities of the parties to control. Here are some examples of operations of law that normally terminate an agency relationship: when an agent dies, when either party becomes insane, when the principal becomes bankrupt, when the agent becomes bankrupt and that bankruptcy affects the agent's ability to serve the principal, when the agency can no longer possibly be performed (as might be the case, for instance, when crucial documents were destroyed by fire), when an unforeseeable change in circumstances destroys the purpose of the agency relationship, and when a change in law makes it illegal to complete the agency relationship (as was the case for liquor sales representatives when prohibition became the law after World War I).

In the past, an agency relationship was also automatically terminated by the death of a principal. However, such immediate, automatic termination often caused the agent undue hardship, particularly when an agent completes a transaction without realizing the principal for whom he or she works has died. Many states now allow immediate termination only if no undue hardship for the agent will result.

SOME PRACTICAL ADVICE

Why is it important that a businessperson know anything about agency relationships and agency law? And what are the most important aspects of the agency relationship to businesspeople?

First off, most businesspeople are either principals or agents. Indeed, a person or business may be a principal in one relationship and an agent in another; it is certainly rarer for a businessperson to be neither than to be both. So what must a businessperson keep in mind about being a principal and an agent?

When you act as a principal in a business, there are clearly some things you need to consider. First, you have to consider whether you're better off hiring someone to work as an employee or as an independent contractor. Both have advantages. You have more control over employees but you also have to be more responsible for an employee—in everything from paying his or her taxes and social security to providing the equipment necessary to do the job. You also are much more responsible for their actions. You don't have to worry so much about those things with an independent contractor, but you also don't have the control over the way that person does the job.

Remember, when you hire an employee, you are making that employee your agent. Given that you are getting into an agency relationship that, as we've seen, is strictly governed by law, it makes sense to be careful and cautious. First, you'll need to define clearly what you expect the relationship with that employee to be. What are the tasks to be performed and under what conditions are they to be completed? If the job is to be completed by an employee, complete details about the scope of and procedures related to the job need to be thought through carefully. However, if you hire a person to work as an independent contractor, you'll have to trust that person's judgment about how best to do the job you want done.

(One particularly important exception to relying on the judgment of an independent contractor is if you're hiring someone for an ultrahazardous activity. If so, you'll want to make sure you specify the extra precautions that will need to be taken to perform the job safely. Get assurance in the contract that the contractor will follow those precautions and any others that are appropriate for the type of work being done.)

There are, it's true, a number of established duties the law says you can expect from employees who are your agents. Nevertheless, it is always best to spell those out right at the beginning of an employer–employee relationship; you cannot expect your employees to understand their responsibilities under agency law unless you make those duties clear. Also, let your employees know how much control you expect to exert and how much responsibility you want them to take. That may change as time goes on, but it's best for everyone if you spell out such things at the start of employment and then review them periodically.

But, remember, no matter how much responsibility you give your agent, you are the one who is ultimately responsible for his or her actions. This doesn't mean that agents can avoid responsibility for their own actions—they can't. But, ultimately, you are responsible for the acts of your agents, and you should supervise your agents accordingly.

If, on the other hand, you are entering the business world as an agent, you should make sure your employer spells out the terms of your employment clearly at the start. Be sure to go over all the issues and be sure you get a clear understanding about your pay or other compensation at the outset. And if there are working conditions that don't look right, call your employer's attention to them. Agency law clearly supports your right to know how you'll be paid and that your working conditions are safe. If your employer doesn't mention those things, bring them up yourself. In the long run, the clearer those terms are, the better the relationship is bound to be.

Finally, know from the very start of an agency relationship how long the relationship is expected to last and what, if any, special conditions might cause it to end early. Do you have to give a certain notice? How much notice will be given you? Are you entitled to severance pay? Don't forget, though, that there are circumstances that might cause the relationship to end in spite of anything either party desires—those conditions we term operations of law (such as death, insanity, bankruptcy, the outbreak of war).

ASSIGNMENTS

- Before you watch the video program, be sure you've read through the preceding overview, familiarized yourself with the learning objectives for this lesson, and looked at the key terms below. Then read Chapter 33 of Davidson et al., *Business Law*.
- After completing these tasks, view the video program for Lesson 24.

- After watching the program, take time to review what you've learned. First, evaluate your learning with the self-test which follows the key terms. Then, apply and evaluate what you've learned with the "Your Opinion, Please" scenarios at the end of this telecourse study guide lesson.

KEY TERMS

Before you read through the textbook assignment and watch the video program, take a minute to look at the key terms associated with this lesson. When you encounter them in the textbook and video program, pay careful attention to their meaning.

Agency	Gratuitous agent
Agent	Nondelegable duty
Consensual	Operation of law
Employee	Operative consent
Employer	Principal
Fiduciary duty	Special agent
General agent	

SELF-TEST

The questions below will help you evaluate how well you've learned the material in this lesson. Read each one carefully, and select the letter of the option that best answers the question. You'll find the correct answer, along with a reference to the page number(s) where the topic is discussed, in the back of this telecourse study guide.

1. Which, if any, of the following options describes an agency relationship?

   a. A relationship between a landlord and his or her tenants
   b. A relationship in which a jewelry store is negotiating to buy wholesale diamonds
   c. A relationship in which Bill delivers a package to Alice for Mary
   d. None of the above describes an agency relationship.

2. Which of the following options *best* describes the term nondelegable duty?

   a. A duty that may not lawfully be assigned by a principal to his or her agent
   b. A duty the agent believes goes beyond the established scope of the agency relationship

c. A duty where the task itself can be delegated although the responsibility cannot be

d. A duty where neither the task nor the responsibility may be delegated

3. Which of the four terms below denotes a person over whom a principal has the least control?

a. Gratuitous agent
b. General agent
c. Special agent
d. Independent contractor

4. At a trade show, Melling was asked by a sales representative if he was "an independent contractor." Melling said he was. Assuming he actually is an independent contractor, which of the following options is most likely correct?

a. Melling is always an agent of the principal.
b. Melling is never an agent of the principal.
c. Melling may or may not be an agent of the person who hired him or her.
d. Melling will have many agents working for him.

5. Olivia is participating in her law school's annual legal scavenger hunt. Her team has been told to find a situation in which an agency relationship does *not* exist. Which of the following four relationships is a guaranteed winner?

a. A prospective home builder and the architect who draws up the plans for him or her
b. A business owner and her firm's lawyer
c. A soft-drink bottler and the employee who drives the delivery truck
d. A business owner and the typesetter hired to typeset the text of the annual report

6. Murdock hires independent contractors all the time and worries about being responsible for their actions. Which of the following conditions is *most likely* to make Murdock liable for any damage caused by the negligence of an independent contractor in his employ?

a. The contractor's drunkenness
b. The contractor's use of drugs
c. The extreme hazardousness of the task he assigned to the contractor
d. *None* of the above; Murdock is overly concerned since principals are never legally responsible for the actions of independent contractors.

7. Which of the following duties, though often performed by an agent, is *not* necessarily owed a principal by his or her agent?

a. Segregation of funds
b. Notice of a payment deposited in the principal's account
c. Loyalty
d. Reasonable value for the compensation received

8. Grey is employed by Hollis. Which one of the following duties does Hollis legally owe Grey?

   a. Severance pay and adequate notice upon termination
   b. An obligation of loyalty
   c. An obligation to provide a safe working environment
   d. Grey is clearly the compensated agent of Hollis. Since Grey is not a principal, Hollis, therefore, has no specific duty to him.

9. Which, if any, of the following circumstances would be considered an operation of law and thus would affect a previously established agency relationship?

   a. A court decision that now makes it illegal to complete the agency relationship
   b. The principal moves to another state
   c. The purpose of the agency is completed
   d. None of the above; operations of law never affect existing agency relationships, only the creation of new ones.

10. Harshaw, who had been a faithful, apparently highly competent employee for over thirteen years, was terminated without clear reason. Her firing came shortly before she would have become eligible for company retirement benefits. Which of the following would have given her employer the right to terminate her, had she not contested and won reemployment under the theory of "abusive discharge"?

    a. Agency at will
    b. Fulfillment
    c. Operation of law
    d. *None* of these; there is no doctrine under which an employer can unilaterally terminate an employee's agency relationship.

YOUR OPINION, PLEASE

Read each of the following scenarios and answer the questions about the decisions you would make in each situation. Give these questions some serious thought; they may be used as the basis of the development of a more complex essay. You should base your decisions on what you've learned from this lesson, though you may incorporate outside readings or information gained through your own experience if it is relevant.

Scenario 1

Barbara Allen had worked in Jane Goodsell's retail store for years, but she was (for the first time) asked to manage it for three months while Jane went on a combined vacation and buying trip. Though Barbara appreciated the chance to manage the store, she was resentful that Jane had not asked her to go along on the buying trip. She felt that Jane's failure to give her a raise with her new responsibilities was typical of Jane's thoughtlessness regarding her.

As soon as Jane left, Barbara raised the price on the shop's most popular items by one-third and began featuring the items in various newspaper ads, all without their given prices but with intriguing come-ons. The advertising campaign was highly successful; the merchandise sold very well. However, Barbara recorded the sales at the old prices on the books and kept the increased profits for herself. After all, she reasoned, sales were — in spite of the higher prices — higher than they'd ever been because of her inventive knack at advertising.

Just before Jane returned, Barbara had a special promotion. She reduced the prices on the store's most popular items, although they were still priced higher than the price Jane used to sell them at. As before, the ads contained no statement about the actual prices but were so cleverly done that the sales response was enormous.

Jane returned and saw by the books that Barbara had done very well for her. She admired the clever ads and gave Barbara a 5% raise, promising that if her advertising continued to be so successful she'd pay her an additional commission. Just after Barbara went home for the night, Jane and one of the store's part-time sales clerks sat down for a cup of coffee. In the course of the conversation, Meg said, "Gee, that Barbara is something else! I thought she was crazy when she raised the price on all those items by one-third. I thought they'd never sell. But that just shows what I know about marketing."

The next morning, Jane fired Barbara and sued for recovery of the funds Barbara had taken. Barbara countersued, charging that her discharge was unwarranted. Jane had, Barbara claimed, suffered no damages whatsoever due to her (Barbara's) actions; Jane had, in fact, profited handsomely from the increased sales volume and the traditional mark-up.

What's your opinion? Based on what you know of the situation, did Barbara violate her employment agreement and duties as an agent? Or did Barbara comply with her responsibilities, seeing to it that the store was as profitable as if Jane had stayed in charge?

- Is a court likely to uphold Jane's view of the relationship and require Barbara to return the extra profits?
- What factors support your view?
- What factors might an attorney cite in arguing against your view?
- What steps, if any, might Barbara have taken to prevent a lawsuit in this situation?
- What steps, if any, might Jane have taken to prevent a lawsuit in this situation?

Scenario 2

Bill Thomas had acted as a purchasing agent for the Wilson Gallery for over twenty years, helping it to become one of the most successful art galleries on the West Coast. Though not on the gallery payroll, Thomas had been so successful for the Wilsons—John and Martha—that he had actually given up purchasing for other galleries. He sometimes made his purchases at the direct request of one of the Wilsons, but he usually took his orders from Karl Weatherby, the general manager of the gallery; Weatherby had been with the gallery ever since John took over the gallery from his father thirty years earlier.

During the past year, John had been very disturbed by extravagant purchases ordered by his wife Martha and had instructed Weatherby not to purchase anything on Martha's orders. Martha had been drinking heavily since the death of their only child the year before, and Weatherby, who had been close to the family, understood John's concern. Weatherby, on the other hand, was reluctant to mention such personal matters to Thomas, whom he considered an "outsider." While Weatherby was in the process of deciding what to say to Thomas, Martha personally instructed Thomas to find her a three- or four-foot-tall jade heron, "like one I saw in Hong Kong a few years back. And price is no object." Thomas was a little concerned about this order, for he had realized that Martha had not quite been herself lately. Nevertheless, Martha had placed orders in the past and the gallery always had thanked him for his efforts.

While Thomas was in Hong Kong seeking the heron, Weatherby died of a heart attack. Two days later, when Thomas arrived with Martha's $30,000 jade heron, John Wilson came apart. The stress of recent events was suddenly too much, and he exploded at Thomas. Thomas was confused and shocked. He tried explaining that he had not been told about the prohibition against Martha's purchases, but Wilson yelled that "any fool would know better than to buy a $30,000 trinket for a drunken woman." He screamed that he would not reimburse Thomas for the heron, or even for his expenses in tracking it down. "Furthermore, you're fired," he yelled. "I've had it. I want you out of my sight. You've violated my trust, and you'll never work for me again."

Thomas was dismayed by this rapid turn of events. For one thing, though he had made a great deal of money working for the Wilsons, he could hardly afford to lose $30,000 plus the $4,600 he spent tracking down the heron. He threatened to sue Wilson to recover his money, to which Wilson yelled, "Get out or I'll throw you out!"

Thomas, now quite angry at Wilson (and recognizing that he no longer had any source of income) sued Wilson for both the cost of the heron and a larger sum for Wilson's unlawful termination of their agency relationship.

What's your opinion? Based on what you know of the situation, do you think Thomas can successfully sue for his costs in obtaining the heron and for the termination of the agency relationship? Or will Wilson's actions, even though taken in anger, be upheld by a court?

- Will Thomas be successful in court? Partially successful? Fully successful?

- What factors support your view?
- What factors might an attorney cite in arguing against your view?
- What steps, if any, might Wilson have taken to prevent a lawsuit in this situation?
- What steps, if any, might Thomas have taken to prevent a lawsuit in this situation?

25

Principals and Agents

LEARNING OBJECTIVES

Upon completing your study of this lesson, you should be able to

- Discuss the primary issues involved in determining the liability of principals and agents in an agency relationship.

- Distinguish among *express, ratification, incidental, implied, emergency, apparent* authority, and *authority by estoppel*, and explain the implications of each for determining the liability of a principal.

- Describe the ways in which liability may vary depending on whether the principal is defined as *disclosed, undisclosed,* or *partially disclosed.*

- Discuss the circumstances under which the agent, and not the principal, will be liable for wrongs and losses that result from the agent's actions, and provide an example of a situation that illustrates these circumstances.

- Describe the circumstances in which a principal is held liable for the conduct of an agent and list and explain the six factors included in the Restatement of Agency that help a court determine whether an agent or principal will be held liable for the agent's conduct.

- Explain the concept of *indemnification* and provide at least one hypothetical example showing when this concept might be enforced.

The relationships of principals and agents are sometimes complex, and there are many factors that influence the liability of each. This lesson explains that the principal is responsible for many of the acts of the agent and discusses what a principal can do to lessen the chance of inadvertently assuming unwanted liability. It also examines the situations in which a principal can escape liability for the actions of an agent or, alternately, seek compensation when held liable for an agent's wrongdoing.

OVERVIEW

Agents, principals, and third parties all incur substantial responsibilities when they create a contract, responsibilities that, if not handled correctly, can become liabilities. But it's not a simple matter to decide just who is liable when things go awry. For one thing, the degree of authority of the agent is a major factor influencing responsibilities and liabilities. In fact, when determining the liability of principals for acts of their agents, courts always consider the various—and often overlapping—kinds of authority under which agents act for their principals.

Types of Authority

There isn't just one way in which an agent can act for a principal; there are, in fact, seven different types of authority that an agent may possess: express authority, ratification authority, incidental authority, implied authority, emergency authority, and apparent authority. As we review each of these types of authority, take note of the different relationship between the principal and agent.

Express Authority

Express authority is a direct instruction from a principal to an agent to do something. This is perhaps the most straightforward type of authority: Simmons tells Lucas, "Buy the Vale property for $80,000." Courts usually interpret this type of authority narrowly to cover only those express directions given to the agent by the principal. Thus, an accountant's instruction to a consultant to "Go *find* us a larger office" would probably mean to locate rather than contract for one.

Ratification Authority

Ratification authority, also termed "authority by ratification," occurs when the principal accepts the benefits of an agent's actions even when those actions had not previously been authorized. Perhaps paper buyer Hemming often acts as an agent purchasing paper products for a big corporation, LXR, Inc.; because of his connections in the industry and his excellent past performance, LXR trusts Hemming's judgment. If Hemming comes across 1,000 sheets of plastic transparency film for an exceptionally low price, he might think it a perfect purchase for LXR and order it—even though buying plastic film is not part of Hemming's *express* authority. If, however, LXR accepts the transparency film, Hemming has—retroactively—received ratification authority.

Note, however, that the acceptance of benefits ratifies the entire agreement the agent entered into, not just the part that benefitted the principal. Suppose, for example, that an agent was able to buy 1,000 reams of paper at $2.25 a ream only on condition that 2,000 more reams of paper would be purchased at that price before the end of the year. Under these circumstances, the principal could not use the original reams without being bound to also purchase the remaining 2,000 reams.

Incidental Authority

Incidental authority results from the incidental, customary acts an agent performs in order to do his or her duties. An employee hired to oversee the staff of a company would undoubtedly need to interview, hire, evaluate, and, if necessary, fire employees. The authority to carry out these tasks is the incidental authority needed in order to carry out the functions implied in the job. On the other hand, this person's incidental authority would probably not extend to ordering reams of paper.

Of course, the smaller a business is, the more "hats" any one person is likely to wear. A single person may well have incidental authority for both firing employees *and* purchasing office supplies. Obviously, such situations can quickly become confused and troublesome unless all employees and agents know just how far their incidental authority extends. More than one business has had severe difficulties when the actions taken by an employee as part of his or her incidental authority conflicted with the desires of higher-level managers.

Implied Authority

Implied authority is very similar to incidental authority; the difference is that, whereas incidental authority derives from the tasks implicit in the agent's assignments, implied authority derives from the agent's title and the customary tasks a person in that position would conduct. For example, a private secretary would normally have the authority to make appointments for the principal; that would be an example of implied authority. Ordering paper may well be an incidental authority granted to a personal secretary if the secretary has been assigned the task of keeping the office stocked with supplies, but there is nothing implicit in the title "personal secretary" that automatically conveys the authority to order paper. The difference, however, is relatively subtle.

Emergency Authority

The courts consider express, ratification, incidental, and implied authorities to be *actual authorities*—authorities that are routine and, at least ideally, clearly conveyed. There are, however, less prevalent—but still legally valid—types of authorities that may arise in special situations. For example, *emergency authority* arises from an agent's need to perform *uncustomary* actions because of an emergency situation. Suppose a fire started in a leased store and the only person on duty, a sales clerk, put out the fire. In doing so, however, the water used by the clerk damaged the building's floors and ceilings. Is the principal responsible for the clerk's actions?

Putting out fires is clearly not a customary part of the job of sales clerk. But in an emergency situation like this, the clerk was "given" the authority to put out the fire. When doing this caused damage, the clerk's employer — the principal — became responsible for the clerk's actions, just as if putting out fires had been a customary part — and, thus, an incidental authority — of the sales clerk job. As a result, it would be the principal (or, more likely, the principal's insurance company) who would be liable for the costs of repairing the water damage caused by the sales clerk.

Apparent Authority

Apparent authority occurs when a principal lets a third party believe that someone is acting as his or her agent. Apparent authority is not an actual authority because the principal makes the authority known to the third party, not to the agent. Suppose employer Miller tells customer Jackson, "Check with my assistant Rhodes — she knows the price on those." Jackson calls Rhodes and receives a price quote; unfortunately, Rhodes quotes a price that is much lower than what Miller had expected. Under such circumstances, Miller is bound to sell at Rhodes's price quote, even though Rhodes was perhaps unaware that she had been designated an agent in this transaction.

Let's further suppose that Rhodes makes lots of mistakes. This is the final straw for Miller, and he fires Rhodes. Obviously, Rhodes is no longer expected to be an agent of Miller's. However, even when an agency is *revoked* by the principal, that person may remain an apparent agent in the eyes of third parties. It is, therefore, usually important for the employer to inform the third parties of that *revocation*. Otherwise, there's the danger that the fired agent might continue to "transact business" that the principal could be obligated to fulfill.

Authority by Estoppel

We have, therefore, six different authorities under which an agent can act for a principal. There is one other "authority" that needs to be mentioned, even though it is not really an authority at all. *Authority by estoppel*, or *ostensible authority*, is not a grant of authority by a principal. Rather, it is a grant of authority by a court, after the fact, that prevents a principal from profiting from misleading actions that seemed to create an agency relationship. The legal concept of preventing someone from profiting from misleading actions is called *estoppel*. How might estoppel be applied to an agency relationship? Let's look at an example.

Suppose Janeck was trying to sell her lawnmower and told Edmonds about her efforts. Edmonds subsequently offers Janeck's mower for sale to Wallace for $100, an offer Janeck knew about and did nothing to stop. What if Janeck later gets an offer of $150 for the mower? Can she now refuse to sell to Wallace on the grounds that Edmonds wasn't really her agent? Probably not. The court would likely conclude that Edmonds had ostensible authority because Janeck did not stop or revoke Edmonds's offer to Wallace and "allowed" it to appear as though Edmonds were her agent. Janeck would be *estopped* from now, at this late date, denying the agency so as to profit from the better offer.

The numerous types of authorities described above may seem overly precise, but they all have one thing in common: They usually bind the principal to follow the terms of an agreement made by the principal's agent and a third party. If White is Green's agent, and White strikes a bargain with Brown, then Green is bound to act on that bargain. In other words, in the eyes of both the third party and the law, conducting business with the agent is equivalent to conducting business with the principal.

In fact, a principal may be held liable to a third party for failing to meet obligations even though the agent failed to tell the principal about those obligations. Carson, acting as an agent for York, might sell a gross of shutoff valves to a third-party buyer with delivery guaranteed for May 15 and severe penalty payments if the date is not met. Even if Carson fails to tell York of the obligation to have the valves to the buyer by May 15, a late delivery will cost York money. Perhaps this seems unfair, but there is good logic behind this rule. It is part of an agent's fiduciary duty to relate crucial business information to his or her principal. Thus, knowledge given to the agent is assumed to be known by the principal. Such knowledge is called *imputed knowledge*. York may well have a complaint against Carson for failing to fulfill this fiduciary duty, but that is irrelevant to York's obligation to get the valves delivered on time.

Here's another example. Suppose Blaine is a tenant in MacGregor's apartment house. Upset with the apartment's unsanitary conditions, Blaine tells apartment manager Arnold that she is going to sue for return of her rent if MacGregor doesn't correct the problems. At this point, Blaine has every reason to believe that Arnold will tell MacGregor about the conversation and that MacGregor is now responsible for what happens next. A court would probably agree. What's more, it probably wouldn't make much difference if apartment manager Arnold forgets to tell MacGregor of Blaine's complaint. The principal is responsible for the quality of the agents he or she hires, and third parties have the right to expect those agents to carry out their lawful duties — one of which is advising principals of information obtained in the course of the agency relationship.

Disclosed, Undisclosed, and Partially Disclosed Principals

The liability of parties in an agency relationship also depends on whether the principal is *disclosed*, *undisclosed*, or *partially disclosed*.

Disclosed Principal

A principal is a *disclosed principal* when the agent reveals to third parties that he or she represents a named principal. If Judd's business cards say he is a sales representative for Avondale Products, then Avondale is disclosed as his principal.

This disclosure has some special implications. First, it implies that the principal exists. In Judd's case, the parties to whom the business card is handed have the right to expect that Avondale Products truly exists. Second, the disclosure implies that the person is truly an agent for that principal; you cannot go around claiming you're an agent of General Motors if there is actually no relationship. Finally, disclosure implies that the agent is authorized to enter into this kind of contract for his or her principal; Judd's disclosure of his position as sales representative for Avondale Products implies that a third party can count on his authorization to sell Avondale's products.

An agent will not normally be liable for the disclosed principal's failure to comply with the terms of a contract the agent makes with a third party when the agent had the authority to enter into the contract. Assuming that Judd were authorized to make the contract in the first place, if Judd collected $500 from Dunn for the products Dunn ordered, Judd would not be liable to Dunn if the company failed to ship the merchandise. Avondale Products, as the principal, would normally be the liable party. (If Judd were not authorized to make the contract, however, then Judd himself could be sued by the third party for the damages suffered by the nondelivery.)

From the other perspective, suppose Dunn gave Judd a check for $500 for some products Judd had on hand. While normally Avondale Products would sue if Dunn's check bounced, *either* the company or Judd could sue in this case. In other words, an agent can sue a third party for breach if the agent can show that he or she has an interest in the contract. In the situation above, Judd would have such an interest, since it was from his stock that he took the products that the check was intended to cover.

Undisclosed Principal

Liability is different for the parties when the principal is *undisclosed*, that is, when both the principal's existence and identity are unknown to the third party. When the principal is totally undisclosed, the agent may be sued directly by the third party if the contract is not fulfilled. The reasoning here is that when the contract was made, the agent was the only person with whom the third party knew she or he was dealing. (If the principal subsequently is discovered, however, then the third party can include the principal in the suit.) Conversely, the agent may sue the third party if necessary in cases where the principal is undisclosed. Can the undisclosed principal sue the third party? There is no single answer; the nature of the contract itself influences whether the undisclosed principal, in his or her own name, can sue a breaching third party.

Why would a principal want to remain totally undisclosed? There are many reasons — and some of them are illegal. But often a principal simply wishes to keep his or her presence undisclosed because the disclosure might prove embarrassing. It might, for example, be troublesome (although perfectly legal) for a school teacher to own a tavern. In such circumstances, the teacher might have another person buy the tavern as the teacher's agent.

Partially Disclosed Principal

One can also have a situation where the *existence* of a principal is known, but the *identity* is not. In such situations, the principal is said to be *partially disclosed*. The rules applied when there is a partially disclosed principal are much the same as those applied in an undisclosed principal arrangement. One very important similarity is that the agent can be held personally liable; this can happen when the third party contracted with the agent based on the agent's name and reputation. For example, suppose that wealthy socialite Williams tells agent Vaughn to make purchases of land for a new symphony hall but not to let anyone know that she is behind the purchases. It is perfectly acceptable for Vaughn to say that he is buying the land for a principal who does not want her name disclosed. If, however, a seller agrees to sell based on Vaughn's personal reputation for reliability and a breach occurs, either Vaughn or Williams—or both Vaughn and Williams—might be sued.

The Principal's Liability

Respondeat Superior

Agency relationships frequently have agents engage in physical activities or labor on behalf of the principal. Suppose, for example, Nelson ask Unis to pick up the drive shaft for the company delivery van, or to take the Malitas contract to the attorney.

For a variety of reasons, agents often are placed in situations where they come in contact with "the public." And, unfortunately, agents sometimes act in ways that result in injury to some member of the public. Let's suppose, for example, that on his way to pick up the drive shaft, Unis causes an auto accident. In such situations, the principal often has *vicarious liability* for the wrongs of his or her agent. In other words, Nelson may have to pay for damage caused by Unis's wrongdoing.

In general, the law holds that every person is responsible for his or her own wrongs or torts. Thus, the fact that an agent was working for a principal when he or she committed a tort does not relieve the agent of responsibility. But under the legal doctrine of *respondeat superior*—or "let the master answer"—the principal may also be held liable for torts that happen due to an agent's actions. When the agent and principal can both be held responsible for wrongful acts, the liability is said to be *joint and several*—either party (several) or both parties (joint) may be liable.

It's important to understand that the reason the principal is held responsible has nothing to do with his or her personal involvement in the wrongdoing. Rather, the responsibility is based on the fact of agency; the law presumes that if no agency had existed, the activity would not have occurred and no harm would have resulted. Had Nelson not asked Unis to pick up the drive shaft, Unis could not have caused that particular accident. So, because the principal hired the agent, and the agent erred, the principal may have to pay.

That a principal can be held liable is often of great practical benefit to an injured party. Generally speaking, a principal usually has greater financial assets than the agent — more "deep pockets" filled with money from which to pay for the damages. Nelson's corporation is, for example, likely to have more money to compensate the accident victim than delivery driver Unis. Some worry, however, that this philosophy may have gone too far — that suits are directed against the parties with the greatest chance of being able to pay rather than against the parties most responsible for the wrongdoing. But principals are not always found liable for wrongdoings by their agents. In fact, specific conditions must exist before a principal can be held vicariously liable for the actions of an agent.

Application of Respondent Superior

For the principal to be liable for the actions of an agent based on *respondeat superior*, the agent's wrongdoing must have occurred in the *course and scope of employment*. For example, suppose a hardware store employee on lunch break gets into a heated argument about the merit of a professional football team and strikes another patron at the tavern where he's eating. It's unlikely that the hardware store owner would be responsible should the assaulted patron sue; talking about football while on lunch isn't really part of the course and scope of employment of the hardware store job.

In addition, for a principal to be liable for an agent's actions, it must be shown that the nature of the agent's employment was as a "servant" agent — an everyday employee — rather than as an independent contractor. Deciding whether an agent is a servant agent or an independent contractor is often complicated, but one of the most important distinctions is that the principal has the *right to control* the details of the servant agent's work.

The term "servant agent" may seem odd, but the laws governing such principal–agent relationships derive from the master–servant relationships of earlier centuries and include many concepts that governed such relationships. For example, the principal can give direct orders to a servant agent, but does not have the same right to "order around" non-servant agents. As a result, a court was — and still is — likely to hold the principal less responsible for the actions of those non-servant independent contractors than for the principal's own servant agents. If the guests at the Roosevelts' New Year's party get food poisoning from food prepared by the Roosevelts' long-time cook, the Roosevelts may well be responsible. They are less likely to be responsible if the food was prepared by Rose's Custom Catering, the independent contractor hired for this single occasion.

Determining Liability

Remember, though, that once a master–servant relationship is established, the criterion for determining whether the principal is liable becomes whether the wrongdoing of the agent was committed within the course and scope of employment. As in many other areas of the law, a set of guidelines, this time from the *Restatement of Agency* (see page 610 of textbook), is used to make this decision. Note, however, that no single guideline governs the decision; the complete employment picture is considered when deciding whether any particular act of wrongdoing was or was not within the course and scope of employment.

The following are some, but not all, of the factors identified in the Restatement of Agency that are used to determine whether the conduct of the agent was within the course and scope of employment:

- whether the conduct was the type of action the agent was employed to perform,
- whether it took place on work premises during working hours,
- whether it occurred in an effort to serve the purposes of the principal,
- whether it was the type of conduct commonly done by similar agents,
- whether the principal had reason to expect that the type of conduct would occur, and
- the nature of the previous relation between the agent and the principal.

In applying the Restatement of Agency guidelines, the court often asks: "Did the wrongdoing result from a failure to follow instructions?" and "Did the agent fail to act as instructed?" The court will also want to know if the principal was directly responsible for the wrongful act of the agent. After all, sometimes the agent's tort results directly from the instructions of the principal, while other times it's the result of the agent's method of carrying out a general instruction. Contrast, for example, the difference between "Harvey, I want you to burn these leaves this afternoon in the incinerator" and "Harvey, I want you to get rid of the leaves in the yard" should Harvey's out-of-control fire burn down the house next door.

As should be obvious by now, determining the course and scope of employment is not always a cut-and-dried decision. For example, a truck driver's route may be considered his work premises. But what if the driver stopped for coffee at a friend's house, which was directly on his route? When pulling away from the curb in front of the house after the coffee break, he missed seeing an approaching car and drove right into it. Was the driver still on his work premises? Was he acting in the course and scope of employment? In other words, to what extent would the principal be responsible?

A number of factors enter here. The house was on the regular route, true. But what was the employer's policy on coffee breaks? And was this coffee break in compliance with that policy? Could, in fact, the principal have anticipated that the driver would stop for a coffee break? And, of course, we'd need to know if the driver was at fault for the accident. Why did the driver miss seeing the car? Was he perhaps intoxicated or sleepy? Was the truck driver personally reckless or negligent in a way that the principal could not have foreseen?

All in all, principals are not responsible for all possible torts committed by their agents. Still, they may be held liable even when the wrongs committed by their agents came about because the agent didn't follow instructions or act as directed. This is, perhaps, somewhat difficult to understand. After all, it may seem that giving your agent clear instructions to act in a safe and prudent manner should go a long way toward protecting you from liability if your agent acts otherwise. This helps, to be sure, but it does not remove all responsibility.

For example, the security guards at the Collins National Bank are supposed to fire weapons only in response to life-threatening situations. Suppose, however, that while two guards were controlling some intruders, one accidentally fired her weapon, injuring the fellow guard. Would the employer be responsible for the injuries, even though the guard fired her weapon inappropriately? What if she intentionally fired in the air to scare the intruders, but misaimed and hit one of them? In both of these situations, the employer would most likely be held responsible for the damages caused by the agent's wrongdoing, even though the actions came about from a failure to follow instructions.

Why is this so? Remember that the law tends to look beyond the surface event to see the underlying causes for the wrongdoing. If the bank had not hired that guard, if the bank had had a better training program, if the bank had run better weapons safety classes, or if the bank had more rigorously evaluated the likely performance of their guards in stressful situations — any of these might have kept the wrongdoing from occurring. So even though the incident came about in direct opposition to an instruction from the principal (the bank) to an agent (the guard), the court is likely to recognize that the bank had a contributing role in the wrongdoing.

Sometimes, though, it's even hard to know who the responsible principal is. Let's say that the county is putting sewer lines through a rural area. The work has been going well, and today's schedule has everyone working on the segment that goes through Welch's property. The county has contracted with Macadam Excavators for trenching, and Macadam's employee, Ellis, is operating the backhoe used for digging the trench. Welch is on site to help direct action so the backhoe won't tear up an irrigation line. On one occasion, just as owner Welch signals for operator Ellis to stop, Ellis turns to listen to the county engineer directing his work. He misses Welch's signal to stop, the backhoe continues digging, and the bucket rips through Welch's irrigation line.

Clearly, something has gone wrong, but who should pay? Who was the principal — Ellis's boss at Macadam Excavators? The county? Welch? Under what is called the *borrowed servant doctrine*, the law would allocate responsibility for the loss among the parties by asking the following kinds of questions: Who benefitted most from the work? Who had the power to direct the servant? For whom was the work being done? In our example, the county was clearly benefitting the most by the construction of the sewer line, it was directing the work, and the work was being done for the county. Thus, a court (all other things being equal) would probably allocate the greatest share of the responsibility to the county.

Crimes and Intentional Torts

There are times, however, when an agent's actions constitute an intentional tort (wrongdoing) or a criminal act. If the principal directed the agent to commit an intentional tort, there is no question but that *respondeat superior* could be applied to hold the principal liable for any *civil* damages. But where an agent committed an intentional tort without directions from the principal, courts are more reluctant to apply *respondeat superior* against the principal.

Where the agent's actions constitute an actual crime, and if the crime is also not a tort, *respondeat superior* does not apply; it applies only in civil cases. In other words, responsibility for a crime cannot be transferred. As it turns out, of course, directing someone to commit a crime is, in itself, a crime, so it's difficult for a principal to escape criminal punishment if proof of the direct order is available. But where the principal is not connected to the action that constituted the crime, the principal is not subject to criminal penalties.

To illustrate this distinction, let's look at a nightclub bouncer. If, in the course of a night's work, the bouncer became overzealous and caused serious injury to a patron, both the bouncer and the owner of the club would likely be liable for damages in a civil suit for assault and battery. If the injured patron also attempted to press criminal assault charges, only the bouncer—the person who actually committed the alleged assault—would be charged.

Indemnification

By now, it should be clear that a principal is often held liable for damages caused by his or her agent. The law generally wants to correct a wrongdoing, and that often means holding the principal responsible. At the same time, though, there are many cases where the wrongdoing for which the principal is responsible wouldn't have happened had the agent acted more appropriately on the principal's behalf.

In such cases, the principal may be entitled to *indemnification*, the right to be repaid by the agent. Indemnification recognizes that *respondeat superior* is based not on the principal's personal wrongdoing but on the principal's responsibility for the acts flowing from the agency relationship that the principal initiated. Through indemnification, the principal is allowed to seek "reimbursement" from the actual wrongdoer—the agent.

Suppose the patron assaulted by our overzealous nightclub bouncer wins a sizable settlement in his civil case. Suppose, too, that the nightclub had an exemplary training program to teach its bouncers how to handle customers and that this particular bouncer had been evaluated many times and found to be satisfactory. As it turns out, however, the assaulted patron had just married the bouncer's ex-wife, for whom he still had strong feelings. Under these circumstances, the nightclub could make the case that their agent, the bouncer, acted inappropriately and that it is entitled to indemnification. (As a practical matter, of course, the nightclub may never actually collect much money from the bouncer.)

Conversely, an agent may be entitled to indemnification in some situations. For example, suppose an agent signed a contract to purchase a thoroughbred racehorse for an undisclosed principal. After the initial down payment, the principal failed to provide the necessary cash to finish the transaction. If the agent were sued for breach of contract, the agent could seek indemnification from the principal for any losses the agent suffered.

Another case where indemnification might be appropriate is when a principal misleads an agent into believing that necessary permission has been received for an act the principal hires the agent to perform. Suppose, for instance, that a farmer needs an irrigation ditch in a location that is best reached through a neighbor's property. The farmer falsely informs the construction company hired to dig the ditch that he's obtained permission to drive through his neighbor's fields to reach the digging site. If the neighbor subsequently demands reimbursement for damage to his crops caused by the equipment, the construction company can get indemnification from the principal who contracted for the ditch.

Workers are also entitled to indemnification for injuries sustained on the job. If the injury was sustained because of hazardous conditions that the employer had not told the worker about—particularly conditions that the worker could not reasonably have been expected to detect on his or her own—the owner will almost certainly have to indemnify the worker for payments made for medical care. But if injury occurred due to the worker's negligence, the employer will have some defense.

Suppose, though, that a worker's injury results not from the direct negligence of the employer but from that of another worker. Under common law, the *fellow-worker doctrine* prevented the injured worker from recovering money from the principal. Today, however, most states require *workers' compensation*—medical and wage insurance which pays the medical expenses and salary losses of workers injured on the job. Worker's compensation laws typically make it unnecessary to consider either the common-law fellow-worker doctrine or the issue of whether the worker was a contributing cause to his or her own work-related injury. States that have adopted workers' compensation laws see them as creating an equitable balance between the need to compensate workers for work-related injuries and the need for employers to avoid unlimited liability under *respondeat superior*.

SOME PRACTICAL ADVICE

What are the real problem areas for parties in an agency relationship? What cautions should a businessperson exercise in those relationships, whether as principal or agent or third party? What steps are necessary to guard against or fix liability? Clearly, any businessperson acting as either agent or principal can—through carelessness, thoughtlessness, or simple ignorance—end up with complicated and potentially costly liabilities. How can these responsibilities be controlled?

First, remember that whenever one enters into an employment contract, the courts will look to see whether it establishes a master–servant relationship. Most determinations of liability rest on the assumption that the master is responsible for the actions of the servant. Even so, an employer is not responsible for every action of his or her agent, or for every contract. Thus, it's important for both the principal and agent to see that the terms of the relationship are carefully spelled out and understood. Both parties need to pay special attention to the types of authority bestowed on the agent. A good way to assure this is to spend the time necessary to develop and agree to a thorough written employment contract and job description.

Another point to consider carefully is whether the identity of the principal is to be disclosed to third parties. If the existence and identity of the principal are to be clearly disclosed, the principal alone is bound by any contract he or she authorized — unless the agent has also agreed to be bound by the terms of the third-party contract. Thus, one benefit of a disclosed principal relationship is that responsibility for and determination of liability are fairly clear — to the principal, to the agent, and to the third parties.

There is nothing necessarily illegal or even unethical about undisclosed principals, but agents acting for undisclosed principals should be extremely careful. In particular, be sure that the transaction is not regulated by government rules that demand disclosure. Also consider whether any eventual disclosure will result in ill will directed at the agent or the principal. Many businesspeople rely on the character of the people with whom they consider doing business; if they feel "tricked" upon learning of the existence and identity of an undisclosed principal, it may be quite difficult to maintain good ongoing relationships.

Undisclosed principals also need to remember that they are limited in their ability to sue in their own name if the third party breaches the contract. Thus, the principal needs to make sure that the third-party contract is drawn so as to be assignable by the agent. Likewise, the agent–principal contract should specify that the agent is bound to assign the contract to the principal upon the principal's request.

As the agent in an undisclosed principal relationship, remember that the agent has great exposure — it's the agent who will be sued by the third party for a breach by the undisclosed principal; after all, unless the principal is subsequently disclosed, the agent is the only person the third party believes to be responsible. The agent may, in fact, want a written commitment from the principal to accept assignment of the third-party contract immediately upon signing.

As mentioned, an agent should make sure that he or she is not committing any violation by not disclosing the existence and identity of the principal. The agent should consider having the principal affirm in the employment contract that no regulations are being violated and that the principal will provide legal representation and reimburse expenses if regulations are violated. Also, consider a contract clause that provides for specific indemnification by the principal if the principal breaches the third-party contract or if the third party breaches and the agent is obligated to sue for breach.

Regardless of the type of agency relationship, both principal and agent need to remember that the agent is still responsible for his or her own wrongs. Although the doctrine of *respondeat superior* — when the servant does something wrong, the master has to pay — permits wronged third parties to seek relief from principals, the concept of indemnification allows a principal to seek reimbursement from an agent for the agent's wrongful actions. But from a practical viewpoint, indemnification may well be of more theoretical than practical benefit to a principal. For this reason, it's important to avoid situations in which an agent acts wrongfully.

Agency relationships are at the heart of the business world; it would be impossible for commerce to proceed without them. Still, their prevalence doesn't mean they can be handled carelessly. Since an understanding of the exact scope of authority in an agent–principal relationship is the best defense against problems, the time spent in defining and explaining the role of each party will be well spent.

ASSIGNMENTS

- Before you watch the video program, be sure you've read through the preceding overview, familiarized yourself with the learning objectives of this lesson, and looked at the key terms below. Then read Chapters 34 and 35 of Davidson et al., *Business Law*.
- After completing these tasks, view the video program for Lesson 25.
- After watching the program, take time to review what you've learned. First, evaluate your learning with the self-test which follows the key terms. Then, apply and evaluate what you've learned with the "Your Opinion, Please" scenarios at the end of this telecourse study guide lesson.

KEY TERMS

Before you read through the textbook assignment and watch the video program, take a minute to look at the key terms associated with this lesson. When you encounter them in the textbook and video program, pay careful attention to their meaning.

Actual authority	Indemnification
Apparent authority	Joint liability
Authority by estoppel	Ostensible authority
Disclosed authority	Partially disclosed principal
Emergency authority	Ratification
Express authority	*Respondeat superior*
Fellow-worker doctrine	Several liability
Implied authority	Undisclosed principal
Imputed knowledge	Vicarious liability

SELF-TEST

The questions below will help you evaluate how well you've learned the material in this lesson. Read each one carefully, and select the letter of the option that best answers the question. You'll find the correct answer, along with a reference to the page number(s) where the topic is discussed, in the back of this telecourse study guide.

1. Which of the following kinds of authority is never considered an actual authority?
    a. Authority by estoppel
    b. Emergency authority
    c. Express authority
    d. Implied authority

2. Ostensible authority is another name for
    a. authority by ratification.
    b. apparent authority.
    c. incidental authority.
    d. authority by estoppel.

3. Client Kovacs calls independent stock broker Timmons; Timmons is at lunch but her personal secretary Mills says she'll convey Kovacs's sell order to Timmons. Unfortunately, she forgets to do this and Kovacs's stock drops in value. Kovacs views Timmons as being at fault and threatens legal action to recover his lost money. Does Kovacs have grounds for legal action?
    a. No; Timmons is the principal and that's who the transaction has to be with.
    b. No, but only because Mills isn't a licensed broker; the sell order could have been given to any properly licensed person.
    c. Yes, because Mills is Timmons's agent and the concept of imputed knowledge applies.
    d. Yes, because the company involved in the transaction (never an individual) is always the principal and thus any employee of the company has the requisite authority.

4. If the principal in a transaction is disclosed and the principal fails to comply with the terms of the contract, who is *most likely* to be liable?
    a. Only the agent
    b. Only the principal
    c. Both the agent and the principal

5. The rules applied to contracts in which the principal is partially disclosed are quite similar to
    a. those applied to a contract with a disclosed principal.

b. those applied to a contract with an undisclosed principal.

c. *Both* of the above; the extent of disclosure is not an important factor.

d. *None* of the above; the extent of disclosure is dramatically different for each of the three types of disclosure.

6. In judging whether to uphold a non-competition covenant, the courts

a. consider whether irreparable damage might result for the principal.

b. consider whether the covenant would impose unduly harsh conditions on the former agent.

c. *Both* a and b above.

d. *Neither* a nor b, since the only significant factor is what the two parties themselves agreed to in their original contract.

7. Which of the following three situations is the *best* example of vicarious liability?

a. *All* of the following are good examples of vicarious liability.

b. Employer Jacobs is responsible for injuries sustained by driver Keller in a collision with Jacobs's truck driven by employee Howard.

c. Employee Howard is injured when an improperly maintained boiler in Jacobs's factory explodes.

d. Employer Jacobs illegally removes money from the company pension fund.

8. Which of the following factors is *not* a guideline in the *Restatement of Agency* that helps determine whether an employee was acting within the scope of his or her employment?

a. Was the action the kind of duty the employee is normally expected to perform?

b. Was it the intention of the employee to cause the injury?

c. Was the action taken by the employee expected by the employer?

d. Was the action undertaken to serve the "master"?

9. Principal Blanchard is ordered to pay a third party for damages caused by his agent Locke. Blanchard, however, feels that the injury to the third party was entirely Locke's fault. What legal concept may give Blanchard the right to recover money from Locke?

a. Ratification authority

b. The equal-dignities rule

c. Borrowed-servant doctrine

d. Indemnification

10. The application of the concept of *respondeat superior* has which one of the following four effects?

a. It holds the principal civilly liable for the act of his or her agent.

b. It holds the principal criminally liable for the act of his or her agent.

c. It excuses the agent from civil responsibility for his or her actions.

d. It excuses the agent from criminal responsibility for his or her actions.

YOUR OPINION, PLEASE

Read each of the following scenarios and answer the questions about the decisions you would make in each situation. Give these questions some serious thought; they may be used as the basis for the development of a more complex essay. You should base your decisions on what you've learned from this lesson, though you may incorporate outside readings or information gained through your own experience if it is relevant.

Scenario I

Mountain View High School was a private high school that had a reputation for straightening out "problem kids" who couldn't make a go of it in the public schools. Part of its success may have been due to mandatory physical education classes for all grades and mandatory participation in intrascholastic sports programs. Since the school also had an excellent academic record, it attracted students from a wide range of backgrounds and with a wide range of interests.

Over the years, school officials had received complaints that some teachers might be a little too zealous in straightening out the problem kids. In particular, rumors — supported by letters from some parents — talked about teacher Dan Altman being too tough on students. Altman, however, also happened to be the most successful football coach in Mountain View's history. School officials realized that he was a tough disciplinarian with a hair-trigger temper, but also believed those characteristics were part of what made him a successful coach. They felt he treated all students the same way, so they disregarded what some students had voiced as his negative attitude toward "long-haired creeps" in his classes.

During a break between classes one day, Coach Altman discovered one of his physical education class "creeps" behind the gym having a cigarette. Both he and the student, Tom Nero, knew that smoking on campus was strictly against the rules at Mountain View. Altman was having a bad day, and seeing Nero sneaking a cigarette was the last straw. As he reached over to slap the cigarette from Tom's lips, Coach Altman misjudged the distance and his strength. The force of his slap whipped Tom's head back; it struck the building and Tom crumpled to the ground, unconscious.

Coach Altman was charged in criminal court with assault and battery and found guilty. In a civil action against Altman, the Neros also sued the school principal and the board of directors of the private school, seeking not just normal damages but also punitive damages.

What's your opinion? Based on what you know of the situation, do you think the court will support the Neros' suit against the principal and board of directors as well as against Altman? Do you think the Neros were justified in naming them in addition to Altman in their suit? Does the fact that earlier abuse complaints had been made against Coach Altman have any bearing on this case?

- Is the Nero suit for normal and punitive damages against the principal and board of directors likely to be upheld in court? Why or why not?

- What facts support your argument?

- What factors might an attorney cite in arguing against your view?

- What steps, if any, might Mountain View High School have taken to prevent the lawsuit in this situation?

- What steps, if any, might Tom Nero's parents have taken to avoid this situation?

Scenario 2

Mary Alice Peters, the facilities manager of Samuels and Parker, Inc., was asked by her employer, company president Don Samuels, to locate new office space for the company headquarters. Samuels told her to find a few good prospects and then give the details of the possible arrangements to him.

Peters located a number of prospects but was particularly pleased with an excellent building at a very good price. This building was a real find, but the lease rate was going to increase more than 20% the following week when owner Brody turned over building leasing and management to a realty firm. Unfortunately for Peters, however, Samuels was now on a trek in Nepal and out of communication until after the broker was to assume responsibility for leasing the building.

After consulting with the company vice presidents, Peters decided to call building owner Brody. She informed Brody that she had not been authorized to lease a property, only to locate one, and that her boss was out of town until the end of next week. Peters said that she was confident her boss would want the property but that she could not commit the company to the lease. As a sign of interest, however, she gave Brody a $5,000 company check to hold the property—again emphasizing that even though she had only been authorized to locate the property, she was sure her boss would want it.

When Samuels returned, he was, as Peters expected, quite pleased with the property. Unfortunately, neither Peters nor the company vice presidents had informed the company board of directors about the plans to lease the Brody building. And while president Samuels, as he well knew, had been authorized to negotiate on a building, the final decision to lease had to be the board's. But when the matter was brought before the board, the directors, fearing an impending recession and accompanying drop in company sales, refused to authorize the lease of the Brody building.

Peters then asked Brody to return the $5,000 deposit. Brody refused, saying that the $5,000 had clearly been paid as an option on the building and that she had, in fact, turned down offers from other potential lessees. The Samuels and Parker board sued to recover the money, claiming that Peters was not an authorized agent of the company and, further, that Brody knew it.

What's your opinion? Based on what you know of the situation, was Peters an authorized agent for Samuels and Parker? Did Peters do anything wrong? Is Brody likely to be able to keep the $5,000?

- Is the Samuels and Parker suit likely to be upheld in court? Why or why not?
- What facts support your answer?
- What factors might an attorney cite in arguing against your view?
- What steps, if any, might Brody have taken to prevent a lawsuit in this situation?
- What steps, if any, might Samuels have taken to protect the interests of Samuels and Parker, Inc., in this situation?

26

Real Property

LEARNING OBJECTIVES

Upon completing your study of this lesson, you should be able to

- Define the term *property*, and distinguish between *real* and *personal* property, using examples to illustrate the distinction.

- Explain the concept of *property rights* and discuss seven general rights to which a person is automatically entitled by virtue of property ownership.

- Explain in detail the criteria used in determining whether a given item (e.g., a rug) will be defined as *real* property.

- List and discuss four ways in which an owner can acquire real property.

- Discuss several ways in which an owner may lose real property, and the steps that may be taken to protect real property.

- Explain the general requirements governing the rental or lease of real property and the rights and duties of tenants and landlords.

- List and discuss the forms of joint ownership of real property.

Lesson 26 introduces the legal concept of property and the rights associated with owning it. We'll note the two different types of property that the law recognizes — *real property* and *personal property* — and discuss the sometimes subtle differences between them. The lesson then focuses on real property — land and the things permanently attached to it — and discusses the ways that real property can be acquired, lost, and protected from loss. The rights and obligations of landlords and tenants are also reviewed, as well as the arrangements by which several persons may own property jointly.

OVERVIEW

Property — and the rights associated with its ownership — is central to our legal system. So deeply is the idea of owning property ingrained in us, in fact, that we often take the rights of ownership for granted. As a result, many people are surprised when they first encounter the sometimes confusing legal requirements that limit their rights to use or transfer their property.

But "property" doesn't mean only tangible objects like houses or land. Property may also refer to a package of legal rights connected to an object, such as the lease of a building, which gives the owner of the lease the right to occupy and use the space, or — in many cases — the right to sell or otherwise transfer those rights of use to someone else. Property can also refer to legal rights that are economically valuable but not connected to a physical object, such as copyrights, patents, and trademarks. The name of a business, for example, is considered property.

A Definition of Property and Types of Property

In general, property may be defined as *any valuable asset*. And inherent in the term are legal concepts that specify the ways a person can acquire and transfer ownership of an asset. These legal concepts apply for the two major categories of property — *real property* and *personal property* — although some of the details are different for each category. This lesson focuses on real property — land, interests in land, and things permanently attached to land, including buildings, roadways, and trees. Personal property refers to any other valuable asset, and it is the subject of another lesson.

Property Rights

What does it mean to "own" your home or business? For legal purposes, it means that you have some specific rights:

- You can use that property personally,

- You can give or rent the use of the property to someone else,

- You can improve, sell, or abandon the property, or

- You can use the property as collateral to secure a loan.

If your property is a business — Louisiana Ribs, let's say — then these rights apply to the business name as well as the appliances, tools, supplies, and inventory you have accumulated. These rights also apply to your lease on and improvements to (within limits) the business location. And when you tire of cooking ribs and want to sell your business, you have that right.

If your property is land and the buildings on it, however, you are often further entitled to its continued use and enjoyment *in its present condition*. Does that right mean that you can stop construction of a three-story addition to your neighbor's house because it will block your view of a mountain? Some state courts have ruled that it does. Do you have the right to use your property in *any* way you want? Not exactly, since ownership does not entitle you to put that property to "illegal" use, which includes criminal activity as well as violation of land-use planning and zoning restrictions that a governmental agency may impose.

The rights of ownership may seem simple in the abstract. But as with many areas of the law, applying those rights to real-life situations can be complicated and a fertile ground for misunderstandings and litigation. Distinguishing between real property and personal property when you sell a house, for instance, is one of the areas where misunderstandings may well arise.

Real Property versus Personal Property

Can you take your rugs with you when you've sold your house? Your favorite rosebush? The antique pedestal sink you installed in the bathroom? Real property, remember, is land and things that are permanently attached to it, while personal property is movable goods.

But personal property can become permanently attached to land or buildings. When this happens, what was personal property becomes real property and is called a *fixture* — property that at one time was movable and independent of real estate but is now attached to it. Your throw rugs, for instance, remain personal property. But wall-to-wall carpeting — personal property when purchased in the store — becomes a fixture and is considered real property once it is "permanently" installed in the house. Of course, the wall-to-wall carpeting can, with only moderate effort, be removed; people obviously change carpeting occasionally or decide to refinish the wood floors hidden under the carpet. Nevertheless, it takes effort to turn the property back into movable property and restore the real property (the floor) to a usable condition once the fixture (the carpeting) is removed. For this reason, the wall-to-wall carpeting — along with sinks, overhead light fixtures, and the like — takes on the character of real property and, as such, is called a fixture.

In determining whether property is real or personal, courts will also look at the reasonable expectations most people would have about the property; that is, is it reasonable to think that the property is permanently affixed — that is, a fixture — and secondly, how much damage would be caused if the property is removed? Your pedestal sink, for example, became a fixture of the real property once it was connected to the plumbing since it would require effort to make it movable again. Also, it would cause a considerable amount of damage if it were removed.

What about your rosebush? Once planted, it's no longer readily movable, so it's probably a fixture. Suppose, though, that your property has an acre of walnut trees ready for harvest. The walnuts are currently on immovable trees, but left to themselves, the walnuts are going to fall to the ground, where they'll be extremely movable. Are the walnuts real or personal property? It turns out that in this case, the Uniform Commercial Code addresses the issue directly: if the buyer is going to remove them, the buyer has purchased real property; if the seller is going to remove them, the buyer has purchased personal property. We point this out not so that you'll know how to sell a walnut farm, but as an example of the intricacies involved in determining whether property is real or personal property.

Acquiring Real Property

People may acquire real property through original occupancy, voluntary transfer, and inheritance. Most people acquire real property by inheriting or buying it. But a person may also gain title to real property by means of an outright grant of land by the government (a condition known as *original occupancy*), or gain possession of formerly public land by means of *homestead entry laws*. These methods are less prevalent than they were in the more formative years of the country, but they still exist.

Property gets inherited in two ways. Usually, the owner specifies in his or her will who the property is to be transferred to — that is, who inherits the property. But if a property owner dies without a valid will, the ownership of that person's property will generally be transferred by means of the *intestate succession statute* of the state in which the property is located. In other words, a law in your state says who gets the property — both real and personal — of someone who dies without a will.

The Use of Deeds

Whether the title to land is transferred by grant, inheritance, or purchase, however, the process always requires the use of a written *deed*. A deed describes in detail the land being transferred and generally includes additional information such as the amount paid, any ownership rights *not* transferred, and any promises the buyer makes to the seller. When property is transferred by inheritance, the court system will create the deed that transfers the legal title.

One critical concept to remember is that no voluntary transfer of title is ever possible until a deed is *written* and *delivered*. The fact that rich parent Kaiser tells his son that he can have the family oil well when he turns 21 carries no weight if the promise isn't followed up with a written and delivered deed. Further, in most instances the transfer should be *recorded* by a prescribed government official, usually the county clerk or recorder, in the official land records of the state. This helps ensure that all interested parties can tell who really owns the land, and helps defeat fraudulent claims.

Types of Deeds for Real Property

It might seem that transferring real property is something like writing a contract; one needs to put down on paper the details of the sale and record the contract with the proper government official. Well, it's not quite that simple. Let's create a scenario that, while perhaps not common, is certainly not farfetched.

After looking around, Herbek found the place of her dreams—five acres and a house along a meandering stream. On her real estate agent's advice, Herbek required that the seller, Ramirez, transfer the property by means of a *warranty deed*. As her agent explained it to Herbek, a warranty deed is an "insured" way to transfer land—the deed contains a number of implied promises to the effect that the seller is conveying a good and marketable title. The sale proceeded and Herbek moved onto the property.

But three years after she moved in, Herbek receives a call from Ramirez's ex-wife. The former Mrs. Ramirez claims that, as part of a divorce settlement, she has title to two acres of the property that her ex-husband sold Herbek. Mrs. Ramirez says she'll gladly give up her claims to the two acres—but on condition that Herbek pay her for the two acres and refrain from using them until the transfer is completed. Herbek isn't too happy with that alternative; she's already built a barn on the land in question and, besides, she already paid for the land once. Under the conditions of the warranty deed, is Herbek protected from Mrs. Ramirez's claim?

If Mr. Ramirez had conveyed the property to Herbek with a *quitclaim deed*—in which the grantor simply releases his interest in the property without making any promises about his interest in it—then she probably would have no protection. But since Mr. Ramirez used a warranty deed to convey the property to Herbek, he has broken its covenants and he is therefore required to defend Herbek against his ex-wife's claim. In other words, a deed can be either a warranty deed or a quitclaim deed, and the protections afforded by each differ significantly.

Protection of Real Property

It is necessary for an owner to protect property. Property can be lost by adverse possession, operation of the law, action of the government, easement, or action of nature. In the previous example, regardless of the type of deed, Herbek might have had a clearer claim to the disputed two acres if she were able to counterclaim title under the condition of adverse possession. *Adverse possession* occurs when someone tries to take title and possession of real estate from the owner by openly occupying and using the land as their own. But Herbek had not held the land long enough to qualify for clear title under adverse possession; the laws of her state required a ten-year holding period. Was Herbek out of luck?

Perhaps not, since the laws of her state reduce the holding period to only three years when the adverse possessor (Herbek) takes possession under what is called color of title. *Color of title* refers to the conditions under which the adverse possessor takes possession. Clearly, Herbek thought she had a legal right to take possession of the property; she had a deed from Rameriz, no one had challenged the transaction, everything seemed perfectly normal. What's more, Herbek had also been paying the county real estate taxes on the property, another condition for demonstrating adverse possession. The important point here is not so much to understand everything about color of title and adverse possession (although those are important concepts), but to notice how complicated Herbek's initially straightforward purchase of five acres has become.

Involuntary Transfers by Operation of the Law

Another way people can lose property is by operation of the law. Suppose Miller bought a house, but when she lost her job, she was unable to make the mortgage payments. The bank threatened *foreclosure* proceedings against her, but her uncle loaned her the money to cover what she owed and in return took an interest in the property as security for his loan. Soon after, however, Miller was involved in a traffic accident, the damages from which exceeded her insurance coverage. One of the injured parties gained a judgment against her for that non-covered amount. Miller herself didn't have enough money to pay the judgment, but didn't want the judgment holder to get a court order requiring the sale of her house to pay the judgment. Miller gathered together all the money she had, and then went to her uncle, who again came to the rescue. During that time, Miller was having a barn built on her property, but the costs of the auto accident prevented her from paying the carpenters, who filed a *mechanics' lien* against the property for the value of labor and materials still owing them. Under the laws of the state in which Miller lives, the carpenters weren't able to force a sale of the property to get their money, but they did prevent her from selling the property until she paid them. Miller has only one house, but here we find five parties—the bank, Miller's uncle, the accident victim, the carpenters, and Miller herself—with some interest in the property.

Or consider Polk: His ten acres border a county park that the county commission was interested in expanding. Since government bodies have the right to take private lands for public use (called the right of *eminent domain*), the county wants to acquire Polk's property as an addition to the park. When exercising the right of eminent domain, the governmental agency must pay an owner a reasonable amount for the land and also establish a legitimate public use for the property. What if Polk doesn't want to sell the property? In this particular situation, Polk's normal rights to do what he wants with the property can be overridden.

Another example of operation of the law is provided by Merrick Enterprises; it bought land on which to build a twenty-six-story office tower. As the building was being constructed, city authorities received complaints that the upper stories blocked the view of the city's landmark mountain for several hundred thousand commuters traveling on a main freeway into the city each day. Would Merrick have to reduce the height of its building? Possibly; the commission had to examine the city's *zoning laws* — which restrict how property may be used — to see if the building violated any conditions. There was a thirty-one-story restriction on height — which Merrick met — but nothing to prevent blocking the scenic vista the commuters had enjoyed. As a result, Merrick was allowed to build the building it wanted. However, all of the authorities felt that there *should* have been a restriction on the books to protect this special vista; if it had been there, Merrick would have been limited by the zoning laws in its normal right to do what it wanted with its property.

Easements

An owner can be limited in the use of all or part of property through an *easement*, a legal concept which gives another the right to use an owner's property in a particular manner. Many property owners, sometimes without knowing it, have property with easements to water, gas, and electric utility companies; these easements give the companies the right to use the property for their utility lines and the right to come on the property to maintain the pipes and wires. But some easements are used on a daily basis. Suppose Tewes had once owned a ten-acre parcel but had sold the five acres farthest from the road to Mayer years before. Mayer and Tewes were close friends and Mayer was allowed access to his five acres through Tewes's property. When Tewes died, his five acres from the original ten acres were sold to Jenkins.

Jenkins doesn't have any motivation to continue allowing Mayer to use the old access — now on Jenkins's property. Given that you are usually permitted to do what you want with your land when it doesn't violate statutes and regulations, could Jenkins prevent Mayer from crossing his property? Probably not. Having no other way to get to his property, Mayer would undoubtedly petition the court for an easement *by necessity*. A court would probably grant it, too, especially since Mayer's only access to his property is across Jenkins's land. It also helps Mayer's argument that he originally had an agreement from the initial property owner Tewes and came to rely on it. If Tewes and Mayer had written their agreement of use and met the requirements of a valid transfer, this written "transfer of rights to use" would have been an easement that went with the Tewes property when it was sold to Jenkins — and Jenkins would have been bound by it.

Transfers by Action of Nature

Here is one last example of a threat to a person's normal rights to property. Nash lives on a creek that floods virtually every year; Tucker lives about a mile downstream where the creek widens and flows more slowly. Every year, the flooded creek washes away part of Nash's land and deposits the soil downstream on Tucker's property. In effect, Nash's land is shrinking while Tucker's is growing. Can Nash do anything about this? Not from a legal perspective; the situation is changing slowly enough (and by an "act of God" at that) that Nash wouldn't be allowed to, say, hire a dump truck and loader and go recover his land from Tucker. In effect, Nash no longer owns the land. (On the other hand, if a windstorm blew Nash's canoe into the creek and it floated down to Tucker's property, the rapid nature of the event wouldn't cause any transfer of ownership and Nash could recover the canoe.)

Renting Property

As mentioned, one of the rights of property ownership is the right to rent or lease the *use* of the property to another person. When real property is rented or leased, the property owner is referred to as the *landlord*, the property renter is called the *tenant*, and the legal relationship of landlord and tenant is called a *tenancy*. These same terms apply whether the rental agreement applies to a commercial tenant renting space to operate his or her business or a residential tenant renting an apartment in which to live.

Most arrangements in which a tenant is using the property of a landlord can be classified as one of four types of tenancies — distinguished according to the length or nature of the use of the rental property: tenancy for years, periodic tenancy, tenancy at will, and tenancy by sufferance.

The two most common tenancies are tenancy for years and periodic tenancy. When Fong signs a rental agreement to use Young's store for a set period of time, with a specific starting and ending date, they have created a *tenancy for years*. This period of time can be any length — two months, five years, ninety-nine years, etc. (Note, incidentally, that the Statute of Frauds in most states will require landlord and tenant to put the rental agreement in writing if the rental period is to be for longer than one year.)

On the other hand, Fong may not want to commit for a specific period of time — perhaps she's unsure of how successful her business will be and doesn't want to commit to, say, a five-year rental agreement. In this case, she might prefer a *periodic tenancy*, a rental agreement that has a fixed starting date but no fixed termination date. In a periodic tenancy, the rental period continues for successive periods (such as a month) until terminated by the landlord or the tenant after proper notice. The rental period is usually specified in the rental agreement, as is the amount of notice — often sixty or ninety days — required to terminate the tenancy.

The other two types of tenancies, tenancies at will and tenancies by sufferance, aren't as common. *Tenancies at will* can be thought of as day-to-day tenancies. They allow the landlord or tenant to terminate the agreement at any time — not the most stable arrangement from either a landlord's or a tenant's perspective. A *tenancy by sufferance* describes the landlord–tenant relationship when a tenant wrongfully continues in possession of the rented property after the expiration of any rental agreement. The tenant is in possession only at the sufferance of the landlord — until the landlord initiates legal action to evict the tenant.

Rights and Duties of Landlords and Tenants

But regardless of the sort of tenancy that exists, the rights and duties of landlords and tenants in commercial real estate transactions remain generally the same. Let's look at the relationship between Iwasaki and his landlord Baker, who owns the building Iwasaki rents and the two buildings on either side of it. As with most commercial tenancies, by signing a year's lease on the building for his photography business, Iwasaki has gained the *right to exclusive possession and control* of the building. Baker, however, retains the *right to enter the premises in case of an emergency*.

Iwasaki will have to install certain fixtures in order to carry out his business, including dark-room equipment; the tenancy permits this. According to the lease, those fixtures remain Iwasaki's property if they are removed before the end of the lease, but if the removal causes any damage, he will generally be held responsible. Baker can expect Iwasaki to conduct a business compatible with the overall nature of the building, while Iwasaki can expect Baker to keep the building in good condition. (In the case of residential housing, in fact, some state courts have held that a lease implies a *warranty of habitability*. This means that, by offering to rent the property, the landlord promises that the premises will be fit for living.)

Another implied condition that states recognize is that the owner will protect the tenant's right to quiet enjoyment or use of the premises. Should Baker rent the building next to Iwasaki's to a rock band whose ear-splitting practice sessions interfere with Iwasaki's work, and should Baker refuse to stop the activity, Baker's actions might be interpreted by some courts as constituting *constructive eviction*. This means that the photographer can probably move out without any further liability to pay rent on the balance of his lease.

Baker has the right to retake possession at the end of the lease's term, and—in most leases—the landlord usually reserves the right to terminate the lease if the tenant breaches any promises, including the promise to make the lease payments on time. Thus, if Iwasaki does not pay for the space, Baker may sue him for unpaid rent, start eviction proceedings, place a lien on Iwasaki's personal property on the premises, and perhaps even lock Iwasaki out of the building. The landlord also has the right to collect for any damages—beyond normal wear and tear—that tenants and their clients or guests may cause. For protection against such damages, landlords often collect a *security deposit*.

Now suppose that Iwasaki's photography studio isn't catching on and, thinking the grass greener elsewhere, he takes his equipment (causing some damage during its removal) and leaves town. Landlord Baker now has an empty building and six months more time on the lease with Iwasaki. Should he go ahead and try to lease the building as is or attempt to repair the damage Iwasaki caused? And what will happen if Iwasaki changes his mind in two weeks and returns, expecting to use the remaining time on his lease?

Things could get pretty complicated pretty fast, so first off, Baker needs to confer with his lawyer, so he doesn't do anything that would get him in any deeper problems. And what the lawyer will probably suggest is that Baker first try to verify that Iwasaki is gone for good, that he does not want to continue the lease. After that, however, Baker's next responsibility is to *mitigate damages*. That is, Baker must look after his own best interests, keeping the damage from the apparent breach of the lease as small as possible.

For example, in most commercial real estate tenancies, landlords have the obligation to diligently try to re-rent the property. This means they must exert good-faith efforts to quickly locate a new tenant and obtain a lease that is the most favorable as possible to them. Thus, if the abandoning tenant is found to have wrongfully abandoned the lease, the money collected under the lease with the new tenant will be applied against the money the former tenant owes the landlord. A landlord who does not attempt to mitigate damages cannot expect that the court will force the abandoning tenant to pay every cost. In our example, for instance, Baker cannot expect the court to order Iwasaki to pay six months of rent for the building unless Baker diligently tries and fails to get another tenant. Simply letting the building sit empty assuming that Iwasaki will eventually have to pay his full lease obligation would be a poor decision by Baker.

Some of the concepts underlying commercial tenancies also pertain to residential tenancies. However, the specific laws regulating the rights and responsibilities of residential landlords and tenants are often very different. The residential statutes are more protective of tenants' rights than are the laws governing commercial leases. For example, in most states, landlords of residential property cannot lock tenants out of the housing or hold personal property as security against tenants' wishes—even if the tenant is behind in paying the rent. Note, too, that the applicable laws vary from state to state, so it is not a safe assumption to think that the rights and responsibilities of landlords and tenants in Oregon are the same as those in Florida.

Co-Ownership of Property

So far we've talked about the rights and duties of *a* property owner. In practice, however, it's often the case that more than one person owns the real property in question. And, not surprisingly, there are many different business and personal reasons why people would choose to co-own property and many different objectives that they would have for the property. To accommodate this diversity, the law recognizes four different forms of joint real property ownership.

The four forms of co-ownership are joint tenancy, tenants in common, tenants by the entirety, and community property ownership. They have some points in common; for instance, they usually allow each owner the *undivided right to use* the whole property, even though some of the owners may have contributed more money or talent or work in acquiring the property and "own" a greater percent of the value of the property. But the differences among the four forms of co-ownership are significant, a principal one being the amount of freedom an owner has to transfer his or her interest to a third party.

Consider the case of Carlos and Reina, brother and sister. After serving as senior designer in a big New York company, Reina wants to return home. She persuades Carlos, an account manager for a public relations firm in their home town, to join with her to open their own design firm. Reina has the money to back the company and the design skills honed by her years in New York. Carlos has the local contacts and personality to bring in both the big and the promising small accounts. They consider renting office space in a large office building but instead decide to buy an old Victorian house in the newly developing "arts" section of town. But before concluding the purchase, they have to decide how they will co-own the property.

Tenants in Common

They might choose to become *tenants in common*. Here, a number of individual owners—or "tenants" as they are called—own the property together. Each has a right to use the whole property, even when the tenants' interests in the property are not equal. Each tenant in common may sell, assign, will, or give away his or her legal share of the property. What's more, a creditor of an individual owner may lay claim only to that tenant's interest in the whole property. Given that Reina apparently has more money than Carlos, this might be the preferable form of co-ownership.

Joint Tenants with Rights of Survivorship

They could also be *joint tenants with rights of survivorship*. This form varies from tenants in common in that each tenant has an equal interest in the property, and when one tenant dies, his or her interest passes to the remaining co-tenants. In effect, the tenant who outlives the other co-tenants will eventually own the property alone. In fact, even if a joint tenant sells or gives away his or her interest in the property, the buyer or transferee would *not* receive the survivorship rights of a joint tenant. Carlos and Reina may have no problem with the idea of the house passing to the other but, remember, Carlos will have to have an equal interest in the property—something that may not reflect the amount of money he can contribute to the purchase of the house.

Tenants by the Entirety

The remaining two forms of co-ownership require that the two tenants be husband and wife. The form called *tenants by the entireties* has ownership passing to the surviving spouse upon the death of the other, the same as for joint tenancy. Unlike joint tenancy, however, one spouse is generally not allowed to dispose of his or her partial interest unilaterally unless they obtain a legal separation or divorce.

Community Property

But tenancies by the entireties are not recognized in the handful of states that are *community property states*. The concept of *community property* is based on the idea that a marriage is a *financial* partnership and that one-half of all property accumulated during marriage belongs to each spouse, regardless of how the property came to be owned. Community property (which, like tenants by the entireties, applies only to husbands and wives) does not have a survivorship feature. As a result, either spouse may will his or her share to someone other than the surviving spouse. In fact, each spouse might well be perceived—at least theoretically—as owning half a toaster, half a blender, half a sofa, and, perhaps, half a house.

Community property ownership does not, however, give a husband the right to sell his half-interest in the toaster to another party, nor could the wife decide to sell her half of the house to her brother *while the marriage still exists*. But once the marriage is dissolved, either by divorce or the death of one spouse, the separate-but-equal-interest concept becomes applicable. In other words, while the wife cannot sell her half of the house to her brother while the marriage exists, she may be able to will it to him. In practice, however, the laws of community property states vary from state to state, and there are restrictions on what can be done and what counts as community property during the course of the marriage.

SOME PRACTICAL ADVICE

What are the most important things to keep in mind when buying, selling, or renting property? First, it's useful to remember that—for legal purposes—property is defined as any valuable asset, including land and buildings as well as legal rights that are not connected to an object, such as a business name. In fact, people sometimes own property—an easement, copyright on a textbook, or rights to season tickets for a pro football team—that they don't think of as property. Property also carries with it a set of specific legal rights; remember, ownership of property usually entitles a person to use, rent, improve, abandon, give away, or pledge the property.

Whether you are buying, selling, inheriting, or giving away property, however, it's useful to keep in mind the distinction between *real property* and *personal property*. Whether property is defined as real or personal depends on whether it is permanently affixed to land or a building; personal property is generally movable. This concept becomes important if you are going to "improve" property that you own or rent. Your improvements were probably personal property when you bought them, but in the course of the improvement activity they became affixed to the real property. This makes them "fixtures" and they are now part of the real property. This means that they stay with the real property when you vacate it unless you specifically contract otherwise. Renters—commercial and residential—need to understand this distinction and find out—before they sign a lease or make improvements—whether they will be compensated for the value of their improvements once the lease is over.

Remember, too, that transfers of real estate, by most states' Statute of Frauds, must be in writing to be enforceable. The most common written instrument for transfer is a deed—either a warranty deed, grant deed, or quitclaim deed. The type that provides the most protection for a buyer is a warranty deed; if you aren't receiving a warranty deed in a real estate transfer, be especially careful to check the seller's ability to convey a good and marketable title. (And, as you probably know, you can usually obtain *title insurance* for a real estate transaction; while title insurance doesn't affect any of the underlying legal principles, it does transfer the financial responsibility for a clear title from buyer and seller to the title insurance company.)

Property ownership does, in a general sense, convey the right to retain and use the property as the owner wishes. Recognize, though, that there are many legally sanctioned threats to that freedom. Failure to make required payments on a mortgage or a loan secured by the property, failure to pay a legal judgment, or failure to pay workers who supplied labor or materials for the construction or improvement of the real property can all cause the loss of ownership. But since all of these transfers occur after a full legal hearing with notice to the owner, it should not come as a surprise to the property owner.

Occasionally more surprising are the effects that government bodies can have on property ownership. Private land necessary for public use can be "taken" by the government against the owner's wishes—so long as the owner is paid a reasonable amount for the land. Use of property can be (and, in most cities, usually is) restricted by zoning and planning laws. When government intends to regulate private property, however, elaborate procedures allowing for public and interested-party participation must be followed. Unfortunately, some property owners don't pay proper attention to these events. Wise property owners will know what plans governmental agencies have for their own and adjacent property. (It is particularly important to check on these matters prior to acquiring a new piece of property; it's entirely possible that, due to government restrictions, the property may already be unsuitable for the use planned for it.)

Like ownership, tenancy carries with it a host of restrictions. As a landlord, for example, don't assume that because you "own" the property, you can do as you please. In fact, this is very far from the truth. And as a tenant, don't lose sight of the numerous obligations you've undertaken. Keeping good landlord–tenant relations and living with a lease is most importantly a matter of communication—letting the other party know what's on your mind and what's going "wrong" with the building or relationship. Remember, though, that this lesson has focused principally on landlord–tenant relationships where the tenant was renting commercial property—not residential property to serve as the tenant's home. Very special laws apply in residential landlord–tenant situations, and anyone considering becoming a residential landlord should get detailed guidance from a lawyer.

Finally, if you are considering purchasing real property with another person, consider the different types of co-ownership arrangements under which title to the property can be held. Each has its own set of benefits, rights, and limitations, and how each will affect you is governed chiefly by the laws of the state in which the property is located and the laws of the state(s) in which you and the proposed co-owner reside. Legal counsel would also be helpful here.

In fact, regardless of how you become involved with real property, it's wise to become acquainted with the applicable state and local statutes. There are occasionally classes and seminars that discuss these matters, and sometimes trade associations, business groups, and government agencies publish relevant documents. Or, spend a short amount of time with a lawyer to learn the basics of what's expected of you. The rights of ownership and tenancy can become tangled and complex—

and are more likely to become so for persons who are ignorant of the applicable laws and regulations than for those who know ahead of time how to arrange their affairs.

ASSIGNMENTS

- Before you watch the video program, be sure you've read through the preceding overview, familiarized yourself with the learning objectives for this lesson, and looked at the key terms below. Then, read Chapter 49 of Davidson et al., *Business Law*.
- After completing these tasks, view the video program for Lesson 26.
- After watching the program, take time to review what you've learned. First, evaluate your learning with the self-test which follows the key terms. Then, apply and evaluate what you've learned with the "Your Opinion, Please" scenarios at the end of this telecourse study guide lesson.

KEY TERMS

Before you read through the textbook assignment and watch the video program, take a minute to look at the key terms associated with this lesson. When you encounter them in the textbook and video program, pay careful attention to their meaning.

Adverse possession	Mechanics' lien
Color of title	Periodic tenancies
Community property	Personal property
Constructive eviction	Quitclaim deed
Easement	Real property
Fixture	Right of eminent domain
Foreclosure	Tenancies at sufferance
Grant deed	Tenancies at will
Homestead entry laws	Tenancies for years
Joint ownership	Tenants by the entirety
Joint tenants with rights of	Tenants in common
survivorship	Warranty deed
Lease	Warranty of habitability

SELF-TEST

The questions below will help you evaluate how well you've learned the material in this lesson. Read each one carefully, and select the letter of the option that best answers the question. You'll find the correct answer, along with a reference to the page number(s) where the topic is discussed, in the back of this telecourse study guide.

1. For only one of the four objects given below would there be much dispute over whether it is real or personal property. Which one is not clearly one or the other?

   a. The drapes covering a bay window
   b. A ceiling-mounted light fixture
   c. A dried flower arrangement designed for the entry of the house
   d. A tall ladder needed to clean the second-story windows

2. Deeds and documents that transfer important property interests should be in writing. Which of the following would *least likely* need to be written?

   a. A gift of land to a relative
   b. The refinancing of a first mortgage by a private investor
   c. The trade of a station wagon for a pickup truck
   d. A board of directors' motion for the corporation to purchase a building lot for its new headquarters

3. Which of the following four people is likely to be living on land acquired through *original occupancy*?

   a. Boone, whose great-great-grandfather was the first to plant crops on his sixty-five acres of Ohio farmland
   b. Michaels, the first person to live on a lot in the newly developed Waterhouse subdivision
   c. Bekins, whose house in Massachusetts was built the year the United States declared independence
   d. Bothel, whose California family winery was first started on a land grant from the Spanish government

4. Durbin is the only surviving relative of his grandfather, a successful silver miner. Further, the old miner has said that he wants Durbin to have control of the silver mine when he dies. The old miner dies on July 23. On July 24, Durbin receives a lucrative offer for the mine from a large mineral company. Can he sell the mine now?

   a. No; Durbin doesn't have any rights to the mine.
   b. Maybe; if the miner died without a will, the mine is now Durbin's. (If there is a will, Durbin will have to wait to see if he inherited the mine.)

c. Maybe; if the miner lived in a community property state, the mine is now Durbin's. (If not, Durbin will have to wait while a court verifies that there are no other relatives.)

d. Yes; the oral expression of the miner's desire for Durbin to have the mine is adequate, especially if the statement was witnessed.

5. Reynolds hired Dollin Building to construct a sunroom addition on her house. Dollin finished the work, but Reynolds isn't happy with it, so she doesn't pay the final payment due Dollin. Which of the following would Dollin likely resort to to protect his interests?

a. Adverse possession
b. A mechanic's lien
c. Eminent domain
d. A quitclaim deed

6. A person with an invalid warranty deed who is occupying real property is most likely occupying the property

a. as a squatter.
b. under a grant deed.
c. under color of title.
d. as a tenant at sufferance.

7. Marples owns an office building; Fowler is her tenant. Fowler's lease states that either party can terminate the tenancy with sixty days' notice to the other party. Marples wants Fowler to vacate and gives him notice. Five days later, Fowler calls, demanding that Marples correct some defects in the building's wiring. Need Marples make the repairs at this time?

a. No; since she's severing her agreement with Fowler, she can wait to see if the next tenant requests the repairs.

b. No; a tenant is usually responsible for fixing faults in the building that develop after the tenant assumes occupancy.

c. No; since the lease gives Fowler the right to leave with proper notice, he could just vacate the premises if the defects troubled him, leaving Marples to find a new tenant. (Of course, this point is moot now that she's told Fowler to leave, but that doesn't make Marples responsible.)

d. Yes.

8. Ken and Sue were married and purchased a house together. Ken later died in an airplane crash. Who owns the house now?

a. Only Sue
b. Sue owns half and the person named in Ken's will (who may well be Sue) owns the other half
c. Sue owns half and the person next to Sue in her state's intestate succession statute owns the other half
d. Either a or b might be correct

9. Edwin and Joan are cousins, and the two of them hold a considerable amount of real estate as joint tenants with rights of survivorship. Edwin, who borrowed a lot of money for which he used his interest in the property as collateral, dies in an accident. Who of the following would *most likely* receive Edwin's interest in the property?

    a. Joan
    b. Edwin's brother, Harold
    c. Edwin's creditors
    d. It would depend entirely on the statutes of the state where the property was located

10. There are *least likely* to be disputes over community property

    a. when one or both spouses have been previously married.
    b. when a spouse dies intestate.
    c. when one moves from a non-community property state to a community property state.
    d. when the property involved is real property.

YOUR OPINION, PLEASE

Read each of the following scenarios and answer the questions about the decisions you would make in each situation. Give these questions some serious thought; they may be used as the basis for the development of a more complex essay. You should base your decisions on what you've learned from this lesson, though you may incorporate outside readings or information gained through your own experience if it is relevant.

Scenario I

Johnson rented an office for her graphic design company, signing a year's lease with landlord Simpson and paying the first and last months' rent in advance as well as a security deposit of $200. During Johnson's first month, Simpson has been in and out of the office several times, coming unannounced and using his passkey to let himself in when no one is there. Johnson tells him that he has no right to continue entering the premises without permission, but Simpson argues that he has to complete some repairs and can't always come at her convenience. After three months, Johnson buys a phototypesetter that requires developing equipment, but then discovers that the solutions from the processor will not drain properly. Unfortunately, she learns of the problem only when the tenants below her notice the liquid stains on their ceiling.

When Simpson comes to investigate the problem, he notices that the entry door has been damaged. Johnson says that it was damaged when she moved in, but Simpson vows to hold her responsible for repairs. He promises to fix the sink, but first must attend to the ceiling below. Another month passes. Then Simpson rents the adjacent office to a printing firm; the considerable noise from their printing equipment makes it very difficult for Johnson to work. She complains to Simpson, but Simpson merely points out that printing equipment is likely to make some noise and there's nothing he can do about it.

Johnson can't take anymore, so she finds another office to rent and moves out the following week without notifying Simpson; he only discovers that she has gone when he comes to fix the sink several weeks later. On inspection, he finds that a large section of the office carpet has been damaged from the developing solution, as has the wallboard behind where the processor was located. He manages to find Johnson's new address and demands that she honor the rest of her lease as well as pay him for the cost of repairing the damages, which greatly exceed her security deposit.

Johnson's lawyer, however, demands that Simpson return her security deposit, since the damages weren't her fault. The lawyer also demands that Simpson return the last month's rent that Johnson had paid in advance, since his leasing of the adjacent office to the noisy printing company constituted constructive eviction. This, the lawyer argued, gave Johnson the right to move out without any further liability to pay rent. The attorney adds that Simpson had breached the terms of the lease in the first month anyway due to his unannounced and unwelcome visits to Johnson's office. Simpson responds by threatening to sue to get the money he feels he was owed.

What's your opinion? Was Johnson unreasonable or within her rights? What right, if any, did Simpson have to enter the office and ignore Johnson's complaints about the noise? Was the damage Johnson's fault as Simpson maintains?

- Based on what you know of the situation, do you think Simpson's suit is likely to be upheld in court? Why or why not?
- What factors support your answer?
- What factors might an attorney cite in arguing against your view?
- What steps, if any, might Johnson have taken to protect her rights in this situation?
- What steps, if any, might Simpson have taken to protect his rights in this situation?

Scenario 2

In 1980, Ramone sold his house and city lot to Warren. Ramone received a large down payment and carried the contract for the balance owing, so that Warren made monthly payments directly to Ramone. Five years later, after Warren had failed to make monthly payments for six months in a row, Ramone advised him that he was about to institute foreclosure proceedings and retake possession of the real estate. He further advised Warren that he intended to resell the house, and threatened to bring suit against Warren for any amount still owing him that he could not recover from the sale. And since the price for homes in the area had dropped dramatically in the past five years, it seemed likely that a sale would, in fact, be for less than what Warren still owed Ramone.

As an alternative, Warren asked for permission to try for six months to sell the house himself. He added that if he failed, he would not fight the foreclosure action, which could tie up the house for months in court, but instead would execute a quitclaim deed giving Ramone his interest in the house. Ramone agreed to this arrangement, and when Warren failed to sell the house he executed and delivered the deed to Ramone.

When Ramone found a buyer for the house, however, a search of records by the escrow officer charged with handling the sale revealed that Warren had granted an easement for a driveway through Ramone's property. The easement had been given to a neighbor on the adjacent street so that the neighbor wouldn't have to exit onto his busy and dangerous street. The neighbor had paid Warren $3,000 for the easement, and their agreement was expressed in a contract. Ramone has threatened to sue Warren for the $3,000 easement fee in order to buy back the rights from the neighbor. He has also argued that the neighbor has no right to use the easement because Warren did not have the right to sell it to him. The neighbor argues that he purchased the easement in good faith and has the right to use it. And Warren argues that he cannot be held liable for the easement because his quitclaim deed made no promises about the extent of his interest in the property or any encumbrances on it.

What's your opinion? Based on what you know of the situation, do you think a court will uphold Ramone's suit on the basis that *any* deed must list any ownership rights that are *not* included in the conveyance, such as easements? Does the fact that a quitclaim deed makes no promises about the grantor's interest in the property support Warren's position? What about the neighbor? Do you think a court will force him to sell his easement back to Ramone?

- Is Ramone's suit likely to be upheld in court? Why or why not?
- What factors support your answer?
- What factors might an attorney cite in arguing against your view?
- What steps, if any, might Ramone have taken to protect his interests in this situation?
- What steps, if any, might the neighbor have taken to protect his interests in this situation?

27

Personal Property

LEARNING OBJECTIVES

Upon completing your study of this lesson, you should be able to

- Define *personal property* (as distinguished from *real* property).
- Distinguish between *tangible* personal property and *intangible* personal property, using examples to illustrate the distinction.
- List and discuss several ways in which an owner can acquire title to personal property.
- Discuss several methods — legal and illegal — by which one can lose personal property, and the steps that may be taken to protect personal property.
- Define *bailment* and, using examples, discuss the three different classes of bailments.
- Explain the duties and liabilities of a bailee of personal property, and discuss circumstances in which bailees' attempts to limit their liability will not be upheld by the court.

Perhaps you think that some aspects of business law might not pertain to you. Maybe so, but no one can say that they don't have any reason to learn about personal property; after all, we all acquire and give up personal property on a daily basis. This lesson defines personal property and points out the differences between the two types of personal property—intangible and tangible. This lesson also explores the ways in which one may acquire, lose, and protect title to personal property. Finally, we'll look at the duties and liabilities of persons who have temporary possession and/or use of the personal property of another person.

OVERVIEW

Has your car ever been damaged in a parking garage? Ever had your baggage lost by an airline? Have you ever given a gift that you later wanted back? Your car, your baggage, and the gift you purchased are all items of personal property. A whole body of law exists that sets out a personal property owner's rights and the liabilities that others assume when they have temporary custody or use of another's personal property. If you've experienced any of the situations just described—or others along the same vein—it will be interesting and useful to understand this body of law.

The Nature of Personal Property

In the previous lesson, we discussed the fact that property—defined as any valuable asset—is also a legal concept with an accompanying bundle of rights and obligations. Some of these specify the ways in which a person can acquire and transfer his or her assets. We also discussed the fact that there are two types of property—*real property*, which is land, interests in land, and everything permanently attached to it, including buildings and roadways, and *personal property*—everything that can be owned that is not real property. In business, most transactions (as you might guess) involve personal rather than real property.

But even though there's a clear difference between real and personal property, the components—or rights—of ownership are the same for both. Thus, ownership of personal property includes the rights to use, give, sell, rent, abandon, or improve the property. Ownership also includes the right to physical possession or custody and title to the property. *Title* is a legal concept that pertains to the written evidence of ownership, including the name of the current legal owner and the method of acquisition.

Tangible and Intangible Personal Property

Unlike real property, though, personal property is divided into two categories. *Tangible* personal property can be moved, felt, tasted, or seen; items such as books, cars, and paper clips are tangible personal property. *Intangible* personal property, on the other hand, cannot be evidenced by physical possession. Exactly what constitutes an item of intangible personal property is sometimes difficult to imagine, but it includes such things as copyrights, accounts receivable, or corporate good will.

As an example of intangible property, consider the copyright to a novel. While the author may have physical possession of the manuscript that she or he created, that represents (at least initially) only a few cents worth of used paper. It's the right to use the text of the novel that is the valuable item of property. If the author has sold this "right" to a publisher, the publisher can choose to reproduce the words of the novel. The publisher will produce books containing the valuable words with the intention of selling them for more than the combined cost of production and payment to the author.

We now have both tangible personal property (the original manuscript) and intangible personal property (the rights to the novel). In fact, this intangible property is much more valuable than the tangible original manuscript—although the original manuscript might later become valuable property if the author is or becomes famous. But regardless of whether personal property is intangible or tangible, the process of acquiring ownership is the same.

Acquiring Title to Personal Property

In general, there are three ways in which a person may acquire title to personal property. First, you can be the original owner; this is called, logically enough, *original ownership*. Second, you can receive it voluntarily from the person with title to it; that person is called the *donor* and the process is called *voluntary transfer*. Third, you can sometimes acquire title by exercising control over property in the absence of the donor; this is called *involuntary transfer*.

While this third method of acquiring ownership is called an "involuntary" transfer by the owner, this doesn't always mean that the owner was present and protesting at the time control over the property was exercised. As we discuss each way of acquiring title—and the subcategories within each type—note how there are many different ways (some better than others) in which parties can react in situations where there is a possibility of legal disputes.

Original Possession

Original possession occurs when an individual *creates* the ownership instead of receiving it from another person; it also occurs when an individual takes possession of something that has never been owned before. The first situation is pretty clear-cut. When a person creates property—for example, when an artist paints a picture—there is usually little room for dispute about who actually owns it; the artist is the original owner.

But when a person claims title—ownership—to something that hasn't been owned before, the possibility for dispute exists. Consider the case of two deer hunters, each unaware of the presence of the other. Both have sighted their prey. They fire at the same time, and the deer goes down. One hunter arrives first and claims possession. But who owns the deer? There are, certainly, ways to decide; the bullets could be examined, for example. The point, however, is that there are ways in which disputes can arise even from original ownership—and it's the most straightforward of the three ways property gets transferred.

Voluntary Transfer

As mentioned, a person can gain title to property by receiving it in a voluntary transfer from its original owner. This voluntary transfer could be by means of a purchase, a gift, gifts *causa mortis*, inheritance, or intestate succession.

Purchase. Acquiring property by purchase from an original owner doesn't often result in ownership disputes. A purchase occurs when the buyer gives up one form of property, usually money, in exchange for another form of property, such as a used car. Trading one car for another, however, is also a form of purchase. And exchanging services for property—such as swapping house painting for a used car—is also a purchase; trading goods for goods or services for goods is known as *bartering*.

So long as the terms of the exchange are well understood, there is fairly little possibility for dispute over ownership—unless it is a dispute over when ownership transfers. Especially when the trade is one of services for goods, it's important to make clear whether ownership of the goods changes hands when the service begins, when it ends, or at some other time.

Gifts. When ownership of property is transferred as a gift, however, the potential for dispute increases. For one thing, there are three requirements that must be satisfied before a valid transfer of ownership by gift can take place. First, the previous owner—the donor—must *intend* to make a gift. Determining whether the donor intended to give—rather than sell or loan—the property to the other party (the *donee*) can sometimes become difficult.

Take the case of Marshall, for example, who gave $1,000 to her fiance, Tepper, several months before he broke off their engagement. When the wedding plans were called off, Marshall demanded that Tepper return the $1,000. He refused, claiming that she intended the money as a gift, not a loan. Does Tepper need to return the money? It's a close call; a court deciding the issue would want to see proof that Marshall *intended* to make a gift. Similar disagreements also arise when a donor dies and others claim that they were donees for certain gifts. Daughter Jane says that Mother gave her the silverware; daughter Nancy says she didn't. Mother is not there to settle the issue, so Jane will probably have to prove that Mother intended that she have the silver.

Second, to acquire property by gift, the donor must also *deliver* the property to the donee. When there is *actual delivery* of the property—when the donor physically hands the property over to the donee—there usually is no problem in proving the delivery requirement for an effective gift. But suppose Mother said that Jane could have the silverware after she died. There was no physical transfer of the property, so the question of whether a gift was made is still in doubt.

But when actual delivery isn't possible or simply doesn't happen, a process called *constructive delivery* will often be sufficient to satisfy the delivery requirement. In constructive delivery, there is no actual transfer of property, but there is some physical evidence of delivery. For example, Tranh's grandmother is confined to a nursing home. She's been rethinking her will and has decided to give Tranh some family heirloom jewelry. On one of Tranh's visits, her grandmother decides that this is the day to give Tranh the jewelry. If she has the jewelry at the nursing home, she can just hand it to Tranh, effecting delivery. That's actual delivery and clearly gives Tranh possession of the property.

But if the jewelry is elsewhere—say in her safe deposit box in the bank—she can give Tranh the key to the safe deposit box and a note allowing her access to it. Giving Tranh the key and note is constructive delivery of the gift. (Note, however, that in our earlier example we don't have any evidence of a constructive delivery of Mother's silverware to daughter Jane. And if Jane can't produce any evidence of delivery of the silverware—constructive or actual—she's going to have a hard time proving she was given the silverware as a gift.)

Finally, for a valid transfer by gift, the receiver must *accept* the gift. While this isn't usually a problem, people sometimes refuse gifts—perhaps because they fear that acceptance might obligate them to the donor.

Gifts *causa mortis*. A special type of gift is a gift causa mortis. This occurs while the property owner is still alive but is making the gift because he or she expects to die soon. For these gifts to be valid—and claimable in court—they must be made in contemplation of death, and the donor must die from the contemplated cause. If the donor does not die or dies from another cause, the gift may be revoked by the donor or his or her estate.

As an example of the complications that may arise with gifts *causa mortis*, let's return to Tranh and her grandmother's jewelry. Let's change the scenario to say that Tranh's grandmother had suffered a series of strokes and feared that she would die from another at any time. Because she wanted to be sure that—if she did die—Tranh would receive her jewelry, she gave Tranh the safe deposit keys and the note allowing access to her box and possession of the jewelry. Should Tranh's grandmother take a turn for the better and subsequently decide to give someone else the jewelry, she would be entitled to get it back from Tranh because she did not die as anticipated. The other condition placed on gifts *causa mortis* would come into play should Tranh's grandmother die from a fall rather than a stroke. In that case, the grandmother's estate could claim the jewelry because the grandmother did not die from the contemplated cause.

Should Jane get Mother's silverware under the concept of gifts *causa mortis*? It's unlikely. A gift *causa mortis* has more conditions for the transfer of ownership, not fewer. So having a gift be a gift *causa mortis* does nothing to eliminate the need for the gift to be delivered. Instead, it adds the restriction that the donee must die from the expected cause. Even if Jane's mother *had* actually given Jane the silverware because she expected to die soon, she could ask for the silverware back if she did not die.

Inheritances. A person can also receive property from the estate of someone who dies. If the person had a valid will, the person specified in the will receives the property through inheritance.

Intestate succession. Property can also be voluntarily transferred by intestate succession. This occurs when a person dies without leaving a valid will. The property is transferred to recipients who are specified in the state intestate succession statute.

Involuntary Transfers

The third manner in which property can be acquired — by means of an involuntary transfer — is based not so much on the affirmative actions of the donor but on the actions and desires of the receiver. And, as you might suspect, since involuntary transfers are not the direct result of intentional actions by the previous owner, the potential for disputes about ownership is great.

There are four possible ways in which involuntary transfers may occur — through accession, by confusion, by abandonment, or when property becomes lost or mislaid. Each has different conditions and applies in different situations. Still, they all have the same effect — the transfer of property to a new owner without the donee intending to make the transfer.

Accession. This occurs when a person takes property that she or he does not own and adds to it. For instance, a carpenter takes plywood belonging to another person and makes a stereo cabinet. The carpenter can be said to have added to the plywood by turning it into a piece of furniture. Who owns the cabinet — the carpenter or the original owner of the plywood? In general, the person who took the property will not acquire title to the enhanced property. But this is not always the case — under some circumstances title to the enhanced property may pass to the property enhancer.

Courts usually decide ownership by trying to determine whether the enhancer claiming ownership *knew* that she or he had no right to take the property. Let's look at an example. Higgins is a sculptor who has noticed a nice piece of granite in the vacant lot on the other side of her neighbor's house. Thinking that her neighbor owned the vacant lot, she asks about the granite. Her neighbor says, "It's yours if you'll haul it away," and Higgins promptly hauls it to her studio. During the next few months, she turns the granite block into a bust of Hobart Potter, a local banker who had commissioned Higgins to do the piece for $5,000. Later, Louis, the owner of the lot next to Higgins's neighbor, comes to town, notices that the granite is gone, and traces it to Higgins. When Higgins explains what's happened, Louis demands the return of the granite — even though it has been transformed into a bust of Hobart

Potter. Who is now the rightful owner of the granite—Higgins, Louis, or (because he purchased the bust from Higgins) Potter?

Under the most general rule, title to the granite would remain with Louis, the original owner. It would not be transferred to Higgins or Potter simply by virtue of the work Higgins did to it. But in looking at whether Higgins knew she had no right to the property, we see that Higgins may be what's called an *innocent trespasser*—a laborer who took property she *thought* she had the right to use. In our case, Higgins thought she had the right to use the granite because it was a gift from her neighbor. Because of this she may well be granted title to the sculpture (which she could then transfer to Potter).

An innocent trespasser, however, must meet three conditions to obtain title to the enhanced property. First, the property must have lost its original identity because of the enhancement. Given the difference between a block of raw granite and the bust of local banker Potter, a court might well say this condition was met. Second, there must be a great difference in the relative values between the original property and the new property. This condition appears to exist for Higgins's sculpture—the value of the raw granite block is much less than that of the sculpture. Finally, a completely new type of property must be created by the enhancement, with the innocent trespasser having done most of the work to create the new property. With Higgins's sculpture, this condition also seems to have been met—a work of art is a different type of property than is a rock, and Higgins did all the work that transformed the rock into the art piece. Given that all three conditions have been met, it's possible that Higgins acquired title to the granite by accession. (And even if she did not meet all three conditions, she may still be entitled to some compensation for the enhancement she provided.)

The counterpart to the innocent trespasser is the *willful trespasser*—one who *knows* he or she has no right to the original property. Not only can't a willful trespasser acquire title to the property, the enhancer will not be paid for his or her labor in making the enhancement or paid for the increased value of the property. In fact, the willful trespasser could have to pay the owner damages if his or her enhancements make the property less suitable for its rightful owner. These "penalties" are imposed to deter willful trespassing onto another's property.

Confusion. This is a second manner in which property may be "acquired" without the donor actually agreeing to the change in ownership. Confusion occurs when the property of two or more people is mixed together and cannot be identified and separated into what belonged to each person prior to the mixing. Title changes in the sense that the whole mixture is now owned *jointly* by the parties, rather than each party having title to the specific pieces they put into the mixture.

An example will help here. Farmer Smith has 500 gallons of milk that he loads into the dairy's tanker truck. The tanker truck, however, already contains 500 gallons of milk from Farmer Jones's place down the road. It's clear that the milk from one farm is now indistinguishable from the milk of the other farm. Farmer Smith, instead of owning *the* 500 gallons that came from his cows, now simply owns one-half of the 1,000-gallon shipment—he has "acquired" an interest in what was Jones's milk and has "given" Jones an equal interest in what was previously his own milk.

Obviously, confusion doesn't happen whenever all similar types of goods are put together. Confusion only occurs when the property involved is *fungible*; that is, of such a nature that one item of the property is indistinguishable from any other item of the same type of property. Wheat, milk, gravel, corn flakes, ice cubes, and the like are examples of fungible property. But 1959 Chevrolets are not fungible property; when put together on a parking lot, they are still readily distinguishable from each other.

Now, with Farmer Smith and Farmer Jones knowing that they would each be loading milk into a common dairy tanker truck, there really doesn't seem to be much problem with this "confused" ownership. With voluntary confusion, each party knows what is happening, and each will receive a proportion of the money received for the milk equal to the proportion of the milk contributed to the total load.

But at times, one party may intentionally or accidentally mix his or her property with like fungible property without the knowledge of or against the wishes of the other property owner(s). If the resulting mixture lowers the value of the property of the innocent property owner(s), the wrongdoer will be punished by getting a reduced value—or perhaps even losing all title to—the property he or she added. Suppose, for example, that a gasoline tank truck half-full of Brown's premium gasoline pulls up to Green's refinery. By mistake, an employee fills the tanker with Green's regular gasoline. The value of Brown's share of the resultant product is now substantially less than before the confusion. As a result, the odds are that the wrongdoer (Green) will have to compensate Brown for the lower value of the combined tanker load by accepting a reduced value for his portion.

Lost or mislaid property. Title can also be acquired by another when the current owner misplaces or loses property. *Lost* property was unintentionally left someplace—and the owner does not know where it was left or where it may be retrieved. On the other hand, *mislaid* property was intentionally set somewhere—and then forgotten about. To obtain title in either case, the finder of the property needs to follow certain fairly detailed procedures set out in state statutes. These procedures usually require giving public notice of having found the property and specifying where the property is now located (usually with the police for safekeeping). There is also a waiting time within which the owner can reclaim possession of the property. Title does not pass to the finder of the property—or to a public body authorized to receive lost or abandoned property—until the specified procedures are completed.

Abandoned property. Property is abandoned when the owner throws it away or relinquishes it without intending to reclaim it. The key phrase here is intent to surrender and abandon—and, at least at the start, the owner knows where the property was left.

Threats Against the Ownership of Personal Property

The preceding sections focused on ways in which a party may acquire property. Sometimes, as with original ownership, there is no donor; other times, the donor knows about and agrees to the acquisition. These billions of forthright property transfers—encompassing everything from Porsches to macaroni—comprise the vast majority of transactions. As a result, it's easy to think that ownership and transfer is pretty straightforward.

Unfortunately, there are other, much more adversarial, ways in which ownership of property is changed. In such situations, one party—directly, knowingly, and against the expressed wishes of the other party—*takes* property that they know another party exerts claim over. To the person holding the property, the issue is not whether the party seeking control of the property has a lawful claim to the property; the person with possession of the property simply doesn't want to give up the property.

Conversion

One way in which an owner may lose title to property is called *conversion*. This occurs when an individual takes unauthorized control of the owner's property. At its simplest, conversion is the civil equivalent of crimes such as theft or embezzlement. And while the government might institute criminal proceedings to punish the wrongdoer, in cases of conversion, the property owner may also sue the taker for the return of the property or for money to replace it.

However, conversion can also occur when the property owner voluntarily releases use of property to another person who then uses the property in a manner different from what the owner authorized. How could such a voluntary release cause problems? Remember, the owner of the property is often responsible for damages if in the course of use the property is damaged (by the user or a third party) or if the user causes damage to third parties.

It's not always that straightforward, however. Suppose, for example, that Thompson rented a pickup truck from a rental company. Although Thompson said that he would be moving furniture around town, he in fact used the pickup to haul firewood cut illegally in the national forest. When a ranger stopped and arrested Thompson, the ranger—after moving the truck off the road—did not set the parking brake securely. While the ranger was putting Thompson into the patrol car, the truck rolled down a hill into a motorhome parked in a campground; both vehicles were severely damaged. Who would be liable here? The ranger (or the ranger's employer), the rental company, or Thompson? The rental company may escape liability since Thompson made unauthorized use of the property. Further, the rental company can probably successfully sue to force Thompson to return the pickup truck to the same condition as when it was rented.

Escheat

The second way in which an owner can lose title to property is through *escheat*. When the rightful owner cannot be located, property will escheat—or be given—to the government. This tends to happen when a person dies and heirs or relatives cannot be located, or when people forget about small bank accounts or other assets. There's an important principle here: the state is more deserving of the property than anyone but its rightful owner. Suppose, for instance, that you have been storing an elderly neighbor's pristine 1953 Cadillac in your garage. When the neighbor dies and his heirs cannot be found, you might think that you can keep the car. It's likely, however, that the car would escheat to the state instead. Regardless of how you viewed the favor you were doing your neighbor, in the eyes of the law you're no more deserving of the car than anyone else.

Judicial Sale

A person can also lose title to property through a *judicial sale*—the forced sale of property to pay off a debt that the court has determined you owe. Suppose you are a small businessperson whose employee won a civil lawsuit against you for unpaid wages. If you fail to pay off the judgment (the court order saying how much you owe and to whom), the employee can get a writ of execution—that is, an order to seize property—from the court. With this order confirming the existence of an unpaid judgment, the sheriff can seize your property and sell it, giving to the employee the amount necessary to pay the judgment against you and, after taking out costs for the sale, giving you any money left over. Depending on state law, you may have a limited period in which to redeem (or buy back) the property, even if it has been sold to a third party, but otherwise the title to the property goes to the purchaser at the sale.

Repossession

A property owner can also lose title through the similar process of *repossession*. If you borrow money from a bank to purchase equipment for your restaurant, the bank will usually create a security interest in the equipment. This security interest, which recognizes the bank's claim to the property, will allow the bank to repossess or retake that equipment if you do not repay the loan under the terms of the contract. The bank would then sell the property to recover its cash. But repossession can only take place by peaceful means—the bank could not break into your restaurant or get the movers to forcibly restrain you as they came for the equipment. If property cannot be repossessed peaceably, then the bank or creditor must go to court to sue for the value of the debt or the recovery of the property.

Bailments

So far, we've been looking at the ways in which individuals can gain or lose owner-ship of personal property. But many situations arise where you *entrust*—loan or give temporary custody of, that is—your property to someone else. This occurs, for example, when you loan, rent, or *warehouse* (store under someone else's control) your property. This temporary transfer of possession is called a *bailment*; the owner of the property is called the *bailor*, the person with temporary possession is called the *bailee*.

For a bailment situation to exist, the owner must retain title to the property while possession of the property is given to another party. Conversely, that party, the bailee, must accept possession and temporary control of the property for a specific purpose. Finally, both parties must intend that the property will be re-turned to or reclaimed by the bailor (or perhaps another person the bailor has named). You might be surprised at the number of times you've been a bailor or bailee without knowing it; a bailment exists, for example, each time you let your neighbor borrow your lawnmower or leave your cat with a friend while you're on vacation.

As the preceding examples show, some bailments benefit the bailor (having your cat cared for while on vacation) while others benefit the bailee (your neighbor can mow his lawn without having to buy a lawnmower). Still other bailments benefit both parties. These different types of bailments are, logically enough, respectively termed *bailor benefit bailment*, *bailee benefit bailment*, and *mutual benefit bail-ment*. In any particular situation, the issue of who benefits from the bailment has a lot to do with allocating the responsibilities and liabilities if something goes wrong while property is in the hands of the bailee.

Duties and Liabilities in a Bailment

Disputes usually arise in bailment situations when property is damaged. In general, the bailee has two main responsibilities: first, to take proper care of the property during the time of possession and, second, to return the property at the termina-tion of the bailment. These responsibilities are qualified by a number of factors, however.

Proper Care

If you were to sue because your property is damaged while in the custody of a bailee, a court would decide whether the bailee took "reasonable care" of the property. But the amount of care that is "reasonable" depends most of all on the *type* of bail-ment situation. When a bailment is established solely for the benefit of the *bailor*, the bailee is responsible only for *gross negligence*. If you asked a neighbor to drop off your stereo tape deck at the repair shop next door to his office one morning, would your neighbor be responsible if the tape deck were damaged when he braked suddenly to avoid a child who had run into the street? Probably not, especially if the neighbor had otherwise been paying attention while driving. The bailee in a bailor benefit bailment situation is responsible only for damages due to his or her gross negligence—and braking in time to avoid a child who ran unexpectedly into the street is certainly not gross negligence.

In a bailee benefit situation, on the other hand, the bailee will usually be held responsible for even *slight negligence*. Suppose you loan your tape deck to your neighbor when hers breaks down. Since this bailment has been created solely for the benefit of the bailee (your neighbor), she needs to exercise special care in assuring that your property remains in good condition. If she puts the tape deck under a hanging plant and water from overfilling the plant spills into the equipment and damages it, she would probably be held liable for repairs. (What happens in a mutual benefit bailment situation? If you loan your tape deck to your neighbor in return for the use of her television, for example, each party will usually be held to the same level of care as the other exhibits.)

The second factor that determines the degree of care that the bailee must take is the contract that establishes the bailment. Within certain restrictions established by the courts and state statutes, the terms of this contract may increase or decrease the liability of the bailee. A *quasi-public bailee*, one which offers services to the public—a bus company, airline, hotel, or restaurant, for example—will generally not be allowed to limit liability in a contract unless specifically permitted to do so by statute. A *private bailee*, on the other hand, can—through the contract—restrict liability for damage to the property, but only if the restriction does not conflict with the purpose of that contract.

Suppose that Yount Electronics repairs stereo tape decks. You take yours in for repair and, in doing so, create a bailment situation. Yount might be allowed to have a contract that said they would not be liable for your tape deck if their building burned down while your property was in it. On the other hand, they certainly could not get away with a contract clause that said they weren't responsible if the tape deck was ruined by their attempts to repair it; that would defeat the purpose of the repair contract which created the bailment.

If you rent your garage to a friend for storage of his car, for instance, you are allowed to draw up a contract that limits your liability for damages caused by any number of factors, including floods or illegal entry. A public establishment, on the other hand, is usually considered an absolute insurer of a bailor's property except where limits on liability are allowed by statute. Have you ever read the notice on the back of the door into many hotel rooms? That card, in so many words, says "Since you're a guest here and your possessions are in our hotel, a bailment situation has been created that would normally make us responsible for them. On the other hand, the legislature of our state didn't think it was fair for us to be responsible for everything, so they placed some limits on how much and what events we're liable for. So if your diamond necklace is stolen from this room, we're probably not responsible for its full value due to state statute. Note, however, that if you give us the necklace to put in our hotel safe, the statute says we'll remain liable for the entire value."

Return of the Property

Besides the duty to provide appropriate care to the entrusted property, a bailee also has the responsibility to return the property to the bailor. This responsibility can be modified by several factors. If the property is lost, destroyed, or stolen through no fault of the bailee, the bailee won't be held responsible. And, obviously, if the property is taken away by legal process — such as a sheriff's sale or if the property is claimed by someone with a better legal title than the bailor — then the bailee has no duty to return the property to the bailor. Suppose, for example, that on the day of your divorce you put the prized family moosehead into a warehouse to keep your soon-to-be-ex-spouse from getting it. You've created a bailment situation that normally would require the warehouse owner to return the moosehead to you upon request and in good condition. Nevertheless, if your former spouse shows up with a court order saying, "Turn over the moosehead; it's part of my divorce settlement," the bailee can (and should) do so.

SOME PRACTICAL ADVICE

As a businessperson, what are the most important things to consider when acquiring, protecting, or transferring title to personal property? What should you keep in mind when warehousing or loaning property, and what actions can you take if your property is damaged while in someone else's possession?

First, when acquiring personal property, remember that the rules are sometimes different from those governing the transfer of real property. For one thing, the process for transferring real property is much more formal. We all worry about having the paperwork all in order when we buy a house, farm, or office building; we don't, however, call for a written contract each time we transfer ownership of a half-gallon of milk or a pound of nails. In other words, many personal property transfers are routine and done without much thought about the legal ramifications. That's acceptable; besides, there's not much alternative if you want to participate in modern commerce. The trick is to figure out when the property — and the duties and liabilities associated with the property — is important enough to warrant formality. Both a $100,000 computer system and a box of paper clips are personal property, but any sensible businessperson will expend considerable effort worrying about the proper transfer of ownership of the computer while not giving the box of paper clips a second thought.

There are also more ways to acquire personal property than real property. You can, for example, acquire title to personal property through original possession. You do so by creating the property by means of physical or mental labor (e.g., writing a computer program), or by taking possession of something (e.g., a chinook salmon) that has never been owned before. The potential for disputes about ownership in such cases is small, as it is when acquiring property by purchasing it.

Acquiring property as a gift is more likely to cause problems. If you are the donor, make sure that you intend to make a gift (rather than sell or loan the property) and that you deliver the gift, either by actual delivery or by making such delivery as is possible (constructive delivery). Of course, you also need to know that the receiver (or donee) actually accepts the gift. Remember, once a gift has satisfied those requirements, it's usually not possible to take it back. (Also remember that giving away special types of personal property—such as negotiable instruments like money orders or the right to bring legal action—requires that specific procedures be followed; always consult an attorney if you have any doubts.)

Gifts and purchases are voluntary transfers of property, but a businessperson can also acquire title when the transfer is not entirely conscious or intended on the part of the current owner. These types of transfers—including accession, confusion, abandonment, and lost or mislaid property—often present complex legal issues that affect the new owner's right to claim title. Courts tend to resolve such ownership disputes based on the particular facts of each situation, so you should plan on consulting an attorney before attempting to claim or exercise title through involuntary transfers.

By the same token, an owner of personal property must be aware of the ways in which title to the property may be taken by another individual. When someone takes unauthorized control or use of your property, you can usually sue successfully for its return—or for the money to replace it. But what if you voluntarily release your property to someone who then makes use of it in a manner different from what you authorized? In such cases, courts will usually try to determine how greatly the actual use differed from what you authorized before awarding you the cost of any damages that have occurred. Not surprisingly, the better job you have done of specifying in writing the conditions of the voluntary transfer, the better your rights will be protected.

The two biggest legal threats to your business property, however, probably come from repossession (when you fail to make payments on property in which the lender has created a security interest) and from judicial sale of the property ordered by a court to satisfy a judgment made against the business. Obviously, the surest way to avoid problems is to avoid situations where your property is exposed to creditors. But many modern businesses cannot operate that way; company assets have to serve as security for lenders. A less trite, more helpful piece of advice is to attend carefully (probably with the help of a lawyer) to any agreement which exposes business assets — or personal assets, for that matter — to creditors. And if you are having problems meeting your obligations, talk to your creditors to attempt to modify the payment arrangements. Don't just be silent, waiting for attempted repossession or lawsuit. And if you or your company are ever sued, *never ignore the suit*; the outcome that develops without your involvement will almost certainly be worse than what would develop with it.

Finally, a businessperson should be aware of the liability of a bailee (one who assumes temporary custody of another's personal property) when property is lost or damaged while in the bailee's possession. Whenever loaning or storing your own property—or, on the other hand, when borrowing or storing someone else's property—keep in mind that the bailee always has two main duties: to take proper care of the property and to return it at the termination of the bailment. A business-person loaning or holding another's property would be smart to understand (with the help of a lawyer, if necessary) what type of bailment situation has been created and how much care needs to be supplied by the bailee. (And since most businesses are covered by insurance, it's always a good idea to know how your policies treat loaned and borrowed property.)

ASSIGNMENTS

- Before you watch the video program, be sure you've read through the preceding overview, familiarized yourself with the learning objectives for this lesson, and looked at the key terms below. Then, read Chapter 50 of Davidson et al., *Business Law*.
- After completing these tasks, view the video program for Lesson 27.
- After watching the program, take time to review what you've learned. First, evaluate your learning with the self-test which follows the key terms. Then, apply and evaluate what you've learned with the "Your Opinion, Please" scenarios at the end of this telecourse study guide lesson.

KEY TERMS

Before you read through the textbook assignment and watch the video program, take a minute to look at the key terms associated with this lesson. When you encounter them in the textbook and video program, pay careful attention to their meaning.

Accession	Lost property
Bailee benefit bailment	Mislaid property
Bailment	Mutual benefit bailment
Bailor benefit bailment	Original possession
Confusion	Ownership
Conversion	Possession
Escheat	Private bailee
Executed gift	Quasi-public bailee
Fungible property	Repossession
Gifts *causa mortis*	Tangible personal property
Innocent trespasser	Title
Intangible personal property	Willful trespasser
Judicial sale	

SELF-TEST

The questions below will help you evaluate how well you've learned the material in this lesson. Read each one carefully, and select the letter of the option that best answers the question. You'll find the correct answer, along with a reference to the page number(s) where the topic is discussed, in the back of this telecourse study guide.

1. Which of the following is *not* personal property?

   a. Cash
   b. A newly installed bathtub
   c. A business's reputation for outstanding service
   d. The software code for a popular computer game

2. Some craft fairs boast that all wares are sold by the craftspeople who actually made the property. Thus, at the time the event begins, everyone would hold title to their wares through

   a. original possession.
   b. intestate succession.
   c. adverse possession.
   d. accession.

3. There is an ongoing argument over whether the action of giving your car to a parking lot in exchange for money results in a bailment or a lease of space. Why would the parking lot company prefer that you were leasing space as opposed to creating a bailment?

   a. They could not accept money for a bailment.
   b. Continuous leasing of their space helps protect their property from adverse possession.
   c. They would be more likely to be held responsible for what happens to your car if a bailment is created.
   d. Regular parking in their lot could create an issue of accession if it were a bailment, but accession is not an issue with a lease.

4. Harris gives some valuable personal property to Schmidt; there is some chance that Harris gave Schmidt a gift. Three of the following four actions are requirements for the transfer of ownership of the gift; one is not. Which one of these is *not* a mandatory condition of the gift?

   a. Harris must clearly intend to make the gift.
   b. Schmidt must accept the gift.
   c. Schmidt must actually take delivery of the gift.
   d. There must be written evidence of the transfer.

5. Redmond learns that some of his cousin's property will be in a "sheriff's sale." What implication could Redmond accurately draw from this information?

    a. His cousin is attempting adverse possession of property.

    b. His cousin has lost a civil suit.

    c. His cousin is now (or is about to be) in jail for a long enough period that he will not be able to look after his property.

    d. His cousin has acquired and enhanced property which didn't belong to him.

6. Only one of the following four options is always associated with the concept of *bailment*. Which one?

    a. Consideration

    b. A written agreement

    c. Reasonable care of property

    d. Transfer of title

7. Against company policy, Worloski loaned his company's pickup truck to some good friends over the weekend so they could move their belongings to another house. While loaded with his friends' belongings, the engine broke down. The repairs have been estimated at $800. If a dispute over paying for repairs arose, a court would *most likely* rule that

    a. Worloski's friends must pay for repairs; they were using the truck when it became damaged.

    b. Worloski must pay for repairs; he borrowed the truck and thus assumed responsibility first.

    c. The truck's owner (Worloski's company) must pay for repairs; since neither Worloski nor his friends were negligent, it's just coincidence that Worloski was involved when the truck broke down.

    d. The cost of repairs would be split between Worloski and the company; Worloski could try to get his friends to pay some of his share, but they are under no legal obligation to do so.

8. Jenkins borrowed Andrus's car, promising to return it that same afternoon. She drove downtown and parked on the street. While she was having some dental work done, the car was repossessed. Andrus holds Jenkins responsible for the car's being taken. Is she?

    a. Yes; a bailee benefit bailment was created and that makes her responsible for almost everything that happens to the car.

    b. Yes; since Jenkins did not specify where the car would be taken, this is a case of conversion for which she can be held responsible.

    c. No; a bailee benefit bailment was created, but the repossession of the car takes precedence over Jenkins's responsibility to return the car.

    d. No; no bailment was created.

9. Carol and Clyde Forsythe loaned three of their antique Oriental carpets to the city's art museum for a show of Persian art. The rugs were stolen from the gallery during the exhibit. The museum's insurance company is refusing to cover

the loss of the carpets, saying the rugs weren't covered. What would be the *most likely* decision a court would reach in the case?

    a. The insurance company must pay Carol and Clyde for the stolen carpets even though the museum is completely blameless.

    b. Since the museum has no interest in the rugs, neither the museum nor its insurance company are liable for the loss.

    c. The museum is liable for the loss of the carpets and thus its insurer must pay for them.

    d. The decision will hinge on the specifics of the theft; the museum would be responsible only if it can be proved that the museum was guilty of gross negligence.

10. Three of the following four situations are bailments; one is not. Which is *not* an example of a bailment?

    a. A proprietorship leases a building from a commercial property investor

    b. A corporation office rents a copier from an office products dealer

    c. A partnership lets a good customer borrow the company's delivery truck for the weekend

    d. A corporation receives a "loaner" generator while its own is being repaired

YOUR OPINION, PLEASE

Read each of the following scenarios and answer the questions about the decisions you would make in each situation. Give these questions some serious thought; they may be used as the basis for the development of a more complex essay. You should base your decisions on what you've learned from this lesson, though you may incorporate outside readings or information gained through your own experience if it is relevant.

Scenario I

Kidder has rented a small cargo van from a local company to move some furniture of her mother's from one town to another. She has agreed to pay a per-day rate for the van as well as twenty cents a mile. She has further agreed to return the van with a full gas tank (or to pay the company for filling it). She has signed a rental agreement with many other clauses and restrictions, including several that spell out who will be responsible for damages under certain conditions. The company has warranted that the van is in good condition.

Nevertheless, in the early stages of the 100-mile trip from her mother's, the van develops a transmission problem and Kidder has to leave it on the highway full of furniture and hitch a ride to the nearest town. Kidder calls the emergency phone number on her rental agreement, but gets an answering service that merely takes a message without promising any help. Since it is a Sunday and no buses are running, she takes a cab back to her home. On Monday, the company sends a tow truck to retrieve the van, but the tow truck driver notices that the rear door has been broken into and the furniture removed. The loss is reported to Kidder.

Kidder threatens to sue the company for the loss of her furniture and for the cab fare home, pointing out that the van clearly was not in good condition or it would not have broken down, that the breakdown forced her to take the cab, and that it also put her furniture at risk. The rental company argues that Kidder did not exercise "reasonable care" of the van when she left it on the highway and made only the single telephone call. The transmission problem, it argues, could not have happened that suddenly and, if she had been having problems, she should never have left her mother's. The rental company says it might be willing to absorb the cost of the tow and repairs to the rear door, but it certainly will not pay for Kidder's furniture or her cab fare. Kidder responds by filing suit.

What's your opinion? Based on what you know of the situation, is the rental company fully responsible, so that all subsequent losses should be covered by them? Who actually is responsible for the loss of Kidder's furniture?

- Is Kidder's suit likely to be upheld in court? Why or why not?
- What factors support your answer?
- What factors might an attorney cite in arguing against your view?
- What steps, if any, might Kidder have taken to protect her furniture in this situation?
- What steps, if any, might the rental company have taken to protect its rights in this situation?

Scenario 2

Butler has purchased a solid oak dining room table from Fremont, a furniture maker, for $1,000. Fremont built it from lumber he had milled and dried himself, cut from oak logs that he had found along a public roadway. Since Fremont didn't know who had dropped the logs — they had been laying there for several weeks before he finally picked them up — he felt justified in using them.

Several months later, however, a representative of a local lumber company contacted Fremont. A man living near the road where Fremont found the logs had identified him as the finder, and the lumber company demanded their return. Fremont explained that he had cut up the logs and used them to build the dining room table for Butler. The lumber company thereupon contacted Butler and demanded the return of the materials in his table. Butler tells them that's impossible; of what use is a dining room table to a lumber company? Besides, he bought the table from Fremont in good faith for a reasonable price. The lumber company must deal with Fremont if they want compensation. The lumber company files suit against Fremont and Butler, demanding return of its logs.

What's your opinion? Based on what you know of the situation, do you think the logs were lost or mislaid property? Has Fremont acquired ownership by accession? Was he an innocent trespasser? Can Butler legally refuse to return the table? Can Fremont simply pay a reasonable value to the lumber company for the logs? Or would a court be likely to award the finished table to the lumber company as compensation for its loss of the logs?

- Is the lumber company's suit likely to be upheld in court? Why or why not?
- What factors support your answer?
- What factors might an attorney cite in arguing against your view?
- What steps, if any, might Fremont have taken to avoid a lawsuit in this situation?
- What steps, if any, might Butler have taken to protect his title to the table in this situation?

28

Government Regulation

LEARNING OBJECTIVES

Upon completing your study of this lesson, you should be able to

- Discuss the historical evolution of government regulation, beginning with the early *laissez-faire* economy, through the growth of regulation during the Industrial Revolution and beyond, to the current movement toward deregulation in some areas.

- Explain how the U.S. Constitution grants government its regulatory power.

- Explain how a broad interpretation of the commerce clause can expand the scope of the government's regulatory power to encompass business dealings, consumer protection, environmental protection, labor, and unemployment.

- Discuss how and why various administrative agencies enforce government regulations.

- Define the concept of *due process*, and relate this concept to enforcement of government regulations through various agencies.

- Discuss the importance of antitrust legislation in preserving competition within the marketplace.

- Describe the important provisions of several specific instances of antitrust legislation: the Sherman Act, the Clayton Act, and the Federal Trade Commission Act.

Prior to the Industrial Revolution, most Americans were self-employed, regardless of the nature of their work. Many, of course, were involved in agriculture. Such companies as did exist tended to be small and localized. Few — no matter what their methods of operating — had more than a nominal impact upon either the welfare of the American worker or the environment as a whole.

With the Industrial Revolution, all that changed. Today, most products and services are provided by companies, not individuals. By far, the majority of American workers work *for* someone else; those who do not often manage companies of their own. Thus, the way individual companies conduct their business now has major impacts on workers and consumers, on competitors within each industry, and on the economic and environmental welfare of us all.

Largely as a result of this impact, government has taken an ever-greater role in regulating business as a means of preserving the social and economic welfare of our society. Today's business manager makes few decisions — whether involving hiring, manufacturing, borrowing money, labor negotiations, or marketing — that are not, to some extent, controlled by government regulation at the local, state, or federal level.

Of course, not everyone applauds this situation. Many persons see it as a downright nuisance, an intrusion, an interference with free commerce. How can businesses grow and expand effectively, they argue, if they must spend all their time and energy untangling governmental red tape? Those who hold this view tend to favor deregulation. And even those who generally oppose deregulation will often admit that advocates of a more laissez-faire philosophy have a valid point.

But deregulation has its dark side, too. Even if unregulated, some companies would undertake their dealings with the highest social and ethical standards, never compromising integrity, quality, or safety for the sake of higher profits. Unfortunately, other companies will inevitably put profits first. History has shown us that, in the absence of government regulation, corporate empires tend to be quite oppressive toward both their workers and societal concerns such as clean water, clean air, and clean government. Corporate empires tend to see competitors as threats to the existence of the company and thus enemies to be vanquished. Any technique designed to conquer these enemies and reduce competition becomes of paramount concern.

But when competition is destroyed, the motivation to produce better products and services often dies with it. Profiteering, graft, and corruption become commonplace, and often the least scrupulous emerge as the most powerful. To protect the interests of both more ethical businesses and the consuming public, and to create an economic climate in which fair competition can thrive, the government has established some regulations by which all companies must abide.

In this lesson, we'll consider the nature and scope of government regulation of business in America, from both historical and current perspectives. We'll look at how the government derives its power to regulate business and how it currently exercises that power.

OVERVIEW

Deregulation is a hot topic on the American political scene these days. Those who want the red tape cut hold that excessive government intervention is bad for American business and that it hampers our ability to compete effectively in the world marketplace. They cite the extraordinary amounts of time, money, and other resources devoted to just *reporting* compliance with regulations. Many are also quick to point out that consumers ultimately bear the brunt of this costly "inefficiency" (as they view it) since delays, form completion, inspections, safety provisions, and repair or replacement of outdated or dangerous facilities and equipment all take time and money — money that companies have to recover by charging more for their products and services. If these resources were put directly into production, say the "deregulators," not only would productivity rise, but costs to consumers could be cut — so *everyone* would benefit from the new freedom. Besides, they ask, cost aside, how can government — operating from a distance — realistically and effectively manage private businesses?

Consider Wagner, who runs a company specializing in mineral resource exploration. Surely Wagner, who is on-site every day and who has years of technical training and experience, knows more about the needs and goals of his company than some distant government agency, however well meaning. It's hard to debate the logic of this perspective. But from the government's standpoint, that specialized knowledge does not earn Wagner the right to reshape the environment for his own purposes, to infect the land or waterways with dangerous chemicals, or to destroy wildlife habitats in his search for oil deposits. The government says it's fine for Wagner to make a profit, *so long as he does not do so at the expense of others*. In short, he can make whatever profit current compliance with regulations will allow.

Historical Evolution of Government Regulation

It's important to understand that regulation hasn't always been with us. Relatively speaking, it's a rather novel idea if one takes the long historical view. America's founders believed in a *laissez-faire* — or "hands-off" — approach to the regulation of business. Business leaders took care of business, politicians took care of government, and the two groups left each other alone. *Caveat emptor*, "let the buyer beware," was the byword of the marketplace in the 1800s. Moreover, there was little room for "friendly competition" in nineteenth century business transactions. With limited markets, hard-to-get supplies, and few production shortcuts, the business that hoped to survive often felt pressured into taking a fairly ruthless approach — wiping out competitors wherever opportunity permitted and taking full advantage of consumers not sufficiently wily to protect their own interests.

But by the late 1800s, too many competitors and consumers had fallen victim to unscrupulous business practices. Public opinion turned decidedly against the business tycoons, and this new philosophical tone set the stage for more aggressive laws that sought to intervene in the marketplace. Despite widespread public support, however, early efforts at reform were not as successful as advocates had hoped. It was not until the late 1930s that it became generally accepted by lawmakers and the courts that the Constitution did allow Congress fairly wide latitude in regulating commerce.

In fact, today's ongoing discussions about the proper amount of governmental regulation are only the latest round in a debate—and, at times, fight—that is unlikely to end. Typically, business leaders insist that government interference does more harm than good. But many workers and citizens point to abuses of the past and present as proof of the dangers of unregulated industry. In general, legislators and federal agencies now try to balance the ideal of the free marketplace with the less altruistic realities of human nature.

Most observers these days agree that *some* form of government control is necessary. But where and how to apply that control has never been an easy issue to resolve. Few persons want to return to the days in which consumers took their chances in a marketplace where profiteering was an integral part of shrewd business management; yet, at the same time, almost no one favors the insufferable hovering of a government that involves itself in even the least momentous of decisions.

The Sources of Government Regulatory Power

City, county, state, and federal administrative agencies together have created a web of regulations that govern how and under what circumstances a company is allowed to transact business, sell securities, set loan terms, ship freight, use resources, hire and fire employees, compete with rival firms, or negotiate labor contracts. You name it, and there's probably some type of regulation to govern it.

The government derives most of its power to regulate business from the U.S. Constitution's "commerce clause," which states that "*The Congress shall have power . . . to regulate commerce among the several states.*" This clause—together with the Constitution's Article I, Section 8, which empowers Congress to levy taxes—are the twin pillars on which government regulation rests.

The terse phrase *among the several states* allows some latitude in interpretation, and this has resulted in changes over time in the allowable scope of government control. At various points in its history, the commerce clause has been given a narrow interpretation; at other times, the interpretation has been considerably more expansive. At the heart of the issue is the debate over what constitutes *interstate* commerce (from *inter*, meaning *between*) versus *intrastate* commerce (from *intra*, meaning *within*). If the Supreme Court interprets "interstate" commerce to include only the transportation of goods from one state to another, this is quite different from an interpretation that considers "interstate" commerce to be business practices in one state (that is, intrastate) that affect business practices in another state. This distinction between *intra-* and *inter*state commerce is critical because the commerce clause allows Congress to regulate only that commerce that is *among* the several states.

The Early Years of Regulation

Early in the nineteenth century, the Supreme Court interpreted the commerce clause very broadly, giving the government power to regulate not only commerce that passed between states, but also "local" transactions that in some way "affected" interstate commerce. But this broad interpretation had little impact; since Congress left business pretty much alone to do as it wanted, the fact that the Supreme Court would permit broad regulation made little difference. As we noted earlier, however, by the end of the Civil War, workers and social advocates became increasingly upset with the overreaching practices of business, and Congress became more involved in attempting to regulate business practices. The passage of laws outlawing child labor and sixteen-hour work days were major examples of this initial regulation.

As Congress began to intervene in business practices this way, however, the Supreme Court also began to reevaluate its interpretation of the commerce clause. It came to believe that federal power could only extend to those business transactions that in fact moved from one state to another — only these transactions met the definition of *interstate* commerce. It concluded that all other business transactions — even if their influence extended beyond a state's boundaries — were part of *intrastate* commerce and, as such, beyond the reach of the federal government to regulate. So, ironically, as Congress became interested in passing regulatory law, the Supreme Court came to see those efforts as potentially unconstitutional. This conflict between what the public and Congress wanted and what business and the Supreme Court said the Constitution would allow continued until the late 1930s. But around that time, the Supreme Court again reevaluated its interpretation of the commerce clause and concluded that Congress had the power to regulate any transactions by businesses that organized themselves on a national scale, not just those transactions that crossed state lines.

The Current Regulatory Environment

Today, the Supreme Court continues to reflect this broader reading of the commerce clause, bringing it in line with the opinions held by the earliest Supreme Court views. Put simply, the current view is that *the federal government can constitutionally not only regulate commerce that passes through or is transacted across two states, but also commerce that affects business in other states.* Let's consider an example to see how this works.

Let's say that Sharpe, a street vendor of chocolate-chip cookies, uses some questionable business practices to undercut his competitors in the Seattle business district cookie market. At this point, he is probably violating only local fair-business ordinances. But suppose Sharpe instead distributed packages of cookies to be sold in Seattle supermarkets; if Sharpe's dubious practices are cutting into national markets, Sharpe may be charged with violating federal regulations — even though his is not a national company. Similarly, when business booms and Sharpe expands to form Northwest Cookies, a larger interstate company, he must either abandon his crafty methods of competition or risk running afoul of federal regulations.

Administrative Agencies

The war against improper business dealings is, for the most part, fought by government agencies created by Congress to oversee specialized segments of commerce. Agencies like the Federal Communications Commission, Securities and Exchange Commission, Environmental Protection Agency, and Federal Trade Commission wield considerable power. In fact, in the eyes of many observers, they form an unofficial fourth branch of government with the authority to enact rules and regulations (*quasi-legislative* power) and the power to hold hearings to determine whether those rules have been violated (*quasi-judicial* power). This power is delegated by Congress and can be withdrawn at any time; without the laws that authorize their actions, the agencies could not exist within our system of government, and whatever rules they made or hearings they held would have no legal effect.

The due process clauses of the Fifth and Fourteenth Amendments govern the way in which these congressionally created agencies must conduct themselves. First, they are required to guarantee each person or business who is charged with violation of agency rules or regulations *procedural due process*. This includes the right to an attorney, the right to summon witnesses, the right to cross-examine witnesses for the other side, and various other rights. In other words, the government requires that each agency develop a procedure that is *fair* in its dealings with individual or corporate "persons."

Let's pretend that Congress creates the Defense Contract Honesty Administration (DCHA) to monitor the pricing practices of American defense contractors. This agency, we'll suppose, is empowered to examine contracts, conduct independent price surveys, and generally look for evidence of abnormally high pricing, influence peddling, or corruption. Now let's say the DCHA discovers that Superior Widget, Inc., has been charging the Air Force $1,493.66 for widgets that are available in any hardware store for $1.29.

Under the rules of procedural due process, Superior Widget will be summoned to a hearing. But they must be told what charges are leveled against them, given an opportunity to prepare and present their side of the case, allowed to call any witnesses who can testify in support of Superior's pricing policies, and given the opportunity to cross-examine witnesses who might testify, for example, that the hardware store widgets are comparable to those offered by Superior.

The concept of *substantive due process* refers to the content of the rules and regulations set forth by each agency. An agency's rules must be relevant to the primary function for which the agency was created and the area over which it is authorized to regulate. In other words, an agency authorized to monitor and regulate the content of food products could not properly issue rules governing the rubber content of tires. If it tried to do so, a challenge to the agency rules would undoubtedly succeed; the rules would be found to exceed the substantive authority of the agency.

Judicial Review

A company or individual who is dissatisfied with the result of an agency hearing may request a court review. But here's a critical point to keep in mind: Generally, an agency decision will be upheld by the reviewing court if the court can find any evidence to justify the agency decision. If the reviewing court finds that there is evidence to support the agency decision—even if there's also evidence to support a contrary decision—the agency decision will stand. The *substantial evidence rule* means that the reviewing court will not weigh the evidence anew, but will look to see if there is enough evidence to support what the agency decided.

A person who is unhappy with the *procedures* the agency followed in making the decision can also ask for a judicial review of the decision, but this review is also limited. If the court finds that certain procedures were incorrect—and that those incorrect procedures may have made a difference in the outcome—the court will generally order that another agency hearing be held; the court will normally not just redecide the case itself.

Briefly, a person can seek a judicial review by alleging one of the following points:

1. Violation of procedural due process,
2. Violation of substantive due process,
3. Violation of Constitutional rights, or
4. There was an action in which the agency has exceeded its appointed authority.

For example, suppose Barnes, the owner of an interstate trucking company, is charged with violation of Interstate Commerce Commission (ICC) regulations governing permits for long-haul trucking. On the day he is served with notice of the alleged violation, Barnes also is told that his company's permit for interstate hauling is revoked effective that day. Since that revocation occurred without either prior notice or the opportunity to defend his company against the charges, Barnes would be within his rights to seek immediate judicial review of the revocation action. He would, in fact, most likely be successful in getting a temporary reinstatement of his permit; from a procedural standpoint, the ICC has not acted properly in withdrawing his license without giving him the opportunity to face and rebut the charges against him.

However, let's shift the circumstances a bit and suppose that Barnes is given sufficient notice to seek legal counsel and prepare the best possible defense. He summons several witnesses, all of whom have an opportunity to speak on his behalf; and his attorney is given a chance to cross-examine witnesses for the other side. All to no avail, however. The facts—in the eyes of the regulators—speak plainly enough: There is sufficient evidence that Barnes did violate the regulations and should have his trucking company's permit withdrawn. Will Barnes now be successful if he asks a court to review the agency action? From a procedural and a substantive standpoint, it is probable that the court will uphold the ICC action revoking Barnes's permit. While the court might agree that Barnes has some valid points, it is not likely to require a review since the regulators appear to have acted appropriately.

Antitrust Legislation

Once Congress decided in the late 1800s that it wanted—and needed—to regulate business, government leaders faced the monumental task of figuring out exactly what they should regulate and, equally important, how to go about it. These two questions sparked an intense debate that has yet to subside. Still, despite wide-spread controversy, Congress has been able to agree on several vital pieces of legislation, acts whose power has continued to shape government regulation right up to the present.

The Sherman Antitrust Act

The key to all the government's regulatory policy is one of the most significant pieces of legislation ever passed in this country: the *Sherman Antitrust Act*. Try to imagine Congress passing a bill that made many of American industry's most lucrative business practices illegal. The unlikelihood of such legislation—passed in 1890, when big business had an even a stronger influence on Washington politics than it has today—may help us appreciate the remarkable nature of the Sherman Act.

Indeed, by the late nineteenth century, America's corporate giants were virtually a law unto themselves. Workers had no rights; working conditions, even for children, were frequently dirty, dim, and dangerous. Workers who didn't like their jobs could do little but quit, and there were always more workers ready to take their place if they did so. Any attempts to unionize—or protests of any sort—were grounds for termination and, sometimes, criminal prosecution. Yet out of this decidedly probusiness climate emerged the Sherman Antitrust Act of 1890. The Sherman Act was Congress's response to growing public demands for protection from business grown too big, too unruly, too unwieldy, and too insensitive to the community that had fostered it.

Section 1: Restraint of trade. The Sherman Act essentially prohibits business combinations or actions that *restrain trade* or attempt to *monopolize* any area of commerce. The act has several significant sections.

Section 1 of the Sherman Act is simplicity itself: "*Every contract, combination in the form of trust and otherwise, or conspiracy in restraint of trade or commerce among the several states, is hereby declared illegal.*" Yet this wording, ostensibly so clear-cut, is far from simple to interpret. It has been the subject of much debate—and of much litigation.

Early on, the courts interpreted the section very narrowly, pointing out that a too-literal interpretation would, in effect, outlaw virtually every type of business transaction—since almost every contract between two parties restrains the ability of a third party from trading with one of the two. This interpretation had its own problems, however, for if the act were not given *some* literal interpretation, it was difficult to apply at all.

The courts first came to interpret the section under what was called the *rule of reason*. According to this rule, not every contract would be forbidden—only those that would *unreasonably* restrain trade. If a firm could show that its behavior was reasonable, it could use that argument as a defense in court. Of course, reasonableness is often in the eye of the beholder—as the courts rapidly discovered. Nearly any business dealing, however self-serving from one perspective, can look "reasonable" given the right vantage point.

Recognizing this problem—and attempting to more closely approximate the perceived intentions of those who drafted the Sherman legislation—the courts next determined that certain actions would be defined as *per se violations*. Under this theory, certain practices, by virtue of having been committed, were determined to constitute automatic violations of the Sherman Antitrust Act. Per se violations are acts so totally lacking in social value that, from the court's perspective, they are not considered defensible no matter how "reasonable" they may seem to the violators.

Per se violations include the following:

1. *Horizontal price-fixing*—agreements on price among competitors;

2. *Vertical price-fixing*—the granting of special prices to customers by companies or to companies by suppliers;

3. *Horizontal market divisions*—agreements among competing firms regarding who can sell in which region;

4. *Group boycotts*—agreements among competitors not to sell to a particular buyer or not to buy from a particular seller.

Of course, per se violations are usually subtle. Company managers these days do not get together in open meetings to propose price-fixing arrangements. Rather, they tacitly agree, through their behavior, to drive prices up by using pricing strategies that would not normally be dictated by demand. Often, the courts are able to discern that such agreements exist only through the conduct of the parties involved.

Deliberate attempts to fix prices, known as *conscious parallelism*, are in violation of the Sherman Act; conscious parallelism, together with some other factual evidence, will often provide grounds for conviction. However, deliberately fixing prices is different from using good marketing skills to set prices that maximize profit to the company. How does the court determine the difference? Sometimes, it's almost impossible. But an example may help illustrate the nuances in behavior and motivation that a court looks for in attempting to sort out the differences.

In a *pure-competition* economy, supply and demand establish the price of most goods and services. For instance, let's say that Gagnier operates a kennel that specializes in the breeding of golden retrievers. Heckel, on the other side of town, raises bulldogs. In their sports-minded, outdoors-loving community, where hunting is highly popular, the demand for retrievers is high. Bulldogs—generally regarded as watchdogs with minimal hunting skills—have enjoyed little popularity as pets. Thus, the going price for retrievers is, say, $200, while that for bulldogs is about $100. All this can change, of course; supply and demand are always in flux.

For instance, let's say that a rising crime rate (well publicized by the media) makes some citizens decide that having a guard dog is more important than having a good hunting dog. Given this new public perspective, perhaps bulldogs will now sell for $200, and the price of retrievers will drop to, say, $175. So far, supply and demand are dictating how the prices will go.

Heckel, as an established local breeder of bulldogs, might be looked on as the community's price leader in this particular area of commerce. If Kirby, who also raises bulldogs, sets up her kennel in competition with Heckel, it would only be good business for her to investigate current pricing and set her prices accordingly. If Heckel is charging $200 for his dogs and Kirby sets her prices at $300, she isn't likely to make many sales. But she might set her price at $225 and justify it by saying that her dogs are better. Still, she's letting the current market set some reasonable limits, acknowledging the power of her competitor, Heckel. Heckel's strategy is, to this point, an example of *price leadership*.

Now let's spice up this scenario by injecting a bit of conspiracy. Suppose that Kirby and Heckel get together to discuss the current market situation and determine that they're selling ten dogs a month at the going rate of $200 apiece and they expect demand to increase even further. They reason that they can boost demand even more by creating an artificial "shortage" — putting customers on waiting lists and breeding fewer dogs rather than more. In this newly manipulated supply–demand picture, they feel they can raise the going price for a bulldog puppy to $400 — well over current levels. At this new price, they'll make more money with less effort and less expense. They agree also that neither will undercut the other and that neither will raise or lower prices without the knowledge of the other.

Notice that there is no "price leader" in this scenario. Rather than responding to the existing market, the players are manipulating the market to suit themselves, "fixing" both supply and demand. In effect, Kirby and Heckel are no longer competitors; they're operating as if they were members of the same company. Since they're "partners," there is little motivation for one to treat customers better than the other or to produce better bulldogs. As a result, consumers suffer, getting less but paying more. This is *conscious parallelism*, and — were Kirby and Heckel to affect interstate commerce — it's a violation of Section 1 of the Sherman Act. It's precisely the sort of conspiratorial arrangement — admittedly on a small scale — that the writers of the Sherman legislation wanted to discourage.

By the way, you may be wondering whether Heckel and Kirby could be convicted of conscious parallelism simply on the grounds that their prices were identical. The answer is no. Identical prices *can* be the result of coincidence. They can also be, and often are, the result of marketplace competition. Two hot-dog vendors located right next to one another may have identical prices; to the extent that consumers view their hot dogs as a uniform product, they're likely not to patronize the higher-priced vendor. As a result, the price is likely to stabilize at the level that produces the optimum combination of profit and volume. Moreover, the *conscious* part of *conscious parallelism* implies a need for direct intent to match prices — a difficult thing to prove.

Note that it's impossible for a single company or individual to run afoul of any portion of Section 1. There is, after all, no way to have a conspiracy within one company; conspiracy, by definition, requires that multiple entities act in concert. For example, let's say three small companies all sell pig iron. One is headquartered in Oregon, one in Washington, and one in California. The three are in direct competition with a national producer, which sells to all three states. The three smaller companies make a secret agreement to sell only in their respective home states, the better to compete with the big producer. Prior to the agreement, each minor competitor controls 10% of the total pig-iron market in the three-state area. Afterward, by focusing their marketing efforts in a smaller area, each is able to seize 15%, cutting the major producer's market share substantially. Have the three conspiring companies violated the Section 1 rules prohibiting horizontal price-fixing? Probably so, because three supposedly independent companies have agreed to restrain their marketing efforts in order to hurt the sales of a fourth company.

But what about Clark, Martin, and Windsor, all salespersons employed by the Big Boar Pig Iron Company of Peoria? Say the three agree that one will sell in Illinois, one in Indiana, and one in Ohio, the better to compete with their archrival, the multistate Megasmelt Pig Iron, Inc. In this case, the arrangement is perfectly legal, because Clark, Martin, and Windsor all work for the same company.

Section 2: Monopolies. Section 2 of the Sherman Act states that "*Every person who shall monopolize, or attempt to monopolize, or combine or conspire with any other person or persons to monopolize any part of the trade or commerce among the several states, or with foreign nations, shall be deemed guilty of a misdemeanor.*"

This section is designed to keep companies from gaining monopoly power, which, for legal purposes, is defined as more than 70% control of a given industry. Bear in mind, however, that simply *having* monopoly power does not necessarily constitute violation of Section 2. The key questions here are, How was that monopoly power acquired? And what steps—if any—does the company take to maintain a monopoly position, once gained?

Take the case of the Kwik-Kut Automatic Lawnmower Company, which develops a lawnmower with features that put it decades ahead of its time. The Kwik-Kut Self-Propelled 2000 obeys voice commands to automatically cut and vacuum the grass and edge the borders. Advanced safety features ensure that the mower poses absolutely no hazard to pets or children. Better still, through its computerized automated assembly techniques, Kwik-Kut is able to build its mower at about half what it costs competitors to assemble conventional mowers. Retailing for less than $200, it captures 93% of the American lawnmower market in a matter of months.

Kwik-Kut's competitors are, naturally, a little upset; they can't sell their mowers at any price. But would they be able to persuade the government to sue Kwik-Kut for monopolizing, under Section 2 of the Sherman Act? Probably not. As the government—or the competitors' own attorneys—would point out, Kwik-Kut didn't set out to capture monopoly power; it simply had a good product that was so successful it took over the market. While others in the industry may hate to admit it, Kwik-Kut has captured the market through improved design, increased market awareness, and better engineering—what some people would call good old American ingenuity. And there's nothing illegal about that, even if it puts the competitors who can't keep pace out of business.

On the other hand, suppose Kwik-Kut really doesn't have such a revolutionary product after all. Let's say that the 2000 mower doesn't actually have the safety features it is said to have; Kwik-Kut simply made those claims to increase its market share, hoping the claims would not be readily disproved. Further, Kwik-Kut takes every opportunity to undercut competitors' prices through constant "specials" that become, in effect, its regular price. Let's further suppose that Kwik-Kut offers discounts on other merchandise to dealers who agree to carry the 2000 exclusively and advertise it heavily, or that it gives away mowers to influential media managers in order to get favorable news reports or unpaid-for advertising from local radio stations or newspapers. Such conduct would more clearly reveal Kwik-Kut's *intention* to gain monopoly power through whatever means — even to the extent of compromising quality, falsely advertising the product, manipulating customers, or taking unfair advantage of competitors. In the eyes of the law, winning through cheating is *not* the same as winning through excellence, and legal action against Kwik-Kut might well succeed.

The Clayton Act

The Sherman Act is essentially remedial in nature. It's designed to correct injustices after the fact, and to ensure that a company doesn't profit once a wrong has been committed. But in 1914, attempting to take a more active approach in *preventing* problems before they arose, Congress created the *Clayton Act*, legislation intended to nip illicit business practices in the bud.

The Clayton Act has four major provisions, each addressing a different potential problem:

- Section 2 prohibits *price discrimination*,
- Section 3 forbids *exclusive dealing contracts* and *tying arrangements*,
- Section 7 prohibits mergers of any type that tend to have a *negative effect on any line of commerce*, and
- Section 8 prohibits *interlocking directorates*.

Let's take a closer look at each of these.

Section 2. Section 2 of the Clayton Act makes it illegal for a seller to discriminate among buyers in setting prices unless the price difference is justified by some difference in the cost of doing business. For example, Berg, a textile merchant, cannot sell a given fabric at one cost to Park and at another cost to Moench. The price to both must be the same unless a difference in Berg's costs of selling to Park justify a different price than for Moench.

This section of the Clayton Act created a considerable disturbance among merchants when it was first enacted. Regular purchasers often expected and got favored pricing as a kind of reward for continuous and substantial business. When the favors were discontinued, they sometimes threatened to take their business elsewhere, putting merchants in the uncomfortable position of either risking violation or risking substantial — sometimes financially fatal — loss of business. In order to make things more equitable and put some responsibility for ethical conduct on the heads of the purchasers, Congress passed the Robinson–Patman Act, which prohibited buyers from knowingly accepting a discriminatory price. Now buyers — like sellers — faced liability for favoritism in pricing.

Section 3. Section 3 of the Clayton Act prohibits *tying arrangements*, agreements in which one party — usually, but not always, the seller — refuses to buy or sell one product or service unless the arrangement includes a second product as well. It also prohibits *exclusive-dealing contracts* in which one party requires that a second party buy or sell exclusively from or to them. The anti-tying arrangement provision is a good example of how the government attempts to restrain potential monopolies, because for a company to be in a position of forcing a tying arrangement on a customer, the seller has to be in an extremely powerful market position. For instance, if Ralph's Friendly Lawn Care tells Green Valley Country Club that they must buy *all* their gardening supplies from Ralph's, or else Ralph's will not sell them anything, chances are that Green Valley will simply take their business to another store. Ralph's, a local business with a small market share and few if any exclusive products or services, lacks the business clout to set up an exclusive-dealing contract — even if it were legal to do so.

However, suppose that a single semiconductor manufacturer, Beta Corporation, makes 70% of the memory chips used in microcomputers. Since the rest of chips are made by small companies unable to consistently supply chips in sizable volumes, the computer manufacturers almost always have to by some chips from Beta. If Beta announces that they will sell chips only to the computer manufacturers who buy *all* their memory chips from them, Beta is probably violating the Clayton Act's exclusive-dealing provision. Its dominant market position has put the company in the position where it could, unlike Ralph's Lawn Care, successfully engage in monopolistic practices.

Tying arrangements are similar in intent, but they're designed to help a merchant unload a less-popular product to a buyer who's eager to buy another, more-popular product. Suppose that Beta Corporation is the only source of the processing chip that computer manufacturers need to use if their machines are to run any of the generally available software. If Beta announces that they will sell this processing chip only to the computer manufacturers that also buy equivalent numbers of their overpriced, less well-regarded graphics display chip, they may well be violating the Clayton Act's anti-tying provision. Now it's the popularity of a product — the processing chip — that has put the company in the position where it could engage in detrimental monopolistic practices.

Section 7. Section 7 of the Clayton Act covers proper and improper mergers. An improper merger is one designed to "substantially lessen competition or create a monopoly." For instance, suppose that in our ongoing scenario, Ralph's Friendly Lawn Care provides the only local outlet for Kwik-Kut products. As it happens, Ralph's also has a number of lucrative lawn-care accounts, including Green Valley Country Club and Green Acres City Park. Kwik-Kut has had, until now, a very limited market share in the service end of the lawn-care industry. But recent corporate decisions have caused it to embark on an aggressive expansion of its service division. In looking at its customers, it notes that Ralph's market share is quite high; buying out Ralph's would not only expand its own market share but eliminate its major competitor in the area. It makes Ralph's an offer: merge with Kwik-Kut or lose the right to sell the very popular Kwik-Kut mower. Without an alternate supplier available, Ralph's has no real choice. And Kwik-Kut, give its powerful position, can probably set the price to suit itself, ensuring that Ralph's will dissolve into the new company with scarcely a ripple.

Is this a violation of Section 7? Based on these facts, yes. The merger is designed specifically to give Kwik-Kut the monopoly power it craves and to eliminate competition. Further, Ralph's is coerced into joining forces; it's hardly a mutually desirable arrangement. But suppose Ralph's were on the verge of bankruptcy, just about to go under. In that case, a merger with Kwik-Kut might be most welcome — and even sought after — as a way of preserving the company, even if Ralph's identity were totally lost in the process.

Obviously, mergers take place every business day, and the vast majority are perfectly legal. What Section 7 tries to prevent are mergers that seriously harm competition in the marketplace. For example, a horizontal merger — one between two competitors — that gives the resulting company more than 20% of the market is likely to be scrutinized very closely by government regulators. Vertical mergers — between a firm and one of its major suppliers or customers — are also frowned upon if they deny competing firms access to major markets.

Similarly, conglomerate mergers — between firms in two noncompetitive industries — meet with disfavor if they are likely to diminish competition in both industries by reducing the number of firms in each. To illustrate, suppose a major oil company merges with an automobile manufacturer. The gigantic, newly formed company might have sufficient power to virtually eliminate competition in both of the original industries. The clear purpose of such an arrangement might well be to create a monopoly — in direct opposition to the intent of the Clayton Act.

Section 8. Section 8 of the Clayton Act is aimed at preventing *interlocking directorates*, situations where the same people sit on the boards of directors of competing firms. Say Barnard is the chairman of the board at the Bank of Happy Valley. He is also a member of the board of Happy Valley Savings and Loan and is soon to be named to the board chairmanship of Happy Valley Trust. Given the potential for price fixing (e.g., via increased interest rates on loans) and division of markets if all three competing banks were, to a significant extent, controlled by the same person, it's highly unlikely that federal regulators would allow Barnard to sit on all three boards.

The Federal Trade Commission Act

In 1914, the year the Clayton Act became law, Congress also passed the *Federal Trade Commission Act*. This act did two important things: it created the Federal Trade Commission to enforce the Clayton Act and other antitrust laws, and it closed many of the loopholes left by existing antitrust legislation.

The wording of the FTC Act is intentionally broad. It prohibits "unfair methods of competition" and "unfair and deceptive trade practices." The purpose of this deliberately nonspecific language is to give the FTC enough discretionary power to act against any business that is engaging in questionable business practices that do not fit neatly within the more explicit definitions set forth in other legislation. In the absence of the FTC Act, such businesses might readily escape prosecution because *technically* they were not violating the more specific antitrust statutes—even though there might be a very clear violation of the spirit of those statutes. Clearly, the FTC must exercise considerable judgment in determining which practices are or are not unfair—restrictive to free trade, that is. And the FTC Act gives the agency power to do just that.

If, after appropriate procedural steps, the FTC determines that a business practice is unfair or deceptive, it will issue a *cease and desist* order. If the target company disobeys, it faces a fine of $5,000 per violation. This may sound small, but bear in mind that *each day* the order is ignored is treated as a separate violation. That's $35,000 a week in fines, or $1.8 million per year. And while such a sum is still relatively small to a large publicly held company, the publicity that would accompany such fines would be very damaging indeed.

In recent years, the FTC has focused considerable attention on two undesirable advertising practices: deceptive advertising and bait-and-switch advertising. Let's first consider deceptive advertising.

Deceptive advertising. Say the Peaches 'N' Cream Wrinkle Remover, which retails at $80 per precious ounce, claims it can restore "even the oldest, most weathered skin to blushing, youthful radiance." Despite its price, it enjoys staggering sales. But to the dismay of purchasers, the product has no such effect.

Because of its broad mandate, the FTC has the power to insist on corrective advertising—advertising with a public-awareness intent. In this case, Peaches 'N' Cream could be required to inform both past and future consumers about the prior deceptive claims and take steps to remove any false beliefs placed in the public mind by dishonest advertising claims. However uncomfortable it might be, Peaches 'N' Cream would probably be required to withdraw their miraculous claims and admit that their wrinkle remover was really no more effective than a $2 moisturizing lotion. If it saw fit, the FTC could require the company to continue broadcasting its disclaimers until it had spent as much on corrective advertising as it had originally gained through sales of its misrepresented product.

Bait and switch. Bait-and-switch advertising involves the practice of enticing customers into the store by advertising one product and then talking the customer into buying another, more-expensive product—claiming, for instance, that the original product advertised is out of stock or is unsuited to the customer's needs. Let's say that Weitzel sells high-tech electronics products. He advertises a certain car stereo for $200—an outstanding price on the product as he represents it. When Gwynn comes in to buy the stereo, however, Weitzel tells him that the specially discounted stereo is—most unfortunately—not the best model for use with his particular automobile. Gwynn would be much better off, he is assured by Weitzel, purchasing another model that retails at $400—a heftier investment to be sure, but a product he's sure to be far more satisfied with in the long run. Notice how this approach not only nets Weitzel a bigger profit but allows him to pose as if he's acting in Gwynn's best interests as he does so. The FTC has the power to investigate and take corrective action against those companies accused and proven to have engaged in bait-and-switch practices.

Protection of rights. The FTC also acts as a kind of guardian agency for the rights of those who develop and wish to protect special products, procedures, services, strategies, or whatever makes their business prosper. Let's consider several examples of this guardian function.

First, the FTC regulations prohibit *palming off*—the advertising, designing, or selling of goods as if they were the goods of another. For instance, the local bakery cannot buy loaves of bread at volume discount from a national company, repackage them, and sell the bread as its own. Sometimes, palming off involves patent, copyright, or trademark infringements. A shoe store could not, for example, use the name of a famous sport shoe maker to advertise an inexpensive copy of the shoe.

Palming off could also involve trade secrets. *Trade secrets* are the processes or formulas developed by a company in the course of its work. They are as important to the success of the company as any product or service produced by that company and must be treated with the same confidentiality and right to protection. An employee who discloses trade secrets may be held liable for any damages that result— that is, for lost business or profits. The competitor who takes advantage of the trade secrets, by the way, shares liability with the employee who passed on the information; in short, the court treats this behavior as a form of conspiracy.

Finally, the FTC is interested in protecting *trademarks*, *patents*, and *copyrights*. A trademark is a mark, symbol, or name used to identify a particular brand or product. It cannot be used or imitated legally by anyone else. A copyright is an exclusive right to the profits generated by a book, play, song, work of art, or similar item. Such works cannot be reproduced for profit by anyone else. A patent is a federally created and protected monopoly power given to inventors. Patents allow inventors to retain exclusive rights to produce, use, and sell their inventions for a period of seventeen years.

SOME PRACTICAL ADVICE

It is vital that any business owner or manager be familiar with the legislative requirements of the Sherman Antitrust Act, the Clayton Act, and the Federal Trade Commission Act—along with any other legislation that affects his or her particular industry. Keep in mind that government regulation is pervasive; it touches virtually every aspect of business life and refuses to be ignored. Further, the penalties for violation are often severe, and can—in extreme cases—threaten the very existence of a business. Thus, it is not only wise but essential to be informed.

Government-appointed agencies, such as the Environmental Protection Agency, derive their power from Congress and cannot act beyond the power accorded them by Congress. But when they are granted the power to issue rules and regulations, and when they issue rules and regulations within the scope of their authority, their rules and regulations are nearly always enforceable. Agency decisions made in keeping with properly adopted rules and regulations are usually upheld if challenged by judicial review. Further, though these agencies do not make laws, the distinction between a law and a government regulation—from the businessperson's point of view—is a fine one indeed. Assuming an alleged violator is treated with due process (as defined under the Constitution) and is found after examination of the facts to be in violation, the violator may be subject to substantial fines or other penalties, and may also be required, through injunction, to cease the behavior in question. In short, it is foolhardy to assume that government agencies—because they are not true legislative or judicial bodies—lack the power to control one's business fate. Not so.

Of course, rules and regulations governing business are both numerous and complex—a good argument for seeking the experienced counsel of a lawyer who specializes in the laws particularly affecting your business. But in addition, it's helpful to remember that in the area of trade and competition regulation, most government rules pertaining to business have one overriding purpose—to maintain the free market and discourage monopolies that smother competition and ingenuity. Therefore, the wise businessperson will ask of any potential decision, What is its likely impact on the market as a whole? Does it promote and strengthen competition? Or does it simply promote the growth of one business alone—at the potential expense of the industry or the larger marketplace? The answers to these key questions do not tell the businessperson all he or she needs to know about antitrust and anticompetition regulations, but they offer a good clue as to how the government is likely to view any questionable business practice.

ASSIGNMENTS

- Before you watch the video program, be sure you've read through the preceding overview, familiarized yourself with the learning objectives for this lesson, and looked at the key terms below. Then, read Chapters 45 and 46 of Davidson et al., *Business Law*.

- After completing these tasks, view the video program for Lesson 28.

- After watching the program, take time to review what you've learned. First, evaluate your learning with the self-test which follows the key terms. Then apply and evaluate what you've learned with the "Your Opinion, Please" scenarios at the end of this telecourse study guide lesson.

KEY TERMS

Before you read through the textbook assignment and watch the video program, take a minute to look at the key terms associated with this lesson. When you encounter them in the textbook and video program, pay careful attention to their meaning.

Bait-and-switch advertising
Caveat emptor
Cease-and-desist order
Conglomerate merger
Conscious parallelism
Copyright
Corrective advertising
Due process
Exclusive-dealing contract
Failing-company doctrine
Horizontal merger
Interlocking directorates

Interstate commerce
Intrastate commerce
Laissez-faire economy
Monopoly
Per se violation
Price leadership
Pure-competition economy
Trademark
Trade secrets
Tying arrangement
Vertical merger

SELF-TEST

The questions below will help you evaluate how well you've learned the material in this lesson. Read each one carefully, and select the letter of the option that best answers the question. You'll find the correct answer, along with a reference to the page number(s) where the topic is discussed, in the back of this telecourse study guide.

1. A laissez-faire economy is best described as one in which

   a. large corporations control supply and demand.
   b. business management is heavily dominated by unions.
   c. the government closely controls every aspect of interstate trade, though local business is left to private control.
   d. the government interferes as little as possible in business practices.

2. The government's power to regulate business derives *mainly* from

   a. the commerce clause of the United States Constitution.
   b. popular consent.
   c. the Sherman Antitrust Act.
   d. the judicial power of the Supreme Court.

3. History shows that, overall, the most satisfactory approach to regulation seems to be

   a. total deregulation with absolute separation of government and business concerns.
   b. minimal regulation that guards against especially harmful practices, but largely leaves businesses alone.
   c. an intermediate approach that regulates many, but by no means all, business matters.
   d. heavy government regulation that specifies how to handle most business matters.

4. Houser Dairy, located just outside San Francisco, does all its business in the Bay Area. It controls 4% of the local dairy market there but has no measurable impact on the market share of national distributors. If Houser is involved in a vertical price-fixing scheme, is the company likely to be prosecuted for violation of the Sherman Act?

   a. Yes, because vertical price-fixing is a per se violation, and no defense for these actions is allowed if the violation is shown to have occurred.
   b. No, because 4% isn't a large enough market share to give Houser monopoly power — and only monopolies can be prosecuted under the Sherman Act.
   c. Yes, but only if the government can prove that their action was meant to increase their market share.
   d. No, probably not, because Houser's actions, so far as we can tell, have no apparent effect on interstate commerce.

5. After a lengthy investigation, elaborate preparation of testimony, and presentation of cases by both parties, Wilson–Wright, Inc., is convicted of violating the Environmental Protection Agency's regulations and fined $1.5 million. Based on the information given, if Wilson–Wright were to seek judicial review of its conviction, which of the following arguments would likely succeed in overturning the conviction?

   a. The EPA did not give Wilson–Wright adequate time to prepare a case.
   b. The specific rule on which Wilson–Wright's conviction is based is not authorized by EPA legislation.
   c. The EPA regulators did not interpret the evidence in the correct manner.
   d. *Any* of the above would be appropriate grounds for overturning the decision.

6. According to the lesson, a *pure-competition economy* is one in which

   a. there is no government regulation and businesses are free to run themselves as they see fit.
   b. nearly every contract is viewed as a restraint of trade and therefore outlawed.
   c. monopolies are viewed in a positive way and encouraged by consumers and the courts.
   d. no single business has enough power to affect either supply and demand or pricing in a major way.

7. Which of the following scenarios is *least likely* to be a successful defense under the Sherman Act's "rule of reason"?

   a. That an agreement on sales territories among three competing firms was necessary to avoid losing market share to a fourth larger firm.
   b. That a firm was forced to set prices similar to a competitor's to avoid a price war it could not survive.
   c. That the practice of offering "volume discounts" to large buyers and charging more for the same merchandise to low-volume buyers is justified by the different costs incurred in the production runs.
   d. That a group boycott among several buyers is necessary because an important supplier has begun to use unscrupulous business tactics.

8. The overriding purpose behind passage of the Clayton Act was to

   a. prohibit the kinds of business practices that restrain free trade.
   b. close the many loopholes created by the Sherman Act.
   c. outlaw horizontal market divisions and group boycotts.
   d. monitor businesses' advertising practices.

9. Under provisions of the Clayton Act, which of the following is *least likely* to be illegal?

   a. Aero Autocar Company, which manufactures the extremely popular Aero 8000, requires that each retailer also buy one of the less-popular Aero 7000s for each 8000 it supplies.
   b. Promethius Computers, which makes the highly successful Metro personal computer, begins manufacturing software as well — then tells purchasers they will receive no more computers if they buy software from any other supplier.
   c. Roadstar Interstate Trucking is about to file for bankruptcy when it is acquired by Bob's West Coast Freight, which then controls 38% of the west coast market.
   d. Fergus O'Reilly, chairman of the board at Monolithic Motor Corporation, is elected to the board of directors at Paragon Auto Supply Parts.

10. Bork Brewing Company runs a series of television ads in which it claims that Bork Beer actually "has a noticeable impact on weight loss." If subsequent tests show that Bork Beer has the same number of calories as regular beer and no perceptible weight-loss benefits, is Bork Brewing likely to be found in violation of the FTC Act's deceptive trade practices statutes?

    a. No; they never claimed their product would help consumers *lose* weight — only that it would *affect* their weight loss.
    b. No, because even though the wording of the ad is tricky, no reasonable person would believe that anyone can lose weight drinking beer.
    c. Yes, absolutely; the wording of this ad creates a "fair possibility" of deception, and Bork may well be required to run corrective advertising.
    d. We cannot say without knowing whether Bork intended the ads seriously or was making a humorous claim that no one could take seriously.

YOUR OPINION, PLEASE

Read each of the following scenarios and answer the questions about the decisions you would make in each situation. Give these questions some serious thought; they may be used as the basis for the development of a more complex essay. You should base your decisions on what you've learned in this lesson, though you may incorporate outside readings or information gained through your own experience if it is relevant.

Scenario 1

Rogers Pharmaceutical Supply is a large drugstore supply wholesaler based in Chicago. It has about $200 million in annual sales in Indiana and Ohio. Its chief competitor is Jones-Grey Corporation, the largest drugstore supply wholesaler in the country. Jones-Grey also has about $200 million in annual sales in the two-state area. A third company, Pelman Supply, based in Cincinnati, has about $80 million in annual Indiana and Ohio sales.

In an effort to increase its market share in the Midwest, Jones-Grey decides to acquire Rogers Pharmaceutical. Rogers is financially overextended, and without the strong infusion of capital Jones-Grey has promised to provide, Rogers may have to file for bankruptcy. Rogers stockholders agree in principle to the merger, pending regulatory approval.

If Jones-Grey merges with Rogers Pharmaceutical, the resulting company will control more than 80% of the Indiana–Ohio drugstore market. Many large drugstore chains, which need a wide variety of supplies in large quantities, will have no choice but to do business with them. Pelman Supply files suit to block the merger, arguing that it would violate both the Sherman and Clayton Acts. Jones-Grey argues that Rogers Pharmaceutical is on the verge of collapse, so that without the merger there will be chaos in the Midwest marketplace.

What's your opinion? Based on what you know about the situation, do you think the courts would uphold Pelman's contention that the proposed merger would result in a dangerous monopoly? Is the acquisition a sound business dealing? Or will the resulting situation cause more chaos than would be the case if Rogers simply collapsed?

- Is Pelman's suit likely to be upheld in court? Why or why not?
- What factors support your answer?
- What factors might an attorney cite in arguing against your view?
- What steps, if any, might Jones-Grey have taken to prevent a lawsuit in this situation?
- What steps, if any, might Pelman have taken to protect its position in this situation?

Scenario 2

In the year 2024, Urbana Miracle Materials develops and patents a substance called Plastisteel. Plastisteel is a thick fluid that, poured into molds, hardens in a few minutes into a substance stronger than alloy steel and lighter than foam. Using very large molds, it is possible to construct huge skyscrapers, stadiums, and manufacturing facilities from unified shells of Plastisteel, structures that seem to defy the laws of gravity because of the extreme lightness of the material. Plastisteel is cheaply synthesized from natural, renewable materials using a patented, closely guarded, secret manufacturing process, and sells for about the same price as concrete. Manufacturing the material produces no pollution, and Plastisteel components that are no longer needed can be degraded into a nontoxic slurry by the application of a harmless solution of special Plastisteel-eating bacteria.

Within three years, Plastisteel is the main building material used on the planet, and Urbana controls 89% of the American construction materials market. The situation continues for more than a decade, until finally a rival materials firm patents Technolite, a substance that, when dry, is even lighter, cheaper, and more durable than Plastisteel. Moreover, Technolite has the capacity to absorb and store solar power. Within a year, Technolite seizes one-quarter of the building materials market.

Publicly, Urbana Miracle Materials remains serene, claiming it welcomes the competition and that there's plenty of room in the market for both firms. Privately, however, it commissions several intensive studies of Technolite. Each study eventually uncovers the fact that Technolite has a tendency to crack and weaken after prolonged exposure to ultraviolet radiation. These findings, made public through "independent laboratory testing," result in an immediate drop in Technolite sales and a concurrent resurgence in Plastisteel sales.

Technolite, Inc., maker of Technolite, quickly discovers the truth—that the research studies were ordered by Urbana Miracle Materials. They threaten to file suit against Urbana, alleging a violation of the Sherman Act's prohibitions against monopolizing, unless Urbana immediately pays them $3 billion in reparation for lost sales. Urbana refuses, on the grounds that it acquired its monopoly legally by developing a superior product; besides, Urbana spokespeople add, the charges that Technolite is dangerously defective are true—regardless of who commissioned the tests.

What's your opinion? Based on what you know about the situation, do you think the courts will uphold Technolite's suit on the grounds that Urbana is monopolizing? Does the fact that Urbana's charges are true—and Technolite makes no attempt to deny them—justify the fact that Urbana commissioned the studies in an effort to retain its huge market share? Or do Urbana's actions violate the anti-monopolizing statutes?

- Is Technolite's suit likely to be upheld in court? Why or why not?
- What factors support your answer?
- What factors might an attorney cite in arguing against your view?

- What steps, if any, might Urbana have taken to prevent a lawsuit in this case?
- What alternative approaches, if any, might Technolite have used to protect its market share in this case?

29

Consumer and Environmental Protection

LEARNING OBJECTIVES

Upon completing your study of this lesson, you should be able to

- Describe, in general terms, the evolution of consumer protection legislation, beginning with the increased awareness of limited consumer protection in the mid-1960s.

- Explain the primary purposes of consumer protection legislation as it exists today.

- Describe the specific areas of concern covered by consumer credit legislation and product safety legislation.

- Discuss the purposes for and potential impact of environmental protection legislation, using specific examples of environmental abuse to illustrate the need for such legislation.

- List the primary areas of concern covered by the National Environmental Policy Act, and explain — using general examples — the intended impact of this act on each area of concern.

When Horace Greeley gave his legendary entrepreneurial advice—"Go west, young man"—he probably didn't add, "But as you do so, take care not to harm the environment or infringe on the rights of consumers." Neither of these issues was high on the nineteenth-century business agenda. That situation—as we shall see in this lesson—has changed fairly dramatically.

These days, businesspeople no longer have free rein in conducting their business affairs without regard for the impact on consumers or their natural surroundings; in short, profit potential alone is insufficient grounds for business decisions. What has brought about this change? Although it would be nice to give credit to an enlightened ethical sensitivity on the part of business managers, much of the change is, in truth, due directly to the impact of consumer and environmental protection laws.

The purpose of this lesson is to examine these laws and their impact on business behavior. But wait a moment, you may be saying: How are consumer protection laws related to environmental impact? What's the connection here; why study them together? The link is a simple one: both have to do with the overall quality of life. Much new legislation in the latter half of this century, in fact, relates directly to this broad theme: making life better—more livable—for all of us. In this lesson, we'll consider the ways in which laws recognizing consumer rights, as well as those regulating the use of the environment, affect the quality of life.

OVERVIEW

In recent years, Congress has passed many laws intended to protect the consumer from unfair or confusing business practices and dangerous products, and to protect our natural environment. While such laws are intended—as we've noted—to improve the quality of life, they often restrict the way businesses may operate. Sometimes, in fact, the financial impact of complying with such laws can be significant and may limit a business's power to function as it has in the past. In extreme cases, the impact may affect the business's ability to continue functioning at all.

Consumer Protection

Concern for the rights of consumers is not new, but never before in the history of our country has it received so much emphasis or such strong legislative support. During the nineteenth century, *caveat emptor*—"Let the buyer beware"—was the prevailing attitude among merchants. In a nation intent on enhancing its economic future, laws tended to foster commercial development, not protect the consumer.

By the middle of the twentieth century, however, consumers felt that business needs had been given too much preferential treatment—often at the expense of consumers' rights. No doubt millions of individual consumers had previously held this view at one time or another, but now—for the first time—consumers were gaining a sense of their identity as a group and, with that identity, a sense of their growing power. Consumer activists began to convince local, state, and federal governments to pass laws that would reevaluate priorities and give consumers the protection they felt they needed and deserved. In addition, the media—notably television—provided a highly visible forum for consumers who were no longer willing to put up with unfair treatment or inferior, defective, or dangerous products.

The consumer movement's message proved persistent and forceful, and Congress responded. First came federal legislation to encourage product safety. Later federal laws protected consumers in their everyday business transactions. How much of a difference have such laws made? To better appreciate their impact, let's consider a hypothetical scenario as it might have been played out just a few decades ago, and as it might unfold now.

Imagine for a moment that it's the mid-1950s. Cooper, a typical consumer of that era, wishes to purchase an expensive new console television. He does not have enough money to pay cash, so he asks to buy the television on credit. Clearly, this represents a convenience for Cooper, because it allows him to buy the television now, rather than waiting until he's saved up enough to pay cash. But what may be less obvious is that credit also benefits the seller; it not only encourages the sale of more TVs but also, through interest payments, boosts the ultimate purchase price of each product, enhancing the seller's long-term gain.

Of course, this gain is not without some risk. The seller recognizes that if he complies with Cooper's request and extends credit, Cooper will have the television in his home and the seller will have less cash on hand than if the television were sold outright. Later, if Cooper doesn't come through with the agreed-on monthly payments, the seller may never recover the fair value of the merchandise—which by then will be used and worth less. So, to protect the business, the seller may refuse to extend credit at all; and he may or may not give Cooper a reason for this decision. If he does decide to extend the credit, he'll probably ask Cooper to sign an agreement drawn up by the seller specifying how and when Cooper will pay off the debt.

Remember, this is the 1950s; this means that the seller is pretty much in control of the situation. He can decide whether to extend credit to Cooper in the first place, determine exactly what the finance charges will be, and draw up the contract to suit himself—even if some of the language is confusing or misleading to Cooper. Cooper, for his part, can sign or not; if he wants the television—and doesn't have the cash—his options are few. Again, this being the 1950s, the law is primarily on the side of the merchant.

Let's say Cooper does get the credit. A few months go by, and Cooper—who runs a bit short of cash—fails to make a timely payment. The seller can, at his discretion, pursue a number of options. He can attempt to collect the debt himself, come to repossess the television, or turn the case over to a debt collector. Whether trying to collect the debt himself or through a debt-collection agency, the tactics may include talking with Cooper's employer about the situation, calling Cooper at all times of the day or night, verbally or in writing harassing him about the debt, asking neighbors if they know why it is Cooper doesn't pay his debts, or otherwise finding ways to embarrass or pressure Cooper into paying.

If such tactics seem unconscionable to us today, we can thank those whose advocacy of consumer rights has broadened our awareness of the consumer's perspective and reduced our tolerance for behavior that protects business interests at consumers' expense. While businesses have a right to demand payment from purchasers of their goods and services, the law now stipulates that their means of doing so must fall within certain boundaries that society has defined as fair. Consumer protection legislation is designed in part to define what society believes is fair, to make the consumer more equal to the businessperson in commercial transactions, and to make consumer rights more comparable across the states. Businesses that violate such rights will be subject to sanctions, depending on the nature of the violation.

Take Cooper with his television purchase, for instance. These days, he could expect things to go quite differently. If he applied for credit with the seller of the television, the seller would be required to either extend the credit or provide a legally acceptable explanation for refusing to do so (more on this later). If the seller decided to extend credit to Cooper, he would be required to fully document the terms of their credit agreement in writing. Not only would the seller be required to inform Cooper of any finance charges, but he would be required to specify an *annual percentage rate*, or APR, for the transaction, and to show how this was calculated. Should Cooper default on a payment, the seller would have the right to demand payment—and perhaps even to recover the merchandise, if Cooper continued to skip payments. The seller could not, however, take such action without appropriate notice. Nor could he levy any monetary charges not specified in the credit agreement, hire an unscrupulous debt collector to harass Cooper, or openly discuss Cooper's financial situation with his employer, friends, or neighbors.

Consumer Credit Legislation

More than ever before, the consumer is on an equal footing with the business merchant. Current legislation is aimed at ensuring that the consumer enters each business transaction reasonably well informed to be able to make a sound purchasing decision, that each consumer is granted the credit to which he or she is entitled by law. Let's look now at some of the specific legislation under which these consumer rights are granted in the area of consumer credit.

The Federal Consumer Credit Protection Act: The Right to Disclosure of Terms

In 1968, Congress passed the Federal Consumer Credit Protection Act (FCCPA), which states that consumers have a right to know and understand the terms of credit agreements. After all, it's hard to know whether to accept a particular credit arrangement if you do not know what the terms are and can't compare them to terms offered by other credit arrangements. Under this act, creditors have a duty to disclose—and, if necessary, explain—the terms of any credit agreement to consumers. The requirements of the act are explicit. Consumers must be told *when* finance charges are to be imposed—immediately, after thirty days, after three months, or whatever. They must be told precisely *how* these charges have been calculated; for instance, if the amount of the finance charge varies with the nature of the purchase, the size of the debt, or the length of time over which credit is extended, such facts must be disclosed. In addition, the finance charges must be expressed as an annual percentage rate (APR) so a customer can tell, and compare with other arrangements, exactly how much interest he or she will really be paying.

The act in no way relieves the consumer of the responsibility to pay once the credit agreement is signed; it only regulates the way businesses communicate credit terms to the consumer. Businesses that violate the act and do not make the proper disclosures can be sued for money. And because of the way the act allows these "damages" to be calculated, they are likely to be higher than the profit the business expected to make from the loan agreement. In other words, this legislation tries to make it worthwhile for a business to be "up-front" with its customers.

The Fair Credit Billing Act: The Right to Question Problems

Undoubtedly you've heard the expression "The customer is always right." While the saying is an old one, the customer's side of things was, in previous decades, not always given much serious thought. True, many successful businesses may have "catered" to customers by offering particularly courteous treatment or by striving to provide the services or products that customers said they wanted, But sometimes things weren't as easily handled if things went wrong after the sale. In a society geared more to business interests, it was difficult—sometimes futile—for consumers to raise questions over apparent discrepancies with bills or accounts.

To illustrate, let's go back to the 1950s for a moment. Suppose Barnes has a charge account with the Santos Department Store. When her monthly bill arrives, she finds she has been charged for $1,500 worth of merchandise she did not buy. What are her options? Unfortunately—in the 1950s—they're quite limited. She can complain to the department store, and if she's lucky, they may acknowledge their error. On the other hand, if they believe the error is hers, they can continue to try to collect from Barnes. If she does not pay the bill, Santos may report her to the local credit bureau, and Barnes may have difficulty getting credit in the future. Or, they may suspend use of her Santos charge card. Perhaps only by hiring a lawyer could Barnes get sufficient attention from Santos to stop the collection process until the discrepancy was cleared up. Not very happy alternatives.

The Fair Credit Billing Act of 1975, however, put an end to such hard-line tactics. This act specifies first that Santos—or any creditor—must tell the consumer in writing *exactly* how to register a complaint about alleged errors in billing. So, keeping the basics of our scenario the same, let's bring Barnes back to the present, to see how differently things might go for her now. Chances are, today, that if Barnes looks over her bill from Santos carefully, she will find instructions that will tell her precisely how to question the $1,500 overcharge. If she acts within the specified time period, when she phones or writes explaining the error, the creditor (Santos, in this case) is required to either correct the error within a reasonable time or explain why, from their point of view, there is no error. Until the dispute is resolved,

Barnes will continue to be treated like any other customer in good standing. Santos may not try to collect the debt, may not limit Barnes's right to make other purchases (unless there is some other, unrelated reason for a change in Barnes's credit status—loss of employment, for instance), and may not report to others that Barnes has fallen behind in her payments. With this incentive to straighten matters out, Santos likely will soon get to the bottom of the billing dispute.

The Equal Credit Opportunity Act

In a society where car dealers proudly proclaim "No credit record? No problem!", it's possible to get the idea that credit is automatically extended to everyone who asks for it. Advertising hyperbole aside, however, a wise business will not extend credit to consumers who have no apparent means of income, for example, or who have a history of not paying for goods or services. In order to protect their own interests, businesses are allowed to refuse credit for such legitimate reasons.

In the past, however, some businesses have denied credit for reasons that had little direct relationship to the consumer's ability to pay—age, sex, or race, for instance. The Equal Credit Opportunity Act makes it illegal to deny credit on the basis of gender, marital status, race, color, religion, national origin, or age. When a company denies credit to a person, it now must give the reasons, and those reasons must relate directly to ability to pay for purchases. Thus, Santos Department Store cannot deny credit to Bailey because she is young, or to Hermann because she is divorced, or to Manikoski because he is a member of a minority group.

Fair Credit Reporting Act

Businesses, of course, have rights, too. In particular, they have a right to know, before extending credit, whether a person is likely to be able to make the required payments. Answering this question requires a sometimes extensive search into the credit histories of applicants. Thus, each time a consumer makes a major purchase—a house or automobile—or opens a checking, savings, or credit account, information relating to that activity will probably be entered into a credit report intended to summarize the way in which that consumer manages his or her business affairs.

Credit reports are very succinct. They do not tell all there is to know about a consumer's purchasing habits, by any means. But they do hit many of the high points: employment history, major credit purchases (house, car, etc.), credit accounts held or closed, checking and savings accounts, and possibly even creditors' complaints regarding unmade or overdue payments. Clearly, such information could be very useful to creditors in determining a consumer's future ability to pay.

But what if the information contained in a consumer's credit history is inaccurate or distorted? Or suppose a consumer goes through a difficult financial period early in life and defaults on a credit payment, but otherwise has a very commendable credit history; should that early isolated incident continue to influence future credit ratings?

The Fair Credit Reporting Act of 1970 addressed these questions. The FCRA is designed to ensure that the information recorded in a person's credit history is accurately recorded, kept confidential, and used in a reasonable manner. Under the act, consumers have a right to have obsolete material deleted from their files, so that past financial problems do not haunt them forever. Consumers also have a right to know what is in their credit report, where the information comes from, and who asks to see it. If a consumer believes information in the file is incorrect, the information can be questioned and the reporting company must reinvestigate. Inaccurate information must be corrected. If, after further examination, the company still believes the information is correct, the consumer must be notified and allowed to submit a written explanation of his or her view of the matter. The credit reporting company must keep this written explanation as part of the consumer's file and include it in all future credit reports.

For instance, remember Santos Department Store, the company that billed Barnes for $1,500 worth of merchandise she had never purchased? How unfair if—on top of this unsolicited debt—Barnes's credit rating were to suffer when Santos reported that she had defaulted on her credit payments. To avoid this double penalty, Barnes could request a reinvestigation of the situation. Following that reinvestigation, what if Santos stubbornly insists that their $1,500 charge is accurate? In that case, Barnes can attach to the report a letter explaining her side of the matter. And while Santos may continue to report that Barnes defaulted on her $1,500 payment, at least Barnes has the satisfaction of knowing that any future creditor who looks at the report can see both sides of the issue.

The Fair Debt Collection Practices Act

When consumers fail to pay bills, businesses sometimes turn to professional debt collectors and collection agencies for assistance. Debt collectors do not extend credit; their sole job is to collect on unpaid bills. In the past, these companies occasionally used intrusive and embarrassing methods to make consumers pay, such as calling at odd hours, telling the debtor's friends, colleagues, and employers about the unpaid debt, and even threatening the debtor.

Such methods are forbidden under the Fair Debt Collection Practices Act of 1977. Collection agencies may no longer employ techniques that are considered unfair, deceptive, or harassing. Let's say that Firenze owes money on an automobile. The auto dealer may hire a collection agency to try to recover the money from Firenze and other consumers from whom money is owed. But the agency cannot visit Firenze's house at midnight, yell at him through the window, send reports to his employer, or threaten him with bodily injury if he doesn't come up with the money by Friday. Further, if Firenze has an attorney and so informs the collection agency, the agency must immediately stop contacting Firenze directly. All communications from the agency about the debt must be with the attorney, not with Firenze. If the collection agency violates any of these rules, Firenze can sue for damages—and he may well collect more in damages than is due on the original debt.

Product Safety Legislation

The second area included in consumer protection involves product safety legislation. Our society has become increasingly concerned with the dangers presented by defective products sold to consumers—and rightly so. Each year, consumers are killed or injured by poorly designed or constructed merchandise or by products that do not function as intended. Not surprisingly, this is one area in which consumers tend to be very vocal in expressing their concerns. Where once the buyer had to beware, we now want manufacturers, inspectors, and merchants to take primary responsibility for worrying over our welfare. We expect our automobiles to carry us safely down the highway and to hold up reasonably well. We expect our children's toys to be safe and durable—not to poison them with toxic paints, poke them with concealed points, or choke them with small, removable parts. We expect our tools and appliances to operate as intended—not to set our kitchens ablaze or jolt us with short-circuited wiring. The law now recognizes that, as consumers, we're entitled to this kind of confidence.

Two laws passed by Congress give consumers protection at the federal level from defective products; additional protection is also provided through common law and state statutes. The Magnuson-Moss Warranty Act–Consumer Product Warranty Act requires sellers to tell the buyer about all warranties and limitations on warranties when the product is sold. For example, if Ferguson buys a lawnmower from Lou's Lawn and Garden, Lou's must tell Ferguson exactly what warranty rights are provided by Lou's and by the manufacturer and what limitations exist. If a "full-year" warranty is offered, for instance, it must be explained. Does it cover only the motor or also the handle, the gear shift, the cutting blade, and the blade housing? If the handle and gear shift fall off within the first six months, the cutting blade grows prematurely dull, or the blade housing rusts through, Ferguson will need to know what is and isn't covered by the warranty. What's more, any limitations need to be disclosed *before* making a purchase, when the consumer still has the opportunity to buy elsewhere.

The 1972 Consumer Product Safety Act grew out of concerns over dangerous products. The Act set up the Consumer Product Safety Commission, which specifies safety standards for some consumer goods, conducts research on product safety, and provides information to consumers on the relative safety of consumer products. For example, reports that toasters manufactured by Nelson Electric Products tended to short out and cause fires might trigger an investigation that could result in the product being redesigned or taken off the market altogether. Such an investigation could also spur new standards for other, similar products. Numerous safety features on automobiles—from safety-glass windshields to center-mounted brake lamps—have resulted from investigations relating to the cause and preventability of automobile accidents.

The emphasis on research into the causes and prevention of accidents and injuries is significant because out of such research grow standards that may improve the production of a whole line of products—not just one isolated piece of merchandise. It is of little value, for instance, to ban the sale of flammable sleepwear for infants if the company that produced the sleepwear replaces it with a product that causes skin rashes. In other words, we cannot hope to generate legislation rapidly enough to cover every potential danger. What's needed, then, are standards of excellence that ensure that all products will—to the extent possible—meet consumers' needs while not threatening their safety or health.

All this is not to suggest, of course, that manufacturers are out to kill or cripple their consumers and that only fear of legal retribution prevents them from doing their worst. In truth, most are acting in good faith. But those who do not should not be able to succeed at the expense of consumers, and regulations and legislation that set industry standards and requirements for products help to ensure that they won't.

Nor is our discussion meant to suggest that consumers can blithely abdicate all responsibility for their own safety. They cannot. Courts will not necessarily blame manufacturers or sellers when injuries result from the inappropriate or careless use of a product. But the handling of products and the inherent safety of those products themselves are two separate issues under the law. The law states that the manufacturer has a duty to ensure that any given product will meet safety standards and be safe given appropriate use and handling.

Enforcement and Remedies

Consumer protection laws are intended to regulate business behavior, not to enrich the injured consumer. Each statute, consequently, sets out the types of remedies available for a consumer and against a violator of the statute. In some instances, the individual consumer can sue for monetary damages that may represent actual damages suffered or may be fixed by a formula in the statute, such as $1,000 for each violation or twice the finance charge of the consumer credit purchase. At times, the statute will also allow the aggrieved consumer to ask that the business be charged for the costs of the consumer's lawyer. In other instances, however, the consumer may only be able to get a court order stopping the wrongful practice. And in some instances, the consumer's only role is to serve as the initiator of an agency investigation—to complain to the government agency and hope the agency will investigate and, if warranted, fine the wrong-acting business.

Each consumer protection statute is unique and must be consulted separately to see what recourse it gives to the consumer. Remember, however, that when regular common-law remedies are also appropriate—such as damages for fraud, deceit, misrepresentation, or negligence—all the remedies and damages normally available in such a case can be claimed in addition to the remedies specified in the consumer protection statue.

We've now considered several of the laws that make business transactions safer for consumers. Let's turn our attention to those laws intended to preserve and restore the natural environment so that it can be enjoyed by generations to come.

Environmental Protection

Environmental protection is not a new concern. In fact, laws regulating pollution of the waterways date back to the 1880s. However, the focus of this issue has both shifted and intensified in the last half of the twentieth century for several reasons.

First, while it may once have seemed that ours was a country of unlimited resources, we now recognize the shortsightedness of that perspective. We *can* run out of lumber and minerals, fuel sources, clean water — even of clean air itself. In the past few decades, it has become increasingly apparent that we must preserve — and where we can, even *improve* — the finite resources we have.

But in addition, we're much more cognizant these days of the damaging effects pollution is likely to have on the environment. Before the 1960s, a relatively small number of people were even aware of the damage we were doing to our environment. Today, thanks in part to those early environmentalists and conservationists, most people are at least aware of the fact that air doesn't have to be polluted and that business doesn't have to dump chemicals into lakes and rivers. Environmental practices that were tolerated as sensible ways of conducting business in previous years are now, to put it bluntly, illegal.

Because businesses are so visible, and because they are responsible for much environmental harm, Congress has passed a number of laws regulating what effects industry can have on the environment. But in reviewing this legislation, we must remember that, while the law may seem to take direct aim at major industries, in reality it affects each of us in both major and minor ways. We now drive automobiles that use "cleaner" unleaded gasoline. Some of us live in areas that prohibit nonreturnable bottles, or that limit woodburning fireplaces because they add to air pollution. But in addition, we are *indirectly* affected by environmental legislation that controls the design and production of our merchandise, the availability of certain products, and ultimately even what we pay for the products we buy and the lifestyle we live. To understand this better, let's examine some specific laws that attempt to regulate environmental quality.

The National Environmental Policy Act

The National Environmental Policy Act (NEPA) of 1970 is the most important of the environmental laws. It has two major components. First, it established the Council on Environmental Quality (CEQ) as an advisory body. The CEQ does not make or enforce laws. Rather, through investigation and observation, it notes compliance with various laws affecting the environment and reports its findings regularly to the President. Actual enforcement falls to the Environmental Protection Agency (EPA).

Second, the NEPA has established a requirement that before the federal government may take any major action that could have significant environmental consequences, an *environmental impact statement*, or EIS, detailing the project's anticipated effects on the environment must be completed. An EIS is also necessary before approval of any private action that occurs on government land or requires a government permit. The environmental impact assessment component of NEPA is crucial because it represents the federal government's first comprehensive attempt to evaluate the potential environmental impact of a project *before* the project itself is initiated—and the environment is affected.

Each environmental impact statement, or EIS, must

- describe the general impact of the proposed project on the environment,
- describe the *unavoidable* consequences of the project,
- examine possible alternatives for achieving the same goals,
- detail both long-term and short-term effects on the environment,
- describe resources that will be consumed by the project, and, in particular,
- identify those resources that, if consumed, cannot be replaced or replenished.

Before completion of a *thorough* and *detailed* environmental impact statement, the proposed action cannot be finally approved. Even when the EIS is complete in every detail, however, approval is not automatic.

Once the EIS is completed, the likely effects of the proposed action are discussed. During this period, local governments or citizens' groups may voice their views or concerns regarding the project. As one might imagine, the adequacy of the EIS is often an issue—and one that can be challenged in court. In fact, many a project has been postponed because of citizen challenges to the adequacy of the EIS; such challenges often result in courts ordering new EISs to be completed, EISs that address factors undervalued or ignored in the earlier EIS.

The public comment and EIS deliberation procedure allows the federal government time and opportunity for responsible, informed decision making about projects that will affect the environment. During this period, the government will judge whether the probable benefits of the project outweigh any anticipated environmental problems. Note that it is not essential for a project to be without adverse impact to be approved; approval will normally depend on the extent of the adversity and also the relative benefits offered by the project.

While the NEPA is often considered the most significant piece of environmental legislation thus far, other laws have had significant impact as well.

The Clean Air Act

When Congress passed the Clean Air Act in 1963, pollution was viewed primarily as a local problem, though admittedly one with far-reaching consequences. Congress initially hoped that local and state governments could monitor the problem within their own respective areas. It became apparent, however, that some federal action was needed to give the act both clout and consistency in enforcement. Thus, over the years, increasing concern about air pollution has resulted in repeated amendments to the original Clean Air Act. At first, the intent of this legislation was to *correct* existing problems—to get rid of air pollution (particularly from automobiles) that seemed to pose a direct and immediate threat to health.

Gradually, as some improvements were realized, the emphasis shifted to *maintaining* air quality that met federal standards and *improving* the quality of air that failed to meet federal standards. This might seem to be a minor distinction, but in fact it represents a significant breakthrough in attitude—a gradual realization that, through effective legislation, we can not only rid ourselves of problems but actually effect *improvements* in the quality of the environment.

While many of the act's regulations relate specifically to automobile exhaust, others deal with aircraft emissions, smokestack emissions, use of woodburning stoves—anything that affects the air we breathe. Note, too, that regulations affect both consumers—who in some areas must, for example, drive only cars that meet certain emission-control standards—and manufacturers—who, for example, must produce automobiles meeting both general federal standards and more stringent area-specific standards.

The Clean Water Act

The Clean Water Act of 1972 was designed to clean up America's waterways: to make them safe for swimming and other recreational use, to preserve and protect the many types of wildlife that depend on these waterways, to eliminate use of lakes and rivers as dumping grounds, and to require that industries use the best available technology in amending the water pollution problem.

While remarkable progress has been made in reclaiming certain rivers and lakes in the United States, the progress to date has not been all that was hoped for. Nonetheless, as communities come to recognize the valuable asset that clean waterways represent, more are working to reclaim their own waterways. And, as with the Clean Air Act, the Clean Water Act has paved the way for further environmental legislation.

Protection of Public Lands

The federal government is the largest landowner in the United States. About 725 million acres—including national parks, forests, and monuments—are owned or controlled by the government. Land owned or occupied by the government is said to be in the *public domain*. The implication here—and it's an important one—is that these "public" lands belong to all of us as a group, not to one political administration or individual in particular. Accordingly, when someone wants to use public lands for private purposes or when the government wants to give private individuals or corporations special access to public lands, the individuals must apply for and receive a government permit allowing the use.

For example, Swanson may wish to lease a tract of government land on which he and his family can live for a certain number of years. Swanson will need to check with the government to see what resources he and his family are free to use. For instance, it may be well within government regulations for him to catch whatever fish the family can eat, or to cut enough wood to keep his own fireplace going. However, Swanson cannot use the land for commercial purposes—by mining the land, for instance, or harvesting the timber for sale to a lumber mill just because he and his family live on the land. Requiring permits and limiting the use of federal land is the government's way of ensuring that resources will be preserved for the use of all citizens, not consumed for the financial gain of just a few.

In addition to the regulations affecting federal lands, the government has passed a number of regulations affecting the ways in which so-called "private" lands can be used. In part, the government's power to issue these regulations comes from the realization that no land is really "private" in that what happens on it will affect more people than just the current owner.

The Toxic Substances Control Act

This legislation has two purposes. The first is to control the use of substances that are known to be toxic (poisonous). The second is to encourage the testing of chemicals *prior* to their use to determine whether they are toxic and in need of special regulation.

For example, suppose Formula Motor Products wishes to market a new car-washing detergent. Before Formula can put this new product on the market, it must test it to ensure that it is not toxic to the user or to the environment — since, presumably, much of it will eventually find its way into the waterways. This advance-testing requirement gives consumers the security of knowing that the products they buy have been investigated and found to be at least reasonably safe.

Recent efforts to adopt "right-to-know" legislation at the federal and state levels seek to expand the range of groups who are to be told of potentially dangerous chemicals. Worker *right-to-know* legislation gives employees the right to be told about any harmful chemicals or toxic substances to which they will be or are exposed to on the job, the effects of such exposure, and emergency first-aid treatment in case of accidental exposure. Employers cannot, for example, ask farm workers to treat fields with pesticides and other chemicals without first informing them of the nature and risk of the work, providing proper protection and safety training programs, and adopting first-aid procedures. Community right-to-know legislation gives citizens the right to know of any potential effects resulting from the use of toxic substances by local businesses or industries in their community. For example, a business using or manufacturing a substance that could cause increased cancer risks would have to publicly announce this hazard and adopt special community-oriented safety programs.

The Federal Insecticide, Fungicide, and Rodenticide Act

When Wallace discovers that rats are nesting in the wall between his living room and garage, chances are that the last thing he'll worry about is whether the poison he uses to exterminate the intruders will harm the environment. But the government has enacted legislation designed to do the worrying ahead of time, and to ensure, in effect, that when Wallace kills the rats, he doesn't do in his wife, children, and neighbors in the process. Note that this legislation, the *Federal Insecticide, Fungicide, and Rodenticide Act*, does not make the use of all toxic substances illegal; such an approach would have many more disadvantages than benefits.

Rather, it is designed to ensure that substances are identified as toxic and that those that are approved for use are labeled as toxic and bear instructions for appropriate and "safe" use.

The law does, however, make the use of *unapproved* products illegal; theoretically, all products available for sale have been tested and approved for sale. Even so, some approved products are still toxic, and the consumer is given much of the responsibility for ensuring that they are used appropriately. If, for example, Neville's dog gets sick from eating grass sprayed early that afternoon with a weed killer that had been clearly labeled with a warning that pets should not be allowed anywhere near the grass for forty-eight hours, the fault is with Neville, not the manufacturer of the weed killer.

The Solid Waste Disposal Act

Every human society has a problem with waste disposal. The more affluent the society, the more there is to "throw away" — and the more difficult it becomes to find new and *suitable* places to dispose of the waste or transform it to other usable products. The Solid Waste Disposal Act confronts these problems by encouraging recycling and developing new ways to dispose of waste that cannot be recycled.

For example, if Innovative Industries invents a method for reprocessing fast-food containers and turning them into durable and effective insulating material, it may be eligible for government support to help finance the project. Similarly, investigations into nonpolluting incineration of waste and better landfill techniques are supported by the provisions of this legislation.

SOME PRACTICAL ADVICE

As we've seen, achieving a higher quality of life is not without its personal, social, and business costs. Let's revisit the two sides of the issue we've explored in this lesson.

First, consider environmental regulation — a complex issue involving potentially conflicting interests. Standards that benefit the environment may be devastating to certain businesses. For example, the use of some pesticides is now illegal. The newer, safer products that have replaced them may not pollute the soil or water — but they may also be less effective in killing pests and providing society with the type of "perfect, unblemished" fruits and vegetables it has come to expect. And new, high development costs are included in the newer products' purchase prices. Thus, the farmers who need these pesticides may find they have lower crop yields due to insect damage and that it costs them more to produce this less-bountiful harvest. Consumers, in turn, are likely to face higher prices for produce that looks as if it should cost less, since it is neither so perfectly colored nor so well-shaped as what they're used to.

The result? Both farmers and consumers are temporarily unhappy; they may not readily recognize the long-term benefit society gains from the reduction of very toxic chemicals in the soil and water. And what if sales of the product decline because of the higher cost? The frustrated farmer may see only a tough choice: risk noncompliance to keep income up or go out of business. The chemical company that produces the new insecticide may not be able to recover its development costs, while the company that produced the old, less-safe product has lost a reliable source of income; both may face financial difficulties.

Nevertheless, the public, through Congress and the regulatory agencies that enforce the laws, has made a policy decision that the long-term benefits to society as a whole outweigh both the short- and long-term difficulties and adjustments of the farmer, the chemical companies, and disgruntled consumers. The point is, both pollution and pollution control have consequences and cost money. As a result, many businesses have had to face the reality that compliance with government regulation often means reduced profits.

As a businessperson, you may regard environmental legislation as the ultimate form of consumer protection—which, perhaps, it is. Keep in mind, however, that in today's marketplace, the consumer has considerable legal support in relation to everyday transactions as well. As we've seen in this lesson, merchants who hope to profit by taking advantage of consumers are likely to find themselves in serious legal difficulty. Federal law now guarantees consumers the right to know the nature of the products they buy, the warranties provided for those products, the terms of credit, the procedures to follow in the event of a billing problem, and a host of other matters. In addition, credit cannot be granted or denied whimsically or on factors other than the ability to pay. And when credit is denied, the consumer has the right to know why.

Further, consumers are entitled to expect that the products they buy will be safe when used as intended. For the businessperson, this means careful attention to the design and testing of every product marketed, together with realistic warranties that give consumers confidence. It also means, for many businesses, a serious commitment to research in the event that problems are discovered. Simply removing a dangerous product from the shelves, after all, is a kind of band-aid approach to consumer safety. Today's consumers want—and expect—safety standards that apply to all products, and recompense when a product fails to meet safety standards.

Admittedly, we live in an imperfect world. No one, including those who make the environmental and consumer protection laws, expects it to be otherwise. However, it's realistic to say that merchants and manufacturers are increasingly being asked to use the full benefit of existing technology to make the consumer's immediate environment and natural environment safer, more functional, more trouble-free than it has ever been. Both the tone and content of recent legislation deliver a definite message to the businessperson: When it comes to dealing with the consumer or the environment, shortcuts do not pay.

ASSIGNMENTS

- Before you watch the video program, be sure you've read through the preceding overview, familiarized yourself with the learning objectives for this lesson, and looked at the key terms below. Then, read Chapter 47 of Davidson et al., *Business Law*.

- After completing these tasks, view the video program for Lesson 29.

- After watching the program, take time to review what you've learned. First, evaluate your learning with the self-test which follows the key terms. Then, apply and evaluate what you've learned with the "Your Opinion, Please" scenarios at the end of this telecourse study guide lesson.

KEY TERMS

Before you read through the textbook assignment and watch the video program, take a minute to look at the key terms associated with this lesson. When you encounter them in the textbook and video program, pay careful attention to their meaning.

Administrative Procedures Act
Clean Air Act
Clean Water Act
Consumer protection
Consumer Product Safety Act
Environmental impact statement (EIS)
Environmental protection
Environmental Protection Agency (EPA)
Equal Credit Opportunity Act
Fair Credit Billing Act
Fair Credit Reporting Act
Fair Debt Collection Practices Act
Federal Consumer Credit Protection Act (FCCPA)

Federal Insecticide, Fungicide and Rodenticide Act
Noise Control Act
Magnuson-Moss Warranty Act– Consumer Product Warranty Act
National Environmental Policy Act (NEPA)
Quality of life
Resource Conservation and Recovery Act
Solid Waste Disposal Act
Toxic Substances Control Act
Uniform Consumer Credit Code (UCCC)

SELF-TEST

The questions below will help you evaluate how well you've learned the material in this lesson. Read each one carefully, and select the letter of the option that best answers the question. You'll find the correct answer, along with a reference to the page number(s) where the topic is discussed, in the back of this telecourse study guide.

1. Under the Federal Consumer Credit Protection Act, creditors are required to put information regarding finance charges in the form of an annual percentage rate, or APR. The *most likely* reason for this is that

    a. other means of expressing the same information could be misleading.
    b. one year is the standard limit on the time for which most companies will extend credit.
    c. most consumers require at least a year to complete credit payments, so it has become customary to give total costs for that period.

2. Zippo Discount gives credit to eligible customers who wish to make purchases at the store. As Zippo evaluates the eligibility of its credit applicants, which of the following situations would provide Zippo with the *most legitimate* grounds for denying credit?

    a. Sabin, a dental hygienist, is recently divorced.
    b. Tanaka, a 22-year-old graduate student, has just accepted his first job.
    c. Ciani, a corporate vice-president, has a history of not promptly paying his credit card charges.
    d. Dover, an administrative assistant in an insurance firm, defaulted on a car loan twenty years ago.

3. The *main* purpose of the Fair Credit Reporting Act is to

    a. ensure that credit information is never shared with employers.
    b. expand the kinds of information that can legitimately be included in a consumer's credit report.
    c. ensure that credit information on *every* potential consumer is made public.
    d. protect consumers from the unfair effects on credit decision making of false, misleading, irrelevant, or outdated information.

4. Danson wishes to purchase an apartment building, and the real estate company through which he's making the purchase wishes to have Danson's credit investigated. Before they can begin the investigation, the real estate company is required to

    a. notify Danson in writing that an investigation of his credit rating will be conducted.
    b. request Danson's permission to investigate his credit rating.

    c. notify Danson's attorney (if he has one) and his employer (if he has one) that an investigation of Danson's credit will be conducted.

    d. *None* of the above; the company is not required to give notice to anyone.

5. A debt collection agency has been pressuring Ferrarro to pay an outstanding bill. Under the Fair Debt Collection Practices Act, the agency may do any of the following *except one*. In attempting to collect the debt, the agency is *not* allowed to

    a. send repeated letters to Ferrarro summarizing the situation and asking that she pay the debt.

    b. talk to Ferrarro's employer to discuss Ferrarro's wages and withholdings.

    c. phone Ferrarro's home to ask that the debt be paid.

    d. talk to Ferrarro's attorney about the situation.

6. Which of the following *best* describes the *main* purpose of the Magnuson-Moss Warranty Act–Consumer Product Warranty Act? The *main* purpose of this act is to

    a. ensure that all products sold with warranties include *unconditional* written warranties.

    b. ensure that consumers are given full disclosure regarding the type and extent of warranty protection for each product.

    c. extend the types of warranty coverage available for various types of products.

    d. outlaw hidden disclaimers in warranties.

7. The overall purpose of current legislation protecting consumers' rights is *best* described as an attempt to

    a. give consumers *some* protection, however minimal, in a business world still dominated by merchants' interests.

    b. provide remedies for *injured* consumers, though in reality, few laws are aimed at protecting the general consumer population.

    c. help put the consumer and merchant on more equal footing, so that neither benefits at the expense of the other.

    d. protect consumers' interests even when that means compromising merchants' rights.

8. Which of the following *best* describes the general trend in federal legislation involving environmental law over the past few decades?

    a. It has grown tremendously in recent years.

    b. It has grown slightly, though the environment is still not a major area of concern for lawmakers.

    c. The amount of emphasis has remained amazingly constant since the middle of the nineteenth century.

    d. Legislative focus on the environment has, in fact, declined, with many problems apparently correcting themselves as the result of past legislation.

9. Suppose that the Council on Environmental Quality (CEQ) discovers that a local oil exploration company is violating federal regulations governing offshore drilling. Under the National Environmental Policy Act, the CEQ is empowered to

   a. close down the oil company pending further investigation of their conduct.
   b. file suit against the company on behalf of the U.S. government.
   c. enforce the regulations—through injunction or fine, if necessary.
   d. report the company's conduct to appropriate enforcement agencies.

10. An environmental impact statement (EIS) *must* include all of the following *except*

    a. a description of the anticipated impact of the proposed project on the environment.
    b. descriptions of possible alternatives for achieving the same goals.
    c. detailed cost estimates for the proposed project and the two best alternatives for achieving the same goals.
    d. a comparison of long-term and short-term environmental effects resulting from the project.

YOUR OPINION, PLEASE

Read each of the following scenarios and answer the questions about the decisions you would make in each situation. Give these questions some serious thought; they may be used as the basis for the development of a more complex essay. You should base your decisions on what you've learned from this lesson, though you may incorporate outside readings or information gained through your own experience if it is relevant.

Scenario I

Shiroishi, a graduate student in economics, desperately wishes to purchase a computer system to do both word processing and statistical analysis. After careful research, she has identified the equipment and software packages suited to her needs—but she cannot afford the $3,500 price unless she can qualify for credit. Though she has only a part-time job, she is confident that with some careful planning and curtailment of movies and meals out, she can just meet the $90 monthly payments. The importance of this computer system to her graduate studies makes the sacrifice seem worthwhile. Feeling assured by the friendliness and encouragement of the Better Systems Computer staff, Shiroishi fills out a credit application. She accurately notes her monthly income and the fact that she has no current outstanding debts—a point she hopes will work in her favor.

After several weeks, having heard nothing from Better Systems, Shiroishi calls to check on the status of her credit application. Much to her surprise, she is told that she has been turned down and that she will receive a letter to that effect within a few days. When she asks the reason for the rejection, the Better Systems representative says she is sorry, but Shiroishi simply "does not meet the store's qualification requirements." Shiroishi asks for a further explanation but is told that confidential information cannot be shared over the phone. Shiroishi's visit to the store the next day, however, produces no more concrete information or a change in the credit decision.

Shiroishi is about to give up on the situation when she learns a week or so later through casual conversation, that a fellow graduate student, McConnell, has applied for and been granted credit at Better Systems. McConnell, who is also employed part-time, has an income not much higher than Shiroishi's. Convinced its treatment has not been equitable, Shiroishi determines to file a complaint against Better Systems for violation of the Equal Credit Opportunity Act.

What's your opinion? Based on what you know of the situation, does Shiroishi have sufficient grounds to file such a complaint? What will be the most likely outcome? Can Shiroishi hope to collect damages if the store is found to be in violation?

- Is Better Systems likely to be found in violation of the Equal Credit Opportunity Act, based on the information in this scenario?
- What factors support your answer?
- What factors might an attorney cite in arguing against your view?
- What steps, if any, might Better Systems have taken to avoid a complaint in this situation?
- What additional steps, if any, might Shiroishi take *now* to improve her credit status with Better Systems and with other creditors in the future?

Scenario 2

Omega Industries proposes to build a hydroelectric plant at the point where the Frelow River enters Sylvan Lake. The site is privately owned and will be leased by Omega, but it borders national forest land. Consequently, as part of its development process, Omega is obliged to conduct an environmental impact study, detailing the pros and cons of the project. The study is very complete in its detail of the plant's projected impact on the natural environment, an impact that the EIS describes as only "minimally disruptive." The EIS also outlines several other energy alternatives, but none are presented as having the "nominal environmental impact" of the proposed hydroelectric plant. The study points out the plant's economic benefits to the community as a whole (e.g., new jobs, cheaper power, more power for local industry, recreation attraction of the reservoir), but makes no mention whatever of its effect on Northland Retreat Resort, which occupies the south shore of the lake, just opposite the hydroelectric site.

Kirby, owner–manager of Northland Retreat, is infuriated by the whole situation and sees it as nothing short of devastating to his livelihood. As the environmental impact study itself acknowledges, the building of the plant is likely to "somewhat reduce" the amount of wildlife inhabiting the wilderness areas around the lake. Further, the fish population of both the river and the lake will be disrupted. Both factors, Kirby points out, will reduce the recreational appeal of the site to vacationers. Further, he believes that despite the intentions of the company to "restore" the construction site through natural landscaping, the plant itself will be an eyesore. What's more, the plant will create sufficient noise to disrupt the peaceful nature of the wilderness setting—and it's the peaceful setting that Kirby believes attracts people to the resort. Based on the threat to his livelihood, Kirby files suit for an injunction to stop construction of the hydro plant and require revision of the EIS to include the impact of the proposed plant on his business and the character of the area.

What's your opinion? Based on what you know of the situation, does Kirby have sufficient grounds to obtain an injunction? Do you think Omega is remiss in not including some consideration of the plant's impact on Kirby's resort business in their EIS, or does such information go beyond the scope of what an EIS is intended to do? What about the effect on the scenic and wilderness qualities of the area? Based on what you know, if the plant were built, do you think Kirby might have sufficient grounds to file a common-law suit for damages? Why or why not?

- Is Kirby likely to win his suit for an injunction to halt construction of the hydroelectric plant? Why or why not?

- What factors support your answer?

- What factors might an attorney cite in arguing against your view?

- What steps, if any, might Omega have taken to prevent a lawsuit in this situation?

- What additional steps, if any, can Kirby take to protect his own interests in this situation?

30

Labor and Employment Practices

LEARNING OBJECTIVES

Upon completing your study of this lesson, you should be able to

- Discuss the influence of labor and employment practices on the way that a business must operate.
- Using specific hypothetical examples, show the scope of labor legislation in governing employer–employee relationships and practices.
- List and discuss the three major labor acts that affect businesses today.
- Identify and discuss major statutes affecting employment and employment practices within seven major categories: fair employment practice, occupational safety and health, Social Security, unemployment insurance, workers' compensation, wages and hours, and retirement.

In 1786, a group of Philadelphia printers went on strike to increase their weekly wages to $6. Their action marked the first recorded instance of an organized effort by labor to influence the actions of management. Since that time, countless groups have organized — recognizing how numbers increase their strength — to demand not only higher wages, but better working conditions, job security, benefits, and a host of other things.

The union voice was small, just an isolated whisper, in the beginning. In fact, society and government opposed most early unionization efforts. But by the 1940s, unions had gained considerable power, enough power that many felt the balance had been dramatically tipped in favor of the unions, with decreased attention to or concern for the management side of things. Such inequity — regardless of which side currently had the upper hand — was viewed by many persons as a real threat to objective negotiations between employee and employer. The U.S. Congress, in particular, was sensitive to the need for a balance of power between the two sides and thus enacted legislation that attempted to achieve this balance. These days, many years, statutes, and legal debates later, it is difficult for either side to *legally* take a position that is totally insensitive to the needs of the other.

Still, unless we find ourselves in the midst of a confrontation between labor and management, we're unlikely to be very aware of or concerned about the laws that govern and guide employee–employer behavior. For a businessperson, however, such ignorance is a mistake; failure to comply with the applicable legislation can result in heavy fines and penalties, or worse. Equally important, though, is the fact that knowledge of and sensitivity toward employment laws and regulations can create a more productive and pleasant place to work.

The purpose of this lesson is to give you a sense of the general intent and spirit of labor- and management-related legislation, and an understanding of the appropriate — and inappropriate — economic weapons labor and management may use in maintaining that balance. And while there is not space here to explore each crucial piece of legislation in depth, you should leave this lesson with a good understanding of what the law expects of both employers and employees.

OVERVIEW

As anyone who runs a business of any sort quickly discovers, the law sets forth specific rules and regulations governing many aspects of that business, including advertising, product management and display, provision of services, contracts, bookkeeping, investments, taxes — and, of course, employment. And, as common sense would suggest, the larger the business, the more complicated the issues relating to compliance. Let's look at a hypothetical example to see how legal restrictions affect a business, focusing particularly on the issue of employment.

The Influence of Labor and Employment Practices

Suppose Wheeler runs a dry cleaning business. Let's say he lives in the same building from which he runs his business, and he has only two employees—himself and his wife. Having everything in the family makes things about as simple as they ever get for an employer. If business is light, for instance, Wheeler can suggest to his wife that she take the afternoon off. If things pick up, he can suggest that they both keep the store open an extra hour, or that they begin working Saturday mornings. Communication is simple, and since both parties have a vested interest in the success of the business, there isn't much to negotiate. When Wheeler suggests that they work on Saturdays, for instance, we don't expect his wife to respond by walking out, striking for overtime pay, or picketing the business for "unfair labor practices."

But now let's complicate our scenario by making Wheeler's enterprise a booming success. Wheeler and his wife cannot begin to keep up with the consumer demand for clean, pressed clothes, so Wheeler takes on an employee, Craft. Soon, even the three of them cannot keep pace, so Wheeler takes a bold step and opens another store across town, with Craft managing two new employees. At this point, Wheeler's whole business perspective must change. A person who operates a business that employs even one person outside of the immediate family must comply with a host of statutes regarding fair employment practice. These statutes relate, for instance, to the terms of employment, safety on the job, provisions for retirement, workers' compensation, and unemployment insurance.

Who determines what's fair in relation to employment practices? When just Wheeler and his wife are involved, they do. If they decide it will be "fair" for the two of them to work eighty hours apiece per week in order to make the business thrive, that is their option. But when Wheeler begins employing persons outside his family, the law determines what will or will not be viewed as "fair" from society's perspective. For example, Wheeler and his wife have a direct interest in the profitability of the company, while Craft and the other employees probably do not. The law would certainly not consider it "fair" to expect Craft to work Saturdays without pay, even though that may make perfect sense for the Wheelers.

This fairness principle also requires that decisions related to employees aren't made arbitrarily. Wheeler must be able to demonstrate that he has policies that he intends to apply equally to all employees. For instance, he will need to establish uniform policies and procedures regarding holidays, vacations and other benefits, cost-of-living increases, insurance, workers' compensation, and so forth. (The uniformity is important; he can't, for example, decide to give the Friday following Thanksgiving as a day off with pay to Meyers but not to Nelson.) He may also need to consider establishing a pension plan, and if he does, he'll need to be careful about how the money to fund that plan is invested and who has responsibility for that decision. In short, the law gives Wheeler's employees certain rights and, as an employer, Wheeler has the responsibility for knowing the law and abiding by it.

Sometime down the road, if Wheeler's business expands even further, his employees may decide to join a union. If they agree on this issue and vote the union into power, they are, in effect, asking that union to serve as their representative, a kind of bargaining agent who will represent their views to Wheeler, the employer. Such organization gives employees a great deal more power than any one of them might have alone. For instance, if Wheeler decides that his shops will remain open on Saturdays from 9 A.M. to 9 P.M., some employees may be very unhappy about that decision. A single employee alone, however, takes a risk in objecting to such a request since Wheeler might feel it would be easiest simply to replace the objecting employee. On the other hand, if the union—representing *all* employees—objects, the situation looks quite different. The union may tell Wheeler, for instance, that his request for twelve additional hours of work on Saturday exceeds the bounds of fair employment practice, and that workers demand extra wages before they will comply. When workers speak with one voice, they're likely to be more influential. If Wheeler is like most employers, he won't want to alienate his entire crew; he'll either go along with their request or offer a compromise.

In our simple example with Wheeler—who's a pretty amiable sort, despite his workaholic tendencies—we must not overlook the fact that the negotiation process itself is governed by law. In other words, the union too must comply with regulations defining fairness. Unions cannot simply go about making demands without justification or grievance, expecting employers to cave in. The unions must show good faith—a reason for the demand or request, and a willingness to negotiate fairly. Further, the union is required to behave in a socially responsible and ethical manner. Union representatives cannot, for instance, encourage members to threaten Wheeler if he doesn't give in, nor may the union distribute untrue statements about Wheeler's products or business practices. To better understand what's allowable and what's required, let's get a little more specific—first about the scope of labor legislation in governing employer–employee relationships, and then about some of the federal labor statutes that have had the greatest impact on business.

The Scope of Labor Legislation

The scope of labor legislation is impressive. Taken together, the various labor statutes cover *most* employers and employees. Agricultural and domestic workers, independent contractors and supervisors, and federal, state, and local government employers are sometimes excluded from those laws. Even so, government workers who wish to have representation as a group can organize themselves under the authority of Executive Order 11491, entitled "Labor Management Relations in the Federal Service." In addition, approximately two-thirds of the states have now enacted laws permitting collective bargaining in the public sector for state and municipal employees. All in all, the number of employees covered by the various regulations is much greater than the number unaffected.

As noted previously, the scope of labor legislation is impressive—and extensive. Elements covered under labor law include:

- The procedure to be used when employees select their bargaining representative;

- The legitimate practices that both labor and management can employ during the organizing campaign;

- The specific charge that bargaining must be done in good faith over wages, hours, and other terms and conditions of employment; and

- The right to require either side to cease and desist from any unfair labor practice that has accompanied bad-faith bargaining.

The law is very specific about the procedures that must be followed by employees in selecting a bargaining representative. First, there must be some indication of employee interest. It is not fair, for instance, for the union, on behalf of a small minority of employees, to coerce a larger group of employees into seeking union representation.

Once sufficient employee interest is indicated, the employer can voluntarily recognize the union as the bargaining agent for employees. If the employer does not do so, however, the union can petition for an election to prove that employees want it to be designated as the bargaining agent of the employees. The National Labor Relations Board (NLRB), established under the the National Labor Relations Act—commonly called the Wagner Act—reviews procedures to determine whether the election has been conducted validly; if everything seems to be in order, it certifies the union as the *exclusive bargaining representative* of the employees. This means that the employees *must* bargain through the union they've selected; they cannot bargain first through one union and then through another.

An employer who isn't happy with this situation may seek to *decertify* the union—declare its representation invalid, that is—by claiming that the employees do not constitute an appropriate bargaining unit. Sometimes, this is a valid claim. An *appropriate* bargaining unit is one in which the employees have similar duties, skills, and responsibilities. Remember Wheeler and his dry cleaning business? It's easy to imagine that his employees would do similar kinds of work and would therefore have similar needs and concerns. This is likely to be the case with any small or highly focused business. But in a larger business, especially one that deals in diverse products or services, the picture could be very different. Assembly line workers, advertising copy writers, and traveling sales staff likely have many interests that relate only to their special working circumstances. The law agrees, therefore, that it is inappropriate for these various groups to band together to represent the special interests of one. To put it another way, a specific union does not exist to represent the overall rights of workers in general. Rather, each union represents the specific concerns of a focused group of workers who share common interests.

Once the bargaining representative has been recognized, the law demands *good-faith* bargaining by both the employer and the union. Though it is difficult to pin down precisely what is meant by good-faith bargaining, it generally implies a willingness to meet and discuss issues openly and with every effort to be objective. It also suggests a spirit of cooperation on both sides and some demonstration of real willingness to resolve differences. Further, each side is expected to state its position clearly, to voice its specific objections to the other side's position, and to offer any information that may be helpful to the other side in reaching an informed decision.

What topics are open to discussion? The Wagner Act says that anything that affects the terms and conditions of employment is a legally recognized subject for negotiation. Those things that do not have any direct impact on employees are left to the discretion of the employer. For instance, if Wheeler, our dry cleaner, decides to hire a person to answer the telephone, there is no reason for him to sit down and negotiate that decision with the union; it has no direct bearing on employees' working conditions or on the terms of their employment. Similarly, he might decide to install new carpeting, advertise in a different newspaper, run a weekly special offering discount dry cleaning, put in a soft drink machine for the convenience of customers who are waiting for clothes or service, or do a host of other things that would not affect employees directly. In addition, Wheeler would not need to bargain about a decision to sell his dry cleaning business. He might, however, legitimately be asked to bargain about a wide range of related employee concerns, such as the amount of notice to be given employees prior to termination, the amount of severance pay to be allowed, and so on.

Wheeler would, if requested by the union, also have to negotiate such things as whether to allow employees free parking, whether to offer medical insurance, whether to grant cost-of-living increases, or whether to consider seniority in making promotions. Such issues would directly affect employees' working lives; thus, the law takes the position that the employees, through their union, have a right to make these types of concerns known to their employer.

The rules governing good-faith bargaining do not rule out the right of each side to exert economic pressure in making its case. Thus, Wheeler's employees could go on strike to emphasize their request for higher pay on Saturday shifts. Wheeler, in turn, would not be violating the rules of good-faith bargaining through a *lock-out* — a store closure during bargaining.

On the other hand, the National Labor Relations Board (NLRB) can require either side refusing to bargain in good faith to start to do so, and to desist from any unfair labor practice. For instance, if Wheeler threatened to fire those employees who persisted in striking for higher Saturday wages, the NLRB could require him to withdraw that threat and reinstate any employee who had been unfairly discharged. It's important to note, however, that the NLRB's powers are limited. Essentially, it is an interpreting and mediating body. Its requests become law only when they are imposed by a federal circuit court of appeals, which — because of the great backlog of cases relating to fair employment practices — may be slow in doing so.

Because of this delayed reaction, some employers and unions might feel that they are, in practice, rather free of supervision and may do as they please. Not so. If the court becomes involved in settling a labor dispute, it is very likely to consider the responses and recommendations of the NLRB in reaching its decision. Thus, the "freedom" to engage in bad-faith bargaining is likely to carry with it serious legal consequences.

Federal Labor Statutes Affecting Business

As mentioned, the vast majority of employers and employees are affected by Federal labor statutes. Surprisingly, though, much of this influence comes from just three major labor acts. These are

1. The Wagner Act (or National Labor Relations Act) of 1935,
2. The Taft-Hartley Act (or Labor–Management Relations Act) of 1947, and
3. The Landrum-Griffin Act (or Labor–Management Reporting and Disclosure Act) of 1959.

The Wagner Act. Prior to the 1930s, the federal position on labor relations had been pretty much "hands-off." The idea was to let employers and employees work out their own differences, free of regulation, through reasonably peaceful means. The employer had the power to hire and fire, and the employees could picket, boycott, or strike (although their legal right to do so hadn't yet been established). But labor-management relationships weren't always trouble-free. On the contrary, there was a great deal of labor unrest and, occasionally, violent actions and reactions by employers and employees.

In 1935, however, Congress took a much more proactive position by passing the Wagner Act, an act that (in Section 7) approved the rights of employees to organize themselves and "to form, join, or assist labor organizations, to bargain collectively through representatives of their own choosing, and to engage in concerted activities for the purpose of collective bargaining or other mutual aid or protection." This legislation, in other words, supported employee participation in unions, an activity that Congress had come to view as one means of helping ensure that employees' just grievances would get fair hearing and a mechanism through which employees and employers would work together in setting goals for the future.

The Wagner Act also lays out (in Section 8) a number of unfair labor practices which are forbidden to employers, such as firing persons for their union participation or refusing to hire persons who indicate union loyalty. Similarly, employers are expressly forbidden from refusing to engage in good-faith bargaining. The act also established a new agency, the National Labor Relations Board, or NLRB, whose primary functions would include overseeing union elections and investigating and remedying unfair labor practices.

The Taft-Hartley Act. The support derived from the Wagner Act had an important effect on unions and their membership. In fact, as a result of that legislation, unions grew increasingly powerful, to the point where some observers felt that the unions had become too powerful. In 1947, hoping to strike a different balance between employee and employer, Congress passed the Taft-Hartley Act, a deliberate effort to curb union excesses.

Recall that Section 8 of the Wagner Act had specified the unfair labor practices in which *employers* could not engage. The Taft-Hartley Act now modified Section 8 by spelling out unfair labor practices that would henceforth be forbidden to *un-*

ions. These included refusing to engage in good-faith bargaining; conducting secondary boycotts or strikes (that is, strikes against someone other than the employer); forcing an employer to hire, promote, or otherwise favor persons who supported union membership; "featherbedding" (charging an employer for services never provided); and recognitional picketing (attempting to force recognition of some union other than the elected representative). In addition, the Taft-Hartley Act stripped the NLRB of its power to prosecute in unfair labor practices cases, rendering this five-member board primarily a decision rendering and arbitrating body.

In general, the Taft-Hartley Act was an effort to cause a more conciliatory approach to negotiations on both sides. While it came down hard on unions that employed what Congress considered to be unfair practices, it also encouraged freedom of speech on both sides. Employers could freely express their disapproval of unions, so long as such expression did not include any threats against employees who disagreed. Employees, in turn, could engage in informational picketing—picketing to inform the public that an employer does not have a contract with or hire members of a union—without fear of retaliation.

Finally, the legislation established a "cooling-off" period of eighty days when the President believed the potential strike might jeopardize national safety or health. That is, if the work of the union's employees was sufficiently important to the national interests, the President could, in effect, forbid them from striking for an eighty-day period. The hope was, of course, that the negotiations conducted during this period would bring about a settlement that would eliminate the need to strike at all.

The Landrum-Griffin Act. In the beginning, unions had been formed to help end abuses against employees. By the mid-1950s, however, unions themselves had been found guilty of numerous abuses, including embezzlement of union funds by their own officers and unfair treatment of members. Those days, the news was full of stories of inappropriate—and sometimes clearly illegal—actions by union officials.

The Landrum-Griffin Act of 1959 attempted to curb these abuses by establishing more stringent guidelines to govern union conduct. The act requires, among other things, detailed reporting of each union's financial affairs and provides for civil and criminal sanctions in the event of financial abuses. It also provides a "bill of rights" for union members.

Clearly, the Landrum-Griffin Act, the Taft-Hartley Act, and the Wagner Act did much to establish and maintain a good and fair balance in employer–employee relationships. Still, strikes, boycotts, lockouts, and other actions regulated by this legislation are a *reaction* to an existing problem. There was also a desire to ensure good working conditions and fair employment practices for all employees in the first place. In short, more legislation was needed to encourage the kinds of working environments and employment practices that would provide for better relations without the need for strikes and boycotts. Let's look now at a few of the pieces of legislation that have, over the past decades, changed the face of American employment.

Statutes Affecting Employment Practices

Since the mid-1960s, a number of federal and state statutes have endeavored to provide equal employment opportunity for persons who historically have not enjoyed such opportunity. Perhaps the best-known of these is the Civil Rights Act of 1964. Title VII of that law prohibits discrimination in employment *on the basis of race, color, religion, sex, or national origin*. That is, an employer cannot legitimately use any of these factors in making decisions about hiring and firing, or use such factors in making decisions about promotions, compensation, benefits, working conditions, responsibilities, or privileges of employment.

Title VII. It should be noted that Title VII of the Civil Rights Act of 1964 is expansive. It doesn't apply just to employers, but also to unions and employment agencies. An employment agency, for instance, that referred only men for positions in police work or that referred only women for positions in elementary education could be guilty of violating Title VII requirements. Of course, if the employment agency had no male applicants who met the requirements for the position in elementary education, there might be no choice but to refer only women for the position. But the agency might at some point be asked to show that it had vigorously attempted to identify other qualified applicants and that indeed none were available. In addition, the agency might be required to demonstrate that male applicants actually were not qualified for the job at hand. In summary, the intent of Title VII is to ensure that employment decisions are made on the basis of job skills and qualifications and not on other factors unrelated to job performance.

This whole issue of qualifications, by the way, is not so cut-and-dried as one might think. Let's say that a local fire department has an opening for a firefighter. If the employer prefers to have a man in this position rather than a woman, he might state as part of the qualifications that the applicant must be at least 5'10" tall and weigh 175 pounds. This restriction, of course, would not rule out all female applicants, but it would definitely slant things in favor of male applicants—who would be *more likely* to meet these height and weight restrictions. Now the crucial question is, Are the height and weight requirements important to the job?

Well, given that the prospective firefighter might well have to rescue unconscious people from burning buildings, it may be possible to argue that physical size will present an advantage—or even that it's essential. But notice that the job qualification isn't really being a certain physical size; it's being able to get people out of burning buildings—an action more associated with strength than physical size. A better approach, therefore, would be for the employer to specify something like "The applicant will be required to lift and carry 225 pounds a distance of 100 feet." Admittedly, a higher percentage of men would meet this requirement than women, but since the requirement is now directly related to the job that needs to be done, it is acceptable.

But what if the job being advertised isn't for a firefighter but rather for a dispatcher? In that event, the employer would be in violation of Title VII regardless of the wording of the job requirement. Why? Because both the physical size and the lifting ability qualifications are unrelated to the job of dispatching fire trucks.

Indeed, both requirements would have the effect of preventing qualified individuals from obtaining the job.

Violations of Title VII tend to be subtle. Employers don't typically end their advertisements with blanket statements like "Women and minorities need not apply." If their preferences are biased, they tend to look for screening mechanisms such as test scores, degree requirements, or grade-point averages that they *believe* may favor one group over another. But the employer who uses this approach takes a risk. Unless the employer can show a direct relationship between on-the-job performance and the requirements, applicants who suspect bias will have a strong case in suing for damages. It might be quite legitimate to ask applicants for an accounting position to pass a complicated math test, for instance; but asking applicants for a position as bus driver to pass the same test might be highly questionable.

On the other hand, discrimination based on religion, sex, or national origin is permitted where one of these characteristics is a *bona fide occupational qualification* (BFOQ). For instance, it is not a violation of Title VII to advertise for a woman to fill a female role in a play. In that case, the sex of the applicant is a crucial factor in job success. Nor would it be discriminatory to advertise for a Moslem to present a seminar on what it's like to be a Moslem in the United States. Note, however, that in both examples, the "discrimination" arises from a legitimate job qualification; one could not, for example, do a credible job of telling what it's like to be a Moslem without being a Moslem. But an advertisement specifying a Moslem to teach an introductory course in Moslem philosophies would violate Title VII; many non-Moslems would have both the knowledge and the skill necessary to teach the course.

The Civil Rights Act is administered by the *Equal Employment Opportunity Commission*, the EEOC. This commission is authorized to act either on its own or in response to complaints of discrimination by applicants or employees. As a result of its investigations, it may bring action against violators in the federal courts. Victims of discrimination may be entitled to financial compensation; violators may be fined or may have *affirmative action* plans imposed to remediate the situation for the future.

The underlying purpose of affirmative action — deliberate efforts to recruit larger numbers of qualified women and minorities for job placement — is to increase employment opportunities for persons who have frequently been denied such opportunities in the past. Ideally, the EEOC would like to have the percentage of minorities in a given segment of the workforce approximate the percentage of these groups in the population as a whole. In some cases, this means that special steps are necessary to recruit women and minorities for particular jobs.

While affirmative action has important goals and clear benefits, there are those who believe it may sometimes go too far. Concerted efforts to fill certain slots with minority candidates may seem to close doors for qualified male and white applicants — who sometimes, as a result, charge the employer with *reverse discrimination*. This can be a difficult charge to disprove if the majority applicant can demonstrate that he or she is better qualified than the minority candidate chosen to fill the position. Meanwhile, the employer is caught in the middle — with no simple way out. On the one hand, he or she is trying to fulfill the requirements of Title VII and maintain an appropriately balanced workforce. At the same time, deliberately overlooking or displacing qualified candidates because they are not minorities seems to some to undermine the very spirit and intent of Title VII. Obviously, this is a sensitive and complex issue, and one not likely to be fully resolved in the near future.

The Equal Pay Act of 1963. This act requires the employer to pay employees of both sexes equally for performing the same or similar jobs that require equal skill, effort, and responsibility. The employer may differentiate on the basis of seniority, merit, actual amount of work performed (pages typed, circuit boards inspected, etc.), or any other incentive-based system. Differentiation based solely on the sex of the employees, however, is prohibited.

Let's say Wilson hires two administrative assistants, Ted Franks and Marge White. If they are hired at the same time (so neither has greater seniority) and their job descriptions, skills, and duties are virtually identical, Wilson has no choice but to pay them at the same rate. Over time, however, let's suppose that Franks proves to be far more skilled at greeting the public, keeping track of messages, getting work done on time, and generally managing the affairs of the office. He types faster than White, and with a lower rate of errors. At that point, Wilson would be within his rights to increase Ted Franks's pay on the basis of *merit* — even though Franks's duties and White's would remain virtually the same. If White objected, though — as well she might — Wilson would be well-advised to have some means of documenting the differences in their performance, and thus justifying the different rates of pay.

On the other hand, let's suppose that Marge White is working simply because she likes the job — her husband is a successful trial lawyer and her children have all graduated from college — while Ted Franks is the sole support of his wife and six children. When Franks's wife has her seventh child, he asks for a raise. Assuming his job is the same as White's and that he performs it no better, can he be paid more by Wilson? It's hard to say. At the moment, the employer could argue that the two are paid differently because they have different financial needs, needs that might, for example, force Franks to quit to go to a higher-paying job. Therefore, Franks's higher pay is just a matter of offering the raise necessary to keep him at the company. That would, in theory, be acceptable. In practice, however, unless the employer were able to show that females in the company received equivalent raises in equivalent circumstances, there would be a definite question of discrimination.

Equal pay requirements are most often enforced on behalf of a class of employee — all female university professors or all female insurance agents, for example — rather than for individuals. It is, in other words, unlikely that anything could be done to guarantee that any two people are paid equitably. But such a disparity is certainly a signal that there might be broader inequitites in the company's policies. And if there is demonstrable evidence that one sex or the other has been underpaid, the employer can be required to make payments to rectify the past inequity — potentially a very costly settlement.

The Age Discrimination in Employment Act of 1967. This act protects workers age 40 and up from discrimination based on age. In other words, suppose Wilson (from our previous example) decides he'd like to terminate Marge White, who is 62. He cannot use her age as a reason, given the nature of her work. He'll have to show some other justification. Of course, if White had been hired as a rodeo rider, her age might legitimately disqualify her for continued employment at that job—but only because her advancing age would affect job performance.

In other words, for those rare jobs where age may present a personal health risk or dramatically affect performance, some "discrimination" is permissible. We don't expect to see 68-year-old professional hockey players, for instance, nor do Air Force fighter pilots stay fighter pilots for all time. But a 68-year-old accountant may be extremely competent—even more so by virtue of her experience. And the law says that such a competent accountant cannot be discharged—or fail to be promoted— on the basis of age alone. In short, using age as a limiting factor across the board is quite likely to invite charges of unwarranted discrimination; remember, the burden of demonstrating the connection between the job and the age requirement falls to the employer.

The Rehabilitation Act of 1973. This act requires federal contractors to take affirmative action with respect to otherwise qualified handicapped persons. Such contractors are required by law to make "reasonable accommodations" to the limitations of handicapped persons. For instance, a contractor who worked in a building with three front steps could not reasonably deny a position to a qualified applicant in a wheelchair on the grounds that the applicant did not have ready access to the building. Chances are, the law would require the employer to make some adjustments—probably by building a ramp to permit building access. Notice, however, that this provision currently applies only to *federal contractors*; there is no federal legislation that prohibits widespread discrimination against handicapped persons in the general workplace.

The Occupational Safety and Health Act of 1970. This act attempts to ensure that all working men and women will be able to enjoy safe, healthful working conditions. It applies to all businesses that affect interstate commerce, even those with only one employee. Remember our earlier example with Wheeler and his dry cleaning business? As you may recall, so long as he worked only with his wife, he couldn't be forced to, say, install a special guard on a folding machine. Once Wheeler took on employees, however, all that changed; an employer is responsible for the health and safety of employees while they are in the working environment. This means that the employer must make a conscious effort to keep informed of any potential dangers, and to correct any problems as rapidly as possible. The emphasis of the act is on *prevention* of hazards, not just on remediation.

One of OSHA's most powerful elements is its authorization of on-site inspections of the workplace without prior notice. If the employer objects to the inspection, however, the inspector must obtain a warrant—something that is generally very simple to do, particularly if an employee has alleged a complaint or requested a general inspection. And sometimes the employer will request the inspection just to verify compliance or learn what's needed to be in compliance. With employer-requested inspections, OSHA is somewhat more lenient about violations. Provided the employer takes care of the problem quickly, OSHA is likely not to impose penalties. Penalties for intentional or repeated violations, however, can be severe and may involve both fines of up to $10,000 *per incident* and imprisonment.

Certainly OSHA is intended to provide better working conditions for employees of each particular business, but beyond this immediate intent, the legislation is also intended to serve the general public interest. Tens of thousands of dollars are lost each year through work-related illness and injury that increase business expenses, diminish productivity, and cause unforeseen delays in delivery of services or products. A safe, healthful working environment, therefore, does much more than make life pleasant for employees—worthy though that goal may be in itself. It actually increases the productive potential of the business, thereby benefitting the public interest and—incidentally—the business itself.

Social Security. In 1935, Congress passed the Federal Insurance Contributions Act. The legislation was one of the most important elements of a dramatic increase in the role of the federal government in U.S. social policy during President Franklin Roosevelt's administration. While most of us know about FICA—more commonly called social security—as a form of retirement benefits, the act also provides disability insurance and payments to the blind and disabled. Benefits are computed on the basis of an employee's work record and total earnings.

To be fully insured under social security, a worker must work a minimum of ten years, and must, during that ten-year period, earn a certain minimum gross income from which social security payments are deducted. The longer a person works, and the higher the income, the greater the social security benefits the employee will receive on retirement or disability—up to a designated ceiling. Even at the highest level, though, benefits may increase as the cost of living goes up. The important point to keep in mind here is that the computation of social security benefits is highly complex, and depends on age, date of retirement, disability (if any), and work history.

Social security contributions are unique in that they are made equally by employer and employee. Most everyone knows that they have a FICA contribution deducted from their gross pay, but every employer with employees contributing to social security makes a matching contribution.

Unemployment insurance. Through the Federal Unemployment Tax Act (FUTA), the social security program also provides unemployment insurance. Funds to support this system come from taxes—primarily employers' contributions; the employers, in effect, buy insurance for their employees. In some states, however, employees also contribute through taxes on their salaries and wages. The purpose of this insurance is to provide some security to persons who are temporarily unemployed. There is, of course, a limit to the total benefits a worker can receive, the limit being related to that worker's history of employment and amount of previous contributions.

In keeping with the overall intent of the program to promote regular employment, some states offer special premium rates to employers who have relatively lower rates of involuntary unemployment—in other words, to those employers who tend to lose fewer employees through termination or cutbacks. The idea here is to encourage employers to seek out employees who are truly qualified for the work they do, and then to keep them employed. By the same token, there are incentives for workers, too. Unemployment payments are not to be viewed as a kind of subsidized leave of absence from work, but only as a form of temporary assistance. Thus, unemployment benefits may be denied to workers who are dismissed for cause, to those who quit a job without cause, or to those who refuse to seek or accept work for which they are qualified.

Workers' compensation. Workers' compensation is a means of reimbursing workers or their families for work-related injury or death. While laws vary from state to state, such compensation (where available) is, like unemployment, computed on the basis of wages and length of employment. In a sense, the system acts as a kind of legal shortcut, providing a means of remediation to an injured employee without requiring the employee to sue the employer. In other words, the employer is directly liable in the event of work-related injury or death. The employee (or beneficiaries) can collect directly from the employer's insurance according to their particular arrangement, and there is no need for a costly, time-consuming lawsuit to establish liability in the first place. Ideally, both sides benefit from the speed and convenience of this arrangement. (Disputes over the degree of compensation *are* common, but they start from a position of assumed employer responsibility if the injury is work-related.)

In workers' compensation systems, in order to be covered, the employee must be performing the ordinary duties of his or her work when injured, and not acting as an independent contractor. For instance, let's suppose that Bloom works for J&B Plumbing. While unloading a shipment of pipes, Bloom slips on some wet leaves and is seriously injured when some piping strikes him on the head. This is a pretty clear-cut case, and Bloom will likely collect workers' compensation. By the way, Bloom will be eligible even if he contributed to the accident through his own negligence — say, he wasn't watching what he was doing, or he was showing off, trying to unload the piping with one hand behind his back. The employer cannot use Bloom's carelessness as a defense; he'll have to pay.

On the other hand, though, suppose Bloom decides to make a little extra money over the weekend by helping his neighbor install a bathtub in his second-story bathroom. This work is not requested or authorized by J&B Plumbing. If Bloom slips on the stairway and injures his back while carrying the bathtub upstairs, can he collect workers' compensation? Not likely. He was performing the normal duties of a plumber, true, but he was doing the work on his own, as an independent contractor, not as an employee of J&B; therefore, the employer is not liable in this case.

Employee Retirement Income Security Act. In 1974, Congress passed the Employee Retirement Income Security Act (ERISA). Its purpose was to curb underfunding or mismanagement of pension funds, with a resulting loss of benefits to long-term employees who had entrusted a company to manage their contributions wisely. The act does not require that a company have a pension plan — and many smaller companies do not. It does require, however, that companies that offer such a plan as part of a benefits package meet certain minimum requirements in managing that plan effectively. The company must show, among other things, that decisions regarding the investment of pension funds are fully informed and made by the appropriate, authorized decision makers (who are sometimes the employees themselves), that no more than 10% of the total amount invested is reinvested in the assets or securities of the employer, and that there is sufficient income in the fund to cover employees who qualify for pension benefits.

For example, suppose Shields Manufacturing offers a pension plan to employees who have been with the company a minimum of five years. Shields might invest its pension contributions in a variety of ways — purchasing bonds or mutual funds, for instance. But suppose the board of directors for Shields suddenly decides to invest the entire pension fund in a piece of real estate overseas. Under ERISA, they could be in very serious trouble for such a decision. ERISA views the relationship between Shields and its employees as a fiduciary relationship — one of implied trust, that is. Therefore, Shields — or its designated decision maker (say, a professional investment firm) — has a legal responsibility not to violate that trust. The investment must pass muster as a good use of pension funds; the overseas property investment must be something that investors in general would consider safe and profitable.

Through careless, uninformed decision making, a company can jeopardize the economic security of its employees — a grave charge, to say the least. Company-managed pension funds are, therefore, subject to considerable regulation and paperwork, enough that some small businesses go without company-sponsored pensions rather than tackle the complicated compliance process. Most feel, though, that the safeguards provided by ERISA more than offset the increased inconvenience to employers.

SOME PRACTICAL ADVICE

Clearly, the interaction between employer and employee is affected by a wide variety of legislation and regulation. To summarize the implications of the law, let's look at employment laws from both sides — first the employee's side, then the employer's.

"Know the law" is pretty broad advice, but it's crucial here. An employee or job applicant who does not know when his or her legal rights are being violated can't help improve the situation. During the past several decades, the law has taken some strong positions in favor of employees' and applicants' rights — as we've attempted to show in this lesson. But employees themselves must usually take the initiative in seeing that those rights are upheld.

Under Title VII, remember that as an employee seeking promotion or as a new job applicant, you can expect that the qualifications you're asked to demonstrate are in fact essential to the job or promotion you seek. An employer who cannot show this basic relationship is likely to be found guilty of discrimination.

In addition, you have a right to question whether the pay you receive is equal to that given to others with the same qualifications, duties, and responsibilities. If it is not, the employer must show legitimate cause for the difference; appropriate reasons for the difference would include such things as seniority or merit, but not your gender, race, religion, or national origin.

Finally, if you work for a company that offers a pension plan, find out who makes the investment decisions and on what basis. You have a right to this information. Under ERISA, your pension funds are protected, and the relationship of trust that your contribution to such a fund establishes with your employer must not be violated.

What about the employer's side of things? Perhaps you've gotten the idea by now that there are numerous pitfalls to be avoided. That's so. But remember that the overall intent of the law is to create better, more productive conditions for both sides. Here are a few crucial things to keep in mind if you are an employer.

First, should your employees elect a union representative, your attitude toward this arrangement is key to good negotiations. An adversarial sort of relationship can undermine many opportunities for compromise. On the other hand, if you look on the union as a vehicle for getting necessary issues out in the open, negotiations are likely to be more productive.

The requirements under Title VII of the Civil Rights Act necessitate care in hiring, promoting, and reassigning employees. It is essential, for instance, to define the qualifications required for each position with the utmost rigor, and to make sure that those qualifications are not only related to successful job performance, but are, in fact, the criteria by which applicants are actually selected. Remember, discrimination can be a subtle thing — sometimes even unintentional. If you require a test or any other sort of screening in filling a position, be sure that you can demonstrate the manner in which performance on that test is related to performance on the job. If you cannot demonstrate that relationship, it's a good idea to drop the requirement.

Remember, too, that in most circumstances, you must provide equal pay for equal work. Two persons who hold the same position cannot receive different rates of pay based on race, religion, national origin, or gender. By the way, a difference in job titles is not likely to provide a justification for unequal rates of pay if the lower-paid employee can show comparability in responsibilities and effort.

Similarly, it's wise to examine your attitudes toward older workers. Their rights to remain in the workforce are protected by law, except with respect to positions in which age might represent a health or safety hazard to the employee, or where production would clearly be affected. The vast majority of jobs, however, do not entail such risks, and an unwarranted, outdated assumption that "older people just aren't as productive" will not provide you any defense whatsoever.

The importance of creating a safe, healthful environment cannot be overemphasized. There is little need to go into specifics here, since most concerns are fairly obvious, and further, potential hazards and problems tend to differ from one business to another. One point to remember, though: Keep in mind that the emphasis of the law is on *prevention*. Courts do not look kindly on a business that takes little action until after employees' complaints have been registered. Employers who take an aggressive approach toward minimizing risks tend to find favor with the law, whereas those who consistently try to avoid providing safe working conditions are subject to harsh penalties.

Finally, make decisions about pension plans carefully. The ERISA regulations aren't meant to discourage you from offering an employee pension program as a benefit. They do, however, impose requirements that many small companies find difficult to meet. (You will, for example, likely need professional assistance in documenting your plan and getting it approved.) All this regulation, though, is meant simply to ensure that workers' full pensions are available as promised. This, in turn, means that decisions about how the pension funds will be invested must be carefully made. It is generally wise to either leave the decisions to employees themselves or to designate a highly qualified and experienced professional with a proven track record. It is, frankly, impossible to be too cautious regarding these decisions; the potential for liability is staggering.

ASSIGNMENTS

- Before you watch the video program, be sure you've read through the preceding overview, familiarized yourself with the learning objectives for this lesson, and looked at the key terms below. Then, read Chapter 48 of Davidson et al., *Business Law*.
- After completing these tasks, view the video program for Lesson 30.
- After watching the program, take time to review what you've learned. First, evaluate your learning with the self-test which follows the key terms. Then, apply and evaluate what you've learned with the "Your Opinion, Please" scenarios at the end of this telecourse study guide lesson.

KEY TERMS

Before you read through the textbook assignment and watch the video program, take a minute to look at the key terms associated with this lesson. When you encounter them in the textbook and video program, pay careful attention to their meaning.

Bona fide occupational qualification (BFOQ)
Civil Rights Act of 1964
Employee Retirement Income Security Act (ERISA)
Equal Employment Opportunity Commission (EEOC)
Informational picketing
Landrum-Griffin Act

Lockout
Occupational Safety and Health Act (OSHA)
Picketing
Recognitional picketing
Reverse discrimination
Secondary boycott
Social security (FICA)
Taft-Hartley Act

Title VII   Wagner Act
Unemployment insurance   Workers' compensation
Unfair labor practices

SELF-TEST

The questions below will help you evaluate how well you've learned the material in this lesson. Read each one carefully, and select the letter of the option that best answers the question. You'll find the correct answer, along with a reference to the page number(s) where the topic is discussed, in the back of this telecourse study guide.

1. During the nineteenth century, the general attitude of both courts and employers toward labor unions could *best* be described as

   a. hostile.
   b. neutral.
   c. moderately pro-union.
   d. overwhelmingly pro-union.

2. Which of the following is *not* presently a responsibility of the NLRB (National Labor Relations Board)?

   a. Overseeing union elections
   b. Investigating unfair labor practices
   c. Helping interpret federal labor statutes
   d. Prosecuting unfair labor practice cases

3. Ordinarily, employees who seek to form a union or union local will be regarded as constituting an "appropriate bargaining unit" provided they

   a. all favor unionization.
   b. have similar skills, duties, and responsibilities.
   c. can demonstrate that the employer is guilty of unfair labor practices.
   d. all work for the same employer.

4. Under the Wagner Act, *all* of the following *except one* are likely to be considered mandatory bargaining subjects for good-faith bargaining. Which of the following would probably *not* be considered a mandatory bargaining subject?

   a. Terms of and requirements for promotion
   b. Vacation policies
   c. A decision to take on a new product line
   d. Rates for overtime pay

5. Federal and state statutes designed to ensure equal employment opportunity for persons historically foreclosed from the workplace generally date back to

   a. the mid-1960s and thereafter.
   b. the mid-1920s.
   c. the late 1800s.
   d. the early 1800s — and even before.

6. The *main* function of the EEOC (Equal Employment Opportunity Commission) is to

   a. create new legislation to expand Title VII.
   b. mediate labor negotiations between employers and union representatives.
   c. inspect workplaces to ensure compliance with health and safety regulations.
   d. serve as a review and enforcement agency for cases involving unfair employment practices.

7. Sometimes, even under Title VII, discrimination on the basis of a normally impermissible criterion may be legal if the job at hand "demands" that an individual from one special group be hired for the job. Which of the following is *most likely* to be a just and appropriate application of a BFOQ (bona fide occupational qualification)?

   a. A male actor is hired to play the title role in *MacBeth*.
   b. A person of the Catholic faith is hired as a bus driver for a Catholic girls' school.
   c. A female is hired as a telephone operator.
   d. A native of Italy is hired to teach a class in Italian.

8. In 1970, Congress passed the Occupational Safety and Health Act (OSHA). At the federal level, the *primary* motivation for enacting this legislation was to

   a. create consistency among working environments nationwide.
   b. minimize financial losses resulting from employee illness and injury.
   c. promote better health practices among American workers.
   d. increase employers' awareness about the relationship between good health and productivity on the job.

9. An OSHA inspector can inspect a workplace without the employer's permission *if*

   a. he or she obtains a warrant.
   b. there is evidence of a violation.
   c. the request for the inspection comes from an employee.
   d. *None* of the above; the inspector must *always* have the employer's permission.

10. Unemployment benefits are funded *primarily* through

    a. employees' contributions.
    b. employers' contributions.

c. government grants.

d. federal taxes.

YOUR OPINION, PLEASE

Read each of the following scenarios and answer the questions about the decisions you would make in each situation. Give these questions some serious thought; they may be used as the basis for the development of a more complex essay. You should base your decisions on what you've learned from this lesson, though you may incorporate outside readings or information gained through your own experience if it is relevant.

Scenario I

Apex College, which has a strong affirmative action policy, decides to offer a course in Native American history during its winter term. In advertising the position, Apex calls for "teaching experience, knowledge of the subject, and familiarity with Native American culture." It also notes the fact that the college is "an affirmative action employer." Out of twelve applicants, the screening committee finally narrows the selection to two. The first is a white female, age 32, named Reed. Reed has a doctorate in Native American studies and has published several books on Native American culture. She also has five years of junior college teaching experience.

The second applicant is a Native American male, age 38, named Stone. Stone is a poet and novelist with a master's degree in anthropology and a bachelor's degree in history. He has spent several years giving seminars on "multicultural approaches to history," but has no classroom teaching experience.

When Apex finally selects Stone for the position, Reed is outraged and charges the college with sex and race discrimination. The college counters that Stone's Native American heritage is a BFOQ in this case, a significant factor likely to contribute to his success on the job. Further, they allege, they are fulfilling their affirmative action commitment. Reed counters that despite her own white heritage, she has spent a much greater time studying Native American culture than Stone, and is generally better qualified for the job. She decides to sue the college.

What's your opinion? Based on what you know of the situation, do you think Reed can successfully build a case based on her charge of "reverse" discrimination? Or is Apex correct either in asserting that Stone's ethnic heritage is a BFOQ in this case or that affirmative action concerns give the college the right to select the ethnic minority applicant?

- Is Reed likely to win a suit based on claims of discrimination?

- What factors support your answer?

- What factors might an attorney cite in arguing against your view?

- What steps, if any, might Reed have taken to prevent a lawsuit in this situation?
- What steps, if any, might Apex College have taken to prevent a lawsuit in this situation?

Scenario 2

Langer, a journeyman electrician, works for Hughes Lighting and Sound, residential contractors who specialize in lighting and sound systems for private homes. He has been recognized repeatedly for his outstanding work, given numerous promotions and raises, and in other ways cited for excellence. When J. L. Hughes, owner and manager of the firm, decides to build a new home, he asks Langer if he would be willing to contract independently to do the work. Langer agrees readily since, in view of his reputation, he is able to command an excellent fee, which will be paid to him directly and separately, apart from his usual salary.

The wiring of the house is extensive, and Langer projects the work will take him approximately a week, during which he will take earned vacation from the job at Hughes. The third day on the job, Langer is seriously injured when an improperly secured joist on the second floor of the Hughes residence gives way and he falls eight feet to the floor below. The doctor tells him that he'll be unable to return to work for at least six months. Langer requests workers' compensation, but Hughes denies the request, stating that Langer was not doing his regular work and therefore does not qualify.

Langer, however, argues that in this instance, the wiring of the Hughes residence should be considered a logical extension of his regular work, even if performed while on vacation. The contract with Hughes, Langer argues, is really no different from any other company contract except that he agreed — at Hughes's request — to do the wiring personally. Langer thereupon asks the state Workers' Compensation Board to rule that he receive the workers' compensation he believes he is owed.

What's your opinion? Based on what you know of the situation, do you think Langer is entitled to workers' compensation? Is he right in arguing that the work on the Hughes residence is simply an extension of his regular work on the job? Or is he, in fact, an independent contractor? Is the decision affected in any way by the unsafe working conditions at the job site? Why or why not?

- Is Langer likely to receive the workers' compensation he feels he is owed?
- What factors support your answer?
- What factors might an attorney cite in arguing against your view?
- What steps, if any, might Langer have taken to prevent a dispute in this case?
- What steps, if any, might Hughes have taken to prevent a dispute in this case?

Answer Key

1. b (Page 4* and Study Guide Lesson 2)

2. a (Page 4) The primary purpose of law (Option D) is *not* to control citizens, but to protect them and to guard their rights. Control, however, is one component of this protective function.

3. d (Page 4) Under our system, we do have procedural laws (Option C), but they are still laws, not rules. Rules are unenforceable under law—but *administrative rules and regulations*, correctly adopted by a government agency, are part of our laws and thus are enforceable.

4. b (Page 9) Some persons might heartily wish that Option C were true, but it is not. Options A and D are also false. Courts *presume* knowledge of the law, even though such an assumption is admittedly unrealistic. The courts have no official responsibility for instructing citizens in the law except within the context of individual court cases.

5. c (Pages 10ff.)

6. a (Pages 12–13) Under the freedom of contract doctrine, contracting parties are free to establish their own arrangements so long as there is no violation of contract law and the provisions of the contract are not unconscionably unfair to one party. True, we do not know the actual value of each party's services (Option C), but unconscionability is not likely to be an issue here so long as the two parties are happy with their arrangement; it might be different if Stillwell were required under the contract to provide piano lessons for the remainder of McCary's life and the life of his children.

7. b (Page 16) Laws created through legislative action are known as statutes.

8. d (Page 16) There is nothing currently existing in the law books to reflect McDuff's new ruling; nevertheless, her decision, based on interpretations of earlier cases and rulings, may help guide future decisions. Judges in England and the U.S. have the opportunity to "make law," as McDuff is doing here.

---

*Page numbers refer to pages in Davidson et al., *Business Law*, where the topic is discussed.

9. a (Pages 16ff.) The word *passive* can be misleading since it suggests that the judge sits quietly by, letting the trial take its course regardless of how things are going. The judge does oversee the proceedings and may intervene if the testimony of a witness requires clarification, if there are questions about evidence or proof, or if it is important to clarify the law for jurors or others. The judge does not, however, typically take a leading role in directing court proceedings. That is generally left to the attorneys — although there are exceptions.

10. a (Pages 22–25) The Supreme Court's powers are extensive, and it can declare virtually any act of the executive or legislative branches of government unconstitutional. It cannot, however, appoint its own membership; that is the president's job. Appointees are nominated by the president and confirmed by the Senate.

3 — BUSINESS CRIMES AND BUSINESS TORTS

1. b (Pages 40 and 61)

2. d (Pages 64–65)

3. d (Pages 62ff.) The point here is that Donahue did not follow through. Had he done so, he would have been guilty of the crime of robbery. Intentions without any criminal action do not in themselves add up to any criminal liability. If the storekeeper saw that Donahue had a gun and believed Donahue was threatening him, Donahue could be liable under the tort of assault. Under the circumstances, though, there is no liability.

4. a (Page 65)

5. b (Page 70) The key to a defense of justification is that whatever the defendant does to harm the plaintiff must be less than the harm intended by the plaintiff — or at least what the defendant has reason to believe is intended. In other words, Peterson would not be justified in shooting Flores because he caught Flores digging up his prize rose bush. But if Flores attacked Peterson's wife or child, the shooting might be justified.

6. c (Page 41)

7. a (Page 42) Option A is the only one in which the defendant can be held liable even if there is *no* evidence of harmful intent and *no* evidence of negligence. The point here is that the situation is so dangerous in itself that Freemont will be responsible for any resulting injuries even if he does exercise due care and even if he does not mean for anyone to be hurt.

8. d (Page 43) Both are equally serious, so Option C is incorrect. And neither has to do with violation of contract, as suggested in Option B.

9. d   (Page 45) Remember that an action's status as a crime or tort is dependent on statutes and society's perception of acceptable behavior. Shooting rabbits with a pistol in rural Wyoming is likely to be perfectly legal; it is probably not legal in the courtyard of a New York City condominium. (Note, however, that if Kincaid's shooting damages someone else, he could well be liable even though his underlying action was not a crime.)

10. a   (Pages 48–50ff.) All options are important, but in establishing negligence, the court will ask, overall, what would be expected of a reasonable and prudent person in the same situation. Thus, a person could be negligent without intending harm (Option B) or really anticipating harm to anyone, much less the plaintiff in particular (Option D). Option C may be relevant, but there's a crucial point to remember: Under the law, the duty of a person to exercise due care does not extend to personal threat of life and limb. In other words, the law only expects one to go so far. Individuals are expected not to create or contribute to hazardous situations, but they are not expected (under the law) to risk their own safety, health, or lives in order to eliminate hazards or prevent harm to others.

4 — THE NATURE OF CONTRACT LAW

1. a   (Page 125) Most adults will, at some point, do at least one of the following: write a check, use a charge card, take a job, or marry. All these things are, in some respects, contractual in nature and are therefore subject to contract law. Even when no formal contract is drawn or signed, an agreement may be viewed by a court as a contract and the elements of that agreement enforced or interpreted accordingly.

2. b   (Pages 126ff.) Option D, incidentally, would be contrary to the UCC's major purpose.

3. d   (Page 127)

4. a   (Page 127) Contracts need not be in written form (Option B), nor need they be either formal or drawn up by an attorney (Option D). Economic benefit (Option C) is common within contracts, but is by no means a necessary element; a marriage contract, for example, may offer little or no economic benefit to either party, and even if it does, that benefit is not today usually the basis of the contract.

5. d   (Pages 127–128) An agreement that calls for violation of law or public policy is never considered a valid, enforceable contract and will not be upheld by a court.

6. b   (Pages 128–129) One element of a legal contract is clear specification of the terms of performance and compensation. While we might assume that

both parties hold the terms of the contract to be fair and equitable (Option D), that is not a necessary element. It is, however, critical that the two parties enter the contract willingly and both agree at the outset what each will give and receive.

7. a   (Page 129) Option D is not necessarily correct; certainly, a simple oral contract to wash the windows of a house would be easier to renegotiate than a complex, multiparty, multiyear business transaction, even though this latter contract is in writing. Options B and C are simply false. Courts *will* often uphold oral contracts, but clearly defining the terms of an oral contract is tricky at best, and straightening out a disputed oral contract is extremely difficult.

8. d   (Pages 130ff.)

9. a   (Pages 130–131) Option D is partially correct, but misses much of the point. The doctrine of unconscionability applies to cases of extreme unfairness. For example, a person whose skills would seem to command a higher salary than he is receiving could not sue his company under the doctrine of unconscionability. It must be shown that one party is benefitting unjustly because the other party really was not in a position to negotiate freely and reach a commercially viewed "fair" or acceptable contract.

10. a   (Pages 131ff.)

5 – CONTRACT REQUIREMENT: THE AGREEMENT

1. a   (Page 142)

2. d   (Page 143) Option A is not relevant. The point of the objective theory of contracts is not whether the persons involved are behaving in an emotional manner; it's how the situation would look to an uninvolved observer who had no vested interest in either side's position. The court cannot consider what is inside each person's mind.

3. c   (Page 144) Smith's response (Option B) is, for the moment, irrelevant. The point is, there is no definiteness to Bayliss's offer. How large a raise? When? How will Smith's attitude be measured? These and other details need to be supplied before a true offer exists.

4. b   (Pages 146–148)

5. c   (Pages 148ff.) The point in this scenario is that regardless of whether Ruckles made a general public offer, Larson didn't know about it and so, technically, wasn't responding to the offer by returning the cat. (Option B is false.)

6. c   (Pages 148ff. and 157)

7. c (Page 149) Option B may seem the fair and tactful thing to do, but it's not a legal obligation.

8. a (Pages 149–151)

9. d (Pages 149–150) Options A, B, and C are all incorrect. Under common law, there is no limit on how quickly an offer can be revoked after it has been extended. There also is no requirement that the word "revoke" be used in revoking an offer, so long as the *intention* to revoke is clear—as it was in Samantha's conversation with Joyce. And so long as Beverly even indirectly hears about the intent to revoke, as she did through Joyce, the revocation is valid.

10. b (Pages 152 and 157–158)

6—CONTRACT REQUIREMENT: CONSIDERATION

1. d (Pages 164ff.)

2. b (Pages 165ff.) Options A, C, and D may all be true at various times, but none of them is necessarily true. Consideration is whatever is bargained for and given in exchange for a promise from the offeror.

3. c (Pages 165–166ff.) In this example, Knott is the offeror. What he is bargaining for is the restriction of Wilson's dog to Wilson's own property. He offers (that is, promises) the use of the pool in exchange.

4. b (Page 167) Adequacy of consideration (whether what's given in exchange is "worth" what's promised in return) is not the court's worry; that determination is left strictly to the parties to the contract. The court is likely to take the position here that since Beale did agree to the $100, and has in fact received it, he owes Miles four more months' worth of car washes—like it or not.

5. c (Page 169)

6. b (Page 170)

7. d (Pages 171ff.) In effect, Ready Repair and Langley have struck a new bargain, in which Ready offers to cancel the debt if Langley will pay $50. Thus, the $50 is consideration for dismissal of the whole debt. (However, the offer *and* agreement to accept the $50 in full settlement is called a composition agreement.)

8. a (Pages 172ff.) There is no consideration here. The pilot is bound by preexisting duty to fly Reese (or any passenger) safely and somewhat comfortably. He cannot charge extra for "safe" trips.

9. c   (Pages 174–176) Option B is false; promises made out of moral obligation are *rarely* enforced. But the issue here is that what might be looked upon as "consideration"—Evans's years of good service—is really only past consideration, and thus doesn't provide a sound basis for current bargains.

10. c   (Pages 171–177) It isn't likely that Evans's position would be supported by the court, but there is one chance. Perhaps she can show that when she retired from Blackwell's firm she relied on his promise and didn't look for another job to supplement her retirement income and, further, that she has now lost this opportunity to be financially secure. If so, she may win. Promissory estoppel is used in situations like this where injustice will result because a promise that was reasonably relied on is now being broken. In such circumstances, promissory estoppel takes the place of the consideration that would otherwise be required to create a contract. Options A, B, and D will be of no help whatever.

7—CONTRACT REQUIREMENT: CONTRACTUAL CAPACITY

1. b   (Page 184) Option A is partially correct, but contractual capacity is not a matter of legal age alone. Option C is irrelevant; the court will view the terms of the contract as the business of the contracting parties. And, in any case, one's *capacity* to contract has nothing to do with whether one is currently involved in a contract. Similarly, Option D—though important in contract law—has nothing to do with capacity.

2. a   (Page 184)

3. a   (Pages 185–192) In the case of necessaries, a minor cannot disaffirm a contract, although the actual contract he or she signed will not be the one the court enforces, because the minor still lacked full capacity to contract. However, the court will attempt to assure the same result by creating a *quasi contract* in line with the original contract. A minor *can* disaffirm a contract even if the loss to the other party is considerable (although the minor may be required to return the consideration, or the financial equivalent of that consideration, to the other party). If there is an adult cosigner (Option C), that person will be held financially liable if the minor disaffirms the contract; having a cosigner does not, however, prevent the minor from disaffirming the contract.

4. b   (Page 187) Once a minor reaches the age of majority, the period during which a previously signed contract can be disaffirmed is limited. It is up to the courts to determine what will be considered "reasonable."

5. c   (Page 186)

6. a (Page 186) Option B would fulfill the duty of restitution. Option C calls for more than is required.

7. c (Pages 185–191)

8. c (Page 189) Given that necessaries are broadly defined as "anything that directly fosters the minor's well-being," the court could take the position that investments fit within this category. On the other hand, the court might take the position that the value of a painting as an investment is in itself arguable, so that a painting purchased in the hope that its market value will rise cannot be termed a necessary. Further, the court would not decide one way or the other without knowing more about Brad's situation. The point is, the definition of a necessary is highly variable and dependent on circumstance.

9. a (Page 191) Options B, C, and D are completely false.

10. b (Page 185) Option A is of some help, but keep in mind that ratification only becomes effective once the minor reaches majority and, until such time, the minor can disaffirm even a ratified contract. Option C isn't helpful; a minor's promise to restore isn't legally binding. Similarly, the court will establish its own definition of necessary (Option D), based on circumstance, and there's no guarantee that the car would be found a necessary.

8 – CONTRACT REQUIREMENT: LEGAL PURPOSE

1. a (Page 198)

2. b (Pages 199, 209) Did you choose Option D? This comes close, since by implication, the sign suggests that there will be no one to guard patrons' cars or property after 10 p.m. However, the sign does not explicitly state exculpation or freedom from responsibility—as does the sign in Option B.

3. d (Page 199) A bargain that violates public policy is by definition illegal, but may be enforced—at least in part—if the court deems that upholding the bargain will better serve public interest in the long run than voiding the bargain.

4. d (Page 201) An agreement that violates public policy or that is in violation of state statues may, in certain instances, be upheld despite the violation—though one should not conclude from this that the courts support or encourage such violation. Agreements to commit a crime, however, are never upheld.

5. b (Page 201)

6. b (Pages 202–203) Option C is really irrelevant here—though if injury *did* result, Wells could sue the dentist on that basis. But the issue here is whether the dentist had the right to be operating as a dentist—which he did not. All states demand that dentists be licensed professionals; therefore, this "dentist" is in violation of state statutes, and the contract between him and Wells is void.

7. **b**   (Pages 206–208) Courts do sometimes blue-pencil restrictive clauses, but this way of dealing with the situation is relatively rare. The more common approach is to void the restrictive clause but uphold the remainder of the agreement. Note too that the decision in this case rests on the fact that the clause was construed as "unreasonably restrictive and designed only to protect Acme from competition." Had that not been the case, the clause would likely have been enforced.

8. **a**   (Page 209) Many issues are weighed in making such a judgment when there is no statute or clear precedent already providing an answer. When this is the case, the main issue considered by the court is whether the party initiating the agreement has superior bargaining power—which is another way of saying that the party agreeing to the exculpatory (nonresponsibility or nonliability) clause really has little choice in the matter. In many cases, it's a take-it-or-leave-it sort of agreement, nonnegotiable. It is not necessary that the agreeing party stipulate that agreement in writing (Option B), though obviously, if a suit does arise, a written agreement helps provide evidence that in fact an agreement exists. Options C and D are probably both relevant to an extent, but do not carry the weight of Option A—which is the main issue.

9. **b**   (Page 211) Option C is irrelevant here. All that matters in this case is whether Martha knew about the situation. If she had known, she would have been equally guilty, from the court's perspective, and probably could not have recovered her wages. But since she did not, the court will not hold her responsible for the situation.

10. **d**   (Page 211)

9—CONTRACT REQUIREMENT: GENUINENESS OF ASSENT

1. **b**   (Page 216)

2. **a**   (Page 217)

3. **b**   (Page 217)

4. **d**   (Pages 217ff.)

5. **c**   (Pages 217–218ff.) While the basement happened to be flooded at the time of the inspection trip, we do not really know whether on a different day the basement problem would have been discoverable. What's more impor-

tant is whether Brown knew about the basement flooding prior to the close of the sale and either made efforts to conceal the truth or did not tell Kilbeck about the true condition of the basement.

6. a (Pages 217–218ff.) Most courts now encourage openness and full disclosure, even when the plaintiff does not seek specific information. Clearly, it would not be in Riles's best interests to purchase a restaurant with a faulty ventilation system. And because the building is vacant, it is likely that visits to the scene would not disclose the ventilation problem even if it could have been determinable had the restaurant been open. Though we might consider Riles a little careless for not asking about the ventilation, the trend is for courts to overlook his oversight and place liability on Toffel.

7. b (Page 220)

8. a (Pages 222–223)

9. b (Pages 221ff.) Option C raises a good point; but even if Fields had authorization to bind the company to a contract, the main point is that Fields did not know she was signing a contract. She merely meant to acknowledge delivery of goods. The contract was presented to Fields in a deceptive and misleading way; Rickles's company has not acted in good faith.

10. b (Page 227) Option A might sound correct, but it is not. While we might feel that misusing a relationship of trust to gain advantage is "unconscionable," such situations may not always meet the fairly high legal standards for voiding a contract on grounds of unconscionability. (Additionally, contracts can be voided for unconscionability in circumstances that do not involve a relationship of trust.) Undue influence, however, always involves misusing a relationship of trust.

10—CONTRACT REQUIREMENT: PROPER FORM

1. b (Page 243)

2. c (Pages 244ff.) Even though Option C doesn't involve much money, it is a transaction involving land and must therefore be expressed in writing.

3. a (Page 249) Regardless of any previous oral agreement, a written confirmation to which a merchant makes no written objection within ten days will usually be upheld by the court as evidence of a binding contract. The phone call was a fine start, but Clark needed to do more than phone Handywrite. If he didn't want the Handywrite pads, he should have written to the company disaffirming the notice immediately.

4. b (Page 249) Option C is incorrect. Even though court cases are obviously individual and open to interpretation, judges are bound by the statutes that apply to the case. In this case, the promise is not enforceable because it was clearly a promise given in consideration of marriage and was not put into writing. The Statute of Frauds is very clear about such cases.

5. d   (Page 244)

6. d   (Pages 244–245) Option B raises an important point, too. The bank must sue Hawkins unsuccessfully before it can sue Larson. However, it cannot take that step unless Larson has agreed in writing to be responsible for the loan.

7. c   (Page 245)

8. c   (Page 246) Under the *doctrine of part performance*, it is possible that the court will take the position that a contract exists. Henley is living in the house, paying rent, and improving the property. To avoid the unjust enrichment of the seller, the court is very likely to conclude that an enforceable contract exists in this case—but there are no guarantees; normally, contracts involving land must be in writing.

9. b   (Pages 246–247) Option C raises an important point, but the agreement here does not involve the purchase of specific supplies. Rather, it is an agreement to do business with one company exclusively. The main point here is that this is a contract that cannot be concluded within a year; in fact, it's specifically set up not to be concluded within a year. Therefore, it is not enforceable unless it exists in writing.

10. a   (Pages 249–250)

11—INTERPRETATION OF CONTRACTS

1. d   (Pages 234ff.) While Options A, B, and C are all good suggestions, there is simply no way to guarantee that no misunderstandings or ambiguities will ever arise. That is the whole point of interpretation.

2. b   (Pages 235 and 241ff.) Option C goes too far; parol evidence is admissible under some circumstances. Options A and D are false.

3. c   (Page 236)

4. a   (Page 237) It would be nice if we could be sure Option D would be true; but again, there are no guarantees. Option B, incidentally, is more applicable to a partially integrated agreement—as is Option C.

5. b   (Pages 237–238)

6. a   (Page 238) One established rule of interpretation states that handwritten words will control printed ones.

7. d (Pages 237–238 and entire reading assignment)

8. c (Page 239)

9. a (Pages 239–240) This may read like a condition subsequent, but it is more likely to be interpreted by the court as a condition precedent. In effect, what the condition says is that RidPest will uphold their part of the agreement as long as Brown continues to have yearly inspections; one part of the agreement is contingent (dependent, that is) on the other.

10. b (Pages 241ff.)

---

12 – RIGHTS OF THIRD PARTIES

1. a (Page 256)

2. a (Page 259) The sidewalks are clearly intended as a direct benefit to the residents — whether the residents particularly like having sidewalks or not. The residents are probably not mentioned (even as a group) in the contract; but they are still the intended beneficiaries (together with the city as a whole).

3. c (Pages 259ff.)

4. d (Pages 259–260) Though Menefee's housemate has a vested interest in the contract, from the facts given none of the options will help her if Menefee or the insurance company cancels the contract because the premiums weren't paid. (On the other hand, if Menefee named a new beneficiary or cancelled the contract, Nettles might — in some states and under certain circumstances — have grounds for suit under beneficiary law.)

5. b (Pages 259–260)

6. a (Pages 259–263)

7. b (Pages 262–263 and entire reading assignment) The answers to Options A and C could both be "No," and yet the person could still be a third-party beneficiary. But to be a third-party beneficiary, a person or agency must — if nothing else — be affected by the contract. (There are, of course, other factors that must also be present before someone who is affected by a contract gains the status of third-party beneficiary.) (Option D is a bit nonsensical; third-party beneficiaries are those affected by the contract who did *not* sign the contract.)

8. c (Page 263)

9. d (Pages 264–265) The donation is probably a gift — but it might not be. For instance, let's say that Pickwick agreed to hire Jensen's son as an understudy for one season; that would be consideration. Or Jensen gets the best seat in the house. Or extra tickets for friends. In these cases, Jensen and Pickwick may well have a contract. If Jensen is receiving no consideration — as is likely to be the case — then the donation is a gift.

10. a   (Page 265) Note, however, that under the *first-to-give-notice* rule (English Rule), the money would go to Platt since they gave notice before Pickwick.

---

13 — PERFORMANCE AND DISCHARGE

1. a   (Page 276)

2. d   (Pages 276–277)

3. c   (Page 278) Releases frequently involve the exchange of consideration — here Sullivan agrees to help locate a replacement — but need not. Similarly, they need not be in writing, although a prudent businessperson *will* make sure to get the release in writing. And a release can occur at any time after contract signing. Only Option C is correct.

4. d   (Page 279)

5. b   (Page 279) By requesting, and subsequently agreeing, to increase the quantity of feed in the order, the parties have, by implication, rescinded the original contract. They have now substituted a new contract — for the increased quantity and price.

6. c   (Pages 276ff.)

7. a   (Page 280)

8. b   (Page 280) Consideration must be provided to the original creditor — in this case, VastVision. Whatever consideration (Option C) is provided to Mindset (probably use of the hall) isn't relevant to the discharge of the VastVision–Ely contract, although it's clear that unless all three parties are agreeable to the proposed change, a novation would not occur. This is not, incidentally, a case of accord and satisfaction (Option D), so the agreement will become legally binding *before* performance. (Option A is a practical, not a legal, issue; from what we know, if Ely is going to get out of the agreement, it has to let VastVision rent the hall to Mindset.)

9. c   (Pages 281–282) Courts are reluctant to recognize impossibility as a valid means of discharging contractual obligations except in cases of "objective" impossibility — where there truly is nothing any contractor could do about the situation. Passage of a new law making the previously legal terms of a contract illegal is one such situation. In such a case, the court recognizes that there simply is no way that *anyone* could legally fulfill the terms of the contract.

10. a   (Pages 285–286) Failure to meet a condition discharges the obligation of the other contracting party. Thus, none of the other three options—all of which still obligate Hanes to buy the car—is correct.

14—CONTRACTUAL REMEDIES

1. b   (Page 291)

2. a   (Pages 293ff.)

3. a   (Page 292 and entire reading assignment)

4. d   (Pages 293ff.) In this case, Collins is suing for costs directly associated with the failure to perform, and recovery of those costs will place her in the same economic position she would have enjoyed had the contract been performed.

5. c   (Pages 294ff.) Options A, B, and D all provide some relevant information, and courts are open to considering all circumstances relating to a case. But to collect consequential damages, Collins must show that future opportunities were jeopardized as a direct consequence of the breach. Inconvenience (Option D), though important from the plaintiff's perspective, is not sufficient grounds for receiving consequential damages.

6. d   (Page 296) In assessing damages, courts will ask whether the injured party took steps to mitigate the damages. In this case, for example, if Collins immediately tried—albeit unsuccessfully—to reschedule the training session or get other consultants to do the needed training in time to bid on the contract, her case will be stronger.

7. b   (Pages 296–297) Option D is nearly correct, because punitive damages are *rarely* awarded in such suits. However, the court will make an exception if it seems in the public interest to make an example of the defendant. Option C is absolutely false; just the opposite is true.

8. c   (Pages 298–299ff.) Options A and B are wrong—punitive and treble damages (by definition) are money. Option D isn't applicable.

9. a   (Pages 298–299)

10. b   (Page 302) Option A is a definition of waiver of breach; Option C is specific performance; Option D is liquidated damages.

15 — SALES AND SALES CONTRACTS

1. c (Page 311) Options A, B, and D are all partially correct, but the notion of movability is essential to the definition. Goods do not, for instance, include real estate, which is not transportable from seller to buyer.

2. b (Page 312) Remember, a merchant is someone who regularly deals in the relevant goods, who is an expert in the field, or who employs an expert in the field. Only Wilkes qualifies under that definition; Nathan and Holly are operating out of their respective territories.

3. d (Pages 313–314)

4. a (Page 314) The shipment is a response to the offer. Mulberry has in fact accepted the offer but has provided nonconforming goods — something other than what was described in or requested through the contract.

5. b (Pages 315ff.) Option A would be true if neither party had specified any terms relating to shipping. Since Garcia has proposed a plan, and since the intention of his contract form is the same, his specifications are looked on by the UCC as "proposed additions" to the original contract; they will become part of that contract unless Malone objects within a reasonable time. Option C cannot be correct since Malone's form specifies nothing about shipping.

6. b (Page 318)

7. d (Pages 318–319)

8. d (Pages 312ff.) Remember that the phrase *commercially reasonable* is interpreted somewhat differently from the *reasonable person* perspective often applied under common law. What's important here is not so much what any given hypothetical reasonable person or company might do (Option C), but what is commonly practiced day in and day out among merchants having similar business dealings. Their conduct becomes the guideline for establishing what is fair. Option A is important, obviously, but some conduct that is legal may still not be considered commercially reasonable. Option B could create some real problems. The time to determine what is "fair" is during early contract negotiations; the court is unlikely to analyze the "fairness" of the agreement.

9. a (Pages 322ff.) Options B, C, and D are all false. Incidentally, if Forkner did try to claim an exorbitant price, Gluth might successfully sue for rescission of the contract on grounds of unconscionability.

10. b (Page 323)

16—PASSAGE OF TITLE AND RISK OF LOSS

1. b   (Page 345)

2. a   (Pages 345ff.) Option D is sometimes correct, but not all sales transactions involve negotiable documents. Option C makes no sense since reservation of title is an attempt by the seller to retain title. Option B is a necessary— but insufficient—condition for transfer of title.

3. a   (Pages 346–349) A buyer gains an insurable interest from the moment goods are identified to the contract, even if those goods are nonconforming. After all, Output may well decide to keep the computers, and it has a right to protect its interests during shipment.

4. c   (Page 349) Insurable interest is the right to purchase insurance in order to protect one's property rights and interests. Buyers and sellers have insurable interest either when they currently own goods or when there is likelihood that they will gain or regain ownership—in other words, any time they stand in a position to suffer a financial loss if the goods are stolen, damaged, destroyed, or lost.

5. d   (Page 348) Arnold, who is not a merchant, purchased the clock in good faith—and the law will uphold her right to keep it. On the other hand, a merchant—such as Harvey's Clock Shop—is not free to simply dispose of other people's goods in arbitrary fashion without their knowledge or consent. Though the law will protect Arnold's right to keep the goods she purchased in good faith, it will also provide remedies to Blake, who expected to get his clock back. Blake can sue Harvey's, but cannot sue Arnold, who has acted in good faith. By the way, though Option C is obviously exaggerated, and consumer protection laws generally prevent the kind of conduct shown here by Harvey's, it must be acknowledged that Blake did assume *some* risk in entrusting his clock to another party, even though that party was a reputable merchant. (There is no evidence that Harvey's committed fraud—Option B.)

6. b   (Page 351) Option C has a small element of truth. However, if a destination contract is not specified, the court is likely to treat the contract as a shipment contract. Besides, in this case, it is made very clear that the seller expects the buyer to assume risk of loss from the moment of shipment; that is characteristic of a shipment contract.

7. d   (Page 352)

8. a   (Pages 350 and 353) A bailee takes responsibility for holding goods until negotiations between buyer and seller are concluded—for instance, until the seller delivers a negotiable document to the buyer or completes whatever performance is called for by the contract. The bailee does not, however, assume risk of loss; that relationship exists between buyer and seller.

9. d   (Page 354) The intent and performance of the merchant are more important considerations than the amount of merchandise per se. For instance, a business that sold a third of its inventory in a routine, albeit larger-than-usual, transaction, might not be looked on by the UCC as engaging in a bulk transfer sale. Conversely, a shoe manufacturing business that sold all its machinery, desks, chairs, telephones, and other equipment would probably be engaging in a bulk sale even if — because most of their assets were represented by shoes in warehouses — they were only selling 20% of the value of the business. Remember, the UCC rules governing bulk transfer sales are designed mainly to protect the interests of unsecured creditors whose financial welfare may be threatened when a business trades hands or when there is an apparent attempt to avoid responsibility for the business's debts. If our shoe company is going out of business, its creditors are entitled to protection.

10. b   (Page 355) Options A, C, and D are all false. The UCC deliberately makes the buyer responsible because the seller could not reasonably be counted on to work (possibly) against his or her own interests; and creditors often lack the power or opportunity to ensure that debts owed to them are paid.

17 — PERFORMANCE OF A SALES CONTRACT

1. c   (Page 328)

2. a   (Pages 328–329)

3. a   (Page 329) The lesson makes the point that the simpler the arrangement, the lower the chance of difficulty. However, any of the other options (B, C, or D) *could* create problems. Keep in mind, though, that the UCC regulations are specifically designed to handle the kinds of problems noted in Options B and C. (The way around Option D is usually to elect a method of delivery that best suits the goods.)

4. b   (Page 333) The destination contract is advantageous to the buyer because it places loss of risk on the seller until the goods are delivered to the specified destination.

5. b   (Pages 333–334)

6. b   (Page 334) Recall that in a C.O.D. contract, the buyer *must* pay for the merchandise prior to inspection. Therefore, Miller has acted appropriately. Further, his payment does *not* constitute acceptance because he is required to pay before inspection — and a buyer is always entitled to inspect goods before accepting. In other words, Miller has not yet accepted the goods,

and if he notifies Happy Trails promptly of the mistake, they are obligated to cure the defect—to provide the correct boots, that is—at their expense.

7. d (Page 334) Option A isn't a right; short of receiving a gift from someone, you're expected to pay for the goods you receive. Indeed, buyers who accept merchandise are automatically obligated to pay by virtue of that acceptance. The buyer *may* elect to do either Option B or C—at his or her own risk or expense. But the intervening right of the buyer is that which occurs between the seller's duty to perform and the buyer's duty to perform, which is what Option D describes.

8. a (Page 335) Option C is irrelevant in this case because the defect already existed prior to purchase; it was not the result of damage that occurred during transit. The key point here is that the defect was not readily observable and could not be detected under normal circumstances. Though this case obviously demands some interpretation (for example, shouldn't Doig have insisted that he get to drive the car on a freeway?), it is probably fair to say that the court would not expect that every potential buyer test-drive a car at speeds exceeding 60 mph. Therefore, Doig is likely entitled to demand that Klein cure the defect.

9. d (Page 339) Williams is free to use the goods in the way intended and to keep them for the full period of the contract. At any time during the ten days, she may return them, even if they conform fully to the contract. But if she does not return them at the close of the ten-day test period, or subjects them to misuse, she is responsible for paying the full contract price.

10. d (Page 341) The term *without reserve* simply means that the auctioneer must accept the good-faith highest bid, even if it is not acceptable to the seller. What is more important in this situation is that the seller's behavior here is not ethical, and thus Rowan has the option of either not buying the rocker or of buying it at the last good-faith bid she made before the seller began bidding against her.

18—WARRANTIES AND PRODUCT LIABILITY

1. a (Page 360) A warranty is best thought of as a promise; the nature of that warranty can vary from one situation to another.

2. b (Pages 361ff.) Option B is a statement of fact; it's either true or it isn't. Option C, on the other hand, is just an opinion and there is no way of proving it. Not everyone uses the same criteria for judging comfort, nor will any given shoe likely be comfortable on all buyers. Option C is an example of what is sometimes called "puffery."

3. d   (Pages 362–363, 366–367)   The seller may provide an express warranty, written or oral, that allows for return or replacement, but is not required by law to do so. But there is no implied warranty implicit in the purchase of goods that gives this protection to the buyer.

4. a   (Page 364)   Merchantability is assumed as part of a set of implied warranties guaranteed by law. These warranties are always present unless restricted by the seller (e.g., when goods are purchased "as is"). To be merchantable, goods must meet standards of quality set within the industry and by government regulation. Given that all coffee-bean growers would be subject to the same variability in harvest as Richroast and that Richroast hasn't claimed either consistency or any higher standard, Option A seems the best answer.

5. c   (Pages 364–365)   A chicken bone cannot be considered a "foreign" object in a dish made of chicken. However, whether a reasonable person should expect to find chicken bones in chicken and dumplings is probably a matter of interpretation, and may rest on precedents and what is commonly expected of others in the industry.

6. a   (Pages 365–366)   The point here is that Rodmann has recommended a product for a particular use to which that product is clearly not suited—the manufacturer's label provides that evidence. But Rodmann has not violated the warranty of merchantability because there's no evidence that the tires didn't work well for the purpose for which they were intended. In other words, the tires did not perform well on wet pavement, just as the manufacturer warned. The seller, however, did make such a claim and the buyer relied on it. Further, the buyer made his purpose clear and also stated specifically that he was relying on Rodmann's recommendation.

7. b   (Pages 366–367)

8. b   (Pages 367–368)   Option A is partially correct since the buyer must make clear the purpose for which he or she intends to use the goods and must rely on the seller's judgment in making a selection. However, the catch is that a merchant could very easily create a warranty of fitness for a particular purpose without intending to do any such thing—simply by advising the buyer on what to buy.

9. a   (Pages 369ff.)

10. c   (Pages 369ff.)   Many products can be dangerous if misused. A suit based on negligence must demonstrate that the danger to the consumer results from the manufacturer's (or seller's) negligence—improper production, failure to inspect, improper packaging, mislabeling, and so forth—although with inherently dangerous materials the standard of due care to which the manufacturer will be held and judged is quite exacting.

19—REMEDIES FOR BREACH

1. d (Page 376)

2. b (Pages 376–377ff.) Numerous factors can influence the nature and number of available remedies, including the contract itself (which may provide remedies not normally provided through law) and the nature of the situation. But generally speaking, unless the parties have included special provisions within the contract, the overriding factor will generally be the time at which the breach occurs—whether before or after acceptance. And for either buyer or seller, more remedies are available if a breach occurs prior to acceptance.

3. a (Pages 377–378) Option B would be correct were it not for the fact that Arnold has already paid for the goods. That is the key factor here; Handy cannot withhold goods merely on the basis of Arnold's general insolvency if Arnold has found a way to pay for them.

4. a (Page 378) Options B, C, and D are not required.

5. d (Page 379) Suits for lost profits are most likely to arise out of circumstances in which the seller risks designing or manufacturing goods for a specific person or a specific use and those goods are then rejected. The problem the seller faces is that such goods have a very limited market and cannot readily be resold. Note the contrast, for instance, with Option C. (In Options A and B, the seller caused the breach; if profits are lost, it's the seller's own fault.)

6. c (Page 379) Option C is the best definition. (Remember, too, that indirect costs relating to the contract may usually be added to the total for damages; expenses saved are subtracted.)

7. b (Page 380) Option D makes no sense. If the breach occurs after acceptance, obviously it's too late to stop shipment. Attempting to reclaim the goods (Option B) is tricky at best. Suing for the price of goods (which should include lost profits) is the most common remedy—and will theoretically succeed unless the buyer is insolvent.

8. a (Page 382)

9. c (Pages 384–385)

10. b (Page 386) This is an instance of recoupment, and it is one remedy open to the buyer—with the seller's approval. But if the store objects, Norwich cannot simply automatically deduct the money, at least not from a purely legal point of view. Still, this seller probably wouldn't object; selling damaged merchandise at discount may seem a better alternative than not selling it at all. The store's other obvious alternative is to offer to cure the defect—probably by replacing the saw. If Norwich objects to having the saw replaced, he can still sue for damages related to the scratches — but his un-willingness to cooperate in the seller's effort to cure will work against him in court. (Besides which, you'd have to wonder about anyone who decides to sue for $20 or so when they've been offered new merchandise.)

20 — FUNCTIONS AND FORMS OF COMMERCIAL PAPER

1. **d** (Page 394) Order paper and promise paper are the two forms of commercial paper.

2. **b** (Page 394) A negotiable instrument can be a substitute for money, but it is not really a *form* of money (Option A). Negotiable instruments *can* be used to extend credit (Option C), but that is not their only use. Similarly, Option D is too limited in scope.

3. **b** (Pages 394ff.) Option C is irrelevant. Option A is false; all negotiable instruments are contracts, but the reverse is not true.

4. **d** (Page 395)

5. **d** (Pages 395ff.)

6. **d** (Page 397) Options A, B, and C are all false.

7. **b** (Pages 397–398)

8. **b** (Page 398) Prepayment clauses are common in many installment notes, which are a form of promissory note. Unfair though it may sometimes seem, whether Hendricks was aware of the clause at the time of signing (Option C) is irrelevant. He has responsibility for ensuring that he understands the terms of the instrument *before* signing.

9. **d** (Page 400) Kunderson is the one *making* the promise; the installment note is a form of promissory note. The role of maker combines the roles of drawer (Option B) and drawee (Option C), but neither term is sufficient alone to define Kunderson's role here.

10. **d** (Page 401 and entire reading assignment) Option A is false. Option B is partially correct, but too limited; negotiable instruments serve more purposes than simply extending credit and, further, the need for credit is not recent. Option C is not correct; businesses will, of course, accept cash — readily. But most customers do not have sufficient cash to use in paying for all purchases. Option D is the best answer here. Safety is a factor too.

21 — NEGOTIABILITY

1. d   (Pages 404–405ff.)

2. d   (Page 406) It is the intention of the maker that counts most here. If the maker intends to create a signature affirming an order or promise, the mark or symbol is likely to be so interpreted, whether it is handwritten, printed, or typed — and regardless of what the signature or symbol represents. It could, for example, be an X, an official seal, or an individual's name; there is no need for anything "official" (Option C).

3. a   (Pages 406–408) Options C and D are both incorrect. Option B is somewhat true; however, it's incorrect to assume that imposing a condition will necessarily make a situation ambiguous. That doesn't usually turn out to be the case. The primary reason for requiring unconditional promises is so that business can move forward, so that holders need not wait for conditions to be met or verified before collecting their money. While conditional promises are quite permissible within a contract, they would negate much of the benefits of negotiable instruments as a substitute for money.

4. b   (Page 411) Option C is irrelevant. Postdated instruments are negotiable, if the date can be determined from information contained within the document itself. In this case, the date is specific, all right, but there is no way to determine it by looking at the instrument; it would be necessary to verify Ted's age from another source. The draft *would* be negotiable if Reynolds had named the specific date on which Ted would turn 21 — e.g., payable on December 2, 1994.

5. c   (Page 408) Checks may be charged to ongoing accounts without compromising negotiability. Negotiability is impaired, however, if only certain funds — rather than the general assets — of the company can be used to satisfy the debt.

6. c   (Pages 408–409ff.)

7. d   (Page 409) The words *subject to* are key in Option D. It is all right, for instance, to draft a promissory note that reads "as per our contract." It isn't the reference itself, in other words, that defeats negotiability, but the fact that the instrument is subject to, or governed by, another document. Remember, such wording makes it necessary to look outside the instrument to determine all conditions for payment.

8. b   (Page 410) What individuals are willing to accept as payment is irrelevant to the definition of "money" when determining negotiability; it is perfectly all right for McPhee to pay LaRose off in grain or cattle or bricks — if LaRose agrees — but that does not make these items "money" under the UCC. Money must be a common, agreed-on medium of exchange throughout the business community of a given society.

9. a   (Page 410)

10. a   (Pages 412–413)

22—NEGOTIATIONS AND HOLDERS IN DUE COURSE

1. a   (Pages 419–420ff.) Option D is irrelevant in this case; Fremont cannot be a holder in due course — or even a holder — because he is in possession of a check not properly endorsed over to him.

2. d   (Page 420) Remember, it is the drawer who "demands" that his or her bank make payment to the payee (Option A), not the payee. Options B and C are both false. Wheeler cannot retain title, and with this blank, unqualified endorsement, he is accepting secondary liability.

3. d   (Pages 423–424)

4. b   (Pages 423–424) Option D is illegal except with the permission of the drawer and subsequent endorsers, and even then, opens the way for a real defense should the instrument be dishonored. In short, when a change is necessary, it is best to issue a new instrument; such change cannot be effected through endorsement. Options A and C are false.

5. a   (Page 421) An endorsement creates a contract between the endorser and the transferee.

6. d   (Pages 425–426)

7. d   (Pages 429–430)

8. b   (Pages 431–433) Options C and D are false; both are inaccurate descriptions of the situation. Millstone is not a thief, nor is he guilty of fraud in the execution. He is, however, obligated to deliver the table before he can transfer the check. Even though he has it in his hands, in the court's view, the check has not truly been delivered until the conditions for its being issued in the first place have been met.

9. a   (Page 441) Option A is an issue in establishing holder in due course status, but not in determining secondary liability.

10. d   (Pages 450–451)

23 – BANK–CUSTOMER RELATIONS

1. a (Page 457) Options B, C, and D are all false. Liability (Option C) is not really an issue if the checking account is well managed. And since much of the real management is done by the bank, Option D is a real exaggeration. In fact, checking accounts are more popular than ever, and the nature of American business would change dramatically if we were suddenly to find ourselves without them.

2. b (Pages 458ff.) Option C is inaccurate; an oral stop-payment order is valid for fourteen days. Option D is incorrect; banks do not ask about, and then evaluate, the merit of the reasoning behind a stop-payment order. (It is true, however, that a bank usually won't be liable for damages if – because of an error or misunderstanding – it pays a check with a stop-payment order on it when the person being paid the money would have been legally entitled to the money anyway.)

3. a (Page 457)

4. d (Page 458)

5. a (Page 458)

6. d (Pages 458ff.)

7. d (Page 460) The customer is responsible for providing the bank with the most complete description possible of the check covered by the stop-payment order. All three options in this question are important elements for identifying the check.

8. a (Page 461) Option D is required of the bank, not the customer. The bank will expect the customer to do both Options B and C, but neither of these has directly to do with reconciling the statement; Option A is the best answer here.

9. c (Page 463) The ten-day period helps speed commerce by allowing checks written shortly before a person's death to be cashed in the expected course of business, even after a person's death. If this period were not allowed, people holding checks from the deceased would have to make claims against his or her estate, a much more complicated process than cashing a check.

10. d (Page 464) Option A has the principal and agent roles reversed, Option B is incorrect, and Option C – dealing with the issue of damages – is irrelevant to this situation. Option D is correct; in acting in such an abrupt fashion, the bank breached several duties to Loretta. First, it returned duly authorized checks for which the account had money when it had no indication that Loretta would suddenly become a bad credit risk. Second, there is no evidence that Loretta herself breached any terms of the contract, thus justifying the cancellation. Finally, the bank's duty to act in good faith demands that a customer with a well-maintained account receive advance notice that the account will be cancelled.

24 — CREATION AND TERMINATION OF AGENCY

1. c   (Pages 570 and 582)

2. c   (Page 571)

3. d   (Page 572)

4. c   (Pages 573–574)

5. d   (Page 574)   Option D is the correct option. An architect who designs a home and doesn't supervise its construction is probably acting only as an independent contractor and not as an agent. Option B describes a clearcut agency relationship because of the position of special trust a lawyer occupies. Option C describes another obvious agency relationship; employees are always agents of their employers. Option D describes a situation that is clearly not an agency relationship; the typesetter is an independent contractor.

6. c   (Pages 574–575)   While Option D is generally accurate, a principal retains responsibility when the tasks to be performed can be classified as *ultrahazardous*.

7. d   (Pages 576–577)   Although few agents remain in the principal's employ for long if they fail to give reasonable value for the money, this is not a legal duty owed to a principal.

8. c   (Page 578)

9. a   (Page 580)   Option C affects an agency relationship by terminating it, but it is not an operation of law; Option A is. Option D is backward; operations of law terminate existing relationships.

10. a   (Pages 578–579)   Agency at will allows—assuming proper notice—legal termination of an agency relationship at the desire of either party. (Fulfillment and operation of law, Options B and C, also terminate agency relationships, but they do not pertain to this situation.) Option D is completely inaccurate.

25 – PRINCIPALS AND AGENTS

1. a   (Pages 588–593) Express and implied authority are actual authorities. Emergency authority can flow out of either actual or apparent authority, being called forth to meet emergency needs. But authority by estoppel is granted by a court after the fact to stop a principal from benefitting from his or her earlier misleading actions.

2. d   (Page 593) Ostensible authority is that which never really existed at the time the third party thought it did. The principal led the third party to believe the supposed agent had authority so the principal could benefit. But, as explained above, the court estops the principal from benefitting from the earlier misleading actions.

3. c   (Page 594) Though Options A, B, and D are simply false, Option C does a good job of explaining the situation. Mills is the agent of Timmons, and the implicit authority that comes from her job (and probably specific express authority as well) likely gives her the authority to convey messages to her principal. Remember, too, that one portion of agency law theory rests on the assumption that an agent tells all important information to the principal. This in part is the basis for holding the principal liable for acts and contracts of the agent – the principal "knows" what the agent is doing and can control the agent's actions. And even if the agent doesn't tell the principal all the important facts, the principal still will be held liable because he or she has "imputed knowledge" of the agent's actions. All in all, client Kovacs probably had every right to expect that his sell order would be properly executed.

4. b   (Pages 595–596) The agent is normally not liable for the principal's failure to comply with terms of the contract where the principal is fully disclosed.

5. b   (Page 599)

6. c   (Pages 599–601)

7. b   (Pages 607–608) Vicarious liability defines a situation in which one person is liable for an action just because it occurred, not because it is the fault of that principal. It applies in agency law because the master is considered responsible for the servant's acts. If no agency existed, no act of an agent could have been committed. Only Option B describes a situation where the wrongdoing wasn't the fault of the principal Jacobs.

8. b   (Pages 610–611)

9. d   (Pages 616–617) When a principal pays for losses caused by an agent, it is not necessarily because the principal has committed a wrong. The principal often pays because the principal is responsible for the agency relationship; if there had been no agency, no wrong could have been committed by an agent. But where the principal has committed no wrong, it is only

fair that he or she should be allowed to try to recover from the agent; indemnification is the legal concept that allows this recovery. Options A, B, and C all refer to other legal concepts present in agency law, but they do not apply to the principal's right to seek recovery from a wrong-acting agent.

10. a   (Pages 607–608, 614–617) Options B and D are wrong; *respondeat superior* does not apply in criminal law. Option C is not correct, either. Although *respondeat superior* will allow a principal to be held civilly liable for the actions of an agent, it won't allow the agent to escape from his or her own wrongdoing; agents must answer for their own wrongdoings.

26—REAL PROPERTY

1. a   (Page 894) The flower arrangement and the ladder are not the least bit attached to the real property; how well they "go with the house" is irrelevant. The ceiling *fixture* is clearly a fixture. The drapes could be a tough call; they are relatively easy to remove, but because they are specially fitted to one particular window in one particular house, they might well be considered attached to that house. In practice, most house sale agreements make a special point to mention what happens to the window coverings.

2. d   (Page 895) Unlike all the other options, Option D doesn't actually transfer any property. There is no legal requirement that the intent to engage in the transfer of property be in writing.

3. d   (Page 895)

4. a   (Page 897) To transfer real property, the grantee must deliver the deed; it's the delivery of the deed that shows the intention to transfer the property. The miner's oral statements (Option D) aren't adequate. It is, of course, likely that Durbin will inherit the mine, either through the miner's will or the action of the court (Option B), but none of this will have taken place by July 24. (The mention of a community property state in Option C is irrelevant; that only affects joint ownership between husband and wife.)

5. b   (Page 898)

6. c   (Pages 900–902) A person with what turns out to be an invalid deed who nevertheless thinks that his or her occupancy is appropriate is said to have "entered under color of title."

7. d   (Pages 904–905) A landlord has a duty to protect tenants and their guests. While Marples might not have been responsible for a hidden (latent) defect she didn't know about, Fowler's notification requires that she make the repairs. The fact that Marples has given Fowler notice (Option A) doesn't change the fact that he's still her tenant. Option B is incorrect, as

is Option C; the fact that a tenant has a right to end a tenancy doesn't reduce the landlord's obligation to keep the premises safe.

8. d (Pages 906–907) We don't know whether Sue and Ken held title to the house as joint tenants with rights of survivorship (which would make Option A correct) or as tenants in common (which would make Option B correct). Option C is irrelevant; if Ken died without a will, Sue would almost certainly receive the house through intestate succession.

9. a (Pages 906–907) In this tenancy arrangement, when one tenant dies, his or her interest does not pass to that person's heirs. Similarly, while Edwin's creditors quite possibly would have been able to attach his interests while he was alive, all of Edwin's rights to the property passed to Joan on his death. (This does not, incidentally, mean that the debt is erased; Edwin's creditors can sue Joan to get their money, but they don't get the property.) Option D has a point—there are differences in how some types of ownership are treated among states—but joint tenancy with rights of survivorship is pretty standard.

10. b (Pages 908–910) In community property states, community property will pass to the surviving spouse if the other spouse dies intestate (Option B); the death of a spouse therefore makes the issue of what was separate and what was community property moot. Option D is incorrect; disputes can arise over both real and personal property—and frequently do. And Options A and C probably would *increase* disputes since property would have been accumulated under two different situations and, unless rigorously accounted for, would tend to become commingled.

27 — PERSONAL PROPERTY

1. b (Page 915) A bathtub is a fixture and hence is considered real property. A business's reputation is a component of its goodwill, which is personal property. The software code and the cash are both tangible personal property.

2. a (Page 916)

3. c (Page 918) Regardless of the type of bailment, the bailee has to care for the property received. What's more, if the bailee benefits from the bailment—and a parking lot owner being paid for the space is certainly benefitting—the level of care has to be even higher. Since the parking lot owners probably don't want to care for your car any more than they have to, they'd prefer that you were just leasing space.

4. d (Pages 917–919) While written evidence of the transfer of property never hurts, it is not a mandatory element of a gift. The other three options are.

5. b   (Pages 926–927)

6. c   (Page 928)

7. b   (Pages 924–930) Worloski's friends were using the truck in the manner authorized by Worloski. They are, therefore, not liable. However, Worloski's loan of the vehicle could be challenged by the company and treated as conversion. Therefore, Worloski could be held responsible for the repairs, even though the company would have been responsible for repairs if the truck had been used in an authorized manner.

8. c   (Pages 929–930) Option C is a succinct summary of the situation; all other options are completely inaccurate.

9. c   (Pages 927–930) A bailment existed here, one that probably would be viewed as established solely for the benefit of the museum. Since Carol and Clyde were not receiving any financial benefit from the loan of their property, the museum would be responsible for even slight negligence in allowing the theft. It would be up to the court to decide whether the museum had taken totally adequate measures to provide for the carpets' security—although one can hypothesize that it was probably somewhat at fault, given that the theft was committed. (None of the other answers is correct, however, so Option C is clearly best.)

10. a   (Pages 927–931) Bailments concern personal—not real—property, so the lease of a building is not a bailment.

28—GOVERNMENT REGULATION

1. d   (Page 821) The term *laissez-faire* literally means "hands off," and it is used to describe the prevailing attitude of the early nineteenth century that businesses operate best when left alone by government.

2. a   (Page 822) The *primary* power derives from the commerce clause, which specifically states that "Congress shall have power . . . to regulate commerce with foreign nations, and among the several states." The other options are partially true, but only because of the commerce clause.

3. c   (Page 822 and entire reading assignment)

4. d   (Pages 823 and 834) Option D is correct because federal regulation covers only interstate commerce or activities that adversely affect interstate commerce, and Houser conducts all its business in the San Francisco Bay Area. It is important to keep in mind, however, that according to current interpretations of Section 1 of the Sherman Act, *local* businesses can be viewed as adversely influencing interstate commerce—though that does not appear to be the case with Houser; Option A would be correct if there *were* an impact on interstate commerce. Option C, by the way, is totally false; there is nothing illegal about simply trying to increase one's market share. That, after all, is the purpose of being in business in the first place. Option B is also false; companies guilty of per se violations need not be monopolies in order to be prosecuted.

5. b (Pages 826–827) Both procedural irregularities (as in Option A) and an improper rule (Option B) are reasons for a court to overturn an administrative agency decision. But from the information given, Wilson–Wright clearly had time to—and did—present a defense. A court cannot, however, overturn an order properly reached on the basis of a valid rule simply because it would have evaluated the evidence differently than did the agency (Option C). If there is substantial evidence to support the agency decision, the court must let it stand.

6. d (Page 833)

7. a (Pages 834–835) This is a modestly tricky question. The group boycott (Option D) normally would not be defensible. But in this particular case, where the company being boycotted caused the need for the boycott through its unscrupulous activities, it might be successfully argued that the boycott was necessary to avoid economic ruin. Both Options B and C are allowable defenses under Section 1, so only Option A would not be a successful defense.

8. a (Pages 837ff.) Option B is partially true, but only Option A expresses the main impetus behind the Clayton Act, which was to nip problems in the bud. Option C covers practices forbidden under the Sherman Antitrust Act, not the Clayton Act. Deceptive advertising practices are primarily monitored under the Federal Trade Commission Act of 1914, which itself was passed to close loopholes in both the Clayton Act and the Sherman Antitrust Act.

9. c (Pages 838–841) The failing-company doctrine (Option C) provides a suitable defense for horizontal mergers if one of the companies involved is on the verge of bankruptcy. All the other options show clear potential violations of the Clayton Act.

10. c (Page 842) Admittedly, some advertisements use absurdly humorous claims as part of the presentation, and there's nothing wrong with that. But the merchant who makes potentially plausible claims on the theory that he'll later claim it's all a joke is playing a dangerous game; "joking" is not a proper defense to deceptive advertising. Keep in mind too that if there are different interpretations possible—one honest, one deceptive—the FTC has the right to treat the ad as deceptive. It could readily be argued in this case that the ad was worded in a way that would encourage at least some consumers to infer that Bork Beer promoted weight *loss*. Obviously, what Bork could truthfully say is that its product promotes weight *gain*—but since it is hardly in their best interests to say this outright, they

attempt to get around the problem with ambiguous wording. The FTC generally frowns on such strategies, however cleverly employed.

29 – CONSUMER AND ENVIRONMENTAL PROTECTION

1. a (Pages 849–850) Suppose Bailey Mercantile sells Winslow a lawn tractor and requires weekly payments of $50 for the first six weeks, followed by weekly payments of $65 for the next three months, then monthly payments of $215 for six months, and so on. Winslow is likely to have a difficult time indeed determining what percentage of these payments go to paying for the tractor itself and what percentage go to financing the credit extension. The Federal Consumer Credit Protection Act says that Winslow has a right to know, in clear terms, precisely what his finance charges will be on a percentage basis – no matter how elaborate or confusing Bailey's schedule of payments.

2. c (Pages 851–852) Poor credit history – not an isolated incident – is proper grounds for rejecting a credit application. Marital status, age, and outdated credit information do not provide appropriate grounds for such rejection.

3. d (Page 852)

4. a (Page 852) Notice is required. It must be in writing and provided to the consumer prior to the beginning of the investigation. The company is not, however, required to contact Danson's attorney; and contacting his employer might be quite inappropriate. (Option B is a bit tricky, since Danson cannot keep the real estate company from performing the credit check if he wants to buy the building; Danson could, on the other hand, avoid the credit check by deciding not to pursue purchase of the building further.)

5. b (Pages 852–853) The agency may certainly notify Ferrarro by phone or letter and request that the debt be paid. That, after all, is their job. Such behavior does not constitute harassment unless they contact Ferrarro at odd hours or so frequently that the communication constitutes a nuisance. If Ferrarro has an attorney, it is proper for the agency to deal with Ferrarro *through* that attorney rather than deal with her directly – and the agency must do this if Ferrarro says to. It is highly improper, however, to involve Ferrarro's employer or business associates – or friends, family, or neighbors, for that matter – in this private situation.

6. b (Page 853) Option D is true, but it is too limited in scope to describe the full purpose of the Act. There are definite and explicit laws governing warranty coverage to which merchants and manufacturers must adhere. The law does not require that all warranties be unconditional (Option A); most, in fact, are not. It does require, however, that the extent of warranty coverage be fully disclosed to the buyer at the time of the sale. Hidden disclaimers are certainly discouraged. Similarly, a dealer cannot say to the consumer, "Don't worry—this product is well covered. We'll mail you the written warranty in a week." Consumers have a "right to know" about coverage before purchasing a product.

7. c (Page 853 and entire reading assignment) The purpose of current consumer legislation is not to enrich consumers, nor is it focused strictly on those consumers who have suffered injury at merchants' hands. Rather, it is (1) aimed at all consumers and (2) intended, so far as possible, to create a balance of power between merchant and consumer, so that each must consider the interests of the other while having their own interests protected.

8. a (Page 854 and Study Guide Lesson 29) Options B, C, and D are all false. Focus on the environment, both in Congress and among the public at large, has both grown and intensified, particularly in recent decades, and there are no signs that this trend will reverse itself.

9. d (Pages 854ff.) The CEQ is not an enforcement agency. It can report its findings, but really is not empowered to do more. The Environmental Protection Agency has the enforcement power.

10. c (Pages 854–855)

30—LABOR AND EMPLOYMENT PRACTICES

1. a (Page 865)

2. d (Pages 865–866ff.)

3. b (Page 867) Option C is really irrelevant. Employees can and often do seek union representation even if there is no real grievance. Option A is inaccurate; unions often represent some members who do not support the union. And Option D is both insufficient and, occasionally, wrong; some bargaining units cover employees doing the same job for different locations (for example, meat cutters for a number of supermarkets in a city). What's required is that the employees have similar jobs so that their needs and concerns are also likely to be similar. Otherwise, it is impossible for the union to effectively represent them as a unit.

4. c (Page 868) Option C is the only one that would not directly affect employees' working conditions or terms of employment. Some decisions are considered the province of the employer—including decisions to relocate or expand the business or even to go out of business (despite the fact that employees are obviously affected by such decisions)—and are not mandatory topics for negotiation.

5. a   (Pages 870–871)

6. d   (Page 871)

7. a   (Page 874) The question here is, is the qualification in fact essential to the job? Or is it just "seen" as related because of traditional practices or prejudice? While an audience may not know that a woman is playing the role of Hamlet because of good makeup and acting, acting is one of the very few areas in which a sex-based job qualification is generally allowed (Option A). In all the other options, *requiring* a certain religion, sex, or national origin of job applicants would violate Title VII. For example, with Option D, while a native of Italy may well bring some "pluses" to the job—and could be evaluated as such—it would be illegal to require that the person hired be Italian. Issues such as teaching skill, fluency in and understanding of the Italian language, a knowledge of Italian literature and customs, and any number of other matters are undoubtedly more relevant to one's ability to successfully teach a class in Italian than is the fact that someone is a native of Italy. Options B and C are quite easy to dismiss—there is nothing inherent in the job of telephone operator that suggests that it can be better performed by one sex than the other, nor is religion closely related to bus driving skill.

8. b   (Page 877) Obviously, a large concern here was to provide a safe and healthful working environment for workers—and Options C and D are logical offshoots of that broad concern. But the overriding concern at the federal level was to cut down on the large financial losses to the public and to businesses themselves that occur when employees lose time from work through illness or injury.

9. a   (Page 877) Demanding that the inspector obtain a warrant is the employer's right; it is, realistically, only a postponement of the inevitable since such warrants are not difficult to obtain. Without a warrant, however, the inspector must have the employer's permission to inspect.

10. b   (Page 882) Employees do contribute in some states; primary funding still comes from employers, however.